THE CLASSICAL AGE
A STUDY IN FEUDALIZATION

The Classical Age
A Study in Feudalization

SHANKAR GOYAL
M.A., Ph.D., D.Litt.
Professor of History (retd.)
Jai Narain Vyas University, Jodhpur

Foreword by
ROMILA THAPAR
Professor Emerita of History
Jawaharlal Nehru University, New Delhi

Preface by
KUMKUM ROY
Professor of History
Centre for Historical Studies
School of Social Sciences
Jawaharlal Nehru University, New Delhi

ADITYA PRAKASHAN
New Delhi

First Edition, 2022

ISBN 978-81-950961-4-5
Rs.1200

Published by Aditya Prakashan, 2/18, Ansari Road, New Delhi – 110 002.

Email: contact@adityaprakashan.com
Website: www.adityaprakashan.com

Printed at Thomson Press (India) Ltd.

To the cherished memory

of

my papa

PROFESSOR S.R. GOYAL

(1932-2015)

Foreword

Shankar Goyal's latest book, *The Classical Age : A Study in Feudalization*, draws on his many earlier studies of the period of the Guptas and Harsha together with some new material and ideas. It is useful to have these up-dated and collected into one book. The book is dedicated to the memory of his late father S.R.Goyal. This is a fitting tribute. His father's much-read and frequently quoted work was, *A History of the Imperial Guptas*, published in 1967. It was part of many studies that he carried out on the Gupta period.

Coming half a century after his father's study, Shankar Goyal's book is not just an incorporation of the many studies of that period done in the last half-century. His range is wider with an extensive study of the Vākāṭaka dynasty, the high points associated with Gupta rule and including the reign of Harshavardhana of Kanauj. But more importantly he refers to and discusses many of the new perspectives that have illuminated this history. His use of the term 'feudalization' in the title is an indication of this.

In order to explain the use of this term in the title he begins with a summary of the views of Marxist historians or those influenced by some aspects of Marxist thinking on history, and refers to the debates on the feudal mode of production that their analyses generated. The most wide-ranging has been that on whether or not there was a period of feudalism in India and if so can this be dated to the later first millennium continuing onto the second millennium A.D. The current debate outside India in places where advanced medieval history is taught, focuses on the term itself and its feasibility in determining historical periodization. The debate remains inconclusive but has resulted in registering a wide typology for the term. It can no longer be used as a single uniform category applied to most parts of the world. It has to be qualified by its particular form and usage.

It has encouraged the idea of categories of historical forms some of which are closer to and others more distant from what was earlier taken as feudalism. A detailed typology would be helpful with reference to Indian history as well. There are similarities but also differences in the way states were either formed or underwent change in what is now referred to as the early medieval period. In Indian history it led to perhaps the most intense debate on early medieval India. The argument for or against a period of feudalism led to many new areas being opened up and therefore new sources and fresh ways of posing the required questions.

I cannot go into details in a short foreword but I shall mention some of the items that have been discussed in this book and possibly a few others items that pertain to the period of history covered in this book. I have elsewhere described this period as 'threshold times', since there are some aspects that are continued from earlier times and others that are innovations and have a continuity into later times.

For instance, the period between the Mauryas and Guptas saw many major changes in various parts of the sub-continent. Many more detailed sources are available in the form both of inscriptions and texts. The first category provides information on the functioning of various administrative innovations such as shifts in the administrative forms from the earlier period. A noticeable feature is the induction of many more persons of the *brāhmaṇa varṇa* into administrative offices.

Economic prosperity opened up and this has to be explained. It was in part the result of opening up new areas through grants of land largely to *brāhmaṇas* and the consequent extension of agriculture. It was also the result of the increase in commercial income with the trade that was linked to two areas : one was Central Asia with Northern India being linked to the trade from China to the Eastern Mediterranean through Central Asia, and the other was the opening up of trade with places in South-east Asia. The first was an overland trade and the second was maritime.

Contacts with other cultures and peoples, whether through trade or through migration inevitably resulted in the creation of new cultures. Many of the major changes of these times resulted from such situations. The Kushāṇa period saw migrations of people and ideas into India and from India into Central Asia and China. Buddhism for example, that began to decline in India with patronage going to Brāhmaṇism, nevertheless prospered elsewhere in Central, Eastern and South-eastern Asia. In fact for many centuries it was virtually an all-Asia religion. In the period subsequent to this, South-east Asia also saw the imprint of Hinduism and Buddhism and it was again Buddhism that made the more lasting impact in the area.

In the northern part of the sub-continent this was the period that saw the emergence of what is now called Purāṇic Hinduism, namely, the Hinduism of the *Purāṇas.* This was mainly in the form of Vaishṇavism and Śaivism and later the Tāntric religion. In some ways this was a departure from what had been the dominant religions earlier, namely, Vedic Brāhmaṇism and Buddhism. Buddhism had less patronage but remained an important religion until the later part of the first millennium A.D.

It is important to keep in mind all that existed prior to this period as well as that which was characteristic of this period. Classicism is not an unexpected outburst of excellence in various aspects of cultural life. It is the culmination of various processes of change that have had a long gestation period. We tend to treat them as the achievements of those that form the elite in society. But given the historical studies that are being made these days we have to recognize that it is the entire society — both the elites and the non-elites who contribute together to the making of a civilization. A discussion of the achievements of Classicism has to also give attention to the contribution of those that were not the dominant groups and the elite, but who nevertheless, made their contributions to the material and other cultures, and to the social functioning of the society of that period.

It was a period of some complexity with many changes and developments. I am glad to see that Shankar Goyal has not avoided these complexities. He has not tried to pass them off with simplistic answers. He has instead addressed them and discussed them with care and in some detail. As is always required of a good historian he has backed his statements with reference to relevant sources. His insistence on giving due attention to the sources, in what they say and what they imply, is to be highly commended. I am sure the book will have the extensive and interested readership that it deserves.

December 30, 2020

Romila Thapar
Professor Emerita of History
Jawaharlal Nehru University, New Delhi

Preface

Shankar Goyal is amongst those scholars who have a deep interest in early and early medieval Indian history, combined with an ability to engage with a variety of sources, as well as with historiographical debates. In this volume, consisting of 17 essays and an introduction, he covers some of the themes that has attracted his attention for decades, weaving these together to provide insights into what has been recognized as a crucial period in Indian history, namely, the mid- first millennium CE.

The introductory essay provides the framework for the rest of the volume. Here Goyal offers a detailed survey of Marxist historiography on the theme, focusing on both the commonalities as well as the divergences that are apparent within this vast and complex body of scholarship. For his part, he highlights the evidence or lack of evidence on coinage, as well as the indications of a possible decline in urban centres, to argue for feudalization. While both these lines of argument have been interrogated and qualified by scholars such as B.D. Chattopadhyaya and Ranabir Chakravarti, amongst others, Goyal reiterates his position, drawing on a range of textual, epigraphic, numismatic and archaeological evidence.

From this Goyal moves on to a survey of the historiography of the Vākāṭakas, painstakingly documenting shifts in foci that have emerged over a century and more. Thus, earlier concerns with chronology, and dynastic history have given way to a more critical evaluation of the epigraphic evidence and the implications of land grants, most notably in the work of K.M. Shrimali, and have been widened to include religious and cultural developments in the contributions of Hans Bakker. In charting these trends Goyal alerts us to the rich potential of the field, and the various ways in which it has and can be further investigated. Appendices to the chapter offer further critical discussions that are likely to be addressed in future scholarship.

The discussion on historiography leads on to a more detailed consideration of political structures and processes within the Vākāṭaka polity, which is followed up by an analysis of the economy. Contextualizing the discussion within the framework of and in relation to the Gupta polity, Goyal steers a course through the complicated question of understanding the presence/ paucity of numismatic evidence and its implications. He then goes on to examine the epigraphic evidence of land grants, and their significance for the agrarian economy, including the changes in the settlement pattern that may be correlated with these developments.

Goyal next turns to the better-known contemporaries of the Vākāṭakas, the Guptas, often regarded as epitomising the golden age. In a long historiographical essay, devoted to highlighting the contributions of S.R. Goyal to our understanding of the Guptas, the author unpacks historiographical debates in all their detail, drawing attention to the ways in which a range of sources has been interpreted in order to reconstruct the history of the dynasty. He follows this up by re-examining the possible relationship between the Guptas and the Vākāṭakas, cautioning against overemphasizing the dominance of the former. A short but illuminating discussion on the representation of the Vaishṇava ideal of the *chakravartī* in Gupta coinage opens up a fresh dimension that is useful.

This leads on to an ambitious attempt to compare and contrast developments in medieval Europe with those in early medieval India. For Goyal, this is a period of decline—of decentralized polities, economic stagnation, evident in the decline of towns and long-distance trade, the growth of an overly ornate set of cultural practices, the emergence of regional polities with their distinctive culture, growing social fragmentation being amongst the most evident signs of this. More recently, many of these formulations have been called into question and qualified, with several scholars drawing attention to the efflorescence of regional traditions and the consolidation of regional identities during this period. Obviously, this remains an area that is open to further debate, and, in stating his position with clarity, Goyal lays out the possible grounds for such an engagement.

The next set of essays deal with a theme that is perhaps closest to Goyal's heart: Harsha and his times. After an excursus on the need to revisit political history, Goyal opens up the rule and role of Harsha to an intense scrutiny, based on a close examination of textual and epigraphic sources, including the account of the Chinese Buddhist pilgrim Yuan Chwang. Goyal unpacks the complicated and even messy dynastic details, discusses the possible extent of Harsha's kingdom, administrative apparatus, religious and cultural developments, to provide an overall assessment that is likely to stand the test of time.

Goyal provides, amongst other things, a detailed and thoughtful assessment of Bāṇabhaṭṭa and his classic composition, the *Harshacharita*. He attempts to sift the plausible from the imaginary, and provides an explanation for the incorporation of both. Bāṇabhaṭṭa's life, as well as the literary and cultural context within which he wrote are opened up to scrutiny, enabling the reader to understand the specific cultural practices that shaped the writing of what was ostensibly a biographical work, better understood in terms of its literary significance.

Also valuable is the critical assessment of Yuan Chwang's account. Goyal analyses the information that this yields, but instead of accepting it at face value, argues for treating it with caution, keeping in mind the perspective of the author. This strategy enables Goyal to use the material effectively, pointing out the limitations of relying on Yuan Chwang for reconstructing political history, but also highlighting the significance of many of the observations that the Chinese pilgrim made on the economic, social and cultural conditions in the subcontinent. He also weighs the evidence about the religious beliefs of Harsha, to argue for his continued allegiance to Śaivism, even as he extended support to Buddhism and to the Chinese pilgrim. These lead on to an attempt to understand and describe Harsha as a person, an interesting exercise in analyzing a complex personality from the past.

The last set of articles revisit some of the themes laid out in the earlier ones. These include a discussion on the changes and complexities within the social order, where the emergence of *sāmantas* or feudatories led to shifts within the caste categories. Administrative structures, the nature of the army as well as the state of the kingdom under Harsha are also explored, once again through a painstakingly detailed survey of the evidence from a range of sources. Finally, Goyal draws attention to the state of education and the arts during the period under consideration. A set of useful genealogical tables is included, that would enable the curious reader to keep track of the lineages that were significant during the period under study.

Overall, the reader who is interested in this crucial juncture in north Indian history will find much that is of value. Goyal's willingness to engage with the nitty gritty of sources, whether epigraphic, textual or numismatic, enables him to reconstruct an account that is rich in detail. Also in evidence is an acknowledgement of a wide range of historiographical trends; Goyal summarises these with care, and then goes on to present his responses, agreements, and disagreements, which are set out with precision and clarity. These enable further discussions and debates. While Goyal does not shy away from polemics, it is a polemics that is generally tempered with a careful reliance on sources, which enriches the discussion. Students of ancient and early medieval history will benefit from the wide range of themes that have been covered. These range from the details of dynastic history, to reflections on economic changes, social transformation, to cultural developments. Whether or not the readers agree with Goyal's assessment of the significance of these changes, they will find, within this volume resources that will enrich their understanding, and enable a reasoned engagement with the issues that have animated scholarly discussion. This is, therefore, a welcome addition to the volume of scholarship that continues to attract the attention of lay persons as well as those within academic circles, and will be of value to all those who are interested in probing beyond the surface of so-called historical controversies. In enabling readers to understand what is designated as the classical age in all its complexity, Shankar Goyal makes a substantial contribution that is likely to stand the test of time.

February 2021

Kumkum Roy
Professor of History
Centre for Historical Studies
School of Social Sciences
Jawaharlal Nehru University, New Delhi

Author's Preface

The title *The Classical Age : A Study in Feudalization* is used in its widest sense. Besides political histories of the period, it also covers social structure, polity, economy, religion, art, education and ideology. All these are treated in the context of feudalization, suggesting a directional change, and situate the change in its contemporary context. Some of the essays selected for this work were published earlier, and others are being printed for the first time. Though I have revised and updated all the published essays for publication in this book, I could not remove all the repetitions and other defects, for which I crave the indulgence of my readers.

I take this opportunity to thank my friends who have advised me to write this book. To those who took the trouble to read the manuscript and offer their comments I am most grateful. That this monograph carries a foreword from the pen of Professor Romila Thapar, Professor Emerita of History, Jawaharlal Nehru University, New Delhi, is something inestimably precious for me. Her affection and academic encouragement have been great assets of my life for the last three decades or so. Her suggestions have always stimulated my academic thinking which is also reflected in my writings. Needless to say, her dedication to the Indological studies constantly instils in me an urge to work. I would also like to thank Professor Kumkum Roy, Professor of History, Centre for Historical Studies, School of Social Sciences, Jawaharlal Nehru University, New Delhi, for her help throughout. She has also contributed a learned preface to this book. I cannot thank her enough. I am also indebted to Professor K.M. Shrimali, Professor of History (retd.), University of Delhi, Delhi, for his kind courtesy in providing me the material on Hui Chao.

I am equally thankful and obliged to the late Professor R.S. Sharma who was unquestionably one of the best minds of the Indological world. When alive, he was always concerned with my writings, especially on Harsha and the early medieval phase of Indian history, which is evident from his many letters written to me in the last two decades or so.

I also remember with a heavy heart the late Professors A.M. Shastri, an eminent historian of the age of Vākāṭakas, and V.S. Pathak and D. Devahuti, both great authorities on Harsha and his times, who, when alive, always treated me with great affection. To these legends of ancient Indian history, I bow my head with greatest regards.

While writing this preface I remember with a heavy heart my esteemed papa, the late Profesor S.R. Goyal, former Professor and Head, Department of History, Jai Narain Vyas University, Jodhpur, whose scholarly guidance is reflected in every chapter of this work. He was indeed a literary genius, an institution by himself. His loss of life hurts me non-stop. How I wish he were alive today ! With utmost respect I dedicate this work to cherish his memory.

Jodhpur **Shankar Goyal**
January 14, 2021

Contents

Abbreviations

ABORI	*Annals of the Bhandarkar Oriental Research Institute*, Poona.
AHD	*Ancient History of the Deccan*, by G. Jouveau-Dubreuil. Pondicherry, 1920.
AIG	*The Age of the Imperial Guptas*, by R.D. Banerji. Benaras, 1933.
AISIHC	*Ancient India and South Indian History and Culture*, Vol. I, by S. Krishnaswami Aiyangar. Poona, 1941.
AIU	*The Age of Imperial Unity*, ed. by R.C.Majumdar and A.D. Pusalker. Bombay, 1953.
ĀMMK	*Āryamañjuśrīmūlakalpa*, ed. and trans. by K.P. Jayaswal as *An Imperial History of India*. Lahore, 1934.
Arch. Sur. West. Ind./ASWI	*Archaeological Survey of Western India*.
ASI, AR	*Archaeological Survey of India, Annual Reports*.
Aspects	*Aspects of Indian History and Civilization*, by Buddha Prakash. Agra, 1965.
A V	*The Age of the Vākāṭakas*, ed. A.M. Shastri. New Delhi, 1992.
Bayana Hoard	*Catalogue of the Gupta Gold Coins in the Bayana Hoard*, by A.S. Altekar. Bombay, 1954.
BMC, AI	*Catalogue of Coins of Ancient India* (*in the British Museum*), by John Allan. London, 1936.
BMC, GD	*Catalogue of the Coins of the Gupta Dynasties and of Śaśāṅka, King of Gauḍa* (*in the British Museum*), by John Allan. London, 1914.
BSOAS	*Bulletin of the School of Oriental and African Studies*, London.
CA	*The Classical Age*, ed. by R.C. Majumdar and A.D. Pusalker. Bombay, 1962.
Coinage	*The Coinage of the Gupta Empire*, by A.S. Altekar. Varanasi, 1957.

Comp. Hist. Bihar	*A Comprehensive History of Bihar*, Vol. I, ed. by B.P. Sinha. Patna, 1974.
Comp. Hist. Ind.	*A Comprehensive History of India*, Vol. II, ed. by K.A.N. Sastri. Calcutta, 1957; Vol. III, ed. by R.C. Majumdar and K.K. Dasgupta. New Delhi, 1981.
Corpus / CII	*Corpus Inscriptionum Indicarum.*
DKA	*The Purāṇa Text of the Dynasties of the Kali Age*, by F.E. Pargiter. Varanasi, 1962.
Eco. Life	*Economic Life of Northern India in the Gupta Period*, by S. K. Maity. Calcutta, 1958.
EHD	*Early History of the Deccan*, by R.G. Bhandarkar. Poona, 1927.
EHDPP	*Early History of the Deccan : Problems and Perspectives*, by A.M. Shastri. Delhi, 1987.
EHDY	*Early History of the Deccan*, by G. Yazdani. Oxford, 1960.
EHI	*Early History of India*, by V.A. Smith. Oxford, 1957.
EHNI	*Early History of North India*, by S. Chattopadhyaya. Calcutta, 1958.
EI	*Epigraphia Indica.*
GE	*The Gupta Empire*, by R.K. Mookerji. Bombay, 1948.
Giles, Travels	*The Travels of Fa-hsien*, by H.A. Giles. London, 1928.
HB	*Harsha and Buddhism*, by S.R. Goyal. Meerut, 1986.
HC	*Harshacharita*, by Bāṇabhaṭṭa.
HHAH	*History and Historiography of the Age of Harsha*, by Shankar Goyal. Jodhpur, 1992.
HIG	*A History of the Imperial Guptas*, by S.R. Goyal. Allahabad, 1967.
HIL	*A History of Indian Literature*, by M. Winternitz, 3 Vols. Delhi, 1981, 1983, 1985.
Hist. Gup.	*A History of the Guptas*, by R.N. Dandekar. Poona, 1941.
Hist. Ind.	*History of India, 150 A.D. to 350 A.D.*, by K.P. Jayaswal. Lahore, 1933.
HK	*History of Kanauj*, by R.S. Tripathi. Delhi, 1959.
HMHI	*History of Mediaeval Hindu India*, Vol. I, by C.V. Vaidya. Poona, 1921.
HNEI	*The History of North-Eastern India*, by R.G. Basak. Calcutta, 1934.
IA	*Indian Antiquary*, Bombay.
IC	*Indian Culture*, Calcutta.
IE / Ind. Ep.	*Indian Epigraphy*, by D.C. Sircar. Delhi, 1965.
IG	*The Imperial Guptas : A Multidisciplinary Political Study*, by S.R. Goyal. Jodhpur, 2005.

IHQ	*Indian Historical Quarterly*, Calcutta.
IHR	Indian Historical Review, New Delhi.
IMC	*Catalogue of the Coins in the Indian Museum, Calcutta*, Vol. I, by V.A. Smith. Oxford, 1906.
INC	*Indian Numismatic Chronicle*, Patna.
JA	*Journal Asiatique*, Paris.
JAIH	*Journal of Ancient Indian History*, Calcutta.
JAOS	*Journal of the American Oriental Society*, New Haven (U.S.A.).
JAS	*Journal of the Asiatic Society*, Kolkata.
JASB	*Journal and Proceedings of the Asiatic Society of Bengal*, Calcutta.
JBBRAS	*Journal of the Bombay Branch of the Royal Asiatic Society*, Bombay.
JBORS	*Journal of Bihar and Orissa Research Society*, Patna.
JBRS	*Journal of the Bihar Research Society*, Patna.
JESHO	*Journal of the Economic and Social History of the Orient*, Leiden.
JESI	*Journal of the Epigraphical Soceity of India*, Mysore.
JIH	*Journal of Indian History*, Trivandrum.
JNSI	*Journal of the Numismatic Society of India*, Varanasi.
JOI	*Journal of the Oriental Institute*, Baroda.
JOR	*Journal of the Oriental Research*, Madras.
JPS	*Journal of Peasant Studies*, London.
JRAS	*Journal of the Royal Asiatic Society of Great Britain and Ireland*, London.
JRASB(L)	*Journal of the Royal Asiatic Society of Bengal : Letters*, Calcutta.
JUG	*Journal of the University of Gauhati*, Gauhati.
KCMP	*King Chandra and the Meharauli Pillar*, ed. by Munish Chandra Joshi, S.K. Gupta and Shankar Goyal. Meerut, 1989.
Life	*The Life of Hiuen-Tsiang*, by S. Beal. New Delhi, 1973.
MASI	*Memoirs of the Archaeological Survey of India.*
Mbh.	*Mahābhārata.*
NHIP/ VGA	*A New History of the Indian People*, Vol. VI: *The Vākāṭaka-Gupta Age*, ed. by R.C. Majumdar and A. S. Altekar. Lahore, 1946.
Num. Chro. (*NC*)	*Numismatic Chronicle.*
Num. Suppl. (*NS*)	*Numismatic Supplement.*
PHAI	*Political History of Ancient India*, by H. C. Raychaudhuri. Calcutta, 1953.
PIHC	*Proceedings of the Indian History Congress.*

POC	*Proceedings of the All-India Oriental Conference.*
QRHS	*Quarterly Review of Historical Studies*, Calcutta.
Records	*Si-Yü-Ki* or *Buddhist Records of the Western World*, by S. Beal. Delhi, 1969.
Sel. Ins./SI	*Select Inscriptions bearing on Indian History and Civilization*, Vol. I, ed. by D. C. Sircar. Calcutta, 1942.
Studies	*Studies in Indian History and Civilization*, by Buddha Prakash. Agra, 1962.
Suc. Sat. Low. Dec.	*The Successors of the Sātavāhanas in the Lower Deccan*, by D. C. Sircar. Calcutta, 1939.
Travels	*On Yuan Chwang's Travels in India* (A Translation of Hsüan-tsang's *Hsi-Yü-Chi*), by T. Watters. Delhi, 1961.
Vākāṭaka Rājavaṁśa	*Vākāṭaka Rājavaṁśa kā Itihāsa tathā Abhilekha* (in Hindi), by V.V. Mirashi. Varanasi, 1964.
VIJ	*Vishveshvaranand Indological Journal*, Hoshiarpur.
VSH	*Vākāṭakas : Sources and History*, by A.M. Shastri. New Delhi, 1997.

INTRODUCTION

Marxist Histories of the Classical Age and the Debates they Generated

I

A paradigm shift in the understanding of historical change in India was introduced by Marxist interpretations that began as historical debates with B.N. Dutta[1] and S.A. Dange[2], but till the late fifties and sixties it did not get momentum. That is why in the *Historians of India, Pakistan and Ceylon*, published in 1961, A.L. Basham could observe that 'Marxists are only just beginning to study ancient India' and that books of S.A. Dange, Walter Ruben and a few articles by D.D. Kosambi 'are the only significant Marxist contributions to ancient Indian history that I know of (1956)', and in the same work R.S. Sharma could complain that no work on Indian history written with a Marxist approach is included in the bibliographies appended to the volumes on *The History and Culture of the Indian People* published by the Bharatiya Vidya Bhavan.[3] But with the

[1] B.N. Dutta, *Studies in Indian Social Polity*, Calcutta, 1944; idem, *Dialectics of Land Economics in India*, Calcutta, 1952. Taking a long view of the socio-economic developments throughout the ancient period, Dutta spoke at length of the class struggle and growth of feudalism in ancient India.

[2] S.A. Dange, *India from Primitive Communism to Slavery*, Bombay, 1949. It was the first work of some importance on ancient Indian history written with a Marxist approach. But it was not accepted as an authoritative exposition of Marxist interpretation of ancient India, even by Marxist historians. D.D. Kosambi described it as a "painfully disappointing" work, "full of fundamental errors of facts and reasoning that fill the book from cover to cover with endless confusion". In Kosambi's view, "*Because of the caste system, India had helotage not slavery.* Thus, Dange's very title is wrong, for his sources contain neither primitive communism nor slavery." (In *ABORI*, XXIX, 1949, pp. 271-77).

[3] In C.H. Philips, ed., *Historians of India, Pakistan and Ceylon*, London, 1961, pp. 292, n. 93; 114.

arrival of D.D. Kosambi,[4] R.S. Sharma[5] and Romila Thapar,[6] the situation began to change. With the historical writings of Kosambi, in particular, an interest in social and economic history rather than dynastic history alone had been initiated and this was now intensified, calling for a different periodization drawing on social change. With Kosambi, Sharma and Thapar many other Marxist historians, notably D.N. Jha,[7] V.K. Thakur[8] and K.M. Shrimali,[9] began to present their perception of the Gupta age also from various angles, specially from the point of view of the interrelated problems of the rise of feudalism, urban decay and economic decline. On the whole, Marxist historians of ancient India look upon the golden age theory as an utopia set in the distant past to bolster up the nationalist sentiments during the freedom struggle. In the words of Kosambi, "far from the Guptas reviving nationalism, it was nationalism that revived the Guptas."

Probably the most important contribution of the Marxist scholars to classical age has been their attempt to determine how much Vākāṭaka-Gupta polity, society and culture were influenced by feudal tendencies. It has led to a spirited discussion among scholars on the definition of feudalism, its distinguishing features, the validity of the use of the term 'feudalism' in the Indian context and its origin and various phases of its growth. Some historians had viewed feudalism as an agglomeration of institutions connected with the support and service of knights and as a system of law, government and military organisation, the central feature of which would appear to be administrative decentralisation. Indian historians seem to have been influenced by this concept of feudalism when they use feudal terms to describe a situation of parcellized sovereignty.[10] For example, in 1923, H.C. Raychaudhuri compared the *māṇḍalika rājās* of the time of Bimbisāra with the earls and counts of medieval Europe.[11] In 1977, A.S. Altekar

[4] D.D. Kosambi, *An Introduction to the Study of Indian History*, 2nd revised edition, Bombay, 1975; also see his *The Culture and Civilisation of Ancient India in Historical Outline*, 7th edn., New Delhi, 1982.

[5] R.S. Sharma, *Indian Feudalism*, Calcutta, 1965; also see his *Perspectives in Social and Economic History of Early India*, New Delhi, 1983, Chs. 9, 10.

[6] Romila Thapar, *A History of India*, I, Harmondsworth, 1966; idem, *Ancient Indian Social History*, Hyderabad, 1978.

[7] D.N. Jha, ed., *Feudal Social Formation in Early India*, Delhi, 1987. In his Introduction he gives a brief outline of Marxist literature on Indian feudalism.

[8] V.K. Thakur, *Historiography of Indian Feudalism*, Patna, 1989.

[9] K.M. Shrimali, *Agrarian Structure in Central India and the Northern Deccan (A.D. 300-500) : A Study of Vākāṭaka Inscriptions*, New Delhi, 1987.

[10] D.N. Jha, *op.cit.*, p. 29.

[11] H.C. Raychaudhuri, *Political History of Ancient India*, Calcutta, 1923, p. 184.

spoke of the feudatories and feudatory states in ancient India.[12] Earlier in 1967, T.V. Mahalingam identified locally powerful warriors as feudatories paying tribute to the Pallavas in token of their vassalage.[13] All these scholars seem to assume the existence of a decentralised polity as fundamental to feudalism. Obviously, it was in this sense that in 1928 Beni Prasad described the Gupta empire as a 'feudal-federal' organisation.[14]

Against the concept of feudalism as a system of government, Marxist historians have equated the feudal phenomenon with a mode of production based on 'feudal rent' which subsumes the existence of a class of landlords (landed intermediaries), a basic class of producers (peasants) with a special connection with the land which, however, remains the property of the former, and of the overwhelmingly self-sufficient agrarian economy with little scope for the functioning of a market system. The study of feudalism within this frame of reference focuses attention on serfdom and various other forms of constraints on peasant freedom.[15]

II

D.D. Kosambi emerged on the scene of Indian scholarship first as a mathematician and numismatist and then as a Marxist historian. As a Marxist historian he first published some papers which immediately attracted the attention of scholars. Initially in 1956, he came out with his *An Introduction to the Study of Indian History.*[16] Later on, it was supplemented by his *Myth and Reality : Studies in the Formation of Indian Culture*[17] and *The Culture and Civilisation of Ancient India in Historical Outline.*[18] According to him, the simple structure of the closed peasant economy was disturbed during the early centuries of the Christian era when the kings began to transfer their fiscal and administrative rights over land to their subordinate chiefs who thus came into direct relation with peasantry, a process he terms "feudalism from above". It reached an advanced stage of development during the period of the Guptas and Harsha. Kosambi holds that at a later stage "a class of landowners developed within the village between the stage and the peasantry, gradually

[12] A.S. Altekar, *State and Government in Ancient India*, Delhi, 1977, pp. 302-08.

[13] T.V. Mahalingam, *South Indian Polity*, Madras, 1967, pp. 317, 320-23.

[14] Beni Prasad, *The State in Ancient India*, Allahabad, 1928, p. 285.

[15] D.N. Jha, *op.cit.*, p. 30. B.D. Chattopadhyaya (in *Recent Perspectives of Early Indian History*, ed. Romila Thapar, Bombay, 1998, pp. 318-56) has also asserted that the two main concepts which explain the framework of state and economy in north India, from 400-1200 A.D., are 'feudalism' and 'medievalism'. He concedes that it is rather a simplistic generalisation but it dispenses with the conventional ways of periodisation of Indian history.

[16] Bombay, 1956.

[17] Bombay, 1962.

[18] London, 1965.

to wield armed power on the local population"—, a process he calls "feudalism from below".[19] As is obvious the first stage of feudalism envisaged by Kosambi more or less corresponds to the traditional view of feudalism as a system of government. Further, according to him, idelogical background for feudalism was provided by the *Gītā.*

III

R.S. Sharma, who initially wrote a paper on the origins of feudalism in India in 1958, produced his much discussed monograph *Indian Feudalism* in 1965.[20] He does not contest the two stage theory of Kosambi but he apparently does not believe in it. According to Sharma, during the period c. 300-700 A.D., which witnessed the origin and first phase of feudalism, its broad features noticeable were, "the granting of both virgin and cultivated land, the transfer of peasants, the extension of forced labour, the restriction on the movements of the peasants, artisans and merchants, the paucity of coins, the retrogression of trade, the abandonment of fiscal and criminal administration to the religious beneficiaries, the beginnings of remuneration in revenues to officials, and the growth of the obligations of the *sāmantas.*" They appear in the Gupta period, but are especially noticeable from the post-Gupta period onwards.[21]

R.S. Sharma also initiated the theory of an urban decay in the Gupta period. It began with his paper, 'Decay of Gangetic Towns in Gupta and Post-Gupta Times', published in the *Proceedings of the Indian History Congress,* in 1972.[22] Later on it was developed in his work *Urban Decay in India* (c. 300-c. 1000).[23] In its elaborate form the thesis of urban decay envisages two stages in urban decay, the first in the second half of the third or in the fourth century and the second after the sixth century. The urban decline is attributed to several factors such as natural disasters, political changes, foreign invasions, feudal wars and religious preferences. It has also been argued that social crisis as reflected in the description of the Kali

[19] D.N. Jha, *op. cit.*, p. 30. For Kosambi's historiography see D.N. Jha in *Historians and Historiography in Modern India,* ed. S.P. Sen, Calcutta, 1973, pp. 121-32; also articles on him in *Indian Society : Historical Probings in Memory of D.D. Kosambi,* ed. R.S. Sharma in collaboration with D.N. Jha, New Delhi, 3rd edn., 1984; also cf. Romila Thapar, *Readings in Early Indian History,* Oxford, 2013, pp. 21-44; K.M. Shrimali, *Itihāsa, Purātattva aura Vichāradhārā,* Delhi, 2021, pp. 281-96.

[20] R.S. Sharma, 'The Origins of Feudalism in India', *JESHO,* I, Pt. 3, 1958; idem, *Indian Feudalism,* Calcutta, 1965; idem, *Early Medieval Indian Society : A Study in Feudalisation,* Kolkata, 2001. He also wrote several papers on feudalism.

[21] R.S. Sharma, *Indian Feudalism,* pp. 76, 265-67.

[22] In *PIHC,* 33rd Session, 1972, pp. 92-104.

[23] Delhi, 1987; also see V.K. Thakur, *Urbanisation in Ancient India,* New Delhi, 1981.

Age in the third-fourth centuries Purāṇas was an important factor in the urban decline. It is said to have hit the collection of taxes from the peasants, reduced the purchasing powers of town-dwellers, destroyed local markets and undermined artisanal activities in towns. The confirmation of the theory of urban decay is sought in the travel accounts of Fa-hsien and Yuan Chwang, testimony of the *Bṛhatsaṁhitā* and the indications provided by the thinner habitation deposits at the urban sites of the fourth-sixth centuries, as compared with those of the preceding three centuries, the poverty of costly objects such as glass goods, ivory objects, beads of precious and semi-precious items and refined pottery, the poor quality of habitational structures and the use of building material of the earlier period in their construction. The gap between the cultural deposits of the Kushāṇa and Sultanate periods suggests desertion of a town in question.

In his *Ancient India*, published from New Delhi in 1990, R.S. Sharma has expressed his ideas on the golden age model also. But on this question at least here he has, as it were, avoided giving any categorical answer. He observed that the Gupta period is called the golden age of ancient India. This may not be true in the economic field because several towns in north India declined during this period. But the Guptas possessed a large amount of gold, whatever might be its source, and they issued the largest number of gold coins.[24] In matters of detail also Sharma's attitude is different from that of D.N. Jha. He gives the impression of not being dogmatic anywhere. Though he is quite critical of the social inequalities and condition of women, but he also notes the spheres where their condition seems to have improved. He points out to the decline of trade but appreciates the Gupta achievements in the realm of arts and literature.

R.S. Sharma also brought out his *Early Medieval Indian Society : A Study in Feudalisation.*[25] In this work, besides social structure, polity, economy, religion and ideology are also covered. All these are treated in the context of feudalisation. Sharma highlights the feudalisation of the socio-economic structure of India in early medieval times and attributes the rise of land grants to the *varṇa* conflict and the decline of trade. His panoramic sweep takes in the situation of the peasants and he underlines their loss of control over production due to the dominance of landlords. Sharma also examines the traditional *varṇa* system and reveals how it was adjusted to the landed hierarchy. The work also includes a discusion of the influence of tribals on Brāhmaṇism and the proliferation of the Śūdra and other castes. Sharma argues that the presence of landed magnates altered ways of thinking in legal, social and religious matters.

[24] R.S. Sharma, *Ancient India*, New Delhi, 1995, p. 162.
[25] Kolkata, 2001.

IV

Romila Thapar was among the first Marxist historians who expressed their ideas on the golden age issue. She has not written on the Gupta period in detail but she has published a few short discussions on it — two in her own *A History of India*, Vol. I,[26] and *The Penguin History of Early India*,[27] and the other in A.L. Basham's *A Cultural History of India*.[28] Her writings are different from those of other Marxist historians. On feudalism she does not say much. However, she notes the difference in Maurya and Gupta political organisations and the role of land grants in Gupta administration.[29] Unlike D.N. Jha, she does not indulge in provocative comments, and unlike D.D. Kosambi, does not shoot out new ideas as if from a shotgun at the same time running over thousands of years in breathless haste. While D.D. Kosambi uses the terms 'history' and 'culture' in a sense very different from what other historians generally understand by them, Romila Thapar uses the terminology generally acceptable to others. For example, in a recent study she admits that "the classicism of the Gupta period is not an innovation emanating from Gupta rule but the culmination of a process that began earlier."[30] Similar is our view. As shown by us elsewhere, a cultural trend might have a long history before it finally emerges as a definite form and likewise might continue to exist in a changed form for some time even after it has apparently ceased to exist. This being so, we may concede that the age of the Guptas marked the efflorescence and culmination of earlier tendencies, many of which go back to the Maurya period, and that much of its glory continued for about two centuries more after the fall of the Gupta empire.[31]

Romila Thapar also does not seem to share fully R.S. Sharma's perception regarding urban decay in the Gupta age. She observes that with the opening of new routes and the rise in the political status of provinces, cities which had only a local interest now came into prominence. By the time of Harsha, Pāṭaliputra, once the capital of most north Indian dynasties, lost its status, and instead, Kanauj (in western Uttar Pradesh) came to dominate the Ganges plain. Mathurā became a centre both of the textile trade and temples, as also did Banaras. Thanesar acquired a strategic importance, controlling the upper Ganges plain. Hardwar became a centre

[26] Romila Thapar, *A History of India*, I, pp. 133-66.

[27] Romila Thapar, *The Penguin History of Early India*, New Delhi, 2002, pp. 280 ff.

[28] Romila Thapar, 'Aśokan India and the Gupta Age', in *A Cultural History of India*, ed. A.L. Basham, London, 1975, pp. 38-50.

[29] Romila Thapar, *A History of India*, I, pp. 144, 145-46.

[30] Romila Thapar, *Early India*, pp. 281-82.

[31] Shankar Goyal, *Harsha : A Multidisciplinary Political Study*, Jodhpur, 2006, p. 239.

for pilgrimage. It is evident from excavations, where Gupta levels show a greater frequency of better techniques and quality in the objects found, and from descriptions in contemporary literature, that the standard of living was high. The prosperous urban dwellers lived in comfort and ease with a variety of luxuries in the way of jewels and clothes.[32] She also candidly admits that the abundance of copper and iron objects in addition to spouted pottery found in houses would suggest that a degree of comfort in the urban centres at any rate was not restricted to the upper classes alone.[33]

V

M.G.S. Narayanan seeks to turn the theory of Kosambi of the two stage development of feudalism upside down. According to him, "apart from being in disagreement with known facts today, Kosambi's position was also contrary to his professed Marxist view in which the economic order was basic, the political order being a part of the superstructure. Therefore, it goes without saying that Kosambi was taking an un-Marxist position by suggesting that feudalism first developed in the political field and then it appeared in the social and economic fields as a separate phenomenon, if not as a consequence."[34] On the bases of the researches of R.S. Sharma and D.N. Jha, Narayanan has drawn the inference that the "feudal formations in economy and society had already become prevalent though not dominant in the period of imperial Gupta rule. In view of this marked shift in chronology predating the vital feudal tendencies in economy in the context of north India the present writer would also place before the scholarly world for consideration the possibility of reversing Kosambi's order of designating "feudalism from above", i.e., feudal tendencies in the political system, as the first stage and "feudalism from below", i.e., feudal tendencies in economy and society, as the next stage. In the present stage of our knowledge it would be possible to suggest that the feudal political formations reflected in the Allahabad *praśasti* were posterior to and as such reflecting the changes in economy and society starting with the post-Maurya Sātavāhana age."[35]

VI

D.N. Jha emerged as historian of the Gupta period with his *Revenue System*

[32] Romila Thapar, *A History of India*, I, pp. 150-51.

[33] *Ibid.*, p. 151.

[34] M.G.S. Narayanan, in *Śrī Dineśacandrikā*, ed. B.N. Mukherjee et al, Delhi, 1983, p. 293.

[35] *Ibid.*, pp. 289-90. In this para of Narayanan there is some confusion, probably due to oversight, for here Narayanan obviously means that 'feudalism from below' was the first stage (not the next stage, as is said in the para) and 'feudalism from above' the next stage (not the first, as the para reads).

in Post-Maurya and Gupta Times, published from Calcutta in 1967. But his polemics against the golden age model are contained in chapter 7 entitled 'The Myth of the Golden Age' of his *Ancient India : An Introductory Outline* published from New Delhi in 1977.[36] In a Hindi work *Prāchīna Bhārata kā Itihāsa*, published in 1981, his arguments on this topic have also been reproduced in brief in its chapter 12 contributed by Meenakshi Sahaya.[37] Jha attempts to stand the golden age on its head and substitutes it by its counter-image—iron age model. He points out that the eulogy of the Gupta rulers is found only in their epigraphs, especially in the Prayāga *praśasti* of Samudragupta. He further points out that in the nineteenth century, when Prinsep and some other epigraphists and historians studied these epigraphs, nationalist historians deliberately made use of them to prove that the Gupta period was the golden age of Indian history. No extant court drama or poetical work directly refers to any Gupta ruler. In the Purāṇas they are grouped with barbarous (*mlechchhaprāya*) rulers. He argues that due to the emerging feudal conditions in the economic sphere the peasants were reduced to the position of agricultural slaves and were shattered by forced labour, exactions and excessive taxes and that the shrinkage in trade led to the decline of urban centres. However, he uses his choicest barbs against the social and religious institutions of the age. He attacks the general decline in the status of women, the prevalence of several forms of female prostitution, including temple prostitution, the approval of *satī* by several jurists, the proliferation of castes, the increasing degradation of the untouchables, the discrimination in the social order against the Śūdras, the use of religion to legitimise the social inequalities inherent in the *varṇāśramadharma*, and the fact that popular Vaishṇavism—however much it "fulfilled the needs of all sections of society"—also "substituted faith for logic". Jha stresses that the authors of ornate Sanskrit literture patronised by the royal court often found their richest pastures in man's passionate physical love for woman and their works could by no means be understood by the "uneducated masses" and reached their highest expression in theatrical works in which "the leading male characters of high social status—speaks polished Sanskrit and those of low status and all women speak Prakrit." He concedes that Fa-hsien, the Chinese Buddhist pilgrim-scholar, who came to India during the reign of

[36] Its revised and enlarged edition under the title *Ancient India in Historical Outline*, appeared from New Delhi in 1998.

[37] *Prāchīna Bhārata kā Itihāsa*, eds. D.N. Jha and K.M. Shrimali, published by the University of Delhi, 1981, pp. 333-35. On this, also see my paper, 'A Critique of Professor D.N. Jha's Evaluation of the Classicism of the Gupta Age', in *Reappraising Gupta History for S.R. Goyal*, eds. B.Ch. Chhabra, P.K. Agrawala, Ashvini Agrawal and Shankar Goyal, New Delhi, 1992, pp. 61-73. Though we do not support D.N. Jha fully on this issue but there is much substance in his basic idea.

Chandragupta II, tells us that the people were generally happy. But Jha feels that only the upper classes were happy and prosperous, and lived in comfort and ease, as can be judged from the contemporary order. Social inequities and tensions continued and religion was used as an instrument for maintaining the *varṇa* divided society. He sarcastically remarks, "For the upper classes all periods in history have been golden; for the masses none. The truly golden age of the pople does not lie in the past, but in the future."

Jha also raises objections on the question of accepting Gupta culture as 'Hindu' for, he argues, many of its achievements were the contributions of the Buddhist, Jainas (especially in art and literature) and even Greeks and Romans (as in astronomy).

Finally, D.N. Jha builds up the thesis that the Gupta age cannot be described as the golden age of India because it was not an age of intellectual rebirth or revival. In literature and art it merely saw a further development of literary forms and styles which were evolving in earlier periods. The Purāṇas had existed much before the Gupta age; now they were only finally compiled and given their present form. Similarly, basic tenets of Vaishṇavism and Śaivism go back to earlier times; now they merely became more popular. "The much publicised Hindu renaissance (of the Gupta age) was," he concludes, "in reality, not a renaissance, much less a Hindu one."

VII

V.K. Thakur is one of those Marxist historians who have by and large supported the analysis of R.S. Sharma and D.N. Jha on the questions of feudal formation and the description of Gupta period as one of the Hindu renaissance and the golden age of Indian history. His publications include *Urbanisation in Ancient India*,[38] *Historiography of Indian Feudalism*,[39] *Social Dimensions of Technology: Iron in Early India c. 1300-200 B.C.*,[40] *Towns in Pre-Modern India*,[41] *Peasants in Indian History I : Theoretical Issues and Structural Enquiries*,[42] *Science, Technology and Medicine in Indian History*,[43] and *Social Roots of Buddhism*.[44] As early as 1976 Thakur supported the view of D.N. Jha that the much publicised Hindu renaissance was, in reality, not a renaissance, much less a Hindu one. Another historiographical error created by the nationalist historians, he feels, is the

[38] New Delhi, 1981.
[39] Patna, 1989.
[40] Patna, 1993.
[41] ed., Patna, 1994.
[42] ed., Patna, 1996.
[43] ed., Patna, 2000.
[44] Patna, 2000.

concept of golden age in general, and its application to the Gupta period, in particular. The creation of this myth probably had a political justification when we were fighting for our independence, but the same does not hold good for the post-1947 historiography, even that little justification is no longer there. Jha rightly points out that only upper classes had achieved an all-round progress during this period, a fact which is equally true for all periods in history.[45]

On the question of the urban decay in the Gupta age Thakur has come to the conclusion that while most of the towns of the Gandhāra region, Kashmir, Punjab, Haryana, Delhi, Rajasthan, H.P., U.P., and Bihar, which thrived during the Kushāṇa period, either completely decayed or started showing signs of decline in the post-Kushāṇa period while the towns of northern–most Bihar and Bengal continued to thrive. The latter group of town flourished especially during the priod of Pāla supremacy.[46] In 1997, he elaborated his thesis of the urban decay in the core areas of the Gupta empire and the emergence of a different situation in the peripheral regions. The regional context of the urban form from the Gupta period underlines the centrality of the ecological crisis, so poignantly textualised as the *Kaliyuga* crisis in the contemporary texts, in the transition from the ancient to the feudal mode of production. The upper and the middle valleys of Ganga felt the full impact of this crisis, but the peripheries, that had just entered the phase of complex social formations, remained beyond its influences. The exhaustion of the material base of the core area of the civilisation catalysed a process leading to the emergence of regional networks in the erstwhile peripheries. In other words, regions like Bengal, Madhya Pradesh, Gujarat, etc., witnessed the process of state formation and other related developments during this period. This historical reality gets ignored in most of the current writings on this theme as most of these attempts are addressed to the agenda set by R.S. Sharma's construct of Indian feudalism. Obsessive adherence to the deduction of a complete negation of towns as one of the prime variables of this model by most of its opponents wherein the regional specifications are projected as standard practices and even scattered references are blown out of proportion in order to demolish the feudal paradigm. It needs restatement in this context that the evidence for urban continuity in the peripheral zones, instead of negating the emergence of a feudal mode of production in early medieval India, underlines the pattern of regional differentiation, a point that requires better appreciation in the context of attempts to impose a standardised and homogenetic concept of feudalism

[45] V.K. Thakur, 'The Marxist View of Ancient Indian History', in the *Journal of the Bihar Research Society*, Vol. LXII, Pts. 1-4, 1976, pp. 260-61.

[46] V.K. Thakur, *Urbanisation in Ancient India*, p. 295.

on the entire Indian subcontinent.[47]

Thakur has also produced a work on the historiography of Indian feudalism. One of its most interesting portions is appendix II wherein the social roots of the *Gītā* are discussed.[48] Contrary to the generally prevalent view, he suggests that it was composed sometime between 150-350 A.D., "nearer the later then the earlier date probably in order to relate his interpretation of those elements of this text which in his perception are the reflection of feudal tendencies in society with the feudal formation in the Gupta age. Between 150-300 A.D. the tendency of leaving the administration of the donated areas completely in the hands of the beneficiaries which began in earlier period, was further strengthened which paved the way for the feudalisation of not only administrative machinery but the society at large. Thus, by c. 350 A.D., when the *Gītā* was composed, feudal beginnings had been made in India. This text was sung for the upper class with a distinct bias, against the lower orders of the society including woman, Vaiśyas and Śūdras. Thakur argues that the use of the terms such as *mahārathīs* indicates the feudal graded relationship and the description of the war between the Kauravas and Pāṇḍavas as *dharmayuddha* reminds one of the feudal wars known as crusades. The *bhakti* and *śraddhā* doctrines of the *Gītā* involving complete devotion and surrender to the Lord also suited the feudal ideology perfectly which required unflinching loyalty to the overlord. Similarly, the doctrine of *karma*, a deterministic philosophy taught by the *Gītā*, which aimed at maintaining the status quo, breeding helpless submission, illusory happiness even with one's pathetic condition and explaining the lot of the individual by his previous deeds, proved to be a boon for the feudal lords in exploiting the masses without any compuction.

VIII

K. M. Shrimali's work entitled *Agrarian Structure in Central India and the Northern Deccan (c.A.D.300-500): A Study of Vākāṭaka Inscriptions* gives for the first time a systematic study of the economy of the Vākāṭakas on the basis of their inscriptions.[49] Before him only R.S. Sharma has discussed the economy of the Vākāṭakas only briefly. According to Shrimali, the large-scale mechanism of land grants and the absence of money reflect an economy characterized by "burgeoning rural settlements and contraction of urbanism". These features, he argues, lead to the conclusion that "the Vākāṭaka territory was the matrix of the earliest articulated tendencies of

[47] V.K. Thakur, 'Decline or Diffusion : Constructing the Urban Tradition of North India during the Gupta Period', in *The Indian Historical Review*, XXIV, Nos. 1-2, 1997-98, pp. 20-69.

[48] V.K. Thakur, *Historiography of Indian Feudalism*, pp. 104-18.

[49] New Delhi, 1987.

feudal beginnings." Shrimali also provides the cartographic representation of the chronological and geographical distribution of the Vākāṭaka inscriptions, the villages donated, settlements other than donated villages and the geographical configuration of the administrative divisions. The statistical data given in his work is indicative of the fact that in the pre-Pravarasena II phase the concentration of activities was in the eastern half of the dominion while in the Pravarasena II and post-Pravarasena II phases there was a westward expansion. In the Vatsagulma dominion the economy had intimate trade links, whereas the Nandivardhana dominion gave agrarian orientation to the economy. According to Shrimali, the Vākāṭaka settlements, mentioned in defining the boundaries of the donated land, were mostly rural, as indicated by suffixes attached to their names. Further, some of the rural settlements seem to have come up "for the first time under the Vākāṭakas in general and Pravarasena II in particular." Also, excavations are analysed to show a decline in the character of the settlements.

IX

With reference to the Marxist interpretation of the history of Vākāṭakas, we have also produced several papers and a monograph titled *175 Years of Vākāṭaka History and Historiography* with this approach.[50] We have thoroughly investigated Hans T. Bakker's suggestions on the art and culture of the Vākāṭakas and refuse to accept his thesis that the kingdom of the Vākāṭakas is to be seen "on a par with the Gupta world". To us it appears to be somewhat exaggerated proposition. Most historians have accepted the importance of the Vākāṭaka age in central India and the Deccan within the Gupta empire. Even Hans Bakker in his 'Preface' to *The Vākāṭaka Heritage* has categorically stated that at the crossroads of the Indo-Aryan north and Dravidian south, the northern culture of the Gupta kingdom reached the Deccan and developed a character of its own.[51] In our Presidential Address delivered to the XXXVIIth Annual Congress of the Epigraphical Society of India on 24-26 February, 2012, we have examined the feudal nature of Vākāṭaka economy and the question of the existence of their coins.[52] We find it difficult to endorse the views of A.M. Shastri, Hans Bakker, Ellen M. Raven and some others who attribute some copper coins to the Vākāṭakas.

[50] Jodhpur, 2009.

[51] Hans T. Bakker, ed., *The Vākāṭaka Heritage : Indian Culture at the Crossroads*, Groningen, 2004, p. v; also see his *The Vākāṭakas : An Essay in Hindu Iconology*, Groningen, 1997, pp. 2-3.

[52] Shankar Goyal, 'An Investigation into the Feudal Nature of the Vākāṭaka Economy : A Study of the Epigraphic Evidence', my Presidential Address delivered to the XXXVII Annual Congress of the Epigraphical Society of India at M.S. University, Baroda, 24-26, February, 2012, published in the *Journal of the Epigraphical Society of India*, XXXVIII, 2013, pp. 1-38.

Our conclusion is different from Bakker's who finds economic prosperity in the Vākāṭaka kingdom which is not quite visible. A study of the known inscriptions of the Vākāṭakas indicates the comparative paucity of coins resulting in the large-scale mechanism of land grants, growth of small village settlements and relatively declining urban economy.

With regard to the Marxist interpretation of the age of Harsha, there is no full-length study on it. However, we have studied the age of Harsha against the background of the strengthening of feudal tendencies of the seventh century which for the first time became manifest in the Vākāṭaka-Gupta age, or even earlier. Our D.Litt. work *Harsha : A Multidisciplinary Political Study* is essentially a new political biography of Harsha in the light of the decline of classical culture, rise and growth of feudalism and transition to the medieval period.[53]

Political history in our analysis is not a simple study of dynastic changes but a configuration of varying social and economic forces. Thus the rise of the dynasty of Harsha against the background of the twilight of Gupta imperialism and political traditions giving emphasis on the factors that influenced the history of all the major dynasties of this period is a matter of great concern. The major external causes of the decline and fall of the imperial Gupta dynasty were undoubtedly the onslaughts of the Aulikaras of Mandasor and the Hūṇas, but the main internal factors were the rise and growth of feudalism and the impact of the other-worldly pacifist ideology of Buddhism on the dynasty. Actually the political structure of the royal dynasties in north India which arose in the sixth century and continued to dominate the scene in the later centuries was marked by stronger feudal elements than was the case in the earlier period.[54]

Working broadly within the paradigm of Indian feudalism, our another work titled *The 'Medieval' Factor and the Age of Harsha: A Cultural Study*[55] provides an account of society, economy and cultural developments during the reign of Harsha, defining it as a crucial period in the transition to the medieval. While the picture of India in the seventh century did correspond broadly to that of Europe after the decline of the Roman Empire, yet owing to important variations, such as, the presence of caste system in India, Indian feudalism was different in important respects from its European counterpart. There were similarities in the emergence of politcial decentralisation, sub-infeudation of land rights, and regionalisation of culture, while a major

[53] Jodhpur, 2006.

[54] Shankar Goyal, *Harsha Revisited : A Re-interpretation of Existing Data*, Delhi, 2018, p. 5. On this, also see my Presidential Address, Section I : Ancient India, 78th Session, Jadavpur University, Kolkata, 28-30 December, 2017.

[55] Jodhpur, 2016.

point of differences in the absence of serfdom in India by an increasing rigour in the caste system.

Our recent-most study titled *The Significance of Yuan Chwang in the Context of the Seventh Century : A Critical Assessment* [56] not only examines the credibility of the Chinese pilgrim as a source of history, but also discusses his testimony on social organisation and social life, economic life and activities, Indian religions and religious condition, education and learning, and art and literature, taking into consideration the distinctive feature—feudalism—of the age wheresoever possible.

How far Yuan Chwang's observations about the social organisation and social life of the Indians, in general, correspond to the growing rigidity of the social hierarchy and other social dogmas of feudal age have been our major concern. This brings to light that Yuan Chwang, though not concerned to explain the changing social patterns under Indian feudalism in its technical terms, has definitely referred to the growing stagnation and confinement of social status of the people of India with the practice of intercaste marriages and abstention from inter-dining with the peoples of different castes, particularly with lower castes, and also that communities who were considered outcasts not allowed to interact directly with the persons belonging to so-called upper castes. On the other hand, Yuan Chwang has also gone on to mention about the upward social mobility in the political domain, as he observes that though the rulers belonged to the Kshatriya caste only there could be persons of any caste rising to the status of kingship, as was the case with the Pushyabhūtis itself and a Śūdra king in Sindh. Then he also gives indication of the growing merger of the Vaiśya community with the Śūdras, as both are said to have engaged in agriculture, a feature which has been generally understood by many a scholar in terms of increasing rights of the Śūdras in the growing feudal scenario.

One of the major feudal characteristics of the economy is reflected in Yuan Chwang's admiration of great grants to the Brāhmaṇas and other religious recluses and institutions as well as to the administrative retinue in the form of land or village grants. Though all this was said in praise of Harsha but Yuan Chwang's descriptions are more than a testimony also of the feudal character of kingship more concerned with fanfare and show business than genuine build up of infrastructure for the economic growth and general prosperity of the people. From all what Yuan Chwang has narrated about allocations from the royal exchequer, the nature of Harsha's military expeditions and the great religious assembly at Kanauj and also the quinquennial grants and gifting at Prayāga it is amply displayed that all

[56] Delhi, 2018.

these were more an extravaganza and personal aggrandizement on the part of the emperor telling much upon the state treasury and implying serious economic distress at the end.

X

Thus, Marxist histories of the Gupta age have brought to focus the interrelated problems of the rise and growth of feudalism, golden age theory, urban decay and economic decline. Though the conclusions about the existence of feudalism in the Gupta age have been contested by D.C. Sircar[57] and some others, now even non-Marxist historians tacitly assume the emergence of some sort of feudalistic structure in the Gupta age. For example, in 1965, Buddha Prakash[58] spoke of the struggle between the merchants and the landed aristocracy in the fifth century and of the ultimate victory of the latter. In 1967, S.R. Goyal[59] also spoke of the rise of a class of the Brāhmaṇa feudatories which came into existence as a result of the practice of giving land grants to the Brāhmaṇas (and also to the temples, monasteries, civil servants and private individuals) as a factor in the decline of the Gupta empire.

The Marxist histories also reinforced the case of the critics of the golden age model. The arguments of the Marxist historians have been answered by many non-Marxist historians believing in the golden age model;[60] but the significant point here is that just as the people of the Gupta age such as Kālidāsa were dazzled by the cultural progress and the appearance of gold coinage in their society, we modern historians are no less overwhelmed by the fact that one of our ancient dynasties ushered in a veritable golden age in our country. But in our enthusiasm we generally overlook the limitations of this achievement of the Gupta age. We usually forget that the gold coinage of the Guptas is really not so abundant. Leaving aside sporadic finds we have so far only about 20 hoards, only one of which, namely the Bayana hoard, originally contained about 2100 coins. Other hoards have yielded only about *650 coins in all*! These figures appear impressive against the 'no gold coinage' numismatic impression of ancient India but are woefully meagre if we compare them with the finds of the gold coins of the Roman and other ancient empires. Probably, more gold coins of

[57] D.C. Sircar, *Landlordism and Tenancy in Ancient and Medieval India as Revealed by Epigraphical Records*, Lucknow, 1969, pp. 32-38; idem, *Political and Administrative Systems*, Delhi, 1974, p. 32.

[58] Buddha Prakash, *Aspects of Indian History and Civilization*, Agra, 1965, Ch. 1.

[59] S.R. Goyal, *A History of the Imperial Guptas*, Allahabad, 1967, pp. 299-301.

[60] E.g., for example, Lallanji Gopal, Xinru Liu, A.M. Shastri, T.P. Verma and M.K. Dhavalikar. Vide my *Contemporary Interpreters of Ancient India*, Jaipur, 2003, pp. 256 ff.

Rome have been found in India alone than the total number of gold coins of the imperial Guptas themselves. This fact assumes further significance if we recall that so far only one gold coin of the imperial Guptas has been found outside the frontiers of India—it was found from Java. All this goes against the supposed affluence of a society which, it is believed, was enjoying unprecedented prosperity.

The theory that a general trend of decline in urban life took place in the later part of the Gupta age cannot be dismissed altogether.[61] As has been mentioned earlier, it is suggested by the thinner habitational deposits of the fourth-sixth centuries as compared with those of the preceding three centuries, the poverty of costly objects such as glass goods, ivory objects, beads of precious and semi-precious stones and refined pottery, the poor quality of habitational structures and the use of building material of the earlier period in their construction, *but above all by the decline of the Gupta coinage after Skandagupta.* In the heartland of the Gupta empire evidence of urban decay can be seen at many places. For example, at Vaiśālī the Gupta structures are less impressive than those of the earlier period. So is the case with Pāṭaliputra (modern Patna). When Yuan Chwang came to India, the city had already dwindled to a village. Vārāṇasī also showed evidence of decline during the Gupta age.

The urban decay, which resulted in the decline of the Gupta gold coinage is usually explained as having been caused by the decline of India's long distance trade. The inflow of Roman coins stopped after the early Christian centuries and the Roman empire itself crumbled a little later. Trade with the Eastern Roman (Byzantine) empire continued until about the middle of the sixth century. Around this time the Byzantines learnt from the Chinese the art of growing silk worms. This adversely affected India's commercial contacts with the West. According to Ptolemy, in the international economic life of the sixth century the Byzantine empire played a role so important that all the nations carried on their trade in Roman *nomisma.* This Roman *nomisma* was regarded with approval by all men to whatsoever kingdom they belonged since there was no other country in which the like of it existed. Even the king of Ceylon honestly conceded the superiority of the Roman *nomisma* to the Persian *drachma.* This was in sharp contrast to what was happening with the Gupta gold currency.

The economic decline in the later part of the Gupta age is usually explained in terms of the emergence of feudal tendencies. As pointed out by R.S. sharma, during the period 300-700 A.D. which witnessed the origins and first phase of feudalism, its certain broad featuers were : "the granting

[61] Cf. my *The 'Medieval' Factor and the Age of Harsha : A Cultural Study*, Ch. 1.

of both virgin and cultivated land, the transfer of peasants, the extension of forced labour, the restriction on the movements of the peasants, artisans and merchants, the paucity of coins, the retrogression of trade, the abandonment of fiscal and criminal administration to the religious beneficiaries, the beginnings of remuneration in revenues to officials, and the growth of the obligations of the *sāmantas*." They appeared in the Gupta age, but were particularly noticeable from the post-Gupta period.

From the point of view of material prosperity the Pushyabhūti empire also presents a very dismal picture. As is well known, Harsha is regarded as a great conqueror of early India and is known to have issued gold coins as well, but so far only one gold coin of his has been found, despite the fact that he ruled for at least four decades. Both Bāṇa and Yuan Chwang say nothing about the grandeur of the cities of his empire. In the accounts of Yuan Chwang as well as of Bāṇa the royal palace of the Pushyabhūtis is hardly mentioned. The religious assembly at Kanauj was also held probably in a wooden pavilion for it caught fire suddenly. In his travels Harsha used to stay in grass huts. Gold coins are indeed mentioned especially by the Chinese pilgrim, but mostly in connection with charity or when these were given as gift to Yuan Chwang himself.

ONE

Vākāṭaka Historiography : From the Stage of a Chronological, Dynastic Study to the Study of Agrarian Expansion and State Formation under the Main Branch

I

The imperial Guptas (from the last quarter of the third century to the middle of the fifth century A.D.) and the Vākāṭakas (from the middle of the third century to the last decade of the fifth or the beginning of the sixth century) are probably the greatest beneficiaries of the modern epigraphical researches. But till the early years of the nineteenth century the Vākāṭakas were altogether unknown; even their name had not come to light. Their existence was revealed for the first time when the Siwani grant of Pravarasena II was discovered in Madhya Pradesh in 1836.[1] Vindhyaśakti, the founder of the dynasty, has indeed been mentioned in the Purāṇas,[2] but owing to textual misconstruction, he was believed to have belonged to the Yavana or Greek race. Even as late as 1862, after the decipherment of the inscription in Ajanta Cave XVI, which gives the genealogy of the Vākāṭakas (of the Basim branch, the separate existence of which was not known at that time) from the earliest times to the last king Harisheṇa, Bhau Daji remarked that 'the Vākāṭakas were a dynasty of the Yavanas or Greeks'.[3] It was probably the reason why there is not a single word about the Vākāṭaka dynasty in the *Early History of the Deccan* of R.G. Bhandarkar, first published in 1884. Later on, it was noted that the founder of the dynasty has been described in an inscription as a *dvija* which usually means a Brāhmaṇa. It was also noted that the *gotra* of the family was Vishṇuvṛddha, a Brāhmaṇa *gotra*, and that Pravarasena I performed some

[1] *JASB*, V, 1836, pp. 726-27.

[2] Cf. F.E. Pargiter, *The Purāṇa Text of the Dynasties of the Kali Age*, London, 1913, pp. 49-50.

[3] *JBBRAS*, VII, 1861-63, pp. 69-70.

sacrifices which were exclusively meant for the Brāhmaṇas. Thus, it was well-established that the Vākāṭakas were not Yavanas but a Hindu dynasty of the Brāhmaṇa origin.

The period during which the Vākāṭakas flourished also remained uncertain for a long time. Unlike the Guptas, they did not start any era but dated their grants in regnal years.[4] Their age had, therefore, to be conjectured from the script of their inscriptions. Almost all the Vākāṭaka grants are incised in box-headed characters, which soon became stereotyped. But early scholars differed on the question of their general period. For example, Bühler[5] referred to the Vākāṭaka grants to the fifth century A.D. while Fleet[6] and Kielhorn,[7] whose opinion Sukthankar cited with approval,[8] assigned them to the eighth century. The latter view was based on the identification of *Mahārājādhirāja* Devagupta, the maternal-grandfather of Pravarasena II mentioned in the Vākāṭaka grants, with *Mahārājādhirāja* Devagupta of Magadha, the son of Ādityasena, mentioned in the Deo-Baranark inscription, who flourished towards the close of the seventh century. The Vākāṭakas were, therefore, believed to have ruled in the seventh and eighth centuries. However, the Poona plates of Prabhāvatīguptā, discovered in 1912, which K. N. Dikshit first briefly noticed in the *Indian Antiquary* [9] and later on edited fully in the *Epigraphia Indica* explicitly mention that Prabhāvatīguptā, the chief-queen of the Vākāṭaka king Rudrasena II and mother of the crown-prince Divākarasena, was the daugther of the Gupta *Mahārājādhirāja* Chandragupta II (known dates 376-412 A.D.).[10] This evidence has placed the Vākāṭaka chronology on a sound basis and proved that Pravarasena II must have flourished sometime in the early decades of the fifth century. Armed with these facts V.A. Smith, who had not written a single line on this dynasty in his *Early History of India* (third edn., published in 1914), wrote a long article 'The Vākāṭaka Dynasty of Berar in the Fourth and Fifth Centuries'

[4] The theory that the Chedi era starting in 248-49 A.D. marks the establishment of the Vākāṭaka power (K.P. Jayaswal, *History of India : 150 A.D. to 350 A.D.*, Lahore, 1933, pp. 108-11; Govind M. Pai, 'Genealogy and Chronology of the Vākāṭakas', *JIH*, XIV, 1935, 1-26, pp. 165-204), if correct would had given us a fixed starting point; but the untenability of the theory is proved by the fact that not a single Vākāṭaka inscription is dated in this era; all of them refer to the regnal years of the grantors.

[5] *ASWI*, IV, 1883, p.119.

[6] *Corpus Inscriptionum Indicarum*, Vol. III : *Inscriptions of the Early Gupta Kings and Their Successors*, Calcutta, 1888, Intro., p. 15.

[7] *EI*, III, 1894-95, pp. 258-62.

[8] *Ibid.*, XVII, 1923-24, pp. 12-14.

[9] *IA*, XLI, 1912, pp. 214-15.

[10] *EI*, XV, 1919-20, pp. 39-44.

in the *Journal of the Royal Asiatic Society* (1914), setting forth the available evidence of copper-plate grants and stone inscriptions, and giving a history of the dynasty based on it.[11] Later on, J. Dubreuil[12] and H. Heras[13] threw more light on the history of this royal family. On the importance of the dynasty Dubreuil opined:

> Of all the dynasties of the Deccan that have reigned from the third to the sixth century, the glorious, the most important, the one that must be given the place of honour, the one that has excelled all others, the one that has the greatest influence on the civilization of the whole of the Deccan is unquestionably the illustrious dynasty of the Vākāṭakas.[14]

II

It was, however, K. P. Jayaswal who in his book *History of India, 150 A.D. to 350 A.D.* (1933) to which he gave the significant name 'Nāga-Vākāṭaka Imperial Period', brought the Vākāṭaka dynasty into prominence. Since then it has been realized by scholars that a major part of the history of the Vākāṭakas is the history of their relations with the imperial Guptas. Jayaswal was highly critical of the view of Smith who had, in the last edition (1924), as well as in the earlier editions of his *Early History of India*, declared :

> The period between the extinction of the Kushān and Āndhra dynasties, about A.D. 220 or 230, and the rise of the imperial Gupta dynasty, nearly a century later, is one of the darkest in the whole range of Indian history.[15]

Commenting on the opinion of Smith, Jayaswal declared :

> The statement that there was no paramount power before the Imperial Guptas is thoroughly incorrect and cannot be maintained for a moment. The history of the Imperial Hindu revival is not to be dated in the fourth century with Samudra Gupta, not even with the Vākāṭakas nearly a century earlier, but with the Bhāra Śivas half a century earlier still.[16]

Jayaswal tried to show that imperial rule and paramount sovereignty had been in the hands and the keeping of the Vākāṭakas for full sixty years before Samudragupta.[17] According to him, Pravarasena I evolved a clear political thesis:

> His thesis was a Hindu Empire for the whole of India and enthronement of the śāstras. Secondly, a great literary movement in favour of Sanskrit begins

[11] *JRAS*, 1914, pp. 314-15.

[12] J. Dubreuil, *Ancient History of the Deccan*, trans. from French by V.S.S. Dikshitar, Pondicherry, 1920, pp. 71-72.

[13] H. Heras, 'Relations between Guptas, Kadambas and Vākāṭakas', *JBORS*, XII, 1926, pp. 455-65.

[14] Dubreuil, *op.cit.*, p. 71.

[15] V.A. Smith, *Early History of India*, Oxford, 1924, p. 292.

[16] Jayaswal, *op. cit.*, p. 4.

[17] *Ibid.*, p. 5.

> about 250 A.D. and in fifty years reaches a pitch at which the Guptas take it up. ... Thirdly, revival of *Varṇāśrama dharma* and Hindu orthodoxy is emphasized very pointedly; it was the cry of the time. The society under the Vākāṭaka imperialism was seeking to purge the abuses crept in under the Kushan rule. It was a Hindu Puritan Movement which was greatly fostered, and which received a wide imperial implication under Pravarasena I. ... Fourthly, under the Vākāṭakas the art of sculpture and the graphic art of Ajaṇṭā which lay under their direct government, were vivified. ... The credit of this revival of Hindu art which had been universally attributed by the present-day writers wholly to the Guptas, like the credit of Sanskrit revival, really belongs to the Vākāṭakas.[18]

Many of Jayaswal's suggestions about the Nāgas, Vākāṭakas and Pallavas have now been shown by sober criticism to be untenable. His theory of the empire of Samudragupta being just a take over of the Nāga-Vākāṭaka empire overlooked the contents of the Allahabad pillar inscription which clearly show that Samudragupta did not face any empire but actually a congeries of states in the Gangetic Valley.[19] But there can be no doubt that Jayaswal's powerful advocacy of the Vākāṭakas made the modern historians investigate the achievements of this dynasty more intensively.

Further progress in the knowledge of the history of the Vākāṭakas was made in 1939 when the Basim grant of the Vākāṭaka ruler Vindhyaśakti II came to light which was edited by V.V. Mirashi.[20] It showed for the first time that after Pravarasena I the Vākāṭaka kingdom was divided into at least two parts, northern (ruled by Pravarasena I's grandson Rudrasena I and his successors) and southern (ruled by Pravarasena I's younger son Sarvasena and his successors). Consequently, it was proved that the genealogy of the Vākāṭakas as given in the inscription of Ajanta Cave XVI was the genealogy of the Basim branch.

III

In 1941 S. K. Aiyangar published a collection of his papers giving a detailed history of the Vākāṭakas, specially with reference to the Vākāṭaka-Gupta relations.[21] He was of the opinion that king 'Chandra' mentioned in the Meharauli iron pillar inscription was no other than Chandragupta I and consequently the first Gupta *Mahārājādhirāja* was the paramount ruler of

[18] *Ibid.*, pp. 95-97.

[19] B.P. Sinha, in *Historians and Historiography in Modern India*, ed. S.P. Sen, Calcutta, 1973, p. 93.

[20] *EI*, XXVI, 1941-42, pp. 137-55.

[21] S.K. Aiyangar, *Ancient India and South Indian History and Culture*, Vol. I, Poona, 1941, pp. 91-92. Cf. also his article 'The Vākāṭakas and Their Place in the History of India', *ABORI*, V, 1924, pp. 31-54.

almost the whole of India. His views on the early history of the Vākāṭakas were vitiated by this basic presumption.

IV

In 1946 was published *A New History of the Indian People*, Vol. VI *(The Vākāṭaka-Gupta Age)*, edited by R.C. Majumdar and A.S. Altekar, which contains a detailed chapter entitled 'The Vākāṭakas' written by Altekar himself. In this work Majumdar and Altekar tried to rationalize the exaggerated claims of Jayaswal regarding the achievements of the Vākāṭakas. They state :

> The title of the volume was selected for the sake of convenience only. It is not claimed that the political or cultural achievements of the Vākāṭakas were comparable to those of the Guptas and sufficiently important to justify their association with the name of the age.[22]

But the chapter of A. S. Altekar in *The Vākāṭaka-Gupta Age*, written with what may be described as nationalist approach, was a landmark in the Vākāṭaka historiography. It was the first detailed and systematic exposition of the chronology, genealogy and history of the Vākāṭakas. He rightly rejected Jayaswal's suggestion that the Kalachuri-Chedi era was founded by the Vākāṭaka king Vindhyaśakti I. The scheme of the Vākāṭaka chronology suggested by Altekar[23] has generally been adopted with minor modifications by other scholars except R. C. Majumdar and D. C. Sircar. A. S. Altekar opposed Jayaswal's theory regarding the original home of the Vākāṭakas and opined that the village Vakāṭa, to which they originally belonged, was rather to the south than to the north of the Vindhyas. He also did not agree with Jayaswal's view that Pravarasena I was the lord paramount of almost the whole of India and Chandragupta I, and in the beginning even Samudragupta, were his feudatories. He also vehemently opposed Jayaswal's view that Samudragupta defeated and killed Rudrasena I Vākāṭaka[24] but supported the theory of considerable Gupta influence on the Vākāṭaka court during the regency of Prabhāvatīguptā. According to him, during the reign of Narendrasena the Vākāṭakas were invaded and defeated by the Nalas of South Kosala, but very soon recovered the lost ground so much so that the king of Mekalā and

[22] *A New History of the Indian People*, Vol. VI: *The Vākāṭaka-Gupta Age*, Lahore, 1946, Editorial Preface, p. ix.

[23] According to Altekar, Vindhyaśakti I ascended the throne in *circa* 255 A.D., Pravarasena I in *circa* 275, Rudrasena I in *circa* 335, Pṛthivīsheṇa I in *circa* 360 and Rudrasena II in *circa* 385. After him Prabhāvatīguptā ruled as regent upto *circa* 410, and then Pravarasena II ruled upto *circa* 440, Narendrasena upto *circa* 460 and Pṛthivīsheṇa II upto *circa* 480.

[24] Cf. also his papers 'Were the Vākāṭakas Defeated by the Guptas in *circa* 350 A.D.?', *IC*, IX, 1942-43, pp. 99-106; 'Some Alleged Nāga and Vākāṭaka Coins', *JNSI*, V, 1943, pp. 111-34.

the Gupta feudatory of Mālava region accepted his suzerainty. His son Pṛthivīsheṇa II faced the invasion of the Traikūṭakas successfully. Altekar also gave an outline of the history of the Basim branch of the Vākāṭakas.[25]

V

In 1947 R. C. Majumdar published a significant paper in which he proposed quite different dates for the accession of Pṛthivīsheṇa I (*circa* 375 A.D.), Rudrasena II (*circa* 400 A.D.), Divākarasena (*circa* 420 A.D.), Dāmodarasena (*circa* 435 A.D.), Pravarasena II (*circa* 450 A.D.), Narendrasena (*circa* 480 A.D.) and Pṛthivīsheṇa II (*circa* 505 A.D.).[26] This chronology is based on the evidence of the Rithapur plates issued in the nineteenth regnal year of Pravarasena II, which describe the dowager-queen Prabhāvatīguptā as *sāgra-varsha-śata-diva-putra-pautrā*. According to Majumdar, this passage means that Prabhāvatīguptā lived for more than a hundred years and had sons and grandsons living at that time. If she lived for more than hundred years she must have survived her brother Kumāragupta I whose reign came to an end in 455 A.D. According to Majumdar, this fact is quite significant, for it implies that Prabhāvatīguptā was born not later than 365 A.D., that Pravarasena I ascended the throne not much before 440 A.D. and that Prabhāvatīguptā became a widow in *circa* 420 A.D. when she was not less than 55. Hence, the generally accepted view that Rudrasena II died in *circa* 390 A.D. during the life-time of the Gupta emperor Chandragupta II is not correct. On the basis of his chronology of these Vākāṭaka rulers Majumdar determined the date of Vindhyaśakti I, the founder of the dynasty, as 250 A.D. and put the reign of its last king Pṛthivīsheṇa II between 505 and 540 A.D. Majumdar also opines that Prabhāvatīguptā had three sons : Divākarasena (420 A.D.) for whom Prabhāvatīguptā ruled as regent for at least 13 years, Dāmodarasena (*circa* 435 A.D.) who ruled before Pravarasena II and Pravarasena II himself. D. C. Sircar[27] has followed Majumdar closely but has placed the death of Rudrasena II in *circa* 400 A.D. and the reign of Pravarasena II in the middle of the fifth century A.D. In between he places the period of the regency of Prabhāvatīguptā and a 'fairly long reign' of Dāmodarasena.[28]

[25] A. S. Altekar also wrote a chapter on the Vākāṭakas in *The Early History of the Deccan*, ed. by G. Yazdani, Oxford University Press, London, 1960. Its account of the political history of the Vākāṭakas is essentially similar to the one given in *The Vākāṭaka-Gupta Age*.

[26] *JRASB (L)*, XII, 1947, pp. 1-5.

[27] *Ibid.*, pp. 71-72; *ibid.*, XIII, ii, 1947, pp. 75-79; *Select Inscriptions*, Vol. I, Calcutta, 2nd edn., 1965, p. 440, n. 2 and 3; *The History and Culture of the Indian People*, Vol. III: *The Classical Age (CA)*, Bombay, 1954, pp. 180-81.

[28] In *Political History of Ancient India* H. C. Raychaudhuri briefly discusses the relations of the Gupta emperors with their contemporary Vākāṭaka kings. At least, that is the position

VI

1954 saw the publication of another edited work entitled *The History and Culture of the Indian People*, Vol. III : *The Classical Age* by R. C. Majumdar and A. D. Pusalker in which D.C. Sircar gave a systematic exposition of his studies on the Vākāṭakas in the chapter 'Deccan in the Gupta Age'. The importance of his chapter lies in the fact that it reconstructs the history of the Vākāṭakas on the basis of the chronology adopted by Majumdar and Sircar. According to Sircar, the fact that the family is not called *Samrāḍ-Vākāṭaka* with reference to any ruler after Pravarasena I may be due to the waning of their power as a result of the division of the empire.[29] But he does not believe that Rudrasena I was defeated by Samudragupta. "It is possible", he opines, "that Rudrasena I flourished before the victorious advance of Samudragupta in central India."[30] But he accepts that "it is not improbable that the Vākāṭaka king (that is, Pṛthivīsheṇa I) was ousted from his central Indian possessions by the Guptas and that he contracted the matrimonial alliance in order to stem the tide of Gupta advance towards the Deccan."[31] He also accepts the possibility that the Guptas received considerable help from the Vākāṭakas against the Śakas.[32]

VII

In 1955 K. A. Nilakanta Sastri gave a brief history of the Vākāṭakas in his *A History of South India*.[33] Both in respect of chronology and history he broadly followed the outline of Altekar. For example, he believed that Rudrasena I was helped by Bhavanāga in his internal troubles, that the conquests of Samudragupta did not affect the Vākāṭakas, that the Guptas contracted matrimonial alliance with the Vākāṭakas to strengthen the Gupta position 'in execution of their plans against the Śakas', that Prabhāvatī gave considerable help to her father in the Śaka war, and so on.[34]

---

in the sixth edition of the work published by the University of Calcutta in 1953. As the earlier editions of this work published respectively in 1923, 1927, 1931, 1938 and 1950 are not easily available, it is very difficult to know his earlier views on the subject.

[29] *CA*, p. 177.

[30] *Ibid.*, p. 178.

[31] *Ibid.*, pp. 179-80.

[32] *Ibid.*, p.180.

[33] K.A.N. Sastri, *A History of South India*, Madras, 1966, pp. 107-10. For a critical assessment of K.A.Nilakanta Sastri's contribution to ancient Indian history vide Shankar Goyal, 'Historiography of Professor K.A. Nilakanta Sastri', in *Journal of Indian History and Culture*, Vol. XII, Chennai, 2005, pp. 36-50.

[34] Also see Shankar Goyal, *Recent Historiography of Ancient India*, Jodhpur, 1997, p. 408.

VIII

In 1957 V. V. Mirashi produced his Marathi work entitled *Vākāṭaka Nṛpati āṇi Tyāṁcha Kāḷa* of which an enlarged English version was published in 1963 under the title *Inscriptions of the Vākāṭakas (Corpus Inscriptionum Indicarum,* Vol. V*)*. Mirashi's *Corpus* represented the cream of his deep study of the Vākāṭaka history and epigraphy. In it he has given a brilliant study of twenty-seven Vākāṭaka epigraphs along with a detailed introduction containing the political and cultural history of the dynasty. The scheme of the Vākāṭaka chronology as given by Mirashi[35] generally agrees with that fixed by Altekar and differs from the one suggested by Majumdar and Sircar. Mirashi was opposed to Jayaswal's suggestion that the Vākāṭakas were a north Indian dynasty and tried to prove that their original home lay in southern India. On the Vākāṭaka-Gupta relations his views are nearer to those of Altekar. According to him, as a result of the conquests of Samudragupta in the eastern Deccan Rudrasena I's kingdom came to be confined to northern Vidarbha which lay between the Narmadā and the Indhyādri range. As Mirashi puts it :

> Though Rudrasena I's kingdom was thus much reduced in size, he maintained his independence and did not submit to the mighty Gupta Emperor. Perhaps Samudragupta, like Alexander, grew wiser by the resistance he encountered in his southern campaign, and avoided a direct conflict with the Vākāṭaka king. He may also have thought it prudent to have friendly relations with his southern neighbour who occupied a strategic position with regard to the kingdom of the powerful Western Kshatrapas, whom he had not yet subdued. In any case, there are no signs of Gupta supremacy in the Vākāṭaka records of the age.[36]

Mirashi also agreed with the view originally propounded by Smith that Chandragupta II had sought the alliance of the Vākāṭakas against the Western Kshatrapas and cemented it by giving his daughter Prabhāvatīguptā in marriage to the Vākāṭaka prince Rudrasena II. The combined strength of the Guptas and the Vākāṭakas was sufficient to wipe out the Western Kshatrapas. On the history of Prabhāvatīguptā's regency, the reign of Pravarasena II and his successors as well as the history of the Basim branch his views differ from those of Altekar only slightly. However, he has tried to show that Daṇḍin's *Daśakumāracharita* "appears to have preserved a living tradition about the last period of Vākāṭaka rule."[37]

[35] Mirashi gives the following genealogy (with the approximate dates of accession): Vindhyaśakti (250 A.D.), Pravarasena I (270 A.D.), Rudrasena I (330 A.D.), Pṛthivīsheṇa I (350 A.D.), Rudrasena II (400 A.D.), Divākarasena (405 A.D.), Dāmodarasena-Pravarasena II (420 A.D.), Narendrasena (450 A.D.) and Pṛthivīsheṇa II (470 A.D.).

[36] *Corpus Inscriptionum Indicarum*, Vol. V : *Inscriptions of the Vākāṭakas*, Ootacamund, 1963, p. xxii.

[37] *Ibid.*, p. xxxii.

IX

In 1967 S. R. Goyal critically examined the Gupta-Vākāṭaka relations in his celebrated doctoral work entitled *A History of the Imperial Guptas*. In 1969 he produced another work in Hindi entitled *Gupta evaṁ Samakālīna Rājavaṁśa* in which he gave a detailed account of the political history of the Vākāṭakas in over forty pages (its revised version under the title *Gupta aura Vākāṭaka Sāmrājyoṅ kā Yuga* appeared in 1988). As regards the Vākāṭaka chronology, Goyal, with minor modifications, supports Altekar's scheme and gives several new arguments to prove its correctness. But his reconstruction of the history of the Vākāṭakas is significantly different from that of Altekar and Mirashi in several respects. He has criticised both Mirashi and Altekar on the question of the original home of the Vākāṭakas. He has pointed out that there could not have been any connection between the 'Vākāṭaka householder' of the Amarāvatī inscription and the royal dynasty of the Vākāṭakas. He has also pointed out that the titles and the technical terms found in the Vākāṭaka records, to which attention has been drawn by Mirashi, are all found only in the epigraphs of the Basim branch which flourished in the south and was greatly influenced by the southern traditions; they are conspicuous by their absence in the records of the main branch. Therefore, if it is argued that the occurrence of such titles and technical terms proves the southern origin of the Vākāṭakas, then why their absence in the records of the main branch should not be regarded as a proof of their northern origin?[38]

Goyal gives a new interpretation of the phrase *Bhavanāga-dauhitra* occurring for Rudrasena I in the Vākāṭaka records to show that Bhavanāga and Pravarasena I had forged a scheme by which after them the Nāga and Vākāṭaka kingdoms were to merge and Rudrasena I was to succeed both of them, just as in the north Samudragupta, the *Lichchhavi-dauhitra*, was designated as the successor of both Chandragupta I and the Lichchhavi chief, the father of Kumāradevī. Says Goyal :

> ...as is well-known, Gautamīputra predeceased his father Pravarasena I, for we find that the latter was succeeded by Rudrasena I, the son of Gautamīputra. It is very curious, because after the demise of Gautamīputra Pravarasena I should have been succeeded by the eldest of his remaining three sons,... No scholar has so far felt the necessity to explain this rather unusual fact. We, however, feel that its explanation lies in the correct interpretation of the phrase *Bhavanāga-dauhitra* used for Rudrasena I... Manu says that *dauhitra*, in the absence of (natural) son, inherits the whole property and offers *piṇḍas* both to the natural father and maternal grandfather (if he adopts him as subsidiary son of *dauhitra* category). ... It

[38] S.R. Goyal, *Gupta evaṁ Samakālīna Rājavaṁśa*, Allahabad, 1969, pp. 345-46.

> makes it quite reasonable to believe that in the beginning of the fourth century A.D. Bhavanāga, who probably did not have a male issue to succeed him, gave his daughter in marriage to Gautamīputra, the Vākāṭaka crown-prince, on the understanding that his (Bhavanāga's) daughter's son would be his subsidiary son of *dauhitra* category. Pravarasena I readily accepted his proposal,... (and) when his son Gautamīputra died a premature death, he nominated Rudrasena I, the son of Gautamīputra and the grandson of Bhavanāga, as his own successor as well. For, had Pravarasena I been succeeded by any one of his remaining three sons, the two empires could not be amalgamated. ... Now, how far (this plan succeeded) is another matter,...[39]

This suggestion of Goyal cogently explains as to why in the main branch Pravarasena I was succeeded by his grandson Rudrasena I though his other son Sarvasena was alive.

Goyal differs radically from Altekar and Mirashi on the problem of the Vākāṭaka-Gupta relations also. As opposed to the view of Altekar, Mirashi and others, he is of the opinion that Jayaswal's basic suggestion about the identification of Rudrasena I with Rudradeva of the Prayāga *praśasti* (shorn of his other suggestions regarding the achievements of the Vākāṭakas, their relations with the Pallavas and Maghas, the historical reliability of the drama *Kaumudī-mahotsava*, and so on) should be correct because Samudragupta could not go deep into the south without taming the Vākāṭakas and the Vākāṭakas could not give up their imperial title without having been forced to do so.[40] He also points out that Pṛthivīsheṇa I probably participated in the southern campaigns of Samudragupta, for the Gupta emperor followed the policy of *dharmavijaya* in that region and Pṛthivīsheṇa I is credited in the Vākāṭaka records with *dharmavijaya* though he is not known to have conquered any particular region.

Goyal's view regarding the matrimonial alliance between the two royal houses of the Vākāṭakas and the Guptas is also quite original. He has pointed out that the marriage of Prabhāvatī with Rudrasena II took place more than two decades before the extermination of the Western Kshatrapas by Chandragupta II and that the Śakas were a very weak kingdom in comparison to the mighty successor of Samudragupta.[41] Therefore, it is inconceivable that Chandragupta II gave his daughter in marriage to Rudrasena II in order to get the Vākāṭaka help against the Śakas more than two decades before

[39] S.R. Goyal, *A History of the Imperial Guptas (HIG)*, Allahabad, 1967, pp. 89-92.

[40] *Ibid.*, pp. 41-46. On this suggestion of S. R. Goyal Joanna Gottfried Williams comments: "If Rudradeva of the inscription (that is, of the *Prayāga praśasti* of Samudragupta) can be identified with Rudrasena I, one must note that the Vākāṭakas alone in this first category soon returned to an independent status." (*The Art of Gupta India*, New Delhi, 1983, p. 23, n. 5).

[41] *HIG*, p. 246.

the actual invasion on the Kshatrapas took place.[42]

In the post-Pravarasena II years Goyal has postulated a long-drawn Gupta-Vākāṭaka clash. He has given reasons to believe that the Nalas of South Kosala, who claim to have defeated the Vākāṭakas, were probably the subordinate allies of the Guptas and were helped by their overlords against the Vākāṭakas. That explains the spectacular victories of the Nalas, a minor power, against much more powerful Vākāṭakas. But when the Guptas were facing multiple difficulties at the time of Skandagupta's accession, the Vākāṭakas launched a counter-attack and defeated the Nalas and with the help of the Pāṇḍava ruler Bharatabala of Mekalā, the home of the Pushyamitra tribe, invaded the Gupta empire and for a brief period captured Malwa region also.[43] This theory beautifully harmonizes the data provided by the Rithpur plates of Bhavadattavarman, the Bamhani plates of Bharatabala, the Balaghat plates of Pṛthivīsheṇa II, the *Vishṇu-Purāṇa* and the Bhitari record of Skandagupta.

X

This was the state of the Vākāṭaka historiography towards the close of the seventh decade of the twentieth century. The works of Mirashi (1957 and 1963) and Goyal (1967 and 1969) in a way marked the end of an epoch in the historiography of the Vākāṭakas. After the publication of Mirashi's *Corpus* in 1963, till today about a dozen new Vākāṭaka inscriptions have come to light, though so far no detailed revised history of the dynasty has been published. The work of Shrimali (1987), which represents the cream of his deep study of the Vākāṭaka epigraphical records, underlines certain features of their economy for the first time (cf. *infra*). The works of Ajay Mitra Shastri (1987, 1992 and 1997), Hans T. Bakker (1997 and 2004) and S.R. Goyal (2005 and 2006), however, discuss many a problem of the history of the Vākāṭakas though only briefly (cf. *infra*). In this period Mirashi also wrote a chapter entitled 'The Vākāṭakas and Other Contemporary Dynasties' for *A Comprehensive History of India*, Vol. III, Pt. i, New Delhi, 1981, edited by R.C. Majumdar.[44] Numerous articles and other contributions have also been published from time to time on specific problems of the Vākāṭakas and their contemporaries during this period by many noted scholars and epigraphists including B.Ch. Chhabra, K.P. Jayaswal, G. S. Gai, S. Sankaranarayanan, Shobhana Gokhale, S.V. Sohoni, V.B. Kolte, Ajay Mitra Shastri, S.R. Goyal, Joanna Gottfried Williams, K.M. Shrimali, B. N. Mukherjee, K.V. Ramesh, Devendra Handa,

42 *Ibid.*, pp. 243-45.

43 *Ibid.*, pp. 256-57.

44 The chapter was apparently written much earlier than the date of the publication of the book.

Chandrashekhar Gupta, A.P. Jamkhedkar, Walter M. Spink, Hans T. Bakker, Harunaga Isaacson, Hermann Kulke and Ellen M. Raven.[45]

XI

K. M. Shrimali's work entitled *Agrarian Structure in Central India and the Northern Deccan (c.A.D.300-500) : A Study of Vākāṭaka Inscriptions* [46] is a substantial contribution on the subject. Published in 1987, it gives for the first time a systematic study of the economy of the Vākāṭakas on the basis of their inscriptions. According to Shrimali, the large-scale mechanism of land-grants and the absence of money reflect an economy characterized by 'burgeoning rural settlements and contraction of urbanism'. These features, he argues, lead to the conclusion that "the Vākāṭaka territory was the matrix of the

[45] We have also made some humble contribution in this field. For example, in one of our papers we have shown that the epigraphic data cited by scholars to prove the Gupta influence on the Vākāṭaka court during the reign of Chandragupta II does not prove the point (Shankar Goyal, 'Chandragupta II's Political Influence on the Vākāṭakas : Epigraphical Evidence Re-examined', in *History and Archaeology (Professor H.D. Sankalia Felicitation Volume)*, ed. Bhaskar Chatterjee, Delhi, 1989, pp. 351-56; idem, in *King Chandra and the Meharauli Pillar*, eds. M. C. Joshi et al, Meerut, 1989, pp. 150-56). Later on, in 1997 Ajay Mitra Shastri expressed a similar view regarding the untenability of the suggestion that the Pune plates of Prabhāvatīguptā prove the Gupta influence on the Vākāṭakas (*Vākāṭakas: Sources and History*, New Delhi, 1997, p. 182). Another contribution on our part to the subject has been an endowment lecture entitled 'The Vākāṭakas in the History of the Deccan: A Fresh Appraisal in the Light of Recent Discoveries and New Interpretations' delivered to the XXVI Annual Session of the South Indian History Congress at Bangalore University on March 3-5, 2006 (*Proceedings of the South Indian History Congress*, XXVIth Annual Session, Bangalore, 2007, pp. 689-702). In this lecture we have delineated the changes in the framework of the political history of the Vākāṭakas necessitated by the recent epigraphical discoveries and interpretations of the same by various scholars. In it we have not only discussed afresh the theory of the Gupta influence on the Vākāṭakas but also other problems of the Vākāṭaka history in detail including the question of their original home and the emergence of the Vākāṭakas belonging to the Brāhmaṇa order as a ruling power. Another recent contribution on our part to the subject has been our paper entitled 'The Myth of the Vākāṭaka Coins' read at the 90th Annual Conference of the Numismatic Society of India at Santiniketan on December 1-3, 2006 (revised version published in the *IHR*, Vol. XXXIV, No. 2, July 2007 pp. 1-15) in which we have argued that the question of the existence of the currency of an extensive kingdom, as the Vākāṭaka kingdom was, can not be decided by one or two copper coins. We have pointed out that the coins attributed to the Vākāṭakas have been studied by Ajay Mitra Shastri, Prashant P. Kulkarni and others with the help of photographs only which were supplied to them by the coin-collectors; nobody seems to have ascertained whether these photographs are doctored or genuine. In fact no credence should be given to these coins unless they are obtained from regular archaeological excavations or unless their authenticity is proved by detailed investigation (also cf. fn. 52). Also see my recent study titled *175 Years of Vākāṭaka History and Historiography*, Jodhpur, 2009.

[46] New Delhi, 1987.

earliest articulated tendencies of feudal beginnings."

A merit of Shrimali's work is the cartographic representation of the chronological and geographical distribution of the Vākāṭaka inscriptions, the villages donated, settlements other than donated villages and the geographical configuration of the administrative divisions. The statistical data given in the work is indicative of the fact that in the pre-Pravarasena II phase the concentration of activities was in the eastern half of the dominion while in the Pravarasena II and post-Pravarasena II phases there was a westward expansion. In the Vatsagulma dominion the economy had intimate trade links, whereas the Nandivardhana dominion gave agrarian orientation to the economy. According to Shrimali, the Vākāṭaka settlements, mentioned in defining the boundaries of the donated land, were mostly rural, as indicated by suffixes attached to their names. Further, some of the rural settlements seem to have come up "for the first time under the Vākāṭakas in general and Pravarasena II in particular." Also, excavations are analysed to show a decline in the character of the settlements.

Shrimali argues for the prevalence of serfdom in the Vākāṭaka kingdom. According to him, "the king retained full ownership of land." The Yawatmal plates of Pravarasena II, he points out, do not record the renewal of a grant, but the formal donation of a piece which the donee was enjoying, apparently without any right.

Shrimali also attributes the characteristic developments to the process of Sanskritization in the tribal area. The Vākāṭakas are given tribal origins and some of the place-names are explained as having totemistic origins and traces of tribalism. The channels of Sanskritization, according to him, are to be traced in the matrimonial alliance with the Guptas, the growing brāhmaṇic settlements and the migration of people from western, northern and north-western India.

Thus, Shrimali's work is especially noticeable, for no scholar has discussed the economy of the Vākāṭakas before him, the exception being R. S. Sharma, who, in his *Indian Feudalism* (Calcutta, 1965) has touched it only briefly.

XII

The contribution of Ajay Mitra Shastri, to the epigraphy and history of the Vākāṭakas has been the most significant.[47] He was intimately connected with the discovery and study of the majority of the Vākāṭaka inscriptions discovered after the publication of Mirashi's *Corpus* and dominated the field

[47] Unfortunately Shastri sadly and unexpectedly breathed his last on 11th January 2002. For a recent study of his contribution to Indological studies vide Shankar Goyal, *Contemporary Interpreters of Ancient India*, Jaipur, 2003, pp. 123-45.

of the Vākāṭaka historiography since then.[48] As most of these records had either not been published till then or were reported only in rather obscure publications not easily accessible to historians, in 1987 he wrote a detailed chapter on them in his *Early History of the Deccan: Problems and Perspectives* discussing their contents and historical importance. Summarizing the main points of the contents of these reocrds he observed:

> (These records) have given us the only date for Rudrasena II, narrowed the gap in the shifting of the capital of the main branch from Nandi Vardhana to Pravarapura, helped us in locating Padmapura in the Nagpur-Wardha region instead of in the Bhandara District as believed hitherto, brought us nearer the solution of the riddle concerning the succession after Rudrasena II, thrown a fresh light on the reigns of Narendrasena and his son and successor Pṛithivīsheṇa II, given us the only known Śaka date for Devasena which now forms the sheet anchor of the chronology of the Vatsagulma branch and supplied the hitherto unknown name of Devasena's father, viz. Sarvasena II, and names of two of the officers of Harisheṇa, the last

[48] Apart from writing chapters on the fresh epigraphic evidence on the Vākāṭakas in his *Early History of the Deccan : Problems and Perspectives* (Delhi, 1987), *The Age of the Vākāṭakas* (New Delhi, 1992) and *Vākāṭakas— Sources and History* (New Delhi, 1997) Ajay Mitra Shastri has also translated Mirashi's Marathi work on the Vākāṭaka history and inscriptions into Hindi (*Vākāṭaka Rājavaṁśa kā Itihāsa tathā Abhilekha*, Varanasi, 1964). He has also written numerous important articles on the Vākāṭakas. Among them are included the following: 'A Vākāṭaka Seal from Gorakhpur Ghāṭ' (in collaboration), *JNSI*, XXXV, 1973, pp. 238-40; 'Vākāṭaka Coins', presented at the 10th International Congress on Numismatics, London, 1986 (in absentia); 'Some Observations on the Hisse-Borala Inscription of the Time of the Vākāṭaka King Devasena', *Dr. Umesh Mishra Commemoration Volume*, Allahabad, 1970, pp. 617-27; 'Masod Copper-Plate Charter of Vākāṭaka Pravarasena II, Year 19' (in collaboration), *JESI*, X, 1983, pp. 108-16; 'Thalner Plates of Vākāṭaka Harisheṇa : A Re-Appraisal', *JESI*, XI, 1984, pp. 15-20; 'The Date of the Masod Plates of Vākāṭaka Pravarasena II' (in collaboration), *JESI*, XI, 1984, p. 114; 'The Vākāṭaka Kings Dāmodarasena and Pravarasena II', *JESI*, XIV, 1987, pp. 39-42; 'Māṇḍhaḷ Plates of the Vākāṭakas', presented at the 4th Session of the ESI, Madras, 1978; 'Māṇḍhaḷ Copper-Plate Charter of Vākāṭaka Pravarasena II, Year, 16', *EI*, XLI, 1975-76, pp. 68-76; 'Māṇḍhaḷ Plates of Pṛithivīsheṇa II, Years 2 and 10', *ibid.*, pp. 159-80; 'Yawatmal Plates of Vākāṭaka Pravarasena II, Year 26' (in collaboration), *EI*, XLII, 1977-78, pp. 30-34; 'Some Observations on the Balaghat Plates of Vākāṭaka Pṛithivīsheṇa II', *Śrīnidhiḥ : K. R. Srinivasan Festschrift*, eds. K.V. Raman et al, Chennai, 1983, pp. 445-50; 'Fresh Epigraphic Evidence on the Vākāṭakas', *The Journal of the Bihar Purāvid Parishad*, VI, 1982, pp. 101-36; 'The Original Home of the Vākāṭakas', *Bhāratī* (New Series), II, 1984, pp. 97-105; 'Dvitīya Rudrasenāchā Māṇḍhaḷ Tāmrapaṭa-lekha', (Marathi), (in collaboration), *Saṁśodhanāchī Kshitije*, ed. B.L. Bhole, Nagpur, 1983, pp. 223-29. (Chandrashekhar Gupta is the co-author of all the articles published in collaboration listed above).

known member of the Vatsagulma branch of the dynasty. We have, for the first time, the seals attached to the copper-plate grants issued by Prabhāvatīguptā during the reign of her third son Pravarasena II and those of Pṛithivīsheṇa II, the last known member of the main branch of the family. In addition to these facts mainly relating to political history we also get a good deal of information on the cultural history of the period.[49]

Thereafter, in 1992, Shastri brought out his edited work *The Age of the Vākāṭakas.*[50] It contains twenty-four chapters contributed by various scholars and an appendix entitled 'The Progress of Vākāṭaka Historiography' by the present writer (pp. 297-308). The contents of this volume were arranged thematically into four sections dealing with political history, administration and culture, archaeology and art and also epigraphy and numismatics. In chapter 1 Ajay Mitra Shastri showed that at the moment we have no evidence whatsoever to assume that the original home of the Vākāṭakas lay in the south. Like S. R. Goyal he also pointed out that the use of southern titles in the inscriptions of the Basim branch does not prove the southern origin of the Vākāṭakas, for these titles are not found used in the charters of the Nandivardhana-Pravarapura branch. In chapter 2 B. N. Mukherjee suggests that the original habitat of the Vākāṭakas was in the Vindhya region while in chapter 3 K. V. Ramesh assigns them to Vidarbha. The relations of the Vākāṭakas with the Guptas have been discussed by Sohoni (ch. 5) and Mirashi (ch. 8) and the Vākāṭaka-Kadamba relations have been dealt with by M. J. Sharma (ch. 7).

Other papers contained in the volume cover a very wide range of important issues concerning the age of the Vākāṭakas and throw welcome light on them. They also deal with very valuable recent finds, like those of the Vākāṭaka temples at Ramtek (ch. 14) and recent epigraphic and numismatic discoveries. Over half of the Vākāṭaka epigraphs, some of them highly valuable and informative, have come to light after the publication of V. V. Mirashi's monumental *Corpus* of the Vākāṭaka inscriptions mentioned above. A short supplement incorporating a detailed treatment of their contents and value has been included in this volume (pp. 227-68) and so is an account of the Vākāṭaka coins (pp. 285-94). Both these chapters (21 and 24) have been written by Shastri himself.

The last work of Ajay Mitra Shastri on the Vākāṭakas was *Vākāṭakas—Sources and History.*[51] Published in 1997, it was yet another noteworthy effort on the Vākāṭakas. It is divided into two parts. In part I Shastri analysed the

[49] Ajay Mitra Shastri, *Early History of the Deccan : Problems and Perspectives*, Delhi, 1987, p. 45.

[50] New Delhi, 1992.

[51] New Delhi, 1997.

epigraphic and numismatic source-material on the subject and in part II provided an outline of the Vākāṭaka history. Chapter 1 of part I deals with the epigraphs incorporated by V.V. Mirashi in his *Inscriptions of the Vākāṭakas* published in 1963. A perusal of this chapter would suffice to show that it is much more than a mere abstract and in most cases fresh interpretations have been offered. Chapter 2 takes stock of the recent discoveries of the Vākāṭaka charters which constitute more than 50% of the total volume of the epigraphy of the Vākāṭakas known earlier and with a major portion of whose discovery Shastri was intimately associated. A perusal of it would leave no doubt that it is substantial not only in volume but extremely rich in contents and has helped remove some erroneous notions going round till recently. In chapter 3 Shastri also drew attention of scholars to some coins attributable to the Vākāṭakas.[52] Literary sources, which are constituted exclusively by the Purāṇic references, have not been dealt with in this part as they are discussed at length in part II. Having familiarized the readers with the source-material, in part II Shastri provides a historical outline of the Vākāṭaka dynasty. The critical assessment of the evidence has led him to certain new conclusions some of which may be referred to here : the original Vākāṭaka territory lay in the Vindhyan region of central India wherefrom they immigrated about 300 A.D. under Pravarasena I into Vidarbha to spread their wings far and wide, Kāñchanakā (modern Nachna) was their first dynastic capital, the Vindhyan region continued under the dynasty till the time of Pṛthivīsheṇa I, Dāmodarasena and Pravarasena II were two distinct personages who ascended the throne one after another, Narendrasena's accession was disputed and towards the close of his reign he was deprived of his kingdom by his Vatsagulma cousins, and the Vatsagulma branch of the dynasty aspired to spread its wings in south and west from its very inception.

[52] Recently Prashant P. Kulkarni has reported that a copper coin has come to light from Yawatmal region bearing the full name of the Vākāṭaka ruler Pravarasena (II?). Cf. his article in *Numismatic Digest*, Vol. 25-26, 2001-02, pp. 65-69. The difficulty with Kulkarni seems to be that when he finds some coins he is always eager to label them. No doubt he knows the subject of numismatics well, but when he reads the script of a coin he lets his imagination run wild and in his eagerness to suggest something which no one else had suggested earlier he overlooks other evidences which go against his suggestion and tries to prove a doubtful point by another doubtful point. He seems to be a master in the art of making a mountain out of a mole hill which actually does not exist. He has committed the same error here. For a full discussion on the problem whether the Vākāṭaka coins exist cf. Shankar Goyal, 'The Myth of the Vākāṭaka Coins', paper presented at the 90th Annual Conference of the Numismatic Society of India at Santiniketan, December 1-3, 2006. Also see later portion of fn. 45.

XIII

Hans T. Bakker's *The Vākāṭakas : An Essay in Hindu Iconology* (1997) was the last work published on this subject in the twentieth century. Though certainly a highly valuable piece or research, in it Bakker tries to place the kingdom of the Vākāṭakas 'on a par with the Gupta world'.[53] His work is divided into two parts. Part I titled 'The History and Religion of the Vākāṭakas' is further divided in 3 chapters : 1. A Short History of the Vākāṭaka Kingdom (pp. 9-57); 2. The Hindu Religion in the Vākāṭaka Kingdom (pp.58-79); and 3. The Vākāṭaka Sites (pp. 80-92). In part II titled 'A Catalogue of Vākāṭaka Hindu Sculpture' we find a detailed discussion on plates I to XL (pp. 93-159). Then, there are 3 appendices : 1. The Kevala-Narasimha Temple Inscription (pp. 160-67); 2. Gupta-Vākāṭaka Genealogy (p. 168); and 3. Outline of the Vākāṭaka Chronology (pp. 169-71). Finally, Bibliography (pp. 172-92), Index (pp. 193-211), Plates (pp. 213-60) and Maps (pp. 261-65) are given.

Though Bakker's work builds on the achievements of many earlier scholars, including V.V. Mirashi, S.R. Goyal, Ajay Mitra Shastri, A. P. Jamkhedkar and many others, yet it is different from the works of most of his predecessors. Firstly, Bakker considers it no longer productive to concentrate exclusively on one branch of the Vākāṭakas by ignoring or marginalizing the evidence with regard to the other branch. He writes:

> The kings of Vatsagulma and Nandivardhana made up one family and their history is that of one family for all it is worth: divorce and rapprochement, dominance and submission, peaceful coexistence marred by fits of rivalry, occasionally erupting into downright civil war.[54]

He further writes:

> Not only is the political history of both houses interlocked, but so is their religion and culture. An attempt will be made to show that the art of Ajanta can no longer be detached from the artistic achievements of the eastern Vākāṭakas. On the other hand there is some evidence that important religious groups migrated from Vatsagulma to the eastern kingdom.[55]

Secondly, Bakker endeavours to utilize textual and archaeological sources in combination as far as possible. Explaining his view he states:

> For now more than half a century, scholars of the history of Western art have become familiar with the idea that visual art is embedded in a social and cultural context which imbues it with meaning and as such may be viewed as a source which generates knowledge concerning this context: this again may result in a batter understanding of the artefact itself. This synthetic method of investigation, known under the name of 'iconology',

[53] Hans T. Bakker, *The Vākāṭakas: An Essay in Hindu Iconology*, Groningen, 1997, p. 2.

[54] *Ibid.*, p. 3.

[55] *Ibid.*

> has proved to be of great value in the research of the history of culture. Iconology thus defined is a branch of cultural and—applied to religious material — of religious history; it is the counterpart of philology, which contributes to the same by taking textual material as its main object of study. In order to understand the context—political, cultural, religious—the iconologist assimilates the results of philological research and utilizes them in his understanding of the visual material, which again may serve as an important source for the historiography. Since the present study focuses on this visual material as far as it belongs to the Hindu fold—brought together for the first time in the catalogue of Part II—and the understanding thereof, derived from studying its historic context, is again employed in Part I as an important source for this context, the book carries the subtitle *An Essay in Hindu Iconology*.[56]

Elaborating his approach Bakker concludes thus:

> From textual, i.e. epigraphical, evidence we know that Pravarasena, who confessed to be a Māheśvara, had a large temple complex built, which he used as an official state sanctuary, the Pravareśvaradevakulasthāna. This was probably not a *liṅga* temple, since the archaeology of the Vākāṭaka realm proves that these kings were not *liṅga* worshippers; moreover this is in conformity with the reluctance to accept *liṅga* worship which we note in the Sanskrit literature of the brāhmaṇical elite of this period. The inference that the Mansar image was the idol of the Pravareśvara Temple and consequently that this temple was situated in Mansar, appears logical. Charters issued by this king also tell us that, halfway through his reign, when his dominant mother was growing older, he decided either to rename the old residence Nandivardhana after himself or to build a new one, Pravarapura. The evidence of the Mansar Śiva and its connection with the political context of its time would make it appear plausible that Pravarasena II built his new palace in the vicinity of this state sanctuary, i.e. a little to the west of Rāmagiri and Nandivardhana. It may have sealed the process in which the king broke away from his mother and her Bhāgavata milieu. The Mansar Śiva is thus an important piece of evidence in the reconstruction of the political and religious reality of the time. What does this reality contribute to our understanding of the image ? It could explain why this figure, in the words of Joanna Williams, has no 'exact parallel in iconography'. It represents a Śiva who appears to be more domesticated, showing a benign smile and offering life to his devotees, whereas wild traits, such as the erect phallus, third eye and weapons are absent. One could sense here the influence that the Bhāgavata environment still held over the Māheśvara faith of the king.[57]

In accordance with his line of examination Bakker evaluates all the available material concerning the cultural history of the Vākāṭakas in his book. In order to facilitate his research and to place the history and culture of the

[56] *Ibid.*, pp. 3-4.

[57] *Ibid.*, pp. 4-5, 87-88.

Vākāṭakas in their geographical environment, a map has also been produced which shows, as he states, 'the natural theatre of their achievements'.[58]

XIV

The twenty-first century has so far seen some praiseworthy works on the Vākāṭakas. In 2004 Hans T. Bakker produced yet another noticeable treatise, this time an edited one, entitled *The Vākāṭaka Heritage : Indian Culture at the Crossroads.*[59] The articles included in this volume were presented in a colloquium held at Groningen from 6 to 8 June, 2002. In it Hermann Kulke (pp.1-9) discusses the historical background from which the Vākāṭakas emerged and establishes two different, largely autonomous kingdoms : the Eastern and the Western. He suggests that the Eastern Vākāṭaka state can be seen as a transitional phase to the early medieval kingdoms. Derek Kennet (pp. 11-17) gives a critical assessment of the archaeological material regarding the Vākāṭakas and argues that 'urban decay' in the period may be due to a methodological misconception. Ellen M. Raven (pp. 19-31) addresses the question of the absence of Vākāṭaka gold coinage and calls attention to the relationship of the copper coins ascribed to the Eastern Vākāṭakas with coins found in Eastern Malwa. The Malwa tie up is further amplified in the contribution of Michael Willis (pp. 33-58), who concentrates on Udayagiri and shows how under Chandragupta II, father of the Vākāṭaka queen Prabhāvatīguptā, this hill was reshaped into a holy place. Robert L. Brown (pp. 59-69) reexamines the iconography of several images found in the Eastern Vākāṭaka kingdom and indicates Andhra as a possible source of inspiration. Hans T. Bakker (pp. 71-85) gives an assessment of the excavations in Mansar and ponders on a funerary monument of Prabhāvatīguptā. The Western Vākāṭakas and their main monuments in Ajanta are the subject of three contributions. Walter M. Spink (pp. 87-105) focuses on the doorways of the Ajanta caves and reasons how their development can present us with pointers for a relative chronology. The absolute (short) chronology underlying Spink's work is here questioned in an open letter by Heinrich von Stietencron (pp. 107-08). Leela Aditi Wood (pp.109-31) furnishes an interpretation of Ajanta Cave 17 and shows how the *praśasti* and the art of the Vihāra reflect one another and form an integral whole. The last four contributions address the issue of how the Vākāṭaka heritage continued to live in the sixth century. Joanna Gottfried Williams (pp. 133-41) looks at Mandasor in Western Malwa, L.S. Nigam (pp. 143-56) appraises Vākāṭaka influences in the art of Chhattisgarh (Dakshiṇa Kosala), whereas Donald M. Stadtner (pp. 157-65) examines how this process of cultural diffusion may actually have taken place. Finally, Yuko

[58] *Ibid.*, p. 6.

[59] Groningen, 2004.

Yokochi (pp. 167-78), exhibits on the basis of the Mahishāsuramardinī icon, how a model developed in the Vākāṭaka realm mixed up with a similar model of the Gupta north.

XV

Here, a couple of articles, one, by Hermann Kulke,[60] briefly discussed above, and two, by Nandini Sinha Kapur,[61] published in 2004 and 2005 respectively, deserve consideration. They, probably for the first time, have worked on the subject of state formation under the Vākāṭakas which has not been touched by other scholars before them. Both Kulke and Kapur use the term 'Eastern Vākāṭakas' to denote the main branch of the Vākāṭakas (i.e. the Nandivardhana branch). According to Kulke, the matrimonial alliance with the Guptas raised the status of the Eastern Vākāṭakas and the latter also initiated three important innovations : land donations to the Brāhmaṇas, foundation of a 'state sanctuary' (Ramgiri), and copper-plate inscriptions to legitimatise and strengthen their 'newly acquired status as allies of the dominant power of northern India'. However, Kapur agrees with Kulke only with the first part of his opinion mentioned above and argues that had the Eastern Vākāṭakas initiated three important innovations Pravarasena II would not have shifted royal patronage to Śaivism and would not have highlighted his lineage, *gotra* and central Indian affiliations. According to Kapur, Pravarasena II earned socio-political mileage in central India out of reference to his maternal-grandfather, *Mahārājādhirāja* Devagupta, but never projected the Vākāṭakas as 'subordinate allies' of the dominant power of northern India in his records. Kapur also envisages three tentative phases in the emergence of the state in Vidarbha under the Eastern Vākāṭakas : the first phase coincides with the early Vākāṭaka rulers in the pre-Prabhāvatīguptā regency period, the second phase is that of Prabhāvatīguptā's regency initiating a rupture in the Vākāṭaka dominance over Vidarbha and the third phase ran parallel to Pravarasena II's reign marking intensive territorial and political integrative processes in the Vākāṭaka state formation and legitimation of the Vākāṭaka power. However, both Kulke and Kapur opine that Vidarbha represented a transitional stage of state formation out of which the early medieval kingdoms emerged.

XVI

The twenty-first century witnessed two more significant works under the titles *The Imperial Guptas : A Multidisciplinary Political Study* (2005)[62] and

[60] Hermann Kulke, 'Some Thoughts on State and State Formation under the Eastern Vākāṭakas', in Hans T. Bakker (ed.), *The Vākāṭaka Heritage*, *op. cit.*, pp. 1-9.

[61] Nandini Sinha Kapur, 'State Formation in Vidarbha : The Case of the Eastern Vākāṭakas', *IHR*, XXXII, 2, July 2005, pp. 13-36.

[62] Jodhpur, 2005.

A History of the Vākāṭaka-Gupta Relations (2006)[63] by S.R. Goyal in which he drew a picture of the history of the Vākāṭaka-Gupta relations in the light of recent epigraphical finds including the Mandhal charters of Rudrasena II and other Vākāṭaka rulers, the Miregaon plates of Prabhāvatīguptā and the Ramtek inscription of a daughter of Prabhāvatīguptā. Goyal has also looked into the Vākāṭaka-Gupta relations from the peep-hole of the literary sources as well which, if interpreted correctly, presents a very interesting pattern of their changing relationship.

However, Goyal's recent-most contribution in the form of his *A History of the Vākāṭaka-Gupta Relations* requires special mention here, for so far no historian has written an independent work on the history of the relationship of any two ancient north Indian dynasties of the pre-Rajput period. According to Goyal's analysis, during the first part of the reign of Pravarasena I and Chandragupta I the Vākāṭakas and the Guptas were merely local powers and did not come into intimate contact with each other, friendly or otherwise, though the similarity of the facts that Pravarasena I and his contemporary Chandragupta I both assumed imperial titles and both forged a matrimonial alliance of similar nature with their neighbours (Pravarasena I with the Bhāraśiva Nāgas leading to the recognition of his grand son Rudrasena I as *Bhavanāga-dauhitra* and Chandragupta I with the Lichchhavis securing the right of succession for his son Samudragupta to the Lichchhavi state as *Lichchhavi-dauhitra*) suggest that these events were influenced by each other (chs. 1 and 2).

In the next generation, according to Goyal, Samudragupta emerged as a great conqueror, much more powerful than the Vākāṭakas and succeeded in making the Vākāṭakas his subordinate allies. He probably defeated Rudrasena I, the successor of Pravarasena I (for according to Goyal's view Rudrasena I has been rightly identified with Rudradeva of the Prayāga *praśasti*), who was most likely killed in the Gupta-Vākāṭaka encounter. Even if he is not identified with Rudradeva uprooted by Samudragupta, it can hardly be denied that Samudragupta succeeded in making the Vākāṭakas his subordinate allies. Goyal has discussed the imposition of the Gupta hegemony on the Vākāṭakas in this period in detail (ch. 3, also see *supra*).

Then followed the age of Chandragupta II and Kumāragupta I when, according to Goyal, the relations of the Vākāṭakas with the Guptas based on the friendly subordination of the former under the protective umbrella of the latter were strengthened. Chandragupta II Vikramāditya gave his daughter Prabhāvatīguptā in marriage to Rudrasena II, the son of Pṛthivīsheṇa I. After

[63] Jodhpur, 2006. When one turns to writers such as Raghavendra Vajpaeyi the evaluation of the Vākāṭaka-Gupta relations can sometimes fall into comic absurdity (cf. his article in *Churning the Indian Past*, ed. B.P. Roy, Patna, 2003, pp. 217-27).

the unfortunate death of her husband Rudrasena II Prabhāvatīguptā's minor son Divākarasena ascended the throne and then, after the demise of Divākarasena also, her next son Dāmodarasena became the ruler of the Vākāṭakas. But he also did not rule for long. During the yuvarājaship of Divākarasena, and probably during the early years of Dāmodarasena, Prabhāvatīguptā ruled as their regent and her father Chandragupta II looked after the administration of the Vākāṭaka kingdom strenuously, in the words of the author of the Ramtek inscription as 'the best of the beast of burden'.[64] His influence in the Deccan and the south becomes evident by his description as *Trī-Samudra-Nātha* (Lord of the Three Oceans). It was in this period that Ghaṭotkachagupta, a son of Chandragupta II, and the governor of Kumāragupta I in East Malwa with his headquarters at Tumbavana till at least 435 A.D., as is known from the Tumain inscription of this date, was married to a daughter of Prabhāvatīguptā. The name of the mother of Ghaṭotkachagupta as well as of his Vākāṭaka wife are not known. But it is certain that his marriage with a daughter of Prabhāvatīguptā, that is with his own niece, further cemented the Gupta-Vākāṭaka relations. But sometime after 435 A.D., obviously with the help of the Vākāṭakas, Ghaṭotkachagupta revolted against the authority of his brother Kumāragupta I. But his revolt was crushed and his Vākāṭaka wife had to be rescued by 'force' (*balāt*) by her brother (obviously Pravarasena II, the successor of Dāmodarasena on the Vākāṭaka throne) who brought her to his home. This enraged the Guptas who now offered help to a Nala offensive against the Vākāṭakas. These events occurred shortly before or after 445 A.D. Thus, according to Goyal, ended the period of about a century of the Gupta-Vākāṭaka relations which was marked by friendly subordination of the Vākāṭakas to the Guptas (ch. 4).

The next phase of their relations, Goyal believes, was characterised more by hostility between the two royal houses than by friendship. Towards the close of the reign of Kumāragupta I, a number of calamities fell upon the Gupta empire and Skandagupta had to marshal his whole energies to overcome them. He succeeded in his efforts, but these developments forced the Guptas to abandon their Deccan conquests and enabled Narendrasena, the son and successor of Pravarasena II, not only to retrieve the fallen fortunes of the family by driving out the Nala aggressor (who was now left on his own resources)

[64] For details also see S.R. Goyal, *Ancient Indian Inscriptions : Recent Finds and New Interpretations*, Jodhpur, 2005, pp. 221-25. This monograph of Goyal seeks mainly to acquaint the scholars and researchers with important ancient Indian inscriptions discovered in the last few decades. Among such inscriptions are also included all the recently found Vākāṭaka inscriptions including the Ramtek Prabhāvatīguptā Memorial Stone Inscription which has made a thorough revision of the history of the Vākāṭakas and the Vākāṭaka-Gupta relations imperative.

from his kingdom, but also to avenge the defeat sustained by him at the hands of his enemies by invading their own territories—the Nalas in South Kosala and the Guptas in Malwa. According to Goyal, it is quite likely that sometime between 495 and 500 A.D. Pṛthivīsheṇa II ousted the Guptas from some areas of Bundelkhand-Baghelkhand region. After this, Goyal opines, there is no record of any further direct confrontation between the Guptas and the Vākāṭakas of the 'main branch'. The claim of Harisheṇa of the Vatsagulma branch regarding his invasion on Malwa had nothing to do with the Guptas because by that time the hegemony of the Guptas on Malwa had become a matter of history and the Aulikaras had replaced them as the imperial power there (chs. 5 and 6).

XVII

These are in brief the principal developments and changes which have taken place in our knowledge of the history of the Vākāṭakas. The works of K. M. Shrimali (1987), Ajay Mitra Shastri (1997), Hans T. Bakker (1997) and S.R. Goyal (2006) represent the best scholarship on the Vākāṭakas written so far after V. V. Mirashi's *Corpus* (1963), for they provide a critical exposition of the changes which have taken place in our knowledge of the history of the Vākāṭakas and bring us uptodate in this matter. What is interesting to note is the fact that all these scholars have not only worked on those areas of Vākāṭaka history which had been overlooked by their predecessors but have also extended researches distinctively different from each other: Shrimali discusses the economy of the Vākāṭakas for the first time and focuses on its agrarian structure on the basis of epigraphic evidence. Shastri makes the best use of all the source- material to prepare the stage for a more balanced historical outline. Bakker uses all the evidence and earlier works at his disposal to study art, religion and culture during Vākāṭaka times. Goyal's approach is not "what happend ?" but "why did it happen?" not found in other works on the Vākāṭakas; and he boldly enters every scholarly controversy on the period, sorting out evidence and opinions lively and judiciously giving original interpretations and a novel direction to the subject. As a result, the current historiography of the Vākāṭakas has now advanced from the stage of a chronological, dynastic study to an integral analysis of events during c. 250-500 A.D. and to a detailed study of religion and art to an extensive study of agrarian expansion in central India and northern Deccan and to state formation under the main branch.

APPENDIX ONE

Hans Bakker's Suggestion on Art and Culture of the Vākāṭakas : A Critique

Here, it is worthwhile to discuss Hans Bakker at some length, for the importance of the Vākāṭakas of the classical period of Indian history is a highly controversial issue. His two works, one, *The Vākāṭakas: An Essay in Hindu Iconology* (1997), and the other, *The Vākāṭaka Heritage : Indian Culture at the Crossroads* (2004) may in a way be regarded as the culmination of the Vākāṭaka studies at the beginning of the twenty-first century. From these monographs it is obvious that in recent years the development of the Vākāṭaka historiography has in a sense once again taken the direction, though not quite, which was given to it by K.P. Jayaswal. Firstly, as Hans Bakker has stated in the 'Introduction' of *The Vākāṭakas* :"One may say that from the middle of the sixties the kingdom of the Vākāṭakas has come to be seen as pivotal in the history of India, being essential for our understanding of the development of its art, religion and culture; as such it is on a par with the Gupta world, of which it can no longer be considered to be merely a province."[65] In a way this conclusion is quite near to the belief of Jayaswal in whose perception in the age of Pravarasena I, who assumed the title of Samrāṭ, the Vākāṭakas were the paramount rulers of almost whole of India. It is, of course, true that Jayaswal's thesis regarding the imperial status of Pravarasena I and Hans Bakker's theory of Vākāṭaka's 'pivotal role in the history of India' and his emphasis on the Vākāṭaka's being on a par with the Gupta world are not exactly the same prepositions but it can hardly be denied that both these theories emphasize the status of the Vākāṭakas and their parity with the Guptas which many a historian do not believe. Hans Bakker's belief that the kings of the eastern and western Vākāṭaka kingdoms—of the Nandivardhana and Vatsagulma—made up one family and their history is that of one family for all

65 Bakker, *The Vākāṭakas*, p. 2.

it is worth bestows on them some extra political hallow. It is, of course, true and obvious that looking at the Vākāṭakas as one unit does not make them a great imperial power, but it does compel us to keep a wider area in mind while studying their political and cultural history.

Secondly, Jayaswal had laid great emphasis on the revival of art and sculpture under the Vākāṭakas. The Vākāṭaka empire, the second one according to the reconstruction of their political history by Jayaswal, was so rich that "even a minister of Harisheṇa could excavate and decorate with paintings a beautiful chaitya-building at Ajaṇṭā, Cave No. XVI, adorned, as the donor himself with a rightful pride says, 'with windows, spires, beautiful terraces, ledges, statues of the nymphs of Indra and the like, supported by lovely pillars and stairs'—'a lovely chaitya-building'. A member of the same ministerial family cut the Cave No. XIII, which is called the Ghaṭotkacha Cave, wherein the donor gives his family history."[66] According to Hans Bakker also, "the art of Ajanta can no longer be detached from the artistic achievements of the eastern Vākāṭakas. On the other hand there is some evidence that important religious groups migrated from Vatsagulma to the eastern kingdom.'[67]

Here, we do not intend to reject altogether the significance of Bakker's thesis that the kingdom of the Vākāṭakas is to be seen, 'on a par with the Gupta world'; but to us it appears to be somewhat exaggerated preposition. As is well-known, most historians have accepted the importance of the Vākāṭaka age in central India and the Deccan *within the Gupta empire*. Even Hans Bakker in his 'Preface' to *The Vākāṭaka Heritage* has categorically stated that "at the crossroads of the Indo-Aryan north and Dravidian south, *the northern culture of the Gupta kingdom reached the Deccan and developed a character of its own* (italics ours). The major religions of the times, Buddhism, Bhāgavatism and Maheśvarism, all had important settlements in the Vākāṭaka kingdom; constructions in stone, brick or rock testify to the high standards of the arts reached in central India by the middle of the 5th century."[68]

The prosperity of the Vākāṭaka kingdom, as seen by Bakker, also presents two contradictory aspects. On the one hand, almost total absence of the Vākāṭaka coins, certainly of their gold and silver coins, give the impression that the Vākāṭaka economy was extremely poor. Also, as shown by us in detail elsewhere,[69] a study of the known inscriptions of the Vākāṭakas indicate the comparative rarity of the use of coins resulting in the large mechanism of land-grants, growth of small village settlements and declining urban economy. But the development of Hindu temples on and around the Rāmagiri (Ramtek

[66] Jayaswal, *op.cit.*, pp. 104-05.

[67] Bakker, *op.cit.*, p. 3.

[68] Bakker, *The Vākāṭaka Heritage*, p. v.

[69] Cf. Shankar Goyal, 'The Myth of the Vākāṭaka Coins', *IHR*, Vol. XXXIV, No. 2, July 2007, pp. 1-15.

hill) and the Buddhist caves in Ajanta do testify to the prosperity of the Vākāṭaka kingdom. This contradiction may be resolved if we believe that the Vākāṭakas were under the political and cultural influence of the Guptas and the caves and temples which are the only proofs of this prosperity were the result of their relationship—direct or indirect—with the Guptas. That this cultural florescence in the Vākāṭaka areas had its origins in the influence of the Gupta kings is also conceded by Walter M. Spink.[70] However, his observation that Indian classical culture reached the very highest point in its development during the reign of Harisheṇa who ruled from c. 460 to 477 A.D. is not correct as by the early years of his rule the Gupta dynasty was already on the course of disintegration.[71] However, the cultural history of the imperial Guptas and the Vākāṭakas and the monuments of their period cannot be so precisely dated since it merges at both ends in the continuous development of earlier and later periods. Be that as it may, the fact that the artistic activities of the Vākāṭaka kingdom were the result of the Gupta influence necessitates some rethinking on Hans Bakker's hypothesis that the Vākāṭakas were on a par with the imperial Guptas.

[70] Walter M. Spink, 'The Vākāṭaka Caves at Ajanta and Their Successors', in *Reappraising Gupta History for S.R. Goyal*, eds. B. Ch. Chhabra, P. K. Agrawala, Ashvini Agrawal and Shankar Goyal, New Delhi, 1992, p. 248.

[71] *Ibid.*

APPENDIX TWO

A Criticism of K. M. Shrimali's Article 'Religions in Complex Societies : The Myth of the 'Dark Age' '

In a paper entitled 'Religions in Complex Societies: The Myth of the 'Dark Age' ' published in 2007 K. M. Shrimali has tried to show that the historical sense of K. P. Jayaswal (whom he chooses to describe 'a so-called nationalist historian') was extraordinarily similar to that of V.A. Smith so far as their understanding of the post-Kushāṇa pre-Gupta period is concerned.[72] As we have already noted, Smith had opined that:

> The period between the extinction of the Kushān and Āndhra dynasties, about A.D. 220 or 230, and the rise of the imperial Gupta dynasty, nearly a century later, is one of the darkest in the whole range of Indian history.[73]

This, according to Shrimali, is similar to Jayaswal's perception of this period and in order to prove his supposition he quotes his following words:

> The period 180 A.D. to 320 A.D. is called the DARK PERIOD. I undertake the work with the prayer: '*Lead me from darkness to light.*'[74]

Shrimali takes this statement of Jayaswal to imply that like Smith Jayaswal also regarded the pre-Gupta period from about 180 A.D. to 320 A.D. as a 'blank' or 'Dark Age' in Indian history. In his paper under discussion he categorically states that "following the notions of history adopted by Vincent A. Smith and Kashi Prasad Jayaswal, the post-Mauryan centuries were identified as a 'Dark Age'."[75] This provides us, Shrimali argues, with a glimpse of extraordinary similarity between the historical sense of this nationalist

[72] K.M. Shrimali, 'Religions in Complex Societies: The Myth of the 'Dark Age' ', in Irfan Habib (ed.), *Religion in Indian History*, New Delhi, 2007, pp. 36-70.

[73] Smith, *op.cit.*, p. 292.

[74] Jayaswal, *op.cit.*, Foreword, p. 2; Shrimali, *op.cit.*, p. 37.

[75] Shrimali, *op.cit.*, pp. 62-63.

historian and that of Smith and makes us wonder what could be the compulsions of Jayaswal in reiterating this Smithian notion of the history of this period.

But here Shrimali is grossly mistaken for when Jayaswal wrote that "The period 180 A.D. to 320 A.D. is called the DARK PERIOD", he was not giving expression to his own perception of the history of this period; he was quoting the view of scholars like Smith in order to criticize it. As a matter of fact, Jayaswal wrote his *History of India 150 A.D. to 350 A.D.* precisely to prove that this period was not the 'Dark Age' in Indian history. When he categorically assered that the history of the Hindu revival is not to be dated in the fourth century with Samudragupta not even with the Vākāṭakas nearly a century earlier but with the Bhāraśivas half a century earlier still, and also gave a detailed account of his perception of the glories of the Hindus of that period, how it can be maintained that like Smith he believed that these centuries constituted the 'Dark Age' of Indian History ? Neither there was any compulsion before him to reiterate Smith's view of the history of these centuries nor did he reiterate it. What he did was just the contrary — he tried to prove that this period was an age of great national revival and that we cannot and should not regard it as the 'Dark Age' of Indian history. The whole book of Jayaswal is devoted to prove that the pre-Gupta period of the ascendancy of the Bhāraśivas and then of the Vākāṭakas saw the high tide of Hindu nationalism. The Śaka rule had "aimed at denationalising the Hindus and at the basic destruction of their national system. ...The undertaking to deliver the country from such a national calamity was shouldered by the Bhāraśivas on the Ganges. ... What was the National Cult and Faith with which the Bhāraśivas entered on their mission? We find in that period everywhere — Śiva."[76] Jayaswal becomes eloquent, almost poetic, while describing the achievements and political ideology of the Bhāraśivas and their successors, the Vākāṭakas, who, in his view, created a mighty upheaval throughout the country. "The air is surcharged with the belief that the Destroyer Himself (that is, Śiva) has founded the Bhāraśiva State, that He is the guarantor of the king and the people of the Bhāraśiva kingdom."[77]

Jayaswal divides the age of Vākāṭaka ascendancy into two parts—the Vākāṭaka kingdom (248 A.D. to 284 A.D.) and the Vākāṭaka empire (284 A.D. to 348 A.D.) with an appendix on the Later Vākāṭaka Period (348 A.D. to 550 A.D.). Whether his perception of the history of this Bhāraśiva-Vākāṭaka period is correct or not, is a different matter — probably most of his ideas on the subject are not acceptable to the present generation of historians; we ourselves do not accept them in toto. But at the same time it is a fact that while Smith believed that Indian history of the pre-Gupta period

[76] Jayaswal, *op.cit.*, pp. 48-49.
[77] *Ibid.*, p. 49.

is blank—almost unknown, totally dark—Jayaswal believed that the history of this period may be reconstructed in detail and he did write his *History of India 150 A.D. to 350 A.D.* to prove this point. Therefore, to this extent the belief of Shrimali that Jayaswal followed Smithian notion of the 'Dark Age' in Indian history is not correct; it is positively inaccurate, just the opposite of truth. It does not need any argument to prove that when Jayaswal wrote that "The period 180 A.D. to 320 A.D. is called the DARK PERIOD" he was quoting the view of Smith and the like; he did not mean that in his own view also nothing is known about the post-Maurya centuries of Indian history.[78]

[78] Professor K.M. Shrimali has recently responded to our suggestion in his *Prāchīna Bhāratīya Dharmoṅ kā Itihāsa* (Delhi, 2017, pp. 197-98). This had originally appeared in our work titled *175 Years of Vākāṭaka History and Historiography* (pp. 31-33), but his work reiterates his earlier position. While recognising and appreciating the all-important contributions of Professor Shrimali to the study of the discipline of history, and the academic rigour of his work, we feel that, in this instance, he is palpably wrong. His position, that he has adhered to very strongly, is, we feel, rather problematic. However, we would like to analyse and meet the objections he has raised against our suggestions elsewhere.

TWO

The Vākāṭakas : The Age of Feudal-Federal Polity

I

The Vākāṭakas supplanted the Āndhra-Sātavāhanas as the dominant power in the Deccan around the close of the third century A.D. They played a very important role in the politico-cultural history of the Deccan in particular and that of India as a whole in general. But their entry in the historiographical studies took place quite late.[1] Till the early years of the nineteenth century they were altogether unknown; even their name had not come to light. Their existence was revealed for the first time when the Siwani copper grant of Pravarasena II was discovered in Madhya Pradesh in 1836.[2] Vindhyaśakti I, the founder of the dynasty, has indeed been mentioned in the Purāṇas.[3] But owing to textual misconstruction, he was believed to have belonged to the Yavana race.[4] It was probably the reason why there is not a single word about the Vākāṭaka dynasty in the *Early History of the Deccan* of R.G. Bhandarkar, first published in 1884. Later on, it was noted that the founder of the dynasty has been described in an inscription as a *dvija* which usually means a Brāhmaṇa. It was also noted that the *gotra* of the family was Vishṇuvṛddha, a Brāhmaṇa *gotra*, and that Pravarasena I performed some sacrifices which were exclusively meant for the Brāhmaṇas. Thus, it was established that the Vākāṭakas were not Yavanas but a Hindu dynasty of Brāhmaṇa origin.

[1] Here I have dealt with the progress of the Vākāṭaka historiography in brief. I have critically and exhaustively examined it in my *Recent Historiography of Ancient India*, Jodhpur, 1997, pp. 401-16.

[2] *JASB*, V, 1836, pp. 726 ff.

[3] Cf. F. E. Pargiter, *The Purāṇa Text of the Dynasties of the Kali Age*, Oxford, 1913, pp. 49-50.

[4] *JBBRAS*, VII, pp. 69 ff.

J.F. Fleet,[5] who knew only a few Vākātaka grants, assigned them to the eighth century. His view was based on the identification of *Mahārājādhirāja* Devagupta, the maternal-grandfather of Pravarasena II mentioned in them, with *Mahārājādhirāja* Devagupta of Magadha, the son of Ādityasena, mentioned in the Deo-Barnark inscription, who flourished towards the close of the seventh century. The Vākāṭakas were, therefore, believed to have ruled in the seventh and eighth centuries. However, the Pune plates of Prabhāvatīguptā, discovered in 1912,[6] explicitly mention that Prabhāvatīguptā, the chief-queen of the Vākāṭaka king Rudrasena II and mother of the crown-prince Divākarasena, was the daugther of the Gupta *Mahārājādhirāja* Chandragupta II (known dates 376-412 A.D.).[7] This evidence has placed the Vākāṭaka chronology on a sound basis.

K. P. Jayaswal in his book *History of India, A.D. 150 to 350 A.D.* (1933) brought the Vākāṭaka dynasty into prominence. It is of course true that many of Jayaswal's suggestions about the Vākāṭakas and also about the Nāgas, Guptas and Pallavas have now been shown by sober criticism to be untenable but it is also a fact that he has succeeded in imparting a significant place to the history of the Vākāṭakas in Indian historiography. Meanwhile, further progress about the knowledge of the history of the Vākāṭakas was made in 1939 when the Basim grant of the Vākāṭaka ruler Vindhyaśakti II came to light which was edited by V.V. Mirashi.[8] It showed that after Pravarasena I the Vākāṭaka kingdom was divided into at least two parts, northern (ruled by Pravarasena I's grandson Rudrasena I and his successors) and southern (ruled by Pravarasena I's younger son Sarvasena and his successors). Then in 1946 was published *A New History of the Indian People*, Vol. VI (*The Vākāṭaka-Gupta Age*), edited by R.C. Majumdar and A.S. Altekar, which contains a detailed chapter entitled 'The Vākāṭakas' written by Altekar himself. In this work Majumdar and Altekar tried to rationalize the exaggerated claims of Jayaswal regarding the achievements of the Vākāṭakas. Indeed the chapter of A. S. Altekar in *The Vākāṭaka-Gupta Age* was a landmark in the Vākāṭaka historiography. It was the first detailed and systematic exposition of the chronology, genealogy and history of the Vākāṭakas. 1954 saw the publication of another edited work entitled *The Classical Age* by R. C. Majumdar and A. D. Pusalker in which D.C. Sircar gave a systematic exposition of his studies on the Vākāṭakas in the chapter 'Deccan in the Gupta Age'. The next year K. A. Nilakanta Sastri

[5] J.F. Fleet, *Corpus Inscriptionum Indicarum*, Vol. III : *Inscriptions of the Early Gupta Kings and Their Successors*, Calcutta, 1888, Intro., p. 15.

[6] *IA*, XLI, 1912, pp. 214 ff.

[7] *EI*, XV, pp. 39 ff.

[8] *EI*, XXVI, pp. 137 ff.

gave a brief history of the Vākāṭakas in his *A History of South India.* Both in respect of chronology and history he broadly followed the outline of Altekar. In 1957 V. V. Mirashi produced his Marathi work *Vākāṭaka Nṛpati aṇi Tyāṁcha Kāla* of which an enlarged English version was published under the title *Inscriptions of the Vākāṭakas* (*Corpus Inscriptionum Indicarum,* Vol. V). Mirashi's *Corpus* represented the cream of his deep study of the Vākāṭaka history and epigraphy. In it he has given a brilliant study of twenty-seven Vākāṭaka epigraphs alongwith a detailed introduction containing the political and cultural history of the dynasty. About a decade later, in 1967 S. R. Goyal critically examined the Gupta-Vākāṭaka relations in his celebrated doctoral work *A History of the Imperial Guptas.*[9] Goyal gave a new interpretation of the phrase *Bhavanāga-dauhitra* occurring for Rudrasena I in the Vākāṭaka records to show that Bhavanāga and Pravarasena I had forged a scheme by which after them Nāga and Vākāṭaka kingdoms were to merge and Rudrasena I was to succeed both of them, just as in the north Samudragupta, the *Lichchhavi-dauhitra,* was designated as the successor of both Chandragupta I and the Lichchhavi chief, the father of Kumāradevī.[10]

In recent years the contribution of K. M. Shrimali, A. M. Shastri and Hans T. Bakker to the history the Vākāṭakas has been the most significant. In 1987 Shrimali published his *Agrarian Structure in Central India and the Northern Deccan* (*c.A. D. 300-500*) *: A Study of Vākāṭaka Inscriptions.* In it he gave for the first time a systematic study of the economy of the Vākāṭakas on the basis of their inscriptions.[11] In 1987 Shastri also wrote a detailed chapter on the new Vākāṭaka inscriptions in his *Early History of the Deccan : Problems and Perspectives* discussing their contents and historical importance.[12] In 1992 he brought out an edited work *The Age of the Vākāṭakas.*[13] It contains twenty-four chapters contributed by various scholars on the various aspects of the age of the Vākāṭakas and an appendix on 'The Progress of Vākāṭaka Historiography' by me. The last work of A.M. Shastri on the Vākāṭakas was *Vākāṭakas — Sources and History.*[14] It is divided into two parts. Part 1 deals with the archaeological sources and Part 2 with the short history of the dynasty. In one of its chapters Shastri also drew attention of scholars to some coins attributable to the Vākāṭakas

[9] Also see S. R. Goyal's *The Imperial Guptas : A Multidisciplinary Political Study,* Jodhpur, 2005 (hereafter referred to as *IG*).

[10] Goyal, *IG,* pp. 111 ff.

[11] New Delhi, 1987.

[12] New Delhi, 1987.

[13] New Delhi, 1992.

[14] New Delhi, 1997.

— an attribution with which I do not agree. In 1997 Bakker published his *The Vākāṭakas : An Essay in Hindu Iconology* in which he tried to place the kingdom of the Vākāṭakas 'on a par with the Gupta world',[15] a view which I find difficult to endorse. Moreover, the account of the Vākāṭaka history given by him is rather brief. Therefore, a detailed account of their history on the basis of all the material, old and new, literary and epigraphic, and also the light thrown on it by the history of the contemporary neighbouring dynasties, especially the imperial Guptas, the Śaka Śatrapas, the Āndhras and the Kadambas, is still a desideratum.

II

Much new light has been shed by scholars recently on the question of the original home of the Vākāṭakas. K.P. Jayaswal, following some references in the Purāṇas, had located their original home in the "Vindhyan country" and the place of their rise "on the river or in the locality called Kilakilā", which he connected with the river Kilakilā near Panna in the Ajaygarh-Panna area of Bundelkhand.[16] He suggested the derivation of the name 'Vākāṭaka' from a place called Vākāṭa or Vakāṭa and identified it with Bāgāṭa in the area of Orchha in northern-most part of Bundelkhand.[17] H.C. Raychaudhuri considered Vidarbha or Berar as the "proper Vākāṭaka country".[18] D. C. Sircar opined that the Purāṇic description seems to suggest that Vindhyaśakti, the founder of the first Vākāṭaka dynasty, flourished near about East Malwa (where ancient Vidiśā was located).[19] But A.S. Altekar initiating the view that the Vākāṭakas belonged to south India pointed out that "a third century A.D. inscription from Amarāvatī in the Andhra country refers to a Vākāṭaka pilgrim, who had come to visit the local *stūpa*" and that "this may suggest that the village Vakāṭa, to which he belonged, was rather to the south than to the north of the Vindhyas."[20] This theory was strengthened by V.V. Mirashi who drew the attention of scholars to the similarity between some of the technical terms occurring in the grant portions

[15] Groningen, 1997. Also see his edited work *The Vākāṭaka Heritage : Indian Culture at the Crossroads*, Groningen, 2004.

[16] K. P. Jayaswal, *History of India, 150 A.D. to 350 A.D.*, Lahore, 1933, pp. 66-67 (hereafter *HI*).

[17] *Ibid.*, p. 67.

[18] H. C. Raychaudhuri, *Political History of Ancient India*, Calcutta, Sixth edn., 1953, p. 461 and fn.

[19] In *The Age of Imperial Unity*, eds. R. C. Majumdar and A.D. Pusalker, Bombay, 1953, pp. 217-18.

[20] In *The Vākāṭaka-Gupta Age*, eds. R. C. Majumdar and A.S. Altekar, Lahore, 1946, p. 87 (hereafter *VGA*).

of the Basim copper plates of the Vākāṭaka king Vindhyaśakti II and the Hirahaḍagallī and Mayidavolu grants of the Pallava king Śivaskandavarman.[21] The use of the title *Hāritīputra* for the Vākāṭaka king Pravarasena I and of *Dharmamahārāja* for Sarvasena I, the founder of the Vatsagulma branch, and for his son and successor Vindhyaśakti II in the Basim plates of the latter[22] also suggest the southern origin of the Vākāṭakas as these titles are found with only in the charters of early south Indian dynasties like the Pallavas, the Kadambas and the Chālukyas of Badami and are conspicuous by their absence in the north Indian records. The argument that the title *Dharmamahārāja* was used only for the rulers of the Vatsagulma branch cannot be considered as valid because it has been found used for Vindhyaśakti I and Pravarasena I in the Bidar charter of Devasena and the Thalner plates of Harisheṇa, the last known ruler of the Vākāṭakas.

A couple of records of a ministerial family found at Ajanta (Cave XVI) and the Ghaṭotkacha Cave belonging to the reign of Harisheṇa show that the family in question was known as Vallūra, probably because it hailed from a place of that name which may be, as suggested by Mirashi, represented by modern Velur, about thirty miles north by east of Hyderabad in Andhra Pradesh.[23] Mirashi rightly uses the association of this family with the Vākāṭakas to strengthen his theory of the southern origin of the dynasty.

Recently K.V. Ramesh has sought to strengthen the theory of the south Indian origin of the Vākāṭakas on linguistic grounds.[24] He points out that the name 'Vākāṭaka' is totally inexplicable in Sanskrit whereas its middle portion, *kāṭa*, could actually be the Sanskritised form of the word *kāḍu* which in all Dravidian languages denotes 'a forest' or 'a thicket'. He argues that the postulation that *kāṭa* of Vākāṭaka is the Sanskritised form of the Dravidian or vernacular *kāḍu* is substantiated by the coinage of the place-name Vatsagulma for the new headquarters of the Vatsagulma branch of the Vākāṭakas. The Sanskrit word *gulma*, like *kāḍu*, also means 'a forest' or 'a thicket'. It is further likely that by the time the Vatsagulma branch had become established, the region in which they carved out their kingdom out of the Vākāṭaka territory had become highly influenced by the Brāhmaṇical trends and that a place-name not yielding to Sanskrit etymology would have been literally out of place. Hence also the Sanskritisation of Vākāḍu into Vatsagulma.[25]

[21] V.V. Mirashi, *Corpus Inscriptionum Indicarum*, Vol. V: *Inscriptions of the Vākāṭakas*, Ootacamund, 1963, pp. xi-xx (hereafter *CII*).

[22] *Ibid.*, p. xv.

[23] *Ibid.*

[24] K. V. Ramesh, 'On the Vākāṭakas and Their Inscriptions', in *The Age of the Vākāṭakas*, ed. A.M. Shastri, New Delhi, 1992, pp. 27-32 (hereafter *AV*).

[25] *Ibid.*, p. 30.

The emergence of the Vākāṭakas belonging to the Brāhmaṇa order as a ruling power was the culmination of the process which was going on since the beginning of the post-Maurya period. The most important element of the state structure in ancient India was kingship, and significantly enough we find Manu, the Smṛti writer of the Śuṅga period, declaring that "a Brāhmaṇa who knows the Veda deserves to be made a king, a commander-in-chief, the wielder of power of punishment."[26] That this new principle was concomitant with an actual change in the nature of kingship becomes clear from the fact that almost all the important indigenous ruling dynasties of the post-Maurya period belonged to the Brāhmaṇa order. Pushyamitra, the founder of the Śuṅga dynasty, Vasudeva, the first Kaṇva ruler, Simuka, the first of the Sātavāhana kings and many others—the Kadambas, the Guptas[27] and the Vākāṭakas—were Brāhmaṇas. The history of the Vākāṭakas was deeply influenced by the fact that they belonged to the Brāhmaṇa order, something which scholars have not appreciated so far.

As pointed by S.R. Goyal,[28] in the post-Maurya epoch at various levels of administration Brāhmaṇas were given the place of honour. The echo of this change may be heard in the contemporary literature and epigraphs. In the *Mahābhārata* which, in the period under review, was thoroughly revised by the Bhārgavas[29]—the most militant section of the Brāhmaṇa society—we find a glorified picture of the Brāhmaṇa sages and warriors. They are described as highly arrogant, domineering, unbending and revengeful. The kings of the earth are like vermin before them. The mighty Haihayas tremble before the infant Aurva who blinds them by his effulgence, and they have to beg for mercy on bended knees. King Kuśika grovels at the feet of Chyavana and meekly submits to all varieties of indignities. Rāma Jāmadagnya or Paraśurāma, the Bhārgava hero *par excellence*, described as a perfect warrior (*sarvaśastra-bhṛtāṁvaraḥ*), conquers the whole world, alone and unaided. He frees the earth of the burden of the Kshatriyas thrice seven times and makes the gift of the earth to Kaśyapa, his priest, who distributes it among the Brāhmaṇas.[30] That, he was the ideal and a source of inspiration for the Brāhmaṇa rulers of the Deccan of the post-Maurya period, is proved by the contemporary epigraphs. Take, for example, the case of Gautamīputra

[26] *Manu.*, XII. 100. See P. V. Kane, *History of Dharmaśāstra*, Vol. III, Poona, Second edn., 1973, p. 39.

[27] I subscribe to the view that the imperial Guptas belonged to the Brāhmaṇa order. Cf. my *Problems of Ancient Indian History : New Perspectives and Perceptions*, Jaipur, 2001, pp. 151-52.

[28] *IG*, pp. 80 ff.

[29] V.S. Sukthankar, *Critical Studies in the Mahābhārata*, Bombay, 1944, pp. 330 ff.

[30] *Ibid.*, pp. 327-28.

Śātakarṇi, the Sātavāhana emperor. In the Nasik *praśasti* he is called *Eka-Bamhaṇa,* i.e. the unique Brāhmaṇa, and *Khatiya-dapa-māna-madana,* i.e. the destroyer of the pride and conceit of the Kshatriyas. The expression *Eka-Bamhaṇa* when read along with the expression *Khatiya-dapa-māna-madana* leaves no room for doubt that he not only claimed to be a Brāhmaṇa, but also a Brāhmaṇa like Paraśurāma who humbled the pride of the Kshatriyas. As a matter of fact, the inscription specifically describes him as 'the unique Brāhmaṇa, in prowess equal to Rāma' i.e. Bhārgava Rāma or Paraśurāma.[31]

A more intimate glimpse into the psychology of the militant Brāhmaṇas, specially of south India, which led them to capture political power, is provided by the Talagunda inscription of the Kadamba king Śāntivarman.[32] From it we learn that the Kadambas derived their descent from *Hāritī* — a group of the Bhṛgvāṅgirasa family. Mayūraśarman, the founder of the Kadamba dynasty, was a pious Brāhmaṇa devoted to the study of the Vedas and the performance of the Vedic sacrifices. After a good education he went to the capital of the Pallava ruler along with his guru Vīraśarman to complete his studies. There he had a quarrel with a mounted guard (*aśvasaṁstha*) and in his wrath he thought : "Alas! in this age of Kali, Brāhmaṇahood is helpless against the Kshatra; for what can be more pitiful than this that even after I have given full satisfaction to my gurus and studied my *śākhā* with great effort, the realization of my spiritual aim should depend on the king?" So he gave up the sacrificial ladle and grasped the shining weapons of war, wishing to conquer the world. It may be that the rise of the Vākāṭakas, who belonged to the Vishṇuvṛddha *gotra* of the Bhṛgvāṅgirasa family,[33] and of other *Brahma-Kshatra* dynasties, took place in circumstances of similar nature.

The main feature of the religious renaissance of this period was the rapproachement between the Vedic and the devotional schools and the gradual triumph of the latter. The Bhāraśivas performed ten horse-sacrifices, but they constantly carried on their person the emblem of Śiva. This trend is manifest in the religious attitude of the Vākāṭakas also. The Vākāṭaka emperor Pravarasena I performed a large number of Vedic sacrifices like Bṛhaspatisava, Aśvamedha, Agnishṭoma, Āptoryāma, Ukthya and Atirātra, but his successor Rudrasena I was a devotee of Śiva and latter's grandson Rudrasena II was a worshipper of Chakrapāṇi.[34]

The Brāhmaṇical revival of the Vākāṭaka-Gupta age had many aspects.

[31] Raychaudhuri, *op. cit.*, pp. 413-14.

[32] D. C. Sircar, *Select Inscriptions*, Calcutta, 1943, pp. 475 ff. (hereafter *SI*).

[33] V. S. Pathak, *Ancient Historians of India*, Bombay, 1966, p. 25.

[34] *IG*, p. 97.

Firstly, it was extremely nationalist in character. As it was also the result of a reaction against the dominance of the foreigners who were mostly patrons of heterodox faiths, it was bound to be so. The meaning and significance of this aspect of the movement becomes apparent if we compare the nature of the Maurya empire with the character of its Vākāṭaka-Gupta counterparts which were the product of this movement. It has been recognised that the Maurya government was to a great extent influenced by the Achaemenid and Hellenistic traditions.[35] There is at least some truth in the remark of Rostovtzeff, the learned historian of Hellenism: "If one believes in the historical character and early date of the kernel of the *Arthaśāstra* of Kauṭilya and in the radical centralization of Indian government effected by Chandragupta on "Hellenistic" lines, one may say that Chandragupta did more to Hellenise India than Demetrius and Menander."[36]

In contrast to the Maurya empire, the Vākāṭaka and Gupta states were almost thoroughly Indian in character. If "the Mauryan polity with its bureaucratic and pervasive paternalism was an exception to the norm of ancient Indian state",[37] the Vākāṭaka-Gupta administration was in accordance with the best traditions laid down in the text books on the Hindu polity.[38] The Brāhmaṇical revival was also a great unifying force. In the preceding period, Buddhism, after its brilliant legacy of the Maurya period in the sphere of unification of the country had, under the patronage of the foreigners, played a somewhat reactionary role which hindered the process of integration.[39] In the post-Kushāṇa period, under the impact of the reviving Brāhmaṇism, the forces of disintegration started to become weaker and once again the idea of 'universal empire' (comprising the whole of the country or the *chakravartī-kshetra*) became popular. The *Vāyu-purāṇa* declared that the "*chakravartins* are born in each age as the essence of Vishṇu. They have lived in the ages past and will come again in future. In all the three ages — past, present and future — even in the *Tretā* age other *chakravartins* have been and will be born."[40] A few centuries later Medhātithi, the great commentator on Manu, expressed the idea in this manner : "A king of meritorious conduct could conquer even the land of the *mlechchhas*, establish *chāturvarṇya* there, assign to the *mlechchhas* a position occupied

[35] K.A.N. Sastri (ed.), *A Comprehensive History of India*, Vol. II, Calcutta, 1957, pp. 54-55.

[36] *Ibid.*, p. 55.

[37] *Ibid.*, p. 87.

[38] Cf. R. C. Majumdar and A. D. Pusalker (eds.), *The Classical Age*, Bombay, 1954, p. 351 (hereafter *CA*).

[39] *Ibid.*, p. ix.

[40] Cf. *Vayu-purāṇa*, XLVII, 72-76.

by the chāṇḍālas and render that land as fit for sacrifice as Āryāvarta itself."[41] The Gupta emperors and the Vākāṭaka rulers seem to have lived in accordance to this ideal.

III

Some recently found inscriptions have thrown welcome light on the early history of the Vākāṭakas. For example, earlier scholars were not sure about the political status of Vindhyaśakti I. A.S. Altekar even suggested that Vindhyaśakti I, described as *vaṁśaketu* or 'banner of the dynasty' in some texts, was merely a general as he was never anointed king by any formal coronation.[42] But the recently discovered Bidar plates of Devasena and the Thalner grant of Harisheṇa, the last known member of the Vatsagulma branch, mention him as *Ādi Dharmamahārāja* of the Vākāṭakas (*Vākāṭakānām=ādir= Dharmamahārāja*), leaving no doubt in his being coronated and assuming regal title.

Pravīra (Pravarasena I), the son and successor of Vindhyaśakti, who is generally placed between c. 275 to c. 335 A.D., evidently desired to enlarge his kingdom into an empire. But in the northern direction there was no scope for expansion due to the rise of the Nāgas and the Guptas (both of whom themselves aspired for imperial dignity)[43] and consequently he had to move southward where the Sātavāhanas represented by Śaka Śātakarṇi, Kumbha Śātakarṇi and Karṇa (or Kṛshṇa) Śātakarṇi, known almost exclusively from their coins in the Tarhala (Akola district) hoard, ruled up to about 300 A.D.[44]

But the extent of the empire of Pravarasena has been a matter of controversy. By far the most exaggerated notion of his empire is that of K.P. Jayaswal who believed that Pravarasena was the lord paramount of almost whole of India,[45] a view which is not endorsed now by any scholar. Relying on the *Śrīśaila-sthala-māhātmya* tradition that a daughter of Chandragupta named Chandrāvatī daily offered a garland of jasmine flowers to god Mallikārjuna at Śrīśaila and identifying Chandrāvatī with Prabhāvatīguptā, Altekar concluded that the *tīrtha* (Śrīśaila) was included in the Vākāṭaka empire and that all the territory right up to the Kurnool district fell within the Vākāṭaka sphere of influence, even if not actually under the Vākāṭaka administration.[46] However, this tradition is not reliable in this context,

[41] Quoted in *CA*, *op. cit.*

[42] Altekar, in *VGA*, p. 97.

[43] Cf. that the Bhāraśivas performed ten *aśvamedhas* and Bhavanāga adopted the title *Adhirāja* besides *Mahārāja* on his coins.

[44] Shastri, *Early History of the Deccan*, New Delhi, 1987, pp. 38-44.

[45] Jayaswal, *HI*, pp. 82-94.

[46] In *VGA*, p. 99.

especially because the deity at Śrīśaila is Mallikārjuna *Śiva* whereas Prabhāvatīguptā was a staunch Vaishṇava. It has also been argued by Altekar that the end of the line of Chashṭana after Bhartṛdāman and the accession of Rudrasiṁha II, son of Svāmī Jīvadāman, and the non-assumption of the title Mahākshatrapa by him and by his son and successor Yaśodāman II were due to the interference of Pravarasena I in the affairs of the Western Kshatrapas. It has also been suggested that Pravarasena I incited Rudrasiṁha II against the reigning king Bhartṛdāman assuring him all help provided he, that is Rudrasiṁha II, would accept the Vākāṭaka suzerainty, which explains the non-assumption of the title Mahākshatrapa (which was indicative of independent status) by him and his son all through their reigns and payment of tribute which is represented by the Sonpur (Chhindwara district, Madhya Pradesh) hoard containing, *inter alia*, their coins.[47] But this theory is also difficult to be accepted for the cessation of Chashṭana's line can be easily explained as on account of the failure of a male child after Bhartṛdāman. The cessation of the adoption of the title Mahākshatrapa could indeed have been caused by the Vākāṭaka interference in Śaka politics, but it could also have been due to the Sassanians who had about this time occupied Sind and might have compelled the two Kshatrapas from assuming the higher title.[48]

However, even if Pravarasena I could not establish an all-India empire, his achievements were fairly remarkable and justified the assumption of the title of *samrāṭ* by him. From the position of the king of a petty kingdom he rose to be the ruler of a reasonably big empire; the sphere of his influence was probably wider, though its extent cannot be determined accurately.

Pravarasena I performed numerous *śrauta* sacrifices described in the Purāṇas and epigraphs both. The Purāṇas tell us that Pravīra, that is Pravarasena I, performed several Vājapeyas or Vājimedhas attended with rich *dakshiṇās* (gifts or fee to the Brāhmaṇas) while inscriptions aver that he performed all the Soma sacrifies (*sapta-soma-saṁstha*) and four Aśvamedhas. It may also be reasonably assumed that the imperial title *samrāṭ* (which is used only for him among the Vākāṭakas and among the later Indian rulers was adopted only by Yaśodharman alias Vishṇuvardhana Aulikara) was assumed by him after the completion of some of his campaigns.

From the Purāṇas we learn that Pravarasena I had four sons.[49] The statement is generally accepted as correct[50] because the epigraphs reveal

[47] *Ibid.*

[48] Shastri, *Vākāṭakas—Sources and History*, New Delhi, 1997, p. 169 (hereafter *VSH*).

[49] Pargiter, *op. cit.*, p. 50.

[50] Altekar, in *VGA*, p. 102; Sircar, in *CA*, p. 177; Mirashi, *Vākāṭaka Rājavaṁśa kā Itihāsa tathā Abhilekha*, Varanasi, 1964, p. 24.

the existence of at least one brother of Gautamīputra[51] named Sarvasena who ultimately founded the Vatsagulma branch of the dynasty.[52] Now, it is generally supposed that Gautamīputra predeceased his father Pravarasena I, for we find that the latter was succeeded by Rudrasena I, the son of Gautamīputra. It is very curious and should raise questions in the minds of modern historians because, after the supposed demise of Gautamīputra, Pravarasena I should had been succeeded by the eldest of his remaining three sons, and not by Rudrasena I, the son of Gautamīputra. How and why did Rudrasena I succeed in acquiring the throne to which his uncles had a rightful claim? No scholar has so far felt the necessity to explain this rather unusual fact.[53] However, using the interpretation of the term *dauhitra* suggested by V.S. Pathak in another context,[54] S.R. Goyal has opined that Rudrasena I's description as *Bhavanāga-dauhitra* means that he was *dvayāmushyāyaṇa*, that is, he was the son of *dauhitra* category of Bhavanāga, his maternal grandfather, and also the successor of Pravarasena I, his grandfather. According to Goyal, most likely Bhavanāga, who probably did not have a male issue to succeed him, gave his daughter in marriage to Gautamīputra, the eldest son of Pravarasena I on the understanding that his (Bhavanāga's) daughter's son would also be his subsidiary son of *dauhitra* category.[55] Pravarasena I readily accepted this proposal, for it meant that the son of Gautamīputra, as a *dvayāmushyāyaṇa* would inherit the Vākāṭaka as well as the Bhāraśiva empire. In other words, it meant the amalgamation of these two empires during the reign of the son of Gautamīputra. Pravarasena I did not want the opportunity of this peaceful merger of the two contiguous empires under the rulership of his grandson to slip away; therefore, he nominated Rudrasena I, the son of Gautamīputra and the *dauhitra* of Bhavanāga, and not Gautamīputra himself, as his own successor as well. For had Pravarasena I been succeeded by any one of his remaining three sons, the two empires could not be amalgamated. Now, how far did the plan of Bhavanāga and Pravarasena I succeed is another matter, but S.R. Goyal's analysis leaves no room to doubt that their alliance was not an ordinary political treaty; its aim was far more significant—the ultimate amalgamation of the two empires. As such, it must have been regarded as a source of great danger by the contemporary neighbouring states.

[51] So far scholars generally have not paid attention to the fact that the Vākāṭaka records do not give any proper name for the eldest son of Pravarasena I. The appellation Gautamīputra given to him is only a metronymic.

[52] Sircar, *SI*, p. 407.

[53] Cf. *CA*, p. 178; *VGA*, p. 102.

[54] Pathak, in *JNSI*, XIX, ii, pp. 140-41.

[55] *IG*, p. 114.

Significantly, it was precisely in this period—sometime in the early years of the fourth century A.D.—that the Guptas contracted a matrimonial alliance with their eastern neighbours, the Lichchhavis of Magadha on similar lines making Samudragupta a *dvayāmushyāyaṇa* —the son of the *dauhitra* category of his Lichchhavi grandfather and the direct successor of his father Chandragupta I. Probably the factor that compelled the Guptas and the Lichchhavis to come closer to each other was the chronologically earlier emergence of the Vākāṭaka-Bhāraśiva *entente*. It was thus indeed a veritable politico-diplomatic revolution.

Thus, the achievements of Pravarasena I were highly remarkable and his *santāna-sandhi* with the Bhāraśivas a brilliant stroke of diplomacy which could lead, if all went well, to the creation a powerful empire. But all did not go well, for the ambitious princes in both the contracting royal families did not feel kindly to the dreams of Pravarasena I and Bhavanāga. In the Vākāṭaka kingdom it was certainly opposed by the uncles of Rudrasena I of whom at least one, Sarvasena, became independent while in the Bhāraśiva kingdom it was opposed most likely by Nāgasena, the Nāga contemporary of Samudragupta, for he is described in the *Harshacharita* as a ruler of Padmāvatī.

Be that as it may, the period of Rudrasena I's rule saw momentous events and changes in north India when the great Gupta monarch Samudragupta embarked on a victorious career taking his arms far and wide.[56] He uprooted the Nāga rulers, the relatives of the Vākāṭakas. It has been rightly believed by some earlier historians like K.P. Jayaswal[57] and S.K. Aiyangar[58] that Rudrasena I was himself defeated and killed by Samudragupta and that he is mentioned under the name of Rudradeva among the rulers of Āryāvarta (north India) extirpated by him.[59] This suggestion has been opposed by equally great historians. We feel that Jayaswal's view was basically sound and a logical corollary of the Vākāṭaka-Gupta relations as they developed in the age of Pravarasena I and his successors.

The defeat of the Vākāṭakas at the hands of Samudragupta is proved by the degradation of their political status. It is a well-known fact that after Pravarasena I no other king of the Vākāṭaka family assumed the title of *Samrāṭ*, or any other imperial title. According to Altekar, the title of *Māhārāja*, assumed by the successors of Pravarasena I, "did not at this time indicate any subordinate position in the Deccan, as it did in the Punjab. It was used even by independent

[56] Cf. Shastri, *VSH*, p. 176.
[57] *HI*, pp. 14 ff.
[58] *ABORI*, IV, pp. 30-40.
[59] Cf. *IG*, pp. 192-97.

rulers... ."[60] This is quite true, but the title of *Māhārāja* did not indicate the imperial status either, which Pravarasena I had claimed for his dynasty. The rejection of the theory of the Vākāṭaka-Gupta conflict during the reign of Samudragupta would imply that while the Gupta emperor was encircling the Vākāṭaka state by subjugating its northern, eastern and south-eastern neighbours, the Vākāṭaka ruler slept over the new developments and did nothing to ward off the dangers to which his kingdom had been exposed. It also implies that Samudragupta was totally unaware of the dangers to which he was exposing himself by penetrating deep in the south without bringing the Vākāṭakas within the sphere of his influence; for by virtue of his geographical position, the Vākāṭaka ruler could easily cut Samudragupta's lines of supply and communication by moving the Vākāṭaka armies along the lower reaches of the Godavari and trap the Gupta emperor in Andhra, where the imperial armies, encircled by hostile forces on all sides, could be easily crushed.

Jayaswal believes that "Samudragupta's sole objective in the south was the Pallava army" which could become a source of greatest danger to the Gupta kingdom, had the Pallavas (according to Jayaswal a junior branch of the Vākāṭakas) from the south and the Vākāṭakas from Bundelkhand invaded Bihar.[61] This view, however, rests upon the absolutely unproved assumption that the Pallavas were an offshoot of the Vākāṭaka dynasty. If this was so, one may ask what did the Vākāṭakas do when Samudragupta was threatening the security of the Pallava kingdom?

It is also quite possible that in some campaigns Samudragupta's Vākāṭaka ally Pṛthivīsheṇa I also participated. Pṛthivīsheṇa I, though technically independent, was within the sphere of political influence of the Guptas. Now, it is interesting to note that he is called a *dharmavijayin* in the inscriptions of his successors.[62] As he probably ruled in the period when Samudragupta is known to have followed the policy of *dharmavijaya* in the Deccan and the far south (*grahaṇa-moksha- anugraha*), it becomes a very strong possibility that he participated in some of the southern *dharmavijaya* campaigns of the Gupta emperor and his successors gave their credit to him.

The relationship of Pṛthivīsheṇa I with Samudragupta reminds one of the relationship of the Kachhawaha rulers of Amer who offered their allegiance to Akbar, the Great Mughal, in the medieval age. The Kachhawaha rulers were internally free but had to participate in the distant wars of the Mughals; similarly, the Vākāṭaka monarch was also technically free but participated in the Deccan wars of the Gupta emperor. Of course the two situations are not fully identical, but then history never repeats itself fully.

[60] *VGA*, p. 106.
[61] *HI*, p. 136.
[62] *SI*, p. 444.

IV

It is generally believed that with the marriage of Prabhāvatīguptā and Rudrasena II, the friendly hold of the Guptas over the Vākāṭakas tightened. While Pṛthivīsheṇa I, the father of Rudrasena II, was a devotee of Śiva (*atyanta-Māheśvara*) Rudrasena is said to have been a devout Vaishṇava. This change was due to the great influence exerted on him by his chief-queen Prabhāvatīguptā and/or by his father-in-law.

The theory of Gupta influence was advocated mainly by Mirashi and Altekar and others accepted it almost fully. Their theory was based on the use of the nail-headed script of the Gupta empire found in the Pune copper plates of Prabhāvatīguptā, the occurrence of the Gupta genealogy in the Pune and Rithpur plates and the reference to Devagupta *alias* Chandragupta II in the grants of Pravarasena II. However, the epigraphic evidence cited in support of the Gupta influence on the Vākāṭakas does not prove the point. It appears that even Altekar and Mirashi were somewhat confused on this issue. As I pointed out elsewhere,[63] at one place Altekar opines that the Pune plates of Prabhāvatīguptā were drafted by a Gupta officer imported from Pāṭaliputra.[64] But at another place of the same work he contradicts himself by stating that 'the officers who drafted the Vākāṭaka plates during the regency of Prabhāvatīguptā were bred up in the Deccan tradition.'[65] But the use of a particular variety of a script in a document most likely depended on the training of its scribe.[66] Several inscriptions of the imperial Guptas show southern peculiarities. For example, the Udayagiri cave inscription of Chandragupta II of the Gupta year 82 (=401 A.D.) uses the box-headed variety of Brāhmī which was prevalent in the Vākāṭaka region. Similarly, the Sāñchī stone inscription of the same emperor of the Gupta year 93 (=412 A.D.) is also written in the Late Brāhmī of the Southern Class. If these facts cannot be regarded as a proof of the Vākāṭaka influence on the imperial

[63] Shankar Goyal, in *King Chandra and the Meharauli Pillar*, ed. by M. C. Joshi, S. K. Gupta and myself, Meerut, 1989, pp. 51-56; idem, 'Chandragupta II's Political Influence on the Vākāṭakas : Epigraphical Evidence Re-examined', in *History and Archaeology (Professor H. D. Sankalia Felicitation Volume)*, ed. Bhaskar Chatterjee, Delhi, 1989, pp. 351-56. Later on in 1997 A.M. Shastri expressed a similar view regarding the untenability of the suggestion that the Pune plates of Prabhāvatī prove the Gupta influence on the Vākāṭakas (*VSH*, p. 182).

[64] In *VGA*, p. 112, n. 1.

[65] *Ibid.*, p. 106.

[66] Shankar Goyal, 'Chandragupta II's Relations with the Vākāṭakas during the Regency of Prabhāvatīguptā', in *Proceedings of the South Indian History Congress*, Twenty-fourth Annual Session, Calicut, 2004, p. 129.

Guptas, then why should the use of the nail-headed variety in the Pune plates be regarded as a proof of the Gupta influence on the Vākāṭakas ? Further, the Gupta genealogy given in the Pune and Rithpur copper plates is very defective. These inaccuracies negate the idea that the officers who were responsible for the drafts of Pune and Rithpur plates were imported from the Gupta capital. Moreover, scribes were a very low category of government employees. It can hardly be imagined that Chandragupta II could have felt the necessity of sending Gupta scribes to the Vākāṭaka kingdom when he helped his daughter in the task of administration. Actually, the occurrence of the Gupta genealogy and *gotra* in the Vākāṭaka grants may easily be attributed to the custom current in the Vākāṭaka territory where queens usually introduced themselves with reference to their paternal family. The name of Prabhāvatīguptā has probably been given because she had herself ruled as a regent for a long time, or probably because the authors of the Vākāṭaka grants following the Deccan tradition wanted to give the name of the mother of the ruling king.[67] But as was the tradition in the Deccan, with her name the name of her father was also given. The point becomes obvious by the Balaghat grant of Pṛthivīsheṇa II where the author of the grant refers to Ajjhitabhaṭṭārikā, the mother of Pṛthivīsheṇa II as the daughter of the king of Kuntala (*Kuntalādhipatisutāyām Mahādevyām Ajjhitabhaṭṭārikāyāmutpannasya*).[68]

But the fact that the epigraphical evidence cited by Altekar and Mirashi to show Chandragupta II's influence on the Vākāṭaka court during the regency of Prabhāvatīguptā does not prove the point does not mean that such an influence was impossible or altogether non-existent. Indeed in the circumstances as are known to us some sort of Gupta influence on the Vākāṭakas during the minority of the sons of Rudrasena II may easily be presumed.[69] In this connection the fragmentary Ramtek Prabhāvatīguptā Memorial Stone Inscription, which is as yet not known widely, deposes

[67] *Ibid.*, p. 131.

[68] Mirashi, *CII*, V, p. 80.

[69] Three names of the sons of Prabhāvatī are known to epigraphy — Divākarasena, Dāmodarsena and Pravarasena. Earlier some historians believed that Dāmodarasena and Pravarasena II were not two distinct personages and that Dāmodarasena himself assumed the name Pravarasena II after his illustrious homonymous ancestor Pravarasena I. But the seal-inscription of the recently discovered Miregaon plates of Prabhāvatī issued in the twentieth year of Pravarasena II's reign describe her as the 'mother of two kings' (*Vikrāntayor-jananyās=tu Vākāṭaka-narendrayoḥ/Śrī-Prabhāvatī (ti) guptāyāḥ Śāsanaṁ ripu-śāsanam*). As Divākarasena had died without becoming king, the two kings mentioned here must have been Dāmodarasena and Pravarasena II proving that Dāmodarasena and Pravarasena II were separate individuals and both ascended the throne.

interesting evidence.[70] It was found incised on two rectangular blocks of stone inside the *maṇḍapa* (hall) of the Kevala-Narasiṁha temple at Ramtek, identified with the famous Rāmagiri, immortalised by Kālidāsa in his *Meghadūta.* It belongs to the reign of Pravarasena II of the main branch of the Vākāṭakas and purports to record most probably the erection of the Kevala-Narasiṁha temple and the installation of the image of the man-lion (Narasiṁha) *avatāra* of Vishṇu by a daughter (name lost) of Prabhāvatīguptā to perpetuate the latter's memory. She was in all probability assisted by her brother, perhaps Pravarasena II, in this venture.

The opening stanza of this highly important though fragmentary record is an invocation to god Vishṇu or one of his manifestations, quite likely his man-lion (Narasiṁha) form. The third stanza refers to a sovereign monarch, most likely Chandragupta (mentioned by name in Verse 9) whose feet were touched by the crest-jewels (*chūḍāmaṇi*) of the kings which served as his footstool (*pāda-pīṭha*).

The fifth stanza perhaps refers to his queen, most probably Kuberanāgā, mother of Prabhāvatīguptā. We learn from Verse 7 that after sons (Sanskrit plural number implying at least three) were born to them (that is to Chandragupta II and Kuberanāgā) in succession, their younger sister resembling the lustre of the moon (*chandramasaḥ prabh-eva*) was born. Verse 9 refers to Chandragupta (evidently Chandragupta II Vikramāditya) who is spoken of as of 'perfect character' (*paripūrṇa-vṛtta*), a 'god of gods' (*Dai (de) va-deva*) and, 'the lord of the three oceans' (*Tri-samudra-nātha*). This stanza also seems to have contained a reference to the giving by Chandragupta II of his daughter to Rudrasena II Vākāṭaka in marriage. The record next refers evidently to Chandragupta II, who is described as bearing the entire burden of the great kingdom (that is, the Vākāṭaka kingdom) which was difficult to bear as the best of the beasts of burden. Next is mentioned his son Ghaṭotkachagupta, who is styled as 'king of kings' (*Rājarāja*). It is in perfect consonance with the fact that Ghaṭotkachagupta issued gold coins indicative of his imperial status. He was born after Prabhāvatī (or after her marriage). Verse 13, which is almost fully preserved, refers to his (Ghaṭotkacha's) sister's daughter (*bhāgineyī*), i.e. niece, and to the fact that Ghaṭotkacha did something about her marriage. The wordings of the inscription (*pāṇigrahaṇaṁ chakāra*) literally mean and prove that he actually married her.

[70] Cf. Shastri, *AV*, pp. 253-57; idem, *VSH*, pp. 125-35; S. R. Goyal, *Ancient Indian Inscriptions : Recent Finds and New Interpretations*, Jodhpur, 2005, pp. 221-25. Interestingly, one finds almost complete disassociation between money and land grants in all 40/41 inscriptions of the Vākāṭakas indicating comparative paucity of coins during their rule. It explains why was the Vākāṭaka economy feudal in character.

After this there is a lacuna and then probably an allusion to Ghaṭotkacha, and of these first and last are almost lost for historical purposes. The next Verse most probably alludes to Ghaṭotkacha's demise after which the brother of his wife (obviously Pravarasena II) is said to have brought back his widowed sister to his own house 'forcibly' (*balāt*).

After sometime another calamity is said to have taken place. It was the death of Prabhāvatīguptā which must have occurred sometime after the twenty-third year of Pravarasena II's reign (the date of his Tirodi plates when he did a pious act for his mother's merit). This event must have been described in Verse 20 which is now completely lost. The next stanza refers to the pious act performed by the widow of Ghaṭotkacha in memory of her dead mother which was the execution of an image of 'the Lord of the Universe' (*Loka-nātha*) and the erection of his temple. Verse 24 speaks of the excavation of a tank called Sudarśana. The name Sudarśana seems to have been borrowed from the famous homonymous water-reservoir near modern Junagadh (Gujarat). The rest of the contents of the inscription are not of much political importance.

The testimony of the legible portions of the extant portions of this highly fragmentary record clarify and elaborate numerous points of the Gupta-Vākāṭaka history. It makes it clear that Chandragupta indeed looked after the Vākāṭaka administration during the minority of Prabhāvatīguptā's sons. It also shows that he was believed to have been a *Tri-samudra-nātha* (Lord of Three Oceans), a claim which, on the one hand, indicates that he for sometime exercised at least nominal suzerainty over the Vākāṭaka kingdom and, on the other, tends to strengthen the testimony of the Meharauli record regarding the warlike activities of Chandra (generally identified with Chandragupta II) in south India.[71] The inscription also gives highly significant and interesting information that Ghaṭotkachagupta, a son of Chandragupta II, married his own niece and obviously with the help of his Vākāṭaka in-laws revolted against the authority of his brother Kumāragupta I to whom he was owing allegiance till 435 A.D., the date of his Tumain inscription. The fact that after his death his Vākāṭaka wife was forcibly (*balāt*) rescued by her brother and brought to the Vākāṭaka capital shows that the hand of the Vākāṭakas was behind the revolt of Ghaṭotkachagupta.

V

Sometime in 440/445 Pravarasena II was succeeded by his son Narendrasena. He was a younger contemporary of Kumāragupta I while in his later years

[71] For a full discussion on the identity of the king mentioned in the Meharauli pillar inscription vide *King Chandra and the Meharauli Pillar*, pp. 73-237.

he was a contemporary of Skandagupta. He is probably identical with Narindarāja, born of Ājñākabhaṭṭārikā known from the recently discovered Mandhal plates of Pravarasena II of the year 16.[72] His son, Pṛthivīsheṇa II, is the last known king of the main branch of the Vākāṭakas after whose death the leadership of the Vākāṭakas passed into the hands of king Harisheṇa of the Vatsgulma branch. For Harisheṇa's reign we have as many as four inscriptions. One of them is a copper plate charter of his own and the rest are engraved in the caves at Ajanta (Caves XVI and XVII) and nearby Ghaṭotkacha Cave. Thanks to these records, we have a good deal of information about the reign of this last known member of the Vatsagulma branch. Harisheṇa had a minister named Varāhadeva, son of Devasena's minister Hastibhoja, who got Cave XVI at Ajanta and the Ghaṭotkacha Cave excavated and decorated and whose records have been found in these caves. While the Ghaṭotkacha Cave inscription furnishes an account of his own family from its inception and states that his father was a minister of Devarāja (the same as Devasena) and he himself was a minister of Harisheṇa, the Ajanta inscription gives the history of the Vatsagulma branch from the very beginning including its founder Sarvasena's two predecessors, viz. Vindhyaśakti I and Pravarasena I. With reference to Harisheṇa it states (Verse 18) that he conquered Kuntala, Avanti, Kaliṅga, Kosala, Trikūṭa, Lāṭa and Āndhra. On the basis of this evidence it may be claimed that 'Harisheṇa's supremacy was recognised throughout the Deccan extending from Malwa in the north to Kuntala in the south, and from the Arabian Sea in the west to the Bay of Bengal in the east.'[73] But his hegemony over this vast area must have been shortlived, for he is certainly the last known member of the Vatsagulma branch of the Vākāṭakas as Pṛthivīsheṇa II is of the other branch. Both the branches thus came to an end shortly after 500 A.D., within a few years of one another. With them the age of the Vākāṭaka supremacy in the Deccan came to an end.

[72] *EI*, XLI, p. 74.
[73] *CII*, V, Intro., p. xxxi.

APPENDIX

Hans Bakker on the Early History of the Vākāṭakas

Hans T. Bakker, a well-known European scholar, published his work *The Vākāṭakas : An Essay in Hindu Iconology* in 1997 from Groningen. It is one of the recent-most works on the Vākāṭaka history and culture. In its first chapter Bakker has outlined the political history of the Vākāṭakas in brief. Here, I propose to make some observations on his views on the early Vākāṭaka history.

On the early history of the Vākāṭakas, Bakker's views are quite close to those of S. R. Goyal.[74] Like Goyal, Bakker also believes that the second quarter of the 4th century A.D. saw two power blocks beginning to emerge in India, both consolidated by strategic matrimonial alliances.[75] In the Gangetic plain Samudragupta ascended the Gupta throne, inheriting Chandragupta I's kingdom (comprising the regions along the Gaṅgā, including Magadha, Prayāga and Sāketa) as well as the territories of the Lichchhavis, a patrimony to which he was entitled because of his mother, Kumāradevī. To the south of the northern plains Rudrasena I inherited at least parts of the kingdom of his grandfather, Pravarasena I, as well as the territories of the Bhāraśivas, a branch of the Nāga dynasty that ruled from Padmāvatī. Like Goyal, Bakker opines that Rudrasena's father, Gautamīputra, had died before he could ascend the throne; his mother was a daughter of king Bhavanāga of the Bhāraśiva lineage, who was, it would seem, without male offspring, which made Rudrasena, like Samudragupta, a 'daughter's son heir' (*dauhitra*).[76] But both successions, that of Rudrasena and Samudragupta, were not uncontested, since firstly,

[74] S. R. Goyal, *A History of the Imperial Guptas*, Allahabad, 1967. Goyal presented a revised and enlarged version of his perception of the Vākāṭaka history in his *The Imperial Guptas : A Multidisciplinary Political Study*, Jodhpur, 2005 and *A History of the Vākāṭaka-Gupta Relations*, Jodhpur, 2006.

[75] Bakker, *The Vākāṭakas*, p. 9; Goyal, *A History of the Imperial Guptas*, pp. 93-94.

[76] Bakker, *op.cit.*, pp. 9-10; Goyal, *op.cit.*, pp. 89-94.

several agnate princes of Nāga stock remained to challenge Rudrasena's claims to the Bhāraśiva legacy, and secondly, Rudrasena and Samudragupta both had rivals of 'equal birth' (*tulyakulaja*).

The founder of the Vākāṭaka dynasty was a Brāhmaṇa named Vindhyaśakti (I), who belonged to the Vishṇuvṛddha *gotra*. He was succeeded by his son Pravarasena, 'Pravīra' according to the Purāṇic account. He ruled as an emperor (*samrāj*), and performed four Aśvamedhas, a Vājapeya and several other Vedic sacrifices, at least never duplicated by any Vākāṭaka ruler.

But his dynastic line became divided when the Vākāṭakas and their Nāga allies were confronted with Gupta power. Here, Bakker by-passes the question as to why and how did Rudrasen I, the grand son of Pravarasena I, became the successor of the latter while after the death of Gautamīputra, who was one of the four sons of Pravarasena I, other three sons of the latter were entitled to the throne. Goyal raises this question and gives what is apparently a cogent answer.[77]

In the list of the Allahabad pillar inscription the first king of Āryāvarta, who is said to have been eradicated by Samudragupta, is Rudradeva. Goyal[78] and many historians before and after him have identified him with the Vākāṭaka king Rudrasena I. According to Bakker also, this identification 'does make sense'.[79]

Bakker also suggests that a crushing defeat at the hands of Samudragupta may have forced the Vākāṭakas to leave their homeland: Vindhyasena came to rule in Vatsagulma, his nephew Rudrasena — or, if he did not survive the onslaught, the latter's son and successor Pṛthivīsheṇa I — in Nandivardhana. The power (*śakti*) of the Nāgas, on the other hand, seems to have been curbed.[80]

However, their princess Kuberanāgā was given in marriage to Samudragupta's son Chandragupta II as one of his chief wives (*Mahādevī*). Bakker interprets afresh the terms *Dhāraṇa sagotrā* and *Ubhayakulālaṅkāra-bhūtā* occurring in the Poona and Riddhapur inscriptions of Prabhāvatīguptā. They are usually taken to mean that Prabhāvatī belonged to the Dhāraṇa *gotra*, and that she was "as it were, the ornament of both dynasties."[81] Here, 'both dynasties', Bakker insists, should be taken to refer to the Nāgas and Guptas, not to the latter and the Vākāṭakas. "It seems even likey that her *gotra*, Dhāraṇa, was that of the Nāga family and not, as is usually assumed on the basis of later practice, that of the Guptas."[82] But both these suggestions are highly untenable.

[77] Bakker, *op.cit.*, pp. 10 ff.; Goyal, *op. cit.*, pp. 88 ff.

[78] Goyal, *op.cit.*, p. 142.

[79] Bakker, *op.cit.*, p. 11.

[80] *Ibid.*

[81] *Ibid.*, p. 12.

[82] *Ibid.*

While it is apparently logical and in accordance with social conventions if Prabhāvatī is described as an ornament of the family in which she was born and of the family into which she was married, it would be illogical to assume that she has been described as an ornament of the family of her maternal grand father—and that too by-passing such a reference to her parental family. Similarly, it would also be too much to assume that Dhāraṇa was the *gotra* of the Nāgas and Prabhāvatī claimed it as her own, and forgot all about the *gotras* of her parents and husband.

On the issue of the original homeland of the Vākāṭakas Bakker expresses his agreement with A.M. Shastri who believed[83] that the kings Vindhyaśakti and Pravarasena ruled over the Vindhya area to the north of the Narmadā river. Same is the view of Goyal.[84] According to Bakker, and also Goyal, Shastri's arguments, of which the most significant are the very name of the founder of the dynasty, Vindhyaśakti, and the association of the two kings in the Purāṇic account with the Vindhyas, are well-reasoned and convincing, apart from one, viz. his identification of the king Pṛthivīsheṇa, whom Vyāghradeva has mentioned in his Nachne-ki-Talai and Ganj stone inscriptions as his overlord, with Pṛthivīsheṇa I, son of Rudrasena I.[85]

According to Bakker, around the middle of the 4th century or somewhat later, after Samudragupta had firmly established his authority in Bundelkhand, a group of Vākāṭaka nobles succeeded in carving out another kingdom for themselves in Vidarbha, where they built a new royal residence, named Nandivardhana, at the foot of a prominent hill, the Rāmagiri.[86]

With Mahārāja Pṛthivīsheṇa I (son of Rudrasena I), a glorious era began. The inscriptions of his successors compare his rule with that of Yudhishṭhira. According to them, he was "endowed with the following virtues among others: truthfulness, uprightness, compassion, courage, valour, good policy and conduct, magnanimity as well as wisdom, generosity towards those who well deserved it victoriousness in the *dharma* and purity of mind." And the inscriptions continue, "his son(s) and grandson(s), the lineage, and the accomplishment, viz. authority and wealth, were increasing over a period of one century."

A factor that undoubtedly contributed enormously to the material and cultural flourishing of the eastern Vākāṭakas, Bakker believes, is that Pṛthivīsheṇa I concluded the peace with Chandragupta II, who had ascended the Gupta throne at the beginning of the last quarter of the 4th century. The long-term strategic interests of the Guptas required a reliable and strong ally

83 A.M. Shastri, *The Age of the Vākāṭakas*, New Delhi, 1992, pp. 10 ff.

84 Goyal, *Gupta evaṁ Samakālīna Rājavaṁśa*, Allahabad, 1969, pp. 342-46.

85 Bakker, *op.cit.*, pp. 12-13.

86 *Ibid.*, p. 14.

at the southern borders of their realm. To assure this Chandragupta II gave his daughter from his marriage with the Nāga princess Kuberanāgā to Pṛthivīsheṇa I's son Rudrasena II. Hans Bakker describes this event rather dramatically: "The proud bridegroom", he says, "leading his young Gupta princess to her new home in triumph, across the Vindhyas, along the very route that only two generations before his family had probably taken to escape the Gupta rod, must have afforded a fine spectacle. The bride, the younger sister of several brothers, 'who resembled the lustre of the moon', and whose girl-hood name evidently was Muṇḍā, turned out to be a formidable lady, who became famous under the name of Prabhāvatī Guptā, a name that she may have adopted after her husband's death, when she became acting monarch. She brought with her the Vaiṣṇava Bhāgavata faith and the cultural assets and sophistication of the Gupta court. To judge by her inscriptions, in which seven lines are devoted to the eulogy of her imperial origins and only one line to her Vākāṭaka husband — denoting her father Candragupta as Mahārājādhirāja, her husband as Mahārāja — she might have thought herself far above the family of her in-laws."[87]

However, after a rule of about one decade her husband died in c.405 A.D., leaving her with three boys and at least one daughter. She adopted the regency over her eldest son, *Yuvarāja* Divākarasena, but apparently he too died before he could ascend the throne. Her regency over her two remaining sons may have lasted a few years more, which brought the total duration of the rule of this dowager queen to thirteen or fourteen years, from c. 405 to 419 A.D. Thus, ended the first important phase of the Vākāṭaka history.

Thus, the general outline of the Vākāṭaka history till the regency of Prabhāvatīguptā as reconstructed by Bakker in his *The Vākāṭakas* (1997) is almost similar to that of Goyal as was given in his *A History of the Imperial Guptas* (1967). Goyal, however, introduced necessary changes in this outline in the light of the inscriptions, especially the Ramtek inscription discovered after 1967, in his *The Imperial Guptas : A Multidisciplinary Political Study* (2005) and *A History of the Vākāṭaka-Gupta Relations* (2006). But the new Vākāṭaka inscriptions hardly throw any fresh light on the regency of Prabhāvatīguptā, except the Ramtek inscription which mentions several new facts about the regency period. These facts have been discussed by Bakker and Goyal both. From their comparative study it is obvious that the major difference between the reconstruction of Bakker and Goyal is regarding the chronology of events. Thus, Bakker places the death of Rudrasena II in c. 405 A.D. and the total duration of the regency of Prabhāvatīguptā from c. 405 to 419 A.D.[88] while Goyal suggests that Rudrasena II expired in c. 385/90 A.D.

[87] *Ibid.*, pp. 15-16.
[88] *Ibid.*, pp. 16-23.

and Prabhāvatīguptā ruled as the regent of *Yuvarāja* Divākarasena from c. 385/90 to c. 405/10, of Dāmodarasena from c. 405/10 to c. 410/15 and that Pravarasena II, the third son of Prabhāvatīguptā, ruled from c. 410/15 to c. 445/50.[89]

Goyal begins his calculation with the fact that the last known regnal year of Pravarasena II is 32. Therefore, he might have ruled for about 35 years. Now, from the details regarding the Gupta-Vākāṭaka relations alluded to in the Ramtek inscription, when they are studied in collation with other known facts, it seems that Pravarasena II's reign ended sometimes between 445 and 450 A.D. Therefore, he might have started ruling sometime between 410 and 415 A.D. Before Pravarasena II Dāmodarasena was a minor king, for a short while, say, for about 5 years and earlier still Divākarasena for at least 13 years. Therefore, the demise of Rudrasena II might have taken place sometime between 385 and 390 A.D. It makes a substantial difference in the regency period of Prabhāvatīguptā—Bakker placing it between 405 and 419 and Goyal between 385/90 and 410/15.

[89] Goyal, *A History of the Vākāṭaka-Gupta Relations*, pp.87-88.

THREE

Feudal Nature of the Vākāṭaka Economy

GRADUAL INCREASE IN THE COMPLEXITIES OF FEUDAL SYSTEM

The Vākāṭakas flourished in the Deccan during the period of the ascendancy of the mighty imperial Guptas in the north, quite independently but under the protective umbrella of the latter. The imposition of the Gupta hegemony on the Vākāṭakas was established in the reign of Samudragupta. Whether or not he defeated Rudrasena I, the successor of Pravarasena I,[1] there is no denying the fact that he succeeded in making the Vākāṭakas his subordinate ally, for without having done so he could not venture to invade the Deccan and south India at least upto Kāñchī. The structure of the empire which Samudragupta established was feudal-federal. Samudragupta seems to have placed in one category those feudatories in Āryāvarta who recorded their presence in the imperial court, offered regular tribute and obeyed the imperial orders. He puts in another category the other set of feudatories in distant lands who offered allegiance, made occasional presents of maids and other items and also received charters of rights from the sovereign.[2] Its core area was constituted by those Āryāvarta states the rulers of which were exterminated by the Gupta emperor. Among them was included Rudradeva, identified by many, and in our view rightly, with Rudrasena I Vākāṭaka in his capacity as the master of his Āryāvarta possessions. In the time of Chandragupta II by a matrimonial alliance the Vākāṭakas were placed on a footing of near-equality, though in actuality the Guptas continued to remain the dominating party. The number of various

[1] For a recent discussion on this probem cf. S.R. Goyal, *The Imperial Guptas : A Multidisciplinary Political Study*, Jodhpur, 2005, pp. 192-97.

[2] Cf. M.G. S. Narayanan, 'A Reappraisal of Samudragupta's Digvijaya' in *Śrī Dineśacandrikā* (*Shri D.C. Sircar Festschrift*), eds. B.N. Mukherjee et al, Delhi, 1983, p. 287; also see Goyal, *op. cit.*, pp. 175-81.

categories of vassals continued to increase in the subsequent reigns so much so that in the Kahaum pillar inscription of GE 141 (=461 A.D.) it could be said about Skandagupta that his "hall of audience is shaken by the wind caused by the falling down (*in the act of performing obeisance*) of the heads of a hundred kings."[3] The relationship of the suzerain and vassals also became more and more complex so that in the age of Budhagupta (476-495 A.D.) a *Mahārāja* (Suraśmichandra) could be the governor of *Antarvedī* (in the very heartland of the empire) and could have a *Mahārāja* (Mātṛvishṇu) under him as governor of Airikiṇa.[4] A little later Droṇasiṁha of the Maitraka dynasty was invested in a ceremony of coronation with the rank and title of *Mahārāja* by "the ruler of the whole world."[5] All these are isolated facts but they do indicate to the increase in the complexities of feudal system as also an increase in the prestige of the subordinate kings.

The variety of forms of relationship created an uneven character of socio-economic and political development in different parts of the country from the fourth century onwards. The Allahabad *praśasti* flashes a powerful beam of light across the entire subcontinent in c.370 A.D. revealing at one glance this unevenness of growth in which an imperial state co-existed with regional hereditary monarchies in the east and south, regional republican oligarchies in the west and north-west, foreign kingdoms and nomadic tribal groups on the north and north-west border of India and a good number of forest tribes scattered here and there but mostly in the tribal belt of central India. At one end of the scale was the highly advanced Sanskritized society and polity of the Guptas and at the other end we find the forest and mountain tribes, old and new, groping their way towards the formation of their territorial states.[6] That is how the term feudal-federal, used for the Gupta empire first by Beni Prasad,[7] should be interpreted even if he himself did not realise its significance fully. R.S. Sharma calls the Gupta polity 'proto-feudal'.[8] He has examined the post-Maurya changes in economy and society in the light of literature, epigraphy and archaeology and has brought out the tremendous impact of the land grants beginning with the period of the

[3] J.F. Fleet, *Corpus Inscriptionum Indicarum*, Vol. III : *Inscriptions of the Early Gupta Kings and Their Successors*, Calcutta, 1888, p. 67.

[4] *Ibid.*, p. 89.

[5] Whether he was the Gupta emperor himself or his Hūṇa or Aulikara overlord is not clear.

[6] Narayanan, *op.cit.*, p. 288.

[7] Beni Prasad, *The State in Ancient India*, Allahabad, 1928, quoted by Goyal, *op. cit.*, p. 179.

[8] R.S. Sharma, *Aspects of Political Ideas and Institutions in Ancient India*, 4th revised edn., Delhi, 1996, Ch. 18.

Sātavāhanas to prove that the feudal elements in economy and society had already become prevalent, though not dominant, in the period of the imperial Guptas. That the process of strong feudalization of the state apparatus was set in motion by the practice of making grants of lands to the brāhmaṇas from the first century A.D. onwards is beyond doubt. Although Aśoka's edicts are spread all over the country, they do not speak of any land grants. The earliest epigraphic land grant belongs to the first century B.C.[9] But it does not mention transfer of administrative powers to the beneficiary, which is done for the first time in the grants made to the Buddhist priests by the Sātavāhana ruler Gautamīputra Śātakarṇi in the second century A.D.[10] The land granted to them is described as *apraveśyam* (not to be entered by royal troops), *anavamarśyam* (not to be molested by government officials) and *arāshṭrasamvinayikam* (not to be interfered by the district police). "From the middle of the fourth century A.D. such grants in favour of the brāhmaṇas become frequent. Their two significant features are the transfer of all sources of revenue and the surrender of the police and administrative functions."[11] In the light of this changing economic development it is possible to suggest that the feudal political formations reflected in the Allahabad *praśasti* were posterior to and as such reflected the changes in economy and society starting with the post-Maurya-Sātavāhana age.

Against this background the applicability of the term 'feudalism' to the Vākāṭaka situation needs a closer examination. We, therefore, propose to trace such features in the Vākāṭaka economy in the light of their inscriptions known so far which may legitimately be called feudal. How and why these traits continued to remain in the Vākāṭaka kingdom will be the main thurst of our enquiry.

THE PROBLEM OF COINS IN THE VĀKĀṬAKA ECONOMY

Let us start our enquiry with coins, for the absence of coins in a society is usually regarded as a feature of feudal economy.[12] Further, the study of the sources of metal for coinage may throw considerable light on the economy of a society. For example, the abundance of the gold coins of the Kushāṇas gives rise to the question : 'From where did they get so much yellow metal

[9] D. C. Sircar, *Select Inscriptions*, Vol. I, Calcutta, 2nd edn., 1965, p. 188, 1.11.

[10] *Ibid.*, pp. 192, 194-95.

[11] R. S. Sharma, 'Problem of Transition from Ancient to Medieval in Indian History', in *The Indian Historical Review*, March 1974, Vol. I, No. 1, p.2; also see his *Early Medieval Indian Society: A Study in Feudalisation*, Kolkata, 2001, pp. 16-44.

[12] Idem, 'Coins and Problems of Early Indian Economic History', *JNSI*, Vol. XXXI, Pt. i, 1969, pp. 1-8; S.R. Goyal, *The Coinage of Ancient India*, Jodhpur, 1995, pp. 12-14; idem, *Indigenous Coins of Early India*, Jodhpur, 1994, Ch. 1.

for their coinage ?' According to R.S. Sharma, probably one of their sources were the Roman coins which are found only rarely in north India though scores of their hoards have been discovered in the south.[13] Then there is the question: Why did the Kushāṇas not issue silver coins while their Indo-Greek predecessors are known to have issued coins in the white metal ?' To answer the later question Sharma argues that the silver mines of the Kharagpur hills were out of the reach of the Kushāṇas.[14] The problem 'why did the Guptas not issue many copper coins while the Kushāṇas did ?' is also quite interesting. Sharma suggests that in the Gupta age the growth of self-sufficient economic units precluded the use of coins by rural peasantry making the use of money not so necessary.[15] Sharma also raises the question: 'Why is it so that there is almost complete absence of gold coins and paucity of coins in general in north India in the post-Gupta age for about four centuries though coinage revived in some parts of north India in the 11th and 12th centuries ?' and suggests that these developments were connected with external commercial relations.[16]

The different elements, characteristics and attributes of coins often give information of economic importance.[17] For the Vākāṭaka kingdom the problem of the existence or non-existence or non-availability or paucity of coins is of major concern because the existence of coins in their society would prove that it had advanced from the stage of barter economy when goods were usually produced for immediate exchange whereas comparative paucity or complete non-availability of coins would prove economic decline or backwardness in their territories. Writing as early as in 1963 V.V. Mirashi had rightly observed, "The Vākāṭakas did not strike any coins,"[18] an assertion with which most of the scholars agree. Significantly, despite attempts by some scholars to prove that the Vākāṭakas issued their own coins in copper, what Mirashi wrote about half a century ago still remains true.[19] The claims of Ajay Mitra Shastri, A.H. Siddiqui and Prashant P.

[13] *Ibid.*, pp. 2-3.

[14] *Ibid.*, p. 2.

[15] Idem, *Indian Feudalism : c. 300-1200*, Calcutta, 1965, pp. 63-65.

[16] Idem, in *JNSI*, XXXI, i, p. 6.

[17] L.K. Tripathi, 'Coins as Source of Economic History', *JNSI*, XXXIII, i, 1971, pp. 1-14.

[18] V.V. Mirashi, *Corpus Inscriptionum Indicarum*, Vol. V: *Inscriptions of the Vākāṭakas*, Ootacamund, 1963, p. xiv. He has repeated his view in his *Indological Research Papers*, Vol. I, Nagpur, 1982, p. 84.

[19] Among early historians it was only K.P. Jayaswal (*History of India : c. 150 A.D. to 350 A.D.*, Lahore, 1933, pp. 71-73, Pl. III) who believed that the Vākāṭakas had issued their own coins. He attributed some coins of north Indian fabric to the Vākāṭakas. But nowadays nobody believes in his theory. On the so-called Vākāṭaka coins cf. A.S. Altekar, 'Some Alleged Nāga and Vākāṭaka Coins', *JNSI*, V, 1943, pp. 111-34.

Kulkarni to have read on some small coins found from Wardha, Paunar and Yawatmal regions in base metal, with copper predominating, broken legends such as *(Śri-Ma) haraja Pṛthivī*,[20] *(Na) rendra*,[21] *Jaya*,[22] *Vṛddhi*,[23] *Vṛddah*,[24] *Sarva (sena)*,[25] *Vijhasāti*,[26] and *Pravara (se)nasya rā (jya ?)*,[27] are probably not true,[28] though they themselves hold different views regarding different coins. Firstly, we do not find any reference, direct or indirect, to the Vākāṭaka coins in their fairly numerous inscriptions. Not that these inscriptions did not have any occasion to mention them; they could refer to them in connection with the land grants recorded in them. The inscriptions of the contemporary dynasties too do not contain any reference to the coins of the Vākāṭakas. Secondly, there is not a single word mentioning the Vākāṭaka coins in the contemporary literature and in the literature of the succeeding ages. Thirdly, the coins attributed to the Vākāṭakas have been studied by

[20] Ajay Mitra Shastri, 'A Unique Coin of Vākāṭaka Pṛthivīshena (II ?)', in *Indian Coin Society Newsletter*, No. 4, Nagpur, October 1990, p. 2.

[21] Idem (ed.), *The Age of the Vākāṭakas*, New Delhi, 1992, pp. 287-88. Ellen M. Raven also reports a copper coin from the collection of Jan Lingen found from Paunar that carries the legend *Śrī-Nara* on the obverse and a partly accommodated *chakra* on the reverse ('Kings in Copper', in *The Vākāṭaka Heritage : Indian Culture at the Crossroads*, ed. Hans T. Bakker, Groningen, 2004, pp. 22-23). According to Raven, it 'possibly' refers to the Vākāṭaka king Narendrasena who ruled in Nandivardhana between 457-461 A.D. (*ibid.*, p. 22). Raven also tries to establish the relationship of the copper coins ascribed to the Eastern Vākāṭakas with the numismatic traditions as expressed in the copper coinages of the Nāgas of Padmāvatī, the Mālavas and the early Guptas (*ibid.*, pp. 19-31). Some copper coins of Narendrasena in the collection of R.C. Thakur which were found from Ujjain and Mahidapur included in the Vākāṭaka territory have also been published recently (H.D. Pathak and R.C. Thakur, 'Rare Variety Coins of Vākāṭaka Dynasty', *JNSI*, Vol. LXVII, 2005, pp. 85-87).

[22] *Ibid.*, p. 289.

[23] *Ibid.* After Ajay Mitra Shastri, Pathak and Thakur (*op. cit.*, pp. 85-86) have also claimed to have acquired some copper coins with the legends *jaya* and *vṛddhi* which, according to them, were used for Pṛthivīshena.

[24] *Ibid.*, pp. 289-90.

[25] A. H. Siddiqui, in *Oriental Numismatic Studies*, Vol. I, ed. Devendra Handa, New Delhi, 1996, pp. 99-105.

[26] Prashant P. Kulkarni, 'Coins of the Vākāṭakas', *Numismatic Digest*, Vol. 25-26, 2001-02, pp. 66-69.

[27] *Ibid.*, pp. 69-70.

[28] We have examined this problem in a paper entitled 'The Myth of the Vākāṭaka Coins' (*JNSI*, Vol. LXIX, Pts. i and ii, 2007, pp. 80-90). A thoroughly revised version of it has appeared in *The Indian Historical Review*, Vol. XXXIV, No. 2, July 2007, pp. 1-15. On this, also see our books titled *175 Years of Vākāṭaka History and Historiography*, Jodhpur, 2009, pp. 50-64, and *Ancient India and South Indian History and Culture* (forthcoming).

the above-mentioned scholars usually with the help of photographs supplied to them by the coin-collectors; nobody seems to have ascertained whether these photographs are doctored or genuine. We had an occasion to see at Santiniketan the photographs, published along with the paper entitled 'Vākāṭaka Coins from Washim Excavation' by Pradip Meshram and B.S. Gajbhiye submitted to the 90th Annual Conference of the Numismatic Society of India held there (1-3 December 2006), of which at least one seemed to us to be patently doctored. Here, we would like to submit that for obvious reasons one should take *the claim of the coin-collectors* about the antiquity and genuineness of ancient coins in their possession with more than a grain of salt. Fourthly, these coins usually bear no clear legends displaying the full name of any Vākāṭaka ruler. Partial legends and devices on these coins are at the best only subtle, not definite, pointers to the identity of their issuers.

We think that the question of the existence of the currency of an extensive kingdom like that of the Vākāṭakas cannot be decided by one or two copper coins. In fact, it would not be advisable to give credence to such coins which have not been obtained from regular archaeological excavations and the authenticity of which has not been established by detailed investigation. The present dilemma surrounding the Vākāṭaka coins is very much reminiscent of the times of K.P. Jayaswal, who attributed a coin to Pravarasena, and erected a whole edifice of the Vākāṭaka coinage on its basis. For some time Jayaswal's suggestion was widely discussed but ultimately it was proved that the said coin belonged to Vīrasena, a ruler of non-Vākāṭaka origin. Ajay Mitra Shastri has also attributed two copper coins to Narendrasena and one to Pṛthivīsheṇa, while Prashant P. Kulkarni has attributed one copper coin to Pravarasena. Proving or disproving these assumptions based on insufficient proof is always a tricky affair and the example of the coin of Vīrasena attributed by Jayaswal to Pravarasena shows how hazardous it is to hypothesize on the basis of meagre evidence.

As regards those Vākāṭaka coins that supposedly served the purpose of costlier transactions, the question arises what happened to them if they were issued at all ? Some scholars explain the non-availability of costlier coinage of the Vākāṭakas by arguing that earlier and contemporary costly metal coins of other dynasties were in circulation in the Vākāṭaka kingdom also which served the purpose of their costlier transactions. They tacitly assume that as the Vākāṭakas enjoyed the fruits of the classicism of the Gupta age they also must have enjoyed the fruits of their gold coinage as well. But their reasoning appears to be faulty. Conventionally speaking, a classical age is one where political culture, literature, architecture and fine arts reach a high level of excellence to form a standard for later times.[29] From this point of view, there is nothing to suggest that the Vākāṭaka culture was the golden age of the Deccan. The age of the imperial Guptas is no doubt equated with the classical age of India but the characteristic features typical of their age—such as the imperial ideal of the *chakravartin* rulers, and the cultural efflorescence when norms or standard of values were laid down in different walks of life—were conspicuous by their absence in the kingdom of the Vākāṭakas. Not only that the silver and gold coins of the Vākāṭakas have not been found so far, even the copper coins sometimes dubiously attributed to them are artistically inferior, minute in size, irregular in shape and light in weight. For a dynasty which ruled the Deccan for about 250 years and in the neighbourhood of which were the mighty imperial Guptas who produced abundant coins in every type of metal, this fact needs some explanation. In this situation, those scholars who believe that the Vākāṭakas had their own currency, usually do not elaborate their views on this question.[30] A very recent example is C.S. Gupta. In his Presidential Address entitled 'Select Coinage of Central India' published in the *JNSI*, No. LXXI, 2009, he adopts a similar position while commenting on our paper which exclusively deals with the problem of the Vākāṭaka coins published in the *JNSI*, No. LXIX, 2007. Such scholars base their argument on the Mahāyāna caves of Ajanta and the Śaiva sculptures of Mansar and Mandhal which they regard as the proofs of the prosperity of the Vākāṭaka realm. But these monuments were nothing but the extension of the Gupta influence on the Vākāṭaka territory. As pointed out by S.R. Goyal, it cannot be denied that in some spheres of culture—religion, philosophy, literature, sculpture, coinage, etc. this period was indeed the golden epoch of our history, at least in the north.[31] That this cultural efflorescence had its origins in the influence of the Gupta kings is also conceded by Walter M. Spink.[32] However, his observation that Indian classical culture reached the acme of its development during the reign of Harisheṇa (who ruled from c. 460 to 477 A.D.) does not seem to be correct as by the early years of his rule, the

[29] Romila Thapar, *A History of India*, Vol. I, New Delhi, 1966, p. 157.

[30] Ajay Mitra Shastri, *Vākāṭakas—Sources and History* (hereafter *VSH*), New Delhi, 1997, pp. 137, 213; Kulkarni, *op. cit.*, p. 66.

[31] S. R. Goyal, 'The Myth of the Golden Bird : An Investigation into the Belief of Material Opulence of Ancient and Early Medieval India in the Light of Her Gold Coinage', his Presidential Address delivered to the 90th Annual Conference of the Numismatic Society of India at Santiniketan on December 1-3, 2006, *JNSI*, Vol. LXIX, Pts. i and ii, 2007, p. 15.

[32] Walter M. Spink, 'The Vākāṭaka Caves at Ajanta and Their Successors', in *Reappraising Gupta History for S.R. Goyal*, eds. B. Ch. Chhabra, P. K. Agrawala, Ashvini Agrawal and Shankar Goyal, New Delhi, 1992, p. 248.

Gupta dynasty was already on the course of disintegration.[33] Here, Spink conveniently forgets that the traditions of any culture never die immediately; it takes decades, if not centuries, to loosen their impact on society. As shown by us elsewhere,[34] a cultural trend might have a long history before it finally emerges in a definite form and likewise might continue to exist in a diluted or changed form for some time even after it has apparently ceased to exist. The age of the Guptas also marked the efflorescence and culmination of earlier tendencies, many of which originated in the Maurya period, and much of its glory continued for about two centuries more after the fall of the Gupta empire. Romila Thapar expresses a similar opinion in a recent study through her statement that "the classicism of the Gupta period is not an innovation emanating from Gupta rule but the culmination of a process that began earlier."[35] She also rightly opines that in the Deccan and south India it was the post-Gupta period that saw the evolution of a high level of civilization.[36]

Here, it may also be remembered that in the long history of India, archaeologically, the imperial Guptas were the first indigenous dynasty to issue its own gold coinage. But it cannot be regarded as comparable with the gold coinage of Greece and Rome. Leaving aside sporadic finds we have so far only about 20 hoards, only one of which, namely the Bayana hoard, originally contained about 2100 coins.[37] Other hoards have yielded only about *650 coins in all*! These figures appear impressive against the 'no gold coinage' numismatic impression of ancient India but are woefully meagre if we compare them with the finds of the gold coins of the Roman and other ancient empires. Probably, more gold coins of Rome have been found in India alone than the total number of gold coins of the imperial Guptas themselves.[38] This fact assumes further significance if we recall that so far only one gold coin of the imperial Guptas has been found outside the frontiers of India—it was found from Java.[39] All this goes against the supposed affluence of a society which, it is believed, was enjoying unprecedented prosperity. S.R. Goyal expresses his dismay on the economic condition of

[33] *Ibid.*

[34] Shankar Goyal, *Harsha : A Multidisciplinary Political Study*, Jodhpur, 2006, p. 239.

[35] Romila Thapar, *The Penguin History of Early India*, New Delhi, 2003, p. 281.

[36] Idem, *A History of India*, Vol. I, p. 136.

[37] These figures include the coins which were either melted down or were lost due to some other reason before the content of the hoard was properly recorded. Cf. Shankar Goyal, 'A.S. Altekar and the Bayana Hoard', *JNSI*, Vol. LXVII, Pts. i and ii, 2005, pp. 80-84.

[38] As the figures of the finds of the Roman coins in the north-west are not available, it is not possible to assess the total number of the Roman coins found in India.

[39] N. J. Krom, 'The First Hindu Coin from Java', *JNSI*, Vol. XXX, 1968, pp. 200-01.

ancient and early medieval India as evidenced by the paucity of her gold coinage and poverty of her material remains.[40] According to him, "India never saw an affluent gold coinage from the ancient times to the close of the early medieval period except in the age of the Kushāṇas and the Guptas—and even during the rule of these two dynasties our material prosperity was never very high, never comparable with the affluence of many other countries. It is indicated not only by a comparison of India's gold coinage with the coinage of other countries but also by the poor advancement shown by us in the construction of cities and in the fields of urban secular architecture and sculpture."[41] That these two have almost and everywhere been interrelated phenomena—the gold coinage of a people is usually the expression of its material prosperity and the material prosperity of a people is reflected in its gold coinage—cannot be questioned. Only a prosperous Greece or Rome could produce an abundant gold coinage and only a people having abundant economic resources could invest liberally in the construction of cities and other projects of civilized material life. In the light of this argument the conclusion is inevitable that if the imperial Guptas were economically not as rich as the ancient Greeks or Romans, one should not expect that they had developed a very high and advanced gold coinage. In these circumstances the comparative paucity or complete non-availability of the Vākāṭaka currency may be regarded as something quite natural.

That like any other state the Vākāṭaka kingdom also needed coins both in precious and non-precious metals also cannot be questioned. The coins in precious metals were obviously needed for higher trade and land transactions. The inscriptions of the Vākāṭakas refer to such transactions. For example, the Indore plates of the twenty-third regnal year of Pravarasena II record the purchase and grant of half of a village (*vāṭaka*) by a merchant named Chandra.[42] The Ramtek fragmentary stone-slab inscription mentions the purchase of a piece of land by Prabhāvatīguptā's son for the construction of a temple dedicated to her personal god called Lord Prabhāvatīsvāmin and the excavation of a tank named Sudarśana in her memory.[43] Such transactions must have required costlier coins of silver or gold. Therefore, at least silver coins must have existed in the Vākāṭaka kingdom in appreciable numbers. In ancient India coins once issued continued to remain in circulation for centuries until they lost weight due to their constant use for a long time. The fact that punch-marked silver coins were in circulation till at least the

[40] S.R. Goyal, *op. cit.*, pp. 1-24.

[41] *Ibid.*, p. 21.

[42] Mirashi, *op. cit.*, pp. 38-42; *VSH*, pp. 23-25.

[43] *VSH*, pp. 125-35; S.R. Goyal, *Ancient Indian Inscriptions : Recent Finds and New Interpretations*, Jodhpur, 2005, pp. 221-25.

early medieval period is well-known. They are referred to by the name *purāṇa* in inscriptions and literary works of the second century A.D.[44] and as *nīla-kāhāpaṇa* at least up to the fifth century A.D.[45] At a village called Chik Sandogi in the Kopal *taluka* of the Raichur district in Karnataka, a hoard of 5,534 silver punch-marked coins was found in a copper pot bearing a Brāhmī label datable to about the third century A.D.[46] A hoard of 440 silver punch-marked coins found with an Indo-Sassanian coin now preserved in the Lucknow Museum shows the popularity of these coins in the early medieval age.[47] V.S. Agrawala has rightly concluded that the silver punch-marked coins and the *kārshāpaṇa* tradition continued right up to the medieval period.[48] The Sātavāhana silver coins might also have been in circulation in the Vākāṭaka territory as it was formerly under the Sātavāhanas. Quite a few Sātavāhana silver coins have also been reported from Vidarbha.[49] The Western Kshatrapa coins were also highly valued and hoards and stray finds of these have been reported from various sites included in the Vākāṭaka kingdom. As far as Ranjangaon near Pune in Maharashtra, Petlurapalem in Andhra Pradesh and some places in Karnataka hoards of Kshatrapa coins have been reported, while stray coins and moulds for counterfeiting them have been reported from several ancient sites.[50] A treasure-trove of 36 silver coins of the Kshatrapas has also been reported from Dahigaon in the Malkapur *taluka* of the district Buldhana in Maharashtra.[51] Further, the Gupta gold and silver issues must have been available in abundance. They have been reported from some sites in the Vākāṭaka territories, such as Harda (district Hoshangabad), Sakaur (district Damoh), Ganeshpur (district

[44] The name is mentioned in the Mathura inscription of the Kushāṇa king Huvishka and the *Manusmṛti* both of which are usually dated to the second century A.D.

[45] Buddhaghosha's *Samantapāsādikā* refers to the punch-marked silver coins as *nīla-kāhāpaṇa* for their bluish accumulation in course of time. See C.D. Chatterjee, 'Some Numismatic Data in Pali Literature', *Buddhistic Studies*, ed. B.C. Law, Calcutta, 1931, Ch. XV; idem, 'Some New Numismatic Terms in Pali Texts', *Journal of the U. P. Historical Society*, Vol. VI, 1933, pp. 156-57.

[46] Ajay Mitra Shastri, 'Presidential Address', *Proceedings of the Indian History Congress*, 1978, Vol. II, pp. 968-69; see also his *VSH*, p. 143.

[47] P. L. Gupta, 'Fabrication of Ancient Punch-Marked Coins', *Indian Numismatic Chronicle*, Vol. III, p. 133.

[48] V.S. Agrawala, 'Coin Data in Divyāvadāna', *Indian Numismatic Chronicle*, Vol. III, pp. 148-50.

[49] *VSH*, p. 146; also see I. K. Sarma, *Coinage of the Sātavāhana Empire*, Delhi, 1980, pp. 37-38; Mala Dutta, *A Study of the Sātavāhana Coinage*, Delhi, 1990, Chs. 2 and 4; S. R. Goyal, *The Coinage of Ancient India*, pp. 299-300, 310-14.

[50] *Ibid.*

[51] *Indian Archaeology—A Review*, 1972-73, p. 55.

Jabalpur), Pattan (district Betul), Seoni (district Seoni), Ellichpur and Dhamori (district Amaravati), Khairtal (district Raipur), Tewar (district Jabalpur) and Bhandara (district Chanda).[52] The Traikūṭaka silver coins were also in use during this period as a hoard containing, *inter alia*, ten specimens of Dahrasena's coins have been reported at the village of Dahigaon in the Malkapur *taluka* of the district Buldhana.[53] All these coins must have been in circulation in the Vākāṭaka period.

In view of the availability of the coins issued by earlier or contemporary dynasties, it is generally believed that the Vākāṭakas probably did not feel the necessity of issuing coins of their own in gold and silver. It is also believed that they did not feel the need to issue coins even in cheap metals and the people of their kingdom depended for their day-to-day ordinary transactions on the coins of non-precious metals of the earlier and contemporary dynasties which they probably supplemented by the *cowrie*-currency as was done even in the Gupta empire. We know that the immediately preceding period was characterized by an extensive use of base metal coins for ordinary transactions in the Deccan as in north India. We have the Sātavāhana base metal (copper, lead and potin) coins which have been found in thousands in the whole of the Deccan, including the territory later occupied by the Vākāṭakas, which has yielded enormous quantities of coins, especially in potin.[54] Further, the Kushāṇas and the Maghas, as well as other ruling powers of northern India, are known to have issued base metal coins on an extensive scale.[55] The Chinese traveller Fa-hien, who visited India during c.400-411 A.D., refers to heaps of *cowrie* shells in the markets of the cities of the Gupta empire.[56] Even if the Vākāṭakas had issued their own coins in cheap metals, the coins of other dynasties in cheap metals must also have been in circulation because the Vākāṭakas obviously did not issue a copious currency in cheap metals either.

Ajay Mitra Shastri fell in line with the view that the Vākāṭakas permitted the circulation of older or other contemporary currencies in their kingdom. This is evident from his report on the coin finds from Pauni excavation in 1972 wherein he had made the following observations : "It is

[52] Bal Chandra Jain, *Inventory of the Hoards and Finds of Coins and Seals from Madhya Pradesh*, Varanasi, 1957, pp. 11-14; S. R. Goyal, *op.cit.*, p. 360.

[53] V.V. Mirashi, 'Dahigaon Hoard of Kshatrapa and Traikūṭaka Coins', *JNSI*, Vol. XXXV, 1973, pp. 118-22; idem, *Literary and Historical Studies in Indology*, Delhi, 1975, pp. 180-84.

[54] *VSH*, p. 146; S.R. Goyal, *op. cit.*, pp. 299-300; K.M. Shrimali, 'Some Aspects of the Economy of the Vākāṭakas', in Ajay Mitra Shastri (ed.), *op. cit.*, p. 102.

[55] *Ibid.*

[56] *Ibid.* My father Professor S.R. Goyal told me that even in his childhood, in the 1930s, *cowries* were used in the market of our town.

likely that the Vākāṭakas, having no coins of their own, allowed the use of the coins issued by other contemporary dynasties such as the Western Kshatrapas, the Guptas and the Vishṇukuṇḍins."[57] In this context, K.M. Shrimali argues that "the archaeological evidence is against such a supposition", for "Bhokardan, Arni, Pauni, Peddabankur, Dhulikatta, Ter, Malhar, Kahali, etc., have not yielded any noticeable evidence of the post-Sātavāhana settlements", and that there are no indications, at least in the present state of our knowledge, that the coins of the Sātavāhanas, Western Kshatrapas, Kushāṇas and Guptas, which have been reported from the sites belonging to the Vākāṭaka territory, "*remained in circulation during the two centuries of the Vākāṭaka rule as well.*"[58] According to him, "a viable and meaningful explanation of this characteristic economic phenomenon of the reign of the Vākāṭakas, namely, the absence of money, may be sought in the large-scale mechanism of land grants, growth of small village settlements and relative non-urban economy."[59] Actually, this is a very important conclusion of Shrimali drawn after a study of all the known Vākāṭaka inscriptions. But his view that money was totally absent in the realm of a dynasty which ruled in the Deccan and central India for about 250 years cannot be accepted. Further, Shrimali himself recognizes that earlier and other post-Sātavāhana powers "have indeed left significant numismatic evidence of their regimes."[60] Furthermore, the fact that the Vākāṭakas did not strike any coins is in itself a proof that earlier and other contemporary currencies were in circulation in their kingdom. His argument that there is no 'noticeable evidence' of the post-Sātavāhana settlements in some areas of the Vākāṭaka kingdom does not prove anything, for, as he himself believes, the territory under their jurisdiction "comprised a vast land of over thirty districts of the present Madhya Pradesh, Maharashtra and Andhra Pradesh."[61] Also, the list of the Vākāṭaka territories given by him is highly exaggerated and, going by the extant evidences, the Vākāṭakas had nothing to do with many of them.[62] But, as his inscriptional study suggests, the Vākāṭaka rule in parts of central India and northern Deccan exhibits growth of small village settlements and relative decline of urban economy.[63]

[57] S. B. Deo and Jagatpati Joshi, *Pauni Excavations (1969-70)*, Nagpur, 1972, p. 34.

[58] K. M. Shrimali, *op. cit.*, p. 103; also see his 'Pattern of Settlements under the Vākāṭakas', *Proceedings of the Indian History Congress*, 44th Session, Burdwan, 1983, pp. 101-12.

[59] *Ibid.*

[60] *Ibid.*

[61] *Ibid.*, p. 101.

[62] Ajay Mitra Shastri's 'Editorial Note', in Shrimali, *op. cit.*, p. 112, fn. 4.

[63] For details see Shrimali, *op. cit.*, pp. 101-15; also see his *Agrarian Structure in Central India and the Northern Deccan (c.A.D. 300-500): A Study of Vākāṭaka Inscriptions*, New Delhi, 1987, pp. 84-116.

MECHANISM OF LAND GRANTS IN THE VĀKĀṬAKA ECONOMY

The suggestion that the genesis of the phenomenon of the total absence of the coins of the Vākāṭakas may be sought in the mechanism of land grants[64] seems to be well-reasoned. It elucidates why was the Vākāṭaka economy feudal in character. While the Sātavāhana inscriptions of the second century A.D.[65] speak of huge cash donations and gifts of cows, elephants, horses, etc., as well as donations of villages with various privileges, one finds almost complete disassociation between money and land grants in the inscriptions of the Vākāṭakas indicating comparative paucity of coins during their rule.[66] According to our calculation, all their 40/41 inscriptions account donations of 25/26 villages of which 11/12 figure in the 20/21 inscriptions of Prabhāvatīguptā and Pravarasena II alone.[67] Among the inscriptions of the main branch of the Vākāṭakas, which mention donations of villages by name, are included Mandhal plates (year 5) of Rudrasena II : villages donated Selludraha, Achchhabhallikā, Suragrāmakā and Aragrāmakā; Pune plates (year 13) of Prabhāvatīguptā : village donated Da(or I)ṅguṇa-grāma; Jamb plates (year 2) : village donated Kothuraka, Belora charter (year 11) : villages donated Mahallalāṭa, Mahallamalāṭa(?) and Dīrghadraha, Mandhal plates (year 16 and 17) : village donated Mayasagrāma, Chammak plates (years 18) : village donated Charmāṅka, Siwani plates (year 18) : village donated Brahmapūraka, Miregaon charter (year 20) : village donated Jalapuravāṭaka, Indore plates (year 23) : village donated Viśākhāryavāṭaka, Tirodi plates (year 23) : village donated Kosambakhaṇḍa, and Balaghat plate : village donated Śrīparṇakā, all of Pravarasena II; Bamhani and Mallar charters of the time of Narendrasena : villages donated Vardhamānaka and Saṅgama respectively; and Mandhal plates (year 2) : village donated Kurubhajjaka,

[64] *Ibid.*, p. 104; also see Nandini Sinha Kapur, 'State Formation in Vidarbha: The Case of the Eastern Vākāṭakas' in *The Indian Historical Review*, Vol. XXXII, No. 2, July 2005, pp. 21-25.

[65] Such as **अपावेस अनोमस अलोणखादक अरठसविनयिक सवजात पारिहारिक च** [।] **एतेहि न परिहारेहि परिहरेठ** [।] Cf. Nasik cave inscriptions of Gautamīputra Śātakarṇi (years 18 and 24=c. 124 and c. 130 A.D. respectively); Karle cave inscription of Vāsishṭhīputra Puḷumāvi (year 7=c. 137 A.D.) and Nasik cave inscription of the same ruler (year 22=c. 152 A.D.).

[66] The earliest of such references is found in the Washim plates of Vindhyaśakti II of the Vatsagulma branch of the Vākāṭakas of the later half of the fourth century A.D.

[67] The Vākāṭaka grants are invariably given to the brāhmaṇas for earning religious merit for the donor and his parents. Amongst people to whom these grants are generally addressed are included house-holders, brāhmaṇas, other residents (led by brāhmaṇas), officials of noble birth, soldiers, policemen, peasants and *grāmamahattaras* (led by brāhmaṇas). At least one grant, the Yawatmal plates of Pravarasena II (year 26), is not addressed to the government officials but to the village as a whole.

Mandhal plates (year 10) : village donated Govasāhikā, and Mahurjhari plates (year 17) : village donated Jamalakhaṭaka, all of Pṛthivīsheṇa II. Among the inscriptions of the Vatsagulma branch of the Vākāṭakas, which explicitly record donations of villages by name, include Washim plates (year 37) of Vindhyaśakti II : village donated Ākāsapadda (Ākāśapadra); India Office plate and Bidar plates (year 5): villages donated Yappajja and Velpakoṇḍā respectively both of Devasena; and Thalner grant (year 3) of Harisheṇa : villages donated Bhaṭṭikāpadra and Kumāradāsavāṭaka.

Apart from 25/26 donated villages which are mentioned in the Vākāṭaka inscriptions we are also able to count nine examples (of which eight come from the inscriptions of Pravarasena II) where the measure of donated land in different parts of the Vākāṭaka kingdom is recorded. The remaining one belongs to Harisheṇa. These include Chammak plates (year 18), Masod plates (year 19), Dudia plates (year 23), Wadgaon plates (year 25), Yawatmal plates (year 26), Pattan plates (year 27), Tigaon plates (year 29) and Pauni plates (year 32) of Pravarasena II and Thalner grant of Harisheṇa (year 3). These donations vary from 20 or 20½ *nivartanas* (Thalner grant) to 8000 *nivartanas* (Chammak plates)[68] by the royal measure. That even in the case of a huge grant of 2000 *nivartanas* (Tigaon plates) only four brāhmaṇas are mentioned by name, only 49 brāhmaṇas are mentioned by name for a still bigger donation of 8000 *nivartanas* (Chammak plates), and only one brāhmaṇa figures as a donee of an additional grant (Tigaon plates) further establish the fact that the pressure on land in the Vākāṭaka kingdom was not too much. In comparison to these, one exception was perhaps the grant recorded in the Masod plates of Pravarasena II where 300 'lands' (*nivartanas*) was split up into 25 plots of which two shares were given to a certain Mahāpurusha who is styled *apratigrāhin* (non-acceptor of donations).[69] In addition to Mahāpurusha, 19 other donees are mentioned by name. It appears that some names of the donees are missing here because details account for only 21 plots—2 for Mahāpurusha and presumably one each to the other 19 donees. Thus, each plot appears to have consisted of 12 *nivartanas* and was not of a small size at all. Or, alternatively, some donees might have got slightly bigger shares. Shrimali suggests, and quite rightly too, that the cases where measure of donated land is specified, are perhaps such examples where the responsibility of getting the land cultivated devolves directly on the donee. Since even 25

[68] One *nivartana* of land was about 3/4, 2,2 1/4, 3 or 4 3/4 acres according to different authorities (*EI*, XXVIII, p. 245). It differed in different parts of the country and in different periods of history.

[69] Shrimali, *Agrarian Structure in Central India and the Northern Deccan*, p. 7; also see *VSH*, p. 90.

nivartanas of land (Dudia plates) necessitate more than the family labour, it is not impossible to assume that such donations imply the existence of serfs, a requisite feature of the existence of feudalism anywhere. Further, as Shrimali points out, one of the villages where 60 *nivartanas* were donated (Dudia plates), is named Karmakāragrāma. The use of the word Karmakāra/ Kammakāra in the sense of hired/wage labourers has been prevalent from the days of Kauṭilya and the Pāli texts. These facts further emphatically suggest that the pressure on land was not much in the Vākāṭaka kingdom which could result in the obvious growth of agriculture based rural settlements.

We may also refer to some other inscriptions of the Vākāṭakas which, to some extent, prove our point. For example, the Riddhapur plates of Prabhāvatīguptā (year 19 of Pravarasena II) records the grant of a field together with a farm-house and four residences of ploughmen situated in the Aśvatthanagara included in the administrative division of Kośika. Another recently discovered inscription—the Ramtek Prabhāvatīguptā Memorial Stone Inscription—of the reign of Pravarasena II purports to record most probably some pious acts of a daughter (name lost) of Prabhāvatīguptā.[70] The acts apparently consisted of the erection of the Kevala-Narasiṁha temple wherein the inscribed slabs are found fixed and the installation of the image of the Man-lion (Narasiṁha) manifestation of Vishṇu which is still extant. Among pre-Pravarasena II inscriptions are included an undated Deotek inscription of Rudrasena (I or II) which records the construction of a *dharma-sthāna* (a special place of religious worship or the court of justice) at Chikkamburi and the Nachna-ki-talai and Ganj inscriptions of Vyāghradeva, a feudatory of Pṛthivīsheṇa I which respectively refer to some pious acts (not specified) and the construction of something, most likely a dam to stem the waters of a stream, for the religious merit of his parents. The object of the Hisse-Borala Stone-slab Inscription of the Vatsagulma branch is also to record that a lake named Sudarśana was constructed by a certain Āryya Svāmilladeva, an obedient servant of the Vākāṭaka king Devasena, for the benefit of all the creatures in Śaka 380, corresponding to 457-458 A.D. Among the inscriptions of the ministers and feudatories of the Vatsagulma branch the Ajanta Cave Inscription of Varāhadeva, a minister of Harisheṇa, aims at recording the excavation and decoration with paintings and sculptures of the cave (No. XVI) and its donation to the Buddhist Order. Similarly, his Ghaṭotkacha Cave Inscription, found from the place known as Gulwāḍā, eleven miles west of Ajanta, also relates to Buddhism. The

[70] The name of the daughter of Prabhāvatīguptā is only partly legible in the inscription. Hans Bakker (*The Vākāṭakas : An Essay in Hindu Iconology*, Groningen, 1997, p. 17) reads it as Atibhāvatī.

object of the inscription was evidently to register the excavation of the vihāra presently known as Ghaṭotkacha Guhā and its dedication to the local Buddhist saṅgha. Yet another Ajanta Cave (No. XVII) Inscription of Ravisāmba, a vassal of Harisheṇa, also opens with an adoration of the Buddha followed by an account of the family of the donor of the vihāra. Though such instances have very little to offer as far as the study of the economy of the Vākāṭakas is concerned, but they do prove the existence of the feudal structure in the Vākāṭaka territories and also indicate that perhaps there was no pressure on land in their kingdom.

PRIVILEGES AND OBLIGATIONS OF THE DONEES IN THE VĀKĀṬAKA INSCRIPTIONS

As far as the general pattern of the privileges granted to the donees in the inscriptions of the Vākāṭakas is concerned their earliest account is found in the Washim plates of Vindhyaśakti II of the Vatsagulma branch. It declares:

> **अरट्ठसंव्विणयिक। अलवणकेण्ण क्खनक। अहिरण्णधाण्णप्पणयप्पदेय। अपुप्फक्खिरग्गहण। अपरम्परगोबलिवर्द्द [।] अचारसिद्धिक। अचम्मङ्गालिक। अभडप्पावेस अखट्टाचोल्लकवेणे-सिक। अकरद। अवह। सणिधि। सोपणिधि। सकुतुप्पन्त। समञ्चमहाकरण। साव्वजातिपरिहारपरिहितञ्च [।*]**
>
> (the village) is to be exempt from (*the entrance of*) the District Police; to be exempt from the digging of salt and fermentation of liquor; to be exempt from (*the obligation to make*) presents of grain and gold. It does not entitle (*the State*) to (*the royalties on*) flowers and milk; and to the customary cows and bullocks; it is not to provide pasture, hides and charcoal; it is not to be entered by soldiers; it is not to provide cots, water-pots and servants (*to touring royal officers*); it is exempt from taxes; it is not to provide draught cattle; it carries with it the right to treasures and deposits, to major and minor taxes and to platforms and large fields; and it is exempt with immunities of all kinds.[71]

Though we find some additions and variations in privileges in other Vākāṭaka inscriptions[72] their Prakrit forms recur in most of their Sanskrit land grants. These privileges are also found in the Sātavāhana and early Pallava inscriptions but the list of privileges we find here is admittedly a detailed one.

As far as the obligations of the donees are concerned we find an exceptional example in the Chammak plates (year 18) of Pravarasena II where these are enumerated thus :

[71] Mirashi, *op. cit.*, pp. 97-98, 99.

[72] For full details of such additions and variations in the Vākāṭaka inscriptions cf. Shrimali, *op. cit.*, pp. 8-9.

> **श्शा (शा) सनस्थितिश्चेयं ब्राह्मणैरीश्वरैश्चानुपालनीया [।*] तद्यथा राज्ञां सप्ताङ्गे राज्ये अद्रोहप्रवृन्ता (त्ता) नां [अ*] ब्रह्मघ्नचौरा (र) पारदारिकराजापत्थ्यकारिप्रभृति (ती) नां संग्र (ग्रा) म [म*] कुर्व्वतां अन्यग्राम (मे) ष्वन- ॥ पर (रा) द्धानां आचन्द्रादित्यकालीयः [।*] अतोन्यथा कुर्व्वतामनुमोदतां वा राज्ञः भूमिच्छेदं कुर्व्वन्तः (तः) अस्तेयमिति [।*]**
>
> And this condition of the charter should be maintained by the brāhmaṇas and (future) kings :— (*This grant shall be enjoyed by the brāhmaṇas*) as long as the sun and the moon will endure, provided that they commit no treason against the kingdom consisting of seven constituents (the king, his ministers, ally, territory, treasure, fortress and army) of the (*future*) kings; that they are not found guilty of the murder of a brāhmaṇa, theft, adultery and high treason, etc.; that they do not wage war; (*and*) that they do no harm to other villages. But if they act otherwise or assent to such acts, the king will commit no theft if he takes the land away (*from them*).[73]

The inscriptions of the Vākāṭakas also throw some light on the ownership of land during their period. Though the inscriptions in their conventional verses alert people of dire consequences if the execution of grants is obstructed and the threat of punishment and fine is also made, there are at least three examples where we find villages being donated in exchange for donations made previously. For example, the object of the Tigaon plates (year 29) of Pravarasena II was to record the gift of two thousand *nivartanas* of land in the village Dhu(Dhru)vavāṭaka included in the territorial division of Vāruchcharājya but this land was given in exchange for the village named Vijayavallīvāṭaka which had been previously gifted by Pṛthivīrāja, i.e., Pṛthivīsheṇa I. Similarly, the object of the Balaghat plate of Pravarasena II was to record the grant of the village Śrīparṇaka in the administrative division (*mārga*) of Sundhāti but the grant was made in exchange for the previous gift of the village Mānapallikā which was situated in the administrative division (*mārga*) of Yaśapura. The Pauni plates (year 32) of Pravarasena II registers the grant of a piece of land measuring fifty *nivartanas* by the royal measure. This plot of land was given in exchange for some other land which was situated at Achalapura included in the administrative unit named Kṛshṇāleśālikaṭaka. Incidentally, the Yawatmal plates (year 26) of Pravarasena II aims at recording the renewal by him of the donation of some land along with two house-sites in the village Lāṭakapallī included in the administrative unit named Shaḍgṛśaka. It is averred that the land was being already enjoyed by the donees (i.e., it was in their possession) and that the grant was renewed by Pravarasena II in the form of a copper plate charter. In the whole Vākāṭaka epigraphy this is the only example of

[73] Mirashi, *op. cit.*, pp. 25-26.

its kind, all other charters record fresh grants. Unfortunately, we have no information as to who was the original donor and what made it necessary to renew the grant. However, we have a few other cases when fresh copper plate charters were issued in place of earlier charters, sometimes written on palm-leaves,[74] which were destroyed due to some mishap.[75] The present renewal also must have been due to some such reason. All these instances indicate that the Vākāṭakas kept the ownership of land in their own hands. A study of the Gupta inscriptions of the fifth-sixth centuries from Bengal also indicate the same pattern.[76]

IMPACT OF LAND GRANTS ON THE ECONOMIC CONDITION OF THE VĀKĀṬAKAS : BURGEONING OF THE RURAL SETTLEMENTS

That the mechanism of land grants affected the overall economic condition in the Vākāṭaka territories is confirmed by the burgeoning of rural settlements based on agriculture and animal husbandry.[77] The Sātavāhanas had seen profuse economic activities and a general picture of their wealthy and prosperous life is borne out by the archaeological and art remains. But the archaeological data of the Vākāṭaka phase reveals a different perspective altogether. Explorations and excavations at several Vākāṭaka sites suggest the decline or poor character of the settlements under their regime. According to Shrimali, "at Bhokardan all the five structural phases revealed during the 1972-73 excavations belonged to the Sātavāhana period. But the site 'dwindled' after the Sātavāhanas and was reoccupied only in the medieval period. Even during the next season's excavations the position did not change materially. Excavations at Arni in the Yawatmal district yielded evidence of three habitational phases of which the last belonged to the Sātavāhanas and even this showed signs of degeneration. Other major sites, especially Pauni, Peddabankur, Dhulikatta, Ter, Malhar and Kahali, show a similar pattern. Some other sites where one would expect finds of the Vākāṭakas are : Dhanora, Tekwada, Irle, Kausan, Tripuri, Kaundanpur and Bhamiwara. But the scanty reports on these sites are not very encouraging."[78] To us it

[74] The Kurud plates of the Śarabhapura king Narendra registers the renewal of a grant originally recorded on palm-leaves. See Ajay Mitra Shastri, *Inscriptions of the Śarabhapurīyas, Pāṇḍuvaṁśins and Somavaṁśins*, Part 2, New Delhi, 1995, p. 8, text lines 7-8.

[75] The well-known Nidhanpur plates of Bhāskaravarman were intended to replace the original copper plate grant which was destroyed by fire.

[76] Cf. Toshio Yamazaki, 'Some Aspects of Land-Sale Inscriptions in Fifth and Sixth Century Bengal', *Acta Asiatica*, Bulletin of the Institute of Eastern Culture, No. 42, August 1982, pp. 17-36.

[77] For details cf. Shrimali, *op. cit.*, pp. 10-22.

[78] *Ibid.*, pp. 10-11.

appears that here Shrimali is rather confused, for he further states that "in recent years the excavations at Mandhal, Mahurjhari, Ramtek (Nagpur dist.) and Nagara (Bhandara dist.) have indeed yielded significant evidences about the Vākāṭakas. The temples of Kevala-Narasiṁha, Varāha, Rudra-Narasiṁha and Bhogaram at Ramtek are particularly illuminating in this context."[79] But he contradicts himself when he comments that "If one were to rely on just the archaeological evidence, it would present a very gloomy picture of economy under the Vākāṭakas."[80] It seems to us that here Shrimali is trying to prove 'the decline or poor character of settlements under the Vākāṭakas' though he is impressed by the 'recent significant evidences' of the development of Hindu temples on and around the Rāmagiri (Ramtek hill) and the Buddhist caves at Ajanta indicating to the prosperity of the Vākāṭaka kingdom. But this contradiction—poor character of settlements and the development of Hindu temples—may be resolved if we believe that the Vākāṭakas were under the political and cultural influence of the Guptas and the caves and the temples which are the only proof of this prosperity were the result of their relationship— direct or indirect—with the Guptas. Further, the cultural history of the imperial Guptas and the Vākāṭakas and of the monuments of their period cannot be so precisely dated since it merges at both ends in the continuous development of earlier and later periods.[81]

According to Shrimali, an analysis of the inscriptions of the Vākāṭakas reveals an interesting picture of the settlements in their dominions. His study is based on the place-names in these inscriptions. He lists 134 villages/ settlements of which 83 are found in the inscriptions of Pravarasena II.[82] We may classify most of these settlements into various categories, such as *āhāras, bhogas, bhuktis,* camps (military), donated villages, *mārgas,* places from where the grants were issued, residences of donees, *rājyas, rāshṭras, saṁgamikās, vishayas,* and so on. There are some settlements, namely, Arammi *rājya*, Govasāhikā, Kurubhajjaka/Kurubheñjñaka, Mahallalāṭa/ Mahallamalāṭa, Nandivardhana, Pravarapura, Pravareśvara, Rāmagiri, Śaḍvimśativāṭaka, Supratishṭha *āhāra* and Vatsagulma which figure in more

[79] *Ibid.*, p. 11.

[80] *Ibid.*

[81] The fact that the artistic activities of the Vākāṭaka kingdom were the result of the Gupta influence necessitates rethinking on Hans Bakker's hypothesis that the Vākāṭakas were 'on a par with the Gupta world' (Bakker, *op. cit.*, p. 2). For a critique of Bakker's suggestions on art and culture of the Vākāṭakas cf. Shankar Goyal, *175 Years of Vākāṭaka History and Historiography*, pp. 28-30.

[82] For a full list of 134 Vākāṭaka villages/settlements cf. Shrimali, *op. cit.*, pp. 11-22. However, according to Shrimali, as full details of some inscriptions are not available, these figures are incomplete (*op. cit.*, p. 43).

than one inscription but there are some settlements, such as Vatsagulma, which figure almost throughout their regime.[83] It is to be noted that there are lesser number of settlements (according to Shrimali 14 in all)[84] which can be described as urban on the basis of the use of suffixes, such as *pura, pūraka* and *nagara.*[85] These include Achalapura, Aśvatthanagara, Brahmapūraka, Chandrapura, Gepūraka, Hiraṇyapura, Kollapūraka, Lohanagara, Nandipūraka, Padmapura, Pravarapura, Śailapura, Vaṭapūraka and Yaśapura. In contrast to the suffixes denoting urban settlements, suffixes *pallī,*[86] *kheṭa/kheṭaka,*[87] *vaṭa, vāṭaka, vāṭikā,*[88] *grāma, pāṭaka, padda, kaṭa,*[89] etc. denoting varieties of rural settlements are quite numerous. These settlements include Chinchāpallī, Īshṭākapallī, Lāṭakapallī, Lekhapallikā, Māṇapallikā, Añjanavāṭaka, Aśvatthakheṭaka, Beṇṇakaṭa, Bhojakaṭa, Brāhmaṇavāṭaka, Dhuvavāṭaka, Jamālakheṭaka, Kiṇihikheṭaka, Kumāradāsavāṭaka, Nāṅgarakaṭaka, Ākāsapadda, Aragrāma, Gṛidhragrāma, Kāṁsakārakagrāma, Maṇḍukigrāma, Nāndīkaḍa, etc. Then, there are some settlements with pronounced references to flora, i.e., settlements named after medicinal plants (such as Añjanavāṭaka and Karañjaviraka) or with reference to grassy patches (such as Darbhamalaka, Darbhapatha and Darbhaviraka) and trees (such as Aśvatthakheṭaka, Badarīgrāma (badarī=jujube), Vilavaṇaka (=bilva), Chikkamburi (chikkenna=betelnut tree), Chiñchāpallī (chincha=tamarind), Ekārjunaka (name of a tree as well) and many others), etc. Not only this we have also a Nīlīgrāma where indigo plantation may have been predominant. Similarly, Kṛshṇāleśālikaṭaka most probably derived its name from the cultivation of black transplanted paddy because of its cultivation on the black soil of the

[83] *Ibid.*, pp. 22-23.

[84] *Ibid.*

[85] It was once suggested that the word *nagara* was a derivative of Sanskrit word *lāṅgala*, meaning a 'plough', and that it originally meant a settlement thriving on agricultural activities (Paul Whalley, 'Place Names in U.P., of Agra and Oudh', *Journal of the Uttar Pradesh Historical Society*, II, Pt. 2, 1921, pp. 19-29).

[86] In the *Uttarādhyayana Sūtra* and other Jain canonical texts 'Pallī' means a village of wild tribes.

[87] *Kheṭa* or *kheṭaka*, perhaps a derivative from *kshetra* ("field"), also denotes a small village. As early as the days of Pāṇini *kheṭa* is mentioned in the sense of a small village establishment. It has also been suggested that the original meaning of *kheṭaka* or *kheṭa* was an enclosure into which cattle were driven. Gradually, the pastoral camp grew into an agricultural village (cf. Paul Whalley, *op. cit.*, p. 37).

[88] Suffixes such as *vaṭa, vāṭaka* and *vāṭikā* seem to have been derived from the root *vṛt* which indicates enclosure of a village consisting of boundary of trees.

[89] Similarly, *grāma, pāṭaka, padda, kaṭa*, etc., are also suffixes which signify, in one form or another, a small village settlement.

region.[90]

Thus, it would not be wrong to believe that a greater number of the settlements mentioned in the Vākāṭaka inscriptions belong to the category of rural settlements. Shrimali even argues that some of these settlements "came up for the first time under the Vākāṭakas in general and Pravarasena II in particular."[91] But the detailed references to the names of settlements in delineating the boundaries would suggest that these were already in existence. Shrimali also postulates, and possibly quite rightly, burgeoning of rural settlements in parts of central India and the northern Deccan during the Vākāṭaka rule.[92] According to his conclusion, however, the statistical data suggest that in the pre-Pravarasena II phase the concentration was in the eastern half of the dominion and in the Pravarasena II and post-Pravarasena II phases there was a westward expansion. In the Vatsagulma dominion the economy had deeper trade links, whereas the Nandivardhana dominion gave agrarian orientation to the economy.[93]

DECLINE OF URBAN SETTLEMENTS IN THE VĀKĀṬAKA TERRITORIES

Shrimali attributes the decline of the settlements to the process of Sanskritization in the tribal areas of the Vākāṭaka territories. It is a remarkable suggestion indeed, for not only Samudragupta is known to have made all the āṭavika *rājyas* (forest kingdoms) his servants[94] but some other inscriptions such as the Khoh copper plate inscription of Saṁkshobha (Gupta era 209=529 A.D.) and the Kanas plate of Lokavigraha also refer to *sāshṭādaśāṭavīrājya* (18 forest kingdoms) which are usually located in central India[95] not very far from the territories of the Vākāṭakas. It is quite possible

[90] As shown by Malati Mahajan ('Flora from Place Names in Inscriptions Found in Maharashtra', *Studies in Indian Place Names*, III, 1982, pp. 25-38 and IV, 1984, pp. 90-99), the preponderance of several place-names with *vaḍa/vaṭa* and other prefixes signify banyan tree in the Amraoti, Bhandara, Buldana, Nanded and Parbhani districts of Maharashtra. All these districts except Bhandara formed part of the western half of the Vākāṭaka dominion. Further, in her study, which is based on inscriptions in Maharashtra, she argues that a large part of Maharashtra in ancient times was covered either with natural groves or deliberately prepared gardens and plantations.

[91] Shrimali, *op. cit.*, pp. 25-26.

[92] *Ibid.*

[93] The cartographic representation of the chronological and geographical distribution of the inscriptions, the villages donated, settlements other than donated villages and the geographical configuration of the administrative divisions is the major contribution of Shrimali (*op. cit.*, pp. 44-59) and undoubtedly leads to significant inferences.

[94] S. R. Goyal, *Guptakālīna Abhilekha*, Meerut, 1984, pp. 25, 37.

[95] Sircar, *op. cit.*, pp. 394-95.

that these included some regions of the Vākāṭaka dominion. It is also not impossible that in the beginnings "the Vākāṭakas were untouched by Sanskritic culture of the northern plains."[96] Some of the Purāṇic legends about the beginnings of the Vākāṭakas are indeed revealing, e.g., a king of Vidarbha *stealing* the wife of others. These are, according to Shrimali, features of tribal origins.[97] Some of the names of donees of the Vākāṭaka inscriptions also enable us to trace the process of Sanskritization of the tribal areas, e.g., the donee of the Indore plates is Goṇḍārya (the Gonds still constitute an important element of tribal population in the Vidarbha region). One can also propose that settlements such as Ajakarṇa (Tigaon plates), Gṛidhragrāma (Wadgaon plates), Maṇḍukigrāma (Jamb plates) and Mṛigasima (Tirodi plates) had some totemistic origins.[98] Hints of tribalism are also detectable in place-names such as Kollapūraka (Siwani plates) and Millukadratha (Patna Museum plates) which were possibly inhabited by the Kols and the Bhils.[99] In the context of Sanskritization it may also be stressed that the Washim plates, one of the earliest Vākāṭaka inscriptions, mentions the privileges of doness in Prakrit. When, therefore, Mirashi[100] considered the third of the Tigaon plates as not genuine on the ground that its language contains Prakrit words and affixes it becomes somewhat intriguing. Also, in ancient Indian literature the connotation of a tribe is very frequently linked up with frontier people and the idea of the frontier itself has varied according to the changing concepts of the *Āryāvarta* and the *Madhyadeśa.* Shrimali appears to be right when he states that "the Vākāṭakas would, in all probability, fall outside these hallowed regions and, therefore, their territory would be very congenial for Sanskritisation."[101] Possibly, a detailed enquiry of numerous *gotras* of donees mentioned in the Vākāṭaka inscriptions could throw more light on the problem of agents for this economic transformation. However, the matrimonial alliance between the imperial Guptas and the Vākāṭakas may certainly be considered as one of the major agents for these happenings.

The channels of Sanskritization is also seen in the growing brāhmaṇic settlements in the dominions of the Vākāṭakas and the migration of people from western, northern and north-western India. In this context particular mention is made by Ajay Mitra Shastri to Brahmapūraka (Siwani and Patna

[96] Shrimali, *op. cit.*, p. 27.
[97] *Ibid.*
[98] *Ibid.*
[99] *Ibid.*
[100] *CII*, V, p. 63; Shrimali, *op. cit.*, p. 28.
[101] Shrimali, *op. cit.*

Museum plates) and Brāhmaṇavāṭaka (Tigaon plates).[102] Another interesting feature consists of migration of people from western, northern and north-western India for which support is derived from the settlements such as Pākaṇṇa *rāshṭra* (Belora plates 'B'), Ānarttapura *bhukti* (Thalner plates), Lāṭakapallī (Yawatmal plates), Kuruvajjaka (Mandhal plates 'A' of Pṛthivīsheṇa II) and Kurudambhaka (Mandhal plates of Rudrasena II).[103]

Thus, it is clear that in the Vākāṭaka kingdom urban settlements were not many. This relative paucity is seen not only in relation to the pre-Vākāṭaka phase (that is, the age of the Sātavāhanas) but also in relation to the rural settlements of the Vākāṭaka phase itself. According to Shrimali, "the rural-urban nexus hinges on the role of trade."[104] That the growth of a large number of the Buddhist centres in western and central India were closely linked with the growth of trade and the support offered to them by traders and merchants is a well-recognized fact. The inscriptions of the Sātavāhanas testify to this. As noted earlier, we also have three inscriptions of the ministers and feudatories of the Vatsagulma branch of the Vākāṭakas, namely, the Ajanta cave XVI inscription of Varāhadeva, the Ghaṭotkacha cave inscription of Varāhadeva and the Ajanta cave XVII inscription of Ravisāmba which inform us about donations to the Buddhist Order. In all the available inscriptions of the Vākāṭakas only the Indore plates of Pravarasena II records that a merchant (Vaṇijaka) named Chandra purchased half of a *vāṭaka* (=village) and donated it to the brāhmaṇas.[105] This decline in the Vākāṭaka prosperity, and possibly in their status as well, becomes intelligible when we see dresses and ornaments in the Ajanta paintings. On the basis of this evidence Mirashi was forced to comment that "merchants... generally appear

[102] Cf. Ajay Mitra Shastri, 'Socio-economic Significance of Place-names in Vākāṭaka Inscriptions', a paper presented by him in the Seminar on the Recent Trends in the Study of Socio-economic History of India held at the University of Jabalpur, 27 February-1 March, 1986.

[103] Pākaṇṇa has been taken by Ajay Mitra Shastri to mean a derivative and Prakritised form of Prakaṇva referred to by Pāṇini (VI, 1, 153). V. S. Agrawala takes it to be a country of north-western India beyond Kamboja (*India as Known to Pāṇini*, Varanasi, Second edn., 1963, pp. 38 and 50). Some Jaina works such as the *Prajñāpanā*, Śīlāṅka's *Sūtrakṛtāṅgavṛtti*, the *Bhagavatī Sūtra* and the *Bhagavatīvṛtti* of Abhayadeva mention Pākaṇṇa as an *aṇāriya* (non-Aryan) country. The *Prajñāpanā* uses the word *aṇāriya* as a synonym of *milikkhu*. "Couldn't, therefore," Shrimali argues, "Millukadratha also mean a settlement of non-Aryans ?" (*Op. cit.*, p. 28). Ānarttapura and Lāṭakapallī indicate migration from the Saurashtra-Kathiawar region while Kuruvajjaka and Kurudambhaka easily remind us of the land of the Kurus.

[104] Shrimali, *op. cit.*, p. 28.

[105] Cf. *CII*, V, p. 41, 1.20.

without jewellery on their person."[106] But admittedly trade and industry were not completely absent in the Vākāṭaka kingdom. Here, we would like to comment on the observation of Lallanji Gopal, who, while reviewing the work of Shrimali, wrote that "the case for a decline in trade (in the Vākāṭaka kingdom) is not so well-argued. There is some evidence for the availability of mineral resources and the active working of some industries."[107] It is, in fact, just opposite to the truth. Not only the decline in trade in the Vākāṭaka territories is well argued by Shrimali, we clearly notice a decline in the character of settlements there. These facts—the decline in the character of settlements and the decline in trade—are also complementary to each other. We do not mean to say that there is a complete absence of trade and industries in the Vākāṭaka kingdom. Here, we are only trying to understand the evidence at our disposal. Shrimali himself writes that he does not intend to postulate such a view.[108] According to him, "The donated village of Charmāṅka (Chammak plates) perhaps indicates a settlement of leather workers. Similarly, the donated villages named Kāṁsakāraka and Suvarṇakāra, both mentioned in the Thalner copper plates, may be seen as settlements of bronze workers and goldsmiths respectively. The Pattan plates were engraved by a goldsmith called Īśvaradatta. Settlements such as Kāllāra (Tigaon plates) and Madhukajjhari (Patna Museum plates) could be centres of distillers. Iṣṭākapallī (Mandhal plates 'A' of the year 2 of Pṛithivīsheṇa II) may have been the production centre of bricks. Similarly, place-names such as Hiraṇyapura (Dudia plates), Lavaṇatailaka (Mandhal plates 'A' of Pṛithivīsheṇa II) and Lohanagara (Pattan plates) are again indicative of artisanal settlements noted for economic/commercial products."[109]

The relative decline of urban centres is also corroborated by the archaeological findings. In this context, the history of the Hīnayāna Buddhist stūpa at Pauni is noteworthy. The excavations at the site show amazing prosperity of the establishment from the Maurya age to that of the Sātavāhanas. Many inscriptions found at the site indicate to the support extended to it by traders, merchants, goldsmiths, etc.[110] But the excavators were quite categorical in pointing out that "it is... certain that the monument had fallen into disuse by about the third century A.D. and went into oblivion afterwards, not to be noticed or referred to in subsequent times and accounts."[111] We are inclined to admit that the destiny of Pauni after the

[106] *Ibid.*, Intro., p. 1.

[107] Lallanji Gopal, in *The Indian Historical Review*, Vol. XIV, Nos. 1-2, July 1987 and January 1988, p. 300.

[108] Shrimali, *op. cit.*, p. 29.

[109] *Ibid.*

[110] S.B. Deo and Jagatpati Joshi, *op. cit.*, pp. 25-26, 37-43, 94-96.

[111] *Ibid.*, p. 30.

third century A.D. indicates the relative decline of trade and traders in Vidarbha. This is not impossible that this may have given a further momentum to the growth of rural settlements in the Vākāṭaka kingdom.

CONCLUSION

Therefore, the two and a half centuries of the Vākāṭaka ascendancy in parts of central India and the northern Deccan, with its non-monetary, small-scale village settlements and relatively declining urban economy, presents a *milieu* in which we find some elements of feudalism. The view of Shrimali that "the Vākāṭaka territory was the matrix of the earliest articulated tendencies of feudal beginnings"[112] is rather imperfect, for we can possibly go beyond this assumption and argue that being under the shadow of the imperial Guptas for a major period of their rule the Vākāṭaka economy was bound to show some feudal elements in their kingdom. After all, it was the age of the feudal-federal organization of the mighty Gupta rulers. The Gupta period witnessed strong feudalization of the state apparatus which is not to be found earlier. But it is not at all necessary to assume that every feature of feudalism should be noticeable in the Vākāṭaka territories as Lallanji Gopal seems to think.[113]

[112] Shrimali, *op. cit.*, p. 30.
[113] Gopal, *op. cit.*

FOUR

Situating Gupta History for S.R. Goyal

I

Upto about 1947, the vast majority of historians, who wrote about ancient India, including the period of the imperial Guptas, were divided into two main camps : those who shared a bias in favour of British imperialism and those who opposed it.[1] The imperialists included orientalists, as well as direct imperialists. Opposing them were the nationalists and scientifics. The first work of a Western author in which the imperialist historian's concept of 'oriental despotism', a common key to their interpretation of ancient and medieval south Asian political history, was applied and Gupta history was dealt with in some detail was the *Early History of India* by Vincent A. Smith, the first edition of which appeared in 1904. However, Smith could never explicitly integrate his imperialist bias into a coherent theory.

Smith had his critics, even among Englishmen. Perhaps the most interesting of these was E.B. Havell whose *History of Aryan Rule in India from the Earliest Times to the Death of Akbar* appeared in 1918. He rebuked Smith for his theory that Indians are heirs to untold centuries of 'oriental despotism'. But he himself was the victim of a philosophy called Pan-Aryanism.

It was mainly in the twentieth century that Indian scholars directed their attention to writing the political history of ancient India, partly as a reaction against the prejudiced approach of the Western scholars towards India's past and partly due to the influence of the nationalist movement on

[1] Vide David N. Lorenzen, 'Imperialism and the Historiography of Ancient India', in S.N. Mukherjee (ed.), *India : History and Thought*, Calcutta, 1982, pp. 84-102; idem, 'Professor Goyal's Suggestion on Political History Writing in the Light of Historians and Political History of the Gupta Empire', in *Political History in a Changing World*, eds. G.C. Pande, S.K. Gupta and Shankar Goyal, Jodhpur, 1992, pp. 43-45.

Indian historians. They also regarded the period of the imperial Guptas as the 'golden age' which demonstrated and anticipated the nation's potential for future unity and glory. In 1920, R.G. Bhandarkar, the earliest important indigenous historian of ancient India, brought out his *A Peep into the Early History of India*, a history of India from the beginning of the Mauryan period to the end of the Gupta empire, which was first published in the *Journal of the Bombay Branch of the Royal Asiatic Society* in 1900. Bhandarkar's attitude to history was that of the nineteenth century; he would probably have agreed with Ranke, whose works he may have known, that the task of the historian was to describe the past as it actually was.[2] Many Indian historians of pre-1947 period followed Bhandarkar's advice with varying degrees of success. They were mostly confined to the study of facts as they are, without subjecting them to interpretation in the light of a particular ideology. They differed from each other merely in the degree of reliance which they placed on different types of evidence and on the techniques to utilize them. In 1923, H.C. Raychaudhuri published his well-known work *Political History of Ancient India from the Accession of Parīkshit to the Extinction of the Gupta Dynasty*. In many respects it is still the most important work on ancient Indian history written in the last one hundred years or so.

Other monographs, that appeared immediately after Raychaudhuri's, concentrate on the dynastic history of the Guptas, attempting only a chronological reconstruction of the course of important events and the achievements of the individual rulers. In the chronological order of publication they are : S.K. Aiyangar's *Studies in Gupta History* (1928), R.N. Shastri's *Gupta Vaṁśa kā Itihāsa* (1932), G.P. Mehta's *Chandragupta Vikramāditya* (1932) and Bharat Ram's *Samudragupta*. The last work is probably the first biography of any Gupta king written in any Indian language. The year 1933 saw the publication of *The Age of the Imperial Guptas* by R.D. Banerji. Banerji also believed in the reconstructional aspect of history writing. He laid emphasis on his hypothesis that Chandragupta I liberated 'the people of Magadha from the thraldom of the hated Scythian foreigners', and 'brought independence, self-realization and glory to the people of northern India'.

1933 saw another significant work on political history titled *History*

[2] Vide A.L. Basham, *Historians of India, Pakistan and Ceylon*, ed. C.H. Philips, London, 1961, p. 281; for a wider evaluation of Bhandarkar's historiography cf. S.R. Goyal, *A History of the Imperial Guptas*, Allahabad, 1967, Ch. 1; idem, *The Imperial Guptas : A Multidisciplinary Political Study*, Jodhpur, 2005, pp. 8 ff.; also see A.D. Pusalker, in *Historians and Historiography of Modern India*, ed. S.P. Sen, Calcutta, 1973, pp. 27-45; S.K. Mukhopadhyay, *Evolution of Historiography in Modern India: 1900-1960*, Calcutta, 1981, p. 18.

of India, A.D. 150 to A.D. 350 by K.P. Jayaswal, a lawyer, who was a brilliant Sanskritist and also the chief representative of the nationalist school of Indian historians. It was written to controvert Smith's view that the period between the extinction of the Kushāṇa and the Āndhra dynasties and the rise of the imperial Guptas is one of 'the darkest in the whole range of Indian history'. But Jayaswal was also one of those historians who believed that representative democratic institutions existed in ancient India and that the ancient Indian republican states were in fact little different in constitution from the republics of the contemporary West. In order to prove this thesis he wrote his famous work *Hindu Polity* in 1918. He was, therefore, very conscious of the fact that the Guptas were largely responsible for the destruction of these communities. Towards the close of his *History of India* he condemned them for their imperialism.

After Jayaswal R.G. Basak, who held an eminent position in the field of Indological studies, brought out his *History of North-East India from the Founding of the Gupta Empire to the Rise of the Pāla Dynasty of Bengal, 320-760 A.D.* (1934) in which he devoted about a hundred pages to the Gupta empire. In the next year Vasudeva Upadhyaya brought out his book titled *Gupta Sāmrājya kā Itihāsa* (in two volumes). In 1941, R.N. Dandekar published his *A History of the Guptas* while R.S. Tripathi expressed his views on Gupta history in his *History of Ancient India*, published in 1942. Another work of the period was that of R.N. Saletore, *Life in the Gupta Age*, published in 1943. However, the most important work on the Gupta age that appeared in the pre-Independence era was *A New History of the Indian People*, Vol. VI (*The Vākāṭaka-Gupta Age Circa 200-550 A.D.*), prepared by the Bharatiya Itihas Parishad under the general editorship of R.C. Majumdar and A.S. Altekar.[3] In it is found an elaborate account of the history of the imperial Guptas strictly written on traditional pattern with the golden age model in the mind of the editors and most contributors of various chapters.

In the early years of the Independence era also, Indian historians generally followed the 'what happened' approach for the Gupta age and adopted the classical or golden age model for it which they inherited from Smith, Havell and earlier nationalist historians and which is still a hot favourite among the latest generation of them. For example, R.K. Mookerji's *The Gupta Empire*[4] gives a king-wise narration of the political events and an account of the moral and material progress of the country achieved in the Gupta age and of the various institutions—social, economic and administrative—in which the progress was embodied. It gives a picture of

[3] Lahore, 1946.
[4] Bombay, 1947.

India's civilization 'in some of her best days, the days of national freedom and expansion'.

In 1943, fell the 2,000th year of the Vikrama era which was celebrated by the preparation of a volume titled *Vikrama Volume* [5] containing the articles of eminent scholars on topics connected with the Vikrama era, king Vikramāditya, his nine jewels and his capital Ujjain. But the volume, edited by R.K. Mookerji, could be brought out only in 1948. Now, as many learned contributors to this volume believed in theory that the first Vikramāditya of history belonged to the Gupta age, and that Kālidāsa and some other jewels of Vikramāditya graced the Gupta court, their articles, specially those of H.C. Raychaudhuri, R.C. Majumdar, D.C. Sircar and R.K. Mookerji, are of great relevance for the reconstruction of the history of the Guptas and the culture of their period.

The climax of nationalist interpretation of the Gupta age as the classical age of India was reached in the early fifties when *Gupta Polity* of V.R.R. Dikshitar,[6] *The Glamour about the Guptas* of K.M. Shembavanakar[7] and *The Classical Age* edited by R.C. Majumdar and A.D. Pusalker were published.[8] *The Classical Age* is the third volume of the Bharatiya Vidya Bhavan's multi-volume *History and Culture of the Indian People* series, prepared under the general editorship of R.C. Majumdar, the best known of the older generation of Indian historians. This was the work of nationalist historians writing for their own countrymen at a time when nationalist feeling in India had never been more intense. In his Preface to *The Classical Age* R.C. Majumdar also evaluated the period thus : "The Gupta Age, which forms the subject-matter of this volume, has been described in rapturous terms, as the 'Golden Age', the 'Classical Period' of Indian history, *etc.* And fully does it deserve these appellations. It was during this period that Indian intellect reached its high watermark in most branches of art, science and literature, and Indian culture and civilization reached a unique stage of development which left its deep impress upon succeedings ages. ...The facts recounted above will more than justify the appellation 'Periclean Age of India' which is often applied to the Gupta period. ...As in the case of Periclean Athens, the new era of culture ushered in by the Guptas long survived their political power."[9]

The year 1954 was indeed a very fruitful year for Gupta historiography. It not only saw the publication of *The Classical Age* but also of *The Catalogue*

[5] Ujjain, 1948.

[6] Madras, 1952.

[7] Bombay, 1953.

[8] Bombay, 1954.

[9] K.M. Munshi, his Foreword in *The Classical Age*, Bombay, 1954, pp. xlvi, xlviii.

of the Gupta Gold Coins in the Bayana Hoard [10] and the *Guptakālīna Mudrāyeṅ* [11] of A.S. Altekar and *The Decline of the Kingdom of Magadha* of B.P. Sinha. A.L. Basham's *The Wonder that was India* was also published in this year. Altekar had been the co-editor of *A New History of the Indian People*, Vol. VI (*The Vākāṭaka-Gupta Age*) and had published several articles on Gupta coins and inscriptions. But he had not written a full account of the imperial Guptas anywhere. The two mentioned works on Gupta coins and *The Coinage of the Gupta Empire*, published three years later from Varanasi, provided this opportunity to him. These contain his views in brief on several problems of the Gupta history which he tried to solve with the help of numismatic data.

After mid-fiftees there was a sort of lull in the field of Gupta historiography for more than a decade. In this period in 1955 in his Hindi work *Bhāratīya Kṛshṭi kā Ka Kha Ga*, published from Allahabad, Jayachandra Vidyalankar described the Gupta age as the golden age of Indian culture. Then came out R.K. Mookerji's English text book *Ancient India* (1956) containing a brief account of the Guptas as well, S. Chattopadhyaya's *Early History of North India*[12] having a chapter on the Gupta dynasty and *Samudra Gupta : Life and Times* of B.G. Gokhale.[13] Buddha Prakash produced two monographs, *Studies in Indian History and Civilization* and *Aspects of Indian History and Civilization* from Agra, respectively in 1962 and 1965. This was the state of Gupta historiography before the publication of S.R. Goyal's *A History of the Imperial Guptas* in 1967.[14]

II

In 1967 S.R. Goyal entered the scene of Gupta historiography with an entirely new approach to the subject and startling results of a fresh and thorough investigation in the field. His doctoral dissertation, *A History of the Imperial Guptas* (hereafter *HIG*), published from Allahabad in 1967, immediately earned for him a place among chief interpreters of the Gupta age.[15] As is

[10] Bombay, 1954.

[11] Patna, 1954.

[12] Calcutta, 1958.

[13] Bombay, 1962.

[14] For details see my *Recent Historiography of Ancient India*, Jodhpur, 1997, pp. 242-60; *Prāchīna Bhārata kā Ādhunika Itihāsa-Lekhana*, Jodhpur, 2000, Ch.10; for a serious analysis of the various perceptions of the past cf. also Romila Thapar, *The Penguin History of Early India*, New Delhi, 2002, Ch. I.

[15] Before the supplication of his thesis in 1966 and its publication in 1967, more than a dozen research papers of S.R. Goyal on Gupta history had been published. They include: 'Were the Imperial Guptas Brāhmaṇas by Caste ?' (in Hindi), *Bulletin of the Gorakhpur University*, 1960, pp. 5-9; 'Was Magadha the Original Home of the Imperial Guptas ?',

shown below, this work forms a watershed in the historiography of the Gupta dynasty, for it suggested new solutions to most major problems of Gupta history forcing the scholars to either accept or reject them with the result that the outline of Gupta history as was generally accepted till 1967 gradually became modified usually on the lines suggested by Goyal. Further, now a number of scholars concede that a study of the political events of the Gupta age in their situational context is not only possible but desirable also.

Between 1967 and 2006 S.R. Goyal published as many as ten monographs and numerous research articles on the various aspects of the history of the imperial Guptas. His works included :

1. *A History of the Imperial Guptas* (1967),
2. *Gupta evaṁ Samakālīna Rājavaṁśa* (1969),
3. *Guptakālīna Abhilekha* (1984),
4. *Samudragupta Parākramāṅka* (1987),
5. *Gupta Sāmrājya kā Itihāsa* (1987),
6. *Gupta aur Vākāṭaka Sāmrājyoṅ kā Yuga* (1988),[16]
7. *An Introduction to Gupta Numismatics* (1994),
8. *Indian Art of the Gupta Age* (eds. S.R. Goyal and Shankar Goyal, 2000),
9. *The Imperial Guptas : A Multidisciplinary Political Study* (2005), and
10. *A History of the Vākāṭaka-Gupta Relations* (2006).

Apart from these ten works one more work owes its existence mainly to the researches of S.R. Goyal, and that is, *King Chandra and the Meharauli Pillar.*[17] This book contains the lead paper of Goyal, originally published as a part of his doctoral thesis in which he seeks to identify King Chandra of the Meharauli *praśasti* with Samudragupta, and reaction-papers of twenty-

---

PIHC, 1964 (abstract); 'Was Pāṭaliputra the Capital of the Imperial Guptas?', *PIHC*, 1964 (abstract); 'Samudragupta : the King of the Meharauli Pillar Inscription' (in Hindi), *Nāgarī Prachāriṇī Patrikā*, LXIX, Pt. III, V.E. 2021, pp. 261-77; 'Samudragupta and the North-West', *Proceedings of the Oriental Conference*, Gauhati Session, 1964, pp. 153-68; 'The Problem of Bālādityas in the Gupta Period', *Bhuyan Commemoration Volume*, Gauhati, 1965, pp. 100-14; 'Observations on the Śrī Vikrama Coin of Samudragupta', *JNSI*, 1965, XXVII, Pt. II, pp. 142-45; 'The Date of Kālidāsa : An Old Suggestion Modified', *POC*, XXII, I, 1965, pp. 72-73 (abstract); 'The Date of Vasubandhu and the Identity of His Patron' (in Hindi), *Shri S.N.M. Tripathi Abhinandana Grantha*, Varanasi, 1965, pp. 101-07; 'Attribution of Chandragupta-Kumāradevī Coin Type', *Indian Numismatic Chronicle*, IV, Pt. II, 1965-66, pp. 116-26; 'Attribution of the Coins of Prakāśāditya', *JNSI*, 1966, XXVIII, Pt. I, pp. 17-20; 'Early Chronology of the Gupta Dynasty', *JBRS*, III, Jan. 1966, pp. 55-67; 'Gayā and Nālandā Plates of Samudragupta', *JBRS*, III, Jan. 1966, pp. 68-72.

[16] A thoroughly revised and updated version of No. 2.

[17] Ed. by Munish Chandra Joshi, S.K. Gupta and Shankar Goyal, Meerut, 1989.

four reputed Indologists who have either accepted the suggestion of Goyal, or criticised it. Thus, in the words of Munish Chandra Joshi, former Director-General, Archaeological Survey of India, and the editor of the book, 'the credit for bringing out this book should go to S.R. Goyal'.[18]

III

Many inscriptions of the imperial Guptas, which are the main source of their history, were brought to light, deciphered and interpreted gradually in the last decades of the eighteenth and the early decades of the nineteenth century by the British scholars and their Indian colleagues. The early epigraphists naturally committed numerous errors in their decipherment and interpretation of the Gupta records, and in the absence of any independent evidence on the history of this dynasty, literary or otherwise, they had to grope in the dark for a long time in their efforts to locate it in time and space. But the patient efforts of the epigraphists very soon laid its skeleton bare. In his *Bhilsa Topes* General Cunningham suggested 319 A.D. as the initial year of the era used in the Gupta inscriptions, published a correct translation of the statement of Alberuni on the problem of the Gupta era, and gave a connected account of the history of the Gupta dynasty. The publication of J.F. Fleet's *Corpus Inscriptionum Indicarum*, in which he edited the inscriptions of the imperial Guptas, the Later Guptas and others, was a landmark in the progress of Gupta epigraphy. Its importance may easily be realized from the fact that even after more than a century of its publication and after more than fifty years of Independence it has not been replaced by a better work in English. The most which Indian scholarship has been able to do is the publication of its revised version prepared by D.R. Bhandarkar and edited, after the death of Bhandarkar, by B. Ch. Chhabra and G.S. Gai (1981). But the new editors have deleted all the inscriptions of the dynasties which were contemporary of the imperial Guptas.

Among other works produced in the present century which are notable for the inscriptions of the Vākāṭaka-Gupta age mention may be made of D.C. Sircar's *Select Inscriptions bearing on Indian History and Civilization.*[19] But it does not provide summary or translation of the inscriptions in English.

In 1963, V.V. Mirashi brought out his much awaited Volume V of the *Corpus Inscriptionum Indicarum* containing the inscriptions of the

[18] *Ibid.*, p. x. Here mention may also be made of S.R. Goyal's *Ancient Indian Inscriptions: Recent Finds and New Interpretations* (Jodhpur, 2005) which deals with several inscriptions of the imperial Guptas and their contemporaries and his Hindi monograph on the history of Lichchhavi period of Nepal which corresponded to the Gupta period of Indian history (S.R. Goyal, *Prāchīna Nepāla kā Rājanītika aur Sāṁskṛtika Itihāsa*, Varanasi, 1973.

[19] Calcutta, 1942, Second ed., 1965.

Vākāṭakas which had come to light by that time. The Vākāṭaka records which were discovered after the publication of this work are given (at least a detailed treatment of their contents and importance) by Ajay Mitra Shastri in *The Age of the Vākāṭakas.*[20]

But the most important work on the inscriptions of the Guptas, Vākāṭakas and other contemporary powers is S.R. Goyal's *Guptakālīna Abhilekha* in Hindi published from Meerut in 1984. It contains text, translation, textual comments, comments on important passages and a discussion on the importance of each and every Gupta inscription and select inscriptions of other dynasties—the Vākāṭakas, Hūṇas, Aulikaras, etc. What is more, it gives even meanings of all the difficult and important words occurring in an inscription. Naturally, it has been widely acclaimed as an important contribution to ancient Indian epigraphy. On the other hand, Vasudeva Upadhyaya's *Gupta Abhilekha,*[21] which gives extremely faulty translations of Gupta epigraphs and is full of printing mistakes, has nothing to commend itself.

IV

The study of Gupta coins started even earlier than that of the Gupta inscriptions. The first hoard of the Gupta gold coins, which probably consisted mostly of the issues of the later Gupta emperors, was discovered as early as 1783 at Kalighat.[22] After the decipherment of the Gupta script, it became possible to connect the kings known from their coins with the kings mentioned in the Gupta records. It made the study of the Gupta coins immensely interesting and highly rewarding. In the later half of the nineteenth century and in the early years of the twentieth, apart from stray pieces, a number of new hoard of the Gupta gold coins were found. Prominent among them were those which were found at Bharsar (1851), Jessore (1852), Allahabad (1864), Hugli (1883), Tanda (1885), Kotwa (1886), Basti (1887), Hajipur (1893) and Tekri Debra (1912). Their contents were intensively studied by the leading numismatists of the period and the results of these investigations were summed up by V.A. Smith in his *Catalogue of the Coins of Ancient India in the Indian Museum, Calcutta* (1906) and Allan in his famous *Catalogue of the Coins of the Gupta Dynasties,* published in 1914. Several other hoards came to light during or after the publication of Allan's work—including those found at Kasarva (1912), Mithathal (1915),

[20] New Delhi, 1992, pp. 227-68; also see his *Vākāṭakas : Sources and History,* New Delhi, 1997, pp. 3-135. On this, also cf. my *175 Years of Vākāṭaka History and Historiography,* Jodhpur, 2009, Chs. 2, 3.

[21] Patna, 1974.

[22] J. Allan, *BMC, GD,* pp. cxxiv ff.

Sakori (1914), Kumarkhan (1952) and Bayana (1946). The last is the biggest hoard of the Gupta gold coins so far discovered. Altekar published a separate catalogue of its contents[23] and summed up the knowledge of the Gupta coins todate in his *Coinage of the Gupta Empire and its Imitations*, published in 1957, its Hindi version being *Guptakālīna Mudrāyeṅ*.[24]

S.R. Goyal also also brought out a remarkable work on Gupta numismatics from Jodhpur in 1994, titled *An Introduction to Gupta Numismatics*. This work deals exhaustively with fundamental problems of Gupta numismatics. Divided into four chapters—Genral Features of the Gupta Coins, Gold Coin Types, Silver and Copper Coins of the Guptas and Gupta Impact on Post-Gupta Coins—the work also contains an exhaustive Bibiliography and numerous photographic illustrations and line-drawings. Goyal's work is somewhat unique because it seeks to make a comprehensive but compact study of almost all the aspects of Gupta coins in a scientific manner and includes the results of the latest discoveries and researches. On many numismatic problems it sheds new light and suggests new solutions.

On the attribution of Chandragupta-Kumāradevī coin-type Goyal has argued that these coins were issued either by Chandragupta I or by Samudragupta before he issued the Standard type coins. (pp. 41-46). According to him, the latter alternative seems to be the correct one. The Standard type coins were issued quite late in the reign of Samudragupta, for they bear long legends referring to his conquests indicating that they were not struck in the beginning of his reign; if Chandragupta I had issued the Chandragupta-Kumāradevī type coins it would be rather strange that Samudragupta did not immediately continue to issue gold coins. The assumption that Samudragupta issued Chandragupta-Kumāradevī type coins in the early period of his reign does not create such a difficulty.

The greatest hurdle in the suggestion that the Chandragupta-Kumāradevī type was issued by Samudragupta is the supposed absence of any clue to the identity of the commemorator.[25] To overcome this difficulty V.S. Agrawala argued that they were issued by the Lichchhavis who have been mentioned on the reverse of these coins,[26] while V.S. Pathak has suggested that the obverse legends *Chandraguptaḥ* and *Kumāradevī Śrī* and the device of the marriage-scene may together be taken as meaning *Chandraguptasya Kumāradevyāmutpannasya* while the reverse legend *Lichchhavayaḥ* may be construed as *Lichchhavināmdauhitrasya*. Thus,

[23] *The Gupta Gold Coins in the Bayana Hoard*, Bombay, 1954.

[24] Patna, 1954; for details see my *Ancient Indian Numismatics : A Historiographical Study*, Jodhpur, 1998, Ch. 8.

[25] Altekar, *Coinage*, pp. 28-29.

[26] *JNSI*, XVII, i, p. 119.

legends and devices are subtle pointers to the identity of the commemorator, that is Samudragupta.[27] Sohoni[28] also opines that there is enough indication left by Samudragupta on Chandragupta-Kumāradevī type to indicate a reference to him, viz., names of his parents and of the community which had helped him. Goyal, however, feels that such a twist in the meaning of the legends is not altogether necessary. For, as pointed out by Jayaswal, no Hindu would ever think of celebrating the marriage of his father and mother.[29] It is, therefore, more reasonable to assume that Samudragupta issued these medals in the name of the Lichchhavis who were, after all, the co-rulers of the empire. It is quite likely that when his accession was challenged by his rival brothers, he issued these medals in order to publicize the fact that he, being a *dvyāmushyāyaṇa* had a better title to rule over the amalgamated kingdom of the Guptas and the Lichchhavis which other princes, not connected with the Lichchhavis, did not have. It also explains why these coins are not found in Bihar, the region in which the Lichchhavi state was situated. For, if they were issued to publicize that he had a better title to rule over the amalgamated kingdom, it was only natural for him to circulate them in the region where the rebellious princes 'of equal birth' could hope to find some support. The Lichchhavi state must have been solidly behind him and, therefore, he did not feel the necessity of circulating such medallic pieces there.

On Śrī Vikrama coin of Samudragupta, Goyal has criticised (pp. 103-06) the generally accepted opinion that the solitary coin giving the *biruda* '*Śrīvikrama*' to Samudragupta found in the Bamnala hoard was issued during the reign of Chandragupta II, when the obverse die of the Standard type coins of Samudragupta was inadvertently used with the reverse die of the Archer type of Chandragupta II. It is argued that as no Gupta king used two titles, it cannot be assumed that Samudragupta adopted both the titles *Parākrama* and *Vikrama*. However, Goyal has pointed out that Skandagupta assumed the titles *Kramāditya* and *Vikramāditya* both. Further, according to him, mertrology and other numismatic considerations are in favour of regarding this coin as the issue of Samudragupta.

Another theory of Goyal, which is worth-noting here, is concerned with the coins of Prakāśāditya. (pp. 96-101). In this he has given arguments to prove that Prakāśāditya ruled just after Bhānugupta (known date 510 A.D.). For this he has taken the help of the *Āryamañjuśrīmūlakalpa* which refers to 'Pra' initialled, that is Prakāśāditya as the rebellious son of 'Bha' initialled, that is Bhānugupta.

[27] *Ibid.*, XIX, ii, p. 141.

[28] *Ibid.*, p. 153.

[29] Jayaswal, *Hist.Ind.*, p. 91, fn. 1.

Recently K.S. Shukla has tried to give a new turn to the problem of the identity of Prakāśāditya. He published another specimen of the Horseman-lion-slayer type coin on which he has read the circular legend on the obv. between II and IV o'clock as *Bhānugupta* and between VI and XII as *vijitya vasudhāṁ divaṁ jayati.*[30] His reading was accepted and hailed by the editor of the journal, T.P. Verma.[31] However, Verma rightly pointed out that K.S. Shukla's suggestion that the coin shows that Bhānugupta was the ruling emperor and Prakāśāditya his viceroy cannot be accepted. If Shukla's reading is correct, then Prakāśāditya should be regarded as the title of Bhānugupta. P.L. Gupta and S.R. Goyal accept this obvious conclusion.[32] But lately the testimony of the coin itself has come to be regarded as suspect. Firstly, the original coin seen by Shukla in 1975 with a goldsmith at Nawal (Dist. Unnao, U.P.) has since disappeared and its present whereabouts are not known to anybody. Secondly, the photograph of the coin published in the *JNSI* is very poor and serves no useful purpose. Thirdly, it appears that Shukla's reading of the letters *Bhā, nu* and *gu* is not correct. Jagannath Agrawal rules out absolutely the reading *Bhānugupta* on it.[33] Fourthly, P.L. Gupta later pointed out that in accordance with the norms of the circular legends on the Gupta coins, the coin should have the name of the king with or without his *biruda* just before the existing portion of the legend between V and VIII o'clock, and not between II and IV o'clock.[34]

Thus, the so-called new evidence on Prakāśāditya has proved to be a non-starter and we are back to the square one. After rejecting the testimony of this coin Ashvini Agrawal has reverted to the old theory of the identification of Prakāśāditya with Purugupta, while Goyal finds no reason to modify his original thesis on the subject according to which Prakāśāditya should be placed between Bhānugupta (known date 510 A.D.) and Narasiṁhagupta II, the contemporary of Mihirakula.[35]

[30] *JNSI*, XLII, pp. 120-22.

[31] *Ibid.*, Editorial Note.

[32] S.R. Goyal, *Gupta Sāmrājya kā Itihāsa*, Meerut, 1987, p. 339, n. 1.

[33] Quoted by Ashvini Agrawal, in *Numismatic Studies*, Vol. 2, p. 118. n. 32.

[34] In *Political History in a Changing World*, eds. G.C. Pande, S.K. Gupta and Shankar Goyal, Jodhpur, 1992, pp. 182-83.

[35] My chapter on Gupta numismatography (pp.152-75) in *Ancient Indian Numismatics: A Historiographical Study* (1998) critically examines different approaches on the subject. For P.L. Gupta's contribution to the study of the gold coins of the Guptas cf. my paper, 'Dr. Parameshwari Lal Gupta aur Guptakālīna Suvarṇa Mudrāyeṅ', in *Baḍhate Kadam-Badalte Āyāma : Parameshwari Lal Gupta (80 varsha)*, ed., Sarojini Kulshreshtha, Varanasi, 1995, pp. 271-78.

V

Though the first stage of the Indological studies was dominated by literary antiquarianism, no ancient work containing even an outline of Gupta history was available to the early scholars. Therefore, when the newly discovered inscriptions and coins revealed the existence of the Gupta dynasty, there was a natural tendency among scholars to reconstruct its history with the help of oral bardic legends of highly dubious authenticity. For example, in 1873 Col. J.W. Watson[36] published a tradition attributed to the bards of Kathiawad, according to which a Gupta king, who reigned between the Gaṅgā and the Yamunā, sent his son Kumārapālagupta to conquer Surāshṭra and appointed Chakrapāṇi, the son of Prāṇadatta, to rule as a governor in the city of Wāmanasthalī. But, as was shown by Fleet, this tradition was of a very recent date—it owed its origin to certain speculations of Bhagwanlal Indraji which found their way to the bards through an educational treatise.[37] It furnishes an instance of the hazards involved in reconstructing the history of a dynasty with the help of bardic legends.[38] For the royal genealogies of the post-Mahābhārata period, the historical narratives of the eighteen Mahāpurāṇas are of great value. In 1913, F.E. Pargiter brought together all the historical material from these texts in his *The Purāṇa Text of the Dynasties of the Kali Age.*[39] But unfortunately out of the eighteen Purāṇas only the *Vishṇu*, *Vāyu* and *Bhāgavata* refer to the Guptas directly and that too only in a line or two. Further, these references do not mention any Gupta king by name; they only purport to outline the extent of the early Gupta kingdom. Early scholars like John Allan, H.C. Raychaudhuri, R.C. Majumdar, R.G. Bhandarkar, D.C. Ganguly and others, therefore, rightly used this material mainly to determine the location of the original home of the Guptas.[40] Dasharatha Sharma, however, tried to show that the subsequent lines of the *Vāyu* and *Vishṇu*, while referring to the rule of Devarakshita, Mahendra and Guha, describe the expansion of the empire under Chandragupta II (alias Devagupta=Devarakshita), Kumāragupta I Mahendrāditya (=Mahendra) and Skandagupta (=Guha).[41] P.L. Gupta adopted this suggestion of D. Sharma without even mentioning the name of the great savant.[42]

[36] *IA*, II, p. 313.

[37] *Corpus*, III, p. 50.

[38] *HIG*, p. 23.

[39] Oxford, 1913.

[40] Allan, *BMC, GD*, p. xix; Basak, *HNEI*, pp. 11-12; Raychaudhuri, *PHAI*, p. 53; Majumdar, *NHIP*, pp. 134-35; Ganguly, *IHQ*, XXI, pp. 141 ff.

[41] *IHQ*, XXX, pp. 374 ff.

[42] P. L. Gupta, *The Imperial Guptas*, pp. 114-17.

The only ancient work from which a sort of connected account of the imperial Guptas may be gleaned is the *Āryamañjuśrīmūlakalpa*, a Buddhist Mahāyāna Sanskrit text, composed in c. 800 A.D. In one of its chapters it relates the history of ancient India from Buddhist point of view in 1005 verses of which only about 300 are of some historical value. This material has been edited by K.P. Jayaswal[43] from the Sanskrit original[44] and a Tibetan text brought by Rahul Sankrityayana from Tibet. Some stray references to the Gupta rule are found in the Jaina works as well. For example, the *Harivaṁśa Purāṇa* of Jinasena Sūri composed in 783-84 A.D. informs us that the Guptas ruled for 231 years. The *Tiloya Paṇṇati* of Yati Vṛshabha also states that the Guptas ruled for 231 years but in another context it states that they ruled for 255 years. Some light on Toramāṇa and Harigupta and Devagupta of the Gupta family is also thrown by the Jaina romance *Kuvalayamālā* of Udyotana Sūri (777 A.D.). Among the dramas based on historical events, kāvyas and other literary works, there are several which are said to have references to the Guptas in their *bharata-vākyas*, introductory verses or elsewhere. Among them the *Mudrārākshasa* of Viśākhadatta (which probably mentions king Chandragupta in its *bharata-vākya*), *Harshacharita* of Bāṇa (which refers to the murder of a Śaka king by Chandragupta to save Dhruvadevī in the guise of a female) and the *Kāvya-mīmāṁsā* of Rājaśekhara (which alludes to the Dhruvadevī episode) need special mention. The most important Sanskrit drama which is based on the Chandragupta-Rāmagupta-Dhruvadevī episode is the play *Devīchandra-guptam* of Viśākhadeva, usually identified with Viśākhadatta, the author of the *Mudrārākshasa*. Only some extracts of the *Devīchandraguptam* are now available. A. Rangaswami Saraswati was the first scholar to publish three of them in 1923.[45] Gradually about nine more passages came to light. The first historian to reconstruct the history of Rāmagupta with the help of these extracts was R.D. Banerji[46] though A.S. Altekar pleaded for the historicity of this new Gupta ruler with greater insistence.[47] Very soon numerous scholars accepted the suggestion of Altekar [48] which was later strengthened by the discovery of the copper coins of Rāmagupta and the Durjanpur Jaina image inscriptions of his reign.[49]

[43] K.P. Jayaswal, *An Imperial History of India*, Lahore, 1934.

[44] Ed. by T. Ganapati Sastri, TSS, LXXXIV, 1925, pp. 579-656.

[45] *IA*, LII, p. 182.

[46] *AIG*, pp. 26 ff.

[47] *JBORS*, XIV, pp. 223 ff.; XV, pp. 134 ff.

[48] Mirashi, *IHQ*, X, p. 48; Saletore, *Life in the Gupta Age*, pp. 14 ff.; Heras, *JBRS*, XXXIV, pp. 19 ff.

[49] Cf. *HIG*, pp. 226 ff.; Romila Thapar, *The Past Before Us : Historical Traditions of Early North India*, Ranikhet, 2013, pp. 355 ff.

However, S.R. Goyal interpreted the testimony of the *Devīchandraguptam* quite differently using V.S. Pathak's methodology of interpreting early medieval texts to deduce from them more meaningful and scientific history. In his attempt to weave a coherent story such a poet-historian usually inadvertently left several loose ends which ultimately give a lie to the central tale exposing the motive of the author. Such discrepancies, Pathak argues, become to the modern historian as important, if not more, as the coherent picture itself, for they often reveal a story which is usually more in consonance with archaeological sources. Pathak has applied this method to several early medieval works including the *Harshacharita* of Bāṇa, *Vikramāṅkadevacharita* of Bilhaṇa and *Vikramāṅkābhyudaya* of Someśvara III and has concluded that when a younger prince violated the law of primogeniture and forcibly occupied the ancestral throne, his court-poets usually tried to justify his conduct by arguing, *mutatis mutandis*, that :

(1) their patron was destined by fate to succeed his father;

(2) their patron was favoured and selected by his father for succession;

(3) the elder brother himself declined to ascend the paternal throne or proved extremely cruel and vicious when he became king so that his younger brother, the hero of the poem, had to dethrone him for the welfare of the people and to save the fair name of his royal family; and

(4) sometimes the hero had to dethrone his elder brother at the express command of god.

Applying V.S. Pathak's methodology to Viśākha's drama *Devīchandraguptam*, which is based on historical events, Goyal points out to the discrepacies in the epigraphic and numismatic data on the one hand and the literary evidence on the other : "According to the literary tradition, when Rāmagupta agreed to surrender Dhruvadevī to the Śaka invader, Chandragupta II was merely a prince (*kumāra*). This definitely implies that at that time Rāmagupta was an imperial suzerain claiming his sway over the whole of the empire. ... But the archaeological data militate against this conclusion. For, the Gupta epigraphs quite frequently use the phrase *tatparigṛihita* to describe the relationship of Chandragupta II with his father Samudragupta. It implies a claim on the part of the former to the effect that he ascended the throne with the approval of the latter. This renders suspect *Devī Chandragupta*'s description of Chandragupta II as merely a *kumāra*. Further, the coins attributed to Rāmagupta are found significantly in eastern Malwa only, indicating thereby that his authority was confined roughly to that area. This is against his description as the imperial ruler in the *Devī Chandragupta*. ..."[50] "The fact that the story of the *Devī Chandragupta* is

[50] *HIG*, pp. 227-28.

not consonant with the testimony of the archaeological sources, assumes a new significance and the possibility that Viśākha also suppressed or transmuted those facts which were not in harmony with the purpose of his drama becomes worthy of serious consideration. It is quite likely that, after the death of Samudragupta, Chandragupta II violated the law of primogeniture and somehow became the master of almost the whole of the empire while Rāmagupta, the elder brother of the latter, who may have been the governor of the eastern Malwa during the life-time of Samudragupta, could impose his authority only on that province; but Viśākha, who wanted to whitewash the misdeeds of his master, gave a different colour to the whole episode by showing that Chandragupta II had accepted the accession of Rāmagupta, and that it was the misdeeds of the latter that forced Chandragupta to capture power in his own hands."[51]

The statement of the Gupta epigraphs that Chandragupta II was 'accepted' by Samudragupta is not necessarily against the claim of Viśākha. It may be that in the now lost portion of the drama Viśākha had shown that king Samudragupta wanted his younger son Chandragupta II to succeed him, but the latter, like Vikramāditya VI of the Chālukya dynasty, very magnanimously declined the offer.[52]

But Chandragupta II had not only violated the law of primogeniture, he had also married the widow of his elder brother murdered by him. It might be worthwhile to cite Goyal at some length on this point : "Viśākha rose to the occasion and put forward an ingenious plea in the defence of Chandragupta II. In his drama he portrayed Rāmagupta not as a cruel, wicked or avaricious person; instead, he made him an impotent and cowardly husband, who had shamelessly agreed to hand over his queen Dhruvadevī to the enemy king. In contrast to him was Chandragupta II, the hero of the drama, who had 'charm and beauty to match (his) youth', a lion 'at the very sight of whom the herds of deers flee away', and the matchless hero who did not ever hesitate to endanger his own life in order to save the prestige of his dynasty and of the queen. Thus Viśākha killed two birds with one stone; by the skilful characterization of the hero and the villain he furnished a plausible excuse for the legitimate supersession of the latter by the former and also for the spontaneous love of the heroine for the hero, ultimately leading to their marriage.

"Another device by which Bilhaṇa sought to justify the supersession of Someśvara II by Vikramāditya VI is the plea of divine pre-ordination and command. ...Whether Viśākha employed this motif in his drama or not, is not known. However, the Chakravikrama type coins of Chandragupta II

[51] *Ibid.*, p. 231.

[52] *Ibid.*, p. 231, n. 2.

depose significant evidence in this connection. It is quite possible that these coins, on the obverse of which he is shown as receiving three symbols of the universal sovereignty from Chakrapurusha, were issued to publicize the idea that he achieved royal status as a result of the divine favour."[53]

According to Goyal, the device of depicting the dethroned elder brother as cruel and unworthy of royalty was used even in the early medieval epigraphs. For example, when the Rāshṭrakūṭa ruler Govinda II was overthrown by his younger brother Dhruva, the latter claimed that his fight against his elder brother was not so much to gain the throne for himself as to retain it for the Rāshṭrakūṭas. The later rulers of the family elaborated this claim by characterizing Govinda II as a wicked ruler. The fact of the matter, however, is that Govinda II was indeed a great warrior and cavalry leader. He had great confidence in Dhruva and had entrusted practically the whole administration in the hands of the latter. But Dhruva exploited this confidence and usurped the throne for himself. At a later date king Kṛshṇa III, another ruler of the dynasty, employed this device to organize a successful revolt against his cousin Govinda IV. He also made the claim that the vicious life and lascivious ways of Govinda IV had alienated the sympathy of his subjects and feudatories threatening the very existence of the Chālukya dynasty.

VI

S.R. Goyal wrote his doctoral dissertation in six chapters.[54] In chapter I he has analysed the methods and techniques of studying the various types of data for the reconstruction of Gupta history. Then he has surveyed the approaches of the earlier historians of the Gupta history and has explained

[53] *Ibid.*, pp. 234-35. On this, also see my paper, 'Political Ideology of the Early Guptas as Reflected on their Coins', in *Journal of the Numismatic Society of India*, LXIV-V, 2003, pp. 24-28.

[54] For a useful discussion on S.R. Goyal's works on Gupta history vide A.M. Shastri, 'S.R. Goyal's Contribution to Gupta Historiography', in *Reappraising Gupta History for S.R. Goyal*, eds. B. Ch. Chhabra, P.K. Agrawala, Ashvini Agrawal and Shankar Goyal, New Delhi, 1992, pp. 1-14; P.K. Mitra, 'S.R. Goyal and Modern Historiography of the Gupta Age', in *Reappraising Gupta History for S.R. Goyal*, pp. 15-37; T.P. Verma, 'S.R. Goyal's Contribution to Gupta History', in *S.R. Goyal : His Multidimensional Historiography*, eds. Jagannath Agrawal and Shankar Goyal, New Delhi, 1992, pp. 107-22; David N. Lorenzen, 'Professor S.R. Goyal's Suggestion on Political History Writing in the Light of Historians and Political History of the Gupta Empire', in *Political History in a Changing World*, eds. G.C. Pande, S.K. Gupta and Shankar Goyal, Jodhpur, 1992, pp. 53 ff.; Shankar Goyal, 'Historiography of the Imperial Guptas : Old and New', *VIJ*, Vol. XXIX, Pts. I-II, 1991 (1995), pp. 239-74; idem, *Recent Historiography of Ancient India*, Jodhpur, 1997, pp. 261-315; idem, *Prāchīna Bhārata kā Ādhunika Itihāsa-Lekhana*, Jodhpur, 2000, pp. 198-225.

the necessity of studying political history of this period against the background of various factors operating in society. No other historian of pre- or post-1967 period has made such an attempt to discuss techniques, methodology and approaches of other historians. That is why it has been described as 'imaginative', 'well-written' and 'a model of historiography' by Eleanor Zelliot.[55]

Goyal has devoted his chapter II to the study of the early Gupta age. He has studied the problem of the original home of the imperial Guptas from an altogether new angle and has shown that they originally belonged to the eastern part of the present Uttar Pradesh with Prayāga as the early centre of their power. He has also discussed this problem in the context of various factors leading to the rise of this region. The question of the social *milieu* of the imperial Guptas has been studied afresh and it has been shown that most probably they belonged to the Brāhmaṇa order.[56] In this context Goyal has pointed out the significance of the popularity of the Vedico-Āgamic movement and the predominance of the Brāhmaṇas in the administrative structure and its effects on Gupta history. Then, the emergence of the Gupta dynasty as an imperial power under Chandragupta I is studied against the background of the contemporary political situation and various other factors. In that connection Goyal has dealt with the history of some of the contemporary powers, specially that of the Vākāṭakas. Following V.S. Pathak's interpretation of the term *dauhitra* occurring in the genealogical portions of the Vākāṭaka and Gupta records, he has given a new picture of the Vākāṭaka-Bhāraśiva and Gupta-Lichchhavi alliances. Chapter II also contains three appendices, the first of which deals with the early chronology of the Gupta dynasty. Goyal has shown that the Gupta-Lichchhavi alliance was contracted by Ghaṭotkacha. He has followed P.L. Gupta's suggestion that the Gupta era was founded by Chandragupta II though it was reckoned from the date of the accession of Chandragupta I. (In his Hindi work he, for the first time, gives weighty arguments to show that Samudragupta ascended the throne in c. 350 A.D.). Appendix II is concerned with the problem of the authenticity of the Nālandā and the Gayā copper plate grants of Samudragupta and appendix III with the problem of the attribution of the Chandragupta-Kumāradevī type of coins. New solutions of both these problems have been offered. Agreeing with John Allan, Goyal believes that the Chandragupta-Kumāradevī type of coins were issued by Samudragupta but he disagrees with Allan when he suggests that these were the *earliest* coins issued by him.

[55] In *Essays on Gupta Culture*, ed. Bardwell L. Smith, Delhi, 1983, p. 288.

[56] S.R. Goyal made this suggestion for the first time in *Gorakhpur University Magazine* in 1960.

Chapter III is devoted to the reign of Samudragupta. Goyal has studied the revolt of Kācha against the background of various pulls and pressures that marked the debut of Samudragupta as an emperor. The conquests of Samudragupta in the different parts of the country have been studied in the context of various political, geographical, economic and religious factors. It is for the first time that the contribution of religion to the making of political decisions in this age has been determined with some precision.[57] Goyal has indentified Rudradeva of the Prayāga *praśasti* with Vākāṭaka Rudrasena I who was uprooted by the Gupta emperor. Further, it has also been shown that Samudragupta led more than one expedition in the south, that one of his southern campaigns took place in 359-60 A.D., that Vākāṭaka Pṛthivīsheṇa I participated in these campaigns as his subordinate ally and that the aim of his adventures in that part of the country was the acquisition of wealth.[58] The evidence of the Prayāga *praśasti* on his relations with the north-western foreign potentates has been connected with the tribal movements that took place in Bactria and north-western India in his reign and also with the evidence of the Meharauli pillar inscription. The identity of the King Chandra, mentioned in the Meharauli record, has been discussed in appendix III of this chapter and, for the first time, it was suggested that he was perhaps no other than Samudragupta himself. Other appendices of this chapter are concerned with the place of king Kācha in Gupta history, the relative chronology of Samudragupta's campaigns, the capital of the Gupta empire, the date and patron of Vasubandhu and the date of Kālidāsa. Goyal has placed the great poet in the later half of the fourth century A.D. making both Samudragupta and Chandragupta II his patrons. He has located the early Gupta capital at Prayāga and believes that Samudragupta did assume the title 'Śrī Vikrama' as is evidenced by one of his coins.

Chapter IV deals with the reigns of Chandragupta II and Kumāragupta I. In the reign of Chandragupta II western India became the major stage of the drama of political history. In that context, as seen above, Goyal has studied the problem of Rāmagupta afresh in the light of the methodology suggested by V.S. Pathak for the study of dramas based on historical events and has proposed an entirely new interpretation of the archaeological, numismatic and literary data. Then the causes of the Śaka war of Chandragupta II are analysed and his relations with the Vākāṭakas are discussed and put in their proper historical perspective. Goyal has tried to prove that the Gupta-Vākāṭaka alliance was not motivated by the possibility of the Śaka war and that the Śaka

[57] Cf. also my paper, 'Political Ideology of the Early Imperial Guptas', in *Reappraising Gupta History for S.R. Goyal*, eds. B. Ch. Chhabra et al, pp. 215-23.

[58] M.G.S. Narayanan broadly follows this suggestion of S.R. Goyal (*Śrī Dineśacandrikā*, pp. 283 ff.) So does R.C. Majumdar in *Com. Hist. Ind.*, III, Pt. I, p. 25.

war took place towards the close of the reign of Chandragupta II.[59] He has also shown that the age of Chandragupta II and Kumāragupta I was the period of transformation of the Gupta royalty which lost much of its martial fervour and the repercussions of this change on the political developments have been pointed out. Goyal expresses the view that Chandragupta II almost became a Jahangir of the Gupta age. Then the Gupta invasion of the Deccan towards the close of the reign of Kumāragupta I is studied in the context of the new alignment of powers that took place due to the hostility between the Vākāṭakas and the Guptas. (In his Hindi works Goyal has given reasons to ascribe Part I of the Bihar pillar inscription to the reign of Kumāragupta I and its Part II to the reign of Skandagupta).[60]

Chapter V is devoted to the study of the transformation and decline of the Gupta empire in the period from the accession of Skandagupta to the death of Budhagupta. (In his Hindi works Goyal has shown that the two parts of the Junagadh *praśasti* of Skandagupta are actually two records of different dates and that from the first record it is clearly proved that Skandagupta had ascended the throne and acquired victory in the wars described in this epigraph long before 455 A.D. and before the demise of Kumāragupta I). Goyal believes that the invasion of the Pushyamitras on the Gupta empire and the invasion of the Vākāṭakas on Malwa were connected events and were the results of the aggressive policy of the Guptas against the Vākāṭakas in the preceding reign. The Hūṇa invasion has been studied afresh and the nature of Skandagupta's achievements is more accurately determined. Then the problem of gradual transformation and decline of the empire is taken up and it has been shown, for the first time, that the influence of Buddhism had much to do with the weakening of the central authority in this period. The genesis of the feudal-federal organisation of the empire and its influence on the fortunes of the state are also discussed. In the two appendices of this chapter, respectively the problems of succession immediately after Kumāragupta I and the order of succession after Skandagupta are dealt with. In the later appendix, a new solution of the problem of the place of Bālādityas in Gupta history is proposed according to which there ruled in Gupta dynasty two sets of kings named Kumāragupta and Narasiṁhagupta Bālāditya, one set in between Skandagupta and Budhagupta and other set in the post-Bhānugupta period (that is after 510 A.D.) and that both the kings of each set were related to each other by father-son relationship.

[59] Also cf. Shankar Goyal, *Problems of Ancient Indian History*, Jaipur, 2001, pp. 181 ff.

[60] Also cf. his paper, 'Bihar Stone Pillar Inscription of the Imperial Guptas' *JESI*, Vol. VII, 1980, pp. 49-53.

Chapter VI deals with the disintegration and collapse of the Gupta empire. In this connection Goyal has studied the invasion of the Hūṇas under Toramāṇa and Mihirakula and has given it an entirely new treatment. Further, the expansion of the Hūṇa power has been put in its geographical context and the religious aspect of the Gupta-Hūṇa struggle has been analysed in detail for the first time. Goyal has also shown how the influence of Buddhist ideology and the feudalization of the state structure undermined the central authority and led to the rise of new powers. In the appendix of this chapter, which deals with the order of succession after the death of Budhagupta, Goyal has suggested a new solution of the problem of the place of Prakāśāditya in Gupta history placing him in between Bhānugupta and Narasiṁhagupta Bālāditya II.

VII

The most important power of the Deccan in the age of the Guptas were the Vākāṭakas, who were intimately related with the former. S.R. Goyal critically examined Gupta-Vākāṭaka relations in his *A History of the Imperial Guptas.* In 1969, he produced another work, in Hindi, titled *Gupta evaṁ Samakālīna Rājavaṁśa* in which he gave a detailed account of the political history of the Vākāṭakas in over forty pages (its revised version under the title *Gupta aur Vākāṭaka Sāmrājyoṅ kā Yuga* appeared in 1988). Further, in 2006, he published an independent work, titled *A History of the Vākāṭaka-Gupta Relations*, on the history of the changing relationship of these two north Indian dynasties in the light of recent discoveries of source material, specially the Mandhal charters of Rudrasena II and other Vākāṭaka rulers, Miregaon plates of Prabhāvatīgupta, Ramtek inscription of a daughter of Prabhāvatī, etc., and his own researches, which according to him, necessitated radical changes in its picture generally reconstructed by scholars. As regards Vākāṭaka chronology Goyal, with minor modifications, supports Altekar's scheme and gives several new arguments to prove its correctness. But his reconstruction of the history of the Vākāṭakas is significantly different from that of Altekar and Mirashi in several respects. He has criticized both Mirashi and Altekar on the question of the original home of the Vākāṭakas. He has convincingly shown that the theory attributing a southern origin to the Vākāṭakas is not correct. He has pointed out that there could not have been any connection between the 'Vākāṭaka householder' of the Amarāvatī inscription and the royal dynasty of the Vākāṭakas. He has also pointed out that the titles and technical terms found in the Vākāṭaka records, to which attention has been drawn by Mirashi to prove their southern origin, are all found in the epigraphs of the Basim branch which flourished in the south and was greatly influenced by southern traditions; they are conspicuous by their absence in the records of the main branch. Therefore, if it is argued that the occurrence of such titles and technical terms proves the southern origin of the Vākāṭakas, then why their absence in the records of the main branch should not be regarded as a proof of their northern origin?

S.R. Goyal gives a new interpretation of the phrase *Bhavanāga-dauhitra* occurring for Rudrasena I in the Vākāṭaka records to show that Bhavanāga and Pravarasena I had forged a scheme by which after them Nāga and Vākāṭaka kingdoms were to merge and Rudrasena I was to succeed both of them, just as in the north Samudragupta, the *Lichchhavi-dauhitra*, was designated as the successor of both Chandragupta I and the Lichchhavi chief, the father of Kumāradevī. Says Goyal : "... as is well-known, Gautamīputra predeceased his father Pravarasena I, for we find that the latter was succeeded by Rudrasena I, the son of Gautamīputra. It is very curious, because after the demise of Gautamīputra Pravarasena I should have been succeeded by the eldest of his remaining three sons, ... No scholar has so far felt the necessity to explain this rather unusual fact. We, however, feel that its explanation lies in the correct interpretation of the phrase *Bhavanāga-dauhitra* used for Rudrasena I. ... Manu says that *dauhitra*, in the absence of (natural) son, inherits the whole property and offers *piṇḍas* both to the natural father and maternal grand-father (if he adopts him as subsidiary son of *dauhitra* category). ...It makes it quite reasonable to believe that in the beginning of the fourth century A.D. Bhavanāga, who did not have a male issue to succeed him, gave his daughter in marriage to Gautamīputra, the Vākāṭaka crown-prince, on the understanding that his (Bhavanāga's) daughter's son would be his subsidiary son of *dauhitra* category. Pravarasena I readily accepted his proposal, ...(and) when his son Gautamīputra died a premature death, he nominated Rudrasena I, the son of Gautamīputra and the grandson of Bhavanāga, as his own successor as well. For, had Pravarasena I been succeeded by any one of his remaining three sons, the two empires could not be amalgamated. ...Now, how far (this plan succeeded) is another matter,..."[61]

This suggestion of Goyal cogently explains as to why in the main branch Pravarasena I was succeeded by his grandson Rudrasena I though at least one of his other sons, Sarvasena, was alive.

Goyal differs radically from Altekar and Mirashi on the problem of the Vākāṭaka-Gupta relations also. As opposed to the view of Altekar, Mirashi and others, he is of the opinion that Jayaswal's basic suggestion about the identification of Rudrasena I with Rudradeva (shorn of his other theses regarding the achievements of the Vākāṭakas, their relations with the Pallavas and Maghas, the historical reliability of the drama *Kaumudī-mahotsava*, and so on) should be correct because Samudragupta could not

[61] *HIG*, pp. 89-92.

go deep into the south without taming the Vākāṭakas and the Vākāṭakas could not give up their imperial title without having been forced to do so.[62] He also points out that Pṛthivīsheṇa I probably participated in the southern campaigns of Samudragupta, for the Gupta emperor followed the policy of *dharmavijaya* in that region and Pṛthivīsheṇa I is credited in the Vākāṭaka records with *dharmavijaya* though he is not known to have conquered any particular region.

Goyal's view regarding the matrimonial alliance between the two royal houses of the Vākāṭakas and the Guptas, is also quite original. He has pointed out that the marriage of Prabhāvatī with Rudrasena II took place more than two decades before the extermination of the Western Kshatrapas by Chandragupta II and the Śakas were a very weak kingdom in comparison to the mighty successor of Samudragupta.[63] Therefore, it is inconceivable that Chandragupta II gave his daughter in marriage to Rudrasena II in order to get Vākāṭaka help against the Śakas more than two decades before the actual invasion on the Kshatrapas took place.[64]

In the post-Pravarasena II years Goyal has postulated a long-drawn Gupta-Vākāṭaka clash.[65] He has given reasons to believe that the Nalas of South Kosala, who claim to have defeated the Vākāṭakas, were probably the subordinate allies of the Guptas and were helped by their masters against the Vākāṭakas. That explains the spectacular victories of the Nalas, a minor power, against much more powerful Vākāṭakas. But when the Guptas were facing multiple difficulties at the time of Skandagupta's accession, the Vākāṭakas launched a counter-attack and defeated the Nalas and with the help of the Pāṇḍava ruler Bharatabala of Mekalā, the home of the Pushyamitra tribe. They invaded the Gupta empire and for a time captured Mālava region also.[66] This theory beautifully harmonizes the data provided by the Rithpur plates of Bhavadattavarman, the Bamhani plates of Bharatabala, the Balaghat plates of Pṛthivīsheṇa II, the *Vishṇu Purāṇa* and the Bhitari record of Skandagupta.[67]

[62] *Ibid.*, pp. 141- 46. On this suggestion of S.R. Goyal Joanna Gottfried Williams comments : "If Rudradeva of the inscription (that is, Prayāga *praśasti* of Samudragupta) can be identified with Rudrasena I, one must note that the Vākāṭakas alone in this first category soon returned to an independent status" (*The Art of Gupta India*, New Delhi, 1983, p. 23, n. 5).

[63] *HIG*, p. 246.

[64] *Ibid.*, pp. 243-45.

[65] *Ibid.*, pp. 256 ff.

[66] *Ibid.*, p. 259.

[67] The present writer has also made some humble contribution in this field. See my *175 Years of Vākāṭaka History and Historiography*, Jodhpur, 2009.

VIII

S.R. Goyal's English dissertation does not contain separate chapters on administration, economic life, society and culture of the Gupta age, though in his Hindi work, published in 1987, he deals with all these aspects in detail (chapters 17 and 18). However unlike other scholars, Goyal is neither mainly interested in reconstructing sheer dynastic accounts highlighting only a chronological outline of the course of important events and the achievements of individual rulers nor is he obsessed with personal prejudices resulting in coloured projections which is found in the works of many historians who, while writing on a particular dynasty or region, generally take it to be superior to or more important than other contemporary powers, thereby rendering an objective assessment and scientific reconstruction difficult. On the contrary, he takes an integrated objective view of history wherein geo-political, socio-economic and religious factors interact with and not unoften determine the course of political events and *vice versa*. He not only studies 'what happend' but also 'why and how did it so happen.' While recognizing the all important role played by economic factor in shaping the course of history he keeps himself free from dogmatism characterising the writings of some Marxist historians. Though in his dissertation, which is primarily a political history, Goyal does not refer to the 'golden age' model, he is clearly enamoured with the Gupta empire and seems to be quite emotionally concerned with its growth, integrity and security. For example, he condemns the military negligence of Chandragupta II that prevented the empire's expansion and its logical fulfillment of greatness. He laments : "... he (Chandragupta II) apparently did nothing to carry the policy of annexation pursued in the Gaṅgā Valley by Samudragupta to its logical conclusion by incorporating the Indus basin in his empire. This negligence of his, for which Skandagupta and his successors had to pay so dearly, becomes highly intriguing when we remember that personally he was quite a capable monarch and had enough power and resources to undertake such a project. But evidently he let the opportunity slip from his hands and undertook no programme of expansion for about thirty years after his accession—at least this is what the available evidence suggests."[68]

Goyal notices emphatic nationalist orientation of the Gupta culture itself, particularly of the Brāhmaṇical revival that coincided with the rise of the Gupta empire.[69] In support of this thesis he has frequently quoted from such nationalist historians as R.C. Majumdar and A.S. Altekar. He depicts Samudragupta as a national hero of Napoleonic stature. Not only that, he

[68] *HIG*, p. 250.
[69] *Ibid.*, pp. 62-63.

compares Samudragupta far favourably with Aśoka whose policy had made the country lost to nationalism and political greatness. According to him, Samudragupta is the best answer which the Hindu society gave to the Buddhist ideal and example set by Aśoka.[70]

Despite important similarities with nationalist historians Goyal has also basic differences with the more credulous of them. He criticizes the arch-nationalist K.P. Jayaswal for his bias and ambivalence. On the other hand, he finds the 'dry facts'-seeking Rankean scientism of R.G. Bhandarkar barren and inadequate and puts aside A.L. Basham's advice to look only for 'what happened' in ancient India as not applicable to the Gupta period. He proposes a new 'why and how did it happen' approach aiming at interpretation of facts in the light of the factors operating in society. To achieve the goal of interpretational fulfillment one has to follow a method that takes into account the 'situational contexts' of historical events such as components of political power having 'social, economic and religious bases'. Goyal's new approach also enjoins that 'the different aspects of history cannot be studied in isolation' from one another but 'only as facets of an integrated reality'. Then he asserts that ample material on the Gupta period is now available and quite a good number of aspectual studies have been completed by competent scholars to warrant an integrated study of political history in its contextual relatedness.[71]

David N. Lorenzen, the Mexican Indologist, has described Goyal as one of the five best recent historians of ancient India[72] and as "the best of a new group of conservative historians who have reformulated nationalist historiography" to suit post-Chinese invasion (1962) realities in the sub-continent.[73] He then goes on to argue that Goyal has been writing "quite direct commentaries on contemporary India through implicit comparison between it and the conditions in the Gupta age" and "drawing an implicit moral lesson for contemporary India."[74] Lorenzen feels that two great

[70] *Ibid.*, p. 188.

[71] *Ibid.*, pp. 33-40. For a new awareness in political history writing of ancient India see my papers, 'Political History : The Loss of Innocence' in *Political History in a Changing World*, ed. by G.C. Pande, S.K. Gupta and Shankar Goyal, Jodhpur, 1992, pp. 290-99; 'The Nature of New Political History' in my *Aspects of Ancient Indian History and Historiography*, New Delhi, 1993, pp. 9-13; cf. also, Mahesh Vikram, *India Rediscovered*, New Delhi, 2006, Ch. 10.

[72] Lorenzen, 'Professor S.R. Goyal's Suggestion on Political History Writing in the Light of Historians and Political History of the Gupta Empire', *Political History in a Changing World*, p. 55.

[73] *Ibid.*, p. 53.

[74] *Ibid.*, p. 54.

political controversies, one over the question of the appropriate level of India's military preparedness against threats from China and Pakistan and the other over the question of the extent of federalism in India, have cast their impact on Goyal's treatment of Buddhism and the feudal-federal structure of the Gupta empire respectivly as the two chief causes of the empire's decline and fall.[75] However, it is not at all clear why a researcher working on the Gupta empire should regard that empire as an "unstable aberration" and the small and warring regional states as the more normal order of things in ancient India. Despite such neo-imperialist bias of Lorenzen, his identification of S.R. Goyal as a neo-nationalist historian may be accepted with the modification that Goyal is scientific in approach and nationalist in spirit. Indeed Goyal feels that the distinction between the nationalist and scientific historians is more or less artificial and some sort of nationalist bias is found among historians of all countries when they write about the past of their own people. In support of this statement Goyal quotes R.C. Majumdar who declared that the nationalist bias "is not necessarily in conflict with a scientific and critical study, and a nationalist historian is not necessarily a propagandist or a charlatan."

Goyal accepts the evaluation of the Gupta age as a golden age implicitly in his dissertation and quite explicitly in his Hindi work. But he also adds two major qualifications that overturn any simple emphasis on the role of "foreign" invasions in the break up of the empire. Indeed, as pointed out by David Lorenzen, "Goyal's major theoretical contribution is to develop a more sophisticated understanding of the fall of the empire. Goyal seeks to balance the role of external invasions with internal, endogenous factors. He identifies the feudal-like political decentralization of the empire and the pacifist ideology of Buddhism as two major internal factors that combined with the impact of the new Hūṇa incursion of Toramāṇa to hasten the demise of the empire toward the end of the fifth century."[76] This theory he propounded in 1967 in his *A History of the Imperial Guptas*[77] and repeated it in 1987 in his *Gupta Sāmrājya kā Itihāsa*. In the latter work he writes : "But in the time of Kumāra Gupta I the shadow of the Buddhist religion began to fall on the Gupta dynasty. As a result, the Gupta kings became preoccupied with the acquisition of merit instead of with the dream of conquering the earth. ... As a consequence of the influence of the Buddhist religion, the Gupta king's love of battle, which was necessary

[75] *Ibid.*, p. 53.

[76] David N. Lorenzen, in *Reappraising Gupta History for S.R. Goyal*, pp. 57 ff. S.R. Goyal's objection to the pacifist ideology of Buddhism is also reflected in his *Harsha and Buddhism*, Meerut, 1986.

[77] *HIG*, pp. 292-95.

for the defense of the empire, virtually vanished. We have seen that in the sixth century A.D. because of internal disputes and the Hūṇa incursions, the situation of the Gupta lineage became extremely unsteady. At such a time, reform of the system of empire and of military organization, as well as the firm control of external and internal enemies, were the biggest necessities. But, sunk to the neck in the influence of the Buddhist religion, Narasiṁha Gupta II kept filling his kingdom with *chaityas* and *vihāras*. When Mihirakula attacked, Narasiṁha promptly fled to save his own "worthless body." Even afterwards, when the Hūṇa king had been caught by dependent kings, Narasiṁha demonstrated a terrible lack of foresight when, on the advice of his own mother, he came and released this dangerous enemy for the sake of acquiring merit. What better measure of the harmful influence of Buddhist religion than this?"[78]

According to Lorenzen, in using such arguments "Goyal is drawing an implicit moral lesson for contemporary India. His *bête noir* is not Buddhism itself, nor is he primarily making a plea for Hindu unity against other religions; rather he is directing his criticism against the pacifist propensities of Buddhism. In this is he not implicitly thinking back to the reputedly disastrous effects of Aśoka's Buddhist pacifism and ahead to the political controversies over the appropriate level of military preparedness against perceived threats from China and Pakistan?"[79] Though this emphasis on the influence of pacifist Buddhist ideology seems to Lorenzen somewhat 'overdrawn', one aspect of it is clearly substantial. "This concerns the role of the financial drain represented by permanent donation of tax revenues to Buddhist monasteries, Nālandā being simply the biggest and most famous of hundreds of these institutions. This argument is , as Goyal acknowledges, a key element in R.S. Sharma's theory of the "feudalization" of the early medieval period. Goyal's firm location of the beginnings of this process in the early Gupta age is convincing, but to insist on the preponderant role of Buddhist institutions in this process, as Goyal tends to do, seems less justified. Judging from the admittedly limited evidence of Gupta inscriptions, Hindu temples, Brāhmaṇa *agrahāras* and *brahmadeya* villages may have represented an equal or even greater diversion of tax revenues."[80]

Another aspect of the feudalization thesis, feels David Lorenzen, is the role of political ideology and administrative practice. Goyal notes that the *chakravartin* and *digvijaya* ideals permitted, and even encouraged, the Gupta kings to restore conquered minor kings on their former thrones. This

[78] S.R. Goyal, *Gupta Sāmrājya kā Itihāsa*, (in Hindi), pp. 382-83 (tr. from Hindi original by Lorenzen).

[79] Lorenzen, *op.cit.*, p. 58.

[80] *Ibid.*

legitimized an administrative system in which the emperor in fact was content to exercise only nominal control over most of his empire. Goyal attributes the establishment of this system to Samudragupta himself and claims that it was "the chief cause of the Gupta empire's decline and fall".[81] If the emperor faltered, the subordinate kings would not and did not hesitate to claim independent sovereignty. Lorenzen suspects that "here Goyal—together with such unlikely allies as R.S. Sharma and D.N. Jha—has contemporary Indian conditions implicitly in mind. After all, the great political debate between those who favour a strong central government authority and those who prefer a looser federal structure has dominated much of Indian politics in the post-Independence period."[82]

IX

The dissertation of Goyal on Gupta history was quite well-received by the scholarly world. A.L. Basham described it as 'the best analysis of Gupta history'. R.C. Majumdar wrote: "Anyone who reads the preface of this work, in which the author gives a long list of his own original contributions, may feel sceptic about all that he says. But a perusal of the book leaves no doubt that his claims are certainly based on reasonable grounds. In a subject where available materials are scanty, it would be too much to expect definite conclusions acceptable to all. There is, however, no doubt than on quite a large number of debatable issues in the history of the imperial Gupta dynasty, the author has made a new approach and brought a new outlook, and his conclusions are often very plausible and challenge fresh inquiry and re-examination on the part of scholars."[83]

Be that as it may, Goyal's new approach and its results did create a stir in the world of scholarship and older writers hurried either to refute Goyal's conclusions or modify their own in the light of his suggestions, some choosing the easy expedient of not taking note of them. But younger writers have often been deeply impressed and are sometimes carried away. Naturally, all the solutions offered by Goyal of various problems of Gupta history have not been accepted by all, but his basic approach and ideal of historiography do remain unchallenged.

Anyway, one of the most important results of Goyal's work has been that the interest of Indian historians in Gupta history, which was on the wane, was rekindled. Consequently, apart from numerous research articles and chapters on Gupta history in standard works, several monographs on the subject were produced in the post-1967 period, many of which bear a

[81] See *Gupta Sāmrājya kā Itihāsa*, p. 374.

[82] Lorenzen, *op.cit.*, p. 59.

[83] R.C. Majumdar, in his Foreword to *HIG.*

distinct impress of the influence of S.R. Goyal's historiography. These include : Radhesharan's *Samrāṭ Samudragupta,*[84] P.L. Gupta's *Gupta Sāmrājya,*[85] U.N. Roy's *Gupta Samrāṭ aur Unkā Kāla,*[86] P.L. Gupta's English work *The Imperial Guptas,* in two vols.,[87] S.K. Maity's *Gupta Civilization*[88] and *The Imperial Guptas and their Times,*[89] D.K. Ganguly's *The Imperial Guptas and their Times,*[90] Ashvini Agrawal's *Rise and Fall of the Gupta Empire,*[91] and T.R. Sharma's *A Political History of the Imperial Guptas.*[92] Special mention should be made here also of *A Comprehensive History of India,* Vol. III, Parts I-II, [93] and B.P. Sinha's *A History of Bihar,* Vol. I (ed.), *Dynastic History of Magadha,*[94] *Readings in History and Culture,*[95] and *Twilight of the Imperial Guptas.*[96] All these works are written from traditional point of view dominated by 'what and when happened ?' approach. None of them seems to have adopted the concept of 'New Political History' which is becoming more and more popular in the West and is being advocated persistently by S.R. Goyal in his numerous monographs and papers. In Maurya history also Romila Thapar and many others are making use of it, though in different terms.[97] In the reconstruction of political events on traditional lines also, some of these works seek to avoid a discussion on the latest views by adopting the simple expedient of not referring to them. For example, while B.P. Sinha, R.C. Majumdar, S.K. Maity and most other discuss the suggestions of Goyal on scores of occasions in their respective works quoted above, expressing their agreement or otherwise with him, P.L. Gupta and U.N. Roy nowhere mention his views though their own works were published several years after the publication of Goyal's dissertation.

X

Now we are in a position to assess the changes which have taken place in Gupta historiography in the post-1967 decades. Even a casual study of them

[84] Rewa, 1969.
[85] Varanasi, 1970.
[86] Allahabad, 1971.
[87] Varanasi, 1974 and 1979.
[88] Calcutta, 1974.
[89] New Delhi, 1975.
[90] New Delhi, 1987.
[91] Delhi, 1989.
[92] New Delhi, 1989.
[93] New Delhi, 1981.
[94] New Delhi, 1977.
[95] Delhi, 1978.
[96] Delhi, 1993.
[97] See my *History Writing of Early India,* Jodhpur, 1996, pp. 125-30.

would show that they have occurred mainly as a result of the researches of S.R. Goyal. As pointed out earlier, the outline of Gupta history as was generally accepted before 1967 has become gradually modified largely on the lines suggested by Goyal. A comparison of the framework of the political history of the Gupta dynasty usually endorsed till the early sixties with the framework which is generally acceptable now, that is in the beginning of the twenty-first century, makes it quite clear that while many suggestions of Goyal on Gupta history have already found general or limited acceptance, many others are regarded as worthy of serious consideration.[98] It is also obvious that due to Goyal's researches, scholars have been forced to formulate their problems somewhat differently with the result that their researches have perceptibly or imperceptibly taken a different direction. Let us give a few examples from the works published after the research work of Goyal:

Till the early sixties scholars usually assigned the imperial Guptas to one of the three non-Brāhmaṇa *varṇas* ; only H.C. Raychaudhuri, while commenting on their Dhāraṇa *gotra*, had made a casual suggestion in a line of a footnote that they 'may have been related to Queen Dhāriṇī, the chief consort of Agnimitra'. Raychaudhuri obviously did not raise this casual suggestion to the status of a well-reasoned theory, for he himself must have known that the relationship of a *gotra* with the name of the Śuṅga queen is indefensible. Therefore, this suggestion of his was never taken seriously.[99] On the other hand, Goyal's theory that the imperial Guptas belonged on the Brāhmaṇa *varṇa*, first proposed by him in the *Gorakhpur University Magazine* in 1960, and later in his thesis in 1967, is based on well-reasoned arguments and takes into consideration the Purāṇic references to the Brāhmaṇas of the Dhāraṇa *gotra* and the matrimonial alliances of the Guptas. That is why his suggestion has found endorsement from Raj Bali Pandey, U.N. Roy, A.M. Shastri, Ashvini Agrawal, D.C. Shukla, S.K. Purohit and Radhesharan. T.R. Sharma has also conceded that if their (that is, of the imperial Guptas) Dhāraṇa *gotra* was not borrowed from the *gotra* of their Purohita then they must be described as Brāhmaṇas.[100]

[98] Cf. my *Prāchīna Bhārata kā Ādhunika Itihāsa-Lekhana*, Jodhpur, 2000, Ch. 11; Mahesh Vikram, *India Rediscovered*, New Delhi, 2006, pp. 133-47; Romila Thapar, *The Past Before Us*, New Delhi, 2013, Chs. 8, 13.

[99] Raychaudhuri sometimes threw such casual suggestions. Cf. for example, his suggestion that the Nāga king Chandrāṁśa, about whom we hardly know anything, may be identified with the mighty ruler King Chandra of the Meharauli record.

[100] For references not cited here see my *Recent Historiography of Ancient India*, pp. 261-315 at appropriate places. On this, also see Romila Thapar, *Early India*, New Delhi, 2002, pp. 282 ff.

Before the advent of Goyal on the scene of Gupta historiography it was generally believed that the Guptas originally belonged to Magadha. For this the evidence of I-tsing was usually cited, the bone of contention between scholars being where did king Chi-li-ki-to build a temple for the Chinese pilgrims. Numerous articles were written to answer this question. But Goyal gave a new turn to the problem when he showed that the evidence of I-tsing was not much relevant on this point and suggested that the find-spots of the early Gupta inscriptions and coin-hoard as well as the find-spots of their stray gold coins backed by the analysis of the Purāṇic (and the Chinese evidence itself) lead us to the conclusion that eastern U.P. was the original home of the Guptas. This conclusion of Goyal has been accepted by R.S. Sharma, Vasudeva Upadhyaya, A.M. Shastri, Frederick M. Asher,[101] Ashvini Agrawal, Tej Ram Sharma, Radhesharan, S.K. Purohit, D.C. Shukla and Om Prakash[102] while S. Bandyopadhyaya has conceded that the arguments of Goyal on this point 'demand consideration'.[103] S.K. Maity, though still in favour of locating the original home of the Guptas in Bengal, admits that Goyal has offered weighty arguments in favour of placing the original home of the Gupta dynasty in eastern Uttar Pradesh. B.P. Sinha's conclusion that the original home of the Guptas should be placed in eastern U.P., to the east of Lucknow, is also quite close to Goyal's suggestion.

Formerly it was almost the unanimous opinion of scholars that Pāṭaliputra was the capital of the imperial Guptas. But now R.S. Sharma, V.S. Pathak,[104] Vasudeva Upadhyaya, A.M. Shastri, Radhesharan and many others subscribe to Goyal's theory that Prayāga was the capital or the centre of political power of the imperial Guptas. S.R. Goyal tells us that in a personal communication to him the late V.V. Mirashi conceded that the fact that such an important epigraph as the Prayāga *praśasti* has been found at Allahabad strengthens the theory that this city was the capital of the Guptas. In *A Comprehensive History of India*, Vol. III, Pt. I, R.C. Majumdar also admits that the pillar on which such an important inscription is engraved must have been situated in one of the most important cities of the empire, if not the capital.

Till the early sixties it was generally believed that Kumāradevī inherited her father's dominion and therefore she was a regnant queen and it was to publicize this fact that the Chandragupta I-Kumāradevī type of gold coins were issued. Against this, following the lead of V.S. Pathak, Goyal pointed out that in ancient India a daughter never had any right to inherit her father's throne

[101] Frederick M. Asher, *The Art of Eastern India*, Delhi, 1980, p. 13.

[102] Om Prakash, *Prāchīna Bhārata kā Itihāsa*, p. 250.

[103] In *Journal of Ancient Indian History*, V, Calcutta, 1971-72, p. 283.

[104] Quoted by U.N. Roy, in *K.P. Jayaswal Commemoration Volume*, p. 361.

while according to the Smṛti law her son, in this case Samudragupta, as a *dvyāmushyāyaṇa* could succeed his maternal grandfather as his son of *dauhitra* category. This explanation of the term *Lichchhavi-dauhitra*, called by Trautmann 'Pathak-Goyal hypothesis',[105] has been followed *mutatis mutandis* by P.L. Gupta, M.C. Joshi,[106] V.C. Pandey,[107] B.P. Sinha[108] and many others. It has changed the picture of the Gupta-Lichchhavi alliance and also of the circumstances in which Samudragupta ascended the throne. It has also necessitated a new interpretation of the phrase *Bhavanāga-dauhitra* occurring in the Vākāṭaka epigraphs.

On the reign of Samudragupta, Goyal has proposed many new suggestions some of which have been endorsed by competent scholars. According to R.C. Majumdar, Goyal's suggestion on the Nalanda grant of Samudragupta and on the founder of the Gupta era are plausible. With the problem of the Gupta era is connected the problem of the date of Samudragupta. S.R. Goyal for the first time gave some logical arguments to assume that Samudragupta ascended the throne in c. 350 A.D. Majumdar had also conjectured in *The Classical Age*[109] that Samudragupta ascended the throne between 340 and 350 A.D. but without giving any reasons to support this view. But in the *Comprehensive History*[110] he shows much greater confidence than he had shown in *The Classical Age* for dating the accession of Samudragupta in c. 350 A.D. T.R. Sharma placed the beginning of the reign of Samudragupta in c. 353 and for this he uses the arguments advanced by Goyal.[111]

On the conquests of Samudragupta the most significant contribution of Goyal is his support with new arguments to the old suggestion of K.P. Jayaswal and some others that Rudradeva of the Prayāga *praśasti* should be identified with Rudrasena I Vākāṭaka. This theory has found many supporters including Joanna Williams,[112] Radhesharan and S.K. Purohit. Majumdar has also observed that this suggestion of Goyal cannot be brushed aside as impossible.[113] On the Deccan conquest of Samudragupta also he has endorsed Goyal's view[114] that Samudragupta brought much wealth from

[105] *JRAS*, 1972, I, pp. 2-15.
[106] M.C. Joshi, *Princes and Polity in Ancient India*, Jodhpur, 1986, pp. 170-75.
[107] V.C. Pandey, in *JNSI*, XXXVIII, Pt. I, pp. 61 ff.
[108] *Comp. Hist. Bihar*, II, pp. 11 ff.
[109] *The Classical Age*, p. 16.
[110] *Comp. Hist. Ind.*, III, Pt. I, pp. 36-37.
[111] T.R. Sharma, *op.cit.*, pp. 51-52.
[112] *The Art of Gupta India*, p. 23.
[113] In *Com. Hist. Ind.*, III, Pt. I, pp. 41-42.
[114] *Ibid.*, p. 25.

there which increased his prosperity (*mahābhāgya*). Another scholar who has echoed this suggestion is M.G.S. Narayanan who, modifying the suggestion of Goyal somewhat, maintains that the term "mahābhāgya" in this context means great support in terms of treasury and army from an ally.[115]

In his dissertation Goyal had very forcefully argued that Kālidāsa flourished in the second half of the fourth century A.D. and was patronized by Samudragupta and Chandragupta II both. He is also of the view that the poet composed his *Raghuvaṁśa* in c. 390 A.D. These suggestions of Goyal have not caught much attention of political historians, probably because their acceptance or rejection does not make much difference in the reconstruction of political events. But Ashvini Agrawal obviously agrees with the view that the great poet wrote the description of Raghu's *digvijaya* with the help of the data made available to him by the conquests of Samudragupta and Chandragupta II both. Joanna Williams has also accepted this conclusion of Goyal.[116]

The identification of King Chandra of the Meharauli *praśasti* has been one of the most interesting problems of Gupta history. Before the advent of Goyal on the scene of Gupta historiography King Chandra was usually identified with Chandragupta II though scholars writing on the subject had to contend with the theories of R.C. Majumdar (who had suggested his identification with Kanishka I), R.G. Basak and S.K. Aiyangar (who were advocates of his identification with Chandragupta I) and some others who threw other suggestions of various sorts. But after the publication of Goyal's dissertation on Gupta history, and specially after the publication of the monograph *King Chandra and the Meharauli Pillar* in 1989 containing his lead paper on King Chandra's identification with Samudragupta and reaction papers of other scholars on it, the situation changed, for Goyal's arguments in favour of the identification of Chandra with Samudragupta not only converted many senior scholars such as B. Ch. Chhabra, S.B. Deo, M.C. Joshi, K.V. Raman, R. Nagaswamy and several others of younger generation including the present author, Radhesharan, S.K. Purohit, etc., to his side, but also made many others (who still believe in the identification of Chandra with Chandragupta II) admit that Goyal's arguments are forceful and not easily answerable. At one time even R.C. Majumdar accepted Goyal's suggestion as 'plausible'. Therefore, now if a scholar accepts the older theory he has to answer formidable objections against it raised by Goyal and if he follows the suggestion of Goyal he has no alternative but to reconstruct the history of Samudragupta's reign with its help—specially he has to look at

[115] In *Śrī Dineśacandrikā*, p. 91, n. 11.

[116] Joanna Williams, *The Art of Gupta India*, p. 24.

the history of the north-west in the light of the evidence deposed by the Meharauli record. Even the recently discovered Ramtek inscription also concedes the overlorship of Chandragupta II on the southern peninsula *only in theory*.[117]

One of the most significant points in the history of the post-Samudragupta period which Goyal has made concerns the Rāmagupta episode. After making a meticulous analysis of the literary symbolism used in the *Devīchandraguptam* to reconcile its testimony with numismatic and epigraphic evidence, Goyal suggests that at the death of Samudragupta Chandragupta II, his younger son, occupied the whole empire minus the province of eastern Malwa where Rāmagupta, the legitimate heir to the throne, and may be the governor of the province, declared himself emperor. Shortly thereafter in the wake of the Śaka invasion on eastern Malwa Chandragupta II, on the pretext of the security of the empire, attacked and killed Rāmagupta and married his widow Dhruvadevī. S.K. Maity has accepted this reconstruction as 'very near the truth' while R.S. Mishra has appreciated it as a great help in resolving the differences between the archaeological and literary sources.[118]

On the question of Govindagupta's place in Gupta history Goyal does not feel it safe to draw any conclusion on the basis of available evidence. Joanna Williams supports this position. S.K. Maity and B.P. Sinha also seem to agree on the whole with Goyal.

According to Goyal, Malwa enjoyed a special status in the Gupta empire from the days of Samudragupta where usually the crown-prince or some other important prince was sent as governor. This suggestion has been endorsed by B.P. Sinha and S.K. Maity.

Goyal for the first time postulated a transformation of Gupta royalty in the period of Chandragupta II and Kumāragupta I. In these decades under the impact of 'Gupta Peace' life in the empire became marked by a luxurious enjoyment of art, music, dance, drinking, fashion and gaiety which led to a

[117] The evidence of Pune and Rithpur copper-plates and the recently discovered Ramtek stone inscription cited to prove Chandragupta II's influence on the Vākāṭaka court during the regency of Prabhāvatīgupta do not prove the case. Indeed in the circumstances as are known to us some sort of *Gupta influence* on the Vākāṭakas during the minority of the sons of Rudrasena II may easily be presumed but there is nothing to prove any *Gupta interferece* in the Vākāṭaka areas. Hence there is no need to indulge in wild speculations based on conjectural restoration of the now lost text. For more details see my paper, 'The Problem of Chandragupta II's Influence on the Vākāṭakas : A Revised Study of the Epigraphic Sources', in *Epigraphic Studies*, Selected Papers from the Panel on Epigraphy at the 16th World Sanskrit Conference, 2015, Sanskrit Studies Centre, Silpakorn, University, Bangkok, Thailand, ed. D.P. Dubey, New Delhi, 2018, pp. 129-37.

[118] *Itihāsa-Samīkshā*, 2, Jaipur, pp. 36-37.

marked softening of the martial fervour of the Gupta emperors. He has marshalled a lot of evidence in support of this contention. One of the natural consequences of this increasing degree of luxury was the growth of pleasure-seeking psychology and ease-loving outlook. S.K. Maity agrees with this assessment of Goyal.

According to Goyal, in the last years of Kumāragupta I a sort of diplomatic revolution took place and the Nalas of Kosala, helped by the Guptas invaded the Vākāṭakas. The Vākāṭakas, in their turn allied themselves with the Pāṇḍava rulers of Mekalā, the land of the Pushyamitras, and exploiting the opportunity provided by the difficulties of the early years of Skandagupta, helped the Mekalā king in his invasion of the Gupta province of Malwa. For sometime Malwa was occupied by the enemies of the Guptas. This reconstruction of political history of Malwa has been endorsed by many including S.K. Maity.

Goyal has given an altogether new solution of the riddle of the successors of Skandagupta. It is based on his postulation of the existence of two Narasiṁhagupta Bālādityas each of whom had a son and successor named Kumāragupta Kramāditya. According to Goyal, the first set of these rulers, named Narasiṁhagupta I Bālāditya and Kumāragupta II Kramāditya ruled in between Skandagupta and Budhagupta while the second set of Narasiṁhagupta II Bālāditya and Kumāragupta III Kramāditya flourished after Bhānugupta's known date 510 A.D. After a review of the older theories S.K. Maity has accepted Goyal's reconstruction almost wholly. Joanna Williams also accepts the central idea of Goyal's suggestion.[119]

It is almost universally believed that like most kings of ancient India the imperial Guptas followed a policy of religious toleration. Goyal holds the same view but he also expresses his dissatisfaction with those scholars who keep themselves satisfied with citing instances which prove that a particular king employed the followers of various religions and sects as his ministers, commanders, etc. and permitted the followers of different religions to live with each other peacefully. But religious toleration has several connatotions. On the one hand, it may mean total indifference to all religions and religious rituals and, on the other, it may imply active patronage to a particular sect mixed with a feeling of hostility towards other sects without actually persecuting them.[120] Further, the impact of religion on the state policy could be felt in many ways. Says Goyal : "the impression that the political thinking of the Gupta emperors and their approach towards political problems remained completely unaffected by their religious leanings is

[119] *The Art of Gupta India*, p. 65.
[120] In *Political History in a Changing World*, p. 12.

perhaps not wholly correct. To us it appears a matter of significance that while almost all the Gupta emperors were *Paramabhāgavatas* or great devotees of Vishṇu, most of their rivals e.g. the Nāgas, the Vākaṭakas, the Hūṇas, the Maitrakas and even the king Yaśodharman of Mandasor were staunch Śaivas. ...The Vākāṭaka kings were usually the devotees of Mahābhairava or Maheśvara, ...But Rudrasena II, the son of Pṛithvīsheṇa I and the husband of Prabhāvatīguptā, was an exception. He became a devotee of the lord Chakrapāṇi, a form of Vishṇu. He even claimed that he acquired abundance of glory through the favour of this god (*Bhagavataś-Chakrapāṇeḥ-prasād-opārjjita-Śrī-samudayasya*). Now, Rudrasena II flourished in a period when the Gupta influence on the Vākāṭaka court was at its highest. That is why it is commonly believed that Rudrasena's conversion to Bhāgavatism was the result of the influence of his father-in-law, Chandragupta II."[121]

Goyal also points out that : "the rulers of the Varman dynasty of Kāmarūpa, which owed its origin to Samudragupta, claimed to be staunch Vaishṇavas. According to Yuan Chwang, Bhāskara was descended from Nārāyaṇadeva (Vishṇu). Bāṇa in his *Harshacharita* describes this king as belonging to the Vaishṇava family. Probably the Varmans of Mandasor and the Vishṇu brothers of the Eran inscription of 165 G.E., who also owed their royal glory to the Guptas, were Vaishṇavas. Were not the Guptas more considerate to the families of Vaishṇava affiliation?"[122]

Goyal's suggestion that the religious leanings of the early Gupta emperors played some role, if only as an undercurrent, in their politics got an approving nod from some scholars. According to Joanna Williams, the greatest challenge to Vaishṇava Samudragupta came from the areas which were Śaiva strongholds.[123] A.K. Narain also echoes the arguments of Goyal when he points out that : "Whether or not it was due to the influence of the Imperial Guptas, it is significant to note that almost all the important royal dynasties as well as most of the local chiefs and feudatories in India—North and South, East and West—belonging to the Gupta age were generally swayed by Vaiṣṇavism."[124]

Like Goyal Narain also does not feel satisfied with the current concept of the policy of religious toleration and like Goyal (and probably under his impact) he raises certain questions about the policy of religious toleration followed by the Guptas. He asks : "Was this religious pluralism, the liberalism and catholicity of the kings of the Gupta age, a result of a consciously-followed religious policy? Or, were these kings just trying to behave as ideal kings in

[121] *HIG*, pp. 135-36.
[122] *Ibid.*, p. 138, n. 5.
[123] *The Art of Gupta India*, p. 23.
[124] A.K. Narain, in *Essays on Gupta Culture*, p. 44.

the Indian political tradition? Were they merely a part of the system, or were they innovating? What was meant by toleration? Was it a matter of policy or a matter of the religion itself ? Why and how did they succeed in doing what they did generation after generation?"[125]

Goyal is perhaps one of the first scholars to try to reconstruct the political ideology of the imperial Guptas with the help of their inscriptions, coins and whatever literary data we have at our disposal. For this he has utilized the researches of V.S. Agrawala, B. Ch. Chhabra and others on Gupta coins and correlated their indications with the epigraphic data and evidence of some Vaishṇavite texts. Further, he has pointed out that the political ideology of the later Gupta emperors, many of whom were of Buddhist persuasion, was radically different from that of the early rulers or the dynasty. No scholar seems to have done any work on these lines excepting the present author who has made an humble effort by writing a small paper on the political ideology of the early Guptas.[126]

One of the major contributions of Goyal to the study of Gupta history is a sophisticated explanation of the decline and fall of the Gupta empire. He identifies feudal-federal structure of the empire and the influence of the pacifist ideology of Buddhism as two key factors that combined with the onslaught of the Pushyamitras and the Hūṇas to hasten the demise of the empire. From the later years of Kumāragupta I's rule it was "the life-negating and world-renouncing doctrines of later Buddhism that eventually sucked the Gupta emperors dry of their martial fervour and capacity for administering their subordinates with strength and determination." On this sensitive theory of Goyal several scholars have offered their comments. S.K. Maity, R.C. Majumdar and Ashvini Agrawal have kept silence over it while B.P. Sinha has protested against it. Sinha finds no reason to believe that the influence of Buddhism had anything to do with the loss of the military vigour of the Gupta emperors. Reacting to Sinha's criticism Goyal has asserted in his Hindi work (1987) that the learned scholar has not disproved the evidences put forward by him in support of his theory. After examining the available evidence Joanna Williams[127] concludes : "From such evidence, a picture emerges of both popular and royal interest in ideologies that prescribe an immediate, certain escape from the troubles of this existence in the form of an ascetic way of life." Her conclusion seems to be on the side of Goyal.

Another scholar who has commented on Goyal's theory regarding

[125] *Ibid.*, p. 48.

[126] Shankar Goyal, 'Political Ideology of the Early Imperial Guptas', in *Reappraising Gupta History for S.R. Goyal*, pp. 215-23.

[127] *The Art of Gupta India*, p. 67.

the pacifist impact of Buddhism is David Lorenzen. In his view Goyal's emphasis on the pacifist impact of Buddhism on the martial fervour of the Guptas is 'overdrawn', but he accepts Goyal's argument concerning financial drain caused by permanent donations of tax revenues to the Buddhist monasteries though at the same time he seeks to modify it by giving equal importance to the extensive financial donations to the Brāhmaṇas and Brāhmaṇical institutions. But Goyal has himself acknowledged the role of the Brāhmaṇic ideals and institutions in the feudalization and disintegration of the empire.

From the above discussion it is obvious that in the last five decades or so the general outline of Gupta history has become greatly modified largely on the lines suggested by Goyal. A comparison of the works of P.L. Gupta and U.N. Roy (published in the early seventies), who studiously avoid any reference to Goyal's studies on Gupta history with those of S.K. Maity, Ashvini Agrawal and T.R. Sharma shows what a great change took place in the outline history of the Guptas in the seventies and the eighties and how much that change has been the result of Goyal's contribution in this field. Admittedly, now quite a few scholars have accepted many of his suggestions and their researches have taken the direction indicated by the researches of Goyal. Probably in the 20th century no scholar, excepting of course V.A. Smith and R.C. Majumdar, has made such a deep imprint on the historiography of the Gupta dynasty.

XI

But there are certain areas in which Goyal's suggestions have gone largely unheaded. For example, his initiative in discussing the methodology and approaches of the earlier scholars has not been followed by others. It is true that his chapter on this aspect of Gupta studies has been described by Eleanor Zelliot as 'a model of historiography',[128] but no subsequent scholar is known to have taken the trouble to analyze the methods and attitudes of earlier historians of the Gupta age. P.L. Gupta has indeed claimed to have written a section on the 'historiography' of the Gupta dynasty, but in the name of 'historiography' he has discussed the genealogical and chronological problems and the problems connected with the Gupta era while T.R. Sharma's chapter on the historiography of the Guptas merely enumerates the monographs of his academic predecessors without delving into their methodology and approaches.

Goyal also made a fervent plea for the study of source materials with a new angle. He has pointed out how the epigraphic, numismatic and literary material should be analyzed and made to yield more than what is known only

[128] In *Essays on Gupta Culture*, p. 288.

from a mere description of coins and literal translation of inscriptions and ancient texts. In this connection he has rightly drawn the attention of scholars to the suggestions of V.S. Pathak for the study of the attitudes of early medieval court-historians and authors of the *praśastis* found in inscriptions. But no subsequent scholar is known to have followed the methodology of V.S. Pathak and S.R. Goyal for the study of the original sources.

Before the publication of Goyal's doctoral dissertation, the study of political history of ancient India was marked by 'what and when happened' approach and disintegrate aspectual studies. In his dissertation, Goyal for the first time advocated 'why and how did it happen' approach and an integrated study of an aspect as it was related to the whole context. Later on he wrote a paper on this approach on which over fifty scholars were invited to write reaction papers. All these reaction papers along with Goyal's theme paper were published in the form of a book.[129] From a perusal of these papers it is obvious that Goyal's vision of a 'New Political History' has been much appreciated by scholars. "As far as I am able to see", writes J. Gonda, "it will indeed imply a new definition of political history. It will probably mean a turning-point in the study of Indian history." (p. 370). A.K. Narain concurs with Goyal by stating that "One cannot agree more with Goyal that by and large history and historians in India have become stagnant." (p. 23). A.K. Warder enthusiastically welcomes the prospect of the disappearance of Anglocentric or Eurocentric studies. (p. 32). To Alois Wurm "Goyal's epoch-making contributions to scientific consciousness of history are not only an appropriate new definition of political history but also, and especially, a concerned appeal to all scholars to resurrect the phoenix of political historiology from the ashes of its suicidal self-complacence." (p. 34). A.M. Shastri feels that "the need to widen and transform the outdated attitudes to history cannot be seriously disputed, and a historian cannot now afford to remain content with finding out only 'what happened'; he must also try in earnestness to find out 'why did it happen' wherever possible." (p. 36). David N. Lorenzen opines that the call of S.R. Goyal, "for a new style of political history of ancient India deserves wholehearted support from all historians engaged in this enterprise." (p. 44). According to Vivekanand Jha, "Goyal deserves credit for stressing the need for change and improvement in ancient Indian political history and for his readiness to discard the stale and the puerile and to receive and welcome the best from both West and East, old and new." (p. 63). Many other scholars such as K.D. Bajpai, B.P. Sinha, Lallanji Gopal, B.N. Mukherjee, J.P. Sharma, Sibesh Bhattacharya and S.D. Singh have *mutatis mutandis* expressed their

[129] *Political History in a Changing World*, Jodhpur, 1992.

agreement with the basic approach of Goyal.[130]

But despite a theoretical appreciation of Goyal's vision of 'New Political History', so far no scholar seems to have followed it in practice. True, it has not been rejected outright by any subsequent historian, but it is also a fact that it has not been accepted with the same earnestness in the monograph of any subsequent researcher as Goyal has shown in his doctoral dissertation or as above-mentioned scholars have theoretically conceded.

The only scholar known to us who seems to has adopted the view-point of Goyal is M.G.S. Narayanan who has made a re-appraisal of the *digvijaya* of Samudragupta with this angle.[131] Though he mistakenly observes that in the study of Goyal it is only geo-political factor that figures prominently which he dismisses as 'inadequate', what he himself preaches is not dissimilar from the approach of Goyal involving a study of political events against the background of socio-economic, religious and other factors operating in society. Virtually the whole dissertation of Goyal is a study of the political history of the Gupta dynasty with this approach. Therefore, M.G.S. Narayanan merely echoes the attitude of Goyal when he says that he is probing the "socio-economic implications of the statements found in the Allahabad *praśasti* with a view to suggest (*sic.*) a possible correlation between the changes in the political structure and those in the social structure" and that the relations of Samudragupta with other states were "determined by various factors like distance from the Gangetic Valley, socio-political development of the region, economic prospects and the power of the central government to administer the newly acquired provinces."[132] But that is precisely what has been advocated by Goyal. The only difference between his and Goyal's approaches is that while Goyal has taken religious factor also into consideration, Narayanan has not.

However, the fact still remains that barring such exceptions, by and large the present Indian scholarship is not making the concept of 'New Political History' of the imperial Guptas a practical preposition. Probably that is the reason why "Goyal is yet to lead a school of historiography, although his achievements and his philosophy of (ancient Indian) history

[130] Also see my papers, 'Research Methodology in History and Allied Disciplines', *Journal of the All-India Philosophy Association*, Year 38-39, 1993, pp. 98-106; 'Ancient Indian Historiography: Some Problems', paper read in a seminar organized by the Department of Sociology, J.N.V. University, Jodhpur on March 10, 1995.

[131] In *Śrī Dineśacandrikā*, p. 283. We have ourselves made an humble effort to follow S.R. Goyal's methodology and approach in our study of the age of Harsha. See our *History and Historiography of the Age of Harsha*, Jodhpur, 1992; *Harsha : A Multidisciplinary Political Study*, Jodhpur, 2006; *Harsha Revisited*, Delhi, 2018.

[132] *Śrī Dineśacandrikā*, pp. 283-84.

warrant such a possibility."[133]

As regards Goyal's attitude to the description of the Gupta age as the golden age of India, in this respect he has himself followed the footsteps of his illustrious academic predecessors, for almost throughout the twentieth century Indian savants (and Western scholars also, if only for different reasons) have been admiring the Gupta age as the golden age of India. Goyal also belongs to this category though he has restricted the classicism of the Gupta period to northern India alone.[134]

XII

In his *Gupta Sāmrājya kā Itihāsa* (Meerut, 1987)[135] S.R. Goyal points out that Marxist historians do not use the term golden or classical age in the generally accepted sense of an age where literature, architecture and the fine arts reach a high level of excellence to form a standard for later times. D.N. Jha for example uses it in the sense of 'revival' or 'resurgence'. This is obviously to circumvent the logical conclusion which emerges from his own observations that the Gupta culture represents the culmination of earlier tendencies and in several spheres became a standard or norm for the subsequent ages, which is what one means by the term 'classical age'. Jha is quite aware of the fact that in several fields great achievements were made in the Gupta age which became ideal or norm for the subsequent ages. For example, he concedes that "In literature, as in art and architecture, the Gupta period witnessed an efflorescence...", that "Earlier developments in plastic arts seems to have culminated in the Gupta period... The crowning achievement of the Gupta sculpture is noticeable in the numerous seated and standing images of the Buddha and bodhisattvas from Sarnath...", that "The Gupta period may be said to be a landmark in the development of philosophical ideas...", and that "Sanskrit language and literature, after centuries of evolution, through lavish royal patronage, reached what has been described as a level of classical excellence." In view of these observations of his own he should have had no hesitation in concluding that the Gupta age was the golden or classical age of ancient India. He does not do so because he deliberately proceeds from the wrong assumption that a classical age or the golden age should be an age of revival, and not an age of efflorescence which sets norms or ideals for subsequent ages. But who has ever claimed that the

[133] P.K. Mitra, 'S.R. Goyal and Modern Historiography of the Gupta Age', in *Reappraising Gupta History for S.R. Goyal*, p. 37.

[134] S. R. Goyal, 'The Myth of the Golden Bird : An Investigation into the Belief of Material Opulence of Ancient and Early Medieval India in the Light of Her Gold Coinage', his Presidential Address delivered to the 90th Annual Conference of the Numismatic Society of India at Santiniketan on December 1-3, 2006, *JNSI*, Vol. LXIX, Pts. i and ii, 2007, p. 15.

[135] S.R. Goyal, *Gupta Sāmrājya kā Itihāsa*, pp. 419-26.

age of ranaissance in Europe or of the nineteenth century renascent India was the golden age of these regions? R.N. Dandekar neatly points out to the difference between renaissance and efflorescence when he observes: "The Gupta age thus witnessed not the renaissance or revival but the acme or efflorescence of Sanskrit literature."[136]

Thus, D.N. Jha's illogicality is that he first defines the term 'classical' wrongly as 'a period of revival' (while its correct and generally accepted meaning is 'a period of efflorescence') and then goes on to argue that as the Gupta period saw an efflorescence of culture, not its revival, it cannot be described as the classical age of Indian history. Now what one can say to such a patently illogical absurdity?

Raising his voice against the argument of Jha that the prosperity of the golden age was not evenly distributed among all the regions and all the sections of Indian society, Goyal asks, when did it happen that the fruits of a classical or golden age were enjoyed by all sections of society throughout the length and breadth of a country? It happened neither in Periclean Athens, nor in Rome of Augustus and nor in England of Elizabeth.

According to Goyal, Jha has viewed the Gupta age with the eyes of a 'sanitary inspector', for while evaluating it as a golden age he lists only those aspects which appear to him defective. India is a country of caste system with its drawbacks quite well-known. But is it fair to ignore the great achievements of our ancestors of a particular period on this plea? Does it mean that no period of Indian history may be called 'golden' or 'classical', because the caste system existed in India of the Vedic age and exists even now?

Goyal agrees that the literature of the Gupta age does not contain the eulogies of the Gupta emperors. But does it not mean, he argues, that they were not given that importance in Indian society which was given to Alexanders and Caesars in Europe? Does it not prove that the contemporary literature was not 'royal' in inspiration? Does it not make Indian classical age more glorious and relevant for our time? If Jha criticizes the inscriptions of the Guptas for being eulogies of these rulers, then he should admire the Gupta literature for not giving such an importance to them. But he criticizes the epigraphic eulogies of the Guptas for being 'royal' or 'official' in nature, and at the same time argues that the Gupta rulers were not of much importance, for they are not admired in the literature of their own period. It hardly sounds honest, logical and fair.

Jha laments that there is no description of common man in the eulogies of the Gupta emperors. This lamentation is misplaced, for such a description cannot be found in royal edicts. If we want to reconstruct the life of common man, then we should study folk life as depicted in the *Jātakas*,

[136] In *Comp. Hist. Ind.*, III, Pt. I, p. 289.

kathā literature, *Purāṇas*, folk songs, festivals, popular celebrations, folk art in the form of terracottas, the gateway reliefs of Sanchi, the *vedikā* reliefs of Bharhut, etc., and not the royal edicts or court literature or court art. V.S. Agrawala, for example, used such materials for the reconstruction of ancient Indian folk religions, and not the *Vedas*, *Upanishads*, *Gītā* and other religio-philosophical texts.[137] Jha evidently expects material for the study of common man in such sources where, as he himself must be knowing, it does not exist.

Jha raises objection against the use of the term 'Hindu' for Indian culture of the Gupta period[138] for, he argues, many of the achievements of the Gupta age were the contribution of Buddhists, Jainas, Greeks and Romans. But Goyal points out that if one will be guided by this approach there will remain nothing which one would be able to call 'Indian', what to talk of 'Hindu'. As has been emphasised countless times even by the most orthodox 'Hindu' scholars, Indian culture has been, and is, a composite culture and so was the Hindu culture of ancient period. To differentiate between 'Hindu', 'Jaina' and 'Buddhist' cultures in the ancient period of our country's history is, to say the least, a futile exercise, and against the beliefs and psychology of our ancestors. To believe in such an absurdity would be believing that, to quote only one example, *Paramādityabhakta* Prabhākara-vardhana, the Pushybhūti ruler of Kanauj, and his sons *Paramasaugata* Rājyavardhana II and *Paramamāheśvara* Harsha belonged to three different cultures! As regards the contribution of the Greeks and Romans to ancient Indian astronomy, and the acceptance of this contribution as part of Indian astronomical lore, is it a proof of the inherent assimilative strength of Indian culture or a proof of the presumption that the Gupta culture was not 'Hindu'? People like Jha, who give such arguments, criticize the Hindus of the Rajput age for not being able to assimilate foreign elements, but in the present case they cite the assimilation of the Greek and Roman astronomical schools in Indian astronomy only to prove that the Gupta culture was not Hindu ![139] Strange logic!

[137] V.S. Agrawala, *Prāchīna Bhāratīya Loka Dharma*, Ahmedabad, 1964.

[138] Cf., for example, R.N. Dandekar who states that "The Gupta empire can be said to have been essentially Indian—or Hindu—in character", and that the efforts of the Guptas "resulted in a remarkable outburst of the creative activity of Hindu genius" (*Comp. Hist. Ind.*, III, Pt. I, p. 279).

[139] For a criticism of D.N. Jha also see my paper, 'A Critique of Professor D.N. Jha's Evaluation of the Classicism of the Gupta Age', in *Reappraising Gupta History for S.R. Goyal*, pp. 61-73. Though we do not agree with D.N. Jha fully on this problem but his central idea is convincing.

The argument of Jha that the use of the term 'Hindu' for the Gupta culture is erroneous because this term was not in use at that time is curious. Does it mean, Goyal asks, that we should not use the term 'Indian' for our ancestors of the entire pre-British period because they did not use it for themselves?[140]

But all these arguments are not likely to make any difference in the attitude of D.N. Jha because he always adopts the most convenient expedient of keeping mum when he finds it difficult to answer the points raised against his views and continues repeating his suggestions without a reference to their criticism even by such illustrious scholars as S.R. Goyal and several others.

[140] For a detailed discussion on the Marxist trends in Gupta history, vide my *Marxist Interpretation of Ancient Indian History*, Pune, 2000, pp. 59-82; *Contemporary Interpreters of Ancient India*, Jaipur, 2003, pp. 245-73.

FIVE

The Problem of Chandragupta II's Political Influence on the Vākāṭakas : An Analysis of the Epigraphical Sources

The theory of Chandragupta II's political influence on the Vākāṭakas during the regency of Prabhāvatīguptā is mainly based on the testimony of her Pune and Rithpur copper plates. These plates deviate from other Vākāṭaka inscriptions in several respects and supposedly indicate some amount of political influence of the Guptas on the Vākāṭakas during her regency. The comparative recent discovery of the Ramtek Prabhāvatīguptā stone inscription also seems to prove the correctness of this presumption. But in our view the evidence of these documents needs greater critical scrutiny than has been accorded to them so far.

The various arguments given by different scholars to prove Chandragupta II's influence on the Vākāṭakas may be summarised as follows: (1) The characters of the Pune copper plates are mostly of the nail-headed variety having a triangle, with its apex downwards, at the top of the letters, though a few of them are of the box-headed variety in which all other inscriptions of the Vākāṭakas were written. It has, therefore, been suggested that the scribe began to write the present grant in the box-headed characters, but as he was not accustomed to them, he soon changed over to the nail-headed characters with which he was more familiar. It shows that he hailed from north India where the nail-headed characters were in vogue.[1] (2) Though Prabhāvatīguptā describes herself as the Chief Queen of the Vākāṭaka Mahārāja Rudrasena II (*Vākāṭakānām Mahārāja-Śrī Rudrasenasyāgramahishī*) she gives the genealogy of the Guptas, and not of the Vākāṭakas, in the introductory portion of the Pune plates. This is also

[1] V.V. Mirashi (ed.), *Corpus Inscriptionum Indicarum*, Vol. V, Ootacamund, 1963, p. 5.

noticed in her later grant recorded in the Rithpur plates. She was evidently very proud of her descent from the imperial Gupta family.[2] (3) In this connection it is also pointed out that Prabhāvatī refers to her paternal gotra Dhāraṇa (*Dhāraṇa-sagotrā*),[3] instead of Vishṇuvṛddha, the gotra of her husband's family. (4) Unlike his ancestors, who were all Śaivas, Rudrasena II was a devotee of Chakrapāṇi (Vishṇu), to whose grace he ascribed his prosperity (*Bhagavataśchakrapāṇeḥ prasādopārjjita Śrī samudayasya*). According to the current view, this difference in religious creed may have been due to the influence of his wife Prabhāvatī, or/and father-in-law Chandragupta II who were both devotees of Vishṇu.[4] (5) Lastly, it is argued that in the genealogical portion of his own grants Pravarasena II invariably refers to Prabhāvatī's father, Mahārājādhirāja Devagupta (*Mahārājādhirāja-Śrī-Devagupta-sutāyāṁ Prabhāvatīguptāyā-mutpannasya*), obviously Chandragupta II. It may be regarded as a proof of the political help that he must have received from his maternal grandfather during his own minority.

On the basis of these facts the theory of Chandragupta II's influence on the Vākāṭakas during the regency of Prabhāvatī has been built. Scholars generally follow V.V. Mirashi into believing that the use of nail-headed characters and the genealogy of the Guptas given in the copper plates of Prabhāvatīguptā proves that Chandragupta II had sent some of his trusted officers and statesmen to assist his daughter in governing her kingdom.[5] A. S. Altekar suggests that after the death of Rudrasena II, Chandragupta II paid a visit of condolence to his daughter Prabhāvatīguptā. He advised his daughter to assume the reins of administration as regent for the minor king Divākarasena, promising all help, military and administrative.[6] She decided to follow the advice and began to rule as regent. According to P. L. Gupta, the Sanakānīka Mahārāja mentioned in the Udayagiri inscription of GE 88

[2] *Ibid.*, p. 6.

[3] D.C. Sircar, *Select Inscriptions*, 2nd ed., Calcutta, 1965, p. 436, fn. 9; S.R. Goyal, *Guptakālīna Abhilekha*, Meerut, 1984, p. 371; Shankar Goyal, in *King Chandra and the Meharauli Pillar*, eds. Munish Chandra Joshi et al, Meerut, 1989, pp. 150 ff.

[4] Mirashi, *op. cit.*; R.C. Majumdar and A.S. Altekar (eds.), *The Vākāṭaka-Gupta Age*, Lahore, 1946, p. 110; S.R. Goyal, *A History of the Imperial Guptas* (hereafter *HIG*), Allahabad, 1967, p. 244; idem, *The Imperial Guptas : A Multidisciplinary Political Study* (hereafter *IG*), Jodhpur, 2005, pp. 274 ff.; D.C. Sircar, in *The Classical Age*, Bombay, 1954, p. 180; U.N. Roy, *Gupta Samrāṭ aur Unkā Kāla*, Allahabad, 1971, p. 582.

[5] V.V. Mirashi, *op. cit.*, p. xxiv.

[6] A.S. Altekar, *op. cit.*, p. 111. According to P. L. Gupta (*The Imperial Guptas*, Varanasi, 1974, p. 303), the visit of Chandragupta II to east Malwa, recorded in the Udayagiri inscription of his minister Vīrasena, took place when he 'was there on a visit to her daughter'. It is palpably wrong because this inscription explicitly states that he went there 'for the conquest of the whole world' (*kṛtsna pṛthivī jayārthena*).

and general Āmrakārddava mentioned in a Sanchi record of this very period (GE 93) were most likely among the officers, who were deputed by Chandragupta II to look after the Vākāṭaka administration.[7] Altekar even believes that Chandragupta II also took active interest in the training of his young grandsons.[8] For, according to a literary tradition, king Pravarasena wrote a poem *Setubandha*[9] which was revised by Kālidāsa.[10] Altekar identifies this Pravarasena with Pravarasena II, the grandson of Chandragupta II and suggests that probably Kālidāsa was one of the tutors appointed by Chandragupta II to educate the Vākāṭaka princes.[11] S. R. Goyal also admits that this matrimonial alliance proved to be a great boon to the Gupta empire. According to him, "from what we know about Prabhāvatī, it appears that she was a lady with strong personality. On the other hand, her father-in-law Pṛithivīsheṇa I was a man of amiable temperament and her husband Rudrasena II was weak enough to succumb to the pressure of his wife and father-in-law. This personality equation proved to be a very important factor, for it enabled the Guptas to exert some influence on the Vākāṭaka court and its policies."[12]

From the above discussion it is obvious that the theory of Chandragupta II's influence on the Vākāṭakas is mainly based on the use of the nail-headed script in the Pune copper plates of Prabhāvatīguptā, the occurrence of the Gupta genealogy in the Pune and Rithpur plates and the reference to Devagupta alias Chandragupta II in the grants of Pravarasena II. But the use of a particular variety of a script in a document most likely depended on the training of its scribe. Several inscriptions of the imperial Guptas show southern peculiarities. For example, the Udayagiri cave inscription of Chandragupta II of the Gupta year 82 (=401 A.D.) uses the box-headed variety of Brāhmī which was prevalent in the Vākāṭaka region. Similarly, the Sanchi stone inscription of the same emperor of the Gupta year 93 (=412 A.D.) is also written in the Late Brāhmī of the Southern Class. If these facts cannot be regarded as a proof of the Vākāṭaka influence on the imperial Guptas, then why should the use of the nail-headed variety in the

[7] P.L. Gupta, *op. cit.*

[8] A.S. Altekar, *op. cit.*

[9] Some scholars attribute his work to a Kashmirian king of the same name. In any case, Pravarasena II's authorship of the *Setubandha* is doubtful. As pointed out by D.C. Sircar, while the theme of the poem is Vaishṇava, Pravarasena Vākāṭaka was a devotee of Śiva (*The Classical Age*, pp. 182 ff.). Similarly, the tradition as recorded in a verse attributed to the *Kunteśvaradautya*, supposedly written by Kālidāsa, is too confused to be of much historical importance (*ibid.*, pp. 182-83).

[10] *South Indian Epigraphy, Annual Report*, 1914-15, p. 91.

[11] A.S. Altekar, *op. cit.*

[12] S.R. Goyal, *HIG*, p. 244; idem, *IG*, p. 276.

Pune plates be regarded as a proof of the Gupta influence on the Vākāṭakas?

It is also noteworthy that the Gupta genealogy given in the Pune and Rithpur copper plates is very defective. Firstly, both these records make no mention of Gupta, the founder of the dynasty, who has been so mentioned in all the Gupta documents.[13] Rather these grants declare that Ghaṭotkacha was the first king of the Gupta dynasty (*Guptānāmādirājo Mahārāja Śrī Ghaṭotkachaḥ*, Rithpur grant; *Guptādirājo Mahārāja Śrī Ghaṭotkachaḥ*, Pune grant). Secondly, in both these plates Chandragupta I is mentioned with the lower title of *Mahārāja* and not with the imperial title of *Mahārājādhirāja*. Thirdly, some of the epithets used in these grants for Chandragupta II (*Pṛthivyāmapratirathaḥ* ; *Sarvarājochchhettaḥ* ; *Chaturudadhi salilāsvādita-yaśaḥ* ; *anekago-hiraṇya koṭi sahasrapradaḥ*) were actually those of his father Samudragupta. Fourthly, the genealogy of these two records differs not only from the genealogy as given in the Gupta inscriptions, but both these documents differ from each other also. For example, in the Pune plates Ghaṭotkacha is described as *Guptādirāja* while in the Rithpur plates the phrase used is *Guptānāmādirāja*. Further, the Pune plates describe Gupta kings as *satputras* of their respective fathers while the Rithpur grant uses only the word *putra*. Moreover, the Rithpur plates describe Samudragupta as merely a *Māhārāja* while the Pune plates use the usual epithet *Mahārājādhirāja* for him. These deviations are curious and go against the theory that these plates were drafted by the Gupta officers sent to the Vākāṭaka court by Chandragupta II. That is why Altekar, who at one place opines that the Pune plates of Prabhāvatīguptā 'were drafted by a Gupta officer, imported from Pāṭaliputra',[14] was forced to contradict himself in the same work by stating that the 'officers who drafted the Vākāṭaka plates during the regency of Prabhāvatīguptā, were bred up in the Deccan tradition'.[15]

Thus, the idea that the officers who were responsible for the drafts of Pune and Rithpur plates were imported from Pāṭaliputra is negated by the defects in the Gupta genealogy as found in these documents while the theory of the importation of scribes is inherently improbable, for scribes were a very low category of government employees. It can hardly be imagined that Chandragupta II could have felt the necessity of sending scribes

[13] Excepting of course the Supia or Rewa record of Skandagupta (*Select Inscriptions*, p. 317) which also declares that Ghaṭotkacha was the founder of the Gupta family (*Śrī Ghaṭotkachaḥ tadvaṁśe*, etc.). But it is in many respects a unique and exceptional record. For example, it mentions Chandragupta II and Kumāragupta I not by their names but by their respective titles (*Śrī Vikramādityaḥ tatputra Mahārāja Śrī Mahendrādityaḥ*).

[14] A.S. Altekar, *op. cit.*, p. 112, fn. 1.

[15] *Ibid.*, p. 106.

to the Vākāṭaka kingdom even if it is conceded that he helped his daughter in the task of administration. Actually, the occurrence of the Gupta genealogy and gotra in the Vākāṭaka grants may easily be attributed to the custom current in the Vākāṭaka territory where queens usually introduced themselves with reference to their paternal family. For example, Nāgannikā, the Sātavāhana queen, has been described in the Nanaghat cave inscription as the daughter of Mahāraṭhī of Aṅgiya Kula (*bālāya Mahāraṭhino Aṅgiyakulavadhanasa*)[16] while Ajjhitabhaṭṭārikā, the wife of Narendrasena Vākāṭaka has been introduced as the daughter of the Kuntala king (*Kuntalādhipatisutāyām... Ajjhitabhaṭṭārikā-yāmutpannasya*).[17] Therefore, the occurrence of the Gupta family genealogy in the plates of Prabhāvatī cannot at all necessarily mean that her father Chandragupta II exerted any political influence over the Vākāṭakas during her regency. Belief in such a theory should require some other evidence which is as yet not forthcoming. It should also not to be forgotten that the occurrence of the Gupta genealogy in the Rithpur plates cannot be ascribed to the Gupta predominance in the Vākāṭaka court because at the time these plates were issued Prabhāvatī was not a regent and Pravarasena II had already entered his 19th regnal year. By that time Chandragupta II must have been dead and there is absolutely no proof that his successor Kumāragupta I exerted any influence on the Vākāṭakas. A number of grants issued in the earlier years of Pravarasena II are available, but they do not use Gupta genealogy. Therefore, the use of the Gupta genealogy by Prabhāvatī in her grants must be regarded as something *personal* to her or something connected with the local customs of the Vākāṭaka area. We should also remember that all, or most of, the queens when they are known to have described themselves, referred to their parentage, especially when they hailed from great ruling formilies, with justifiable pride. And, therefore, there is noting surprising if Prabhāvatīguptā did so. The reverse would have been more astonishing.

It has been argued that as a result of the influence of Prabhāvatī Rudrasena II gave up his ancestral religion and became a Vaishṇava. But it is also a fact that Pravarasena II, the son of Prabhāvatī, was a Śaiva. If Prabhāvatī could not influence her child-son to become a Vaishṇava, how could she foist her religious ideas on her husband ? The assumption that Śaivism was the family religion of the Vākāṭakas is also not at all sound, for we know that in ancient India there was nothing like a family religion. In the dynasty of Harsha different kings followed different faiths.[18] Even in the Vākāṭaka

[16] D.C. Sircar, *Select Inscriptions*, p. 193; S.R. Goyal, *Prāchīna Bhāratīya Abhilekha Saṁgraha* (*Prāk-Guptayugīna*), Jaipur, 1982, p. 425.

[17] V.V. Mirashi, *op. cit.*, p. 81.

[18] Shankar Goyal, *Harsha : A Multidisciplinary Political Study*, Jodhpur, 2006, Ch. 11.

family a later king Pṛthivīsheṇa II, the grandson of Pravarasena II, was a follower of Vaishṇavism (*Paramabhāgavata*).[19] If he was a Paramabhāgavata of his own accord, there is nothing to imagine that Rudrasena II became a worshipper of Chakrapāṇi because of the influence of her wife or father-in-law, Chandragupta II.

The fact that Pravarasena II refers to his maternal grandfather in the genealogical portion of his grants cannot mean that he had obtained some help from his maternal grandfather Chandragupta II. It is not generally realized that the name of the Gupta emperor in the grants of Pravarasena II occurs simply because he was the father of Prabhāvatīguptā. The Vākāṭaka genealogy as given in these grants does not contain the name of the mother or maternal grandfather of any other king except that of Rudrasena I which has been rightly explained as an instance of 'double inheritance'.[20] The name of Prabhāvatī has been given probably because she had herself ruled as a regent for a long time, or probably because the authors of the Vākāṭaka grants wanted to give the name of the mother of the ruling king. But as was the tradition in the Deccan, with her name the name of her father was also to be given. The point becomes obvious by the Balaghat grant of Pṛthivīsheṇa II where the author of the grant refers to Ajjhitabhaṭṭārikā, the mother of Pṛthivīsheṇa II, as the daughter of the king of Kuntala.[21] Thus, the reference to the maternal grandfather in these records turns out to be a matter of local or regional tradition, instead of being a pointer to the Gupta political influence on the Vākāṭaka court.

Our suggestion was originally published in 1989.[22] Later, A.M. Shastri also showed his agreement with our views by pointing out that Gupta influence on the Vākāṭakas during the regency of Prabhāvatī has been over-exeggerated by historians who feel that even the scribes were imported from her father's kingdom which fact is thought to be responsible not only for the draft of her records but also for the use in one of them of the nail-headed characters instead of the box-headed ones common to the Vākāṭaka charters. Had it been really so, the records would not have contained the serious factual errors from which the genealogical portion suffers. As far as the employment of a particular variety of script is concerned, it depends on the type of training that a scribe receives and the rulers by and large have not much to do with it.[23]

[19] Shankar Goyal, *175 Years of Vākāṭaka History and Historiography*, Jodhpur, 2009, p. 91.

[20] S.R. Goyal, *HIG*, pp. 88 ff.; idem, *IG*, pp. 111 ff.

[21] V.V. Mirashi, *op. cit.*

[22] In Bhaskar Chatterjee (ed.), *Professor H.D. Sankalia Felicitation Volume*, Delhi, 1989, pp. 351-56.

[23] A.M. Shastri, *Vākāṭakas : Sources and History*, New Delhi, 1997, p. 11.

Now, let us mention the relevant portions of the Ramtek Prabhāvatīguptā stone inscription which seem to prove Chandragupta II's political influence on the Vākāṭakas. It was found engraved on two rectangular blocks of stone inside the *maṇḍapa* of the Kevala-Narasiṁha temple at Ramtek, usually identified with the famous Ramagiri, mentioned in the *Meghadūta* of Kālidāsa. A.P. Jamkhedkar[24], Hans T. Bakker[25], Harunaga Isaacson[26], A.M. Shastri[27] and S.R. Goyal[28] were the earlier scholars to study it. The record belongs to the reign of the Vākāṭaka king Pravarasena II and purports to record most likely the erection of the Kevala-Narasiṁha temple with the image of the man-lion (Narasiṁha) manifestation of Vishṇu by a daughter (name lost) of Prabhāvatīguptā to commemorate the latter.

The testimony of the extant portions of this highly fragmentary record clarify and elaborate numerous points of the Gupta-Vākāṭaka relations and the history of the Deccan. Verse 9 of the record refers to Chandragupta (evidently Chandragupta II Vikramāditya) who had 'perfect character' (*paripūrṇa-vṛtta*), was a 'god of gods' (*dai (de) va-deva*) and, what is most important historically, 'the lord of the three oceans' (*tri-samudra-nātha*). That he was believed to have been a *tri-samudra-nātha*, on the one hand, indicates that for sometime he exercised at least nominal suzerainty over the Vākāṭaka kingdom including almost whole of the Deccan and, on the other, tends to strengthen the testimony of the Meharauli record regarding the warlike activities of Chandra in south India.[29] The record next mentions some person who is described as bearing the entire burden of the great kingdom which was difficult to bear and as the best of the beasts of burden. He was obviously Chandragupta II who is believed to have looked after the Vākāṭaka kingdom after the death of his son-in-law Rudrasena II.

[24] A.P. Jamkhedkar, 'A Newly Discovered Vākāṭaka Temple at Ramtek, District Nagpur', in *Shri C. Sivaramamurti Commemoration Volume*, ed. M.S. Nagaraja Rao, Delhi, 1987, pp. 217-23.

[25] Hans T. Bakker, *Ramtek*, Leiden, 1989, pp. 93-94; idem, 'The Antiquities of Ramtek Hill, Maharashtra', in *South Asian Studies*, V, 1989, pp. 79-102; idem, *The Vākāṭakas : An Essay in Hindu Iconology*, Groningen, 1997, pp. 163-68.

[26] Hans T. Bakker and Harunaga Isaacson, 'The Ramtek Inscriptions II : The Vākāṭaka Inscription in the Kevala-Narasiṁha Temple', in *BSOAS*, LVI, Part I, 1993, pp. 46-74.

[27] A.M. Shastri, *Early History of Deccan : Problems and Perspectives*, Delhi, 1987, Ch.5; idem, *Vākāṭakas : Sources and History*, pp. 125-35.

[28] S.R. Goyal, *Ancient Indian Inscriptions : Recent Finds and New Interpretations*, Jodhpur, 2005, pp. 221-25.

[29] Whether Chandra of the Meharauli pillar inscription is Chandragupta II, or his father Samudragupta, is still not certain. For a full discussion on the identity of the king mentioned therein vide *King Chandra and the Meharauli Pillar*, eds. M.C. Joshi, S.K. Gupta and Shankar Goyal, pp. 73-237.

This is all what we know from this inscription regarding our problem. But what do such statements as 'perfect character', 'god of gods' and 'the lord of the three oceans' imply ? The factual position is that the only military achievement of Chandragupta II was his Śaka conquest while this inscription refers to his being 'the lord of the three oceans'. What does it imply ? Does it mean a fresh conquest of the south India by Chandragupta II or does it mean only a reference to his father Samudragupta's conquests of the southern seas ? In our view, this record does not prove that Chandragupta II achieved some significant and fresh successes in the south as a verbal translation would lead us to believe. To us it sounds more logical that *tri-samudra-nātha* and all other such descriptions applied also to Samudragupta, Kumāragupta and Skandagupta are merely conventional descriptions without much historical significance. However, the same cannot be said about the title *ti-samuda-toya-pīta-vāhana* which is applied to Gautamīputra Sātakarṇi, for he controlled a considerable portion of the southern peninsula was difinitely the greatest ruler of it. As regards the Vākāṭakas, there is absolutely no direct hint of Chandragupta II's hegemony over them. This inscription has absolutely nothing to say about any sort of military or administrative support to the Vākāṭakas rendered by Chandragupta II. Even the numerous inscriptions of Chandragupta II himself or of his successors do not inform us about such eventuality. We would like to stress that had Chandragupta II played some role in the Vākāṭaka politics or helped them in any way this fact was bound to get mention in his this or that inscription.

Thus, we observe that the evidence of Pune and Rithpur copper plates and the recently discovered Ramtek stone inscription cited to prove Chandragupta II's influence on the Vākāṭaka court during the regency of Prabhāvatīguptā do not prove the case. We do not mean to suggest that such an influence was impossible. Indeed in the circumstances as are known to us some sort of *Gupta influence* on the Vākāṭakas during the minority of the sons of Rudrasena II may easily be presumed but there is nothing to prove any *Gupta interferance* in the Vākāṭaka areas. Our submission is simple:[30] the evidence cited in favour of this presumption does not prove the point, even the Ramtek inscription only concedes the overlordship of Chandragupta II on the southern peninsula only *in theory.* A.M. Shastri is, therefore, right when he warns us for not indulging in wild speculations based on conjectural restoration of the now lost text.[31]

[30] On this, see Shankar Goyal, 'The Ramtek Prabhāvatīguptā Memorial Fragmentary Inscription', in *Epigraphical Studies*, Select Papers from the Panel on Epigraphy at the 16th World Sanskrit Conference, 2015, Sanskrit Studies Centre, Silpakorn University, Bangkok, Thailand, ed. D.P. Dubey, New Delhi, 2018, pp. 129-37.

[31] A.M. Shastri, *Vākāṭakas : Sources and History*, p. 132. But Shastri is in two minds on this problem. He evidently contradicts his own views at some places in his work.

SIX

The Vaishṇava Chakravartī Ideal

The political activities and attitudes of the imperial Guptas was greatly influenced by their political ideology which was usually a reflection of and conditioned by their religious beliefs.[1] For example, in the case of Narasiṁhagupta Bālāditya, the contemporary of Mihirakula, we know that he came under a strong spell of Buddhism which diminished his martial fervour and love of military adventure. Yuan Chwang records that when Mihirakula raised an army to punish Bālādityarāja, the latter fled 'to conceal his poor person among the bushes of morass' and 'wandered through the mountains and deserts'.[2] The early imperial Guptas were, on the other hand, orthodox, though liberal Hindu rulers, a product of the Brāhmaṇa culture-area[3] and the Brāhmaṇical revival of third-fourth century A.D. They symbolised the tendency of rapprochement between the Vedic and the devotional schools of thought. In that respect they were the product of their age.

Till the beginning of the Gupta age, the *chakravartī* ideal[4] was connected with the performance of the Vedic sacrifices. The Aśvamedha was performed not only to extend and confirm the sovereignty of the performer, but also for going to the heaven or attainment of a son or as a ceremony of expiation for such sins as might have been committed in the prosecution of a

[1] The present essay is a shorter version of the one I wrote for *Reappraising Gupta History for S.R. Goyal*, eds. B.Ch. Chhabra, et al, New Delhi, 1992, pp. 215-23.

[2] S. Beal, *Si-Yü-Ki or Buddhist Records of the Western World*, trans. from the Chinese of Hiuan-Tsiang, Vol. I, repr., Delhi, 1969, p. 168.

[3] We believe that the Guptas originally belonged to the Allahabad region of eastern U.P. For details cf. Shankar Goyal, *Problems of Ancient Indian History : New Perspectives and Perceptions*, Jaipur, 2001, pp. 147-52; idem, *Ancient India : A Multidisciplinary Approach*, Jodhpur, 2006, pp. 119-20.

[4] For a detailed discussion on the conception of a *chakravartī* ruler cf. S.R. Goyal, *Māgadha-Sātavāhana-Kushāṇa Sāmrājyoṅ kā Yuga*, Meerut, 1988, pp. 562-65.

war of conquest or as a symbol of success at the end of one's career. Samudragupta's sacrifice mentioned in the inscriptions and illustrated on his gold coins most probably belonged to the last category. However, as he was the first Indian ruler, after the Mauryas to carve out an empire comprising almost the whole of *chakravartī kshetra*, he performed the horse-sacrifice of elaborate type (*chirotsanna*),[5] and not its abbreviated form which was current in those days. Later on Kumāragupta I also performed an Aśvamedha to assert his *chakravartī* status.

In the Gupta age the conception of a *chakravartī* ruler, performing *digvijaya*, that is to say conquering 'the whole earth', was very popular and was given a Vaishṇava orientation. In the *Vāyu Purāṇa*,[6] for instance, it has been stated that "the *chakravartīs* are born in each age as the essence of Vishṇu. They have lived in the ages past and will come again in future. ... Strength, *Dharma*, happiness and wealth, these wondorous blessings shall characterise these rulers. They will enjoy wealth, plenty, *Dharma*, ambition, fame and victory in undisturbed harmony. They will excel the Ṛishis in their power to achieve results, by their lordliness, by providing plenty and by discipline. And they will excel the gods, demons and men by their strength and self-discipline."[7]

On these lines the influence of the imperial Guptas and of their age is quite distinct. As opposed to the Vākāṭakas and the Bhāraśivas, who were the worshippers of Śiva, the god of destruction and social asceticism, who though a giver keeps no wealth, possesses no material splendour and who is austere and sombre, the Guptas invoked Vishṇu, the king amongst gods, whose emblem if *chakra* — the symbol of imperial dominion — and who is lord of prosperity and growth. The adoption of this cult by a galaxy of great rulers was bound to affect, in turn, the political thinking of the period. Perhaps the author of the lines quoted above from the *Vāyu Purāṇa*, who appears to have been a Bhāgavata, wanted to bring the ideal of *chakravartī* rulers in tune with the polity of the times.[8]

The Vaishṇava orientation of the political thinking of the Guptas is further indicated by the use of such titles as *Achintya* and *Apratiratha* by Samudragupta and Chandragupta II. Though in some inscriptions the epithet *Apratirathaḥ* is applied to both Samudragupta and his son Chandragupta II,

[5] This interpretation of the term *chirotsanna* have been suggested by several scholars such as Jagannath Agrawal (in *Essays Presented to Sir Jadunath Sarkar*, 2, pp. 10-11), A.V.S. Murthi (in *JUG*, XII, pp. 81-82) and V. S. Pathak (*JNSI*, XIX, p. 149).

[6] *Vāyu Purāṇa*, XLVII. 72-76.

[7] R.C. Majumdar, *The Classical Age*, Bombay, 1962, Foreword, p. x.

[8] S. R. Goyal, *A History of the Imperial Guptas*, Allahabad, 1967, p. 136; idem, *The Imperial Guptas : A Multidisciplinary Political Study*, Jodhpur, 2005, pp. 166 ff.

but so far as coins are concerned, it has been used in connection with Samudragupta alone. The Archer type of his gold coins[9] has, on the reverse, the simple legend *Apratirathaḥ* and on the obverse, in addition to the name *Samudra* without any case ending (engraved vertically) the metrical legend: *Apratiratho vijitya kshitiṁ sucharitair= divaṁ jayati.* "It may now readily be admitted that *Apratiratha* stands here as a substantive and not as a mere adjective. Plainly the personality of Apratiratha (Vishṇu) is superimposed (*adhyāropita*, as it may be termed in Sanskrit poetics) on Samudragupta, who is thus presented to us as an embodiment of Vishṇu. ... Harisheṇa, the author of the inscription, seems to have inlaid, as it were, his elaborate composition with astute hints that would indeed make his master appear as the very Vishṇu on earth."[10]

The connection of the early Gupta emperors with the new Vaishṇavite interpretation of the *chakravartī* ideal is almost conclusively established by the unique Chakravikrama type of coin of Chandragupta II.[11] On the obverse of this coin, which was yielded by the Bayana hoard, is shown, inside a big *chakra*, a standing two-armed male figure conferring three round balls on a haloed royal figure in front of him. The reverse shows the figure of Lakshmī standing on a lotus and the legend *Chakravikrama.* It is now almost unanimously believed that the bigger figure inside the chakra represents the *Chakrapurusha* or Vishṇu who is bestowing on the smaller figure of Chandragupta II three symbols of royal power, viz., *prabhu-śakti, utsāha-śakti* and *mantra-śakti* i.e. the kingly virtues of authority, energy and counsel.[12] The symbology of this scene becomes clearer in the light of the data provided by the *Ahirbudhnya Saṁhitā*, a well-known text of the Pāñcharātra Āgama, which 'on the basis of the internal evidence bearing on the religious conditions portrayed in it should be assigned to the Gupta period'.[13] From it we learn that Vishṇu in the form of *Chakra* was held as the ideal of worship for kings desirous of obtaining universal sovereignty. In the words of V.S. Agrawala, it was "a novel and dynamic interpretation compatible with the polity of the times. According to the explanation given in the *Saṁhitā*, the human figure inside the *Chakra* is called *Chakravartī Purusha* both by the people and the wisemen. The king who worships him

[9] J. Allan, *Catalogue of the Coins of the Gupta Dynasties and of Śaśāṅka, King of Gauḍa* (*in the British Museum*), London, 1914, pp. 6-7.

[10] B. Ch. Chhabra, *JNSI*, IX, p. 145.

[11] S.R. Goyal, *The Coinage of Ancient India*, Jodhpur, 1995, p. 393.

[12] A.S. Altekar, *The Coinage of the Gupta Empire*, Varanasi, 1957, pp. 147 ff.; Shivaramamurti, *JNSI*, XIII, Pt. II, pp. 180 ff.; V.S. Agrawala, *JNSI*, Pt. I, pp. 97 ff.; Shankar Goyal, *Aspects of Ancient Indian History and Historiography*, New Delhi, 1993, pp. 47-48.

[13] V.S. Agrawala, *op. cit.*, p. 97.

with a devout heart attains to the rank of a *Chakravartī* ruler in a short time. Those who wish a greater glory (*vipulaṁ śriyam*) should worship the *Chakravartī Purusha*, but specially is this worship enjoined on kings. It was a new conception by which the Pāñcharātra Bhāgavatas utilized the tenets of their religion in the service of the state and thereby greatly influenced the political thought and ideals of kingly power during that period."[14] The *Ahirbudhnya Saṁhitā* clearly states that he who adores the *Chakra Purusha* becomes a Sārvabhauma or Universal Ruler in this world and also becomes a ruler in the other world. Any one who does not pay homage to this deity cannot attain to kingship.[15] It is indeed a welcome addition to our knowledge of the political philosophy of the early imperial Guptas. It is difficult not to believe that Samudragupta, who was himself a great devotee of Vishṇu and was responsible for the adoption of Garuḍa, the *vāhana* of Vishṇu as the emblem of his dynasty, himself subscribed to this new ideology. At least this much cannot be denied that Samudragupta aspired and claimed to be a *chakravartī* ruler.

The Chakravikrama motif of the coins of Chandragupta II probably influenced the Sassanian art of Iran, though the Sassanian artists probably could not grasp its meaning and significance. V.S. Pathak has drawn the attention of the scholars to a decorated ellipsoid in Chalcedony of Sassanian origin. He has described it thus:[16] "A bearded male figure in a domed cap and Iranian dress consisting of full trousers slit at the instep, boots and long skirt tied by a band at the waist the two ends of which are hanging downward, standing right holding a round object in his upraised right hand and another round object in his left hand extended downward, facing another male figure to his right side. The second male figure on the right is also bearded and though not a dwarf is of smaller size. He is likewise robed in Iranian dress, with probably a sword tied at the waist, holds a round object in his right hand and raises his left hand to receive the round object from the principal male figure. A leafy creeper forms the circular border broken a little at the top to make room for the cap of the main figure and at the bottom. An object looking like a shield is at the left side of the smaller male figure. The beard of the male figure is typically Sassanian, aptly described in a similar context by Kālidāsa as 'honey-combed' (*kshaudrapaṭala*). The smaller male figure is likewise bearded and is certainly not a child. The main point, however is three round objects to be gifted away by the divine or heroic figure of higher stature to the man of smaller size. The Sassanian ellipsoid is

[14] *Ibid.*, pp. 99-100.

[15] *Ibid.*

[16] V. S. Pathak, 'Motifs on Gupta Coins and Sassanian Wares', *Numismatic Digest*, Vol. X, 1986, p. 87.

not inscribed, and hence the interpretation of the device may not be conclusive and definite."

Pathak has conjectured that the main figure, as depicted in the ellipsoid under discussion may be Ferdun, the Iranian hero who is described in Pahlvī texts to have bestowed the three portions of his kingdom on his three sons. The three round objects may, therefore, represent the three kingdoms (the three earths) and the man of smaller size may be identified as his son. The identification proposed here, as V.S. Pathak himself concedes, may be right or may entirely be erroneous. But the gift of three round objects by a man of higher stature to a man of lesser size definitely connects it with the Chakravikrama type of coin. The motif of the gift of the three round objects by *Mahāpurusha* can very well be interpreted in Indian cultural context. On the other hand, the motif in the Sassanian ellipsoid does not find any justifiable explanation in the Iranian tradition. Therefore, it may be reasonably concluded that the scene on the Sassanian piece is an imitation of the scene on the Chakravikrama coin type, and not *vice versa.*

In our view, however, the identification of the main figure with Ferdun proposed by V.S. Pathak is difficult to be accepted for the simple reason that if the intention of the Sassanian artist was to depict the scene of the bestowal by Ferdun of three portions of his kingdom on his three sons, he would had depicted three small figures and not just one. It seems to us to be a meaningless imitation of the Indian Chakravikrama motif in which even the halo has been rendered meaningless by its depiction as a leafy creeper.

SEVEN

The Making of Early Medieval Indian Society

That the term 'medieval' implies not only a chronological position intermediate between 'ancient' and 'modern' but also a social and cultural situation different from 'ancient' or 'classical' on the one hand, and 'modern' on the other, and thus connotes that there were certain values and characteristics which were distinctively 'medieval', is a well-recognised fact in European history. But in the Indian context scholars have started talking about these problems only in recent decades.[1] The main questions before us, therefore, are: Do the terms 'classical' and 'medieval' have any connotative or qualitative significance in Indian history? If yes, what were the factors which transformed the Indian 'classical' heritage into 'medieval' culture ? When did these factors begin to operate ? These and such other questions constitute the various facets of the problem of the decline of the classical and the rise of medieval age in India, which we propose to investigate here *with particular reference to the age of Harsha, which we believe constituted a watershed between classical and medieval periods.*

[1] E. g. N. R. Ray, 'The 'Medieval' Factor in Indian History', being the Address of the General President of the Twenty-ninth Session of the Indian History Congress, Patiala, 1967, pp. 1-42; R.S. Sharma, 'Problem of Transition from Ancient to Medieval in Indian History', in the *Indian Historical Review*, March 1974, Vol. I, No. 1, pp. 1-9; idem, *Perspectives in Social and Economic History of Early India*, New Delhi, 1983, Ch. XVI; idem, *Early Medieval Indian Society : A Study in Feudalisation*, Kolkata, 2001, Chs. 1-2; idem, *India's Ancient Past*, Oxford, 2015, pp. 287-98; V.K. Thakur, 'Transition from the Ancient to the Medieval Period', in D. Devahuti (ed.), *Problems of Indian Historiography*, Delhi, 1979, pp. 79-82; B.N.S. Yadava, 'The Accounts of the Kali Age and the Social Transition from Antiquity to the Middle Ages', in D.N. Jha (ed.), *Feudal Social Formation in Early India*, Delhi, 1987, pp. 65-112; Shankar Goyal, *History and Historiography of the Age of Harsha*, Jodhpur, 1992, pp. 243-72; idem, *Harsha : A Multidisciplinary Political Study*, Jodhpur, 2006, pp. 238-68; idem, *The 'Medieval' Factor and the Age of Harsha : A Cultural Study*, Jodhpur, 2016, pp. 1-24.

The question whether or not the term 'classical' and 'medieval' have any qualitative significance in the Indian context, must be answered in the affirmative. The term 'classical' usually means of the first rank or authority, an age in which political culture, literature, architecture and fine arts reach a high level of excellence to form a standard or model for later times.[2] In the European context, which offers a close parallel to the Indian example, the classical tradition chiefly meant the Roman concept of the Universal Empire, the cultural heritage of Greece and Rome and the Roman law and jurisprudence. This legacy was transformed in the medieval period under the impact of the immigration and invasions of the barbarians, growth in the supremacy of the Church, feudalism, triumph of faith over reason, ambivalent attitude towards morals, regionalism in political, economic and cultural life, etc. That is why in the European context the term 'medieval' has not only a chronological but also a connotative and qualitative meaning.

In India the situation appears to have been *mutatis mutandis*the same : the lagacy of the classical age (the imperial ideal of the *chakravartin rulers*, the cultural legacy of the classical age when norms or standards of values were laid down in the different walks of life, and the Smṛti law which formed the basis of socio-political organisation) was transformed by a number of factors and forces. They were almost the same which operated in Europe in the same period excepting of course the supremacy of the Church (for no religion organised in this fashion existed in India; even the Buddhist Church was neither 'universal' nor centralized in the way the Catholic Church was). Then again nothing like the caste system (which provided the basic framework for the Indian society) existed in Europe. Consequently the nature of the medieval society as it emerged in India resembles the European medieval society in a good measure though the difference between the two caused by the differences in their classical heritage and local circumstances are also many.

The transformation of the classical heritage into medieval culture did not take place all at once. It was brought about slowly in the course of several centuries intervening the decline of the Gupta empire and the establishment of the Delhi Sultanate. That is why the culture of this period, on the one hand, seems to have much in common with the classical culture of the Guptas and, on the other, appears to be nearer to the culture of the Sultanate period with the main difference that in the post-Gupta centuries, unlike the Sultanate period, the Muslims were not the dominant political power in northern India. We, therefore, suggest that the beginning of the

[2] Cf. Romila Thapar, *A History of India*, Vol 1, Harmondsworth, 1966, p. 157; also see her *The Penguin History of Early India : From the Origins to AD 1300*, New Delhi, 2003, pp. 280-82.

medieval period in Indian history may broadly be traced from the fall of the Gupta empire itself, though it may be readily conceded that the period of about two centuries, roughly from the fall of the Gupta empire (c. 550 A.D.) and the rise of the Pratihāras (c. 750 A.D.) sheds light on the classical and medieval periods both by a sort of *dehalī-dīpaka-nyāya* (the maxim that a lamp placed on the threshhold illumines both the inside and outside of a room) and thus belongs to both. The age of Harsha formed the focal point of this vast stretch of two centuries.

FACTORS OF CHANGE : FOREIGN INVASIONS

In Europe one of the main factors that led to the transition from classical to middle age was the immigration and invasions of the barbarian nomads. On the one hand it resulted in the barbarization of the classical culture and, on the other, imparted a new vigour to the European society. The immediate consequence of the nomadic pressure, culminating with that of the Huns, was the breaking up of the Roman empire. With this began the process that slowly resulted in the formation of the reginal kingdoms of the Franks, Germans, Lombards, Slavs, Normans, etc. in the early medieval period. The role of the central Asian nomads and other foreign invaders in Indian history, in the centuries preceding and following the fall of the Gupta empire, was almost similar. They belonged to two groups:

(1) The earlier waves of the Yüe-chi, Śakas, Ābhīras and Pārasīkas (including the immigration of the Maga Brāhmaṇas). To them may be added the Bactrian Greeks and the Kidāra Kushāṇas. They all spoke, broadly speaking, languages and dialects belonging to the Indo-European family.

(2) Later waves of the Hūṇas, Turushkas and Gurjaras. They were mainly Indianized Turko-Mongols. To them may be added the Tibetans, Arabs and Turks, the last two being the harbingers of Islam in the country.

The first of these groups was easily merged in the vast ocean of Indian humanity. Then followed a respite for about three centuries and India found time and opportunity not only to put her house in order but also to reach a high level of cultural excellence. The resultant effect was the Gupta empire and its classical achievements. However, the arrival of the ferocious Hūṇas and other kindered tribes which came in their train, shook the very foundation of the Gupta empire just as their western branches had succeeded in disintegrating the Roman empire almost at the same time. Like Rome India also took about a couple of centuries to recover from the shock. But when she came out of the process of readjustment she found, just as Rome did, that her culture had become somewhat different and that the medieval period of her history (the Kali Age of the Purāṇas) had already begun.

The pressure of the foreign tribes not only shattered the imperial fabric of India (which was never fully pan-Indian in the post-Maurya period), it also corrupted her classical values, modified her social and economic institutions and generated a sense of pessimism leading to the theory of social decline in the Kali Age which the post-Gupta literature and epigraphs so vividly describe. On the positive side, the arrival of the foreign tribes imparted a new vigour and vitality to the Indian society, just as the Germanic tribes had done in the decadent Rome. According to N.R. Ray, the emergence of the medieval factor in Indian sculpture and painting was largely due to the impact of the central Asian nomads. In this connection the effeminate and irreligious character of the kings of the sixth century A.D., who have been so roundly denounced by Yaśodharman of Malwa, with vigour and vitality of the Gurjara-Pratihāras of Kanauj offers an interesting comparison. Indeed the age of the imperial Gurjara-Pratihāras has been compared with the period of the Carolingian Renaissance of the medieval Europe. As a matter of fact not only the Gurjara-Pratihāras but several other Rajput dynasties contained some Scythic, Hunnic or Gurjara blood in their veins though many of them, in course of time, became mixed with the indigenous people, specially Brāhmaṇas (who, as a result of the growing feudal tendencies and large-scale land grants bestowed on them, were emerging as one of the most important elements of the ruling aristocracy of the country) and the ancient republican tribes of the Punjab and Rajasthan (which had lost political power only recently in the Gupta age) and probably also the aborginal tribes of Rajasthan, Bundelkhand, etc. (which, when Hinduized, were readily accepted within the pale of the orthodox society). Thus, the *rājaputras* or the Rajputs who emerged as the rulers of the greater part of north India in the post-classical centuries were a profesional class of mixed origin having blood affinities with a number of social groups which were welded into one and infused with new vitality by the new element of the Hinduized foreigners.

ROLE OF FEUDALISM

Another factor that played a significant role in the transformation of the classical society in Europe as well as India was feudalism. But the feudalism of India greatly differed from its European counterpart, so much so that many scholars have doubted its existence in India.[3] But if it is believed that the political essence of feudalism lay in the organisation of the whole administrative structure on the basis of land and its economic essence in a system of self-sufficient local economy in which peasants were attached to the soil held by the landed intermediaries placed between the kings and

[3] Cf. e.g. D.C. Sircar, *Landlordism and Tenancy in Ancient and Medieval India*, Lucknow, 1969.

actual tillers who had to pay rent in kind and labour, then it may be very well argued that the broad features of feudalism emerged in the Gupta age and developed in the post-Gupta centuries. We believe that the differences in the detailed superstructures of European and Indian feudal systems do not mean that the Indian system was not 'feudal' at all. Apparently, a fallacy is involved in first emphasizing the peculiarities of feudalism of Europe and then talking of other feudal systems, for how can one call a non-European society feudal unless possiblities of regional variations in feudalism are recognised ?

Actually, it is very difficult to define the term feudalism. The term is attributed variously to stages of historical development far removed from one another in time and place, such as the interregnum (2475-2160 B.C.) after the Old Kingdom in Egypt and the Chou period in China (c. 1122-250 B.C.); but generally it is applied to European society from the 5th to the 15th century A.D. Fifth to ninth centuries are considered to be the breeding period of feudalism whereas tenth to thirteenth centuries are accepted as its classical age. On its nature also there is divergence of opinion. The central principle of feudalism seems to have been the holding of land in return for services. The king was regarded as the holder of all land, much of which he let out to his feudal barons who, in return for the property, agreed to perform certain services and to make some payments and supplies. This was usually to provide the king with a specified number of soldiers in times of war. The barons, in their turn, let out land to others on similar conditions, and the same process was continued down the scale. When a tenant died, it was usual for his successor to pay a 'fine' to his overlord before he could succeed to his estate. Fines were also paid when the tenant sold or gave any part of his land to a stranger. Payments had again to be made to the master on other recognised occasions such as the knighting of the latter's eldest son and the marriage of his eldest daughter and when he himself had to pay ransom.

Like Europe, the whole of the medieval period of Indian history, including the Turko-Afghan and the Mughal ages, was characterised by a system of feudal assignments. The germs of this system, called the *sāmanta* system in the Hindu kingdoms, are traceable in the Gupta age and even earlier, but it is from the age of Harsha that clear references to the feudal practice of assigning fiefs to officers first appear. Its growth was facilitated by several factors including the pressure of the barbarinas, absence of a strong central power and the Hindu tradition of *dharmavijaya* (righteous conquest) which enjoined on a victor to reinstate the defeated princes. Further, it was concomitant with the trend of economic decline as is evidenced by the paucity and debasement of coins, gradual disappearance of guilds, regionalization of economic structure and decline of cities, trade and industry. As in medieval Europe so in India also, in such a condition there was no other option for kings except to grant lands and estates or income from them to the Brāhmaṇas, Buddhist monasteries, Hindu maṭhas, temples, etc. and also to their officers, army chieftains and others in return for their services.

IMPACT OF FEUDALISM ON SOCIAL, ECONOMIC AND POLITICAL LIFE

Feudalism brought about significant changes in the classical pattern of socio-economic and political organisation. Firstly, in ancient India economic theorists usually believed in the peasant proprietorship of land, although those who advocated royal ownership of land were by no means insignificant. But now feudal chiefs emerged as a third claimant to the ownership. Secondly, in ancient India there is no indication that cultivators were tied to the soil like the European serfs. They enjoyed the freedom to migrate to another state/estate if they were oppressed. But in the post-Gupta age signs of serfdom and quasi-manorial villages are found in some parts of northern India. Thirdly, the rise of feudalism had an adverse effect on the economic system in general. Because of the greed and unscruplousness of the feudal lords (*sāmantas*) and the apathy of the kings the burden of taxation on the people became heavier and the villagers were brought to a very low level of subsistence. The constant feudal wars were responsible for much destruction of the lives and property of people, sacking of cities being a common feature of such wars. Even the march of an army often brought untold misery to the people living in the villages through which it passed. In the *Harshacharita* Bāṇa describes the pathetic condition of the peasants at the time of the march of Harsha's army. Sometimes finding robbery highly profitable, petty feudal chiefs molested merchants who passed through their fiefs.

The impact of feudalism on political institutions and ideals was also quite significant. Feudalism led not only to the fragmentation of political authority but also to its hierarchical gradation as the inscriptions and literary works such as the *Harshacharita* testify. As such the monarch, who was at the apex of the hierarchy, became and began to be viewed more as the lord of the vassal kings, and the *sāmantas* emerged as the real rulers in their respective areas. Thus, the authority of the ruler became more formal than real. He depended for military support on his vassals and *sāmantas*. Yuan Chwang, the Aihole inscription and the *Harshacharita* testify to the feudal nature of Harsha's army. Coupled with the concept of *dharmavijaya* this fact rendered permanent absorption of the conquered territories extremely difficult and made the imperial structure more feudal-federal in character. The tendency began in the Gupta age itself but at that time at least the heartland of the empire was directly administered by the emperor. In the age of Harsha even Matipura and Mathurā, situated close to Kanauj, the imperial capital, could be ruled by the subordinate kings. This phenomenon is found in the history of early medieval Europe also.

The decline in the position of the king is reflected in the changed concept of royalty. In the classical period an ideal king was supposed to be the real head of the state who was always conscious of the duties attending his kingly office and anxious for the welfare of his subjects. But in the post-classical period an ideal king appears more as a private person spending his time in religiosity, pursuits of pleasure and warfare. Even in wars he displays his personal desire for victory for the sake of glory or revenge. Harsha himself is the best example of such an ideal 'feudal' king.

The feudalization and decline of royalty in the post-classical period is also evidenced by the adoption of the vainglorious titles of kings and a more lavish attribution of divinity to them. Now the bards began to weave rich legends of divinity around kings. These tendencies do not prove an increase in the actual power of the rulers; they only indicate to the high pretensions of monarchs under feudal conditions which intellectuals like Bāṇa and Medhātithi highly deplored.

With the feudalization of royalty the state machinery underwent considerable changes. The provincial and local administration was bound to change with the emergence of feudal lords as local centres of power. In the central administration also sometimes the *sāmantas* became the chief counsellers of the king at the cost of ministers who more often that not, displayed greater interest in superstitions and omens rather than in actual statecraft and diplomacy.

IDEAL OF CHIVALRY

One of the by-products of feudalism in medieval Europe as well as India was the ideal of chivalry. Chivalry in medieval Europe consisted of several virtues such as limitless valour, truthfulness, loyalty to the overlord, generosity, etc. It was also associated with romantic love with women. In India though the tradition of bravery was very old, it acquired a new flavour with the accentuation of feudal tendencies. Now a set of chivalric conventions were developed. It emphasized more or less the same virtues which were valued in feudal Europe. Now queens are more often than not described as having been 'bought' by paying the price of valour (cf. the examples of *paurusha parākrama-datta śulkā* Dattadevī, the queen of Samudragupta, and *parākramakrītā* Yaśomatī, the queen of Prabhākaravardhana). Numerous *kāvyas* and dramas describe how the royal hero 'won' the hand of a princess, after defeating other suitors. But with the passage of time the ideal of chivalry degenerated into vanity and arrogance and accentuated the tendencies of family and clannish rivalries and jealousy. Actually, the whole Pṛthvīrāja-Saṁyogitā episode of a later date is the saga of chivalry, romance, clannish rivalry and vanity. Not infrequently such episodes led to futile warfare on smaller or massive scale.

CHANGES IN THE NATURE OF WARFARE

It is quite obvious that the feudal ideal of chivalry could not be very effective in war. Otherwise also, feudalism did not help much in the development of the art of war. Contrary to the practice of the classical period, armies in this age were generally composed of feudal levies. They could swell to huge proportions, but were too heterogeneous to be commanded by the 'overlord' effectively. The practice of maintaining efficient standing armies was given up. Out of the traditional four-fold division of the army chariots almost disappeared in the post-Gupta age. The cavalry was valued but not much was done to improve its technique or to procure horses of good breed from abroad. There was an increasing tendency to construct hill-fortresses and defensive works around cities. The common method of capturing a fortress was actual siege and assault. No special devices appear to have been used for breaking through a fort. The system of espionage, valued in earlier periods, appears to have suffered a decline. The chief weapon in war in the classical period was bow, but now sword became a more popular weapon though archery was not altogether neglected. Much reliance was laid on omens and supernatural support in warfare and a lot of attention was paid to grandeur, show and luxurious living in military camps with the result that the Rajput armies became more or less like the later-day Mughal armies. The earliest picture of such a military camp is preserved in the *Harshacharita* of Bāṇa.

IMPACT OF FEUDALISM ON EDUCATION : EMERGENCE OF 'UNIVERSITIES'

In ancient India *āśramas* or hermitages known as *gurukulas* were the seats of learning. But in the medieval period feudalization of the Buddhist monasteries and Hindu temples resulted in the institutionalisation of education. For the feudal rights enjoyed by the Nālandā Mahāvihāra in the age of Harsha himself, evidence is provided by the Chinese sources. Hui-li, the biographer of Yuan Chwang, records that the king of the country, probably the local ruler of Magadha, or Harsha himself, had remitted the revenues of about 100 villages (the number had increased to 200 by the time of I-tsing), for the endowment of the convent. Two hundred householders of these villages, day by day, contributed several hundred piculs (1 picul=133 1/8 lbs.) of ordinary rice and several hundred catties (1 catty= 160 lbs.) of butter and milk.[4] In the same way clothes, food, beds and medicines were supplied to the inmates.[5]

In the seventh century lavish endowments were made to the Nālandā Mahāvihāra by kings Pūrṇavarman—probably a Maukhari ruler, Harsha, Bhāskaravarman and probably Aṁśuvarman of Nepal.[6] Seals of two Maukhari kings and of Bhāskaravarman have been found at Nālandā. Pūrṇavarman is said to have presented to Nālandā a figure of the Buddha standing upright and made of copper, 80 feet high. He also constructed a pavilion of six stages to cover it. Harshavardhana is usually identified with the king of Mid-India who is mentioned by Yuan Chwang as the builder of one of the largest monasteries there. The construction of the boundary wall around the whole establishment has also been attributed to him. The construction of a large brass monastery built by him was still going on when Yuan Chwang visited Nālandā.

The feudalization of the *vihāras* and their emergence as self-sufficient economic units tended to politicalize their administration.[7] It was but natural for kings, who gave lavish grants and endowments to the monasteries (and temples), to see to it that they behaved in a proper manner. Harsha himself is said to have 'brought the Brethern together for examination and discussion, giving rewards and punishments according to their merit and demerit. Those Brethren who kept the rules of their Order strictly and were thoroughly sound in theory and practice he "advanced to the Lion's Throne" (that is, promoted to the highest place) and from these he received religious instruction; those who, though perfect in the observance of the ceremonial code, were not learned in the past he merely honoured with formal reverence; those who neglected the ceremonial observances of the Order, and whose immoral conduct was notorious, were banished from his presence and from the country.'[8] King Kumāra of Kāmarūpa threatened Śīlabhadra, the Head of the Nālandā Mahāvihāra, that he would demolish the institution in case his request for despatching Yuan Chwang was not complied with. In Kashmir also, the ruler of that kingdom is seen appointing some score of monks headed by Bhadanta Yaśa from among the monks to help Yuan Chwang when the latter stayed there.[9] Incidentally, in China also the

[4] Samuel Beal, *The Life of Hiuen-Tsiang*, Second edn., New Delhi, 1973, pp. 112-13.

[5] *Ibid.* and n. 3.

[6] H. Heras, 'The Royal Patrons of the University of Nālandā', *JBORS*, XIV, 1928.

[7] Cf. S. R. Goyal, *Harsha and Buddhism*, Meerut, 1986, pp. 133-35.

[8] T. Watters, *On Yuan Chwang's Travels in India (A.D. 629-645)*, I, eds. T.W. Rhys Davids and S. W. Bushell, New Delhi, 1961, p. 344.

[9] *Life*, p. 69.

government kept strict control over the Buddhist Church as is evident from the account of Yuan Chwang's life after his return from India.

The transformation of the organisation of the Buddhist monasteries on feudal lines changed the pattern of the Buddhist education also. As pointed out by S. R. Goyal, in earlier periods education in monasteries was intended for monks and nuns only. However, with the feudalization of the monastic life and economy, the monasteries emerged as great organised or corporate centres of higher learning where education was imparted not only to the monks and nuns but to the general public also. In the age of Harsha Nālandā Mahāvihāra was the foremost of such institutions. The emergence of the Brāhmaṇical *agrahāra* villages and temples as centres of learning was the Hindu counterpart of the feudalization of education system. The early medieval temple colleges at Salotgi, Ennariram, Tirumukkuda, Tiruvorriyur, Malakapuram and at many other places and also the Kadiyur Agrahāra, the Sarvajñapura Agrahāra, etc. described by A. S. Altekar were big corporate educational institutions which had their own land and buildings, paid regular salaries to their teachers and sometimes even gave maintenance allowance to students. They could not come into existence without the feudal land grants and endowments. The tradition of these temples and *agrahāras* was continued by the *maṭhas* of the early medieval āchāryas. The feudalized Buddhist monasteries of the Gupta and post-Gupta periods, specially of the age of Harsha may, therefore, be regarded as the forerunners of the later-day corporate educational institutions.[10]

IMPACT OF REGIONALISM AND INSULARITY

As in the early medieval Europe, in India also the rise and growth of feudalism in the post-Gupta age was concomitant and connected with the growth of regional tendencies in life. To some extent foreign tribes which established their own cultural zones (such as the Gurjaradeśa), newly emerging ruling elites (such as the Rajputs who paved the way for the emergence of Rajputana) and feudal system (which thrived on localisation of industries, emphasis on agrarian economy and decline of trade and commerce) stimulated this tendency. In the classical age the farflung corners of the country were linked up through a network of roads and rivers and traders moved from one part of the country to another and also to foreign lands. Consequently, regionalism and insularity were cut across by the hook up of regional economy with the national economic structure. But in the post-classical period the absence of a centralized authority increased localism and insularity in economic life. India's trade with other countries declined leading to a decrease in the total profit from exports, probably even to an

[10] S.R. Goyal, *op. cit.*, pp. 134-35.

unfavourable balance of trade. Indian techniques of ship construction and navigation fell behind those of the Arabs and Chinese. There was decline even in internal trade and industrial production acquired local orientation. The bonds which united the craftsmen of any particular industry slackened, for by this time guilds appear to have become mostly fossilised into occupational sub-castes which retained some form of social control over their members but did not do much in the sphere of economic cooperation. Further, they did not have any organisational connection with their counterparts elsewhere as was the case in the classical age.

The regionalization and decline in economic life is evidenced also by the prevalence of local weights and measures and by the paucity and debasement of coins. As against the originality, excellence and wide variety found in the coinage of the classical period, those of the early medieval age are restricted in number and, with a few exceptions, there is no originality in them. The extreme paucity of gold coins of this period is indeed in sharp contrast to the abundance of the Gupta gold coinage; so far only one gold coin of Harsha has been discovered. According to S.R. Goyal, "India never saw an affluent gold coinage from the ancient times to the close of the early medieval period except in the age of the Kushāṇas and the Guptas—and even during the rule of these two dynasties our material prosperity was never very high,... ."[11] The silver coins of Harsha and others reveal even a more depressing state of affairs. Obviously, like medieval Europe, early medieval India also found barter system more convenient.

The formation of regional cultural units such as Andhra, Assam, Bengal, Gujarat, Karnataka, Kerala, Maharashtra, Orissa, Rajasthan, Tamil Nadu, etc. started from sixth-seventh centuries. Faint beginnings of regional and cultural personality-consciousness are found in other parts of the country also. Bengal was divided into two main units, Gauḍa and Vaṅga, and later the whole region was named after Vaṅga. Yuan Chwang mentions several nationalities. According to R. S. Sharma, the *Mudrārākshasa* of Viśākhadatta speaks of the different regions whose inhabitants differed in customs, clothing and language while the *Kuvalayamālā* (eighth century) notes the existence of 18 major nationalities and describes the anthropological character of 16 peoples, pointing out their psychological features and citing the samples of their languages. Thus, this period seems to have been a watershed in the ethnic history of India.[12]

[11] Idem, 'The Myth of the Golden Bird : An Investigation into the Belief of Material Opulence of Ancient and Early Medieval India in the Light of Her Gold Coinage', his Presidential Address delivered to the 90th Annual Conference of the Numismatic Society of India at Santiniketan on December 1-3, 2006, *JNSI*, Vol. LXIX, Pts. i and ii, 2007, p. 21.

[12] R. S. Sharma, in *IHR*, March 1974, Vol. I, Pt. i, pp. 7-8. Also see his *Perspectives in Social and Economic History of Early India*, pp. 228 ff.

IMPACT OF REGIONALISM AND OTHER MEDIEVAL TRENDS ON LITERATURE AND LANGUAGES

One of the notable developments in early medieval Europe was the growth of regional languages. It was in a way the linguistic aspect of the regionalization of culture and it ultimately led to the emergence of nation states there. A similar tendency manifested itself in early medieval India. In the classical age Sanskrit occupied the position of the *lingua franca* of the country. It enjoyed this position in the post-classical centuries also, though its scope and popularity gradually narrowed down. This phenomenon is comparable to the decline of Latin in early medieval Europe. In India in the early medieval age Sanskrit literature lost touch with the common man and became, by and large, imitative, insipid, artificial, and unnatural. The ornate style in prose and poetry became widely prevalent and strings of adjectives, adverbs and similes are found not only in literary works but also in inscriptions from about the sixth-seventh centuries. The prose style of Bāṇa became a model for the medieval period.

The vacuum created by the decline of Sanskrit in India and of Latin in Europe was filled up by the gradually emerging regional languages. According to S. K. Chatterji, between c. 500 to 900 A.D. the Prakrit languages gradually changed into various Apabhraṁśas and between c. 900 and 1300 A.D. they gradually turned into modern varnaculars or bhāshās of different regions—proto-Hindi, proto-Bengali, proto-Assamese, proto-Gujarati, proto-Marathi, etc. Although it is difficult to fix the beginnings of regional languages, on the basis of the Vajrayāna Buddhist religious writings from eastern India, proto-Bengali, proto-Assamese, proto-Oriya, proto-Maithili and proto-Hindi can be traced back to the seventh century. Similarly, on the basis of Jaina religious Prakrit works proto-Gujarati and proto-Rajasthani are traced back to the same period.[13] The pace of linguistic variation quickened in the country from the sixth-seventh centuries mainly on account of lack of inter-regional communication mobility. Contacts were mainly confined to the march of soldiers and migration of monks and Brāhmaṇas from northern India into the peripheral areas for enjoying land grants.[14]

The local element in languages was strengthened by the insulation of various regions. "On the break-up of the Gupta empire arose several feudal principalities which, in the context of the vast sub-continent, were confined to narrow territorial limits. This naturally hindered countrywide communications. Between the sixth and tenth centuries lack of communication between

[13] *Ibid.*, p. 7.
[14] *Ibid.*

different regions is also indicated by the decline of both internal and foreign trade, which is shown by the striking paucity of coins in this period. It is therefore evident that too many principalities, little trade, and less inter-zonal communication created congenial conditions for the origin and formation of regional languages from the sixth-seventh centuries."[15]

With the regional languages also developed regional scripts out of the parent script of Brāhmī which had so far admitted only regional variations in style. But from the seventh century regional variations became so marked that one has to learn several scripts to be able to read inscriptions of the different regions of the period. Obviously, the regional scripts came into existence due to regional insulation and the availability of the locally educated scribes to meet the needs of local education and administration. There was no central political authority to enforce a common script throughout the country.[16] This not only threatened to compartmentalize the literary and intellectual life of the country but also tended to divide it into small linguistic nationalities, as was happening in the contemporary Europe. Though, because of various other factors, in India separate nationalities did not develop with the same intensity as they did in Europe, yet they certainly hampered the growth of overall unity and the process of centralization in the post-classical period. Viewed in this light, the political confusion created by the warring states assumes a new significance and becomes the manifestation of the tendency of regionalization in political life.[17]

MEDIEVAL TRENDS IN ART

The growing tendency of regionalism reacted on other aspects of culture also, specially art.[18] For about a thousand years, roughly from about the third century B.C. to the seventh century A.D., Indian art admits, despite local variations due to local testes, of a common denominator at each different stage of its evolution. But towards the end of the seventh century A.D. regional spirit began to assert itself. For example, the *Nāgara* style of temple architecture, prevalent roughly in the region between the Himalayas and the Vindhyas, developed regional variations. Such variations were caused by local conditions, different directions in development as well as assimilation of extraneous trends whenever these made themselves felt.

[15] *Ibid.*, p. 8.

[16] *Ibid.*

[17] For a study of the rise of regionalism in early medieval period also see Romila Thapar, *op. cit.*, pp. 221-40.

[18] For details see Shankar Goyal, 'Transition from Gupta Classicism to Medievalism in Indian Art', in *Indian Art of the Gupta Age*, eds. S.R. Goyal and Shankar Goyal, Jodhpur, 2000, pp. 208-21.

In the realm of sculpture and painting the post-Gupta centuries witnessed the emergence of a distinct 'medieval' trend with many regional variations. Plasticity of the fully rounded and modelled form had been the most significant characteristic of classical Indian sculpture and painting both. But now movement started towards summarizing the rounded volume in the direction of flat surface and linear angles.[19] Being essentially three dimensional, sculpture resisted for long the intrusion of this medieval trend while painting, which is essentially two dimensional, offered much less resistance. According to N.R. Ray, this medieval element was the accumulated result of a continuous ethnic fusion of northern racial elements that poured into the plains of north India from central Asia in the centuries preceding and following the fall of the Gupta empire.[20]

Art in the Gupta period (c. 320-550 A.D.), when feudal tendencies had just begun to appear, reflected the vitality and zest of revived Brāhmaṇism which was associated with the emerging socio- economic structure and supported by the rising class of patrons. In the fourth-fifth centuries Vātsyāyana made *nāgarakas* (and not *sāmantas*) the centre of his *Kāmasūtra*. But in the sixth-seventh centuries "the arts patronized by the rich (both the old commercial class and the new feudal lords) reflect aristocratic tastes in their embellishment and in the dignified countenance and elaborate coiffures of both male and female figures. The aristocratic lovers of Badami, Ajanta, Ellora, Deograh, Nachna, etc., indulging in *madhupāna* (drinking of wine) or enjoying music and dance, attended by women with *chauris* or wine-jars, certainly betray the feudal outlook of the age."[21] Commenting on the art of Ajanta Coomaraswamy observed that "despite its invariably religious subject-matter, this is an art of "great courts charming the mind by their noble routine"; adorned with *alaṁkāras* and well-acquainted with *bhāva-bheda*. The *Harṣacarita*, *Kādambarī*, and the works of Kālidāsa and other classic Sanskrit dramatists, and the later Ajaṇṭā paintings all reflect the same phase of luxurious aristocratic culture."[22]

NEW TRENDS IN RELIGIOUS LIFE

The post-classical Indian society was greatly disturbed by the new religious thought-currents also. In this period, as in the classical age itself, Indian rulers generally followed the policy of religious toleration and did not confine

[19] N. R. Ray, *loc. cit.*

[20] *Ibid.*

[21] Devangana Desai, 'Art under Feudalism in India (c. A.D. 500-1300)', *IHR*, March 1974, Vol. I, Pt. i, p. 13.

[22] A.K. Coomaraswamy, *History of Indian and Indonesian Art*, Delhi, 1972, p. 90 and fn.

their partronage to any one particular religion or sect. In the social sphere, the spirit of toleration manifested itself in the spirit of accomodation usually shown by the members of the various sects towards each other, and in the worship of syncretic deities emphasizing the union or identity of the deities of two or more sects. But below the surface one may notice dissensions among various cults which were actually religious manifestions of the socio-economic conflicts of the time.

In the post-classical period the majority of the people of India apparently followed various sects and cults of Paurāṇika Hinduism. The study of the Vedas and Vedic religion were still popular and orthodox Hindus loved to trace all their sects to the ultimate authority of the Vedas, but the cult of sarcrifice existed only as a casual accompaniment of the Paurāṇika Hinduism. The influence of Jainism was restricted in certain areas, specially Rajasthan and Gujarat, while Buddhism, which was declining very fast, almost totally disappeared from the Indian scene by the close of the twelfth century.

The Paurāṇika Hinduism itself was divided into a number of cults and sects. Among them were included Śaivism, Vaishṇavism and Śāktism, not to mention a large number of minor sects and sub-sects centring round the worship of gods like Sūrya, Gaṇeśa, Kārittikeya, Brahmā, etc. Of these probably Śaivism was the most popular one specially among the ruling aristocracy. It had become divided into several branches—Śaiva, Pāśupata, Kāpālika, Kālāmukha, Kaula and many others. Many of these sects became monastic in character. The chief feature of Vaishṇavism of this period was the worship of the *avatāras* (incarnations) of Vishṇu, specially Kṛshṇa, Rāma and Ādivarāha. Śakti or Devī was worshipped under various names—Durgā, Kālī, Chaṇḍī, Bhairavī, etc.

The popular or conventional form of the Hindu sects was characterized by the worship of numerous deities in temples built by kings, *sāmantas* and rich people. They were endowed with grants of land, tolls and taxes. Temple and monastery-building activities, which acquired momentum in the later Gupta age, reached their climax during the eleventh and twelfth centuries. Great temples and monasteries of this period, as noted above, possessed large estates and enormous wealth, with the result that the priestly class, as in medieval Europe, acquired a mighty hold over the people. Even the Jaina priestly class appears to have been organised on quasi-feudal lines.

The wealth and power made the priests of the period greedy and lover of luxury. This psychology was in perfect consonance with and to a great degree the cause of craze for the sensual indulgence which dominated the literature and art of the period. The ritualistic aspect of the Smārta-

Paurāṇika religion, i.e., *pūjā* and *vidhis* was influenced by the Tāntrika elements such as *maṇḍalas, yantras* and *nyāsas.* These Tāntrika elements soon became popular through the patronage accorded by the newly emerging feudal class. As shown by S. R. Goyal, from about the fifth century Tāntrikism underwent changes in its esoteric and *aghorī* (terrible)practices.[23] The Gangadhar inscription of the first quarter of the fifth century A.D. refers to *tantra* and *ḍākinīs.* There was a general belief that the Tāntrikas had knowledge of *rasāyana* (alchemy) and *vājīkaraṇa* (aphrodisiacs) and had gained mastery over magical lore—*shaṭkarma, vaśīkaraṇa, stambhana,* etc. These *siddhis* (achievements) of Tāntrika *āchāryas* were considered useful by kings and feudal chiefs in serving their two dominant interests—war and sex. Hence, the liberal patronage of the Tāntrika *āchāryas* by the new feudal class.[24] In the fifth-seventh centuries many Brāhmaṇas recieved lands in Nepal, Assam, Bengal, Orissa, central India and the Deccan, where Tāntrika texts, shrines and practices appeared about this time. Tāntrikism permeated Jainism, Buddhism, Śaivism and Vaishṇavism, and from the seventh century onwards continued to hold ground throughout the medieval period.

GROWING RIGIDITY OF THE SOCIAL ORDER

The early Indian social organisation was based on the theory of the *chāturvarṇya* which was later on rendered complicated by the emergence of the caste system with further division of labour, functional specialization and social fragmentation. A significant development from about the seventh century A.D. onwards was the proliferation of castes. The *Brahmavaivarta Purāṇa* (Brahmakhaṇḍa, X. 14-136), usually assigned to the seventh century, counts 100 castes including 61 castes noted by Manu, but the *Vishṇudharmottara Purāṇa* (II, 81-2) (c. eighth century) says that thousands of mixed castes are produced by the connection of Vaiśya women with men of lower castes. "In fact, proliferation affected the brāhmaṇas, the Rajputs, and above all the śūdras and untouchables. Increasing pride of birth, characteristic of feudal society, and the accompanying self-sufficient village economy, which prevents both spatial and occupational mobility, gave rise to many castes. The guilds of artisans, which appear in inscriptions from the first century A.D., were gradually hardened into castes for lack of mobility in post-Gupta times. The absorption of the tribal peoples into the brāhmaṇical fold, though as old as Vedic times, was mainly based on conquests. Coupled with the process of large-scale religious land grants, acculturation assumed

[23] S. R. Goyal, *A Religious History of Ancient India*, Vol. 1, Meerut, 1984, pp. 337 ff.; idem, *op. cit.*, Vol. 2, Meerut, 1986, pp. 389 ff.; idem, *Paurāṇika Sects and Cults*, Jodhpur, 2016, Ch. 14.

[24] Devangana Desai, *op. cit.*, p. 12.

enormous dimensions and considerably added to the varieties of the śūdras and so-called mixed castes."[25]

The classical exposition of the caste system is found in the early Smṛti literature which was the Indian counterpart of the Roman law and jurisprudence of Europe. In the post-classical age, however, several factors threatened the very existence of this order. Among them are included political and social confusion created by the fall of the Gupta empire, the pressure exerted by the growing number of foreigners in the Indian society which changed the population texture of the country very fast, specially of the north-western and western regions, and the rise of Tāntrika and other heterodox sects whose attitude was against the very idea of caste organisation. All these factors threatened the traditional social organisation of the country and generated a sense of increasing chaos and decline. In almost similar circumstances in the early medieval Europe, the Church, organised during the later Roman empire, became a bulwork against social chaos. In India, the crisis was faced by making the traditional caste system more rigid with some modifications to meet the new situation. That is why from the sixth century onwards we find that the efforts at the regulation and enforcement of the *chāturvarṇya* accelarated and continued to be so throughout the early medieval period. The inscriptions of the Maukharis and Pushyabhūtis refer to the efforts made by their kings for the proper regulation of the varṇa system. The tightening of the caste rules in the commentaries, digests and the late Purāṇas and the increasing efforts at their enforcement by the rulers of the early medieval period, represent respectively the theoretical and practical aspects of these efforts. The contracting economy of the period with its emphasized agrarian and local character contributed a good deal to this process.

IMPACT OF FEUDALISM AND OTHER DEVELOPMENTS ON CASTE SYSTEM

The emergence of the *sāmanta* hierarchy had a peculiar relationship with the growing rigidity of the caste system. On the one hand it helped in the growing rigidity of the caste system, for in their small principalities petty feudal chiefs found it desirable to enforce the rules of caste rigorously with a view to maintaining the local agrarian set up. The insecurity caused by constant feudal wars also tended to strengthen localism and hereditariness of caste functions. On the other hand, however, feudalism tended to come into conflict with caste system by increasing the process of social mobility. As Sorokin has pointed out, social mobility makes the social structure elastic and breaks caste and class isolation. Also, by creating a new class of feudal

[25] R. S. Sharma, *op. cit.*, p. 6.

barons drawn from all the sections of society, who were gradually accepted within the Kshatriya fold, feudalism posed a new problem for the supporters of rigid caste system. The terms *Brahma-kshatra* and *Vaiśya-kshatra* applied to some ruling dynasties of this period shows that there were some Brāhmaṇas and Vaiśyas who discarded their caste professions for martial pursuits. Though Harsha has not been called a *Vaiśya-kshatra*, yet theoretically he belonged to this category. Yuan Chwang noted that ruling dynasties of the period belonged to all the four varṇas. This tendency ran in direction just opposite to the tendency of the growth in the rigidity of the traditional caste system.

As a matter of fact, the social theorists of the early medieval period had to come to terms with the changing realities not only by making the caste system more rigid, but by giving it a new orientation. This they did by modifying the scheme of the privileges and duties of various castes. For example, with a view to regularizing the fact that a large number of Brāhmaṇas were agriculturists, the social theorists of the period recommended agriculture for the Brāhmaṇas in addition to their six-fold duties. Similarly, the fact that now the Śūdras were forced to work on the fields of their local feudal lords, was also regularized by giving them (the Śūdras) the right to cultivate soil in order to serve the upper castes. That is why we notice a pronounced tendency to lump together the Vaiśyas (small land-owner farmers) and Śūdras in the literature of this period. It seems that in the older settled Brāhmaṇical areas the Vaiśyas lost a good deal of their land rights to the feudal lords. On the other hand, the Śūdras, who were landless labourers, were granted some land and rose in social status. Further, the decline of trade and towns diverted both Śūdra artisans and Vaiśya merchants to cultivation. In this manner the Vaiśyas and Śūdras approximated to each other.[26] This modified Brāhmaṇical order spread from Madhyadeśa into Bengal and south India as a result of land grants to the Brāhmaṇas, many of them migrating from the north from the fifth-sixth centuries. Although the Rajputs emerged as a significant factor in the politics and society of northern India from the seventh century, in Bengal and peninsular India their place seems to have been taken by the landed Brāhmaṇas. In the older inhabited areas the traditional, theoretical fourfold varṇa system did not fit in with the new feudal and social ranks created by unequal distribution of land and military power. From the sixth century attempts began to square up feudal ranks with ritual ranks. The earlier texts regulate the economic life of the people on the basis of their varṇas. But the *Bṛhatsaṁhitā* of Varāhamihira, a work of the sixth century, prescribes varying sizes of houses not only in the varṇa order but also according to the

[26] *Ibid.*, pp. 5-6.

grading of ruling chiefs. This tendency becomes marked in later times in several medieval texts on architecture.[27]

DECLINE OF CITIES AND CHANGING PATTERN OF URBAN AND RURAL LIFE

The foreign invasions, rise and growth of feudalism and regionalization of economy influenced the life of the people both in the cities and villages. In the classical age the growth of industries, finance and internal and external trade contacts had given a great impetus to the development and refinement of urban life, and cities like Pāṭaliputra and Ujjain acquired cosmopolitan or international character. In such cities people belonging to different 'countries' (janapadas), races and religions, wearing strange foreign garbs, and speaking different Indian and alien languages could be easily seen giving rise to what may be called 'universalization of culture'. However, in the centuries immediately following the fall of the Gupta empire, many of the metropolitan and other great cities of north India considerably declined; many of them such as Kanauj were actually sacked several times respectively either by the indigenous enemies or the Tibetans and later on, Muslim invaders. Now their place was taken up by the provincial centres which became the administrative posts of the local feudal chiefs. This tendency is comparable with the decline of urban life in Europe of the same period and in both the regions it led to parochialization of culture. According to R. S. Sharma, "the towns which were active centres of crafts and commerce in the Sātavāhana dominions began to decay from the fourth century A.D. The post-Gupta period proved to be the graveyard of many old commercial cities in northern India. Excavations show that Vaiśālī, Śrāvastī, Hastināpura, Mathurā, Purana Qila (Delhi), and several sites in Haryana and east Punjab, which generally thrived in the Kuṣāṇa age, began to decline from the Gupta period and mostly disappeared in post-Gupta times. Evidently on account of the decline of Indian exports, artisans and merchants living in these towns flocked to the countryside and took to cultivation. The decay and disappearance of urban centres created conditions for the rise of self-sufficient regional productive units, which were prepetuated by the political fragmentation of the country and by restrictions imposed on the movement of artisans and peasants."[28]

[27] *Ibid.*, p. 6.

[28] *Ibid.*, p. 5. For the theory of urban decay in the Gupta and post-Gupta ages see R.S. Sharma, 'Decay of Gangetic Towns in Gupta Times', *PIHC*, 33rd Session, Muzaffarpur, 1972, pp. 92-104; B.D. Chattopadhyaya, 'Trade and Urban Centres in Early Medieval North India', in *IHR*, September 1974, Vol. I, No. 2, pp. 203-19; V.K. Thakur, *Urbanisation in Ancient India*, New Delhi, 1981, pp. 261-91. Vide also R. S. Sharma's *Urban Decay in India* (*c. 300-1000 A.D.*), New Delhi, 1987 and *Early Medieval Indian Society*, Kolkata, 2001.

The system of town-planning and prosperity of the medieval Indian cities are found described in details in the contemporary literature. It must, however, be remembered that much of this literary material is conventional, though some idea of the wealth, prosperity and administrative set up of these cities may be obtained from the combined testimony of inscriptions and later Muslim accounts.

Some material is also available for the reconstruction of the rural life of early medieval India. The villages of this period, as of any other period of Indian history were small. Some of them were caste villages while others had a mixed population. Sometimes they were organised into groups for administrative purposes. Most of the villagers lived in humble dwellings and harrowing poverty. Their misery increased during the times of famine, flood and draught or when an army passed through their village or when their immediate lord chose to be inconsiderate or their local officers became oppressive which was quite often the case. The village chiefs had the tendency of becoming local feudal lords. Village autonomy considerably declined. The villagers of the early medieval period, more often than not, passed their lives groaning under the weight of poverty, feudal conditions and maladministration.

AMBIVALENCE IN MORALS AND GENERAL ATTITUDE TOWARDS LIFE

The interaction of the new religious ideas and the chaotic conditions created by the feudal pattern of political life wrought havoc with the morals of the people. India was traditionally the land of religion and morality, of yoga and upāsanā. It was still so when the classical age came to a close and the famous medieval bhakti movement, intensely moral in character, started gaining strength in the South. But for some time the interplay of the Tāntrika tendencies and feudal culture created an entirely different atmosphere. According to Bāṇa, Pushyabhūti, the founder of Harsha's dynasty, was greatly influenced by a Tāntrika Śaiva from the South. He also describes the

---

However, here it may be remarked that in ancient period new towns and their buildings were constructed with the help of the debris of the older materials. Therefore, it will be hazardous to postulate a decline of urban centres on the basis of archaeological evidence alone. Further, the literary data throws ample light on the urban centres of the Gupta age. And, lastly, the existence of urban centres in early medieval period is not in consonance with the theory of the urban decay in the Gupta age. Vide also Lallanji Gopal, 'Economic Decline in the Golden Age ?', in B. Ch. Chhabra et al, *Reappraising Gupta History for S.R. Goyal*, New Delhi, 1992, pp. 334-41; M.K. Dhavalikar, 'The Golden Age and After: Perspectives in Historical Archaeology', Presidential Address delivered to the Diamond Jubilee Session of the Indian History Congress, Calicut, 1999.

popularity of the Tāntrikas in the court of Prabhākaravardhana.[29]

Many of the new esoteric religious sects reacted against the philosophy of extreme abnegation and austerity and permitted a free rein to the sensual desires of man by enjoyment of meat, drink and damsels. Similarly, feudalism also encouraged love of luxury and sensualism. The perpetually changing kaleidoscope of alliances and struggles among feudal lords, which generated a sense of instability and fickleness, intensified the urge to drink the pleasures of life all at once to the last dreg. As a result of this thinking every standard of modesty and moderation, all the values of decency and refinement were by-passed. That is why we find that in contrast to the classical age, in which kings boasted of their moral decency in literary works, in medieval period kings and barons were immersed in gross sensual excesses and, what is more baffling, they were proud of it ! According to Arnold Hauser, in Europe the courtly culture of the Middle Ages was distinguished by its markedly feminine character. "There is hardly an epoch of Western history," he observes, "whose literature so revels in the description of the beauty of the nacked body, of dressing and undressing, bathing and washing of the heroes by girls and women, of wedding nights and copulations, of visits to and invitations into bed, as does the chivalric poetry of the rigidly moral Middle Ages. Even such a serious work, and one written with such a high purpose, as Wolfram's *Parzival*, is full of descriptions that border upon the obscene. The whole age lives in a state of constant erotic tension."[30] This description applies to Indian society in the age under review. Here also troupes of danceuses, musicians, bards, poets and dwarfs amused the kings, feudatories, officials, chiefs, and sycophants of the royal courts. Bāṇa's description of the birth celebration of Harsha is the typical early example of this atmosphere.[31]

Thus, we observe that most features of the medieval society—feudal political structure, reversion to closed economy, regionalism in languages, art, script etc., proliferation of castes, rigidity in social organisation, ornamentation, emphasis on systematization and lack of originality in literature, adoption of vainglorious titles by kings and feudal lords, growth of the popularity of Tāntrikism, ambivalence in morals, etc. which developed in medieval times may be traced back to the sixth-seventh centuries. R. S. Sharma, therefore, hits on the nail when he concludes that "in these two centuries ancient India was coming to an end, and medieval India was taking shape."[32]

[29] *The Harṣa-carita of Bāṇa*, trans. by E.B. Cowell and F.W. Thomas, Delhi, 1968, pp. 135-36.

[30] Arnold Hauser, *The Social History of Art*, I, p. 220.

[31] *HC*, tr. E.B. Cowell and F.W. Thomas, pp. 111-15.

[32] R. S. Sharma, *op. cit.*, p. 9.

PAURĀṆIKA PORTRAYAL OF THE KALI AGE CRISIS

In recent decades some scholars have tried to show that the Paurāṇika description of the decadence in the Kali Age portrays the transition of Indian society from pre-feudal age of antiquity to the feudal age of the Middle Ages. The Indian idea of Kali Age decadence may easily be equated with that of the decadence which seems to have prevailed in the late classical Europe. The theme of the Kali Age was first touched by R. S. Sharma in his *Śūdras in Ancient India* (Delhi, 1958). It was further discussed by him in 1982 in his article 'The Kali Age : A Period of Social Crisis'[33] in which he highlighted the main features of the Kali Age in the texts assignable to third-fourth centuries A.D. and concluded that "seen in its totality the Kali crisis of the late third and fourth centuries appears as a prelude to the feudalization of Indian society."[34] Meanwhile, B.N.S. Yadava provided a detailed analysis of the concept of the Kali Age to explain the transition from the antiquity to the Middle Ages on the basis of the later Paurāṇika accounts which embody in the ideological garb of prediction "the cognition by the contemporaries or near-contemporaries of the forces and tendencies that were setting off towards the Middle Ages."[35] From all this it has been rightly deduced that the concept of the Kali Age may be profitably utilised to explain the transition from ancient to medieval Indian society.[36] However, more recently there has been an attempt to analyse these changes from a different perspective and some scholars have suggested what they call an integrative polity, rather than a fedual society. In this context it is argued that the formation of states after the Gupta age was itself a different process from the earlier one and, therefore, created a different kind of economy and society. How it is to be interpreted and labelled still remains a matter of debate.[37]

[33] In S. N. Mukherjee (ed.), *India : History and Thought*, Calcutta, 1982, pp. 186-203; also reprinted in D. N. Jha (ed.), *Feudal Social Formation*, pp. 45-64 and *The Feudal Order*, New Delhi, 2002, pp. 61-77; also see R. S. Sharma's *Early Medieval Indian Society*, pp. 45-76.

[34] In D. N. Jha (ed.), *Feudal Social Formation*, p. 60.

[35] B.N.S. Yadava, *op. cit.*, p. 65; also reprinted in D. N. Jha (ed.), *The Feudal Order*, pp. 79-120.

[36] Shankar Goyal, *Probings in Indian History*, Jodhpur, 2009, Ch. 14.

[37] For some relevant discussions also see V.K. Thakur, *Historiography of Indian Feudalism Towards a Model of Early Medieval Indian Economy*, Patna, 1989, pp. 38-40; B.D. Chattopadhyaya, *The Making of Early Medieval India*, New Delhi, 1997, pp. 1-37; R. Champakalakshmi, *Trade, Ideology and Urbanization : South India 300 BC to AD 1300*, New Delhi, 1999, pp. 11-12, 17; Romila Thapar, *The Penguin History of Early India*, pp. 442-48; M.V. Singh, *India Rediscovered : A New Vision of History and Call of the Age*, New Delhi, 2006, Chs. X-XII.

EIGHT

The Age of Harsha and the Further Growth of Feudalism

CURRENT VIEW OF POLITICAL HISTORY

Since the days of Herodotus who in his *Histories* dealt with the theme of Graeco-Persian wars, and Aristotle, who declared that man by nature is a political animal, to the age of Sir John Seeley who defined history as 'past politics', it has been generally assumed that the primary subject-matter of history is politics. But now it appears that political history has lost its popularity and economic, social and cultural history have captured the imagination of historians. Nowadays Seeley's dictum is seldom quoted save to be ridiculed. In the last few decades many noted scholars, such as E. G. Goff,[1] Benjamin Schwartz,[2] Gordon Craig,[3] S. T. Bindoff,[4] and many more, have lamented the decline of political history in the Western world and have tried to analyse its causes with a view to suggesting ways and means for its regeneration, if at all desirable. But in India only a few attempts have been made to study this problem.[5] Most Indian historians working on political

[1] E.G. Goff, 'Is Politics Still the Backbone of History ?', *Daedalus*, Cambridge, Mass., Winter 1971, pp. 1-19.

[2] Benjamin Schwartz, 'A Brief Defence of Political and Intellectual History with Particular Reference to Non-Western Cultures', *ibid.*, pp. 98-112.

[3] Gordon Craig, 'Political History', *ibid.*, Spring 1971, pp. 323-38.

[4] S.T. Bindoff, 'Political History', in *Approaches to History*, ed. H.P.R. Finberg, London, 1962, pp. 1 ff.

[5] See in particular S. Gopal and Romila Thapar, eds., *Problems of Historical Writing in India*, New Delhi, 1963; S. R. Goyal, 'Political History : A Reconsideration', in *Jijñāsā*, A Journal of the History of Ideas and Culture, Jaipur, Volume 2, Number 2, April 1975, pp. 9-26; idem, his lead-paper 'Need of a New Approach to the Writing of Political History of Ancient India', in *Political History in a Changing World*, eds. G.C. Pande, S. K. Gupta and Shankar Goyal, Jodhpur, 1992, pp. 3-17 and reaction-papers on it by 53 eminent historians of India and other countries published therein, pp.19-370.

history are still living in the age of D. R. Bhandarkar, K. P. Jayaswal and R. K. Mookerji, while their discipline has gradually lost its appeal.

The most damaging criticism levelled against the current form of political history in the West is that it is elitist in content, that it lays too much emphasis on kings and heroes, and that it pays too much attention to political events, military conquests and chronology. In the Western world this problem is being solved by transforming the very concept of political history. Now Western political historians do not look upon political history as only a record of the deeds and dates of kings; rather they, by and large, seem to agree with the view that political history is the study of the political aspect of social life. The dictum of Jacques Pirenne[6] that "the true aim of historical research is a knowledge of the factors that control men living in society", will perhaps be acceptable, at least on a tentative basis, to the majority of present-day Western scholars for their investigations. This definition implies that different aspects of history cannot be studied in isolation from one another but only as facets of an integrated reality, and that the focal point of history is not an individual, however great he may be, but society. If this view is correct, political history can be regarded neither as a mere chronicle of events nor only as an account of kings and emperors who strut about the stage trying to attract the attention of the audience. It is basically the study of the political aspect of social life—the study of political activity in its situational context, of the functioning of the centres of political authority with a view to discovering the motivations of political life and recognizing that components of political power have social, economic and religious bases. In brief, it is a study of factors influencing and determining political life, events and developments. Benjamin Schwartz[7] has this kind of integral political history in mind when he argues that a political historian must welcome all the aid which sociologists, economists, demographers, anthropologists and others can provide to help him to understand the situation in which political action takes place.

Thus political history in the West is shifting its focal point from kings to society and making the notion of power and the institutions connected with it its central theme. It is against this background that I am making an effort to delineate and expound this new concept of political history with reference to Harsha and his age in order to show how the decline in the popularity of political history in India may also be arrested and this discipline can be made more relevant with the present-day realities.[8]

[6] Jacques Pirenne, *The Tides of History*, quoted in *Problems of Historical Writing in India*, p. 56; cf. S.R. Goyal, *op.cit.*, p. 8.

[7] Benjamin Schwartz, *op.cit.*, p. 100.

[8] Since the middle of the nineteenth century Harsha has attracted the attention of modern scholars and has been the subject of numerous monographs and hundreds of

HARSHA : A NEW POLITICAL BIOGRAPHY

Among the foremost literary sources of the age of Harsha are included the *Harshacharita* (The Story of Harsha) by Bāṇabhaṭṭa,[9] the *Si-Yü-Ki* or an account of the travels of Yuan Chwang in India, the biography of Yuan Chwang composed by Hui-li, other Chinese official and private writings and the three plays which attribute themselves to Harsha. Among other source materials are included coins of Harsha himself and those of his father Prabhākaravardhana and of the Maukharis whom he replaced in Kanauj, epigraphic material mainly in the form of copper land grants and *praśastis*, i.e. laudatory records of the achievements of contemporary kings and some important socio-political and secular texts. Bāṇa is certainly one of the most celebrated scholars of the age of Harsha : his work is seen not as a source for historical data, but instead as a civilization's many ways of thinking about and writing its history.[10] He is refreshing, realistic and bold in his approach. He transforms the goddess Lakshmī into an untouchable, ridicules the sanctity of royalty and brings to life princes and vagabonds, soldiers and hermits, horses and talking birds. With equal ease he transports the reader into the luxurious city of Ujjayinī or into a forest settlement in the Vindhyas. He is an expert in the art of camouflage through endless punning and metaphor as well as in making the hard and unpleasant truth visible through a barrage of compliments—something a modern historian must remember while using the testimony of his works. Understanding his motivation in writing the biography of Harsha is a difficult preposition.[11] His relationship with Harsha is intriguing in nature, for he himself reports that he was not liked by Harsha and yet claims that in no time both began to like each other immensely. However, he does not disclose the

---

research papers. But they hardly discuss political events of the age of Harsha in the context of socio-economic and cultural changes and do not make any effort to correlate political and dynastic changes with socio-economic and cultural realities. Among the more important publications on Harsha in the last three decades or so are included D. Devahuti, *Harsha : A Political Study*, 2nd edn., New Delhi, 1983 and S. R. Goyal, *Harsha Śīlāditya*, Meerut, 1986; also see my works *Harsha : A Multidisciplinary Political Study*, Jodhpur, 2006 and *The 'Medieval' Factor and the Age of Harsha : A Cultural Study*, Jodhpur, 2016.

[9] One view dates it to c. 620, which is now generally accepted, although others have argued for a slightly later date.

[10] Romila Thapar, *The Past Before Us : Historical Traditions of Early North India*, New Delhi, 2013, pp. 471-96.

[11] For details, see Shankar Goyal, '*Harshacharita* as a Source of History' in the *Papers from the Aligarh Historians Society*, ed. Irfan Habib, 69th Session of the Indian History Congress, Kannur University, Kannur, 28-30 December, 2008, pp. 122-52.

reason of this change. According to S.R. Goyal,[12] he obtained the favour of Harsha by agreeing to write the *Harshacharita* in which he tried to absolve Harsha of the charge of having some hand in the assassination of his own elder brother Rājyavardhana about which rumours were afloat in society. Another important source for the history of Harsha, it is believed, are the plays *Ratnāvalī, Priyadarśikā* and *Nāgānanda* which are said to have been authored by Harsha himself. But there may also be some truth in the ancient rumours that Bāṇa was the actual author of the three plays which were ascribed by him to Harsha for monetary consideration.[13]

Among the Chinese sources for the age of Harsha are included the travel account of Yuan Chwang, the *Life* of Yuan Chwang by Hui-li and some other works based on the material provided by Yuan Chwang. Yuan Chwang's account is regarded as trustworthy because it is from the pen of an impartial foreigner. But Yuan Chwang was highly partial to Buddhism and intensely jealous of his country's cultural greatness. Further, in his account he constantly reveals his own superstitious nature and egotism. Everywhere in his description of India he reveals his superstitious nature which sometimes affects his credibility, and depicts himself as towering head and shoulders above everybody else. Even great kings, including Harsha, cut a sorry, almost pitiable figure in his presence. He depicts Harsha as a great Buddhist ruler, almost as great as Aśoka. But this view has been challenged, and in my view quite rightly.[14] There is no doubt that Harsha remained a Śaiva throughout his life, though, like other Indian kings of the period, he also showed great respect to religions other than his own, including Buddhism. However, Yuan Chwang took the conventional respect shown to Buddhism by Indian rulers, including Harsha, as indicative of their unflinching faith in Buddhism, for one showing respect for a religion different than his own was a phenomenon unknown to him. Here we should also not forget that there are inner contradictions in the Chinese sources as well. For example, the accounts of the Kanauj assembly as given in the *Si-Yü-Ki* and

[12] S. R. Goyal, *Harsha Śīlāditya*, p. 7; idem, *Harsha and Buddhism*, Meerut, 1986, pp. 108-10. R.C. Majumdar (*The History of Bengal*, Volume I : *The Hindu Period*, Dacca, 1943, pp. 76-77) was the first scholar to indicate towards the possibility of Harsha's indirect link with the conspiracy culminating in the assassination of Rājyavardhana by Gauḍādhipa. However, V.S. Pathak's exposition (*Ancient Historians of India*, Bombay, 1966, pp. 45 ff.) of the *Harshacharita* provided a logical support to such a possibility.

[13] Shankar Goyal, 'The Authenticity of the Plays of Harsha', in the *Proceedings of the Indian History Congress*, 69th Session, Kannur, 2008 (Kolkata, 2009), pp. 86-93.

[14] See my paper, 'Religious Analysis of Harsha's Personality', in the *Proceedings of the Indian History Congress*, 68th Session, Delhi, 2007 (Delhi, 2008), pp. 136-48.

Life radically differ from each other.

The rise of the dynasty of Harsha against the background of the twilight of Gupta imperialism and political traditions giving emphasis on the factors that influenced the history of all the major dynasties of this period is a matter of great concern. The major external causes of the decline and fall of the imperial Gupta dynasty were undoubtedly the onslaughts of the Aulikaras of Mandasor and the Hūṇas, but the main internal factors were the rise and growth of feudalism and the impact of the other-worldly pacifist ideology of Buddhism on the dynasty. Actually the political structure of the royal dynasties in north India which arose in the sixth century and continued to dominate the scene in the later centuries was marked by stronger feudal elements than was the case in the earlier period. It was one of the tendencies which I think became the characteristic feature of medievalism in India.

The political ideology of the early Gupta rulers was Vaishṇavite in nature.[15] It was the product of the Brāhmaṇical revival of the third-fourth century A.D. and was characterized by a rapprochement of the Vedic and devotional schools and gradual triumph of the latter. Under the early imperial Guptas the Vaishṇava school became more popular and was accorded royal patronage in the sense that whenever an opportunity or occasion arose to establish subordinate dynasties under them, the Guptas usually chose persons belonging to the Vaishṇava faith for this purpose. However, in the post-Kumāragupta I period many Gupta emperors came under the impact of Buddhism. The later imperial Guptas' dislike for non-violence and their pacifist ideology must have given, by way of reaction, stimulus to the popularity of Śaivism in the war-like royal families of the sixth century, as an under-current at least. Otherwise it would become difficult to explain as to why most kings of the Maukhari, Aulikara, Hūṇa, Gauḍa and Kāmarūpa royal houses were worshippers of Śiva and as to why the worship of Vishṇu and the Buddha shows such a marked decline among them. Even in the Pushyabhūti family not a single king is said to have been the devotee of Vishṇu. In other words, the age of the rapprochement of the Vedic and Paurāṇika schools was still continuing but with a significant difference—now the royal families are found in greater sympathy with Śaivism. It is one of the factors which is necessary to take note of while drawing a picture of the political condition on north India when the Pushyabhūti dynasty rose to power, for it had much to do also with the events of the reign of Harsha himself.

Some rulers of this period professed faith in sun worship as well

[15] Shankar Goyal, 'Political Ideology of the Early Imperial Guptas', in *Reappraising Gupta History for S. R. Goyal*, eds. B. Ch. Chhabra, P. K. Agrawala, Ashvini Agrawal and Shankar Goyal, New Delhi, 1992, pp. 215-23.

(just as Prabhākaravardhana and his two immediate predecessors did) or in some other Brāhmaṇical deity, but their number seems to have been limited. As regards Buddhism, it was patronized mainly by the Maitrakas of Valabhī and in the entire history of the Maukharis only Grahavarman and in the Pushyabhūti dynasty only Rājyavardhana II are said to have been the worshippers of the Buddha. Harsha himself was personally a Śaiva though he showed respect and liberality to Buddhism as well. In a country where religious toleration was almost a rule and devotees of different gods could be found in the same family and kings could pay respect to gods other than their own—this fact may not appear very significant. But I think that this sudden decline in the popularity of Vaishṇavism and rise in the popularity of Śaivism and solar worship etc. in the sixth-seventh centuries in the royal houses of north India demands serious consideration, specially if it is juxtaposed against the similar popularity of Vaishṇavism in the royal houses of the Gupta age.

The role of geographical factor in the history of north India in this period has also not been properly investigated. The shift of the centre of political power to Kanauj was one of the more significant features of the political history of the post-Gupta period and betrays the impact of geographical factor on political history. Actually to a modern student of Indian history a shift in the centre of political power in India from east to west should appear to be gradual but definite. It may be noted that the imperial capital of the Nandas, Mauryas and Śuṅgas was Pāṭaliputra in Bihar. Then followed the age of the invasions of the Yavanas, Śakas, Pahlavas and the Kushāṇas. When another indigenous empire arose, that is the empire of the Guptas, its heartland is found to be not in Bihar, but in eastern U.P., with Prayāga as its early capital.[16] The centre of power shifted further west, to Kanauj, in the post-Gupta age. The final push towards the west occurred in the medieval period when Delhi became the imperial capital. This history of the gradual shift of political power from the east to west makes the emergence of Kanauj as the imperial capital of the Maukharis, Pushyabhūtis and Yaśovarman look quite natural.

The nature of the court culture and religious and feudal atmosphere of the Pushyabhūti kingdom greatly influenced its subsequent history. These factors played an important role not only in shaping the character and ideals of Harsha, to some extent they also conditioned the course of political events. So far historians, mainly occupied as they have been with the reconstruction

[16] Cf. S. R. Goyal, *A History of the Imperial Guptas*, Allahabad, 1967, pp. 41 ff., 210 ff.; idem, *The Imperial Guptas : A Multidisciplinary Political Study*, Jodhpur, 2005, pp. 66-78.

of 'what' and 'when' aspects of political history, have utterly neglected to turn their attention to 'how' and 'why' aspects of political events.[17] But a study of political history from this angle, that is from the point of view of the interaction of various factors operating in society and state, throws a new and welcome light on the course of political events. For example, Harsha (and for that matter any other ruler) could not overlook the fact that his power depended mainly on the militia provided by the feudatories against whom, at least against the powerful ones of them, he could hardly take any action.In feudal polity when high dignitaries of the state were paid not in cash but in the form of land assignments, usually important posts of ministers went to feudal barons or conversely, the important feudal barons became ministers. The same phenomenon of ministers enjoying large feudal holdings and serving in the army is seen *mutatis mutandis* in the Mughal age. That is why even if a minister was basically a scholar or artist he was also a feudal lord and had to serve in the army. Yuan Chwang states that when he visited India, royal lands were divided into four principal parts one of which was meant for providing subsidies to the 'ministers' and 'chief officers' of the state.[18] In such a situation a study of the political atmosphere of the Pushyabhūti court and the role of the various factions active there becomes essential for understanding the course of early history of the dynasty.

In the region of Thanesar (Śrīkaṇṭha *janapada*) people were given to agriculture, but trade and commerce were also becoming important. Bāṇa refers to the flourishing state of agriculture in this *janapada*.[19] Yuan Chwang also says that its soil was rich and fertile and the crops were abundant.[20] But he also noted that "only a few of the inhabitants of the region were given to farming" and that "the majority pursued trade." Probably trade acquired greater importance here after Harsha's western campaigns, when the trade routes of the Arabian Sea became accessible to traders in the interior. The removal of the Hūṇa menace too must have acted favourably on the north-western inland trade with Afghanistan and Persia. But the fact that the ruling family of the region, namely the Pushyabhūtis, belonged to the Vaiśya caste of traders[21] suggests that trade and commerce were in a developed state

[17] Shankar Goyal, 'Political History : The Loss of Innocence', in *Political History in a Changing World*, eds. G. C. Pande et al, pp. 290-99.

[18] T. Watters, *On Yuan Chwang's Travels in India* (henceforth *Travels*), I, Delhi, 1961, p. 176.

[19] *The Harṣa-carita of Bāṇa* (hereafter *HC*), trans. E. B. Cowell and F.W. Thomas, Delhi, 1968, pp. 79-80.

[20] *Travels*, I, p. 314.

[21] See my article, 'Social *Milieu* of the Pushyabhūtis : Significance of Some Hitherto Unnoticed Passages of the *Harshacharita* ', in the *Proceedings of the Indian History and Culture Society*, 3-5 January, 1986, New Delhi, 1986, pp. 167-70.

quite well before the conquests of Harsha enabling the Vaiśya caste to acquire a dominant position in political life. As regards the religious beliefs of the inhabitants of Sthaṇvīśvara, Yuan Chwang, a Buddhist, regretfully notes that non-Buddhists were very numerous and that there were in the capital only three Buddhist monasteries, with over 700 professed Buddhists, all Hīnayānists, as against over 100 Hindu temples.[22] On the other hand, Bāṇa, a Brāhmaṇa, naturally expresses his great admiration for the religious atmosphere of Śrīkaṇṭha *janapada.*[23]

According to Bāṇa, the founder of the dynasty of Harsha was Pushyabhūti who, most likely, flourished in the Gupta age. He does not refer to any immediate successor of Pushyabhūti. However, Harsha's three inscriptions, Banskherea,[24] Kurukshetra-Varanasi[25] and Madhuban,[26] of the years 628, 629 and 631 A.D. respectively, and his Sonepat[27] and Nalanda seals,[28] prove that at least three generations of rulers preceded Prabhākara-vardhana, the father of Harsha. They were: Mahārāja Naravardhana, Mahārāja Rājyavardhana I and Mahārāja Ādityavardhana. Prabhākara, the father of Harsha, was born from Mahāsenaguptā, the queen of Ādityavardhana. According to Bāṇa, he was a lion to the Hūṇa deer, a burning fever to the king of Sindhu, a troubler of the sleep of Gurjaras, a bilious plague to that scent-elephant, the lord of Gandhāra, a destroyer of the lawlessness (or skill) of the Lāṭas, and an axe to the creeper of Mālava Lakshmī (i.e. Mālava fortune or sovereignty).[29] Here it would not be out of place to draw attention to the fact that according to one opinion, in the latter half of the sixth century the Pushyabhūti rulers became subordinates of the Maukhari emperors, though some scholars doubt it. But the overlordship of the Maukharis over the Pushyabhūtis may be very logically argued;[30] nay, it may even be shown that Prabhākara himself accepted their suzerainty till quite late in his life for he is said to have agreed to marry his daughter Rājyaśrī (who was at that time about twelve years old) with Grahavarman, the Maukhari emperor (whom Bāṇa describes as middle aged) obviously

[22] *Travels*, I, *op.cit.*

[23] *HC*, pp. 79-84.

[24] *EI*, IV, 1896-97, pp. 208-09.

[25] *JESI*, XXXI, 2005, pp. 136-46; *EI*, XLIII, Pt. i, 2011, pp. 40-51.

[26] *EI*, I, 1892, pp. 67-75.

[27] J.F. Fleet, *Corpus Inscriptionum Indicarum*, Volume III, Calcutta, 1888, No. 52, pp. 231-32.

[28] *EI*, XXI, 1931-32, pp. 74 ff.; *JBORS*, 1919, p. 302; *ibid.*, 1920, pp. 151-52.

[29] *HC*, p. 101.

[30] This issue is examined in my paper 'Prabhākaravardhana : A New Assessment', *Sri Venkateswara University Oriental Journal*, Volume XLIII, Parts 1 and 2, 2000, pp. 9-31.

because he could not say 'no' to the proposal of the emperor. Further, there are some obvious indications of the influence of the Maukhari political culture on the Vardhana court.[31]

Prabhākara's eldest son was Rājyavardhana II, the elder brother of Harsha. He was murdered by Śaśāṅka, king of Gauḍa, when he (that is, Rājyavardhana II) went to Kanauj to punish the Mālava king who had murdered Grahavarman, the husband of Rājyaśrī. But there are scholars who believe that Harsha was also implicated in the conspiracy hatched to bring about Rājyavardhana's assassination. I find myself in agreement with this view and think that despite the indubitable fact that Śaśāṅka was directly responsible for his murder, very strong indications are available suggesting that Harsha was in some way implicated (or at least it was then believed that he was implicated) in the conspiracy which led to the end of Rājyavardhana's life. Bāṇa also refers to the rumours that Harsha was implicated in such a conspiracy.[32]

It might be useful to analyse the factors and forces in the early career of Harsha with caution who succeeded to the Pushyabhūti throne after the murder of Rājyavardhana II. Here we should not forget that contrary to popular belief the order of events of Harsha's reign as described by Bāṇa is not reliable and that Harsha was never reluctant to ascend the paternal throne. The greatest single factor that influenced his career at this stage was politics of rivalry in the royal court. Immediately after his accession Harsha vowed to destroy the 'vile Gauḍa' who had killed his brother and also resolved to undertake a *digvijaya* campaign. But the description by Bāṇa of Harsha's resolve to undertake a *digvijaya* campaign is not only hyperbolic, but impossible as well. If we remember the precarious condition in which the small kingdom of Thanesar (very small indeed in comparison to the vast Gauḍa empire) was at the time of the accession of Harsha, a sixteen year

[31] *Ibid.*, pp. 19 ff.

[32] S.R. Goyal (*Harsha Śīlāditya*, pp. 79-80) has produced an extremely significant piece of evidence from the *Harshacharita* which indubitably proves that Harsha was accused, in his own days, of complicity in the murder of Rājyavardhana. In the seventh chapter of his *HC* (p. 204) Bāṇa casually mentions that "Like the Lord of the Immortals, he (that is, Harsha) appeared busy in wiping away the stain of his elder brother's slaughter" (*Amarapatirivāgrajabadhakalaṅkaprakshālanākulaḥ*). Now, it is a very important statement, for according to Indian mythology Indra had committed the crime of killing Viśvarūpa, the three headed son of Tvashṭṛ, who was in a sense his *agraja*. Therefore, it was said that Indra had committed the crime of killing his elder brother. Now, if according to Bāṇa Harsha was busy, like Indra, in wiping away the stain of his elder brother's murder then it can only mean that during the reign of Harsha rumours were afloat that he was implicated in the murder of Rājyavardhana.

old inexperienced lad, then it will be impossible to believe that Harsha could make such a resolve and take the risk of annoying the neighbouring kings unnecessarily. The general assumption that Harsha's resolve and declaration for *digvijaya*, his march towards Kanauj, his alliance with Bhāskaravarman and the successful search of Rājyaśrī in the Vindhya region—all took place in 606 A.D., also does not seem to be correct. Such a rapid succession of events no doubt seems to be indicated by Bāṇa. But if we go through his narrative carefully we find that he has given no specific date and has spoken of several time-gaps as well. Actually Bāṇa has introduced the motif of *digvijaya* in order to glorify his patron and has mixed it up with Harsha's vow to take a revenge on the Gauḍas. That is why he describes the campaign of Harsha some time as a project of *digvijaya* and some time as an expedition to punish the Gauḍa ruler(*daṇḍa-yātrā*). Significantly the words which Harsha uses in his vow regarding his revenge on Śaśāṅka do not bind him by any time-limit—he merely says that if 'in a limited number of days' he would not clear the earth of the Gauḍas he would hurl his sinful self into an oil-fed flame. Apparently Bāṇa knew that even by the time he composed his *Harshacharita*, Harsha had not succeeded against the Gauḍa enemy. That is why he did not make Harsha set a time limit for this revenge.

While Harsha was resting at the first encampment during his march on the outskirts of his capital, he met Haṁsavega, a confidential messenger sent by the lord of Kāmarūpa. In his message from his master Haṁsavega told Harsha that "the sovereign of Prāgjyotisha desires with Your Majesty an imperishable alliance." Harsha readily welcomed this offer with reciprocal gesture of goodwill. It is generally believed that the king of Kāmarūpa sought on his initiative a subordinate alliance with Harsha.[33] However, it may be pointed out that Haṁsavega specifically tells Harsha that his master wanted this alliance on the basis of equality, a condition which Harsha accepted. Further, in 606 A.D. Harsha was an ordinary king; he was yet to acquire the status of the Lord Paramount of north India. At that time he was surrounded by enemies and his position was extremely precarious. And then the kingdom of Kāmarūpa (in modern Assam) was far away in eastern India. The vast Gauḍa empire comprising greater part of Bengal, Bihar and U.P. intervened between the two. How could then the Kāmarūpa envoy come and meet Harsha somewhere near Thanesar ? And what advantage could Bhāskara see in an alliance with such a distant and ordinary king ? But it is also a fact that the friendship of Harsha and Bhāskara did materialize, for in 643 A.D. Yuan Chwang himself witnessed it. Therefore the conclusion is inevitable that this alliance was concluded not in 606 A.D. but sometime afterwards

[33] D. Devahuti, *op.cit.*, pp. 86-87.

when Harsha had acquired eminent position in north India.[34] It is, therefore, another instance of Bāṇa's disregard for exact chronology. Most likely at that time Harsha and Bhāskaravarman became friends against Śaśāṅka, Harsha gradually asserting his superiority over Bhāskara.

According to the order of events as narrated by Bāṇa, after sending the Kāmarūpa envoy back Harsha proceeded on his eastward march. Probably halfway between Sthāṇvīśvara and Kanauj he was met by Bhaṇḍi, who had accompanied Rājyavardhana when the latter went to punish the Mālava king. He told him that Rājyaśrī had burst from her confinement, and with her retinue entered the Vindhya forest. Harsha now decided to go in search of Rājyaśrī instead of leading the army, a task which he entrusted to Bhaṇḍi. During his wandering in the Vindhya forest he met Divākaramitra, the boy-friend of Grahavarman. With his help he rescued Rājyaśrī when she was preparing to burn herself by mounting the funeral pyre.

Bāṇa's account of Harshavardhana's successful search for Rājyaśrī is usually regarded as literally true. But the fact that Harsha saved her just before she was about to mount the funeral pyre is too dramatic a conclusion of the search to have been true. Its dramatic quality makes one wonder about its veracity which seems to be further reduced if we remember that Rājyaśrī escaped from the prison quite a long while before Harsha saved her—she escaped long before Harsha met Bhaṇḍi after which Harsha is said to have spent a long time in her search in the Vindhya forest. It becomes, therefore, difficult to believe that Harsha met her just when she was about to mount the funeral pyre. Such dramatic twists are alright for the stories of ancient plays and modern films, but they cannot be regarded as sober history. It does not mean that Harsha did not make a search for his sister or that his search was not successful; actually, his search and its successful conclusion were much less dramatic than Bāṇa asks us to believe. Here I would like to point out that the motivating factor in Harsha's attitude towards Rājyaśrī was also political, not only brotherly affection. This is quite clear from his attitude and subsequent course of events.

Harsha flourished at the fag-end of the Gupta classical age when many unsavoury aspects had developed in the lives of kings and feudal lords and the ideal of *dharmavijaya*, in which the victor reinstated the vanquished foes, had become strengthened by feudal polity which proved to be a powerful check on royal absolutism. The story of Harsha's wars and conquests and the nature of the organisation of his empire prove it, for his empire was feudal-federal in character in which the emperor was the leader of a host of feudal lords on whose support and backing his own position

[34] S.R. Goyal, *Harsha Śīlāditya*, pp. 98 ff.

depended whatever were the outward appearances. He was not the sole ruler of the empire, an *ekarāṭ* like Mahāpadma Nanda or Aśoka. He was a Mahārājādhirāja, a lord (*adhirāja*) of numerous Mahārājās who were in turn overlords of numerous rājās ruling over a large number of sāmantas, big or small. In war the subordinate kings supported the Mahārājādhirāja by their own contingents. An emperor of this age had a comparatively small army of his own and whatever influence he could exercise emanated not from his own military might but usually, if not always, from his personal qualities. Sometimes the emperor had to tolerate gross insolence of his allies/ subordinate allies, as Harsha had to, when he overlooked the ultimatum of Bhāskaravarman of Kāmarūpa to Śīlabhadra of Nālandā situated in Bihar (to send Yuan Chwang to Kāmarūpa or else) which was an important region of Harsha's empire.

The mode of the acquisition of Kanauj by Harsha was greatly influenced by religious factor—by the differences in the religious leanings of the people of Thanesar and Kanauj and by the religious attitude of other contemporary rulers and rivals of Harsha such as Śaśāṅka.[35] The acquisition of Kanauj was also the direct consequence of the situation created by the murder of Grahavarman Maukhari, husband of Rājyaśrī. Somehow the impression has become widely current among scholars that on hearing the news of the arrival of Harsha, Śaśāṅka fled from Kanauj thinking discretion was the better part of valour. But that does not negate the possibility that Śaśāṅka left his representative in Kanauj and Harsha had to remove him before Po-ni suggested his name for rulership.

Here it also needs to be emphasized that Rājyaśrī, what to talk of Harsha, had no claim over the Kanauj throne.[36] In ancient India the claim of a wife, and for that matter of any female member of the family in royal succession, was not recognized. Therefore after the murder of Grahavarman his natural successor was to be his son, and as he had no son, then one of his brothers, cousins or some other male member of his own family. In view of this fact, the existence of 'Su', a son of Avantivarman, and Pūrṇavarman (probably also a Maukhari prince), assumes significance. There might have been other Maukhari princes as well about whom we do not know. But the seal of 'Su' (Suvra ? Suchandra ? Suvrata ?) with full imperial titles has been found from Nālandā. The *Āryamañjuśrīmūlakalpa* also talks of a Maukhari prince 'Suvrata' after Grahavarman. As Bāṇa makes Grahavarman the eldest son of Avantivarman, 'Su' must have been a younger brother of

[35] Vide Shankar Goyal, 'Śaśāṅka and Buddhism' in the *Proceedings of the Indian History and Culture Society*, 10th Annual Conference, 23-25 December, 1986, Varanasi, 1988, pp. 45-50.

[36] S.R. Goyal, *Harsha Śīlāditya*, pp. 102-03.

Grahavarman.[37] Viewed in this light, it must be admitted that Harsha, who himself did not have any valid claim over the Maukhari throne, acquired it after superceding the rightful claim of the Maukhari princes. The assumptions that he 'accepted' it to help his sister to whom 'the kingdom of Kanauj rightfully belonged' and ruled it as her 'Regent' or 'Guardian' and that he did not have any lust for power, are obviously groundless. Harsha must have showed reluctance in accepting the crown of Kanauj only for the sake of appearances.[38] So was his show of consulting the image of the Bodhisattva.[39] It may be noted that despite his being a Śaiva he consulted the image of a Bodhisattva. This was prompted probably by the fact that the people of Kanauj were more inclined to Buddhism. His show of reverence of Avalokiteśvara must have strengthened the hands of people like Divākaramitra and Bhaṇḍi who were on his side and were trying to win over the people to the idea that he become the ruler of Kanauj.

Thus Harsha seems to have usurped Kanauj by diplomacy. It is also possible that he made the ministers of Kanauj offer him the crown and himself made the show of reluctance to gain the sympathy of at least some sections of the Kanauj people. As Rājyaśrī, his sister, was the widowed Maukhari queen, he must have exploited the sympathy of the Kanauj populace by acting as her patron and guardian. That is why in the beginning he did not sit on the royal throne and assumed the title of only 'Kumāra'. The next stage of the usurpation of Kanauj is revealed by the *Shi-Kia-Fang-Che* which was written with the help of the notes of Yuan Chwang. According to this text Harshavardhana carried on the administration of Kanauj with his widowed sister. Then followed its complete usurpation when he became its sole, fullfledged ruler as Yuan Chwang found him during his visit of India. The 'gradualness' of the usurpation only points to the fact that he had to face opposition from some sections of the Kanauj people.

According to some scholars Harsha conquered Magadha, a province of the Maukhari empire, in the beginning of his reign. But Magadha could not come under Harsha before the death of Pūrṇavarman, and Pūrṇavarman died only some time before 637, as Yuan Chwang, who visited Nālandā in that year, refers to an image of the Buddha as 'the work of Pūrṇavarmanrāja'.

Harsha probably attacked Śaśāṅka towards the close of latter's reign. Śaśāṅka's Ganjam copper plate inscription is dated 619 and one of his

[37] R.C. Majumdar (*The Classical Age*, Bombay, 1954, p. 102) suggests that 'Su' might have been a protégé of Śaśāṅka.

[38] Cf. Caesar's show of reluctance in accepting the imperial crown of Rome though he badly wanted to accept it.

[39] See Alexander's show of consulting the oracles though he had already decided to return from the Beas.

Midnapur charters was issued probably in 622. In 637 Yuan Chwang describes him as a 'recent' king. His final overthrow, therefore, took place after 619 and before 637, but probably nearer the former date as after his death but before 637 we have to place Pūrṇavarman's reign and the beginning of Harsha's reign as well.

Orissa seems to have been conquered by Harsha late in his life. When Yuan Chwang visited Koṅgoda (Ganjam region) in 639 it was an independent kingdom. Obviously by that time Harsha had not invaded this region. But in 642 Harsha was in a position to make the offer bestowing the revenue of its 80 villages to the Buddhist scholar Jayasena of Nālandā.

Nowadays scholars generally believe that in his later years Harsha acquired the status of the suzerain of Bhāskaravarman of Kāmarūpa. But known facts only underscore the feudal nature of the relationship between these two rulers in which one took advantage of favourable conditions whenever he could without feeling too much offended if on some other occasion the other did the same. In other words, there was no specificity in the relations between the two.

As regards Harsha's political relations with Kashmir, the view that the tooth-incident (in which Harsha carried away treacherously Buddha's tooth-relic from Kashmir) proves that Kashmir accepted the suzerainty of Harsha, has nothing to support it. It was a treacherous act on the part of Harsha, nothing less nothing more. The incident of tooth-relic must have happened in c. 634, for till September 633 the relic was in Kashmir where and when Yuan Chwang saw and worshipped it, but when the pilgrim visited Kanauj in September 636, it was already housed there.

In the west Harsha is said to have carried his victorious missions against Sindh and the Maitraka ruler of Valabhī. As the kingdom of Sindh extended well up to the point of the confluence of the Punjab rivers not far from the boundaries of Harsha's empire, it may not have been difficult for him to conduct a campaign against it.

Harsha's attack on Valabhī resulting in the marriage of her daughter with the Maitraka ruler seems to have been guided by two motives : to secure a strategic position for his southern campaign and to add to the economic prosperity of his kingdom by controlling a coastal trade centre.

One of the most important military adventures of Harsha was against Pulakeśin II, the Chālukya emperor of Vātāpi. The battle between them recorded in the Aihole inscription seems to have been fought mainly with the help of their respective elephant forces. Pulakeśin may well have encountered Harsha's armies on the banks of the Narmadā, but in this particular battle Harsha was defeated. Pulakeśin's vast resources and military strength, the hazards of fighting on enemy soil in unfamiliar surroundings, and geographical factors such as the formidable Chālukya boundary of hilly forests and a wide river were probably the factors which led to Harsha's defeat.[40]

So far scholars have been assuming that Pulakeśin II fought and defeated Harsha either between 610 and 612[41] or some time before 634,[42] the date of the Aihole record. But none of them has paid attention to the fact that *the struggle between these two great monarchs was going on even in 640 when Yuan Chwang visited Maharashtra.* His testimony proves that (1) the Harsha-Pulakeśin conflict recorded in the Aihole inscription was not desicive, and that (2) this conflict was a protracted one and was going on in 640, for in his record of the journey made in 640 Yuan Chwang explicitly says that by that time Harsha had 'not yet conquered' Pulakeśin.[43]

The problem of the extent of the empire of Harsha, I am sure, cannot be solved easily. In the beginning of the Indological studies historians generally believed that his empire included almost the whole of north India.[44] This view was probably first opposed by R.C. Majumdar.[45] As early as 1923 he opined that Harsha was the master of a much smaller empire which included only U.P., portions of eastern Punjab and Magadha. According to this view, "Harsha's domains were bounded by the Himalayas, the western Punjab, Rajputana, central India and Bengal." As regards Orissa he, at that time, held that Harsha no doubt proceeded as far as Koṅgoda or Ganjam district, "but that does not mean that he conquered it permanently." Later, however, he included Orissa in the empire of Harsha. R. S. Tripathi[46] also believed that the empire of Harsha consisted of "portions of eastern Punjab, almost the whole of the present United Provinces (=Uttar Pradesh) excepting

[40] See my 'Harsha's Relations with the Deccan and the Far South: Some Problems and Suggestions', in the *Proceedings of the Twenty-second Annual Session of the South Indian History Congress*, Thiruvananthapuram, 2002, pp. 135-37.

[41] J. F. Fleet, *Dynasties of the Kanarese Districts*, Bombay, 1899, p. 351, n. 4; R.K. Mookerji, *Harsha*, London, 1926, p. 36; K. C. Chattopadhyaya, in *PIHC*, III, pp. 586 ff.; K.V. Ramesh, *Chālukyas of Vātāpi*, Delhi, 1984, pp. 74-75.

[42] A. S. Altekar, *ABORI*, XIII, pp. 300-06; R.S. Tripathi, *History of Kanauj*, Delhi, 1959, pp. 124-29; G.S. Chatterji, *Harshavardhana*, 2nd edn., Allahabad, 1950, pp. 76-80; D.C. Sircar, in *The Classical Age*, p. 237; D. Devahuti, *op.cit.*, pp. 107-08; Ranabir Chakravarti, *Exploring Early India*, 3rd edn., Delhi, 2016, pp. 319-20.

[43] S.R. Goyal, *Harsha Śīlāditya*, pp. 144-47.

[44] E.g. V.A. Smith, *The Early History of India*, 4th edn., Oxford, 1924, p. 354; K.M. Panikkar, *Śrī Harsha of Kanauj*, Bombay, 1922, p. 22; M.L. Ettinghausen, *Harṣa Vardhana, Empereur et Poéte, etc.*, Paris, 1906.

[45] *JBORS*, IX, Pts. iii and iv, reprinted in *Readings in Political History of India*, ed. S.P. Gupta, Delhi, 1976, pp. 127-37.

[46] R. S. Tripathi, *op.cit.*, p. 119.

Mathurā and Matipura, Bihar, Bengal and Orissa including Koṅgodha or the Ganjam region." More recently D. Devahuti,[47] S.R. Goyal,[48] R. S. Sharma[49] and Romila Thapar[50] have also restricted the extent of the empire of Harsha. But this problem is to be dealt with more discretion.[51] While discussing the extent of the empire of Harsha one should differentiate between the areas directly ruled by him, areas ruled by kings who accepted his suzerainty (real or nominal), areas which were under his sphere of influence, areas which were independent but the rulers of which thought it prudent to maintain friendly relations with him and areas which were independent but were considered 'natural prey' to his ambition. Most scholars do not make such differentiation though some have tried to distinguish between areas under Harsha's direct control and areas within the sphere of his influence. But in that age of feudal-federal polity the relationship of the imperial authority with the various regions was not only of two types — directly controlled regions and regions within the sphere of influence — it could be of several types, the quantum of hold exercised by the imperial authority on them differing from state to state. We should also remember that the nature of the relationship between the imperial authority and a particular state could undergo a subtle change in course of time. Initially, for example, two states could contract an alliance on the basis of equality but later on one of them could emerge as stronger, the other adjusting itself to the changed situation by making a show of respect to its former ally in a suitable manner (as happened with Harsha and Bhāskara-varman). Sometimes the changed relationship was accorded a formal recognition; sometimes no such recognition was deemed necessary. Such changes in the relationship of two powers could take place several times in the long course of their relationship. Sometimes a weak state, though formally independent, had to tolerate the arrogance and even plunder of its border areas by its more powerful neighbour without making any fuss over it (as Kashmir did in the tooth-relic incident). Such weaker states, quite independent for all practical purposes, may be included neither among the subordinate states and nor within the sphere of influence of the more powerful neighbour. We may call them 'natural prey' of the latter.

[47] D. Devahuti, *op.cit.*, Ch. 4 and the map given at the end of her work.

[48] S.R. Goyal, *Harsha Śīlāditya*, pp. 160-62.

[49] R.S. Sharma, *Ancient India*, 5th repr., New Delhi, 1995, p. 171.

[50] Romila Thapar, *The Penguin History of Early India*, New Delhi, 2003, p. 289.

[51] For discussions related to this problem, see Shankar Goyal, 'Yuan Chwang's India and the Problem of the Extent of Harsha's Empire and Sphere of His Influence', in the *Papers from the Aligarh Historians Society*, ed. Irfan Habib, 77th Session of the Indian History Congress, Kerala University, Thiruvananthapuram, 28-30 December, 2016, pp. 104-16.

Viewed thus, we can include in the empire of Harsha only Punjab (of the Indian Union), Haryana and U.P. The kingdoms of Jalandhara, Matipura and Mathurā probably enjoyed more autonomy than other regions. Suvarṇagotra and Kapilavastu were also probably only under his nominal suzerainty. Magadha, parts of Bengal and Orissa were conquered by him in the last ten to fifteen years of his reign. Among these Orissa was quite a late addition. In the east whether trans-Gaṅgā regions were occupied by him or by Bhāskara is difficult to say. Kāmarūpa was never under his suzerainty. The kingdoms of Rajasthan and the region between Yamunā and Narmadā were under his influence. Valabhī accepted his suzerainty but quite late in his reign and renounced it before his death. Kashmir and Sindh were his 'natural prey' but no more. He tried to conquer Maharashtra but did not succeed and the view that he invaded Far South is apparently baseless. These conclusions are different from the conclusions of other scholars and no doubt in the case of several regions it is not possible to form a definite opinion. But in the present state of knowledge, it seems, that is the best one can do and a greater precision in our conclusions is not warranted.

In the age of Harsha contacts were maintained between India and China, including diplomatic exchanges between the two countries. The account of these exchanges has been preserved in the Chinese records though it was Harsha who initiated them. It has been generally held that Harsha established official contacts with China as an indirect result of his contact with Yuan Chwang.[52] But from all accounts it appears that Harsha dispatched first of his six missions to China in 641 A.D. while his meeting with Yuan Chwang took place in 642 or early 643.[53] The Sino-Indian exchange of missions was inspired mainly by commercial and religious motives and, besides, were utilized for cultural exchanges in such fields of knowledge as science and philosophy. From the submissive attitude of Harsha described by Ma Twan-lin it has been inferred that Harsha must have been in great trouble and needed the help of China.[54] But such a conclusion is not acceptable. It is impossible to believe that Harsha could really expect any material help from such a distant country as China of which he knew very little.[55] Intellectual curiosity and desire to get prestige may have been the main factors which guided him in opening diplomatic relations with China. The immediate result of this intercourse was China's increased interest in Buddhism also manifested through the visits of various monk scholars. From the economic point of view exotic articles were exchanged;

[52] M.L. Ettinghausen, *op.cit.*, p. 54; R. C. Majumdar, *The Classical Age*, p. 120.

[53] D. Devahuti, *op.cit.*, p. 251; S.R. Goyal, *Harsha Śīlāditya*, p. 169.

[54] M.L.Ettinghausen, *op.cit.*, pp. 54-57.

[55] R.C. Majumdar, *op.cit.*

from the Indian side 'fire pearl' and turmeric are stated to have been sent with the third mission. Bhāskara 'offered curiosities', it is said, 'and a map of the country', and asked for 'a picture (or statue) of Lao-tzŭ'. He also requested the mission, that was led by Li I-piao and assisted by Wang Hiuen-ts'e, to obtain for him a Taoist text, the *Tao-te ching*, of which a Sanskrit translation was prepared for him. Harsha's third mission took a present of a sapling of the *Bodhi* tree to China. Almost certainly other Buddhist relics and texts were sent through the state embassies. A-lo-na-shun, who was carried to China by Wang Hiuen-ts'e, took with him a scholar Na-lo-mi-si-po-ho, proficient in arts and magic, who knew the secret of longevity. T'ai-tsung was happy to patronize him. One of the important assignments for Li I-piao's mission was to learn the Indian technique of making sugar. I-tsing, who spent twelve years in India (673-85), includes in his records three chapters on medicine. Yuan Ch'ao is said to have returned to India in 664 under imperial orders to collect medicinal plants and make contacts with famous physicians. These exchanges also stimulated in China the study of Indian grammar and philology, architecture and sculpture, painting and music, and so forth. Chinese influence too, in many fields, entered India. Yuan Chwang was entertained with a T'ang period musical composition by Bhāskara in 638 A.D. Some scholars of Chinese civilization presume the influence of Taoism on Indian Tāntric Buddhism.[56]

India's cultural and commercial contacts with Iran in the post-Gupta age were quite close. Sometimes these relations found reflection in political relations also. The Arabs and Iranians sent a large number of merchant ships to China which passed through Indian ports. The westward journey of the *Pañchatantra*,[57] the great Sanskrit book of stories, began in the sixth century A.D. with its translation into Pahlavi, and then into Syriac. Persian and Arabian writers state that chess or Śatarañja (Sanskrit *Chaturaṅga*) came to Persia from India. From Iran the game passed to the Arabians and from them, directly or indirectly, to various parts of Europe.[58] Hindu sciences, notably Āyurveda and Arithmetic, were highly prized in Iran.[59]

Tabari (838-923 A.D.) informs us that in the 36th year of the reign of the Persian emperor Khusru II (590-628 A.D.). i.e. in 626 A.D. (when

[56] D. Devahuti, *op.cit.*, pp. 255-56.

[57] M. Winternitz, *A History of Indian Literature*, Volume III, repr., Delhi, 1963, pp. 294 ff. According to Philip K. Hitti (*History of the Arabs*, first published in 1937, p. 404), the basis of the famous work titled *Thousand and One Nights* was a Persian book which contained several stories of Indian origin.

[58] H. J. R. Murray, *A History of Chess*, published in 1913, quoted in *The Classical Age*, p. 639, n. 2.

[59] See also *The Classical Age*, p. 640.

Harsha was ruling over northern India and Pulakeśin II was the Lord of the Deccan) a king of India, named Prmesh, sent to the Persian ruler ambassadors carrying letters and presents for him and his sons. Noldeke,[60] the translator of this passage, rendered Prmesh as Pulakesha or Pulakeśin. The suggestion of Noldeke was used by Fergusson[61] to support his interpretation of the paintings found in the Cave 1 at Ajanta which represents an Indian king on his throne receiving an embassy or deputation of people. Fergusson assigned the Cave No. 1 to the period between 610 and 630-40 A.D. He also believed that the foreigners depicted in these paintings were Persians. With these facts he combined the suggestion of Noldeke that Pulakeśin II sent an embassy to Khusru in 626 A.D.

However, according to R. C. Majumdar,[62] the Indian embassy received by Khusru II was really sent by Harsha. It may be pointed out that Harsha exerted a great influence in the north-western part of the sub-continent[63]— even more than Majumdar was ready to concede. His hold over Rajasthan is indicated by the prevalence of his era in this region. His political influence in Gujarat is proved by his victory over the king of Valabhī recorded in the inscriptions of the Gurjaras of Lāṭa. His invasion of Sindh has been explicitly recorded by Bāṇa, while his political hold over some parts of the Punjab is proved by the testimony of Yuan Chwang and the Tibetan historian Tārānātha. According to Yuan Chwang Harsha was able to assign the task of taking him safely across the Indian border to the king of Jalandhar and Tārānātha has recorded the story of the persecution of the Mlechchhas near Maulasthāna or Multan at the hands of Harsha.[64] The Mlechchhas of this story were undoubtedly Persians. The story, if correct, makes it highly likely that Harsha had some dealings with the Persian court.

Then, Harsha was not only an immediate neighbour of the Iranian emperor, there is also some likelihood that the former had economic and political relations with the latter. Bāṇa says that the conquest of Iran was regarded by Harsha's *sāmantas* as not so difficult. They boasted that "the land of the Turuṣkas is to the brave but a cubit. Persia is only a span."[65]

[60] *JRAS*, 1879, p. 166, fn. 1.

[61] *Ibid.*, pp. 155 ff.

[62] See R.C. Majumdar, *Readings in Political History of India*, pp.156-57.

[63] For a detailed discussion on this problem see my paper, 'Yuan Chwang's India and the Problem of the Extent of Harsha's Empire and Sphere of His Influence', in the *Proceedings of the Papers from the Aligarh Historians Society*, ed. Irfan Habib, 77th Session, Indian History Congress, Kerala University Thiruvananthapuram, 28-30 December, 2016, pp. 104-16.

[64] Tārānātha, *History of Buddhism*, trans. A. Schiefner, St. Petersburg, 1869, p. 94.

[65] *HC*, p. 210.

Tārānātha's story of the persecution of the Mlechchhas near Maulasthāna or Multan, at the hands of Harshavardhana, even if false, suggests quite a close relationship between India and Persia during Harsha's rule. Bāṇa refers to the fact that Harsha's horses were imported, among other countries, from Persia also.[66] In the *Kādambarī* also we are informed that a horse named Indrāyudha, which was of exceptionally good breed, was sent by the monarch of Iran for the hero of this work.[67] Tārānātha confirms the existence of such contacts by stating that a Persian king presented horses to the king of Madhyadeśa (probably Harsha) and the latter sent to the former in return a few elephants.

DECLINE OF CLASSICAL CULTURE, RISE OF FEUDALISM AND TRANSITION TO THE MEDIEVAL PERIOD

The beginning of the medieval period in Indian history may broadly be traced from the fall of the Gupta empire itself, though it may be readily conceded that the period of about two centuries, roughly from the fall of the Gupta empire (c. 550 A.D.) to the rise of the Pratihāras (c. 750 A.D.) sheds light on the classical and medieval periods both by a sort of *dehalī-dīpaka-nyāya* (the maxim that a lamp placed on the threshhold illumines both the inside and outside of a room) and, therefore, belongs to both. The age of Harsha formed the focal point of this stretch of two centuries.[68] In Europe one of the main factors that led to the transition from Classical to Middle Ages were the invasions of the foreign tribes which resulted not only in the barbarization of culture but also imparted a new vigour and vitality to the Indian society. Another factor that played a significant role in the transformation of the classical society in Europe as well as India was feudalism. It brought about consequential changes in the classical pattern of socio-economic and political organisation. It led not only to the fragmentation of political authority but also to its hierarchical gradation due to which the monarch, who was at the apex of the hierarchy, became and began to be viewed more as the lord of the vassal kings and the *sāmantas* emerged as the real rulers in their respective areas. Coupled with the concept of *dharmavijaya*, this fact rendered permanent absorption of the conquered territories extremely difficult and made the imperial structure more feudal-

[66] *Ibid.*, p. 50.

[67] *Kādambarī*, edn. of Pt. Ramtej Shastri, Varanasi, 1952, pp. 164-65.

[68] For a detailed study of the decline of classical culture, rise of feudalism and transition to the medieval period, see my *Harsha : A Multidisciplinary Political Study*, Jodhpur, 2006, Ch. 9; for further research on the subject, also see my recent-most works *The 'Medieval' Factor and the Age of Harsha : A Cultural Study*, Jodhpur, 2016, and *Harsha Revisited : A Re-interpretation of Existing Data*, Delhi, 2018.

federal in character. The feudalization and decline of royalty in the post-classical period is evidenced by the adoption of the vainglorious titles by kings and a more lavish attribution of divinity to them. These tendencies do not prove an increase in the actual power of the rulers; they only indicate to the high pretensions of monarchs under feudal conditions which intellectuals like Bāṇa highly deplored.[69]

One of the by-products of feudalism in medieval India was the ideal of chivalry. It emphasized more or less the same virtues which were valued in feudal Europe. Now queens are more often than not described as having been 'bought' by paying the price of valour. Numerous *kāvyas* and dramas describe how the royal hero 'won' the hand of a princess after defeating other suitors. But with the passage of time the ideal of chivalry degenerated into vainty and arrogance and accentuated the tendencies of family and clannish rivalries and jealousy. But the feudal ideal of chivalry did not help at all in the development of the art of war. Contrary to the practice of the classical period, armies in this age were generally composed of feudal levies. They could swell to huge proportions, but were too heterogeneous to be commanded by the 'overlord' effectively. The practice of maintaining efficient standing armies was given up. Much reliance was laid on forts, omens and supernatural support in warfare and a lot of attention was paid to grandeur, show and luxurious living in military camps with the result that the Rajput armies became more or less like the later-day Mughal armies. The earliest picture of such a military camp is preserved in the *Harshacharita*.[70]

In the medieval period feudalization of the Buddhist monasteries and Hindu temples resulted in the institutionalization of education. For the feudal rights enjoyed by the Nālandā Mahāvihāra in the age of Harsha himself extensive evidence is provided by the Chinese sources. The feudalization of the *vihāras* and their emergence as self-sufficient economic units tended to politicalize their administration. It was but natural for kings, who gave lavish grants and endowments to the monasteries (and temples), to see to it that they behaved in a compliant manner. All this also changed the pattern of the Buddhist education. Now monasteries emerged as organised or corporate centres of higher learning where education was imparted not only to the monks and nuns but to the general public also. In the age of Harsha Nālandā Mahāvihāra was the foremost among such institutions. The emergence of the Brāhmaṇical *agrahāra* villages and temples as centres of learning was the Hindu counterpart of the feudalization of educational system.

As in the early medieval Europe, in India also the rise and growth of

[69] *HC*, pp. 208-09.
[70] *Ibid.*, pp. 201, 207-08.

feudalism in the post-Gupta age was concomitant and connected with the growth of regional tendencies in life. In the post-classical period the absence of a centralized authority increased localism and insularity in economic life. India's trade with other countries declined leading to a decrease in the total profit from exports, probably even to an unfavourable balance of trade. It is evidenced not only by the prevalence of local weights and measures and by the paucity and debasement of coins but also by the formation of regional cultural units such as Andhra, Assam, Bengal, Gujarat, Karnataka, Kerala, Maharashtra, Orissa, Rajasthan, Tamilnadu, etc. which started from sixth-seventh centuries. Faint beginnings of regional and cultural personality consciousness are found in other parts of the country also. Yuan Chwang mentions several nationalities of India. The *Mudrārākshasa* of Viśākhadatta speaks of the different regions whose inhabitants differed in customs, clothing and language[71] while the *Kuvalayamālā* (eighth century) notes the existence of 18 major nationalities and describes the anthropological character of 16 peoples, pointing out their psychological features and citing the samples of their languages.[72] Thus this period seems to have been a watershed in the ethnic history of India.[73] In the early medieval age Sanskrit literature lost touch with the common man and became, by and large, imitative, insipid, artificial, and unnatural. The ornate style in prose and poetry became widely prevalent and strings of adjectives, adverbs and similes are found not only in literary works but also in inscriptions from about the sixth-seventh centuries. The prose style of Bāṇa became a model for the medieval period. The early medieval age is the age of scholastic elaboration and systematic analysis of commentaries and sub-commentaries of manuals and sub-manuals. The tightening of the Smṛti rules, loss of contacts with the outside world, feudal atmosphere in the courts, and the growth of insular tendency stifled the free spirit of intelligentsia. The vacuum created by the decline of Sanskrit in India was filled up by the gradually emerging regional languages. According to S.K. Chatterji, between c. 500 to 900 A.D. the Prakrit languages gradually changed into various Apabhraṁśas and between c. 900 and 1300 A.D. they gradually turned into modern varnaculars or *bhāshās* of different regions. With the regional languages also developed regional scripts out of the parent script of Brāhmī which had so far admitted only regional variations in style. The growing tendency of regionalism influenced on other aspects of culture also, specially

[71] *Mudrārākshasa*, ed. Alfred Hillebrandt, Part I, Breslau, 1912, 9.

[72] Quoted in Yu. V. Gankovsky, *The Peoples of Pakistan*, Moscow, 1978, p. 103.

[73] R.S. Sharma, 'Problem of Transition from Ancient to Medieval in Indian History', in *The Indian Historical Review*, March 1974, Volume I, Number 1, pp. 7-8; also see his *Perspectives in Social and Economic History of Early India*, New Delhi, 1983, pp. 228 ff.

art.[74] Towards the end of the seventh century A.D. regional spirit began to assert itself. In the realm of sculpture and painting also the post-Gupta centuries witnessed the emergence of a distinct 'medieval' trend with many regional variations. The post-classical Indian society was greatly disturbed by the new trends in religious life also. The popular or conventional form of the Hindu sects was characterized by the worship of numerous deities in temples built by kings, *sāmantas* and rich people. They were endowed with grants of land, tolls and taxes. Temple and monastery-building activities, which acquired momentum in the later Gupta age, reached their climax during the eleventh and twelfth centuries. Great temples and monasteries of this period possessed large estates and enormous wealth, with the result that the priestly class, as in medieval Europe, acquired a mighty hold over people. Their wealth and power made the priests of the period greedy and lover of luxury.

In the post-classical age, several factors threatened the social order based on the four-fold caste system.[75] Among them are included political and social confusion created by the fall of the Gupta empire, the pressure exerted by the growing number of foreigners in the Indian society which changed the population texture of the country very fast, specially of the north-western and western regions, and the rise of Tāntric and other heterodox sects whose attitude was against the very idea of caste organisation. All these factors generated a sense of increasing chaos and decline.

The emergence of the *sāmanta* hierarchy had a peculiar relationship with the growing rigidity of the caste system. On the one hand, it helped in the growing rigidity of the caste system, for in their small principalities petty feudal chiefs found it desirable to enforce the rules of caste rigorously with a view to maintaining the local agrarian set up. The insecurity caused by constant feudal wars also tended to strengthen localism and hereditariness of caste functions. On the other hand, however, feudalism tended to come into conflict with the caste system by creating a new class of feudal barons drawn from all the sections of society who were gradually accepted within the Kshatriya fold. The terms *Brahma-kshatra* and *Vaiśya-kshatra* applied to some ruling dynasties of this period shows that there were some

[74] On this point, see Shankar Goyal, 'Transition from Gupta Classicism to Medievalism in Indian Art', *Indian Art of the Gupta Age*, eds. S. R. Goyal and Shankar Goyal, Jodhpur, 2000, pp. 208-21.

[75] On this, see Shankar Goyal, 'Caste System as Reflected in the Works of Bāṇa and Yuan Chwang', in the *Papers from the Aligarh Historians Society*, ed. Irfan Habib, 71st Session of the Indian History Congress, Gaur Banga University, Malda, 11-13 February, 2011, pp.124-47.

Brāhmaṇas and Vaiśyas who discarded their caste professions for martial pursuits. Though Harsha has not been called a *Vaiśya-kshatra*, yet theoretically he belonged to this category.

In the centuries immediately following the fall of the Gupta empire, many of the metropolitan and other great cities of north India considerably declined; many of them, such as Kanauj, were actually sacked several times respectively either by the indigenous enemies or the Tibetans and later on by the Muslim invaders. On account of the decline of Indian exports, artisans and merchants living in these towns flocked to the countryside and took to cultivation. The decay and disappearance of urban centres created conditions for the rise of self-sufficient regional productive units, which were strengthened by the political fragmentation of the country and by restrictions imposed on the movement of artisans and peasants.

The interaction of the new religious ideas and the chaotic conditions created by the feudal pattern of political life wrought havoc with the morals of the people. Many of the new esoteric religious sects reacted against the philosophy of extreme abnegation and austerity and permitted a free rein to the sensual desires of man by enjoyment of meat, drink and damsels. Similarly, feudalism also encouraged love of luxury and sensualism, with the result that every standard of modesty and moderation, all the values of decency and refinement tended to be bypassed. That is why we find that in contrast to the classical age, in which kings boasted of their moral decency, in medieval period kings and barons were immersed in gross sensual excesses and, what is more baffling, they were proud of it!

The Paurāṇic description of the decadence in the Kali Age portrays the transition of Indian society from pre-feudal age of antiquity to the feudal age of the Middle Ages. That is why many scholars believe that the concept of the Kali Age may be profitably utilized to explain the transition from ancient to medieval period of Indian history. The theme of the Kali Age was first touched by R. S. Sharma in his *Śūdras in Ancient India* (Delhi, 1958). It was further discussed by him in 1982 in his article 'The Kali Age : A Period of Social Crisis'[76] in which he highlighted the main features of the Kali Age in the texts assignable to third-fourth centuries A.D. and concluded that "seen in its totality the Kali crisis of the late third and fourth centuries appears as a prelude to the feudalization of Indian society."[77] Meanwhile, B.N.S.

[76] In S.N. Mukherjee, ed., *India : History and Thought*, Calcutta, 1982, pp. 186-203, also republished in D.N. Jha, ed., *Feudal Social Formation in Early India*, Delhi, 1987, pp. 45-64 and *The Feudal Order : State, Society and Ideology in Early Medieval India*, New Delhi, 2002, pp. 61-77; also see his *Early Medieval Indian Society*, Kolkata, 2001, pp. 45-76.

[77] In D.N. Jha, *Feudal Social Formation*, p. 60.

Yadava[78] provided a detailed analysis of the concept of the Kali Age to explain the transition from the antiquity to the Middle Ages on the basis of the later Paurāṇic accounts which embody in the ideological garb of prediction "the cognition by the contemporaries or near-contemporaries of the forces and tendencies that were setting off towards the Middle Ages." From all this it has been rightly deduced that the concept of the Kali Age may be profitably utilized to explain the transition from ancient to medieval Indian society.[79]

The political culture and administration of the age of Harsha betray several features which were not liked by some of his contemporary thinkers. Even Bāṇa is known to have raised his voice of protest and dissent against some of the ideals and practices of the political culture of his age. For example, he was highly critical of the theory of the divinity of kings—a theory which was widely current in ancient India and which kings deliberately tried to popularize. He was also highly critical of the custom of *satī*. In the accounts of the self-immolation by Yaśomatī and attempt for the same by Rājyaśrī, Bāṇa does not say anything by way of his own opinion; obviously, he could not make any adverse remarks against the actions of the mother and sister of his patron. But in the *Kādambarī* he makes Chandrāpīḍa, the hero of the work, criticize the *satī* custom in no uncertain terms.[80] Another instance where Bāṇa becomes quite critical of the political culture of his age occurs when he makes Haṁsavega, the Kāmarūpa envoy to Harsha, enter upon a diatribe against government servants. It is a bitter invective probably unparalleled anywhere else in Sanskrit literature. The flattery of the royal courtiers, the royal servant soaked in utter selfishness and the haughtiness and proud demeanour of king who behaved with utter contempt have been painted here with a rare fidelity.[81]

[78] B.N. S. Yadava, 'The Accounts of the Kali Age and the Social Transition from Antiquity to the Middle Ages', in Jha, *op.cit.*, p. 65, also reprinted in D.N. Jha, *The Feudal Order*, pp. 79-120.

[79] However, more recently there has been an attempt to analyse these changes from a different perspective and some scholars have suggested what they call an integrative polity, rather than a feudal society. In this context it is argued that the formation of states after the Gupta age was itself a different process from the earlier one and, therefore, created a different kind of economy and society. How it is to be interpreted and labelled still remains a matter of debate. For some relevant discussions on this problem, see V.K. Thakur, *Historiography of Indian Feudalism : Towards a Model of Early Medieval Indian Economy*, Patna, 1989, pp. 38-40; B.D. Chattopadhyaya, *The Making of Early Medieval India*, New Delhi, 1997, pp. 1-37; R. Champakalakshmi, *Trade, Ideology and Urbanization : South India 300 BC to AD 1300*, New Delhi, 1999, pp. 11-12, 17; Romila Thapar, *The Penguin History of Early India*, pp. 442-48.

[80] *Kādambarī*, tr. of C.M. Ridding, Bombay, 1956, p. 156.

[81] V.S. Agrawala, *The Deeds of Harsha*, Varanasi, 1969, p. 207.

Viewed in its totality, the administrative organisation of Harsha seems to have been based on the administrative pattern of the preceding Gupta age, but at the same time it appears to have been much more 'feudalized' and with lesser cohesion. Under the Guptas political unity was characterized by a balance between centralization and regional autonomy. Harsha's empire, however, was a looser federation much more based on diplomatic alliances than on the firm hold over the central authority. Harsha's superiority over his subordinate kings and feudatories depended on his strength which was far lesser than that of the Guptas despite the fact that he is said to have had a very large army, for his army itself was not a 'monolith' controlled by the emperor but a collection of the feudal military units contributed by the *sāmantas*. Actually the growth of the *sāmanta* institution was the greatest single factor which differentiates the administrative organisation of Harsha from the administration of earlier periods.

Harsha was a child of his age, not its maker. His personality was moulded by the tendencies of his time. Of course the same may be said for far greater monarchs like Aśoka and Samudragupta. But they displayed some originality as well, a capacity to influence and to some extent change the spirit of their age, a claim which can hardly be made for Harsha. At the most he may be described as the typical representative of his age. He flourished in a transitional phase of Indian history when the classical period was coming to a close and the early medieval period was unfolding itself. The *Chakravartin* ideal of the Guptas was sought to be emulated by the post-Gupta rulers. In literature as well as arts, specially sculpture, the achievements of the Gupta age had set 'standard' or 'ideal' for the subsequent ages. Kālidāsa is remembered by Bāṇa as well as by the author of the Aihole inscription. But in political sphere the popularity of the ideal of *dharmavijaya* followed by Samudragupta in the Deccan (in which the conqueror appropriated only the glory of the defeated kings, not their kingdoms) greatly weakened the cohesion of the political structure. To some extent the concept of *dharmavijaya* was the sublimation or idealization of the difficulties involved in establishing a centralized political system in a country of sub-continental dimensions, as well as an evidence of the inability of the conquerors to realize the ideal of political unity. Actually the *Chakravartin* ideal based on the concept of *dharmavijaya* and the feudal-federal polity were the two sides of the same coin. Harsha was brought up in the *milieu* of this ideal and was its typical product. On the one hand, he belonged to the twilight period of the classical culture and, therefore, could bask in its aura even of diminished light and, on the other, was greatly handicapped by the growing tendencies of early medievalism.

The disintegration of the Gupta empire, invasions of the barbarians and the rise of feudalism were concomitant with the decline in the popularity of the Vedic rituals, threat to the traditional *varṇa* organisation, rise of Tāntricism and the decline of political morality. That was the reason why in the sixth-seventh centuries A.D. it was the general feeling among the people that they were living in an age of decline when the evils of the Kali Age had become more pronounced. Thus Harsha was born and brought up in an atmosphere which was regarded as decadent by the people of his own age. The feudal atmosphere of the Pushyabhūti court and *harem*, popularity of Tāntricism even in the Pushyabhūti royal family and their capital, feudalization of the Pushyabhūti army with all its concomitant evils, obsession of kings with the idea of their divinity which thinkers like Bāṇa did not like and influence of family members and other contemporaries — all these factors played their role in the formation and evolution of the personality and psychology of Harsha.

The royal courts of the age of Harsha were greatly influenced by the Smārta tradition also which laid emphasis on charity and self-abnegation. The Purāṇas and the *Mahābhārata* extol gifts of land (*bhūmidāna*), etc. The concept of the transience of wealth and material prosperity (*lakshmī*) finds mention frequently in inscriptions and literature. The Kanauj religious assembly and the quinquennial ceremonies held at Prayāga by Harsha, in which he used to give in charity all that he possessed (*sarvasvadāna*), were not something unique with him. Such assemblies, probably on smaller scale, were held by the kings of Kapiśā, Śīlāditya Dharmāditya of Mo-la-po, the Maukhari 'ancestors' of Harsha and Dhruvabhaṭa, his son-in-law. Thus from the psycho-sociological point of view also Harsha was the child of his age — an age in which kings were, on the one hand, given to the evil ways of Kali and behaved in a manner which was amoral as well as immoral, and on the other, extolled the virtue of charity and self-abnegation. Harsha could spend his life in fighting wars of conquests and boast that he appropriated the 'lakshmī' of the king of Sindh, and yet could empty his treasury every five years in charity and in his records sermonize that material prosperity is transient. In other words, bravery and world-renouncing ideology, sensualism and self-abnegation, love of wealth and devotion to charity, self-conceit and deep interest in religious discourses—all these could be found in the character of one and the same person. And in Harsha they are found in abundance.

How much was Harsha influenced by the personalities of his family members and friends, it is difficult to assess. Yet some indications for this are available. If Bāṇa's statement that Prabhākara wanted Harsha to ascend the throne has some truth and was reflected in Prabhākara's behaviour during Harsha's childhood, then one can presume that it might have helped in making Harsha ambitious. It might have produced a latent feeling in Harsha's mind that Rājyavardhana, his elder brother, was an obstacle between him and the paternal throne. Rājyavardhana was interested in the religion of Śākyamuni, but he was also a great warrior and, according to Śaṅkarārya, the commentator of Bāṇa, could be lured by Śaśāṅka by the offer of the hands of his daughter. If at all, Harsha might have learnt from him the lesson that it is the duty of a prince to punish his enemies and enjoy the pleasures of life. Among other characters of the period Siṁhanāda is known to have stimulated Harsha's ambition to become a world-conqueror, and Skandagupta, the commander of elephant forces, taught him the necessity of always remaining cautious. That Harsha was very cautious in his political behaviour (whether or not due to the advice of Skandagupta) is quite apparent. For example, when the news of Grahavarman's murder was received Rājyavardhana became highly angry and left 'the same day' to punish the enemy and as a consequence of his haste was deprived of his life. On the other hand, when the news of Rājya's murder came, Harsha expressed his anger suitably but left to punish the enemy only after making due preparations and settling the affairs of the kingdom properly. Divākaramitra probably taught him how a king might exploit the religious sentiments of his people for political ends, and Bhaṇḍi most likely helped him in political intrigues and art of diplomacy. Bāṇa was merely a court-poet whose sole aim was to get the patronage of the emperor. But in his company (and that of other poets) Harsha's literary tastes might have become more refined. Yuan Chwang entered the life of Harsha very late. He was also too young, by at least ten years, to influence the personality of Harsha. However, Bhāskara, the Kāmarūpa monarch and a friend of Harsha, belonged to his age-group. Both of them were Śaivite and believed in the policy of religious toleration. Therefore it is easy to surmise that probably it was from his love for China and things Chinese that Harsha also became interested in them.

In my view all these aspects of Harsha's personality necessitate a reconsideration of his place in history. The impression that he was the first great conqueror to establish a large empire in the post-Gupta period and was the last great emperor of Hindu India is not true.[82] The empires of Lalitāditya Muktāpīḍa of Kashmir, Yaśovarman of Kanauj, Pāla emperors Dharmapāla and Devapāla, Pratihāra emperors Mihirabhoja and Mahendrapāla, etc. were much more extensive, and some of them definitely much more stable.[83] The achievements of Harsha look bigger because we

[82] Devahuti, *op.cit.*, p. 268.

[83] *JBORS*, IX, Pts. iii and iv and *IHQ*, V, June, 1929, both reprinted in S.P. Gupta, ed., *Readings in Political History of India*, pp. 127-42.

possess more detailed sources for him the study of which creates a false impression about his importance. He ruled for forty years or slightly more but with his death his empire collapsed like a house of cards. He apparently had sufficient time to evolve an administrative structure which could sustain the stresses and strains of adverse circumstances. But he did not or could not do so. His failure to build an infrastructure which could provide permanency to his imperial edifice is rather strange and requires some explanation.

Therefore an overall assessment of the achievements of Harsha is a difficult preposition. He inherited a kingdom which was confined to the Śrīkaṇṭha *janapada*, with some influence over the neighbouring states. At the time of his accession he was over-burdened with problems and difficulties, both internal as well as external. But in the four decades of his reign he made himself the greatest monarch of north India so much so that he could be described by the rival Chālukyas as *Sakalottarāpatheśvara.*[84] By any standard it was no mean achievement. But he could not evolve an administrative structure which could impart even a semblance of stability to the imperial edifice he erected in his life time. He did not take interest in the construction of forts also which were a must in that feudal age. Psychologically speaking, an emperor who lived in grass huts when on tours could hardly think of constructing forts at strategic points for the defence of the empire. He is also not known to have taken any pains for the welfare of his subjects, excepting of course giving regular charities, opening *puṇyaśālās* and the like. He must be praised for these activities but at the same time it must also be pointed out that he is not known to have taken any steps for the betterment of the condition of the peasantry, or for the improvement of trade, commerce, etc. On the other hand, his wars and religious policy proved to be a great burden on the people. His addiction to charities was an extremely poor substitute for the public welfare measures which he could but did not undertake.

That Harsha's personal accomplishments were noble can hardly be doubted. Both Bāṇa and Yuan Chwang praise his personal qualities. Bāṇa virtually makes him an abode of all the qualities which our ancients sought in an ideal king and an ideal hero of an epic. It may also be easily conceded that he was not given to those vices which, according to the epigraphic records of Yaśodharman and the Maukharis, were commonly found in the monarchs of that age. His interest in performing arts is reflected through a reference to his *vīṇā*-playing in the *Harshacharita* and it is said that he

[84] Ranabir Chakravarti, however, wrongly believes that it was a grossly exaggerated claim (*op.cit.*, p. 319).

authored three Sanskrit plays. Though he did not succeed in establishing an administrative organisation which could make his empire stable, but in his own way he did take deep interest in the administrative affairs of his realm. But it is also clear that he suffered from over-ambition; one may even say that he was power-hungry (as is indicated by his possible complicity in the murder of Rājyavardhana and his show of respect to Bodhisattva Avalokiteśvara and use of Rajyaśrī's name to enlist the support of the Kanauj people for the acquisition of the Kanauj throne). He could also take undue advantage of his military superiority (as is evidenced by the Kashmir tooth-relic incident and by the fact that he forced Bhāskara to send the Chinese pilgrim to him), could enlist the support of writers like Bāṇa (or Mayūra) for propaganda on his behalf, and was greatly enamoured of foreign (Chinese) scholars. But these are all usual human failings.

All in all, I find Harsha undoubtedly the most ambitious ruler of his period. But, as already mentioned, he was only a child of his age which was the age of transition dominated by feudal atmosphere; he had no capacity to change the direction of the tendencies of the period. He was interested only in wars and charities, not in evolving a stable political structure or introducing innovative changes in economic and military organisation. The result was complete downfall of his empire as soon as he died. Instances of such complete collapse are not wholly unknown but they are not too many either. Harsha, therefore, cannot be regarded as a great monarch of India of the category of Chandragupta Maurya, Aśoka, Samudragupta and Chandragupta II Vikramāditya. He was an important ruler only in comparison with the lesser monarchs of our country, such as Khāravela of Kaliṅga and Yaśodharman-Vishṇuvardhana of Malwa.

NINE

The *Harshacharita* : A Factual Biography of the Medieval Idiosyncrasy

PERSONAL HISTORY OF BĀṆA

In the history of Sanskrit literature Bāṇa is among those few ancient authors who have left to posterity a reasonably detailed account of themselves in their works. To his *Kādambarī* is prefixed only a brief description of his family while in his *Harshacharita*,[1] we find a much fuller account of his ancestors and himself. Indeed, the first two *uchchhvāsas* of the *Harshacharita* are devoted to the history of Bāṇa's forefathers and Bāṇa himself. His personal narrative is continued even in the third *uchchhvāsa*. From this account we learn that Bāṇa was born in a learned Brāhmaṇa family. His love

[1] In modern times the *Harshacharita* has often been printed and also translated into English and some other Indian languages. However, as against the *Kādambarī*, the other work of Bāṇa, on which several commentaries are available, there is only one Sanskrit commentary available on the *Harshacharita*, namely, *Saṁketa*, written by Śaṅkara who flourished probably sometime before the twelfth century A.D. It is very valuable, particularly for the explanation it gives of obscure words and puns. However, it is very often quite brief and passes over whole pages with scarcely a word of comment. As it has been found in Kashmir, it is usually supposed that Śaṅkara was a native of that region. His father's name was Puṇyakara. But he does not give any other details about himself though at the end of his commentary he informs us that he had followed a tradition in explaining the difficult words of the *Harshacharita* indicating thereby that his commentary was preceded by some other commentaries which are now lost. As far as English translations of the *Harshacharita* and the *Kādambarī* are concerned, the former was published from London as early as 1897 by E.B. Cowell and F.W. Thomas. This translation is extremely well done and is of great merit for understanding the meanings of Bāṇa. The annotated text of the *Harshacharita* with exhaustive notes by P.V. Kane appeared from Bombay in 1918. The *Kādambarī* was translated by C.M. Ridding and published from London in 1896 and edited by P.V. Kane and published from Bombay in 1920.

of mixing with people of all types gave him a boldness of character and a deep but sympathetic knowledge of human nature. His first-hand knowledge of the life of the people of all classes, as well as his access to royal quarters, qualified him for giving a reliable and trustworthy account of events, unless of course he himself chose to do otherwise. Though most of the contents of the *Harshacharita* refer to the earlier part of Harsha's career when Bāṇa had not come into contact with him personally and for such events as Harsha's coming to power, his treaty with the king of Kāmarūpa, or his search for his bereaved sister Rājyaśrī, Bāṇa no doubt depended upon hearsay, but it is evident that because of his inquisitive nature he must have tried to collect reliable information on these topics. It is another matter that his view of history and scant regard for chronology prevented him from describing the events of Harsha's reign as they occurred and exactly when they occurred.

Bāṇa is refreshing, realistic and bold in his approach to life. He transforms the goddess Lakshmī into an untouchable, ridicules the sanctity of royalty, and brings to life princes and vagabonds, soldiers and hermits, horses and talking birds. With equal facility he transports the reader into the luxurious city of Ujjayinī or into a forest settlement in the Vindhyas. He is an expert in the art of camouflage through endless punning and metaphor as well as in the remarkable skill of making the hard and unpleasant truth visible through a barrage of compliments, something a modern historian must remember while using the testimony of his works.[2] The latter is amply exemplified, for instance, in the scene between Rājyavardhana and Harsha, each trying to impress the other with filial devotion and lack of ambition, or in the long exchange between Harsha and the envoy of Kāmarūpa, the latter's anguish at having to seek an unequal treaty of alliance spilling through the text in spite of Bāṇa's efforts to disguise it. However, he always provides numerous peepholes to see through his literary camouflage. If the reader cannot see through the peepholes which the author provides for him, the fault lies with the reader himself. That he enables the reader to see through such devices is a measure of Bāṇa's success in coveying the truth.

But first let us see what Bāṇa says about himself, for it is only rarely that we come across authentic information about the family and academic background of an ancient Indian historian, so necessary for understanding his attitude to history and also his psychology.

Bāṇa descended from a long line of ancestors distinguished for their learning and pious observances of rituals. Vatsa, the progenitor of Bāṇa's family, lived in a village called Prītikūṭa on the banks of the Hiraṇyabāhu,

[2] Shankar Goyal, *History and Historiography of the Age of Harsha*, Jodhpur, 1992, p. 8; idem, *Harsha : A Multidisciplinary Political Study*, Jodhpur, 2006, p. 36; idem, for further details, *Harsha Revisited : A Re-interpretation of Existing Data*, Delhi, 2018, pp. 33-68.

also called Śoṇa. Bāṇa's mother, Rājadevī, expired while he was yet a child. He had the misfortune of loosing his father Chitrabhānu also when he was about fourteen years old. Bāṇa tells us that thereafter he led the wandering life of an *itvara* or vagabond making himself an object of ridicule in the eyes of the elders but acquiring much wisdom, experience and also a widened outlook. During this period, gathering a throng of companions of his own age, he wandered from his home, despite inheriting ancestral wealth quite sufficient for a Brāhmaṇa. When he met Harsha for the first time, he confessed that his youth was not without slight, though not serious, follies for which he felt repentent.

Bāṇa was evidently gifted with sharp intellect and was trained by a renowned teacher in his boyhood named Bhatsu or Bharvu who is singled out for salutation in the *Kādambarī* and whose lotus feet are said to have been worshipped by the two kings of the Maukhari family. He claims to have mastered the Veda with its six *aṅgas* and to have heard lectures on *śāstras*. But his special *forte* was his liking for Sanskrit and Prākrit kāvyas, for he mentions with great respect the author of the *Vāsavadattā*, the prose author Harichandra, the lyric poet Sātavāhana (Hāla), the epic poet Pravarasena, the dramatists Bhāsa and Kālidāsa, the writer of the *Bṛhatkathā* and now an unknown author called Āḍhyarāja.[3]

Bāṇa was endowed with an inquisitive nature. He was always hungry for information about men and things from all sources. As he himself puts it, "any new object or matter draws me irresistibly towards it" (*atiparavānasmi kutūhalena*). While going to meet Harsha with his chamberlain he stopped in the way to have a look at the royal stables and the royal elephant Darpaśāta. The second virtue with him was a penetrating intellect (*svabhāvagambhīradhī*) and a sharp memory on which men and matters with whom he came in contact left vivid and lasting impressions as shown by the intimate pen-pictures in both his works. To these was added a third asset, namely, his experience of the wide world gained by his wanderings. Bāṇa tells us that he attended and actively participated in many kinds of *goshṭhīs* which were then a regular feature of civic life. These were like modern clubs for free association of cultured citizens who took interest in such topics as poetry (*kāvya-goshṭhī*), dance (*nṛtya-goshṭhī*), music (*saṁgīta-goshṭhī*), stories (*kathā-goshṭhī*), fine arts (*kalā-goshṭhī*) and gossip (*jalpa-goshṭhī*). As a result, his mind became further saturated with information about the learning—traditional as well as about the culture of his own times.[4]

[3] U.N. Ghoshal, *Studies in Indian History and Culture*, Second revised edn., Calcutta, 1965, pp. 53-54.

[4] Cf. for details V.S. Agrawala, *The Deeds of Harsha* (*Being a Cultural Study of Bāṇa's Harshacharita*), Varanasi, 1969, pp. 2-3.

BĀṆA'S RELATIONSHIP WITH HARSHA

When Bāṇa first met Harsha the latter was irate; however, before long the former had won an indulgent patron. But the nature of his relationship with Harsha is rather intriguing. Some of his statements about it are obviously not entirely true. For example, according to his own admission he believed that all service is hateful. In the *Harshacharita*, when Haṁsavega, the messenger of Bhāskaravarman, meets Harsha, Bāṇa puts a long speech in the mouth of the messenger describing the evils of servitude—something quite unnecessary and irrelevant at that place and in that situation. It is a bitter invective probably unparalleled anywhere else in Sanskrit literature. The flattery of the royal court, the royal servants soaked in utter selfishness and the haughtiness and proud demeanour of the king who behaved with utter contempt have been painted here with a rare fidelity.[5] In his view the government servants hardly deserved to be called human beings. Similarly, when Bāṇa receives the message of Kṛshṇa, the brother of Harsha, to meet the Emperor immediately, he proudly ponders :

> What shall I do?... all service is hateful, and attendance is full of evils, and a court is full of dangers. My ancestors never had any love for it, I have no hereditary connection with it, — nor is mine the consideration from remembering former benefits... .[6]

In fine, he disclaims any relationship and desire for a connection with royalty for himself and for his ancestors. But what are the actual facts? Even at this particular moment, his above-mentioned pondering was occasioned by the message of Kṛshṇa, the brother of Harsha, to the effect that :

> In thy absence the king was on various occasions prejudiced against thee by the malevolent;... Therefore [60] your highness must repair to the palace without delay.[7]

The fact that Kṛshṇa, the brother of the Emperor, took the trouble of sending the message to Bāṇa, and the message itself, show that Bāṇa had close contacts with the royal house of the Pushyabhūtis, including the Emperor and his brother, and had made friends and enemies both in the imperial court long before this message was received by him. Elsewhere, he records that during his wanderings as a youth he had observed 'great royal court'. In the *Kādambarī* also he states that the feet of his ancestor Kubera were worshipped by the Gupta emperors and his own *guru* Bhatsu was worshipped by the Maukhari emperors and their nobles (*sāmantas*). These facts clearly prove that Bāṇa himself, his family and *guru* — all were

[5] *Ibid.*, p. 207.

[6] E.B. Cowell and F.W. Thomas, *The Harṣa-carita of Bāṇa* (hereafter referred to as *HC*, Eng. tr.), Second edn. Delhi, 1968, pp. 43-44.

[7] *Ibid.*, pp. 41-42.

intimately associated with the contemporary imperial and other royal houses. Therefore, his reaction and expression of abhorrence for court-attendance on hearing the message from Kṛshṇa not only appears to be a piece of false self-adulation but also makes the nature of his relationship with Harsha quite intriguing. When he ultimately went to meet Harsha, we are told, Harsha said to the son of the king of Mālava who was sitting behind : "He is a great rogue" (*mahānayam bhujaṅgaḥ*) and when Bāṇa made a protest he merely said, "So we heard" and did not welcome him to sit down, etc. The next day Bāṇa left the royal camp "and remained for a while in the houses of his friends and relations, until the king...became favourably inclined to him. Then he re-entered again to visit the royal abode; and in the course of a very few days he was received by his gracious majesty into the highest degree of honour springing from kindness, of affection, and of confidence, and shared with him in his wealth, his hours of unbending, and his state dignity."[8] Interestingly, in this whole narration he does not tell us anything about his work or achievement for which he was rewarded with wealth and a cane-seat beside the Emperor. Obviously, by that time he had not even composed the *Harshacharita*. And yet he, who on his own admission did not like court-attendance and had been insulted by the Emperor in the open court, suddenly and inexplicably became such a great admirer of the latter that he broke all records of adulation of royal masters by court-poets and set new precedence and norms for the early medieval poets in this field. How did it happen ?[9] In answer to this question is the key to what Bāṇa does not want to say explicitly.

DATE OF THE *HARSHACHARITA*

Bāṇa's contemporaneity with Harsha is one of the surest landmarks of ancient Indian literary history. But the exact date of the composition of his *Harshacharita* is not known. Most of the scholars including M. Winternitz, U. N. Ghoshal, A. A. Macdonell, P.V. Kane, V. S. Agrawala, V. S. Pathak and D. Devahuti are content with the fact that the contemporaneity of Bāṇa with Harsha is well-established.[10] Some of those who have given a thought to the problem of its more exact date place its composition in c.620 A.D. on no surer ground than the fact that Bāṇa appears to have been a young man

[8] *Ibid.*, p. 69.

[9] S.R. Goyal, *Harsha and Buddhism*, Meerut, 1986, pp. 108-10.

[10] E.g. M. Winternitz, *History of Indian Literature*, III, Part I, Delhi, 1963; A.A. Macdonell, *A History of Sanskrit Literature*, Delhi, 1962; V.S. Agrawala, *Harshacharita: Eka Sāṁskṛtika Adhyayana*, Patna, 1964; P.V. Kane, *The Harshacarita of Bāṇabhaṭṭa*, Second edn., Delhi, 1965; U. N. Ghoshal, *op. cit.*; V.S. Pathak, *Ancient Historians of India*, Bombay, 1966; D. Devahuti, *Harsha : A Political Study*, New Delhi, 1970, Second revised edn., New Delhi, 1983.

when he met his patron and composed his biography.[11] Other scholars usually follow Keith in this respect who has suggested a late date for the *Harshacharita.*[12]

But fortunately now the date of the *Harshacharita* has been almost exactly fixed. There are certain facts the combined testimony of which conclusively proves that this work was written in c. 620 A.D.[13] The first of these facts is provided by Yuan Chwang who, in course of his visit to Fa-la-pi or Valabhī, the capital of the Maitrakas, states that its ruler Tu-lo-po-po-tu or Dhruvabhaṭṭa was "a son-in-law of Śīlāditya, reigning at Kānyakubja."[14] Now, as the Chinese pilgrim visited Valabhī in November 640 A.D. or shortly after it,[15] the daughter of Harsha must have been born not very much after 625 A.D.,[16] and, consequently, the marriage of Harsha himself could have taken place around this date at the latest. But when Bāṇa composed his *Harshacharita,* Harsha was as yet a bachelor. For when the poet visited his patron before the composition of his work he found that at that time the king was observing the vow of celibacy (*gṛhītabrahmacharyamāliṅgitaṁ Rājalakshmyā*).[17] Unfortunately, E.B. Cowell and F.W. Thomas translated the word 'brahmacharyam' as 'vow of austerity' which led Thomas Watters to remark that probably "Harshavardhana in the early part of his life had joined the Buddhist church and perhaps taken the vows of a bhikshu, or at least of a lay member of the Communion."[18] Thereafter, it became a subject of controversy whether or not in the early part of his life Harsha wanted to become a monk and was reluctant to ascend the throne.[19] In the confusion

[11] Vide A.B. Keith, *History of Sanskrit Literature* (Hindi edn.), Delhi, 1960, p. 372.

[12] *Ibid.*, pp. 372-73. Vide G. S. Chatterji, *Harshavardhana* (in Hindi), Second edn., Allahabad, 1950, p. 397; M. C. Byrski, 'Some Remarks about King Harṣavardhana Śīlāditya', *Bhāratī,* 5, i, 1961-62, p. 79.

[13] S.R. Goyal, *Harsha Śīlāditya,* Meerut, 1986, Ch.1.

[14] T. Watters, *On Yuan Chwang's Travels in India* (henceforth referred to as *Travels*), II, First Indian edn., Delhi, 1961, p. 246.

[15] Cf. the chronology of Yuan Chwang's travels as given in A. Cunningham's *The Ancient Geography of India,* Varanasi, 1963, p. 477. Vincent A. Smith has also worked out the chronological order of Yuan Chwang's journeys (T. Watters, *Travels,* pp. 229-44). He has placed the Valabhī visit of the Chinese monk after the rains of 641 A.D. but before 642 A.D.

[16] Note that Rājyaśrī was married when she had become a young woman—*taruṇībhūtā vatsā Rājyaśrīḥ* (P.V. Kane, *HC,* IV, *op.cit.*, p. 13). Unless otherwise stated, here we have used the text of the *Harshacharita* edited by Kane.

[17] *Ibid.*, II, p. 32.

[18] *Travels,* I, p. 346.

[19] Cf. R.S. Tripathi, *History of Kanauj to the Moslem Conquest,* Delhi, 1959, pp. 68 ff.; G.S. Chatterji, *op. cit.*; D. Devahuti, *loc. cit.*, First edn., pp. 11, 79 ff.

created by this dispute the simple import of Bāṇa's statement that Harsha was observing the vow of celibacy (and not of austerity) at the time Bāṇa met him before the *Harshacharita* was written, was relegated into the background.

Some scholars believe that Harsha could have been a married man and the father of a daughter in 606 A.D. though he observed the vow of celibacy after the tragic murder of his brother. But it would imply that although Bāṇa described the marriage of Rājyaśrī in detail, he neglected even to mention the marriage of Harsha, and the birth of a daughter to him. It will be an absurd proposition to adopt. Bāṇa could have hardly failed to describe these events in his narrative had they occurred earlier than the events with which his work ends.

Thus, we conclude that Harsha was the father of a married daughter in 640 A.D. and was, therefore, himself married not later than c. 625 A.D. But, as we have seen, he was a celibate when his biography was composed by Bāṇa. Therefore, the *Harshacharita* must have been composed before 625 A.D. This date thus constitutes the *terminus ad quem* for its composition.

Curiously, the *terminus a quo* for the *Harshacharita* is also provided by the combined testimony of the Chinese sources and the *Harshacharita* itself. According to the *Life*, after the religious assembly held at Kanauj the Chinese pilgrim expressed his desire to return to China. Thereupon, Harsha urged him to accompany him to Prayāga. He is reported to have said, "I have established a great religious convocation every five years, to attend which all the Śramans and Brahmans of the five Indies are invited, and besides these the poor and the orphans and the destitute; on this occasion during seventy-five days the great distribution of alms called the Moksha is attended to; I have completed five of these assemblies and am now about to celebrate the sixth : why does not the Master delay his departure till then ?"[20] Yuan Chwang acceded to his request and in December, 642 A.D. witnessed the great spectacle which was the sixth of its type in which everything which Harsha owned 'except the horses, elephants, and military accoutrements'[21] was distributed. Then, the king begged from his sister an ordinary second-hand garment and gladly put it on.[22] This evidence proves that the practice of holding such quinquennial assemblies at Prayāga, in which Harsha distributed all of his belongings, commenced twenty-five years before 642 A.D., i.e. in 617 A.D. It is significant because by the time the *Harshacharita* was composed one or more such assemblies had already taken place, for while describing the personality of Harsha, Bāṇa explicitly makes a reference

[20] S. Beal, *The Life of Hiuen-Tsiang*, Second edn., New Delhi, 1973, p. 184.

[21] *Ibid.*, p. 186.

[22] *Ibid.*, p. 187.

to *Jīvitāvadhigṛhītasar-vasvamahādānadīkshāchīra*, i.e., the strip of cloth put on to signify the solemn conferring as a special gift of all the prosperity gained during one's whole life.[23] It is apparently a succinct description of the ceremony witnessed by Yuan Chwang in which Harsha distributed all of his belongings (*sarvasvadāna*) and gladly put on a second-hand garment (*dīkshāchīra*). It conclusively proves that the *Harshacharita* was composed after at least the first assembly of this type which was held in 617 A.D.

Thus, we find that the *Harshacharita* was written before 625 A.D. and after 617 A.D., say in c. 620 A.D. This conclusion is supported by another interesting line of evidence. In the *Harshacharita* a reference is made to an official named Skandagupta who is described as Gajasādhanādhikṛta or 'the commander of the elephant troop.'[24] Now, Skandagupta is also mentioned in the Banskhera plate of the Year 22 (=628 A.D.)[25] and the Madhuban plate of the Year 25 (=631 A.D.)[26] of Harsha in which he is described as the *dūtaka* of these grants (a position quite often enjoyed by the royal princes themselves), and also as a Mahāsāmanta Mahāprāmātāra. Apparently, in 628 and 631 he was occupying far more important posts than was the case at the time the *Harshacharita* was composed. It indirectly suggests that the *Harshacharita* should be placed earlier than 628 A.D., the date of the Banskhera grant.

Further, it may be noted that though in the third chapter of the *Harshacharita* Śyāmala, the cousin of Bāṇa, is made to describe many of the great achievements of Harsha including his successful clash with the ruler of Sindh,[27] there is no mention here of Harsha's conquest of Valabhī mentioned in the records of the Gurjaras of Lāṭa. This fact also proves that the *Harshacharita* was composed earlier than the dates of these events.

In the light of the above discussion, the conclusion that the *Harshacharita* was composed in c. 620 should be regarded as almost certain. It is a very important conclusion because it helps us solve several other problems. For example, now it can be asserted with greater confidence that the *Kādambarī* was composed later than the *Harshacharita*, for while at the time of the composition of the *Harshacharita* in c. 620 Bāṇa was

[23] *HC*, II, p. 33.

[24] *HC*, VI, p. 49.

[25] *EI*, IV, 1896-97, pp. 208-11.

[26] *Ibid.*, I, 1892, pp. 67-75. However, the recently discovered Kurukshetra-Varanasi grant of Harsha of the Year 23 (= 629 A.D.) records the name of the *dūtaka* as Mahākshapaṭalādhikaraṇādhikṛta Sāmanta Mahārāja Kṛshṇagupta (cf. our paper 'The Recently Discovered Kurukshetra-Varanasi Grant of Harsha : Year 23', *JESI*, XXXI, 2005, pp. 136-46).

[27] *HC*, III, pp. 40-41.

comparatively a young man, at the time of his death which stopped the completion of the *Kādambarī* he had a major son in Bhūshaṇa Bhaṭṭa to complete it. Further, the conclusion that the *Harshacharita* was composed in c. 620 A.D. gives additional weight to the theory that it is a complete and finished product of literary art.[28] At least now it cannot be maintained that Bāṇa must have been aware of the greater part of the career of Harsha. It is possible that Bāṇa intended to describe only the acquisition of sovereignty by Harsha, as V.S. Pathak has argued, and therefore he summarized all the subsequent events of importance of the life of Harsha which had occurred by the time Śyāmala made his speech.

BĀṆA'S MOTIVE IN WRITING THE *HARSHACHARITA*

Some scholars suggest that Bāṇa wrote his *Harshacharita* in order to absolve Harsha of the charge of having some hand in the assassination of his elder brother Rājyavardhana. R.C. Majumdar was the first scholar to indicate towards the possibility of Harsha's indirect link with the conspiracy culminating in the assassination of Rājyavardhana by the Gauḍādhipa.[29] V. S. Pathak's brilliant exposition of the *Harshacharita* provided a logical support to such a possibility.[30] D. Devahuti was also inclined in favour of this hypothesis.[31] S.R. Goyal has placed this theory on very strong grounds.[32] According to Pathak, in the early medieval period when a prince violated the law of primogeniture by dethroning or killing the elder prince, to save him from the infamy his court-biographers generally used three literary symbols:[33] (1) They tried to show that God himself sent their hero to rule this world. (2) They also tried to show that the father of their patron wanted to appoint him his successor ignoring the claim of the elder son. And (3) they described the elder brother of their patron as either unworthy or disinclined to rule.[34] In the *Harshacharita* of Bāṇa, *Vikramāṅkadevacharita* of Bilhaṇa, *Vikramāṅkābhyudaya* of Someśvara and many other biographical works, and also in the Rāshṭrakūṭa epigraphs, these motifs have been used for propaganda purposes. Goyal has followed Pathak closely and has shown that such claims were usually baseless and were made merely to justify the usurpation of power by the younger brother at the cost of his elder brother.

[28] V.S. Pathak, *loc. cit.*, pp. 30 ff.

[29] R.C. Majumdar (ed.)., *The History of Bengal* (Volume I : Hindu Period), Dacca, 1943, pp. 76-77.

[30] V.S. Pathak, *op. cit.*, pp. 45 ff.

[31] D. Devahuti, *op. cit.*, Second edn., pp. 79 ff.

[32] S.R. Goyal, *op. cit.*, pp. 7-11.

[33] V.S. Pathak, *op. cit.*, Ch. II.

[34] *Ibid.*, p. 62.

Following Pathak he is also of the opinion that in such works events are not described in their true form; rather, they are so moulded as to bring them in harmony with the aim (*phalāgama*). For this end in view even significant events which were not in harmony with the *phalāgama* were deleted and their chronological order was distorted. But while attempting to bring about such harmony the writer sometimes failed to reconcile various events with each other or moulded the character of the hero and others according to the necessities of the *phalāgama*. The analysis of such defying snippets of the story, therefore, is of great value to the historian; for it alone enables him in finding out the real aim behind them. The story that emerges by the analysis of the literary symbols used by Bāṇa (such as Harsha was born to rule,[35] Rājyavardhana II had a dislike for the throne[36] and Prabhākaravardhana wanted Harsha as his successor)[37] and the 'refractory snippets' scattered over the body of the text is entirely different and opposed to the one narrated in the text.

In the light of this analysis and the non-allusion to certain significant events by Bāṇa, such as the coronation of Rājyavardhana, his death under suspicious circumstancs creates doubts against Harsha. The use of the revealing similies by Bāṇa that foretell the death of Rājyavardhana and Harsha's suggestive dreams[38] on the eve of the elder prince's departure for Kanauj strengthen these doubts. In this context Yuan Chwang's statement that 'owing to the fault of his ministers he was led to subject his person to the hand of his enemy'[39] tends to impart the character of certainty to these doubts. Bhaṇḍi, being present on the spot, could have been one of those ministers who were accused by the Chinese pilgrim of negligence in safeguarding the person of Rājyavardhana. He accompanied Rājyavardhana in the latter's campaign against the Mālava king. He was a close associate of Harsha as is indicated by the fact that he stayed with the latter at the time of the Hūṇa invasion. He is probably identical with Po-ni who played a significant role which resulted in the acquisition of the kingdom of Kanauj by Harsha.[40] Thus, in all probability a complex situation existed which consummated in the murder of Rājyavardhana in questionable circumstances. Goyal has rightly pointed out that Bāṇa has also referred to the rumours that the fame of Harsha was sullied by the stain of the accusation

[35] *HC*, Eng. tr., p. 97.

[36] *Ibid.*, p. 170.

[37] *Ibid.*, pp. 155-56.

[38] *Ibid.*, p. 117.

[39] S. Beal, *Si-Yü-Ki* or *Buddhist Records of the Western World*, V, repr., Delhi, July 1969, p. 211.

[40] *Ibid.*, pp. 210-11 (S. Beal's identification of Bhaṇḍi with Po-ni of Yuan Chwang is generally accepted).

that, like Indra, he was implicated in the murder of his elder brother.[41]

PLACE OF THE *HARSHACHARITA* IN THE HISTORY OF SANSKRIT LITERATURE : IMPACT OF THE PURĀṆA MODEL ON BĀṆA

Bāṇa based his *Harshacharita* on the Purāṇa model, at least broadly. The narratives of the Purāṇas are usually put in the form of replies of a sūta or of a sage to the queries addressed by other sages or kings. In the *Harshacharita* also Bāṇa narrates Harsha's life and achievements to his kinsmen in reply to their requests to hear the story of Harsha. He tells us how after his return home from the court of Harsha, one afternoon one of his kinsmen recited an Āryā couplet to the effect that the *Vāyu Purāṇa* is in no way different from the story of the achievements of Harsha and then the youngest of them made a request to him to tell the full story of the king to which Bāṇa responded after a show of reluctance. Thus, Bāṇa's biography of the king is presented before us in the setting of his autobiography. In the *Gauḍavaho*, the *Navasāhasāṅkacharita*, the *Vikramāṅkacharita* and the *Rāmacharita* of later times the poet-chroniclers added sketches of their careers to their works independently either by way of prefatory notice or else of a supplement. Bāṇa's bold and unique plan ensured for his work a unity of design which was not achieved by his successors.[42]

HARSHACHARITA AS AN *ĀKHYĀYIKĀ*

Bāṇa, however, introduces his *Harshacharita* to his readers under the title of an *ākhyāyikā*, while his other work the *Kādambarī* is introduced with the title of a *kathā*.[43] An *Ākhyāyikā* signifies a composition dealing with historical facts while a *kathā* is a work of imagination. In his *Mahābhāshya* Patañjali (middle of the second century B.C.) mentions three *ākhyāyikās* by name, viz. the *Vāsavadattā*, the *Sumanottarā* and the *Bhaimarathī* signifying that the tradition of composing the *ākhyāyikās* started long before the second century B.C. To the same category may be assigned the prose

[41] "Like the Lord of the Immortals, he appeared busy in wiping away the stain of his elder brother's slaughter." (Cf. *HC*, Eng. tr., p. 204). Indra, the Lord of Immortals, is said to have killed Viśvarūpa who was regarded as his *agraja* (elder brother). Following S. R. Goyal we also believe that this statement of Bāṇa clearly points to the fact that like Indra Harsha also had to try to wipe away the stain of the accusation of the murder of his elder brother.

[42] U.N. Ghoshal, *op. cit.*, p. 51.

[43] For a useful discussion on this problem vide U.N. Ghoshal, *op.cit.*, pp. 49-50; P.V. Kane, *op.cit.*, pp. xiii-xxii; V.S. Pathak, *op.cit.*, pp. 36-45; V.S. Agrawala, *The Deeds of Harsha*, p. 6; A.K. Warder, *An Introduction to Indian Historiography*, Bombay, 1972, pp. 38-40; S.N. Dasgupta, *A History of the Sanskrit Literature*, Vol. I : *Classical Period*, Second edn., Calcutta, 1975, pp. 225-39.

composition of Harichandra which is praised by Bāṇa in one of the introductory verses of the *Harshacharita*.[44] All these works are no longer extant. On the other hand, the composition of the *ākhyāyikās* appears to have gone out of fashion after Bāṇa's time, for we have no work of this class of a later date than the *Harshacharita*.

There was a controversy among Sanskrit rhetoricians about the distinctive features of an *ākhyāyikā* and a *kathā*. According to Daṇḍin, in an *ākhyāyikā* it is the hero himself who tells the whole story; while in a *kathā*, the story is told either by the hero or by someone else. An *ākhyāyikā* is divided into sections named *uchchhvāsas* and contains verses in the Vaktra and Aparavaktra metres; while in a *kathā* it is not so. In a *kathā*, such topics as the kidnapping of a girl, battles, separation, the rise of the sun and the moon are described; in an *ākhyāyikā* it is not so. A *katha* is distinguished by possessing certain catch words which the author intentionally puts in. However, Daṇḍin also remarks that no hard and fast line of demarcation can be drawn between the two classes of works, and that these points have not been invariably followed by writers and, therefore, a *kathā* and an *ākhyāyikā* are virtually two names for the same species of prose composition.

Abhinavagupta also distinguishes an *ākhyāyikā* from a *kathā* by saying that the former is divided into sections called *uchchhvāsas* and contains verses in the Vaktra and Aparavaktra metres; while the latter lacks these features. The *Sāhityadarpaṇa* says that a *kathā* contains a fine plot in prose with verses in the Āryā, Vaktra or Aparavaktra metres here and there; a *kathā* is introduced by a salutation in verse and reference is made to the conduct of the wicked, etc. It further says that an *ākhyāyikā* is just like a *kathā* with this addition that the former contains a narrative of the poet himself and of other poets, that its divisions are styled *āśvāsas* and that it contains verses at the beginning of each *āśvāsa* that suggest future events.

According to the *Agni Purāṇa*,[45] an *ākhyāyikā* should comprise a description of the author's family in some detail as also of such calamitous events as abduction or forceful seizure of a maiden, battle, separation, etc., brilliance of style (*rīti*) and expressiveness (*vṛtti*), division of chapters named *uchchhvāsa*, abundance of portions in Chūrṇaka style, presence of Vaktra and Aparavaktra metres. On the other hand, a *kathā* is to consist of only a brief account of the poet, a prologue introducing the main story and the absence of chapter-divisions or in some cases the presence of chapters by the name of *lambaka*. Bāṇa himself often alludes to the two classes of prose compositions. He refers to some peculiarities that distinguished an *ākhyāyikā* from other classes of compositions, viz. the division into *uchchhvāsas* and

[44] U.N. Ghoshal, *op. cit.*, p. 49.
[45] 336. 13-14.

the occurrence of the Vaktra metre. He himself clearly intimates that his *Harshacharita* is an *ākhyāyikā* while the *Kādambarī* was intended to be a *kathā*. It means that he was quite clear in his mind that he *did not* strike out a new path in writing his two prose works. Bāṇa himself classes *ākhyāyikās* not with poetic works such as epics and romances but with such mythologico-historical forms of writing as *ākhyāna*, *itihāsa* and *purāṇa*.[46] The *Mahābhāshya* also groups these four *genres* together.[47] The *Arthaśāstra* of Kauṭilya is more definite, as it explicitly mentions an *ākhyāyikā* along with *purāṇa*, *itivṛtta*, etc., as a constituent part of *itihāsa*.[48]

For Bāṇa the *Mahābhārata*, the greatest *itihāsa* work of India, was an ideal composition.[49] He consciously imitates its plan and style. The Great Epic begins with a description of the Bhārgava Brāhmaṇas, the *Harshacharita* also starts with the history of the Bhārgava-Vātsyāyanas. The narration of the *Mahābhārata* begins by Ugraśravā at the instance of some *ṛshis* led by Śaunaka. Likewise, in the *Harshacharita* Bāṇa describes the deeds of Harsha at the request of Śyāmala in the circle of his kinsmen. Above all, the fact that in the epilogue of his work Bāṇa makes his cousin Śyāmala describe the *Harshacharita* as a second *Mahābhārata*[50] suggests that Bāṇa took the Great Epic as the model for his work.[51]

HARSHACHARITA AS THE FORERUNNER OF THE BIOGRAPHIES OF KINGS (*CHARITA KĀVYAS*)

In the history of Sanskrit literature the *Harshacharita* may also be regarded as the forerunner of a new class of compositions called *charitas*.[52] It is indeed the earliest *charita kāvya* written on a *contemporary* monarch. Probably Bāṇa wanted to make his mark in literature by undertaking this bold experiment. He took for his theme the biography of his great patron Harsha and became for all practical purposes the creator of a new literary *genre* which found many imitators among his successors. It is indeed true that the word *charita*, a part of the name *Harshacharita*, had begun to be used long before the time of Bāṇa as in the *Buddhacharita* of Aśvaghosha and *Paümachariya* of Ravisheṇa.[53] But the *Harshacharita* is the first work dealing with the biography of a *contemporary* ruler. However, it is not a clear-cut

[46] V.S. Agrawala, *Kādambarī : Eka Sāṁskṛtika Adhyayana*, Varanasi, 1958, p. 13.
[47] IV. 2.60.
[48] I, 5.
[49] *HC*, Intro., v. 9.
[50] *Ibid.*, p. 140.
[51] Cf. V.S. Pathak, *op. cit.*, p. 37.
[52] U.N. Ghoshal, *op. cit.*, p. 50.
[53] V.S. Agrawala, *The Deeds of Harsha*, p. 10; S.N. Dasgupta, *op. cit.*, pp. 69-79.

historical text. Bāṇa has composed it with all the literary exuberance of a poet's style including a description of Harsha's life, his personality, some contemporary events, his court and some of the high dignitaries. Daṇḍin has given a definition of a *Mahākāvya* which would follow a conventionalized pattern of describing a city, mountain, ocean, natural beauty of seasons, sun-rise, moon-rise, garden-sports, water-sports, marriage, birth of a son, royal counsellors, march of the army, etc. Bāṇa was fully conversant with this technique of a *Prabhandha Kāvya* and has tried to avail of it, although he was writing in prose.

IS *HARSHACHARITA* AN INCOMPLETE WORK ?

Many modern historians have described the *Harshacharita* as 'fragmentary', a work with an 'abrupt' ending, because it does not deal with the complete life of Harsha and abruptly stops after the meeting of Harsha with his recently widowed sister Rājyaśrī. But we submit that all those who make this point usually forget that in the third *uchchhvāsa* Bāṇa has explicitly stated that he was unable to do justice with the whole career of Harsha and, therefore, would deal only with a portion of it :

> What man could possibly even in a hundred of men's lives depict his story in full? If, however, you care for a part, I am ready.[54]

Logically also, if a court-poet composed the biography of his patron during the latter's life-time he simply could not describe the events of his reign up till his demise; therefore, the *Harshacharita* was bound to depict the life of Harsha only up to a certain point of time, and not till the death of Harsha. Further, as V.S. Pathak argues,[55] from the literary point of view and according to the best bardic tradition it is a complete whole, organically designed and artistically composed for the specific purpose of the union of Harsha with royal glory (*rājyaśrī*) embodied in the person of Rājyaśrī, the sister of Harsha. The *Harshacharita*, according to Pathak, falls into five well-defined stages followed in the works of drama—the beginning (*prārambha*), the effort (*prayatna*), the hope of achieving the end (*prāptyāśā*), the certainty of success (*niyatāpti*), and the end (*phalāgama*). Since the last stage of the end is reached with the recovery of Rājyaśrī—the sister of Harsha but notionally the royal glory—the story ended with it. And lastly (and this in view of Pathak conclusively proves that the *Harshacharita* is a complete work), the autobiography of Bāṇa, in which the story of Harsha's life is emboxed, is resumed in the concluding portion of the *Harshacharita*. There are two stories in the narrative—the account of Bāṇa and his ancestry, and

[54] *HC*, Eng. tr., p. 77; III, p. 41 (कः खलु पुरुषायुषशतेनापि शक्नुयादविकलमस्य चरितं वर्णयितुम्। एकदेशे तु यदि कुतूहलं वः, सज्जा वयम्।))।

[55] V.S. Pathak, *op. cit.*, p. 32.

the history of Harsha. The first was abruptly interrupted by Śyāmala who requested Bāṇa to narrate the glorious deeds of Harsha and thus furnished an excuse for Bāṇa for emboxing the royal biography in the story of his own life. However, towards the conclusion of the book, the thread of the first story is resumed with the statement that

> As he was relating there to his friends the story of the recovery of Rājyaśrī, the sun completed his journey through the heavens.[56]

This reversion to the initial story, which is pursued to the end, is a definite indication that the book is complete.

BĀṆA'S VIEW OF HISTORY

In the early medieval court tradition the meaning of *itihāsa* was narrowed down to an account of events culminating into the achievement of royal glory by the king. Further, because of the romantic spirit of the age, the early medieval poet-historians represented the abstract idea of royal glory in the form of a beautiful princess symbolising the goddess of Royal Fortune, mentioned variously as *Rājya-śrī*, *Nṛpa-śrī* or *Sāmrājya-lakshmī*, whose love the king wins after overcoming numerous difficulties. From the fourth century A.D. this motif of royal glory became widely prevalent. In different forms, it occurs in numerous historical works. Inscriptions of the Guptas, the Pālas, the Pratihāras, the Rāshṭrakūṭas and others make frequent use of this motif. As noted above, according to V.S. Pathak, in such historical narratives the process of the achievement of royal glory by the king is invariably developed in five stages. These stages provide an ordered sequence in the story. However, for the writers of such works notionally the end (*phala*) of the story was the real starting point. Observes Pathak :

> In this reverse process, his (poet-historian's) endeavour is not so much to develop gradually the consequences of a given initial situation as to arrange antecedent events in such a way that they necessarily culminate into the known outcome. Further, since a man can hardly grasp and describe life in all its multifarious aspects, the historian selects only that series of events through which he can explain the end in question.[57]

He further writes :

> In the reverse process of constructing the history of the past, the concern of the historian is not so much to bring out the consequences which would inevitably follow if a person with certain given qualities were placed in the initial situation as to divine in his characters those qualities which make the known outcome appear rational and inevitable. Therefore, besides conditioning the treatment of antecedent events, the end (*phalāgama*) also influences the characterization.[58]

[56] *HC*, Eng. tr., p. 258.

[57] V.S. Pathak, *op. cit.*, p. 45.

[58] *Ibid.*, pp. 47-48.

However, in his attempt to weave a coherent story such poet-historian usually inadvertantly left several loose ends which ultimately give a lie to the central tale exposing the motive of the author. Such discrepancies, Pathak argues, become to the modern historian as important, if not more, as the coherent picture itself, for they often reveal a story which is usually more in consonance with archaeological sources. Pathak has applied this method to several early medieval works including the *Harshacharita* of Bāṇa. He has shown that Bāṇa, who aimed at describing the achievement of universal sovereignty (*rājya-śrī*), personfied in latter's sister Rājyaśrī,[59] not only concocts the story that Lakshmī had herself favoured Pushyabhūti, the founder of the Vardhana royal house, with the boon that a Chakravartin ruler named Harsha will be born in his family, but also puts in the mouth of Prabhākaravardhana the statement which suggests that the dying king wanted his second son Harsha to succeed him. Bāṇa also makes Rājyavardhana to offer the crown to Harsha and deliberately neglects to mention that Rājyavardhana did ascend the throne, a fact which is revealed to us by the epigraphic evidence. From this Pathak concludes that :

> The story which emerges from these discrepancies naturally runs in the opposite direction, cutting across the central tale of the *Harshacharita* at its vital point. If the latter portrays the noble character of Harsha with such an exuberance of pious and affectionate colours that it assumes an aerial nebulosity, the former casts dark shadows of doubt on his intentions towards Rājya. If the central story suggests that there was a noble struggle between Rājya and Harsha, both of whom wanted the other to ascend the throne, the tale of anomalous fragments may be construed to indicate that attempts were made to enthrone Harsha by superseding Rājya. ...
>
> One can even bring oneself to believe in the correctness of the account of the overpowering affection of Prabhākara towards Harsha, to the exclusion of Rājya. But the author outsteps all bounds, when he neglects to mention the accession of Rājya to the throne of Thanesar. The little epigraphic evidence gives a clear verdict against this part of Bāṇa's story.[60]

QUESTION OF THE RELIABILITY OF THE *HARSHACHARITA* AS A WORK OF HISTORY

However, by virtue of his favoured position at the court of Harsha, Bāṇa enjoyed exceptional opportunities for acquiring true knowledge of the contemporary events. It is proved by the fact that quite often his statements are confirmed by independent evidence of reliable nature. Thus, the religious eclecticism attributed to the Pushyabhūti family by Bāṇa who describes

[59] *Ibid.*, p. 49.

[60] *Ibid.*, p. 55. Cf. also Romila Thapar, *The Penguin History of Early India : From the Origins to AD 1300*, New Delhi, 2003, p. 288.

Pushyabhūti as a passionate devotee of Śiva, Prabhākaravardhana as that of Sun, Rājyavardhana as the worshipper of the Buddha and Harsha as a worshipper of Nīlalohita (Śiva) is confirmed by the inscriptions of Harsha himself which do not mention Pushyabhūti but describe Prabhākara, Rājya and Harsha respectively as *Paramādityabhakta*, *Paramasaugata* and *Paramamāheśvara*. The wicked lord of Mālava, who, according to Bāṇa, killed Grahavarman of Kanauj and was subsequently defeated with 'ridiculous ease' by Rājyavardhana has rightly and unanimously been identified with Devagupta of Harsha's records. Bāṇa's vague account of the treacherous murder of Rājyavardhana by the 'wile Gauḍa serpent' (*Gauḍabhu-jaṅga*)[61] is corroborated though only by equally vague reference in Harsha's inscriptions and in the contemporary work of Yuan Chwang. For these reasons the *Harshacharita* has always been accepted as a reliable source for the early history of Harsha's reign and for the history of his immediate predecessors.

But the question of the trustworthiness of Bāṇa has another dimension as well. Though the events of the early history of Harsha's reign as delineated in the *Harshacharita* are intrinsically factual; their order, dates and significance are not necessarily the same as they are said to be in the epigraphs. Let us scrutinize the *relative chronology* of the reign of Harsha as given by Bāṇa which, according to us, is patently unreliable. For example, the account of Bāṇa shows that when Harsha ascended the throne he was a sixteen year old boy of a very small state which was at war with the Hūṇas and was surrounded on all sides by the enemies. Further, his father Prabhākara had died only a short while ago and his brother and brother-in-law were murdered only recently. On the other hand, at that time Śaśāṅka, his enemy, was at the height of his glory. He had, as it appears from the Doobi plates, successfully invaded Kāmarūpa and captured Bhāskaravarman and his brother as prisoners. In the west he had occupied Kanauj after murdering Grahavarman. Thus, he was ruling over a vast empire, which included Kāmarūpa, Bengal, Bihar, U. P. and Malwa. How then, could Harsha proclaim, at the time of his accession, his intention for *digvijaya* by threatening all the rulers of 'the entire earth' and how could Bhāskaravarman, even if he had thrown off the Gauḍa yoke by that time, send an embassy to Harsha with costly presents? Further, how could this embassy cross the vast Gauḍa empire to reach the young Pushyabhūti ruler and what benefit could Bhāskaravarman expect from an alliance with a small ruler as Harsha at that time was ? But the friendship of Harsha and Bhāskara-varman is mentioned by Yuan Chwang as well, though at a later date. Therefore, the

[61] *HC*, p. 47.

conclusion is inescapable that this alliance was contracted at a later date when the victorious arms of Harsha had reached as far as Bengal, but Bāṇa has mentioned it as an event which occurred at the commencement of Harsha's reign.

From the *Harshacharita* we learn that on receiving the news of Rājyavardhana's murder, on exhortation of Siṁhanāda, Harsha vowed: "By the dust of my honoured lord's feet I swear that, unless in a limited number of days (*pariganitareva vāsaraḥ*) I clear this earth of Gauḍas, and make it resound with fetters on the feet of all kings who are excited to insolence by the elasticity of their bows, then will I hurl my sinful self, like a moth, into an oil-fed flame."[62] But here Bāṇa mixes this vow with Harsha's resolve for *digvijaya*, for he says that after this declaration Harsha gave instructions to Avanti, the supreme minister of war and peace, who was standing near : 'Let a proclamation be engraved': "As far as the orient hill (Udayāchala in the east),... as far as Suvela (in Ceylon in the south),... as far as the western mount (Astagiri in the west),... as far as Gandhamādana (in the north),... let all kings prepare their hands to give tribute or grasp swords,... let them bend their heads or their bows, grace their ears with either my commands or their bowstrings, crown their heads with the dust of my feet or with helmets,... let go their lands or arrows,... take a good view of themselves in the nails of my feet or the mirrors of their swords. ..."[63] When the day dawned he called Skandagupta, the commandant of the whole elephant troops (*gajasādhanādhikṛta*) and instructed him that he "must hastily call in the elephant herds out at pasture" and told him that the "hot pain of my brother's defeat forbids even the briefest delay in marching."[64] After sometime a day of marching was fixed with careful astronomical calculations.

This description by Bāṇa of Harsha's resolve to undertake a *digvijaya* is not only hyperbolic, but impossible as well. As S. R. Goyal points out, if we remember the precarious condition in which the small kingdom of Thanesar (very small indeed in comparison to the vast Gauḍa empire) was at the time of the accession of Harsha, a sixteen year old inexperienced lad, then it will be impossible to believe that Harsha could make such a resolve and take the risk of annoying the neighbouring kings unnecessarily.[65] Goyal also rightly points out that the general assumption that Harsha's resolve and declaration for *digvijaya*, his march towards Kanauj, his alliance with Bhāskaravarman and the successful search of Rājyaśrī in the Vindhya region—all took place in 606 A. D., does not seem to be correct. Such a

[62] *Ibid.*, Eng. tr., p. 187.
[63] *Ibid.*, pp. 187-88.
[64] *Ibid.*, p. 191.
[65] S.R. Goyal, *Maukhari-Pushyabhūti-Chālukya Yuga*, Meerut, 1988, pp. 178-79.

rapid succession of events no doubt seems to be indicated by Bāṇa. But if we go through his narrative carefully we find that he has spoken of several time-gaps as well. For example, according to him, after making the declaration for *digvijaya* Harsha first devoted his attention to doing what was needed to stablise the condition of his kingdom (*sakalarājyasthitiśchakāra*).[66] It must have taken some time; indeed it might have taken a few months or even more. Then, some time passed (*atha vyatīteshu keshuchiddivashesu*) before a team of astrologers fixed 'an hour of marching' suitable for *daṇḍayātrā*.[67] Though it will not be proper to assume that such time-gaps, indicated by Bāṇa, were very long; but it is also obvious that they are against the usually accepted view that Harsha started for the conquest of quarters immediately after he had made the declaration of his resolve for *digvijaya*— a declaration which itself was probably never made.

Actually, Bāṇa has introduced the motif of *digvijaya* in order to glorify his patron and has mixed it up with Harsha's vow to take a revenge on the Gauḍas. That is why he describes the campaign of Harsha sometime as a project of *digvijaya* and sometime as an expedition to punish the Gauḍa ruler (*daṇḍayātrā*). When Harsha received the news of his brother's murder he made a resolve 'to clear the earth of the Gauḍas' (*nigauḍāṁ karomi medinīm*) but at the same time he also resolved to undertake the conquest of quarters (*digvijaya*). Then, the astrologers were asked 'to fix the hour of marching' for punitive expedition. At that time his army is also shown talking of the impending Gauḍa war (*Gauḍa vigraha*). But his feudatories are depicted as thinking of conquering the whole world including Persia. Later on, when Harsha met Bhaṇḍi, he ordered him to march with the army against the Gauḍas (*bhavānapikaṭakamādāya pravaṛtatām Gauḍābhimukham*) and he himself went in search of Rājyaśrī. Thus, so far as the narrative of Bāṇa is concerned Harsha's military campaign was meant at least in name for the conquest of quarters but in fact his army marched to punish the Gauḍa king. However, so far the actual result is concerned it achieved neither of these objectives. Bāṇa remains satisfied with using contemptuous epithets like *Gauḍādhama* and *Gauḍabhujaṅga* for the Gauḍa king. His account of the punitive expedition against the Gauḍa monarch ends with Harsha's order to Bhaṇḍi to "advance against the Gauḍas." Actually, Bāṇa nowhere categorically states that Harsha succeeded in defeating Śaśāṅka. Even Śyāmala, who enumerates the achievements of Harsha known at the time the *Harshacharita* was composed, does not include a victory over the Gauḍas among them. Significantly, the words which Harsha uses in his vow regarding

[66] *HC*, Eng. tr., p. 194.
[67] *Ibid.*, p. 197.

his revenge on Śaśāṅka do not bind him by any time-limit—he merely says that if 'in a limited number of days' (*pariganitareva vāsaraḥ*) he would not clear the earth of the Gauḍas he would hurl his sinful self into an oil-fed flame. Apparently, Bāṇa knew that even by the time he composed his *Harshacharita*, Harsha had not succeeded against the Gauḍa enemy. That is why he did not make Harsha set a time-limit for this revenge. Incidentally, this suggestion agrees with the view that the *Harshacharita* was composed in c. 620, for from the Ganjam plates of Śaśāṅka we know that he was ruling with full imperial glory till atleast 619 A.D., the date of this record. It, therefore, follows that when Bāṇa makes Harsha order Bhaṇḍi to invade the Gauḍas, he was only fulfilling the necessity of the story; in reality Harsha did not and, being in the precarious position he was at that time, could not invade the Gauḍas.

While Harsha was resting at one of his camps during his march, in fact the first encampment on the outskirts of his capital, he met Haṁsavega, a messenger (*dūto antaraṅgaḥ*) sent by the lord of Prāgjyotisha (Kāmarūpa), who had reached there with many valuable presents from his master to Harsha. These presents included Varuṇa's umbrella (*chhatra*) named Abhoga which was the symbol of sovereignty over four oceans. This umbrella was especially valuable as it was an heirloom of the Kāmarūpa royal family and was also something of a marvel since it had the property of emitting coolness. In his message from his master Haṁsavega told Harsha that "from childhood upward" it was his master's "firm resolution never to do homage to any being except the lotus feet of Śiva." Emphasizing the importance of the bonds of friendship Haṁsavega told Harsha that "The sovereign of Prāgjyotisha desires with Your Majesty an imperishable alliance." Harsha readily welcomed this offer with reciprocal gesture of goodwill. He asked Haṁsavega to "use his endeavours" so that his "yearning to see the prince may not torment" him for long and sent Haṁsavega away with a load of answering gifts in charge of eminent envoys after the latter had assured him that the Kāmarūpa monarch would meet him within a few days.[68]

It is generally believed that the king of Kāmarūpa sought on his own initiative a subordinate alliance with Harsha. According to Devahuti, it was "perfectly timed to give the latter (that is, Harsha) both the psychological and the strategic advantage over Śaśāṅka."[69] She believes that the fact that Bhāskaravarman surrendered Abhoga, the umbrella of Varuṇa, clearly shows that he was "greatly afraid of Śaśāṅka and most anxious to secure Harsha's support even at the cost of compromising his own status. For Harsha

[68] Cf. D. Devahuti, *op. cit.*, p. 87, n. 2.
[69] *Ibid.*, p. 86.

too the alliance was equally important at this stage. His pleasure and gratification at the offer show up as clearly in Bāṇa's description of his audience with the Kāma-rūpa envoy, as, indeed, does Bhāskara-varman's anguish at having to accept an inferior status in the relationship."[70] Devahuti also opines that the desired meeting between Bhāskaravarman and Harsha may have taken place at the successful termination of the latter's eastern campaign, pushing Śaśāṅka to his native Gauḍa. "It seems that Harsha, in the tradition of paramount sovereigns, used this opportunity formally to instal Bhāskara-varman on the throne of Kāma-rūpa."[71] Bāṇa refers to the anointing of one Kumāra among Harsha's achievements. Cowell and Thomas take *Kumāra* to be a common noun and translate it as 'young prince', but according to Devahuti, "Harsha's achievement would not have been considered worthy of mention if Kumāra in this case did not stand for the king of Kāma-rūpa."[72] Therefore, she not only suggests that Bhāskara offered to become a subordinate ally of Harsha of his own accord, but also argues that the language used by Haṁsavega was full of flattering effects because Bhāskaravarman was afraid that "Harsha might be annoyed at not being offered whole-hearted submission."[73]

But it is difficult to believe that an alliance of this nature between these two monarchs was concluded in 606 A.D. As seen above, in that year Harsha was an ordinary king; he was yet to acquire the status of the Lord Paramount of North India. Further, as we have also noted above, at that time he was surrounded by enemies and his position was extremely precarious. And lastly, the kingdom of Kāmarūpa was far away in eastern India. The vast Gauḍa empire comprising greater part of Bengal, Bihar and U.P. intervened between the two. Then, how could the Kāmarūpa envoy come and meet Harsha somewhere near Thanesar? And that too with such costly presents ? And what advantage could Bhāskara see in an alliance with such a distant and ordinary king ? And what danger could Bhāskaravarman visualize if Harsha became annoyed with him ? A sixteen years old king, whose brother and brother-in-law had been just murdered and whose own sister was in prison of the enemies and who was surrounded by powerful hostile rulers, could not be seen as a friend or foe of great consequence by the far distant ruler of Kāmarūpa, who, according to the Doobi plates, himself had been in the Gauḍa prison only a short while ago.

But it is also a fact that the friendship of Harsha and Bhāskara did materialize, for in 643 A.D. Yuan Chwang himself witnessed it. Therefore,

70 *Ibid.*, pp. 86-87.

71 *Ibid.*, p. 87.

72 *Ibid.*, p. 87, n. 4.

73 *Ibid.*, p. 87, n. 2.

the conclusion is inevitable that this alliance was concluded not in 606 A.D. but when Harsha had acquired eminent position in north India. Most likely at that time Harsha and Bhāskaravarman became friends against Śaśāṅka, Harsha gradually asserting his superiority over Bhāskara. Initially, this alliance must have been concluded at a time when Bhāskaravarman could come to meet Harsha easily after only 'a few days' march, as Haṁsavega put it. In 606 A.D. the king of Kāmarūpa could not come and meet Harsha for the vast Gauḍa empire was a physical barrier between the two. Bāṇa has put the arrival of Haṁsavega in 606 because he wanted to show that Harsha also acquired the *chhatra* named Abhoga which only a Chakravartin could possess. But in 606 Harsha had not become a Chakravartin ruler. Going still deeper, even the *chhatra* motif must have been only a myth for, as we have seen, according to Kalhaṇa's *Rājataraṅgiṇī* (a tradition which Bāṇa probably did not know), Abhoga had been taken back to his abode by its owner Varuṇa in remote antiquity. As regards the *abhisheka* of a certain Kumāra by Harsha, he could not have been Bhāskara. Bhāskara was already an anointed king when Haṁsavega met Harsha.

Bāṇa's distortion of various events of the reign of Harsha is also explicit in his account of Harsha's successful search for Rājyaśrī which is usually regarded as literally true. But the fact that Harsha saved her just before she was about to mount the funeral pyre is too dramatic a conclusion of the search to have been true. Its dramatic quality makes one wonder about its veracity which seems to be further reduced if we remember that Rājyaśrī escaped from prison quite a long while before Harsha saved her—she escaped long before Harsha met Bhaṇḍi after which Harsha is said to have spent quite a long time in her search in the Vindhya forest. It becomes, therefore, difficult to believe that Harsha met her just when she was about to mount the funeral pyre. Such dramatic twists are alright for the stories of ancient plays and modern films, but they cannot be regarded as sober history. We do not mean that Harsha did not make a search for his sister or that his search was not successful. We are only suggesting that his search and its successful conclusion were probably much less dramatic than Bāṇa asks us to believe.

This distortion of the event leads to certain other intriguing questions and throws suspicion on the reliability of the *Harshacharita*. For instance, why did Rājyaśrī not go to Thanesar after her escape from prison ? If after her escape she heard the news of Rājyavardhana's murder, then she must have also heard that Bhaṇḍi was somewhere nearby. Then, why did she not go to him ? Had she heard about the rumours that Bhaṇḍi or some other Pushyabhūti ministers were implicated in Rājya's murder ? One should remember that at that time she was not exactly friendless and resourceless.

saw a number of evil omens such as the deer moving from right to left, a crow facing the sun against its wont and perching on a blighted tree and a naked Jaina mendicant 'all lamp-black as it seemed with the collected filth of many days'. All these points show his credulous nature, not an acumen for scientific history.

Bāṇa had an uncritical belief in magical weapons and ornaments. For example, Bhairavāchārya presented to the king Pushyabhūti the magic sword Aṭṭahāsa. The magic umbrella Abhoga of Varuṇa was presented to Harsha by the ambassador of the king of Prāgjyotisha, while the pearl-wreath *Mandākinī*, was presented to him by sage Divākaramitra. With this may be mentioned Bāṇa's faith in the efficacy of astrology and divination. Of this we have conspicuous examples, in the elaborate description of Harsha's horoscope and prognostication of his future greatness by his bodily marks.[86] Like other ancient Indian author Bāṇa was incapable of differenciating between legend from history. Tracing the family history of the king of Prāgjyotisha his ambassador tells Harsha how Naraka, the son of Vishṇu by the Earth-goddess, was born in hell, and how he wrested the miraculous umbrella Abhoga (thereafter preserved in the family as an heirloom) from the god Varuṇa. Here, Bāṇa's knowledge of the history of this umbrella was not accurate, for we learn from Kalhaṇa's *Rājataraṅgiṇī* that Abhoga was carried back to Varuṇaloka long before the age of Harsha; at least it was so believed.[87]

Tracing his own ancestry Bāṇa begins with a scene in heaven when God Brahmā was engaged in philosophical discussions with the attendant sages, while others were chanting the Vedas. There in a fit of anger the irascible Durvāsā cursed the divine Sarasvatī to be born on earth. Descending to earth Sarasvatī united herself in marriage with the sage Dadhīcha by whom she had a son Sārasvata. How this last became the friend and teacher of Bāṇa's eponymous ancestor Vatsa has been told at another place. Of the miraculous pearl-wreath presented by the Buddhist sage Divākaramitra to Harsha we are told how the moon's tear-drops falling into the sea were swallowed by the pearl-oysters; how Vāsuki, became possessed of these pearls and made of them a single pearl-wreath which became the antidote against all poisons; how Nāgārjuna, being brought to hell by the Nāgas, received it as a gift from Vāsuki; how returning from hell he presented it to the king Sātavāhana; and how in course of time it came into the possession of Nāgārjuna.[88] Such descriptions, and they are several in number, mar the value of the *Harshacharita* as a piece of history.

[86] *Ibid.*, pp. 134-35, 146-48, 176-77, 194-96.

[87] S.R. Goyal, *Harsha Śīlāditya*, pp. 125-26.

[88] *HC*, Eng. tr., pp. 4-30, 216-17, 251-52.

PORTRAYAL OF THE TRANSITION FROM THE CLASSICAL TO THE MEDIEVAL PERIOD IN THE *HARSHACHARITA*

However, the importance of the *Harshacharita* for the cultural history of India is simply immense. It depicts the transition of Indian culture from the classical phase to the medieval phase, for we believe that the age of Harsha constituted a watershed between these two epochs.[89] The transformation of the classical heritage into medieval culture did not take place all at once. It was brought about slowly in the course of several centuries intervening the decline of the Gupta empire and the establishment of the Delhi Sultanate. That is why the culture of this period, on the one hand, seems to have much in common with the classical culture of the Guptas and, on the other, appears to be nearer to the culture of the Sultanate period with the main difference that in the post-Gupta centuries, unlike the Sultanate period, the Muslims were not the dominant political power in northern India. Therefore, the beginning of the medieval period in Indian history may broadly be traced from the fall of the Gupta empire itself, though it may be readily conceded that the period of about two centuries, roughly from the fall of the Gupta empire (c. 550 A.D.) and the rise of the Pratihāras (c. 750 A.D.), sheds light on the classical and medieval periods both by a sort of *dehalī-dīpaka-nyāya* (the maxim that a lamp placed on the threshhold illumines both the inside and outside of a room) and thus belongs to both. The age of Harsha, for which the *Harshacharita* of Bāṇa is the most important Indian text, formed the focal point of this vast stretch of two centuries.

In Europe one of the main factors that led to the transition from the classical to the middle age was the immigration and invasions of the barbarian nomads. This factor does not figure in the history of the period under discussion except in the mention of the Hūṇa war of the Pushyabhūtis, but another factor that played a significant role in the transformation of the classical society in Europe as well as India was feudalism though the feudalism of India greatly differed from its European counterpart, so much so that many scholars have doubted its existence in India.[90] Feudalism led not only to the fragmentation of political authority but also to its hierarchical gradation as the *Harshacharita* and the inscriptions of the age testify. As such the monarch, who was at the apex of the hierarchy, became and began

[89] Cf. R.S. Sharma, 'Problem of Transition from Ancient to Medieval in Indian History', in *IHR*, March 1974, Vol. 1, No. i, p. 1. Also see his *Early Medieval Indian Society : A Study in Feudalisation*, Kolkata, 2001, Ch.1 and *India's Ancient Past*, Oxford, 2015, pp. 287-97.

[90] Cf. e.g. D.C. Sircar, *Landlordism and Tenancy in Ancient and Medieval India*, Lucknow, 1969, pp. 32 ff.

to be viewed more as the lord of the vassal kings, and the *sāmantas* emerged as the real rulers in their respective areas making the authority of the ruler more formal than real. This decline in the position of the king is reflected in the changed concept of royalty and vainglorious titles of kings. In the classical period an ideal king was supposed to be the real head of the state who was always conscious of the duties attending his kingly office and anxious for the welfare of his subjects. But in the post-classical period an ideal king appears more as a private person spending his time in religiosity, pursuits of pleasure and warfare. Even in wars he displays his personal desire for victory for the sake of glory or revenge. As shown in the *Harshacharita*, Harsha himself is the best example of such an ideal 'feudal' king. Now, the bards began to weave rich legends of divinity around kings. These tendencies do not prove an increase in the actual power of the rulers; they only indicate to the high pretensions of monarchs under feudal conditions which intellectuals like Bāṇa highly deplored. In his *Kādambarī* Bāṇa expresses his opposition to it quite explicitly. In this work at one place Śakunāsa, the minister of Tārāpīḍa, teaches Chandrāpīḍa, the crown-prince, some basic principles of pragmatic politics. It is quite a lengthy discourse and may be regarded as representing the ideas of Bāṇa himself on the subject. In this discourse at one place Chandrāpīḍa is taught that only utterly foolish kings believe that they are god incarnate on earth :

> ...though subject to mortal conditions, they look on themselves as having alighted on earth as divine beings with a superhuman destiny; they employ a pomp in their undertakings only fit for gods and win the contempt of all mankind. They welcome this deception of themselves by their followers. From the delusion as to their own divinity established in their minds, they are overthrown by false ideas, and they think their own pair of arms have received (like the four arms of Vishṇu) another pair; they imagine their forehead has a third eye (like the third eye of Śiva) buried in the skin. They consider the sight of themselves a favour; they esteem their glance a benefit; they regard their words as a present; they hold their command a glorious boon; they deem their touch a purification.[91]

With the feudalization of royalty the state machinery underwent considerable changes. The provincial and local administration was bound to change with the emergence of feudal lords as local centres of power. As shown in the *Harshacharita*, in the central administration also sometimes the *sāmantas* became the chief counsellors of the king at the cost of ministers who, more often than not, displayed greater interest in superstitions and omens rather than in actual statecraft and diplomacy.

[91] *Kādambarī*, Eng. tr. of C.M. Ridding, London, 1896, Indian repr., Second edn., Bombay, 1960, p. 95.

One of the by-products of feudalism in medieval Europe as well as India was the ideal of chivalry. Chivalry in medieval Europe consisted of several virtues such as limitless valour, truthfulness, loyalty to the overlord, generosity, etc. In India also though the tradition of bravery was very old, it acquired a new flavour with the accentuation of feudal tendencies. It emphasized more or less the same virtues which were valued in feudal Europe. Now, queens are more often than not described as having been 'bought' by paying the price of valour (cf. the example of *parākramakrītā* Yaśomatī, the queen of Prabhākara-vardhana). It is quite obvious that the feudal ideal of chivalry could not be very effective in war. Otherwise also, feudalism did not help much in the development of the art of war. Contrary to the practice of the classical period, armies in this age were generally composed of feudal levies. They could swell to huge proportions, but were too heterogeneous to be commanded by the 'overlord' effectively. The practice of maintaining efficient standing armies was given up. Much reliance was laid on omens and supernatural support in warfare and a lot of attention was paid to grandeur, show and luxurious living in military camps with the result that Harsha's army became more or less like the later-day Mughal armies. The earliest picture of such a military camp is preserved in the *Harshacharita*. It describes in detail the large kitchens of the king and great nobles, the use of luxurious articles by them in the camp, the carriages of the high born nobles' wives and the troops of their seraglio elephants. Bāṇa notes:

> Donkeys ridden by throngs of boys accompanied the march. Crowds of carts with creaking wheels occupied the trampled roads. Oxen were laden with utensils momentarily put upon them. ... Here groups of elephant men, bachelors, knaves, donkey boys, camp followers, thieves, serving men, rogues, and grooms, sated with an easily acquired meal of plentiful readily pounded remnants of grain, expressed their approval of the camp in bold boisterous jubilation. There poor unattended nobles, over-whelmed with the toil and worry of conveying their provisions upon fainting oxen provided by wretched village householders and obtained with difficulty, themselves grasped their domestic appurtenances,... Here swiftly running in a line,... were the king's hired porters, carrying... golden footstools, waterpots, cups, spittoons, and baths, pushing every one aside in irrepressible pride at being in charge of their sovereign's property with himself at hand : also bearers of kitchen appurtenances with goats attached to thongs of pig-skin, a tangle of hanging sparrows and forequarters of venison, a collection of young rabbits, potherbs, and bamboo shoots, buttermilk pots protected by wet seals on one part of their mouths which were covered with white cloths, baskets containing a chaos of fire-trays, ovens, simmering pans, spits, copper saucepans, and frying-pans.[92]

[92] *HC*, Eng. tr., pp. 201, 207-08.

From the *Harshacharita* it appears that Harsha's army covered about nine miles per day. The plight of the villagers at the time of the march of Harsha's army has also been vividly described by Bāṇa:

> Here, with cries of 'The labour is ours, but when paytime comes some other rascals will appear,' village servants, set to scare on the feeble oxen tripping at every step, were indiscriminately badgering the whole body of nobles. There the whole country side had come in eager haste from both directions out of curiosity to see the king, and fools of grant-holders, issuing from the villages on the route and headed by aged elders with uplifted waterpots, pressed furiously near in crowds with presents of curds, molasses, candied sugar, and flowers in baskets, demanding the protection of the crops: flying before their terror of irate and savage chamberlains, they yet in spite of distance, tripping, and falling, kept their eyes fixed upon the king, bringing to light imaginary wrongs of former governors, lauding hundreds of past officials, [238] reporting ancient misdeeds of knaves. Others, contented with the appointed overseers, were bawling their eulogies:— 'The king is Dharma incarnate'; others, despondent at the plunder of their ripe grain, had come forth wives and all to bemoan their estates, and to the imminent risk of their lives, grief dismissing fear, had begun to censure their sovereign, crying 'Where's the king ?' 'What right has he to be king ?' 'What a king !' [93]

One of the notable developments in early medieval Europe was the growth of regional languages. It was in a way the linguistic aspect of the regionalization of culture and it ultimately led to the emergence of nation states there. A similar tendency manifested itself in early medieval India. In the classical age Sanskrit occupied the position of the *lingua franca* of the country. It enjoyed this position in the post-classical centuries also, though its scope and popularity gradually narrowed down. This phenomenon is comparable to the decline of Latin in early medieval Europe. In India in the early medieval age Sanskrit literature lost touch with the common man and became, by and large, imitative, insipid, artificial and unnatural. The ornate style in prose and poetry became widely prevalent and strings of adjectives, adverbs and similes are found not only in literary works but also in inscriptions from about the sixth-seventh centuries. The prose style of Bāṇa became a model for the medieval period.

In the history of Sanskrit literature early medieval age is the age of scholastic elaboration and systematic analysis, of commentaries and sub-commentaries, of manuals and sub-manuals. The tightening of the Smṛti rules, loss of contacts with the outside world, feudal atmosphere in the courts, and the growth of insular tendency stifled the free spirit of intelligentsia. The poetry and dramas, though cultivated and exclusive, were artificial, unimaginative

[93] *Ibid.*, pp. 208-09.

and out of touch with reality. The device of *ślesha* by which an entire *kāvya* is made to have a manifold meaning applicable to totally different themes was a peculiarity of this period. The verse of Mayūra marks the beginning of this style which soon became widely popular. Historical *kāvyas* were composed, but they smack more of romance than history.

The vacuum created by the decline of Sanskrit in India and of Latin in Europe was filled up by the gradually emerging regional languages. As has been shown elsewhere,[94] between c. 500 to 900 A.D. the Prakrit languages gradually changed into various Apabhraṁśas and between c. 900 and 1300 A.D. they gradually turned into modern varnaculars or bhāshās of different regions—proto-Hindi, proto-Bengali, proto-Assamese, proto-Gujarati, proto-Marathi, etc. Although it is difficult to fix the beginnings of regional languages, on the basis of the Vajrayāna Buddhist religious writings from eastern India, proto-Bengali, proto-Assamese, proto-Oriya, proto-Maithili and proto-Hindi can be traced back to the seventh century. Similarly, on the basis of Jaina religious Prakrit works proto-Gujarati and proto-Rajasthani are traced back to the same period.[95] The pace of linguistic variation quickened in the country from the sixth-seventh centuries mainly on account of lack of inter-regional communication mobility. Contacts were mainly confined to the march of soldiers and migration of monks and Brāhmaṇas from northern India into the peripheral areas for enjoying land grants.[96]

The post-classical Indian society was greatly disturbed by the new religious thought-currents also. Now, there developed a general belief that the Tāntrikas had knowledge of *rasāyana* (alchemy) and *vājīkaraṇa* (aphrodisiacs) and had gained mastery over magical lore — *shaṭkarma, vaśīkaraṇa, stambhana*, etc. These *siddhis* (achievements) of the Tāntrika āchāryas were considered useful by the kings and the feudal chiefs in serving their two dominant interests—war and sex. Hence, the liberal patronage to the Tāntrika āchāryas by the new feudal class.[97] The *Harshacharita* mentions the Tāntrika āchāryas at several places. According to Bāṇa, Pushyabhūti, the founder of Harsha's dynasty, was greatly influenced by a Tāntrika Śaiva from the south. When Harsha returned from hunting to meet his ailing father in the capital he saw :

There young nobles were burning themselves with lamps to propitiate the

[94] Shankar Goyal, *op. cit.*, pp. 253-55; idem, *Harsha Revisited : A Re-interpretation of Existing Data*, pp. 65-66.

[95] R.S. Sharma, *op. cit.*, p. 7.

[96] *Ibid.*

[97] Devangana Desai, 'Art under Feudalism in India (c.A.D. 500-1300)', in *IHR*, March 1974, Vol. 1, No. i, p. 12.

> Mothers (Mātṛkās). In one place a Dravidian was ready to solicit the Vampire (Vetāla) with the offering of a skull. In another an Āndhra man was holding up his arms like a rampart to conciliate Caṇḍī. Elsewhere distressed young servants were pacifying Mahākāla by holding melting gum on their heads. In another place a group of relatives was intent on an oblation of their own flesh, which they severed with keen knives. Elsewhere again [170] young courtiers were openly resorting to the sale of human flesh. Thus the capital seemed polluted with the ashes of cemeteries, encircled by ill-omens, pillaged by fiends, swallowed up by the Kali age, hid beneath mounds of sin, sacked by the raids of demerit, victimized by the taunts of transience, appropriated by the mockeries of fate; vacant, wrapped in slumber, robbed, abashed, deluded, fallen in a swoon.[98]

As in Europe, in India also feudalism also encouraged love of luxury and sensualism. The perpetually changing kaleidoscope of alliances and struggles among feudal lords, which generated a sense of instability and fickleness, intensified the urge to drink the pleasures of life all at once to the last dreg. As a result of this thinking every standard of modesty and moderation, all the values of decency and refinement were bypassed. Bāṇa's detailed description of the birth celebration of Harsha is the typical early example of this atmosphere :

> So proceeded the great birth festival, the order of the royal household gone,... entrance to the harem in no wise criminal, master and servants reduced to a level, young and old confounded, learned and unlearned on one footing, drunk and sober not to be distinguished, noble maidens and harlots equally merry, the whole population of the capital set a-dancing.
>
> From the morrow onwards the wives of the neighbouring kings could be observed in thousands approaching the palace from every side. ... As they danced, the quarters of the heavens rang with jewelled anklets clashing as their feet knocked together.
>
> [144] Thus the festal jubilation gradually blossomed forth. Here young people, of ancient noble houses and unused to dancing, showed by frolics their love for the king. There drunken slave women allured the favourites, while the monarch himself looked on with a secret smile. In one place respectable old feudatories were, much to his amusement, clasping the necks of the intoxicated bawds of the capital in a furious dance. In another place naughty slave boys, set on by a glance from the sovereign, betrayed in songs the secret amours of the ministers of state. Elsewhere wanton water-girls raised a laugh by embracing aged ascetics. Elsewhere again in the eagerness of ardent rivalry throngs of slaves carried on a war of foul language. In another place chamberlains knowing nothing of dancing were, to the entertainment of the maids, violently forced to dance by the king's women. ...

[98] *HC*, Eng. tr., pp. 135-36.

> In this place and in that harlot-women danced to the accompaniment of instrumental music. ...
>
> In other places, where under the terror of chamberlains' wands the people had made room [147] the king's wives essayed the dance, a brilliant throng with a forest of white parasols held above them,... Some, wrapt in loose shawls hanging from both shoulders, swayed as if mounted on play swings. ...
>
> All womankind being thus set dancing, the earth, crimsoned by trickling lac from their feet, seemed rosy with the flush of love. Their round gleaming bosoms made the festival like a mass of auspicious pitchers. ... Even old ladies shouted like maniacs. [148] Old men even lost all shame, as though bewitched. The wise forgot themselves, as if intoxicated. Even hermits' hearts were all agog for a dance.[99]

Thus, we observe that most of the features of the medieval society may be traced back to the age of Harsha so vividly described in the works of Bāṇa. R. S. Sharma, therefore, hits on the nail when he concludes that in these two centuries (of which, we think, the reign of Harsha was the focal point) "ancient India was coming to an end, and medieval India was taking shape."[100]

CONCLUSION

In the light of this analysis Bāṇa, it seems to us, gives the impression of being a typical representative of many Sanskrit authors of his age and his work, the *Harshacharita*, symbolizes a factual biography of the medieval idiosyncrasy. But the text of the *Harshacharita* has often been treated rather innocently by historians, and hitherto very limited endeavour has been made to understand the presuppositions and the literary practices according to which it was written. The result is that Bāṇa's biography even today is looked upon not as a work of art, but directly of history, whereas it is not a straightforward historical text[101] and belongs to the branch of literature called *kāvya* (literature as an art), in which aesthetic aims and methods are regarded as supreme.

[99] *Ibid.*, pp. 111-15.

[100] R.S. Sharma, *op. cit.*, p. 9.

[101] Cf. also R.C. Majumdar, 'Ideas of History in Sanskrit Literature', in *Historians of India, Pakistan and Ceylon*, ed. C.H. Philips, London, 1961, pp. 18-19.

TEN

The Significance of Yuan Chwang in the Context of the Seventh Century

THE CHINESE SOURCES

The study of the history of the age of Harsha is of absorbing interest mainly because of the comparative abundance of contemporary source materials, the foremost among them being the *Harshacharita* by Bāṇabhaṭṭa, the *Si-Yü-Ki* or *Buddhist Records of the Western World* by Yuan Chwang and the *Life of the Master of the Law* (that is, Yuan Chwang) composed by Hui-li. The works of Yuan Chwang first attracted the attention of scholars and translators in the middle of the nineteenth century. S. Julien published his *Histoire de la vie de Hiouen-thsang et de ses voyages dans l'Inde, depuis l'an 629 jusqu'en 645* in 1853, supplemented by *Mémoires sur les contrées occidentales...*, French translations respectively of the *Ta T'ang Ta Tz'u-ên Ssu San-tsang Fa-shih Chuan* by Hui-li and Yen-Ts'ung and of the *Ta T'ang Hsi Yü Ki* by Yuan Chwang, in 1857-58. Then followed their English translations by S. Beal in 1884 and T. Watters in 1904-05. Beal also translated the first five of the ten chapters of the *Life* of Yuan Chwang by Hui-li and Yen-Ts'ung in 1888.

The *Life* of Yuan Chwang by Hui-li and Yen-Ts'ung was composed in ten chapters. The first five chapters dealing with the period 602-645 A.D., from the birth of Yuan Chwang until his return from India to China, were written by Hui-li who died in 670 A.D. and the last five shorter chapters covering the period until the death of Yuan Chwang himself in 664 were later added by Yen-Ts'ung who also edited the entire work and published it in 688 A.D. However, S. Beal's English translation of the *Life* brought out in 1888 consisted of only the first five chapters with a brief concluding summary of the remaining career of Yuan Chwang.

D. Devahuti has published a concise edited résumé of chapters VI to X in the *ABORI*(LXI, 1980, pp. 131-55) along with the correspondence of Yuan Chwang with Prajñādeva and Jñānaprabha of Mahābodhi given in chapter VII. This correspondence is now easily available to English readers.[1] However, the résumé of other contents of the chapters VI to X of the *Life* is still confined to the pages of the above-mentioned journal. We are reproducing in appendix 1 of this chapter the summary of their résumé as given by Devahuti for the benefit of a wider readership.

The *She-Kia-Fang-Che* is also an important Chinese account of India. Its author had taken the description down as he had heard it from Yuan Chwang as was done by Hui-li who composed the *Life*. The *She-Kia-Fang-Che* thus supplements the *Si-Yü-Ki* and the *Life* and at places supplies us with new information not available in those two works.

YUAN CHWANG : HIS RELIABILITY

Yuan Chwang's writings were conditioned by many factors.[2] The tradition of Chinese historiography and his family background of administrative careers gave him a sense of the factual and a perception of detail. His Confucian and Buddhist ethics made him a deliberately honest observer and narrator but prone to exaggeration in the direction of his own biases. He came from a family which was reputed for its administrative talents. His father was an able and quite man who was more interested in his books than high government offices. Early in life Yuan Chwang was initiated into Confucian and Buddhist classics by his father and elder brother. During the seven years of his study and training as a Buddhist, from the age of thirteen to twenty, China saw general political confusion and anarchy resulting in his frequent flights from one monastery to another. Early in life, therefore, Yuan Chwang became acquainted with different aspects of human nature and hardships. No wonder if he was impressed by comparative greater peace he saw in India.

At the age of twenty Yuan Chwang was ordained as bhikshu. He came to India in 629 A.D. and spent nearly thirteen years here, travelling, visiting holy Buddhist sites, studying, collecting curiosities and learned treatises—twenty horse-loads of them—meeting and living with ordinary people as well as kings and scholars, expounding the tenets of Mahāyāna

[1] P. C. Bagchi prepared its English translation which was published by the Viśva-Bhāratī in 1959.

[2] For an account of the life and travels of Yuan Chwang, vide S. N. Sen, *India through Chinese Eyes*, Madras, 1956, pp. 20 ff.; J. Barthelemy Saint-Hilaire, *Hiouen-Thsang in India*, Varanasi, 1965; Shankar Goyal, *The Significance of Yuan Chwang in the Context of the Seventh Century : A Critical Assessment*, Delhi, 2018, pp. 1-31.

and, what is most important for historians, making mental and written notes of his observations. Within three years he took leave of Harsha he had written *Buddhist Records of the Western World*, an account of his travels in India. The material for his biography, the *Life* by Hui-li, was also collected while the memory of events was still fresh. It was finished in 648-49 A.D., two to three years after the *Records* had been completed.

As a Buddhist author Yuan Chwang indulges in wishful thinking on topics like piety or vegetarianism. In connection with Buddhist miracles he displays superstitions of the faithful. Some of his geographical details are obviously inaccurate but we need not criticise him on every instance of an apparent mistake. Apart from the copyists' oversight, the error may sometimes be ours because of the lack in our knowledge of the contemporary geographical facts. Similar may be the case regarding figures of the size of armies, the number of students and monks in a monastery, participants in a conference or an assembly, etc. In Yuan Chwang's account there is also a certain ambiguity in the usage of some terms, such as the "Five Indias", and an apparent contradiction of facts such as those concerning payment of government employees, unpaid labour or meat-eating. He is also usually criticised for being unduly partial to Harsha. In fact Harsha was not the only Indian patron of Yuan Chwang and nor the only Buddhist monarch of his day. Even his Buddhist convictions are under the cloud of doubt. In any case, Yuan Chwang cannot be charged with giving to Harsha attention out of proportion to his stature.

We should remember that Yuan Chwang's account does not at all prove that Harsha as a great Buddhist ruler. The Chinese pilgrim entered India in October 630, but met Harsha for the first time in October 642, and that too at the latter's initiative. The greater part of this long period of twelve years was spent by him in the empire of Harsha. He resided in Kanauj itself for three months (from September to the end of November, 636 A.D.). But apparently he was not sufficiently impressed with the reputation of Harsha as a Buddhist ruler, for there arose no desire in him to meet this Indian king whom he later on sought to portray as another Aśoka. Even as late as 641, when he resolved to return to China, the idea of meeting Harsha did not cross his mind. All this proves that Harsha was not at all famous as a great Buddhist ruler in his own time.[3]

In his account Yuan Chwang constantly reveals his superstitious nature which mars the value of his testimony. The fact that he consulted a Nirgrantha, who was 'skilled in divination' to know whether he will be able to carry successfully the sacred texts and images to China, shows his

[3] S.R. Goyal, *Harsha and Buddhism* (henceforth *HB*), Meerut, 1986, pp. 84-85.

superstitious nature. In the *Records* he constantly mentions supernatural phenomena and miracles which donot deserve any serious consideration from historions. As R. C. Majumdar observes :

> Anyone who goes through the pilgrim's bulky volumes is struck by his enthusiasm, bordering almost on fanaticism in matters concerning Buddhist religion. He was so much blinded by faith and devotion that he even describes supernatural phenomena as happening before his very eyes. He saw everything in India through the spectacles of Buddhism, and regarded its inherent superiority over all other religions as beyond question. The account of such a person about the religious proclivities of Harsha must be accepted with more than usual reserve.[4]

Another important feature of Yuan Chwang's nature is his supreme egotism. Everywhere in his description of India he depicts himself as towering head and shoulders above everybody else. Even great kings, including Harsha, cut a sorry, almost pitiable figure in his presence. In the words of S.R. Goyal:

> Yuan Chwang's vanity and egotism were the academic counterpart of the superiority complex which the Chinese exhibited in the political sphere. Everywhere in their narratives they have given a grossly exaggerated account of their military achievements.[5]

Yuan Chwang took the conventional religious catholicism of the Indian rulers including Harsha as indicating their unflinching faith in Buddhism, for one showing respect for a religion different than his own was a phenomena completely unknown to him. Goyal writes :

> The behaviour of ancient Indians was usually marked by humility, absence of self-adulation and respect for others' sentiments. Like Aśoka, who in his edicts pleaded for paying greatest possible respect to other sects, and the imperial Guptas who were always helpful to the religions of others, most ancient Indian rulers usually extended open-hearted and liberal support to other faiths. But our foreign visitors, brought up in a less liberal atmosphere, could not always understand this attitude. Even in the medieval period European Christian missionaries misunderstood Akbar's quest for religious truth and drew the entirely wrong conclusion that the Mughal emperor was on the verge of accepting Christianity as his personal faith. No wonder if Yuan Chwang could not understand the religious attitude of Harsha properly.[6]

Lastly, the inner contradictions in the Chinese sources—and they are full of them—should not be overlooked. For example, the accounts of the Kanauj assembly as given in the *Records* and *Life* radically differ from each other. The tendency in modern scholars so far has been to mix up the two accounts

[4] R.C. Majumdar, in *The Classical Age* (hereafter *CA*), Bombay, 1954, p. 117.

[5] *HB*, p. 89. Cf., for example, the grossly exaggerated description of the raid of Wang-hiüen-ts'e, the Chinese envoy, who came after the death of Harsha.

[6] *Ibid.*

and prepare a synthetic picture of the events connected with the assembly on the basis of elements taken from the two accounts. But this approach is obviously wrong, for the two accounts do not 'supplement' each other; they are 'contradictory'.[7]

YUAN CHWANG ON THE SOCIAL BACKGROUND OF HARSHA

Yuan Chwang speaks little of the family of Harsha. However, he tells us that Harsha was of Fei-she (Vaiśya) extraction.[8] This information is of vital importance for, among the Indian sources it is only the *Āryamañju-śrīmūlakalpa* which clearly states that the Pushyabhūtis were Vaiśya.[9] According to Tripathi, the suffix bhūti additionally indicates that Pushyabhūti, the founder of the family, was a Vaiśya.[10] Devahuti, in her study of Harsha,[11] also supports the view that Harsha was of Vaiśya extraction. Jayaswal held the same opinion.[12] But many scholars, including Cunningham,[13] Bühler[14] and B.N. Sharma[15] believe that the Pushyabhūtis belonged to the Kshatriya class. Their belief is based on a passage occurring in the *Harshacharita* of Bāṇa according to which the two houses of the Pushyabhūtis and the Maukharis were like the Moon and the Sun (*Somasūryavaṁśāviva Pushyabhūti Mukharavaṁśau*).[16] Commenting on the statement of Yuan Chwang that Harsha belonged to the Fei-she caste, Cunningham also opines that 'it is a mistake'. For, "being a celebrated ruler Harsha must have belonged to the Kshatriya class; probably he was a 'Bais Rajput', in which case he would be a Kshatriya but the word 'Bais' led Yuan Chwang into believing that he was a Vaiśya."[17] This is a remarkable reasoning indeed! For, Cunningham deduces from the statement of Yuan Chwang what the Chinese pilgrim does not say. As Watters states, we must remember that Yuan Chwang had ample opportunities for knowing the antecedents of the Pushyabhūti family, and must have had some grounds for making this assertion.[18] We donot think that one

[7] Cf. Shankar Goyal, 'Recent Historiography of the Age of Harsha', *ABORI*, Poona, Vol. LXXII-LXXIII, 1993, p. 350.

[8] T. Watters, *On Yuan Chwang's Travels in India* (hereafter *Travels*), I, Delhi, 1961, pp. 344-45.

[9] K. P. Jayaswal, *An Imperial History of India*, Lahore, 1934, p. 28.

[10] R.S. Tripathi, *History of Kanauj*, Delhi, 1959, pp. 30-31.

[11] D. Devahuti, *Harsha : A Political Study*, 2nd edn., Oxford, 1983, p. 72.

[12] K. P. Jayaswal, *op.cit.*

[13] A. Cunningham, *The Ancient Geography of India*, Varanasi, 1963, p. 377.

[14] *EI*, I, p. 68, fn. 4

[15] B.N. Sharma, *Harṣa and His Times*, Varanasi, 1970, pp. 89-92.

[16] *Harshacharita* of Bāṇa (hereafter *HC*), P. V. Kane's edn., Delhi, 1965, p. 16.

[17] A. Cunningham, *op. cit.*

[18] T. Watters, *op.cit.*

should have any reservations in accepting the testimony of the author of the *Āryamañjuśrīmūlakalpa* and Yuan Chwang, both of whom categorically state that the family of Harsha was of the Vaiśya caste.[19] The fact that Harsha was a Vaiśya and did not belong to a tribe greatly influenced the subsequent history of the Pushyabhūti kingdom. It played a significant role even after his death, for after his death his family or dynasty remained unsupported by a tribal following as it happened in so many cases when a king belonging to a tribe was supported by his tribal followers in times of distress. Ajit Singh of Jodhpur, so loyally served by Durgadas and the Rathor tribe, is a case in the point.

YUAN CHWANG ON HARSHA'S CONQUESTS

Yuan Chwang describes Harsha's wars and military expeditions in a vague and general manner. At one place he tells us :

> ... as soon as Śīlāditya became ruler he got together a great army, and set out to avenge his brother's murder and to reduce the neighbouring countries to subjection. Proceeding eastwards he invaded the states which had refused allegiance, and waged incessant warfare until in six years he had *fought* the Five Indias (According to the other reading had brought the Five Indias under allegiance). Then having enlarged his territory he increased his army, bringing the elephant corps up to 60,000 and the cavalry to 100,000, and reigned in peace for thirty years without raising a weapon.[20]

In the *Records*, after the description of the assumption of the royal office by Harsha at Kanauj with the title Śīlāditya, the statement of the pilgrim runs thus :

> And now he commanded his ministers, saying, "The enemies of my brother are unpunished as yet, the neighbouring countries not brought to submission; while this is so my right hand shall never lift food to my mouth. Therefore do you, people and officers, unite with one heart and put out your strength." Accordingly they assembled all the soldiers of the kingdom, summoned the masters of arms (*champions*, or, *teachers of the art of fighting*). They had a body of 5000 elephants, a body of 2000 cavalry, and 50,000 foot-soldiers. He went from east to west subduing all who were not obedient; the elephants were not unharnessed nor the soldiers unbelted (*unhelmeted*). After six years he had subdued the Five Indies. Having thus enlarged his territory, he increased his forces; he had 60,000 war elephants and 100,000 cavalry. After thirty years his arms reposed, and he governed everywhere in peace.[21]

[19] Cf. Shankar Goyal, 'Social *Milieu* of the Pushyabhūtis : Significance of Some Hitherto Unnoticed Passages of the *Harshacharita* ', *Essays in Indian History and Culture*, ed. Y. Krishan, New Delhi, 1986, pp. 167-70.

[20] *Travels*, I, p. 343.

[21] S. Beal, *Si-Yü-Ki* or *Buddhist Records of the Western World* (hereafter *Records*), I, Delhi, 1969, p. 213.

In the *Life* also a reference is made to Harsha's success in avenging the murder of his brother :

> He was soon able to avenge the injuries received by his brother, and to make himself master of India. His renown was spread abroad everywhere, and all his subjects reverenced his virtues. The empire having gained rest, then the people were at peace.[22]

Apart from these notices Yuan Chwang also mentions Harsha's struggle against Pulakeśin[23] and his conquest of Koṅgoda.[24]

The chronology of Harsha's campaigns indicated by the testimony of Yuan Chwang is also quite confusing. From his statement, as translated by Watters, it appears that Harsha fought wars for six years and then reigned in peace for thirty years. But (1) Beal renders the same passage to mean that in the first six years Harsha subdued the Five Indias and then "After thirty years his arms reposed and he governed everywhere in peace." It implies a total of 36 years of warfare. (2) But even the rendering of Beal is not free from difficulties because it would mean that after thirty-six years of warfare, ending in 606+36=642 A.D., he ruled peacefully, while we know that he was engaged in constant warfare even after 641 A.D. (3) The sense of Watters' translation is impossible *per se* because "considering the unsettled political condition of the time it would be unreasonable to expect that Harsha could reign in peace for 30 years without any struggle though he had to fight both before and after this period."[25] (4) Ma Twan-lin categorically states that Harsha was engaged in severe battles between 618 and 627.

In view of these facts one must conclude that Yuan Chwang's statement regarding the period when Harsha was engaged in warfare is confused either because the Chinese pilgrim was not given accurate information by his informants or because, which is more likely, some copyists' errors have crept in his wordings in course of time.

YUAN CHWANG ON THE GRADUAL ACQUISITION OF KANAUJ BY HARSHA THROUGH RELIGIOUS DIPLOMACY

Yuan Chwang narrates the acquisition of the sovereignty of Kanauj by Harsha thus :

> The people having lost their ruler, the country became desolate. Then the great minister Po-ni (Bhaṇḍi), whose power and reputation were high and of much weight, addressing the assembled ministers, said, "The destiny of the nation is to be fixed today. The old king's son is dead : the brother of

[22] S. Beal, *The Life of Hiuen-Tsiang* (henceforth *Life*), New Delhi, 1973, p. 83.
[23] *Travels*, II, p. 239.
[24] *Life*, pp. 159-61.
[25] *CA*, p. 108.

> the prince, however, is humane and affectionate, and his disposition, heaven-conferred, is dutiful and obedient. Because he is strongly attached to his family, the people will trust in him. I propose that he assumes the royal authority : let each one give his opinion on this matter, whatever he thinks." They were all agreed on this point, and acknowledged his conspicuous qualities.[26]

But Harsha showed diffidence in accepting the crown. He told them:

> The government of a country is a responsible office and ever attended with difficulties. The duties of a prince require previous consideration. As for myself, I am indeed of small eminence; but as my father and brother are no more, to reject the heritage of the crown, that can bring no benefit to the people. I must attend to the opinion of the world and forget my own insufficiency. Now, therefore, on the banks of the Ganges there is a statue of Avalokiteśvara Bodhisattva which has evidenced many spiritual wonders. I will go to it and ask advice (*request a response*).[27]

Then he went to the statue of the Bodhisattva who is said to have appeared before him in bodily form. On being requested by Harsha for advice the Bodhisattva replied :

> "In your former existence you lived in this forest as a hermit (*a forest mendicant*), and by your earnest diligence and unremitting attention you inherited a power of religious merit which resulted in your birth as a king's son. The king of the country, Karṇasuvarṇa, has overturned the law of Buddha. Now when you succeed to the royal estate, you should in the same proportion exercise towards it the utmost love and pity. If you give your mind to compassionate the condition of the distressed and to cherish them, then before long you shall rule over the Five Indies. If you would establish your authority, attend to my instruction, and by my secret power you shall receive additional enlightenment, so that not one of your neighbours shall be able to triumph over you. Ascend not the lion-throne, and call not yourself Mahārāja." Having received these instructions, he (that is, Harsha) departed and assumed the royal office. He called himself the King's Son (Kumāra); his title was Śīlāditya.[28]

The narrative of Yuan Chwang is somewhat inaccurate and full of difficulties. Yuan Chwang makes Harsha's brother and father the rulers of Kanauj while actually they had been the kings of Thanesar. This mistake was obviously the result of the fact that when Harsha met the pilgrim, he was known as the king of Kanauj and his predecessor there, namely Grahavarman, was also murdered like his brother Rājyavardhana. But the problem of succession related in this narrative certainly pertains to Kanauj because, firstly, at Thanesar Harsha was the natural successor of Rājya;

[26] *Records*, I, pp. 210-11.
[27] *Ibid.*, pp. 211-12.
[28] *Ibid.*, pp. 212-13.

there could be no need of persuation by its ministers to accept Harsha as the new king. Secondly, Harsha is said to have sought guidance from a statue of Bodhisattva Avalokiteśvara situated on the banks of the Gaṅgā which shows that the scene of this episode was Kanauj, and not Thanesar.

Thus from the account of Yuan Chwang it appears that Harsha usurped Kanauj, on which he had no legal right, not by force, but by diplomacy. It is also possible that he made the ministers of Kanauj offer him the crown and himself made the show of reluctance to gain the sympathy of at least some sections of the Kanauj people. As Rājyaśrī, his sister, was the widowed Maukhari queen, he must have exploited the sympathy of the Kanauj populace by acting as her patron and guardian. That is why in the beginning he did not sit on the royal throne and assumed the title of only 'Kumāra'. The next stage of the usurpation of Kanauj is revealed by the *Shi-Kia-Fang-Che*, which was written with the help of the notes of Yuan Chwang. According to this text Harshavardhana carried on the administration of Kanauj with his widowed sister. Then followed its complete usurpation when he became its sole, fullfledged, ruler as Yuan Chwang found him during his visit of India. The 'gradualness' of the usurpation only proves that he had to face opposition from some sections of the Kanauj people.

YUAN CHWANG ON THE INCIDENT OF KASHMIR TOOTH-RELIC

From the account of Yuan Chwang, who stayed in Kashmir for two years from 631 to 633 A.D., it appears that Kashmir was an important kingdom with several dependencies. Yuan Chwang does not refer to the name of its ruling monarch who "hospitably entertained" him, "invited" him "to read and expound the scriptures" and "gave him twenty clerks to copy out manuscripts, and five men to act as attendants."[29] Kalhaṇa's *Rājataraṅgiṇī*, however, provides us with the name of the ruler of this period, Durlabhavardhana. When in Kashmir, the Chinese pilgrim visited in September 633 a famous stūpa to pay homage to 'a tooth of the Buddha in length about an inch and a half, of a yellowish-white colour', which 'on religious days' emitted a bright light.[30] It was obviously the same celebrated relic which was carried away by Harsha a few years later. Yuan Chwang saw it in Kanauj in September 636. It was so revered by the people that Harsha had imposed a tax of one gold coin on its *darśana*. In the *Life*, following the account of the Kanauj assembly held at the end of 642 A.D., we are told that to the west of the king's travelling palace there was a saṅghārāma under the patronage of the king. In this building there was a tooth of the Buddha 'about an inch and a half long and

[29] *Travels*, I, p. 259.
[30] *Records*, I, p. 158.

of yellowish white colour'. It ever emitted sparkling light.[31] A little later the *Life* states:

> In recent times Śīlāditya-rāja, hearing that Kaśmir possessed a tooth of Buddha, coming in person to the chief frontier, asked permission to see and worship it. The congregation, from a feeling of sordid avarice, were unwilling to consent to this request, and so took the relic and concealed it. But the king fearing the exalted character of Śīlāditya,.. found it (*the relic*),.. presented it to the king. Śīlāditya seeing it was overpowered with reverence, and exercising force, carried it off to pay it religious offerings. This is the tooth spoken of.[32]

The Kashmir tooth-incident throws light on the characters of Harsha and Yuan Chwang both. Harsha played a trick on the king of Kashmir and injured the feelings of the Kashmir people by first asking their permission to only see and worship the holy relic and later carried it off by force while Yuan Chwang is guilty of partiality because he accuses the Kashmiri monks, who must have been apprehensive of Harsha's intentions, of 'sordid avarice' when they did not allow Harsha to see the holy relic, but describes the character of Harsha as 'exalted' even when he carried away the tooth-relic by 'force', thereby proving the apprehensions of the Kashmiri congregation as correct. It is obvious that the king of Kashmir was frightened by Harsha's strength rather than by his 'exalted character'.

From the testimony of Yuan Chwang it appears that the incident of tooth-relic must have happened in c. 634 for till September 633 it was in Kashmir where and when Yuan Chwang saw and worshipped it, but when the pilgrim visited Kanauj in September 636, it was already housed there. As it has been there for some time (so much so that the tax of a gold coin had been imposed on those who wished to see it), it must have been brought from Kashmir not much later than 634 A.D.[33] Incidentally, the imposition of a tax as high as a gold coin by Harsha on those who desired to 'see' it, proves the avarice of Harsha, not the exaltedness of his character.

As regards Harsha's political relations with Kashmir, the view that the tooth-incident proves that Kashmir accepted the suzerainty of Harsha is not correct. There is nothing in the testimony of Yuan Chwang to support it. In Tripathi's opinion the expression that Śīlāditya carried off the tooth by force probably means nothing more than that he brought it to Kanauj much against the wishes of the Kashmir people.[34] "Having achieved his aim in a war of nerves Harsha came back from Kashmir, and it does not seem that he had any further political connections with it. There is no indication that

[31] *Life*, p. 181.

[32] *Ibid.*, p. 183.

[33] S.R. Goyal, *Maukhari-Pushyabhūti-Chālukya Yuga*, Meerut, 1988, pp. 210-12.

[34] R. S. Tripathi, *op.cit.*, p. 85.

Durlabha-vardhana, the king of Kashmir, ever visited Harsha's court, or that a treaty was ever concluded between the two."[35] The testimony of Bāṇa regarding the exaction of tribute from the inaccessible land covered with snow has also been used by Mookerji and Devahuti to prove Harsha's occupation of Kashmir. But Bāṇa's statement lacks territorial specificity.

GENERAL DESCRIPTION OF INDIA AND ITS PARTS IN YUAN CHWANG

The general description of India and its parts as provided by the Chinese pilgrim Yuan Chwang is obviously related to the question of the extent of the empire of Harsha. As is well known, in the beginning of the Indological studies historians generally believed that the empire of Harsha included almost the whole of north India. This view is held even now by several scholars. But while discussing the extent of the empire of Harsha certain points should be kept in mind. Firstly, one should differentiate between the areas directly ruled by an emperor, areas ruled by kings who accepted his suzerainty (real or nominal), areas which were under his sphere of influence, areas which were independent but the rulers of which thought it prudent to maintain friendly relations with the emperor, and areas which were independent but were considered 'natural prey' to the ambition of the emperor. Most earlier scholars donot make such differentiation though some historians have tried to distinguish between areas under Harsha's direct control and areas within the sphere of his influence. We, however, believe that in the age of feudal-federal polity the relationship of the imperial authority with the various regions was not only of two types—directly controlled regions and regions within the sphere of influence—it could be of several types, the quantum of hold exercised by the imperial authority on them differing from state to state. Secondly, we should remember that the nature of the relationship between the imperial authority and a particular state could undergo a subtle change without any formal recognition being accorded to that change. Such changes in the relationship of two powers could take place several times in long course of their relationship.

Here it may also be emphasised that we should not draw any specific conclusion about the extent of empire of any ruler from such conventional phrases as "Sakalottarāpatheśvara", "Lord of the Four Oceans", "Trisamudrādhipati" (Lord of the Three Oceans), etc. For example, the description of Śaśāṅka as 'the lord of the entire earth bound by the four oceans' does not mean anything so far as the extent of his empire is concerned. Similarly, Harsha has been described as the lord of the entire Uttarāpatha not because he ruled over the entire north India but simply

[35] D. Devahuti, *op.cit.*, p. 112.

because the authors of the Chālukya records wanted to enhance the glory of Pulakeśin by claiming that he defeated even the lord of entire Uttarāpatha which in their eyes might have been a justifiable exaggeration because Harsha in fact was the most powerful ruler of the north. In the same category we can place the description of Harsha by Yuan Chwang as the "Lord of the Five Indies" because whether this term is taken in its wider sense or in the narrower sense Yuan Chwang has used it loosely. The evidences of such sources as the verse of Mayūra are too vague and hyperbolic to merit any serious consideration.

The meaning of the term 'five Indies' used by Yuan Chwang in connection with Harsha's conquests is somewhat problematical. In the general description of India he applies it to the whole sub-continent saying that "The countries embraced under this term of India are generally spoken of as the five Indies. ... on three sides it is bordered by the great sea; on the north it is backed by the Snowy Mountains."[36] As noted by Thomas Watters, other Chinese travellers also mention that India had five main divisions, north, east, west, central, and south.[37] The indigenous sources, such as, the *Bhuvanakosha* section of the Purāṇas, divide the country into *madhyadeśa*, *udīchya*, *prāchya*, *dakshiṇāpatha*, and *aparānta*, sometimes adding to the list the Himalayan and Vindhyan regions also.[38] Therefore, the use of the term 'five Indies' by Yuan Chwang to denote the whole country was justified. But the pilgrim uses the term in a limited sense also. With reference to his account of Kanauj and Maharashtra he uses it to mean only the territory under Harsha's rule. In his description of Harsha's exploits as the king of Kanauj he states that after six years of warfare he subjugated the 'five Indies', and in describing the conflict between Harsha and Pulakeśin II of Maharashtra, he mentions that the former gathered troops from the 'five Indies'. According to Chatterji, one Chinese text has the variant 'five Gauḍas' for 'five Indias'.[39] Devahuti feels that "this reading fits the context perfectly. There is both literary and epigraphic evidence to show that Gauḍa was used to denote *uttarā-patha*, the north, just as Draviḍa was used as a generic term for *dakshiṇā-patha*, the south, the Vindhyas dividing the two regions. The *Śabda-kalpa-druma* quotes stanzas from the *Skanda-Purāṇa* giving the five divisons of the south- and north-Indian brāhmaṇas, grouped respectively as *pañcha-Draviḍa* and *pañcha-Gauḍa*."[40] However, S. R. Goyal does not feel satisfied with this interpretation because at the

[36] *Records*, I, p. 70.

[37] *Travels*, I, p. 140.

[38] D.C. Sircar, *Geography of Ancient and Medieval India*, Delhi, 1960, p. 73.

[39] G.S. Chatterji, *Harshavardhana* (in Hindi), 2nd edn., Allahabad, 1950, p. 104.

[40] D. Devahuti, *op.cit.*, pp. 97-98.

time Yuan Chwang wrote that Harsha collected troops from the 'five Indias', he had not become the ruler of Orissa, one of the 'five Gauḍas'. He, therefore, believes that the Chinese pilgrim had used the term 'five Indias' and not 'five Gauḍas' and that too figuratively, depicting Harsha as a *chakravartin*. Yuan Chwang was too well aware of what it implied to have credited Harsha with actual dominion over the whole sub-continent. His statement about Harsha's rule over the 'five Indias' should be regarded as symbolic as Bāṇa's description of his patron as the "Lord of the Four Oceans" or of the "Four Quarters".[41]

But instead of depending on such vague references we should rely on the description by Yuan Chwang of the political condition of India as he found it in the last decades of Harsha's reign. But here also we should not be rigid in our interpretation. It is generally believed that those kingdoms whose rulers have not been mentioned by Yuan Chwang were included in the empire of Harshavardhana and those, whose rulers have been mentioned by him, were independent. But this criterion cannot be applied everywhere. For example, the pilgrim mentions the rulers of Mu-t'o-lo (Mathurā) and Mo-ti-pu-lo (Matipura, near Bijnor) though these could not have been independent kingdoms as they were situated in the vicinity of Kanauj. Actually Yuan Chwang describes the kingdoms of India not only by referring or not referring to their kings. Sometimes he mentions a kingdom and its ruler by name along with his dependencies, sometimes he gives the names of the dependencies but not of the king, sometimes he mentions the name of the kingdom along with the number of dependencies but does not give their names. As a matter of fact we should realise that he was not writing a political gazetteer of India following fixed rules for making entries in it; he was trying to give a general description of the country and has recorded the information which appeared to him interesting due to whatsoever reason. It may also be remembered that he could describe a dependent state in greater detail because it could be larger, more important and stronger than its neighbouring independent but much smaller and politically insignificant state.

Let us now make a region-wise survey of the data provided by Yuan Chwang about the nature of Harsha's political relations with various states keeping in mind also his wars and conquests.[42] Here we should remember that, according to Yuan Chwang, the people of Yin-tu (the Chinese name for India) use local appellations for their respective countries, and he himself understands this to mean that the natives of India had only designations of

[41] S.R. Goyal, *op.cit.*, p. 188.

[42] The following analysis about the nature of Harsha's political relations with various states is based on known facts as well as conclusions arrived at and suggestions made in our work *Harsha : A Multidisciplinary Political Study*, Jodhpur, 2006, Chs. 6-7.

their own states, such as, Magadha and Kauśāmbī, and that they were without a general name under which these could be included.[43] Yuan Chwang, of course, must have known that the people had a name for the whole country, such as, Jambudvīpa or Āryāvarta,[44] but he has obviously in mind the common people : that they had no sense of belonging to a country and so no need to use a name for it.[45]

Now let us move on to Yuan Chwang's description of India. He reached Kia-pi-shi (Kapiśā) in May 630. At that time Kapiśā was a strong and independent kingdom situated between the Hindukush and the Indus. It was then ruled by a Buddhist king of Kshatriya caste who every year made a silver figure of the Buddha eighteen feet high and convoked Mahāmoksha-parishad in which alms were given to the poor. His power extended over more than ten of the neighbouring lands.[46] Lan-po (Lamghān), Na-kie-lo-ho (Nagarahāra or Jalalabad), Kien-t'o-lo (Gandhāra) and Fa-la-na (Varana, identifiable with Bannu ?, Bolor ?) were also his dependencies.[47] Apparently, Kapiśā had nothing to do with Harsha. Similarly, the kingdom of U-chang-na (Udyāna) also, situated to the west of the Indus, had no political dealings with Kanauj.[48]

To the east of the Indus Kia-shi-mi-lo (Kashmir) was the first important kingdom. It had Ta-ch'a-shi-lo (Takshaśilā), Sang-ha-pu-lo (Siṁhapura), Wu-la-shi (Urasa, modern Hazara), Pun-nu-ts'o (Punch) and Ho-lo-she-pu-lo (Rājapurī or Rajori) as its dependencies.[49] It was an independent kingdom but weaker than that of Harsha, and was, therefore, his 'natural prey'.

In the Punjab, Tsch-ka or Cheh-ka (Ṭakka) was the largest kingdom situated between the Indus and the Beas with its capital near Śākala.[50] It had

[43] *Travels*, I, pp. 131-32.

[44] Yuan Chwang himself mentions that the 'Brāhmaṇa' country (obviously a rendering of 'Brahmavarta') was a popular name for India (*Records*, I, p. 69; *Travels*, I, p. 140). In this context it has been pointed out that by this interpretation of the name, the identification of the domain of caste-hierarchy with India becomes manifest (Shireen Moosvi, 'The Making of India', her General President's, Address, in the *Proceedings of the Indian History Congress*, 77th Session, University of Kerala, Thiruvananthapuram, 2016, Aligarh, 2017, p.7).

[45] J. S. Grewal, 'Hiuen Tsiang's India', in *India—Studies in the History of an Idea*, ed. Irfan Habib, New Delhi, 2005, p. 62.

[46] *Records*, I, pp. 54 ff.

[47] *Ibid.*, pp. 90-91, 98; II, p. 281.

[48] *Ibid.*, p. 119.

[49] *Ibid.*, pp. 136, 143, 147, 148, 163.

[50] *Ibid.*, p. 165.

two dependencies—Mou-lo-san-pu (Multan ?) and Po-fa-ta (Parvata).[51] It was outside the pale of Harsha's authority.

Yuan Chwang mentions four kingdoms of the eastern Punjab and the hilly region situated to its north-east. They were Chi-na-po-ti (Chīnapati), She-lan-to-lo (Jālandhara), K'iu-lu-to (Kulūta) and She-to-t'u-lo (Śatadru).[52] He does not say anything about their political status. However, about Jālandhara he says that it was 'formerly' ruled by a Buddhist convert who was rewarded by the king of Mid India with the important office of the 'sole inspector of the affairs of religion (*the three gems*) throughout the five Indies'. This 'former king' may be identified with Wu-ti or Udita of Jālandhara, who was charged by a king of Mid India (identifiable with Harsha) to escort Yuan Chwang to the borders of India.[53] According to Devahuti, by his phrase 'former king' the pilgrim means that Wu-ti, at the time of his visit a royal official for the affairs of religion for the 'five Indias', had at one time been the independent king of Jālandhara.[54] And if Jālandhara had come under the suzerainty of Harsha, then the other three kingdoms might also have been forced to do so. But we cannot be certain of that.

Between Jālandhara and Mathurā were situated the kingdoms of Sa-t'a-ni-ssu-fa-lo (Sthāṇvīśvara) and Su-lo-k'in-na (Śrughna).[55] Yuan Chwang does not say anything about their rulers, though we know that Sthāṇvīśvara was the ancestral kingdom of Harsha. The hilly kingdoms of Po-lo-hih-mo-pu-lo (Brahmapura, in Kumaon-Garhwal region), Su-fa-la-na-kiu-ta-lo (Suvarṇagotra, to the north of Brahmapura) and Kiu-pi-shwang-na (Goviśaṇa, corresponding to Kashipur, Rampur and Pilibhit districts)[56] were neighbours of Śrughna. Yuan Chwang does not say anything about their rulers except about Suvarṇagotra which he describes as "the eastern women's country" where husband of the queen was called a king but did not administer the government. The suzerainty of Harsha over these states, though quite likely, cannot be definitely proved.

Now let us consider the kingdoms situated roughly in the present Uttar Pradesh (excluding Uttaranchal) and Bihar. They were Mu-t'o-lo (Mathurā), Mo-ti-pu-lo (Matipura, modern Madawar, near Bijnor in western Rohilkhand), O-hi-chi-ta-lo (Ahichchhatrā, Ramnagar in Bareilly district), Pi-lo-sha-na (Vīraśāṇa ?, identified with Atranjikhera, near Kanauj), Kie-pi-ta (Kapitha or Sānkāśya, modern Sankisa), Kie-jo-kio-she-kwo (Kanauj),

[51] *Ibid.*, II, pp. 274-75.
[52] *Ibid.*, I, pp. 172, 175, 177, 178.
[53] *Life*, pp. 189-90.
[54] D. Devahuti, *op.cit.*, p. 104.
[55] *Records*, I, pp. 183, 186.
[56] *Ibid.*, pp. 198, 199.

O-yu-t'o (Ayodhyā), O-ye-mu-khie (Hayamukha, modern Daunḍiakhera on the banks of the Gaṅgā), Po-lo-ye-kia (Prayāga), Kiao-shang-mi (Kauśāmbī), Pi-so-kia (Viśoka or Vaiśaka, not yet identified), Shi-lo-fu-shi-ti (Śrāvastī), Kie-pi-lo-fa-su-tu (Kapilavastu), Lan-mo (Rāma or Rāmagrāma), Kie-shi-na-kie-lo (Kuśīnagara), P'o-lo-ni-sse (Vārāṇasī), Chen-chu (not yet identified, but possibly Ghazipur), Fei-she-li (Vaiśālī), Fo-li-shi (Vṛjji)[57] and Mo-kie-t'o (Magadha).[58] In the north of Uttar Pradesh and Bihar was the kingdom of Ni-po-lo (Nepal).[59] Yuan Chwang does not mention the rulers of these kingdoms except those of Matipura, Mathurā, Kānyakubja, Kapilavastu, Magadha and Nepal. The king of Matipura was a Śūdra by caste who did not believe in Buddhism and worshipped the *devas* (i.e., the Hindu deities). Mathurā is said to have been governed by a Buddhist king who, with his ministers, applied himself to religious duties with zeal. The kings of Matipura and Mathurā, because of the close proximity of their kingdoms to Sthāṇvīśvara and Kanauj, must have been the feudatories of Harsha. Kanauj was the capital of Harsha himself. In Kapilavastu there was no sovereign, each city had its own chief. As regards Nepal and Magadha we find that Harsha had no jurisdiction over Nepal while Magadha was conquered by him shortly before 637 A.D.

In the eastern direction, between Magadha and Assam, Yuan Chwang places the kingdoms of I-lan-na-po-fa-to (Hiraṇyaparvata, identified with modern Munghyr), Chen-po (Champā, modern Bhagalpur), Kie-chu-hoh-khi-lo or Kiu-chu-wen (Kajaṅgala or Kajughira, modern Rajmahal), Pun-na-fa-t'an-na (Puṇḍravardhana, modern Pabna), San-mo-ta-th'a (Samataṭa), Tan-mo-li-ti (Tāmralipti, modern Tamluk) and Kie-lo-na-su-fa-la-na (Karṇasuvarṇa, corresponding to Burdwan, Birbhum and Murshidabad).[60] To their east was situated the kingdom of Kia-mo-lu-po (Kāmarūpa) ruled byKumārarāja. About Hiraṇyaparvata the pilgrim informs us that "in recent times the king of a neighbouring state had deposed its ruler and given the capital to the Buddhist brethren." This king of the neighbouring state might have been Harsha. No king of Champā is mentioned by Yuan Chwang and about Kajaṅgala he tells us that the native dynasty had been extinguished centuries before his arrival and the capital was deserted. So, king Śīlāditya, during his progress to 'East India', held his court there in temporary grass huts which were burnt when he left the place. As regards Puṇḍravardhana, Samataṭa, Tāmralipti and Karṇasuvarṇa the pilgrim reports that shortly before his visit they were ruled by Śaśāṅka. But after his death,

[57] *Ibid.*, I, pp. 179-240; II, pp. 1-80.

[58] *Ibid.*, II, pp. 82-185.

[59] *Ibid.*, pp. 80-82.

[60] *Ibid.*, II, pp. 186, 191, 193, 194, 199, 200, 201.

sometime between 619 and 637, these regions came under the suzerainty of Harsha and Bhāskara; probably they divided the Bengal regions of Śaśāṅka's empire among themselves as they were won as a result of their joint campaign. The occupation of Karṇasuvarṇa by Bhāskara evidenced by his Nidhanpur plates could have taken place only after the fall of Śaśāṅka while there is no reason to presume that it took place after the death of Harsha. The fact that when Bhāskara came with Yuan Chwang to meet Harsha he brought a large force with him, including twenty thousand elephants and thirty thousand ships, also tends to suggest that Bhāskara was in control of large tracts of Bengal.

To the south of modern Bengal were situated the kingdoms of U-ch'a or Wu-t'u (Oḍra) and Kung-yü-t'o (Koṅgoda, modern Ganjam).[61] Yuan Chwang is silent about the governments of both but he testifies that Harsha conquered them towards the close of his reign, between 639 and 642.

The strongest kingdom to the south-west of Kanauj was Mo-ha-la-ch'a or Maharashtra. It was ruled by Pulakeśin II. According to Yuan Chwang, Harsha had made vigorous efforts to conquer it but had not succeeded till 641. We, however, believe that Harsha-Pulakeśin tussle was a long drawn affair. So far scholars have been assuming that Pulakeśin II had fought and defeated Harsha either between 610 and 612 or sometime before 634, the date of the Aihole record. *But the struggle between these two great monarchs was going on even in 640 when Yuan Chwang visited Maharashtra.* His testimony proves that (1) the Harsha-Pulakeśin conflict recorded in the Aihole inscription was not decisive. (2) This struggle was a protracted one and was going on in 640, for in his record of the journey made in 640 Yuan Chwang explicitly says that at the time of his visit Harsha had 'not yet conquered' Pulakeśin. It, therefore, follows that the conflict which took place before 634 was only one of the numerous battles fought by them. It is, thus, quite possible that the conflict between the two also occurred before the battle recorded in the Aihole *praśasti* of 634, for which no evidence is now available. This analysis renders the question of the date of the Harsha-Pulakeśin war mentioned in the Aihole *praśasti* quite irrelevant. We can safely say that the conflict recorded in the Aihole *praśasti* was in the nature of a battle, not of a war. That is, the Aihole *praśasti* records only one phase of the long-drawn war between Pulakeśin and Harsha, and not the whole war.[62]

On the western coast was the kingdom of Po-lu-kie-ch'o-po (Bhṛgukachchha or Bharuch), identifiable with the Gurjara kingdom of Lāṭa

[61] *Ibid.*, II, pp. 204, 206.

[62] Shankar Goyal, *op.cit.*, pp. 203-08; idem, 'Harsha-Pulakeśin II Struggle : A Collated Sutdy of Epigraphic and Literary Evidence', in *JESI*, XXXVII, 2012, pp. 100-05.

(south Gujarat) whose king Dadda II gave shelter to the king of Valabhī when the latter was invaded by Harsha. Therefore, there is no question of Lāṭa having been under Harsha's subordination. As regards Fa-li-pi (Valabhī), Yuan Chwang tells us that the reigning king T'u-lo-p'o-po-t'a (Dhruvabhaṭa or Dhruvapaṭa) was the nephew of Śīlāditya, the former king of Mālava, and the son-in-law of Śīlāditya of Kanauj. He participated in the religious assembly of Kanauj and quinquennial ceremony of Prayāga. Taking this information along with the evidence of the Gurjara records, we believe that Dhruvabhaṭa (Dhruvasena II of Valabhī records) was invaded by Harsha. He took shelter with Dadda II but later on thought it more prudent to accept the overlordship of Harsha. Harsha won him over by giving his daughter in marriage. Dhruvabhaṭa's status was not equal to that of Bhāskara, as he was not a Mahārājādhirāja and had to taste the might of Harsha, but being the ruler of a big and powerful kingdom and the son-in-law of the emperor his status could not have been very much low either. The fact that his successor Dharasena IV assumed imperial titles in 645-46 A. D., even when Harsha was alive, also shows that Harsha's influence on Valabhī was only nominal.

According to Nogāvā grants of Dhruvasena II, he was ruling over Mālavaka in 639-40. But in the same year Yuan Chwang describes Mo-la-p'o (identified with western Malwa) as an independent kingdom with some dependencies of its own. Probably a tussle for power was going on in that region in c. 640 A.D.

In central India, north of Narmadā, Yuan Chwang also describes three other kingdoms—Wu-shê-yen-na (Ujjain), Chi-ki-t'o or Chih-chi-t'o (Jijhauti ?[63] in Bundelkhand) and Mo-hi-ssu-fa-lo-pu-lo (Maheśvarapura, the region around Gwalior).[64] The rulers of these kingdoms were Brāhmaṇas—those of Ujjain and Maheśvarapura being non-Buddhists and that of Chih-chi-t'o a staunch Buddhist.

Beyond Valabhī to its north was the kingdom of Sin-tu (Sindhu). According to Yuan Chwang, its king, who was of Śūdra caste, was a believer in Buddhism. He had under him three dependencies. The pilgrim does not give any indication of Harsha's suzerainty over it. As regards Bāṇa's statement that Harsha appropriated the fortune of its monarch, it probably refers to some clash in which Harsha's troops plundered the border areas of Sindh.

Now remains the region presently called Rajasthan situated to the north of Gujarat and Malwa, east of Sindh, west of U.P. and south of the

[63] As the name *Jijhauti* or *Jejākabhukti* probably came into existence in the post-Harsha period, this identification may not be correct. But this much is certain that Chih-chi-t'o was situated in the Bundelkhand region.

[64] *Records*, II, p. 271.

Punjab. Yuan Chwang refers to only two kingdoms of this region— Kiu-che-lo[65] (Gurjara) ruled by a Buddhist king of Kshatriya caste and Po-li-ye-to-lo (Pāriyātra, identified with Bairat).[66] It was ruled by a Vaiśya king. He is described as brave, impetuous and warlike. In the *Harshacharita* Pāriyātra is mentioned as a kingdom which Harsha's feudatories wished to conquer. The Gurjara kingdom is generally identified with the Pratihāra kingdom of Mandor. But the Pratihāras of Mandor were Brāhmaṇas and they nowhere call themselves Gurjaras. S. R. Goyal has, therefore, identified the Kiu-che-lo of Yuan Chwang with the Chāpa kingdom of Bhinmal.[67]

Now we are in a position to determine the extent of the empire of Harsha and the sphere of his influence by taking together the testimony of Yuan Chwang and other sources. First of all let us reiterate that we cannot proceed with the assumption that we should regard Harsha as the ruler of only those countries which are specifically mentioned by Yuan Chwang as under his suzerainty. If the description of Yuan Chwang is taken literally one must conclude, as Majumdar[68] has pointed out, that "Harshavardhana was merely the king of Kanauj", for the Chinese pilgrim does not name even one kingdom except Kanauj as subject to the Pushyabhūti authority. But such a conclusion will be against the known facts of Harsha's conquests as known from inscriptions and Yuan Chwang himself. According to Tripathi, therefore, it may be assumed that those territories of north India were included within the empire of Kanauj about the governments of which Yuan Chwang maintains silence.[69] But this line of approach also creates difficulties, for Yuan Chwang mentions the kings of Mathurā (Mu-t'o-lo) and Matipura (Mo-ti-pu-lo) also who, if one follows the reasoning of Tripathi, must be placed beyond the sphere of Harsha's influence. But that is impossible. How could Harsha, the ruler of Thanesar and Kanauj, who carried his victorious arms in Orissa and Gujarat, leave Mathurā and Matipura, both situated in U.P. between Kanauj and Thanesar, as separate independent entities ? The testimony of Yuan Chwang, therefore, should not be analysed in this fashion. It must be kept in mind that he was not writing a political gazetteer. It must be realised that about various states he mentions only those facts which he

[65] *Ibid.*, p. 269.

[66] *Ibid.*, I, p. 179. According to G.S.L. Devra, however, the Chinese pilgrim visited not one or two places but six places during his two visits to Rajasthan. Bhatner, Osian and Chittor were prominent among them (in *Rajasthan Itihāsa ke Abhigyāna Rūpa*, Jaipur, 2010, Ch.2). But his view rests on his own identification of some places which may not be necessarily correct.

[67] S.R. Goyal, *op.cit.*, p. 240.

[68] *JBORS*, 1923, p. 318.

[69] R. S. Tripathi, *op.cit.*, p. 115.

thought were interesting or significant. But he has certainly not followed a set formula. Further, it must be remembered that in that age of feudal polity in which an emperor had his subordinate kings who in turn had their own feudatories, a feudatory of the emperor could be more important than an independent king. Yuan Chwang, therefore, could mention a feudatory king and omit to mention a minor ruler of an independent state. Hence we should determine the nature of Harsha's relations with any particular state by taking into consideration all the known facts about it.[70]

YUAN CHWANG ON THE ADMINISTRATION OF HARSHA

In addition to some records belonging to the preceding and succeeding periods, contemporary literary sources, throw a good deal of light on Harsha's administration. In Yuan Chwang we also find general statements about condition in India and information regarding the political set up and governmental machinery.[71] Viewed in its totality the polity of Harsha seems to be based on the administrative pattern of the preceding Gupta age, but at the same time it appears to have been much more 'feudalized' and with lesser cohesion. Under the Guptas political unity was characterized by a balance between centralization and regional autonomy; Harsha's empire was a looser federation much more based on diplomatic alliances than on the firm hold of the central authority. Harsha's superiority over his subordinate kings and feudatories depended on his strength which was lesser than that of the Guptas despite the fact that he is said to have had a very large army, for his army itself was not a 'monolith' controlled by the emperor but a collection of the feudal military units contributed by the *sāmantas*. Actually, the growth of the *sāmanta* institution, the Indian version of feudalism, was the greatest single factor which differentiates the administrative organisation of Harsha from the administration of earlier periods.[72]

In the feudal polity the success of a king depended largely upon his personal ability and his devotion to work. Therefore, kings like Harsha

[70] For further details, cf. Shankar Goyal, 'Yuan Chwang's India and the Problem of the Extent of Harsha's Empire and Sphere of His Influence', in the *Papers from the Aligarh Historians Society*, ed. Irfan Habib, 77th Session, Indian History Congress, Thiruvananthapuram, 28-30 December, 2016, pp. 104-16.

[71] For details, vide also my paper, 'Feudalization of Polity in the Age of Harsha : An Analysis', in *History and Politics*, ed., Shankar Goyal, Jodhpur, 2015, Ch. 9.

[72] Although hereditary monarchy was the familiar form of government in the seventh century, a faint hint of the pre-Gupta 'republics' was left in Kapilavastu, Buddha's birthplace, where, according to Yuan Chwang, 'each town had its own chief.' But this system seems to be more 'feudal' than 'republican' in character.

worked dedicatedly. Yuan Chwang refers to the busy daily routine of Harsha and his tours of inspection. He says :

> He was just in his administration, and punctilious in the discharge of his duties. He forgot sleep and food in his devotion to good works. ... The king also made visits of inspection throughout his dominion, not residing long at any place but having temporary buildings erected for his residence at each place of sojourn, and he did not go abroad during the three months of the Rain-season Retreat. ... The king's day was divided into three periods, of which one was given up to affairs of government, and two were devoted to religious works. He was indefatigable, and the day was too short for him.[73]

In the age of Harsha the king not only had a council of ministers but also a large secretariat consisting of various departments such as those for revenue, public welfare, interstate relations, army and so forth. In this context Yuan Chwang refers to separate custodians for maintaining official annals and state papers collectively called *nīla-piṭa.* He also records the appointment of an inspector for Buddhist affairs by Harsha.

Harsha's empire was divided into administrative units of different sizes. Yuan Chwang usually mentions the dimensions of the seventy 'countries' he visited in India, but often in 'circuits', a method quite unhelpful in determining the area of the 'country' in question. Some of them were very large, others quite small. Harsha's inscriptions, however, mention the traditional *grāma* (village), *vishaya* and *bhukti* but not the *deśa* of the imperial Gupta epigraphs, although the division may have existed in his time.

The Chinese pilgrim also gives a few details about the military organisation of the period. He informs us that :

> The National Guard (lit. warriors) are heroes of choice valour, and, as the profession is hereditary, they become adepts in military tactics. In peace they guard the sovereign's residence, and in war they become the intrepid vanguard.
>
> The army is composed of Foot, Horse, Chariot, and Elephant soldiers. The war-elephant is covered with coat-of-mail, and his tusks are provided with sharp barbs. On him rides the Commander-in-chief, who has a soldier on each side to manage the elephant. The chariot in which an officer sits is drawn by four horses, whilst infantry guard it on both sides. The infantry go lightly into action and are choice men of valour; they bear a large shield and carry a long spear; some are armed with a sword or sabre and dash to the front of the advancing line of battle. They are perfect experts with all the implements of war such as spear, shield, bow and arrow, sword, sabre &c. having been drilled in them for generations.[74]

[73] *Travels*, I, pp. 343-44.
[74] *Ibid.*, p.171.

Thus, Yuan Chwang reproduces the traditional list which includes chariots. But in fact the chariots had gone out of use even in Gupta times and boats had become an important wing of the army (*mahānau* of inscriptions). Yuan Chwang himself nowhere else refers to the chariots in the armies of contemporary kings.

Harsha had a large standing army. He increased his army from 5,000 elephants, 20,000 cavalry and 50,000 infantry to 60,000 elephants and one lac infantry.[75] Yuan Chang does not give the increased figures of cavalry. These figures may appear exaggerated but, in view of the situation of the period, may not be altogether incorrect. Yuan Chwang states that when Bhāskaravarman came to meet Harsha he brought 20,000 elephants and 30,000 ships (actually large boats) with him. Therefore, the figure of 60,000 for Harsha's elephants may be regarded as not unduly inflated. The elephant corps appears to have received the greatest attention, perhaps because the huge beast could be used to destroy the enemy fortifications. Pulakeśin II also had an exceptionally strong elephant division. The *Harshacharita*, and to some extent the *Records*, contain most interesting information on the ingenious use of elephants in war. Bāṇa also recalls the designations of various officers connected with this wing of the army. Cavalry was not neglected. Horses of good breeds were imported from well beyond the Indian frontiers and the science of steeds was a well developed branch of knowledge. The infantry also played an important part in the battlefield. They could wield a variety of weapons including arrows, javelins and slings, while they protected their bodies with thick unguents and shields made of leather.

Yuan Chwang had all praise for Indian system of taxation. He gives a few details about the fiscal matters in the general description of India :

> As the Government is generous official requirements are few. Families are not registered, and individuals are not subject to forced labour contributions. Of the royal land there is a fourfold division : one part is for the expenses of government and state worship, one for the endowment of great public servants, one to reward high intellectual eminence, and one for acquiring religious merit by gifts to the various sects. Taxation being light, and forced service being sparingly used, every one keeps to his hereditary occupation and attends to his patrimony. The king's tenants pay one-sixth of the produce as rent. Tradesmen go to and fro bartering their merchandize after paying light duties at ferries and barrier stations. Those who are employed in the government service are paid according to their work. They go abroad on military service or they guard the palace; the summonses are issued according to circumstances and after proclamation of the reward the enrolment is awaited. Ministers of state

[75] *Ibid.*, p. 343.

> and common officials all have their portion of land, and are maintained by the cities assigned to them.[76]

Though this description is somewhat idealised, yet it gives an idea of how Harsha conducted the economic affairs of his realm.

Writing about the judicial processes the Chinese pilgrim writes:

> As the government is honestly administered and the people live together on good terms the criminal class is small. The statute law is sometimes violated and plots made against the sovereign; when the crime is brought to light the offender is imprisoned for life; he does not suffer any corporal punishment, but alive and dead he is not treated as member of the community (lit. as a man). For offences against social morality, and disloyal and unfilial conduct, the punishment is to cut off the nose, or an ear, or a hand, or a foot, or to banish the offender to another country or into the wilderness. Other offences can be atoned for by a money payment.[77]

Yuan Chwang also makes a reference to *divyas* or ordeals:[78]

> These are by water, by fire, by weighing, and by poison. In the water ordeal the accused is put in one sack and a stone in another, then the two sacks are connected and thrown into a deep stream; if the sack containing the stone floats, and the other sinks, the man's guilt is proven. The fire ordeal requires the accused to kneel and tread on hot iron, to take it in his hand and lick it; if he is innocent he is not hurt, but he is burnt if he is guilty. In the weighing ordeal the accused is weighed against a stone; and if the latter is the lighter the charge is false, if otherwise it is true. The poison ordeal requires that the right hind leg of a ram be cut off, and according to the portion assigned to the accused to eat, poisons are put into the leg, and if the man is innocent he survives, and if not the poison takes effect.[79]

RELIABILITY OF YUAN CHWANG'S TESTIMONY ON HARSHA'S FAITH IN BUDDHISM

Harsha was personally a devotee of Śiva. The evidence for his faith in the worship of Lord Śiva is quite weighty, diverse and profuse. His Banskhera inscription of the Year 22 (=628 A.D.), Kurukshetra-Varanasi grant of the Year 23 (=629A.D.) and Madhuban plate of the Year 25 (=631 A.D.) definitely call him a Paramamāheśvara. According to the *Harshacharita*, when he started on his campaign he "had with deep devotion offered worship to the adorable Nīlalohita."[80] The golden seal presented to him by the village notary at the time of his first halt was inscribed with the emblem of bull

[76] *Ibid.*, pp. 176-77; D. Devahuti, ed., *The Unknown Hsüan-Tsang*, Oxford, 2001, pp. 135-36.

[77] *Ibid.*, pp. 171-72.

[78] Somewhat differently they are also mentioned by Bāṇa.

[79] *Travels*, I, p. 172.

[80] *HC*, edn. of E.B. Cowell and F.W. Thomas, Delhi, 2nd edn., 1968, p. 197.

(Nandī), the *vāhana* of the Lord Śiva.[81] On his Sonepat copper seal the reclining Nandī symbol is depicted.[82] Similarly, on the reverse of his gold coin Śiva and Pārvatī are shown as seated on Nandī. Yuan Chwang also refers to the worship of Śiva by Harsha at Prayāga as late as 643 A.D.

However, despite these evidences of indubitable nature, Harsha is usually regarded as one of the greatest Buddhist rulers of ancient India. It is held that he set himself to imitate Aśoka so that the narrative of his doings in the later years of his reign 'reads like a copy of the history of the great Maurya'[83] and that his interest in Buddhism, which was quite mild in his youth, acquired more and more intensity with the passage of time ultimately leading to his complete, almost fanatic, devotion to the Mahāyāna form of this religion. But most of the arguments given in support of this theory are merely 'opinions' of modern scholars.[84] For, as seen above, Indian sources are explicit and emphatic in deposing that Harsha was a devotee of Śiva. It is only Yuan Chwang who tends to show that his Indian patron was a believer in Buddhism. It is true that much should not be made of the fact that Harsha is supposed to have written *Nāgānanda*, a play with a Buddhist theme.[85] But it hardly proves his own faith in Buddhism. Firstly, as noted elsewhere in this work, it is not at all certain that Harsha actually wrote this play. Further, in ancient India authors did not pick up a theme for composing a play or a *kāvya* only when it corresponded to their own religious beliefs. Kālidāsa sang the eulogy of Rāma in his *Raghuvaṁśa* and of Śiva in his *Kumārasambhava.*

Yuan Chwang's reference to Harsha's respect for the statue of the Bodhisattva Avalokiteśvara also does not prove Harsha's faith in Buddhism. It may be argued that the predominance of Buddhism in Kanauj and the fact that the people of this city had recently been put to a great trouble by Śaśāṅka, the avowed enemy of Buddhism, the show of respect to the statue of the Bodhisattva Avalokiteśvara by Harsha (who was an ardent worshipper of Śiva) cannot be regarded as more than a diplomatic move to win over to his side the affections of the Buddhist subjects of the Maukhari kingdom.[86] Even nowadays shrewd politicians visit shrines of religions other than their own to prove their large-heartedness. This also makes it quite likely that Harsha erected a number of stūpas on the banks of the Gaṅgā at the request of his Buddhist sister and to please the people of Kanauj who were more

[81] *Ibid.*, p. 198.
[82] J.F. Fleet, *Corpus Inscriptionum Indicarum*, III, Calcutta, 1888, No. 52.
[83] V.A. Smith, *The Early History of India*, 4th edn., Oxford, 1924, p. 197.
[84] For details vide, *HB*, Ch. 9.
[85] R. S. Tripathi, *op.cit.*, p. 181.
[86] *HB*, p. 82.

inclined towards the creed of the Buddha. The same motivation might have been behind the 'forcible' appropriation of the tooth-relic of the Buddha from Kashmir and its subsequent enshrinement in a saṅghārāma in Kanauj.

Yuan Chwang's reference to the erection by Harsha of hospices (*puṇyaśālās*) provided with food, drinks and physicians with medicines for travellers and poor persons also cannot be regarded as indicative of Harsha's faith in Buddhism for it would be assuming that kings belonging to other religions did not do such things for the welfare of their people. Further, what Yuan Chwang has reported is not wholly correct. For example, his statement that king Harsha 'forbade the slaughter of any living thing or flesh as food throughout the Five Indies on pain of death without pardon' is palpably wrong. In the general description of India he explicitly states that in food 'fish, mutton and venison are occasional dainties'.[87] According to the *Life*, Harsha himself gave in gift among other things 'various drinks and meats' to '10,000 of the religious community' (Buddhist monks) in the quinquennial distribution of alms at Prayāga.[88]

There is another consideration which goes against Yuan Chwang's portrayal of Harsha as a great Buddhist ruler. Yuan Chwang entered India in October 630, but met Harsha for the first time in October 642[89] and that too at the latter's initiative. Apparently, he was not sufficiently impressed with the reputation of Harsha as a Buddhist ruler, for there arose no desire in him to meet this Indian king whom he later on sought to portray as another Aśoka. Even as late as 641, when he resolved to return to China, the idea of meeting Harsha did not cross his mind, though he was very much anxious to obtain the help of some king for his return journey. "Does it not prove", S.R. Goyal rightly asks, "that Harsha was not at all famous as a great Buddhist ruler in his own time ?"[90]

From the above discussion it is apparent that Yuan Chwang's testimony does not prove that Harshavardhana had developed a *personal* interest in Buddhism before he met Yuan Chwang. Now, the question arises : did Harsha change his *personal* religion after he came into contact with Yuan Chwang ? Unfortunately, Yuan Chwang is the only source for this phase of Harsha's religious beliefs and the corrective evidence of the *Harshacharita*, inscriptions, coins, etc. is not available.[91] However, an investigation of the inner contradictions in Yuan Chwang's testimony shows that he is not wholly

[87] *Travels*, I, p. 178.
[88] *Life*, p. 186.
[89] A. Cunningham, *op.cit.*, p. 478.
[90] *HB*, p. 85.
[91] *Ibid.*, p. 86.

reliable on things concerning Buddhism. His faith in Buddhism was as fathomless as was his egotism. It may be noted that he does not claim that his influence over Harsha increased gradually. In his usual egoistical fashion he claims that Harsha's devotion to him was instant, spontaneous and complete. The description of the circumstances leading to their meeting as given in the *Life* by Hui-li on the basis of the information supplied by Yuan Chwang himself is the best example of his vanity. He has narrated them in a fashion which leaves in the mind of the reader the impression that the two great kings of India—namely, Harsha and Bhāskaravarman—were vying with each other in soliciting his teachings, and one of them even endangered his own life for the sake of his company. Here, it is significant to note that not only the *Hsi Yü Chi* but other Chinese state records so far known to us including the *Chiu t'ang-shu*, the *T'ang hui-yao*, the *Tz'e-fu yüan-kuei* and the *Wen-hsien t'ung-k'ao* which throw light on the period also use a conventional phraseology to demonstrate the superiority of China over a foreign country, whatever the relative status of the two at a given time. Not only official historians, but even the Buddhist monk I-tsing, who pays tribute to Indian medicine in his records, sometimes indulges in similar sentiments.

The account of the first meeting of Yuan Chwang and Harsha itself is highly coloured. According to the *Life*, Harsha first met Yuan Chwang at Kajaṅgala at the pavilion-of-travel. "On his arrival the king bowed down at the feet of the Master of Law, then scattering flowers before him he regarded him with respect, and uttered his praises in verses innumerable."[92] But it is difficult to believe that Harsha could have shown such respect and could sing 'innumerable verses' in praise of a Chinese priest whom he was meeting for the first time, even if he was a poet of some merit. In his second meeting Yuan Chwang showed Harsha his treatise which was written with a view to restraining the 'wicked doctrine' (viz. the Hīnayāna). After examining it at the very spot, Harshavardhana came to the conclusion that it had destroyed all the other doctrines and established the truth of the Mahāyāna. It was indeed a marvel. Harsha took a cursory look at the book of Yuan Chwang (in the circumstances it could not have been a deeper study) and became absolutely convinced of the superiority of the Mahāyāna over every other creed ! His conviction became so complete that 'the same day'[93] he sent orders for convening a grand all-India assembly at Kanauj to prove its merit!! What is more, his sister became overjoyed when she heard Yuan Chwang demolishing the Hīnayānist creed in which she had been believing for more than thirty-five years !!! Needless to say that such miraculous conversions donot take place in real life.

[92] *Life*, p. 175.
[93] *Ibid.*, pp. 175-76.

There is an inherent contradiction in Yuan Chwang's description of Harsha's faith in the Mahāyāna. For, on the one hand, he strives to show that it was he who was responsible for bringing Harsha and Rājyaśrī within the fold of the Mahāyāna, but, on the other, by referring at other places to Harsha's resolve to consult the statue of Avalokiteśvara and his invitation to the Mahāyāna scholars of Nālandā to face the challenge of the Hīnayānī priests of Orissa, Yuan Chwang gives the impression that Harsha was interested in the Mahāyāna even before he met him. Both these positions cannot be correct.

From Kajaṅgala Yuan Chwang and Harsha went to Kanauj where the proposed religious assembly was held. According to its description in the *Life*,[94] kings of eighteen countries of the Five Indies, 3,000 priests thoroughly acquainted with both Hīnayāna and Mahāyāna, 3,000 Brāhmaṇas and Nirgranthas and about a thousand priests from the Nālandā monastery participated in the assembly. The proceedings of the assembly opened with a huge procession in which a golden statue of the Buddha was carried out on a gorgeously caparisoned elephant. On its right went king Harsha dressed as Śakra (Indra) holding a white chowrie and on the left was Bhāskaravarman, dressed as Brāhma-rāja (Brahmā) with a precious parasol in his hand. When the procession reached the venue of the assembly, the statue was carried into a hall and placed on a precious throne. The worship of the statue was followed by a grand feast and the feast by religious discussions. In the hall of discussion were seated 1,000 Buddhists, 500 celebrated Brāhmaṇas and followers of heretical doctrine (the Hīnayāna) and about 200 of the great ministers of the different kingdoms. Others were seated outside the gate of the hall. Yuan Chwang, who was nominated as the 'Lord of the discussion', began by extolling the teachings of the Mahāyāna and announced a subject for discussion. He also caused a placard to be written and hung outside the door of the place of assembly stating: "if there is any one who can find a single word in the proposition contrary to reason or is able to entangle (the argument) then at the request of the opponent, I offer my head as a recompense." But none dared to challenge him for five days. Then the followers of the Hīnayāna, 'seeing he had overturned their school', plotted to kill him. Thereupon, Harsha issued a proclamation threatening that if 'any one should hurt or touch the Master of Law, he shall be forthwith beheaded; and whoever speaks against him, his tongue shall be cut out'. After this 'the followers of error withdrew' and no one joined the discussion. Therefore, when 18 days had passed and the assembly dispersed, Yuan Chwang was declared victorious and carried out in a procession to proclaim

[94] *Ibid.*, pp. 177-81.

his victory. "The whole multitude was filled with joy on account of the Master's success... the congregation of the Great Vehicle called him Mahāyāna Deva... whilst the followers of the Little Vehicle called him Moksha Deva."

The account of the Kanauj assembly as given in the *Records* [95] differs from the one given in the *Life* on some minor and major points. The most important difference between the two is this : the *Records* does not say anything about the plot to kill Yuan Chwang; instead it refers to the plot of the Brāhmaṇas to kill Harsha himself. According to the version of the *Records*, 'on the day of the separation' of the assembly the great tower built in the hall and pavilion over the gate of the saṅghārāma suddenly caught fire. But it was miraculously extinguished when Harsha prayed : "let the force of my religious conduct destroy this fire; or if not, let me die." Soon after it, when Harsha was surveying the scene of destruction from the top of the stūpa, a strange man, knife in hand, rushed on the king. The man was seized and confessed that he was hired by the heretics who had deliberately set the tower on fire to get an opportunity to assassinate the king. Five hundred Brāhmaṇas, all of singular talent, confessed to their share in the plot, adding that they were "jealous of Śramaṇas whom the king had reverenced and exceedingly honoured." The king punished the chief of them and banished the 500 Brāhmaṇas to the frontiers of India.

From the above account it is clear that while the *Life* refers to the plot of the Hīnayānists to kill Yuan Chwang because 'he had overthrown their doctrine', the *Records* refers to the plot of the Brāhmaṇas to kill Harsha because they were jealous of the favours showered by Harsha on the Śramaṇas. Which of the two accounts is correct ? So far it has been the practice of the historians to mix up the two accounts assuming that both of them are correct.[96] But it is highly unlikely, if not altogether impossible, that two different plots were hatched by two different communities to kill two different persons in the same assembly. It seems that the account of the *Life* represents the true course of events.[97] It should be remembered that the thrust of Yuan Chwang's endeavour was against the Hīnayāna doctrine. It was so earlier also when he was selected by Śīlabhadra to go to Orissa to controvert the Hīnayānist priests there; and it was his declared objective to demolish the Hīnayāna faith in the Kanauj assembly. Actually, the assembly was called by Harsha to examine the treatise composed by Yuan Chwang for refuting the Hīnayāna doctrine. Therefore, the Hīnayānist plot to kill him should be regarded as the rational outcome of the emotional atmosphere

[95] *Records*, I, pp. 218-21.
[96] Cf. *CA*, pp. 118-19.
[97] *HB*, p. 85.

prevailing in the assembly. The reference in the *Records* to the miraculous extinction of fire proves that at least some supernatural elements were introduced in it by Yuan Chwang by his own imagination; in contrast, the account of the *Life* is more human and entirely devoid of supernatural events.

The worship of the image of the Buddha by Harsha and Bhāskaravarman in the Kanauj assembly does not prove Harsha's *personal* faith in Buddhism. It should not be overlooked that the Kanauj assembly was an assembly of the Buddhists and was called in order to give an opportunity to the Buddhist scholars to examine the treatise of Yuan Chwang. In such an assembly the worship of the Buddha was but natural. We should remember that like nowadays, in ancient India also, the Hindus usually did not hesitate to worship the gods of other religions. Harsha, a highly liberal Śaiva, can hardly be expected to have any such objection. If Bhāskaravarman could participate in the worship of the Buddha and yet be regarded as a Śaiva, one wonders why should it be argued that as Harsha had participated in the ceremony of Buddha's worship he must have had given up his *personal* faith in Śaivism.

From Kanauj Yuan Chwang went to Prayāga to participate in Harsha's quinquennial alms-giving ceremony (March 1, 643). According to him, Harsha performed such ceremonies after the example of his ancestors[98] who were certainly not Buddhists. He also states that the quinquennial ceremony in which he himself participated was the sixth such ceremony performed by Harsha. It means that Harsha was holding such ceremonies since 617. But he was definitely a *Paramamāheśvara* till at least 631. It follows, therefore, that these ceremonies had no particular Buddhist affiliation. Bāṇa, who knew Harsha as a believer in Śaivism, also refers to a strip of cloth (*chīra*), which was put on to signify the solemn conferring as a special gift of all the property (*sarvasvadāna*).[99] It at once reminds one of Yuan Chwang's statements that after all was given as gifts, Harsha begged from his sister Rājyaśrī an ordinary second-hand garment to put on.[100]

Actually, Yuan Chwang has given a 'doctored' version of this ceremony in the *Records*.[101] For example, in the *Records* he refers only to the worship of the Buddha[102] while in the *Life* it is explicitly stated that the image of the Buddha was worshipped on the first day, of Ādityadeva (Sūrya) on the second

[98] *Records*, I, p. 214. Such ceremonies were also organised in the eighth century. For example, Hui Chao (732 A.D.) gives an account of the *Wu-che ta hui* ceremony which was held by the ruler of Gandhāra twice a year. *Wu-che* literally means 'without bar', that is, where no one is excluded.

[99] *HC*, p. 60.

[100] *Life*, p. 187.

[101] *HB*, p. 100.

[102] *Records*, I, p. 233.

day and of Īśvaradeva (Śiva) on the third day.[103] The reference to the worship of the Buddha, Sūrya and Śiva by Harsha at Prayāga appears to be correct for Āditya was worshipped by the ancestors of Harsha, the Buddha by his brother and sister and Śiva by Harsha himself. Hui-li could not have invented the names of these three particular gods, which were worshipped by the various members of the Pushyabhūti royal family, out of his own mind. Thus, the evidence of Yuan Chwang himself conclusively proves that Harsha was personally a devotee of Śiva till 643 when the Prayāga ceremony took place— which is one of the last events of his life known so far.

After having worshipped respectively the Buddha, Āditya and Śiva on the first three days Harsha gave gifts to '10,000 of the religious community' (most likely the Buddhist monks) for a day only, while the bestowal of gifts to the Brāhmaṇas lasted for 20 days. Even bestowal of gifts to the heretics (the Jainas, etc. ?) and also to those who came from distant lands lasted for ten days each and to the poor, destitute and the orphans for thirty days. The last, that is the seventy-fifth day, was devoted to the bestowal of Harsha's personal belongings.[104] Thus, out of these 75 days, only one was allotted for the distribution of gifts to the Buddhists and as many as twenty for distributing gifts to the Brāhmaṇas. This fact was also not mentioned by Yuan Chwang in the *Records*, obviously because it was against his portrayal of Harsha as a great supporter of Buddhism and Buddhists.[105]

[103] *Life*, p. 186.

[104] *Ibid.*, pp. 186 ff.

[105] On this, see Shankar Goyal, 'Religious Analysis of Harsha's Personality', in the *Proceedings of the Indian History Congress*, 68th Session, University of Delhi, 2007 (Delhi, 2008), pp. 136-48.

ELEVEN

Strengthening of Feudal Tendencies in the Social Order and Socio-Economic Life

GROWING RIGIDITY OF THE SOCIAL ORDER AND THE PROLIFERATION OF CASTES IN THE SEVENTH CENTURY

The early Indian social organisation was based on the theory of the *chāturvarṇya* which later on became complicated by its transformation into caste system with further division of labour, functional specialization and social fragmentation. A significant development from about the seventh century A.D. onwards was the proliferation of castes. The *Brahmavaivarta Purāṇa* (Brahmakhaṇḍa, X. 14-136), usually assigned to the seventh century, counts 100 castes including 61 castes noted by Manu, but the *Vishṇudharmottara Purāṇa* (II, 81-82) (c. eighth century) says that thousands of mixed castes are produced by the connection of Vaiśya women with men of lower castes. This proliferation affected every segment of society—Brāhmaṇas, Rajputs, Vaiśyas, Śūdras and untouchables. Increasing pride of birth, characteristic of feudal society, and the accompanying self-sufficient village economy, which prevents both spatial and occupational mobility, gave rise to many new castes. The guilds of artisans which appear in inscriptions from the first century A.D. gradually hardened into castes for lack of mobility in post-Gupta times. The absorption of the tribal people into the Brāhmaṇical fold, which began in the Vedic times, was mainly based on conquests. Coupled with the process of large-scale religious land grants, acculturation assumed enormous dimensions and considerably added to the varieties of the Śūdras and so-called mixed castes.[1]

The classical exposition of the caste system is found in the early Smṛti

[1] R.S. Sharma, 'Problem of Transition from Ancient to Medieval in Indian History', in *The Indian Historical Review*, March 1974, Vol. I, Pt. i, p. 6; idem, *Early Medieval Indian Society : A Study in Feudalisation*, Kolkata, 2001, Ch. 1.

literature which was the Indian counterpart of the Roman law and jurisprudence of Europe. In the post-classical age, however, several factors threatened the very existence of this order. Among them are included political and social confusion created by the fall of the Gupta empire, the pressure exerted by the growing number of foreigners in the Indian society which changed the population texture of the country very fast, specially of the north-western and western regions, and the rise of Tāntrika and other heterodox sects whose attitude was against the very idea of caste organisation. All these factors threatened the traditional social organisation of the country and generated a sense of increasing chaos and decline. In almost similar circumstances in the early medieval Europe, the Church, organised during the later Roman empire, became a bulwark against social chaos. In India, the crisis was faced by making the traditional caste system more rigid with some modifications to meet the new situation. That is why from the sixth century onwards we find that the efforts at the regulation and enforcement of the *chāturvarṇya* accelerated and continued to be so throughout the early medieval period. The inscriptions of the Maukharis and Pushyabhūtis refer to the efforts made by their kings for the proper regulation of the varṇa system. The tightening of the caste rules in the commentaries, digests and the late Purāṇas and the increasing efforts at their enforcement by the rulers of the early medieval period, represent respectively the theoretical and practical aspects of these efforts. The contracting economy of the period with its emphasized agrarian and local character contributed a good deal to this process.[2]

The emergence of the *sāmanta* hierarchy in the post-Gupta age had a peculiar relationship with the growing rigidity of the caste system. On the one hand, it helped in the growing rigidity of the caste system, for in their small principalities petty feudal chiefs found it desirable to enforce the rules of caste rigorously with a view to maintaining the local agrarian set up. The insecurity caused by constant feudal wars also tended to strengthen localism and hereditariness of caste functions. On the other hand, however, feudalism tended to come into conflict with caste system by increasing the process of social mobility. As Sorokin has pointed out, social mobility makes the social structure elastic and breaks caste and class isolation. Also, by creating a new class of feudal barons drawn from various sections of society, who were gradually accepted within the Kshatriya fold, feudalism posed a new

[2] For a detailed discussion on the growing rigidity in the social order, impact of feudalism and other developments on caste system and other related issues in the age of Harsha, see Shankar Goyal, *Harsha : A Multidisciplinary Political Study*, Jodhpur, 2006, Ch. 9; idem, *The Significance of Yuan Chwang in the Context of the Seventh Century : A Critical Assessment*, Delhi, 2018, pp. 47-71.

problem for the supporters of rigid caste system. The terms *Brahma-kshatra* and *Vaiśya-kshatra* applied to some ruling dynasties of this period shows that there were some Brāhmaṇas and Vaiśyas who discarded their caste professions for martial pursuits. Though Harsha has not been called a *Vaiśya-kshatra*, yet theoretically he belonged to this category.[3] Yuan Chwang noted that ruling dynasties of the period belonged to all the four varṇas. This tendency ran in direction just opposite to the tendency of the growth in the rigidity of the traditional caste system.

As a matter of fact, the social theorists of the early Indian medieval period had to come to terms with the changing realities not only by making the caste system more rigid, but by giving it a new orientation. This they did by modifying the scheme of the privileges and duties of various castes. For example, with a view to regularizing the fact that a large number of Brāhmaṇas were agriculturists, the social theorists of the period recommended agriculture for the Brāhmaṇas in addition to their six-fold duties. Similarly, the fact that now the Śūdras were forced to work on the fields of their local feudal lords, was also regularized by giving them (the Śūdras) the right to cultivate soil in order to serve the upper castes. That is why we notice a pronounced tendency to lump together the Vaiśyas (mostly small land-owning farmers) and Śūdras in the literature of this period. It seems that in the older settled Brāhmaṇical areas the Vaiśyas lost a good deal of their land rights to the feudal lords. On the other hand, the Śūdras, who were landless labourers, were granted some land and rose in social status. Further, the decline of trade and towns diverted both Śūdra artisans and Vaiśya merchants to cultivation. In this manner poor Vaiśyas and rich Śūdras began to approximate each other.[4] This modified Brāhmaṇical order spread from Madhyadeśa into Bengal and south India as a result of land grants to the Brāhmaṇas, many of them migrating from the north from the fifth-sixth centuries. Although the Rajputs emerged as a significant factor in the politics and society of northern India from the seventh century, in Bengal and peninsular India their place seems to have been taken by the landed Brāhmaṇas. In the older inhabited areas the traditional theoretical fourfold varṇa system did not fit in with the new feudal and social ranks created by unequal distribution of land and military power. From the sixth century attempts began to square up feudal ranks with ritual ranks. The earlier texts regulate the economic life of the people on the basis of their varṇas. But the *Bṛhatsaṁhitā* of Varāhamihira, a work of the sixth century, prescribes varying sizes of houses not only in the varṇa order but also according to the

[3] Shankar Goyal, *Harsha : A Multidisciplinary Political Study*, p. 260.

[4] R. S. Sharma, *op. cit.*, pp. 5-6.

grading of ruling chiefs. This tendency becomes marked in later times in several medieval texts on architecture.[5]

SCENARIO OF CASTE SYSTEM IN THE AGE OF HARSHA

In the seventh century Yuan Chwang found kings belonging to all the four castes. Apart from Kshatriya kings there were Brāhmaṇa kings in central India, kings of Vaiśya caste in Kanauj and Pāriyātra and of Śūdra caste in Sindh and some other states. He states :

> The sovereignty for many successive generations has been exercised only by Kshatriyas : rebellion and regicide have occasionally arisen, other castes assuming the distinction.[6]

Yuan Chwang apparently thought that the sovereign *de jure* was usually of the Kshatriya caste, and it was that caste alone which could lawfully produce a king, but he found instances of men of other castes raising themselves to the throne. According to him :

> There are four orders of hereditary clan distinctions. The first is that of the Brāhmins,... these keep their principles and live continently, strictly observing ceremonial purity. The second order is that of the Kshatriyas, the race of kings; this order has held sovereignty for many generations, and its aims are benevolence and mercy. The third order is that of the Vaiśyas or the class of traders, who barter commodities and pursue gain far and near. The fourth order is that of the Śūdras or agriculturists; these toil at cultivating the soil and are industrious at sowing and reaping. These four castes form classes of various degress of ceremonial purity. The members of a caste marry within the caste,... Relations whether by the father's or the mother's side do not intermarry, and a woman never contracts a second marriage.[7]

This description of Indian castes in the first half of the seventh century A.D. is important because it has been recorded by an intelligent and impartial foreign observer who lived among the people and studied and understood their language.

It is interesting that in the matter of marriage, there is a distinct difference in the remark of Megasthenes (c. 300 B.C.) and that of Yuan Chwang. In c. 300 B.C. Megasthenes had observed that the Brāhmaṇas were allowed to marry wives from the lower castes. "No one is allowed to marry out of his caste or to exchange his profession for another", he observes, "an exception

[5] *Ibid.*, p. 6.

[6] T. Watters, *On Yuan Chwang's Travels in India* (henceforth *Travels*), I, Delhi, 1961, p. 170.

[7] *Ibid.*, p. 168. Yuan Chwang, though a Buddhist, here puts the castes in the order given in the Brāhmaṇa books, but in the Buddhist scriptures the Kshatriyas are usually placed above the Brāhmaṇas.

is made in favour of the philosopher who for his virtue is allowed this privilege."[8] This agrees with the provision of *Manusmṛti* which allows the higher castes to marry into a lower one. In such a case the progeny, when the lower order was immediately next, belonged to the same caste as that of the father. Thus, in the seventh century caste system was still somewhat loose and higher castes were generally allowed to marry in the immediately lower caste without the lowering of the caste of the progeny. Yuan Chwang reports that Harsha's daughter was married to Dhruvabhaṭa of Valabhī and that while the former was a Vaiśya the latter was a Kshatriya.

In the seventh century the occupations of the first two castes remained much the same as in the pre-Harsha period. In the pre-Harsha period the place of the Brāhmaṇas in the society was indispensable as teachers, priests, purohitas and preceptors. All important religious ceremonies in the life of a man beginning from the cradle to his pyre (and even after his death) were performed by purohitas who received gifts and donations for religious performances. Therefore, gifts and donations had become the main source of livelihood of the Brāhmaṇas. Literary and epigraphic sources at our disposal provide us with innumerable instances of these ceremonial gifts. In this respect a very significant and interesting fact has been mentioned by Yuan Chwang which, contrary to the prevailing notion among historians, proves that Harsha was much more pro-Brāhmaṇa than pro-Buddhist.[9] In the *Life* of Yuan Chwang it is said that in the quinquennial assembly held at Prayāga, in which Harsha gave lavish gifts for seventy-five days to the priests, monks, etc., he was extremely partial to the Brāhmaṇas, for he gave gifts to "the religious community" (that is, the Buddhist monks) for a day only, while his bestowal of gifts to the Brāhmaṇas lasted for twenty days. Even bestowal of gifts to the heretics (Jainas, etc. ?) and to those who came from distant lands lasted for ten days each and to the poor, destitute and orphans for thirty days. The last, that is the seventy-fifth day, was devoted to the bestowal of Harsha's personal belongings. Thus,out of these 75 days only one was allotted for distribution of gifts to the Buddhists and as many as twenty for distributing gifts to the Brāhmaṇas.

In her *The Unknown Hsüan-tsang* Devahuti has quoted an interesting passage from a Chinese text which deposes that the Brāhmaṇas learnt the four Vedas. The first is called 'the span of life' (*Āyurveda*), i.e. the nourishing of life and the development of one's nature. The second Veda is called 'sacrifice' (*Yajurveda*), i.e. sacrifice and prayers. The third is called 'evenness/balance/

[8] Cf. J.W. McCrindle, *Ancient India as Described by Megasthenes and Arrian*, Calcutta, 1877, p. 86.

[9] For details, vide S.R. Goyal, *Harsha and Buddhism*, (hereafter *HB*), Meerut, 1986, p. 101.

peace' (*Sāmaveda*). The fourth is called 'arts' (*Atharvaveda*), i.e. extraordinary ability and skills, exorcisms and medicine.[10] According to Devahuti, the Āyurveda was actually a part of the *Atharvaveda* and it is curious that here Yuan Chwang puts it as an independent Veda at the head of the list of Vedas. The pilgrim was no doubt familiar with the *Ṛgveda* as the first Veda.[11] Its complete omission by him in this context is not easy to explain. A possible explanation is that being a Buddhist Yuan Chwang was casual about the Vedas just as he was about the Brāhmaṇic, theoretical class profession equation which he records a little later and where he assigns agriculture to the Śūdras. The *Ṛgveda* was the most authoritative Veda for the Brāhmaṇas and we know that some of its hymns were directly criticized by the Buddha. That probably explains Yuan Chwang's deliberate disregard for it.[12]

According to Yuan Chwang, "Among the various castes and classes of the country the Brāhmaṇas are the purest",[13] and they are "highly esteemed."[14] It was for their excellent reputation that in China the name "Brāhmaṇa-country" (P'o-lo-men-kuo) became "popular for India"[15] The pilgrim was highly impressed by their devotion to learning. He tells us that the Brāhmaṇas lived contentedly, strictly observing ceremonial purity. He writes, 'among the various castes and classes of the country the Brāhmaṇas were the purest, and they were highly esteemed.' Once he met a Brāhmaṇa who was 'super abundant in reasoning and eminent in the Vedas and other śāstras'.[16]

The second varṇa in the social structure was that of the Kshatriyas. According to Yuan Chwang, the Kshatriyas were of 'the race of kings' and 'had held sovereignty for many generations'.[17] They were praised for their 'benevolence and mercy'.[18] The kings of the greater part of India were generally Kshatriyas when Yuan Chwang paid his visit. But he has himself recorded some exceptions. In his general account of the caste system Yuan Chwang observes that it was no longer the exclusive right of the Kshatriyas to rule. As the pilgrim himself tells us, the kings of Matipur and Sindh were of Śūdra stock while the rulers of Kāmarūpa, Ujjain and Jajhoti were Brāhmaṇas by caste, Harsha himself was a Vaiśya and so was the king of

[10] D. Devahuti, *The Unknown Hsüan-tsang*, Oxford, 2001, p. 126.
[11] *Ibid.*
[12] *Ibid.*, p. 128.
[13] *Travels*, I, p. 168.
[14] *Ibid.*
[15] *Ibid.*, p. 140.
[16] Samuel Beal, *The Life of Hiuen-Tsiang*, New Delhi, 1973, pp. 74-75.
[17] *Travels*, I, p. 168.
[18] *Ibid.*, pp. 168 ff.

Pāriyātra (in modern Rajasthan).[19] The Brāhmaṇas were regarded throughout India as the most honourable caste, but they did not always hesitate to take to cultivation as an honest means of livelihood. When once Yuan Chwang and his fellow travellers were running before a band of robbers they came across a Bhāhmaṇa ploughing the field.[20]

The third varṇa in the society was that of the Vaiśyas or 'a class of traders who bartered commodities and pursued gains far and near'.[21] By the seventh century the later names of Vaiśya sub-castes had not yet come into being and communities such as Maheshvaris and Agrawals were then unknown. Their main distinctive appellations or suffixes were gupta and bhūti though some other words were also used such as vardhana. The suffix vardhana, taken by Harsha's family, indicates Vaiśya caste for him and the testimony of Yuan Chwang that Harsha was a Fei-she, or Vaiśya, is conclusive.

Lastly, we have to speak of the Śūdras whose occupation, according to Yuan Chwang, was agriculture.[22] The general condition of the outcastes was not satisfactory. They were segregated and not allowed to mix with the three higher varṇas. Yuan Chwang mentions that butchers, fishermen, public performers, executioners and scavengers 'had their habitations marked by a distinguishing sign' and that 'they were forced to live outside the cities and were required to sneak along on the left when going about in hamlets'.[23]

Yuan Chwang speaks of the mixed castes also.[24] These are described by him as innumerable. Those who called themselves neither Brāhmaṇas nor Kshatriyas, neither Vaiśyas nor Śūdras were probably included by him in these mixed classes. "There are", he observes, "numerous classes formed by groups of people according to their kinds and these cannot be described."[25] Their number indeed, then as now, must have been counted

[19] Samuel Beal, *Si-Yü-Ki* or *Buddhist Records of the Western World* (hereafter *Records*), I, Delhi, 1969, pp. 179, 190, 209; II, pp. 196, 271, 272.

[20] *Life*, p. 73.

[21] *Travels*, I, p. 168.

[22] *Ibid.* The classical varṇa theory in fact did not have any place for a fifth varṇa. As Romila Thapar points out, the basic structure of the fourfold category was theoretically not open to alteration (*Ancient Indian Social History*, Delhi, 1978, p. 129). The distinction that Manu and other lawgivers made between the four varṇas and untouchables like the Chāṇḍālas, however, gave rise in course of time to the concept of the fifth varṇa (cf. for details, Vivekanand Jha, 'Caṇḍāla and the Origin of Untouchability', in *The Indian Historical Review*, Vol. XIII, Nos. 1-2, July 1986 and January 1987, pp. 1-36). On this, also see Shankar Goyal, *The 'Medieval' Factor and the Age of Harsha : A Cultural Study*, Jodhpur, 2016, Ch. 3.

[23] *Ibid.*, p. 147.

[24] *Ibid.*, pp. 147, 168.

[25] *Ibid.*, p. 168.

by hundreds and hence the despairing remark of Yuan Chwang that they cannot be described. Mixed castes with special occupations have been described in several Smṛtis also and each division mentioned therein is again divided into subdivisions according to minor diversities of occupations, gradually increasing their number.

Towns and villages in the seventh century were usually enclosed by high walls. The walls were white washed with *chūnam* and the floors were plastered with cowdung.[26] Yuan Chwang refers to corded benches which were in universal use.[27] The modern *chārpāī*, so common in north India, is obviously the lineal descendant of Yuan Chwang's corded bench or identical with it. Yuan Chwang states, and his statement is confirmed by I-tsing, that "those utensils which are of pottery or wood thrown away after use and those which are of gold, silver, copper or iron get another polishing."[28] He, however, not only refers to strong drinks of different kinds but asserts that the higher castes had their distinctive wines and beverages. Thus, "the wines from the vine and sugar-cane are the drink of the Kshatriyas; the Vaiśyas drink a strong distilled spirit; the Buddhist monks and Brāhmins drink syrup of grapes and of sugar-cane; the low mixed castes are without any distinguishing drink."[29]

Some interesting information about the daily life and character of the people of the various castes of Madhya Deśa is found in the *Ta T'ang Hsi Yü Chi* which Devahuti has partly reproduced in her *The Unknown Hsüan-tsang.*[30] The Kshatriyas and Brāhmaṇas, Yuan Chwang tells us, were of simple manners, clean, frugal and fond of spotless white. The robes of the king and the ministers were quite different. They wore flowers and jewel-adorned headgears and rings, bracelets and pendants. The rich merchants wore only bracelets. Most people went barefoot, few using foot-wear. They stained their teeth red or black, trimmed their hair and pierced their ears. They washed before eating, and cleaned their teeth after eating; everytime they performed the call of nature they took bath and used perfumes of sandal-wood or turmeric. They did not pass dishes, and they did not eat left-overs. The pottery and wooden (bark ?) vessels were destroyed after use; the vessels of gold, silver, copper and iron were rubbed and polished after every meal. The ordinary people were upright, and faithful in their promises. They

[26] *Ibid.*, p. 147; for details, see Shankar Goyal, *The Significance of Yuan Chwang in the Context of the Seventh Century : A Critical Assessment*, Ch. 6.

[27] *Ibid.*

[28] *Ibid.*, p. 152; J.A. Takakusu, *A Record of the Buddhistic Religion as Practised in India and Malaya Archipelago (A.D. 671-695) by I-tsing*, Delhi, 1966, p. 36.

[29] *Ibid.*, p. 178.

[30] D. Devahuti, *The Unknown Hsüan-tsang*, pp. 126-29.

were not crafty in money matters, or deceitful in their conduct. There were nine ways of showing outward respect. The most respectful was 'to make one's prostration on the ground and then to kneel and laud the virtues of the one addressed'.

According to Yuan Chwang, cleanliness[31] among Indians was their conscious habit, not the result of compulsion. They did not allow others to use their own eating utensils. Earthenware and wooden vessels (for food) were thrown away after their first use. Gold, silver, copper and iron vessels were polished every time. After eating they chewed the willow branch (*dātun* of an unidentifiable wood) to clean their mouths and they touched each other only after they finished washing. They washed each time after urination and after emptying their bowels. They smeared perfumes such as sandal (*chandana*) and turmeric on their body. They bathed before religious ceremonies and before they said prayers. Most of these habits have persisted among Indians till today. There were no fixed regulations as to the dress of mourning. It was customary to raise lamenting cries and weep together. The mourners rent their garments and loosened their hair, struck their heads and beat their breasts. The priests were not permitted to lament or cry for the dead, not even for their parents. They simply recited their prayers and recounted their obligations to the dead. There were three ways of doing the last rites of the dead:[32] by cremation, by water, and by desertion. In the first, the body was burnt; in the second, it was thrown into flowing water; and in the third, it was left in a wilderness to be devoured by beasts. No eating was allowed in the house till after the funeral. Those who attended the funeral had to wash themselves. No posthumous titles were given and no death anniversaries were observed. The old and infirm, and those who suffered from serious illness, or wanted to end their life for other reasons, drowned themselves in the Ganges in the hope of being born among the *devas*.

SCENARIO OF SOCIAL LIFE IN YUAN CHWANG

In the age of Harsha marriages were permitted within a *varṇa* though we also find several examples of intercaste marriages. But there is no ground to generalize that intercaste marriages were socially preferred. However, both *anuloma* and *pratiloma* marriages were solemnised. Bāṇa mentions that he had two cousins whom he describes as "Pārśavau", i.e., sons of a Brāhmaṇa father through a Śūdra wife. In this context Yuan Chwang says that "the members of a caste marry within the caste, the great and the obscure keeping

[31] *Ibid.*, p. 126.

[32] Cf. also, J. S. Grewal, 'Hiuen Tsiang's India', in *India—Studies in the History of an Idea*, Irfan Habib (ed.), New Delhi, 2005, pp. 65-66; Shankar Goyal, *The Significance of Yuan Chwang in the Context of the Seventh Century*, pp. 54-59.

apart."[33] But here the pilgrim's account does not appear as fully correct as we have many other examples of intercaste marriages.

As regards clothing Yuan Chwang categorically writes :

> The inner clothing and outward attire of the people have *no tailoring* ; ... The men wind a strip of cloth round the waist and up to the armpits and leave the right shoulder bare. The women wear a long robe which covers both shoulders and falls down loose. ...[34]

The second or upper piece of cloth was used by both men and women sometimes but not necessarily. The dress of ordinary men in ordinary times could not have been anything else but the two white cloth pieces. The custom of wearing garlands on the head like a crown has now ceased entirely, and the turban has been substituted for it. It is probable, therefore, that no third cloth was ordinarily used for covering the head. The difference between the great and the low consisted in the fineness of the cloth and the whiteness of its colour. The Buddhist monks and nuns wore simple cloth coloured red, though in this colour there must have been different shades in different schools.[35] The Jaina recluses affected cloth coloured yellow and the Hindu *saṁnyāsis* used cloth coloured soiled red. The garments were made from cotton, wild silk (*kausheya*), linen, wool, and a sort of wool from the hair of a wild animal much prized. We are also told that the garbs of the non-Buddhists (religieux) are varied and extraordinary.[36] Some people "wear peacock's tails." This is probably about the Jainas.[37] Some "adorn themselves with a necklace of skulls;"[38] some are "quite naked;"[39] some cover the body with "grass or boards;" some "pull out their hair and clip their moustaches;"[40] some "mat their side-hair and make a top-knot coil."[41] This description appears to be true about the people of different sects and schools in India.

The usual food in the age of Harsha, Yuan Chwang informs, consisted of milk, ghee, granulated sugar, sugar-candy, parched grain, and the oil of mustard seed. Fish, mutton and venison were occasional dainties, but flesh of

[33] *Travels*, I, p. 168. It appears that by the time of Bāṇa and Yuan Chwang the institution of *svayaṁvara* had become obsolete. In the accounts of the Chinese pilgrim we do not find a single example of *svayaṁvara* being performed.

[34] *Ibid.*, p. 148.

[35] *Ibid.*, p. 150.

[36] *Ibid.*, p. 148.

[37] We find a similar description of the Jaina monks in Bāṇa's accounts.

[38] They were probably the Pāśupatas.

[39] They were probably the Jaina *sādhus*.

[40] This must have a reference to the *Keśaluñchakas* of the Jaina sect.

[41] *Travels*, I, *op.cit.* Some of these peculiar ornamentations and dresses were also prevalent among the Śabaras and the people of mountainous regions.

ox, ass, elephant, horse, pig, dog, fox, wolf, lion, monkey, and ape was forbidden. Those who ate their flesh were universally reprobated; they lived outside the walls. Those who used onions and garlic in food were expelled beyond the walls of the town. People generally ate from one vessel; mixing all sorts of condiments together; and they ate with their fingers. They had no spoons or cups, and no chopsticks. When sick, they were fed with copper spoons. There were saucepans and stewpans but no steamers for cooking rice. Many vessels were made of dried clay but very few of bronze. The mixed classes and base-born used vessels which were very different "both as to value and material".[42] During Harsha's period wine-drinking was common. There were various sorts of wines and liquors. Yuan Chwang tries to make certain distinctions in the use of wines and other beverages :

> The wines from the vine and the sugar-cane are the drink of the Kshatriyas; the Vaiśyas drink a strong distilled spirit; the Buddhist monks and the Brāhmins drink syrup of grapes and of sugar-cane; the low mixed castes are without any distinguishing drink.[43]

During the times of Harsha betel-chewing was very common. But surprisingly Yuan Chwang does not mention the habit of betel-chewing among the Indians. He only says, "They stain their teeth red or black."[44] These "red or black" teeth were, most probably, due to the constant use of betel.

People were particular about personal cleanliness. In this context Yuan Chwang writes :

> They are pure of themselves and not from compulsion. Before every meal they must have a wash; the fragments and remains are not served up again; the food utensils are not passed on; those utensils which are of pottery or wood must be thrown away after use, and those which are of gold, silver, copper, or iron get another polishing. As soon as a meal is over they chew the tooth-stick and make themselves clean; before they have finished ablutions they do not come into contact with each other; they always wash after urinating; they smear their bodies with scented unguents such as sandal and saffron. When the king goes to his bath there is the music of drums and stringed instruments and song; worship is performed and there are bathing and washing.[45]

Magic was one of the most popular means of amusement among the people of north India. Yuan Chwang writes that the people of Sthāṇvīśvara were "greatly devoted to magical arts and highly prized outlandish accomplishments."[46]

[42] J.S. Grewal, *op.cit.*, p. 64.
[43] *Travels*, I, p. 178.
[44] *Ibid.*, p. 151.
[45] *Ibid.*, p. 152.
[46] *Ibid.*, p. 314.

The slaves (*dāsas* and *dāsīs*)[47] in the age of Harsha were well treated as domestic servants. They were entrusted with all important affairs of the daily family life and enjoyed the affection and confidence of their masters. So far as Yuan Chwang is concerned, he does not make any direct reference to slavery. He indirectly points out that "individuals are not subject to forced labour contributions," and that even in the government service they were "paid according to their work."[48]

We have a few particulars as to the ways in which the people of the age of Harsha treated their sick and dead. Yuan Chwang reports :

> Every one who is attacked by sickness has his food cut off for seven days. In this interval the patient often recovers, but if he cannot regain his health he takes medicine. Their medicines are of various kinds, each kind having a specific name. Their doctors differ in medical skill and in prognostication.
>
> At the obsequies for a departed one [the relatives] wail and weep, rending their clothes and tearing out their hair, striking their brows and beating their breasts. There is no distinction in the styles of mourning costume, and no fixed period of mourning. For disposing of the dead and performing the last rites there are three recognized customs. The first of these is cremation, a pyre being made on which the body is consumed. The seond is water-burial, the corpse being put into a stream to float and dissolve. The third is burial in the wilds, the body being cast away in the woods to feed wild animals.
>
> When the sovereign dies the first thing is to place his successor on the throne in order that he may preside at the religious services of the funeral and determine precedence. Meritorious appellations are conferred on the living; the dead have no honorary designations. No one goes to take food in a family afflicted by death, but after the funeral matters are again as usual and no one avoids [the family]. Those who attend a funeral are regarded as unclean, they all wash outside the city walls before entering [the city].
>
> As to those who have become very old, and whose time of death is approaching, who are afflicted by incurable disease and fear that their goal of life has been reached, such persons are content to separate from this world, and desire to cast off humanity, contemptuous of mortal existence and desirous to be away from the ways of the world. So their relatives and friends give them a farewell entertainment with music, put them in a boat and row them to the middle of the Ganges that they may drown themselves in it, saying that they will be born in Heaven; one out of ten will not carry out his contemptuous views.

[47] Slavery is a social institution the mild form of which was not regarded as important enough in ancient societies to be discussed and commented upon.

[48] *Travels*, I, p. 176. Hui Chao (732 A.D.) expresses similar view.

> The Buddhist Brethren are forbidden to wail aloud (i.e. over a departed one); on the death of a parent they read a service of gratitude; their "following the departed" and "being earnest about his death" are securing his bliss in the other world.[49]

Yuan Chwang witnessed all acts of salutation and reverence with his own eyes. He tells us about the ways of showing respect and doing homage among the people of the age of Harsha. He records :

> There are nine degrees in the etiquette of showing respect. These are (1) greeting with a kind enquiry, (2) reverently bowing the head, (3) raising the hands to the head with an inclination of the body, (4) bowing with the hands folded on the breast, (5) bending a knee, (6) kneeling with both knees (lit. kneeling long), (7) going down on the ground on hands and knees, (8) bowing down with knees, elbows, and forehead to the ground, (9) prostrating oneself on the earth. The performance of all these nine from the lowest to the highest is only one act of reverence. To kneel and praise the excellences [of the object] is said to be the perfection of reverence.[50]

These ways of showing reverence and honour from the fourth to ninth, as given above, seem to have been common in royal palaces. We find a number of instances of such salutation.

Generally speaking, the character of the people is determined by time and place. Therefore, we find variations in the habits, manners, attitudes, behaviour and temperament in the lives of the people in all parts of the country. As Yuan Chwang had travelled widely he gives us valuable information about their general character. According to him, the people of Nagar, Takshaśilā, Matipur, Ahichchhatrā, Kānyakubja, Prayāga, Kauśāmbī, Vārāṇasī, Vaiśālī, Magadha, Puṇḍravardhana, Kāmarūpa, etc., "were of good character, courageous, hospitable, fond of art and literature." But he was displeased to meet the people of Lampā, Gandhāra, Siṁhapura, Jālandhara, Nepal and several other places. They were, as he remarks, mean-minded, ill-mannered, deceitful, etc. In his usual survey the pilgrim sums up the character of the people of India in general. He writes :

> They are of hasty and irresolute temperaments, but of pure moral principles. They will not take anything wrongfully, and they yield more than fairness requires. They fear the retribution for sins in other lives, and make light of what conduct produces in this life. They do not practise deceit and they keep their sworn obligations.[51]

[49] *Ibid.*, pp.174-75; also see, D. Devahuti, *The Unknown Hsüan-tsang*, pp. 134-35.

[50] *Ibid.*, p. 173; cf. also, D. Devahuti, *The Unknown Hsüan-tsang*, pp. 133-34.

[51] *Ibid.*, p. 171; for social behaviour also see, D. Devahuti, *The Unknown Hsüan-tsang*, p. 132; Shankar Goyal, *The Significance of Yuan Chwang in the Context of the Seventh Century*, pp. 59-60.

The pilgrim also states :

> For offences against social morality, and disloyal and unfilial conduct, the punishment is to cut off the nose, or an ear, or a hand, or a foot, or to banish the offender to another country or into the wilderness.[52]

INDIA'S ECONOMY IN THE AGE OF HARSHA AS KNOWN FROM YUAN CHWANG

From the grants of Harsha it is clear that the ultimate owner of the land was the sovereign who could grant the land or the whole village or the group of villages to any one he desired. According to Yuan Chwang, the farmers were his tenants and paid one sixth of the produce as rent.[53] When a tract of land or a village was donated to someone the entire revenue was given to the donee. The income from royal lands was divided into four divisions; one part was used for the "expenses of government", one for the "endowment of great public servants", the third part was reserved for rewarding persons of "high intellectual eminence", and the rest was distributed to various sects for gaining "religious merit."[54]

In the age of Harsha agriculture contributed considerably to the economic progress of the people. Says Yuan Chwang :

> As the districts vary in their natural qualities they differ also in their natural products.[55]

At Lampā the country produced "upland rice" and sugar-cane and it had much wood but little fruit.[56] At Nagar, grain and fruits were produced in abundance and Gandhāra was known for its crops of cereals, fruits and sugar-cane.[57] Kashmir was famous for saffron, fruits and flowers. The people of Jālandhara produced upland rice and other grain and fruits and flowers. The soil of Mathurā, Sthāṇvīśvara and Śrughna was rich and fertile and the crops were abundant but there the majority pursued trade. The country of Ahichchhatrā was also mainly an agricultural one. While describing Kānyakubja, Yuan Chwang tells us that "the inhabitants were well off and there were families with great wealth. The region of Ayodhyā, Prayāga and Kauśāmbī was also very fertile and the main occupation of the people was cultivation. The land about Kauśāmbī "yielded much upland rice and sugar-cane". The regions between Śrāvastī and Kuśīnārā were also

[52] *Ibid.*, p. 172.

[53] T. Watters, *On Yuan Chwang's Travels in India* (henceforth *Travels*), I, Delhi, 1961, p.176. For an extensive discussion on India's economy in the age of Harsha, see my *The 'Medieval' Factor and the Age of Harsha : A Cultural Study*, pp. 82-103.

[54] *Ibid.*

[55] *Ibid.*, p. 177.

[56] *Ibid.*, p. 181.

[57] *Ibid.*, pp. 183, 199.

very fertile and had good crops.[58] However, in that age Kapilavastu was not prosperous and more than ten cities were utterly deserted and ruined. But in Vārāṇasī, "harvests were abundant; fruit and other trees grew densely and there was a luxuriant vegetation". The country of Magadha also yielded "luxuriant crops". In Bengal the land was moist and "crops were abundant. There population was dense and the "farming operations were regular". The country of Kāmarūpa was also "low and moist" and the "crops were regular". In his general survey the pilgrim also summarises his description of fruits with the following words :

> It is impossible to enumerate all the kinds of fruit and one can only mention in a summary way those which are held in esteem among the inhabitants. ... From Kashmir on, pears, plums, peaches, apricots, grapes are planted here and there; pomegranates and sweet oranges are grown in all the countries.[59]

According to Yuan Chwang, sowing, planting and reaping were carried on regularly though all the cultivators were not hard-working and alert. The main agricultural products were rice, wheat, ginger, mustard, melons and pumpkins. From this description of Yuan Chwang it seems that almost the whole of north India was prosperous with its agricultural and natural products. Specially the entire Gaṅgā Valley and the Gaṅgā-Brahmaputra Delta were prosperous areas.

The metal industry showed a high level of development in the age of Harsha. Household utensils were made of brass and copper. All the implements of war such as spear, shield, sword, sabre, arrow, coat-of-mail, etc. were made of iron. At Vārāṇasī the pilgrim saw a t'u-shi (bell-metal ?) image of the Deva "nearly hundred feet high". He does not mention clearly the name of the Deva whose image he saw at Vārāṇasī. According to Watters, however, it was the *liṅgam* of Śiva. At Nālandā, he noticed copper image of the Buddha more than 80 feet high.

Yuan Chwang describes that the third order of Indian society was "class of traders" (Vaiśyas) who "bartered commodities and pursued gain far and near".[60] According to him, majority of the people of Sthāṇvīśvara "pursued trade" and "rarities from other lands were collected in this country".[61] He testifies that international trade was carried on with China, Ceylon, Persia and other countries. He informs us that the city of Charitrapura (Che-li-ta-lo) was "a thoroughfare and resting-place for sea-going traders and strangers from distant lands".[62] The port of Tāmralipti

[58] *Ibid.*, pp. 366, 377.
[59] *Ibid.*, pp. 177-78.
[60] *Ibid.*, p. 168.
[61] *Ibid.*, p. 314.
[62] *Ibid.*, II, p. 194.

was also a noted centre of sea-trade.[63] The inhabitants of Sūrat were traders by profession.[64]

Growth of industries and trade naturally led to the conspicuous growth of city-life. Takshaśilā, Jālandhara, Mathurā, Sthāṇvīśvara, Matipura, Mayūra, Ahichchhatrā, Kapitha, Ayodhyā and Kauśāmbī were some of the more famous and prosperous cities of northern India. Prayāga and Vārāṇasī were highly praised by the pilgrim for their wealth and prosperity. They were densely populated and had "boundless wealth" that included "rare valuables".[65]

However, some of the famous and great Buddhist urban centres were losing their importance. Śrāvastī, Kapilavastu and Vaiśālī, which once had been very famous centres of Buddhism, were in ruined condition. In the province of Kapilavastu there were more than ten deserted cities "all in utter ruin".[66] But Nālandā was at the height of its glory and repute.[67] Champā and Rājamahal were famous towns of Bihar. Sūrat and Valabhī were important trade centres in western India. Puṇḍravardhana, Tāmralipti, Samataṭa and Karṇasuvarṇa were the renowned cities of Bengal. The capital of Kāmarūpa was also in a flourishing condition and there were perpetually running streams and tanks in the towns. There were no big cities in Kāmarūpa. The pilgrim informs us that "the country was a series of hills and hillocks" and it was "without any principal city".

Kanauj, Harsha's capital, impressed Yuan Chwang much. A profuse availability of fruits and flowers in the city and its valuable merchandise draw his comment. He found that its inhabitants were well off and contented.[68] Education was widespread and scholarly life was vigorous. Here, the Buddhist learning involved studies not only in religion but also in grammar, logic, epistemology, and certain sciences. In northern India, Kashmir, Valabhī, Vārāṇasī and Nālandā were the great centres of learning with many lesser ones, such as Kanauj, Prayāga, Jālandhara, etc. A modern Chinese scholar, Liang Chi-chao, has traced in his indigenous sources names of 162 visitors from China to India between the fifth and eighth centuries A.D.[69] Yuan Chwang's detailed account of the Nālandā establishment throws

[63] *Ibid.*, p. 190.

[64] *Ibid.*, p. 248.

[65] *Ibid.*, p. 47.

[66] *Ibid.*, p. 1.

[67] *Ibid.*, pp. 164-70; for the hugeness and magnificence of the buildings of the Nālandā Mahāvihāra, see S.R. Goyal, *Harsha and Buddhism* (hereafter *HB*) , Meerut, 1986, Ch. 13.

[68] D. Devahuti, *Harsha : A Political Study*, Second edn., New Delhi, 1983, pp. 166-67.

[69] *Ibid.*, p. 167.

much light on Indian education of this period.[70] Centres of learning in Kashmir and at Nālandā and Kāñchī attracted as much interest from the outside world as did the Indian centres of trade.[71]

The accounts given above on the whole give an impression of general welfare in Harsha's reign. Yuan Chwang records that the government was "magnanimous". People were contentedly engaged in cultivating their land. Land-tax was no more than one-sixth of the produce. Yuan Chwang first remarks that there was no (regular ?) *corvée* but then adds that it was moderate and that the taxes were light. He says :

> Tradesmen go to and fro bartering their merchandise after paying light duties at ferries and barrier stations.[72]

According to Devahuti, here perhaps he is referring to the provision of labour in lieu of taxes.[73]

Thus, the portrayal of all-round progress and material growth is amply borne out by several references in the *Life* and the *Records*. Yuan Chwang saw many statues of the Buddha made of gold. The common man contributed to the construction of *saṅghārāmas*. Wherever Yuan Chwang went he received open-armed hospitality and was continually offered gifts which, being a scrupulous Buddhist monk, he did not accept.

Yuan Chwang makes three references to forced labour (*vishṭi*), or to the lack of it, in one paragraph on Indian administration. That he persistently remarks on it in connection with military service, construction work, and land revenue is probably due to his background, for in China the state made use of it freely, sometimes even forcing the *bhikshus* to do revenue accounts. With regard to revenue, taxation, and payment for labour in India, he remarks :

> As the government (of Harsha) is tolerant, official requirements are few. There is no registration of households, nor is there *corvée* for individuals. Royal land is divided generally into four parts... [for defraying various expenses]. For this reason, tax and *corvée* are light, and the people are happy to follow the calling of their forefathers. Those who work as tenant farmers on the royal estate, hold land in proportion to the number of persons in the family, and they pay a tax of one part in six. ... Official building does not rely on *corvée*, but people are rewarded according to the work they accomplish. For the purpose of manning defences and military expeditions as well as standing guard at the royal palace [variant : camp] appropriate

[70] Samuel Beal, *The Life of Hiuen-Tsiang* (hereafter *Life*), New Delhi, 1973, pp. 110-13; Samuel Beal, *Si-Yü-Ki* or *Buddhist Records of the Western World* (hereafter *Records*), II, Delhi, 1969, pp. 167-71; *Travels*, II, pp. 164 ff.

[71] D. Devahuti, *op.cit.*, p. 167.

[72] *Travels*, I, p. 176.

[73] D. Devahuti, *op. cit.*, p. 165.

> numbers are invited to join the army, and there is reward (remuneration) waiting to be collected by those who join. ...[74]

The Indian artisan and the cultivator both paid taxes. The latter contributed his share mostly in the form of land produce but, as Harsha's grants point out, might also be required to provide '[objects of] enjoyment, taxes, gold and so forth, and ... service'. As the principle of labour in lieu of taxes was recognized, the service required of the cultivator in Harsha's grants may be expected to have been of a well-accepted and reasonable type. An obvious cursory interpretation of such a practice would be the one that Yuan Chwang presents us with, that forced service was exacted but that it was mild.

Indian sources state that there were eighteen kinds of taxes, of which that on land was the most important, but they do not name the others. A broad term *daśāparādhaḥ*, or 'ten offences', is used in the context of judicial administration and implies crimes or misdemeanours for which fines were payable. They were classified as follows : three offences of the body : theft, murder, and adultery; four of speech: harsh, untruthful, libellous, and pointless; and three of mind: coveting others' property, thinking of wrong, and devotion to what is not true.[75] In view of Yuan Chwang's statement that taxation was light, it may be surmised that Harsha's government probably did not exploit all these sources of income or possibly the Chinese traveller's statement was conditioned by his own national background. He does, however, inform us that 'merchants paid a light tax at ferries and barrier stations'.

ECONOMIC IMPLICATIONS OF HARSHA'S WARFARE AND RELIGIOUS ACTIVITIES : THE EVIDENCE OF YUAN CHWANG

Harsha's reign as a king was marked specially by two types of activities, namely, constant warfare and charities, both having economic implications. Apart from the expenditure incurred on salaries on ministers, public servants and royal household, warfare and charities were the two main items with which his state exchequer was concerned. His religious activities proved to be an immense, probably unbearable, burden on the exchequer.[76] In his general description of India, Yuan Chwang records that the private demesnes of the crown were divided into four principal parts: the first was for carrying out the affairs of the state and providing sacrificial offerings; the second was for providing subsidies for the ministers and chief officers of the state; the third was for rewarding men of distinguished ability; and the fourth was for

[74] Samuel Beal, *Chinese Accounts of India*, Vol. II, Calcutta, n.d., p. 143.

[75] D. Devahuti, *op. cit.*, pp. 236-37.

[76] *HB*, p. 136.

charity of religious bodies, whereby the field of merit is cultivated.[77] A good deal of Harsha's charities went to the Brāhmaṇas. His three extant copper plate grants were issued for the merit and fame of his father, mother and elder brother. They must have been only a very small fraction of the total number of such grants which he must have issued in the four decades of his rule. According to the *Harshacharita*, when Harsha set out for the subjugation of all the four quarters, after worshipping Lord Śiva he "bestowed costly gifts upon Brāhmans".[78] According to the *Life*, "Yearly during three or seven days (or, perhaps, *during three seven-days, i.e., three weeks*) he provided food for the whole body of priests."[79] According to the *Records*, "He built on the banks of the river Ganges several thousand *stūpas*, each about 100 feet high; ... On all spots where there were holy traces (*of Buddha*) he raised *saṅghārāmas*."[80] How much all this construction activity cost the state exchequer is not specified. His benefactions to the Nālandā monastery deserve special mention here. He was probably the builder of one of the largest *vihāras* there. The construction of the boundary wall around the whole establishment has also been attributed to him. The construction of a large brass monastery undertaken by him was still going on when Yuan Chwang visited Nālandā. The Nālandā Mahāvihāra enjoyed a grant of a hundred villages (increased to 200 by the time of I-tsing). Such land grants, it is said, were enjoyed by numerous other monasteries of that period.

The Kanauj religious assembly organised by Harsha was a highly costly affair. In it kings of eighteen (or twenty) kingdoms, three thousand Buddhist priests, three thousand Brāhmaṇas, and one thousand priests of the Nālandā monastery—apart from a large number of ministers and other high officials of the various kingdoms—participated. Use of huge golden statues of the Buddha in procession, scattering of precious jewels on the way, presentation of golden dishes, cups, ewers, staffs, thousands of gold coins, and vestments of superior cotton stuff to the image of the Buddha characterized its proceedings. In this assembly the Chinese pilgrim was also offered 10,000 pieces of gold, 30,000 pieces of silver, 1,000 garments of superior cotton whilst princes of the eighteen (or twenty) kingdoms each presented him with rare jewels.[81] After breaking up the assembly the king handed over to the *saṅghārāma* the golden image he had cast, and the garments and money.[82] The Kanauj assembly, therefore, must have proved quite a burden directly on the treasuries of Harsha and various other

[77] *Records*, II, p. 87.

[78] *Harṣa-carita of Bāṇa*, tr. E. B. Cowell and F. W. Thomas, Delhi, 1968, p. 197.

[79] *Life*, p. 83.

[80] *Records*, I, p. 214.

[81] *Life*, p. 177.

[82] *Ibid.*, p. 183.

kingdoms and indirectly on the people. Here, it may also be recalled that such religious assemblies were convened by him quite frequently. The account of the Kanauj assembly is known to us because Yuan Chwang participated in it.

The Prayāga quinquennial ceremony to which all the Śramaṇas and Brāhmaṇas of the Five Indies were invited besides the poor and the orphans and the destitutes was also a costly affair. It consumed seventy-five days of the emperor, rulers of all the subordinate kingdoms and high officers of the realm—apart from the time which was taken by their journey from and to the capital. And all this happened every fifth year! It means every fifth year about 100 to 120 days were spent by the whole imperial establishment on this ceremony. From the financial point of view it was apparently simply disastrous. Here for seventy-five days the accumulated wealth of five years was given in charity. The result was, on the last day, except the horses, elephants and military accoutrements, nothing remained. Besides these the king gave away his own gems and goods, his clothings and necklaces, ear-rings, bracelets, chaplets, neck-jewel and bright head-jewel. All being given away, he begged from his sister an ordinary second-hand garment to put on.[83] That Harsha gave away everything in charity and put on a second-hand garment is recorded even by Bāṇa in his *Harshacharita.*[84]

Apart from these charitable activities our sources mention several other instances of Harsha's liberality. To Jayasena, a Buddhist scholar, he offered the revenue of eighty large towns of Orissa. When Yuan Chwang left for China he was given 3,000 gold pieces and 10,000 silver coins for meeting his expenses on the road.

From these facts one can easily form an idea of the stupendous liberality of Harsha. Normally, religious and charitable activities of an ancient king receive commendation from historians—and Harsha has also received undiluted praise from modern historians. But, as pointed out by S. R. Goyal, his charities and benefactions should also invite our critical comments because from the point of view of motivation, whatever he did in this field was done to earn religious merit (*puṇya*) for himself or his family members.[85] Nowhere do we find even an oblique reference to his concern for the people as their king. His charities and benefactions involving huge expenditure were all economically non-productive. Nowhere do we find any reference to his attempt for rural, agricultural or commercial development. Despite the fact that perhaps he is the best documented monarch of ancient India, none of our sources make reference to the construction or repairment of roads, or

[83] *Ibid.*, pp. 183-87.

[84] Quoted in *HB*, p. 139.

[85] *Ibid.*

canals (as one finds mentioned in the Hathigumpha inscription of Khāravela, Junagadh inscription of Rudradāman, Junagadh inscription of Skandagupta, etc.) or to steps taken for the betterment of the lot of the people. Even if his charities and benefactions are admired for themselves, one cannot overlook the fact that he overdid them. Goyal, therefore, cannot be blamed if he concludes :

> For a kingdom the treasury of which was completely emptied by its ruler for his personal satisfaction every fifth year and had to sustain the constant demands of his benefactions in between (apart from his huge expenditure on warfare), could not expect to be a stable edifice—even if the subordinate rulers made up the loss from their own treasuries because ultimately they must have replenished their own loss by exacting more taxes from the farmers, traders, etc. In other words, ultimately it was a burden which the common man had to bear for the sake of his king's love of charities to the religious persons and institutions. It was a disastrous policy even from the standard of the age in which it was pursued.[86]

FEUDAL TENDENCIES IN THE ECONOMIC LIFE AS KNOWN FROM YUAN CHWANG

A significant aspect of the economic life of age of Harsha was the strengthening of feudal tendencies which for the first time became manifest in the Gupta age. The empire which Samudragupta established and organised was a feudal-federal structure.[87] Between Samudragupta and Harsha feudal tendencies became more pronounced and strong. These included the practice of granting of both virgin and cultivated land to the Brāhmaṇas, temples, monasteries, public servants, royal favourites etc., the transfer of peasants along with the donated lands, the extension of forced labour, the restriction on the movements of the peasants, artisans and merchants, the paucity of coins, the retrogression of trade, the abandonment of fiscal and criminal administration to the religious beneficiaries, the beginnings of renumeration in revenues to officials, and the growth of the obligations of the *sāmantas.* The Buddhist monastic life was also feudalised in the age of Harsha. This is best exemplified in the transformation of the Nālandā Mahāvihāra.[88]

The magnitude of the Nālandā Mahāvihāra in the age of Harsha is obvious from the fact that according to Hui-li, the number of its students

[86] *Ibid.*, p. 140.

[87] S. R. Goyal, *A History of the Imperial Guptas* (hereafter *HIG*), Allahabad, 1967, pp. 295-96; idem, *The Imperial Guptas : A Multidisciplinary Political Study*, Jodhpur, 2005, pp.379-80; Shankar Goyal, *Problems of Ancient Indian History : New Perspectives and Perceptions,* Jaipur, 2001, pp. 147 ff.

[88] *HB*, p. 123; R. S. Sharma, *Indian Feudalism,* Calcutta, 1965, p. 76.

"always" reached the figure of 10,000 counting "the priests belonging to the convent or strangers residing therein,"[89] though from Yuan Chwang himself and I-tsing this figure seems to vary between three thousand and four thousand[90]—still a staggering number for an ancient religious-cum-educational institution. If Hui-li is to be believed, out of the total number of 10,000 monks, as many as 1,510 were teachers—1,000, who could explain twenty collections of the *sūtras* and *śāstras*; 500, who could explain thirty collections; and 10, who could explain fifty collections. The Mahāvihāra provided all its students free of cost their four requisites of clothes, food, bedding and medicine.

But that is not all. The standard of living of the Nālandā monks was very impressive and proves that the monastery possessed immense wealth and resources. Yuan Chwang reports that he was lodged in the monastery built by Bālādityarāja where he was entertained by Buddha-bhadra for seven days. Subsequently, he lived in the abode of Dharmapāla. Here, he was served each day with 120 jambiras (a fruit), twenty areca nuts, twenty nutmegs, an ounce of camphor, and a peck of the finest variety of rice called Mahāśāli, which grew only in Magadha. Besides these provisions he was provided with two menial servants and a riding elephant. Significantly, it is said that the Head of the Mahāvihāra entertained "a myriad priests after this fashion,"[91] an obvious exaggeration.

The emergence of the Nālandā Mahāvihāra (and also other *vihāras* and Brāhmaṇical temples in the age of Harsha) as self-supporting economic units was actually one of the incidental results of the feudalisation of the state structure and administrative organisation of the Gupta and post-Gupta periods.[92] The early Pali texts refer to the villages donated to the Brāhmaṇas by the rulers of Kosala and Magadha, but they do not refer to the delegation of administrative rights by the donors. In the Gupta period the rulers not only surrendered police and administrative rights over the lands granted by them, they also gave up control over almost all sources of revenue including pasturage, hides, mines for production of salt, forced labour and all hidden treasures and deposits.[93] Commenting on the term *brahmadeya*, Buddhaghosha, who flourished in the fifth century A.D., states that the *brahmadeya* grant carried with it judicial administrative rights.[94] It was

[89] *Life*, p. 112.

[90] J. A. Takakusu, *A Record of the Buddhistic Religion as Practised in India and Malaya Archipelago (A.D. 671-695) by I-tsing*, Delhi, 1966, p. 154; *Records*, II, p. 170.

[91] *Life*, p. 110.

[92] *HIG*, p. 295.

[93] R. S. Sharma, *op. cit.*, pp. 2 ff.

[94] *Ibid.*, p. 4.

indeed a very significant development. Of the seven organs of the state power mentioned in literature, taxation system and coercive power were rightly regarded as two vital elements. If they were delegated, the state disintegrated. This was actually the position created by the grants made to the Brāhmaṇas and monasteries. As a result of this process the monasteries and temples developed as semi-independent areas enjoying immunities on religious grounds, and were gradually transformed into medieval *maṭhas.*[95]

"The accounts of Fa-hsien and I-tsing leave no doubt that the monasteries got their lands cultivated by temporary tenants. I-tsing gives some idea about the nature of the tenure on which the cultivators were assigned land. He states that the *Saṅgha* provided the bulls and fields, and generally received one-sixth of the produce. I-tsing does not indicate whether the cultivators were also provided with ploughs, seeds, manure and other equipments for agriculture. It seems that the tillers of the soil were not hired labourers receiving wages, as in former times, but were semi-serfs or temporary tenants paying rental to the landowners. If a temple or a monastery was the landowner, it had no payment to make to the state."[96]

By the middle of the eighth century serfdom became fairly common, as is attested by the following extracts from a Chinese account of Hui Chao of 732 A.D. :

> According to the law of the Five Indies, from the king, the royal consort and the princes down to the chiefs and their wives all build monasteries separately in accordance with their respective capacities and abilities. Each of them builds his own temple, but does not construct it jointly. They say when each person has one's own meritorious virtues, what is the necessity of joint effort ?
>
> Whenever a monastery is built, village and its folk are immediately offered to support the Three Precious Ones. ...
>
> As to rich commoners, though they have no village to donate, they try their best to build temples and manage these by themselves. Whenever they obtain things, they offer them to the Three Precious Ones. As in the Five Indies, no human being is sold; so there are no female slaves. Villages and their inhabitants could be donated if wanted and necessary."[97]

From this account, which may be regarded as applicable to the seventh century as well, it is obvious that the practice of donating villages along with

[95] *Ibid.*, p. 46.

[96] *Ibid.*

[97] Jan Yun-Hua, 'Hui Chao's Records on Kashmir', *Kashmir Research Biannual*, No. 2, 1962, pp. 119-20, quoted by R. S. Sharma, *op. cit.*, pp. 58-59; also cf. K.M. Shrimali, his foreword in *Hye Ch'o kā Yātrā-Vṛttānta : Āṭhavīn Sadī kā Bhārata*, Hindi translation of *The Hye Ch'o Diary : Memoir of the Pilgrimage to the Five Regions of India* (1984) by Jagdish Chandrikesh, New Delhi, 2007, pp. 21-23.

their inhabitants to the monasteries by kings, queens, princes and chiefs was as common as that of building them by these dignitaries. There was no dearth of donations because not only the kings and queens but also the princes and chiefs possessed their own villages and village folk whom they could dispose of freely.

"This Chinese account," Sharma concludes, "established a significant link between the breakdown of slavery and emergence of serfdom. Speaking of donations to the Buddhist monasteries it points out that human beings are not sold in the Five Indies, and adds that there are no female slaves. Although the statement reminds us of the one made by Megasthenes that there were no slaves in India, it implies that there were some male slaves in the seventh century. But the absence of slavery in general did not raise any difficulty, because, "villages and their inhabitants could be donated if wanted and necessary." Since inhabitants were transferred to the monasteries for cultivating the villages granted to them, the beneficiaries did not experience the lack of labour power."[98]

[98] R. S. Sharma, *op. cit.*, p. 59.

TWELVE

Religion and the Medieval Trends in the Religious Activities of Harsha

HARSHA WAS A CHILD OF HIS AGE, NOT ITS MAKER

Harsha is usually regarded as one of the greatest rulers of India.[1] But a religious study of his personality[2] suggests that he was a child of his age, not its maker.[3] He flourished in a transitional phase of Indian history when the classical period was coming to a close and the early medieval period was unfolding itself.[4] He was brought up in the *milieu*

[1] Since the middle of the nineteenth century Harsha has attracted the attention of modern scholars and has been the subject of numerous monographs and hundreds of research papers. But they hardly discuss political events of the age of Harsha in the context of socio-economic and cultural changes and do not make any effort to correlate political and dynastic changes with socio-economic and cultural realities. Among the more important publications on Harsha in the last five decades or so are included D. Devahuti, *Harsha : A Political Study*, 2nd edn., New Delhi, 1983; 1st edn., Oxford, 1970; S.R. Goyal, *Harsha Śīlāditya*, Meerut, 1986; Shankar Goyal, *Harsha : A Multidisciplinary Political Study*, Jodhpur, 2006; idem, *The 'Medieval' Factor and the Age of Harsha : A Cultural Study*, Jodhpur, 2016; idem, *Harsha Revisited : A Re-interpretation of Existing Data*, Delhi, 2018.

[2] For an indepth analysis of Harsha's religious outlook cf. S.R. Goyal's *Harsha and Buddhism* (henceforth referred to as *HB*), Meerut, 1986.

[3] We have adopted a similar approach in the study of the psycho-sociological analysis of the personality of Harsha and presented a research article at the Sixty-fourth Session of the Indian History Congress, held at Mysore, December 28-30, 2003. See its published version 'Psycho-Sociological Analysis of Harsha's Personality', in *Journal of Indian History*, Vols. LXXVI-LXXVIII, Thiruvananthapuram, 2004, pp. 7-14.

[4] For the transformation of the classical heritage into medieval culture vide our papers 'Rise of Medievalism in Indian History', in *Annals of the Bhandarkar Oriental Research Institute*, Vol. LXXVIII, Pts. i-iv, Poona, 1997, pp. 13-40 and 'Factors in the Making of Early Medieval Society in India', in *Journal of Indian History and Culture* , Vol. XI, Chennai, 2004, pp. 25-52.

of the ideal of *dharmavijaya*— an ideal in which the conqueror appropriated only the glory of the defeated kings, not their kingdoms — and was its typical product. He was born and brought up in an atmosphere which was regarded as decadent by the people of his own age. He had grown up in an age in which kings, on the one hand, were given to the evil ways of Kali and behaved in a manner which was amoral as well as immoral, and on the other, extolled the virtue of charity and self-abnegation.[5] Being a child of his age Harsha was no exception. Therefore, in the present chapter we have tried to look upon his religion and religious activities against the background of various factors and forces operating in society.

RELIGIOUS SIDE OF HARSHA'S PERSONALITY : HE REMAINED A ŚAIVA THROUGHOUT HIS LIFE

Contrary to the prevalent view that Harsha was a Buddhist, we believe that he was personally a devout Śaiva, though like other rulers of ancient India he also patronized other faiths such as Buddhism as well. The positive evidence for his faith in the worship of Lord Śiva is quite weighty, diverse and profuse. His Banskhera inscription of the Year 22 (=628 A.D.) and Madhuban plate of the Year 25 (=631 A.D.) definitely call him a Paramamāheśvara. His recently discovered Kurukshetra-Varanasi grant of the Year 23 (=629 A.D.) also calls him a Paramamāheśvara.[6] According to the *Harshacharita*, when he started on his campaign he "had with deep devotion offered worship to the adorable Nīlalohita."[7] The golden seal presented to him by the village notary at the time of his first halt was inscribed with the emblem of bull (Nandī), the *vāhana* of the Lord Śiva.[8] On his Sonepat copper seal the reclining Nandī symbol is depicted.[9] Similarly, on the reverse of his gold coin Śiva and Pārvatī are shown as seated on Nandī. Yuan Chwang also refers to the worship of Śiva by Harsha at Prayāga as late as 643 A.D.

There are some circumstantial evidence also which strongly indicate that Harsha must have been a Śaiva. Such circumstantial evidence may be understood if it is analysed against the background of the religious atmosphere in the region around Sthāṇvīśvara. That Harsha was a Śaiva,

[5] Shankar Goyal, in *Journal of Indian History*, *op.cit.*, pp. 7-9.

[6] For a detailed analysis of this inscription cf. our paper 'The Recently Discovered Kurukshetra-Varanasi Grant of Harsha : Year 23', in *Journal of the Epigraphical Society of India*, Vol. XXXI, Mysore, 2005, pp. 136-46.

[7] *The Harṣa-carita of Bāṇa* (hereafter *HC*), trans. by E.B. Cowell and F.W. Thomas, London, 1929, Second edn., Delhi, 1968, p. 197.

[8] *Ibid.*, p. 198.

[9] J.F. Fleet, *Corpus Inscriptionum Indicarum,* Vol. III, Calcutta, 1888, No. 52, pp. 231-32.

not a Buddhist, by faith is consonant with the fact that the ascendancy of Śaivism in the homeland of the Pushyabhūtis was beyond doubt. As regards the religious beliefs of the inhabitants of Sthāṇvīśvara, Yuan Chwang, a Buddhist, regretfully notes that non-Buddhists were numerous and that there were in the capital only three Buddhist monasteries, with over 700 professed Buddhists, all Hīnayānists, as against over 100 Hindu temples.[10] On the other hand, Bāṇa, a Brāhmaṇa, naturally expresses his great admiration for the religious atmosphere of Śrīkaṇṭha janapada and the devotion of Pushyabhūti and his people to Śiva.[11] This probably explains the emergence of Pushyabhūti, a Vaiśya by caste and a Śaiva by faith, as its ruler.[12] This also explains the fact that Harsha, like his predecessors, who are called Paramādityabhaktas, i.e. great devotees of the Sun, was a follower of Brāhmaṇical religion and gave donations to the Brāhmaṇas and his faith in Śaivism was something quite *personal* with him. That Brāhmaṇical religion was very popular in the homeland of the Pushyabhūtis is also evident by the fact that Rājyavardhana II, the elder brother of Harsha, who is called a great devotee of Sugata, i.e. Buddha, and who ruled for a very short period just before Harsha, was treacherously murdered by Śaśāṅka of Gauḍa, who was known to be a great champion of orthodox faith, with the help of Harsha and his ministers, who were staunch followers of Śaivism. Though the exact nature of this help is still shrouded in mystery yet the alliance of Śaśāṅka and Harsha explicitly prove not only the popularity of Śaivism in the royal family of the Pushyabhūtis beyond doubt but it also explains the common factor of friendship between the two, resulting the conspiracy which led to the end of Rājyavardhana's life.[13]

However, despite these evidences of indubitable nature, Harsha is usually regarded as one of the greatest Buddhist rulers of ancient India. It is held that he set himself to imitate Aśoka so that the narrative of his doings in the later years of his reign 'reads like a copy of the history of the great Maurya'[14] and that his interest in Buddhism, which was quite mild in his youth, acquired more and more intensity with the passage of time ultimately leading to his complete, almost fanatic, devotion to the Mahāyāna form of this religion. But most of the arguments given in support of this theory are

[10] T. Watters, *On Yuan Chwang's Travels in India*, Vol. I, Delhi, 1961, p. 314.

[11] *HC*, tr. E.B. Cowell and F.W. Thomas, pp. 84-85.

[12] Shankar Goyal, *History and Historiography of the Age of Harsha*, Jodhpur, 1992, pp. 124-27.

[13] For a detailed discussion on the murder of Rājyavardhana II cf. Shankar Goyal, 'The Rājyavardhana Murder Case', *Heritage of India : Past and Present* (Professor R.K. Sharma Felicitation Volume), eds. P.K. Mishra and S.K. Sullerey, Delhi, 1994, pp. 579-90.

[14] V.A. Smith, *Early History of India,* 4th edn., Oxford, 1924, p. 197.

merely 'opinions' of modern scholars.[15] For example, it is only the opinion of R.S. Tripathi[16] that the 'mighty religious transformation' in Harsha's life leading to the adoption of Buddhism as his *personal* religion was brought about by his fondness for his brother Rājyavardhana and sister Rājyaśrī; but there is nothing to prove or disprove this assumption. One should remember that Rājyavardhana was murdered when Harsha was only sixteen years old and Rājyaśrī was only fourteen years old when, as a result of the murder of her husband Grahavarman, she began to live with Harsha. Similarly, the suggestion that protracted campaigns of Harsha led him towards the non-violent creed of the Buddha[17] is also a matter of personal opinion. If it is supposed that protracted wars are incompatible with belief in Buddhism, then one can easily conclude that Harsha never became a Buddhist, for he was waging wars of conquest as late as 641, and there is no evidence to show that he gave them up even after this date. And if it is assumed that faith in Buddhism and waging wars are not incompatible with each other, then how can one argue that protracted wars made Harsha a believer in the religion of the Buddha ?[18]

The supposed influence of the Buddhist sage Divākaramitra over Harsha[19] is also a matter of personal opinion. Harsha met him for the first time when he was roaming in search of Rājyaśrī. The sage is mentioned in no other source and nowhere else in the *Harshacharita*. Harsha's promise to him that 'At the end, when I have accomplished my design, she and I will assume the red garments together'[20] was apparently made to console Rājyaśrī. He is not known to have made any attempt to fulfil it. The contention of Byrski that Harsha had accepted Divākaramitra as his *guru*,[21] is baseless. Addressing sages and saints of whatever faith as one's *guru* was a form of Indian etiquette of those days. In his conversation with Yuan Chwang and Śīlabhadra of Nālandā both, Harsha called himself their 'disciple'. Bhāskaravarman of Kāmarūpa, though a Śaiva by faith, presented himself to both Śīlabhadra and Yuan Chwang as their 'disciple'. He called himself a

[15] For details vide, *HB*, Ch. 9. Similar is the attitude of R. S. Sharma who in a recent study *opines* that "A Śaiva in his early years, Harsha gradually became a great patron of Buddhism" but does not substantiate his views (*India's Ancient Past*, Oxford, 2015, p. 262).

[16] R.S. Tripathi, *History of Kanauj to the Moslem Conquest*, Delhi, 1959, pp. 163-64.

[17] *Ibid.*

[18] *HB*, *op.cit.*, pp. 78-79.

[19] G.S. Chatterji, *Harshavardhana* (in Hindi), 2nd edn., Allahabad, 1950, p. 252.

[20] *HC*, tr. E.B. Cowell and F.W. Thomas, p. 258.

[21] *Bhāratī*, Vol. V, Varanasi, 1961-62, p. 77.

'disciple' of Śīlabhadra even when he wrote a threatening letter to him.[22]

Much should not be made of the fact that Harsha is supposed to have written *Nāgānanda*, a play with a Buddhist theme.[23] Firstly, it is not at all certain that Harsha actually wrote this play. Secondly, in ancient India authors did not pick up a theme for composing a play or a *kāvya* only when it corresponded to their own religious beliefs. Kālidāsa sang the eulogy of Rāma in his *Raghuvaṁśa* and of Śiva in his *Kumārasambhava*.

Yuan Chwang's reference to Harsha's respect for the statue of the Bodhisattva Avalokiteśvara also does not prove Harsha's faith in Buddhism. It may be argued that the predominance of Buddhism in Kanauj and the fact that the people of this city had recently been put to a great trouble by Śaśāṅka, the avowed enemy of Buddhism, the show of respect to the statue of the Bodhisattva Avalokiteśvara by Harsha (who was an ardent worshipper of Śiva) cannot be regarded as more than a diplomatic move to win over to his side the affections of the Buddhist subjects of the Maukhari kingdom.[24] Even nowadays shrewd politicians visit shrines of religions other than their own to prove their large-heartedness. This also makes it quite likely that Harsha erected a number of stūpas on the banks of the Gaṅgā at the request of his Buddhist sister and to please the people of Kanauj who were more inclined towards the creed of the Buddha. The same motivation might have been behind the 'forcible' appropriation of the tooth-relic of the Buddha from Kashmir and its subsequent enshrinement in a saṅghārāma in Kanauj.

Yuan Chwang's reference to the erection by Harsha of hospices (*puṇyaśālās*) provided with food, drinks and physicians with medicines for travellers and poor persons also cannot be regarded as indicative of Harsha's faith in Buddhism for it would be assuming that kings belonging to other religions did not do such things for the welfare of their people. Further, what Yuan Chwang has reported is not wholly correct.For example, his statement that king Harsha 'forbade the slaughter of any living thing or flesh as food throughout the Five Indies on pain of death without pardon' is palpably wrong. In the general description of India he explicitly states that in food 'fish, mutton and venison are occasional dainties'.[25] According to the *Life*, Harsha himself gave in gift among other things 'various drinks and

[22] Samuel Beal, *The Life of Hiuen-Tsiang*, London, 1911, Second edn., New Delhi, 1973, pp. 170-71.

[23] R.S. Tripathi, *HK*, p. 181. *Contra* Shankar Goyal, 'The Plays Ascribed to Harsha', in *Annals of the Bhandarkar Oriental Research Institute*, Vol. LXXV, Poona, 1994, pp. 273-80.

[24] Vide Shankar Goyal, 'Acquisition of the Maukhari Empire by Harsha', in *Journal of the Asiatic Society*, Vol. XLV (2), Kolkata, 2003, pp. 53-62.

[25] *Travels*, I, p. 178.

meats' to '10,000 of the religious community' (Buddhist monks) in the quinquennial distribution of alms at Prayāga.[26]

There is another consideration which goes against Yuan Chwang's portrayal of Harsha as a great Buddhist ruler. Yuan Chwang entered India in October 630, but met Harsha for the first time in October 642[27] and that too at the latter's initiative. Apparently, he was not sufficiently impressed with the reputation of Harsha as a Buddhist ruler, for there arose no desire in him to meet this Indian king whom he later on sought to portray as another Aśoka. Even as late as 641, when he resolved to return to China, the idea of meeting Harsha did not cross his mind, though he was very much anxious to obtain the help of some king for his return journey. "Does it not prove", S.R. Goyal rightly asks, "that Harsha was not at all famous as a great Buddhist ruler in his own time ?"[28]

From the above discussion it is apparent that there is no conclusive evidence to believe that Harshavardhana had developed a *personal* interest in Buddhism before he met Yuan Chwang. Now, the question arises : did Harsha change his *personal* religion after he came into contact with Yuan Chwang ? Unfortunately, Yuan Chwang is the only source for this phase of Harsha's religious beliefs and the corrective evidence of the *Harshacharita*, inscriptions, coins, etc. is not available.[29] However, an investigation of the inner contradictions in Yuan Chwang's testimony shows that he is not wholly reliable on things concerning Buddhism. His faith in Buddhism was as fathomless as was his egotism. It may be noted that he does not claim that his influence over Harsha increased gradually. In his usual egoistical fashion he claims that Harsha's devotion to him was instant, spontaneous and complete. The description of the circumstances leading to their meeting as given in the *Life* by Hui-li on the basis of the information supplied by Yuan Chwang himself is the best example of his vanity. Actually, he has narrated them in a fashion which leaves in the mind of the reader the impression that the two great kings of India — namely, Harsha and Bhāskaravarman — were vying with each other in soliciting his teachings, and one of them even endangered his own life for the sake of his company. Here, it is significant to note that not only the *Hsi Yü Chi* but other Chinese state records so far known to us including the *Chiu t'ang-shu*, the *T'ang hui-yao*, the *Tz'e-fu yüan-kuei* and the *Wen-hsien t'ung-k'ao* which throw light on the period also use a conventional phraseology to demonstrate the superiority of China

[26] *Life*, p. 186.

[27] A. Cunningham, *The Ancient Geography of India*, Varanasi, 1963, p. 478.

[28] *HB*, p. 85.

[29] Shankar Goyal, *The Significance of Yuan Chwang in the Context of the Seventh Century*, Delhi, 2018, Ch. 1.

over a foreign country, whatever the relative status of the two at a given time. Not only official historians, but even the Buddhist monk I-tsing, who pays tribute to Indian medicine in his records, sometimes indulges in similar sentiments.

To return to Yuan Chwang, the account of his first meeting with Harsha itself is highly coloured. According to the *Life*, Harsha first met Yuan Chwang at Kajaṅgala at the pavilion-of-travel. "On his arrival the king bowed down at the feet of the Master of Law, then scattering flowers before him he regarded him with respect, and uttered his praises in verses innumerable."[30] But it is difficult to believe that Harsha could have shown such respect and could sing 'innumerable verses' in praise of a Chinese priest whom he was meeting for the first time, even if he was a poet of some merit. In his second meeting Yuan Chwang showed Harsha his treatise which was written with a view to restraining the 'wicked doctrine' (viz. the Hīnayāna). After examining it at the very spot, Harshavardhana came to the conclusion that it had destroyed all the other doctrines and established the truth of the Mahāyāna. It was indeed a marvel. Harsha took a cursory look at the book of Yuan Chwang (in the circumstances it could not have been a deeper study) and became absolutely convinced of the superiority of the Mahāyāna over every other creed! His conviction became so complete that 'the same day'[31] he sent orders for convening a grand all-India assembly at Kanauj to prove its merit!! What is more, his sister became overjoyed when she heard Yuan Chwang demolishing the Hīnayānist creed in which she had been believing for more than thirty-five years!!! Needless to say that such miraculous conversions do not take place in real life.

There is an inherent contradiction in Yuan Chwang's description of Harsha's faith in the Mahāyāna. For, on the one hand, he strives to show that it was he who was responsible for bringing Harsha and Rājyaśrī within the fold of the Mahāyāna, but, on the other, by referring at other places to Harsha's resolve to consult the statue of Avalokiteśvara and his invitation to the Mahāyāna scholars of Nālandā to face the challenge of the Hīnayānī priests of Orissa, he gives the impression that Harsha was interested in the Mahāyāna even before he met him. Both these positions cannot be correct.

HARSHA'S ROLE IN THE KANAUJ ASSEMBLY

From Kajaṅgala Yuan Chwang and Harsha went to Kanauj where the proposed religious assembly was held. According to its description in the *Life*,[32] kings of eighteen countries of the Five Indies, 3,000 priests

[30] *Life*, p. 175.
[31] *Ibid.*, pp. 175-76.
[32] *Ibid.*, pp. 177-81.

thoroughly acquainted with both Hīnayāna and Mahāyāna, 3,000 Brāhmaṇas and Nirgranthas and about a thousand priests from the Nālandā monastery participated in the assembly. The proceedings of the assembly opened with a huge procession in which a golden statue of the Buddha was carried out on a gorgeously caparisoned elephant. On its right went king Harsha dressed as Śakra (Indra) holding a white chowrie and on the left was Bhāskaravarman, dressed as Brāhma-rāja (Brahmā) with a precious parasol in his hand. When the procession reached the venue of the assembly, the statue was carried into a hall and placed on a precious throne. The worship of the statue was followed by a grand feast and the feast by religious discussions. In the hall of discussion were seated 1,000 Buddhists, 500 celebrated Brāhmaṇas and followers of heretical doctrine (the Hīnayāna) and about 200 of the great ministers of the different kingdoms. Others were seated outside the gate of the hall. Yuan Chwang, who was nominated as the 'Lord of the discussion', began by extolling the teachings of the Mahāyāna and announced a subject for discussion. He also caused a placard to be written and hung outside the door of the place of assembly stating: "if there is any one who can find a single word in the proposition contrary to reason or is able to entangle (the argument) then at the request of the opponent, I offer my head as a recompense." But none dared to challenge him for five days. Then the followers of the Hīnayāna, 'seeing he had overturned their school', plotted to kill him. Thereupon, Harsha issued a proclamation threatening that if 'any one should hurt or touch the Master of Law, he shall be forthwith beheaded; and whoever speaks against him, his tongue shall be cut out'. After this 'the followers of error withdrew' and no one joined the discussion. Therefore, when 18 days had passed and the assembly dispersed, Yuan Chwang was declared victorious and carried out in a procession to proclaim his victory. "The whole multitude was filled with joy on account of the Master's success... the congregation of the Great Vehicle called him Mahāyāna Deva... whilst the followers of the Little Vehicle called him Moksha Deva."

The account of the Kanauj assembly as given in the *Records* [33] differs from the one given in the *Life* on some minor and major points. The most important difference between the two is this : the *Records* does not say anything about the plot to kill Yuan Chwang; instead it refers to the plot of the Brāhmaṇas to kill Harsha himself. According to the version of the *Records*, 'on the day of the separation' of the assembly the great tower built

[33] Samuel Beal, *Buddhist Records of the Western World* (A translation from the Chinese of Hiuen Tsiang's *Si-Yü-Ki*), Vol. I, London, 1884, repr., New Delhi, 1969, pp. 218-21.

in the hall and pavilion over the gate of the saṅghārāma suddenly caught fire. But it was miraculously extinguished when Harsha prayed : "let the force of my religious conduct destroy this fire; or if not, let me die." Soon after it, when Harsha was surveying the scene of destruction from the top of the stūpa, a strange man, knife in hand, rushed on the king. The man was seized and confessed that he was hired by the heretics who had deliberately set the tower on fire to get an opportunity to assassinate the king. Five hundred Brāhmaṇas, all of singular talent, confessed to their share in the plot, adding that they were "jealous of Śramaṇas whom the king had reverenced and exceedingly honoured." The king punished the chief of them and banished the 500 Brāhmaṇas to the frontiers of India.

From the above account it is clear that while the *Life* refers to the plot of the Hīnayānists to kill Yuan Chwang because 'he had overthrown their doctrine', the *Records* refers to the plot of the Brāhmaṇas to kill Harsha because they were jealous of the favours showered by Harsha on the Śramaṇas. Which of the two accounts is correct ? So far it has been the practice of the historians to mix up the two accounts assuming that both of them are correct.[34] But it is highly unlikely, if not altogether impossible, that two different plots were hatched by two different communities to kill two different persons in the same assembly. It seems that the account of the *Life* represents the true course of events.[35] It should be remembered that the thrust of Yuan Chwang's endeavour was against the Hīnayāna doctrine. It was so earlier also when he was selected by Śīlabhadra to go to Orissa to controvert the Hīnayānist priests there; and it was his declared objective to demolish the Hīnayāna faith in the Kanauj assembly. Actually, the assembly was called by Harsha to examine the treatise composed by Yuan Chwang for refuting the Hīnayāna doctrine. Therefore, the Hīnayānist plot to kill him should be regarded as the rational outcome of the emotional atmosphere prevailing in the assembly. The theory that the Kanauj assembly was marked by the antagonism between the Mahāyānists and the Hīnayānists is proved to be right by the letters exchanged between Yuan Chwang and the Indian monks Jñānaprabha and Prajñādeva of the Mahābodhi monastery between 652-54 A.D.[36] In one of the letters Yuan Chwang reminds Prajñādeva that during his stay in India he had the honour of meeting Prajñādeva in the convocation of Kānyakubja where "we engaged in a debate and argued out our respective view-points in the presence of princes and thousands of

[34] Cf. R.C. Majumdar and A.D. Pusalker (eds.), *The Classical Age*, Bombay, 1954, pp. 118-19.

[35] *HB*, p. 95; for a detailed discussion on this problem vide Shankar Goyal, *The Significance of Yuan Chwang in the Context of the Seventh Century*, pp. 29 ff.

[36] D. Devahuti, *op.cit.*, pp. 281-96; S.R. Goyal, *op.cit.*, pp. 56-67.

devotees. As one of us expounded the tenets of the Mahāyāna school, the other advocated the aims of Hīnayāna. In the course of debate our arguments unavoidably got heated. In order to defend the truth, there was scant regard for personal feelings. Thus, there were clashes."[37] Yuan Chwang also makes it clear that in the debate Prajñādeva was not defeated because in this very letter written in 654 A.D. he is still pleading that Prajñādeva gives up his 'persistence in unbelief ' and embraces Mahāyānism.[38] It clearly shows that the Kanauj assembly was marked by the Mahāyāna-Hīnayāna rivalry and Yuan Chwang was not an unchallenged victor of the contest. Not only that the reference in the *Records* to the miraculous extinction of fire also proves that at least some supernatural elements were introduced in it by Yuan Chwang by his own imagination; in contrast, the account of the *Life* is more human and entirely devoid of supernatural events.

The worship of the image of the Buddha by Harsha and Bhāskaravarman in the Kanauj assembly does not prove Harsha's *personal* faith in Buddhism. It should not be overlooked that the Kanauj assembly was an assembly of the Buddhists and was called in order to give an opportunity to the Buddhist scholars to examine the treatise of Yuan Chwang. In such an assembly the worship of the Buddha was but natural. We should remember that like nowadays, in ancient India also, the Hindus usually did not hesitate to worship the gods of other religions. Harsha, a highly liberal Śaiva, can hardly be expected to have any such objection. If Bhāskaravarman could participate in the worship of the Buddha and yet be regarded as a Śaiva, one wonders why should it be argued that as Harsha had participated in the ceremony of Buddha's worship he must have had given up his *personal* faith in Śaivism.

To us it appears that Yuan Chwang could not understand the religious attitude of Harsha properly. His vanity and egotism were the academic counterpart of the superiority complex of the Chinese which they exhibited in the political sphere. It is comparable with the grossly exaggerated account of the raid of Wang-hiuen-ts'e, the Chinese envoy, who came after the death of Harsha. It was their incessant practice to represent the customary presents brought by foreign envoys as the tribute paid by the vassal state and to misinterpret ordinary marks of courtesy and politeness as acts of submission. Ma Twan-lin states that when a Chinese envoy presented himself in the court of Harsha in 641 A.D., Harsha "received the imperial decree with bended knees, and placed it on his head." No sensible person can accept it as a fact. On the other hand, ancient Indian rulers like Aśoka, Samudragupta and Skandagupta usually extended unselfish and generous support to other faiths. Even in the medieval age European Christian

[37] Quoted in *HB*, pp. 98-99.

[38] *Ibid.*, p. 99.

missionaries misread Akbar's pursuit for religious truth and drew the entirely wrong conclusion that the Mughal emperor was on the verge of accepting Christianity as his personal faith.

HARSHA'S ADDICTION TO CHARITY : THE PRAYĀGA QUINQUENNIAL CEREMONIES

From Kanauj Yuan Chwang went to Prayāga to participate in Harsha's quinquennial alms-giving ceremony (March 1, 643). According to him, Harsha performed such ceremonies after the example of his ancestors[39] who were certainly not Buddhists. He also states that the quinquennial ceremony in which he himself participated was the sixth such ceremony performed by Harsha. It means that Harsha was holding such ceremonies since 617. But he was definitely a *Paramamāheśvara* till at least 631. It follows, therefore, that these ceremonies had no particular Buddhist affiliation. Bāṇa, who knew Harsha as a believer in Śaivism, also refers to a strip of cloth (*chīra*), which was put on to signify the solemn conferring as a special gift of all the property (*sarvasvadāna*).[40] It at once reminds one of Yuan Chwang's statements that after all was given as gifts, Harsha begged from his sister Rājyaśrī an ordinary second-hand garment to put on.[41]

Actually, Yuan Chwang has given a 'doctored' version of this ceremony in the *Records*.[42] For example, in the *Records* he refers only to the worship of the Buddha[43] while in the *Life* it is explicitly stated that the image of the Buddha was worshipped on the first day, of Ādityadeva (Sūrya) on the second day and of Īśvaradeva (Śiva) on the third day.[44] The reference to the worship of the Buddha, Sūrya and Śiva by Harsha at Prayāga appears to be correct for Āditya was worshipped by the ancestors of Harsha, the Buddha by his brother and sister and Śiva by Harsha himself. Hui-li could not have invented the names of these three particular gods, which were worshipped by the various members of the Pushyabhūti royal family, out of his own mind. Thus, the evidence of Yuan Chwang himself conclusively proves that Harsha was personally a devotee of Śiva till 643 when the Prayāga ceremomy took place—which is one of the last events of his life known so far.

From the description of Yuan Chwang it is also apparent that in alms-giving Harsha was somewhat partial to the Brāhmaṇas, not Buddhists, as is generally supposed to. According to the *Life*, at Prayāga, after having

[39] *Records*, I, p. 214.

[40] *HC*, tr. E.B. Cowell and F.W. Thomas, p. 60.

[41] *Life*, p. 187.

[42] Cf. *HB*, p. 100.

[43] *Records*, I, p. 233.

[44] *Life*, p. 186.

worshipped respectively the Buddha, Āditya and Śiva on the first three days he gave gifts to '10,000 of the religious community' (most likely the Buddhist monks) for a day only, while the bestowal of gifts to the Brāhmaṇas lasted for 20 days. Even bestowal of gifts to the heretics (the Jainas, etc. ?) and also to those who came from distant lands lasted for ten days each and to the poor, destitute and the orphans for thirty days. The last, that is the seventy-fifth day, was devoted to the bestowal of Harsha's personal belongings.[45] Thus, out of these 75 days, only one was allotted for the distribution of gifts to the Buddhists and as many as twenty for distributing gifts to the Brāhmaṇas. This fact was also not mentioned by Yuan Chwang in the *Records*, obviously because it was against his portrayal of Harsha as a great supporter of Buddhism and Buddhists.[46]

Here, it may be pointed out that the royal courts of the age of Harsha were greatly influenced by the Smārta tradition also which laid emphasis on charity and self-abnegation. The Purāṇas and the *Mahābhārata* extol gifts of land (*bhūmidāna*), etc. The concept of the transience of wealth and material prosperity (*lakshmī*) finds mention frequently in inscriptions and literature. The Kanauj religious assembly and the quinquennial ceremonies held at Prayāga by Harsha, in which he used to give in charity all that he possessed (*sarvasvadāna*) were not something unique with him. Such assemblies, probably on smaller scale, were held by the kings of Kapiśā, Śīlāditya Dharmāditya of Mo-la-po, the Maukhari 'ancestors' of Harsha and Dhruvabhaṭa, his son-in-law.

It is also to be noted that in the records of the Sino-Indian missions in the age of Harsha the reception of the envoys was most cordial. However, we have detailed account only of Harsha's reception of the Chinese deligations. It is comparable to the welcome accorded to high foreign dignitaries in modern times. The arrival of such visitors was treated as a festive occasion. Streets were decorated, incense was burnt, citizens turned out to watch the procession, and the king and his ministers ceremoniously received the envoys. Their credentials, official messages, and presents were accepted with traditional gestures of courtesy and politeness. T'ang emperor T'ai-tsung, too, is mentioned in the *Chiu t'ang-shu* on one occasion to have "treated the (Indian) envoy with great courtesy... seeing that his land was far away." The accomplished Indian scholars who accompanied the missions were often put up in the royal palace or in the best official establishments. We know that Na-lo-mi-si-po-ho, a scholar in arts and magic, was invited to live and work in the palace under the charge of the Minister of War. Such

[45] *Ibid.*, pp. 186 ff.

[46] *Contra* D. Devahuti, *op.cit.*, pp. 180-82. Her suggestion that the Prayāga quinquennial ceremony in which Yuan Chwang participated was held in the Buddhist tradition is obviously not logical.

illustrations ascertain that Harsha's reception of Yuan Chwang was not an unprecedented occurrence. It was also not related with the religious faith of the Indian monarch.

CONCLUSION

The above discussion makes it clear that the religion and religious activities of Harsha was affected by the growing tendencies of his time. This was the period of the decline of political and religious morality. This was the period of following *a double standard* in public life. That is why Harsha could spend his life in fighting wars of conquests and boast that he appropriated the 'lakshmī' of the king of Sindhu, and yet could empty his treasury every five years in charity and in his records sermonize that material prosperity (*lakshmī*) is transient. In other words, bravery and world-renouncing ideology, sensualism and self-abnegation, love of wealth and devotion to charity, and self-conceit and deep interest in religious discourses—all these could be found in the character of one and the same person. And in Harsha such contradictions are found in abundance. That Harsha's political and religious ideas were highly amoral is indicated by the possibility of his complicity in the murder of Rājyavardhana, his show of respect to Bodhisattva Avalokiteśvara and use of Rājyaśrī's name to enlist the support of the Kanauj people for the acquisition of the Kanauj throne, his trickery in acquiring the Kashmir tooth-relic, use of his superiority in forcing Bhāskara to send Yuan Chwang from Kāmarūpa to his court, etc. And yet it is also a fact that he was not greatly given to the vices usually found in other contemporary rulers and took delight in charity, religious discussions and company of scholars.

Thus, this study establishes indubitably that Harsha, whose personality was moulded by the tendencies of his time, continued to remain a Śaiva throughout his life. But he showed tolerance and liberality to Buddhism and extended traditional Indian courtesy to the foreign visitor which his guest misunderstood, probably deliberately, as Harsha's conversion to his own faith but Harsha never gave up his *personal* faith in Śaivism.[47]

[47] *Contra* R.S. Sharma, *op.cit.*, pp. 262-63.

THIRTEEN

The Feudal Mind : A Psycho-Sociological Study of Harsha's Personality

DETERMINANT FACTORS OF HARSHA'S PERSONALITY

The psycho-sociological study of the personality of Harsha reflects his feudal character. He is usually regarded as one of the great est rulers of India. But a psycho-sociological study of his personality suggests that he was a child of his age, not its maker. His personality was moulded by the tendencies of his time. Of course the same may be said for far greater monarchs like Aśoka and Samudragupta. They were also products of their respective ages and their policies and personalities may be understood only against the background of the tendencies of their own respective periods. But they had originality as well, a capacity to influence and to some extent change the spirit of their age. Such a claim can hardly be made for Harsha. While to Mahāpadma Nanda, Aśoka and Samudragupta one can reasonably apply the dictum *rājākālasyakāraṇam* (king determines the spirit of the age), even if in a limited sense, Harsha at the most may be described as the typical representative of his age.[1]

[1] Shankar Goyal, *History and Historiography of the Age of Harsha* (henceforth referred to as *HHAH*), Jodhpur, 1992, Ch. 14; idem, *Harsha : A Multidisciplinary Political Study*, Jodhpur, 2006, pp. 296-301.

Since the middle of the nineteenth century Harsha has attracted the attention of modern scholars and has been the subject of numerous monographs and hundreds of research papers. But they hardly discuss political events of the age of Harsha in the context of socio-economic and cultural changes and do not make any effort to correlate political and dynastic changes with socio-economic and cultural realities. However, among the more important publications on Harsha in the last five decades or so are included D. Devahuti, *Harsha : A Political Study*, 2nd edn., New Delhi, 1983; 1st edn., Oxford, 1970; S.R. Goyal, *Harsha Śīlāditya*, Meerut, 1986; Shankar Goyal, *Harsha : A Multidisciplinary Political Study*, Jodhpur, 2006; idem, *Harsha Revisited : A Re-interpretation of Existing Data*, Delhi, 2018.

CONTRADICTORY PSYCHO-SOCIOLOGICAL TRENDS OF THE AGE OF TRANSITION

Harsha flourished in a transitional phase of Indian history when the classical period was coming to a close and the early medieval period was unfolding itself.[2] It was really the period of the twilight of Gupta classicism when some tendencies of the classical culture had disappeared, many had become weak and many persisted even if in a weak form in the subsequent ages. When Harsha began his empire-building activities, the Gupta empire had become a thing of the past, but its memory was still lingering on. In his *Kādambarī* Bāṇa recalls that the feet of his ancestor Kubera were worshipped by the Gupta emperors. The *āditya* titles of the Guptas had become quite popular; Harsha himself was known by his title Śīlāditya. Specially the title Vikramāditya of the Guptas had acquired the same popularity in India which was enjoyed by the title Caesar in Europe.[3] The chakravartin ideal of the Guptas[4] was sought to be emulated by the post-Gupta rulers. In literature as well arts, specially sculpture, the achievements of the Gupta age had become 'standard' or 'ideal' for the subsequent ages.[5] Kālidāsa is remembered by Bāṇa as well as by the author of the Aihole inscription. But in political sphere the popularity of the ideal *dharmavijaya* followed by Samudragupta in the Deccan (in which the conqueror appropriated only the glory of the defeated kings, not their kingdoms) greatly weakened the cohesion of the political structure. To some extent the concept of *dharmavijaya* was the sublimation or idealisation of the difficulties involved in establishing a centralised political system in a country of sub-continental dimensions as well as of the inability of the conquerors in the realization of the ideal of political unity. Actually, the chakravartin ideal based on the concept of *dharmavijaya* and the feudal-federal polity were the two sides of the same coin. Harsha was brought up in the

[2] For the transformation of the classical heritage into medieval culture vide our paper 'Rise of Medievalism in Indian History', *Annals of the Bhandarkar Oriental Research Institute*, Vol. LXXVIII, Pts. i-iv, Poona, 1997, pp. 13-40.

[3] The Russian title Czar and the German title Kaisar were really the variants of the title Caesar.

[4] In the Gupta age the conception of a *chakravarti* ruler, performing *digvijaya*, that is to say conquering 'the whole earth', was very popular and was given a Vaishṇavite orientation. Cf. our paper 'Political Ideology of the Early Imperial Guptas', in *Reappraising Gupta History for S.R. Goyal*, eds. B. Ch. Chhabra et al, New Delhi, 1992, pp. 215-23.

[5] However, the story of the art of the Gupta age which begins with the emergence of classicism and the transformation of the Kushāṇa art into Gupta art comes to a close with the decline of classicism and the emergence of medieval factor in Indian art. Vide our chapter 'Transition from Gupta Classicism to Medievalism in Indian Art', in *Indian Art of the Gupta Age*, eds. S.R. Goyal and Shankar Goyal, Jodhpur, 2000, pp. 208-21.

milieu of this ideal and was its typical product. On the one hand, he belonged to the twilight period of the classical culture and, therefore, could bask in its aura even of diminished light and, on the other, was greatly handicapped by the growing tendencies of early medievalism.

The disintegration of the Gupta empire, invasion of the barbarians and the rise of feudalism were concomitant with the decline in the popularity of the Vedic rituals, threat to the traditional varṇa organisation, rise of Tāntricism and the decline of political morality. That was the reason why in the sixth-seventh centuries A.D. it was the general feeling among people that they were living in an age when the evils of the Kali Age had become more pronounced. Yaśodharman refers to the evil ways of the contemporary kings. The Haraha record of the Maukharis and the *Harshacharita* of Bāṇa mention the evils of the Kali Age at several places. The Paurāṇic accounts of the Kali Age composed in this period portray the decline of public morality. Thus, Harsha was born and brought up in an atmosphere which was regarded as decadent by the people of his own age. Elsewhere we have delineated the picture of the feudal atmosphere of the Pushyabhūti court and *harem*, popularity of Tāntricism even in the Pushyabhūti royal family and their capital, feudalisation of the Pushyabhūti army with all the concomitant evils[6] and the obsession of the kings with the idea of their divinity which thinkers like Bāṇa did not like.[7] All these factors played their role in the formation and evolution of the personality and psychology of Harsha.

But the royal courts of the age of Harsha were greatly influenced by the Smārta tradition also which laid emphasis on charity and self-abnegation. Buddhism also greatly valued them. The Purāṇas and the *Mahābhārata* extol gifts of land (*bhūmidāna*), etc. The concept of the transience of wealth and material prosperity (*lakshmī*) finds mention frequently in inscriptions and literature. The Kanauj religious assembly and the quinquennial ceremonies held at Prayāga by Harsha, in which he used to give in charity all that he possessed (*sarvasvadāna*) were not something unique with him. Such assemblies, probably on smaller scale, were held by the kings of Kapiśā, Śīlāditya Dharmāditya of Mo-la-po, the Maukhari 'ancestors' of Harsha and Dhruvabhaṭa, his son-in-law. Thus, from the psycho-sociological point of view Harsha was the child of an age in which kings, on the one hand, were given to the evil ways of Kali and behaved in a manner which was amoral as well as immoral, and on the other, extolled the virtue of charity and self-abnegation. They, on the one hand, expressed their pride in capturing and

[6] *HHAH*, Chs. 12 and 13.

[7] There are some passages in Bāṇa's *Harshacharita* and *Kādambarī* which certainly echo his voice of protest and dissent against some traditional beliefs and institutions and contemporary administrative system. Vide *HHAH*, pp. 291-300.

enjoying the wealth and women of their enemies and, on the other, bestowed *agrahāras* to the Brāhmaṇas and Buddhist monasteries and rendered help in the marriages of Brāhmaṇa girls. Rājyavardhana could declare his intention to become a monk and then, in the very next moment, could resolve to go to punish the wicked Mālava king. Harsha could spend his life in fighting wars of conquests and boast that he appropriated the 'lakshmī' of the king of Sindhu, and yet could empty his treasury every five years in charity and in his records sermonize that material prosperity (*lakshmī*) is transient. In other words, bravery and world-renouncing ideology, sensualism and self-abnegation, love of wealth and devotion to charity, and self-conceit and deep interest in religious discourses—all these could be found in the character of one and the same person. And in Harsha they are found in abundance. That Harsha's political ideas were highly amoral is indicated by the possibility of his complicity in the murder of Rājyavardhana,[8] his show of respect to Bodhisattva Avalokiteśvara and use of Rājyaśrī's name to enlist the support of the Kanauj people for the acquisition of the Kanauj throne,[9] his trickery in acquiring the Kashmir tooth-relic,[10] use of his superiority in forcing Bhāskara to send Yuan Chwang from Kāmarūpa to his court,[11] etc. And yet it is also a fact that he was not greatly given to the vices usually found in other contemporary rulers and took delight in charity, religious discussions and company of scholars.

HARSHA'S ADDICTION TO CHARITY

Harsha was greatly addicted to alms-giving. Yuan Chwang describes his quinquennial alms-giving ceremony (March 1, 643). According to him, Harsha performed such ceremonies after the example of his ancestors.[12] He also states that the quinquennial ceremony in which he himself participated was the sixth such ceremony performed by Harsha. It means that Harsha was holding such ceremonies since 617. Bāṇa also refers to a strip of cloth (*chīra*), which was put on to signify the solemn conferring as a special gift of all the property (*sarvasvadāna*).[13] It at once reminds one of Yuan Chwang's statements that after all was given as gifts, Harsha begged

[8] *HHAH*, pp. 162-65.

[9] *Ibid.*, pp. 187-93.

[10] *Ibid.*, pp. 203-04.

[11] *Ibid.*, pp. 199-201.

[12] Samuel Beal, *Buddhist Records of the Western World* (A translation from the Chinese of Hiuen Tsiang's *Si-Yü-Ki*), Volume I, London, 1884, reprinted, New Delhi, 1969, pp. 214 ff.

[13] *The Harshacharita of Bāṇa*, trans. by E.B. Cowell and F.W. Thomas, London, 1929, Second edn., Delhi, 1968, p. 60.

from his sister Rājyaśrī an ordinary second-hand garment to put on.[14]

From the description of Yuan Chwang it is also apparent that in alms-giving he was somewhat partial to the Brāhmaṇas, not Buddhists, as is generally supposed to. According to the *Life*, at Prayāga Harsha gave gifts to '10,000 of the religious community' (most likely the Buddhist monks) for a day only, while the bestowal of gifts to the Brāhmaṇas lasted for 20 days. Even bestowal of gifts to the heretics (Jainas etc. ?) and also to those who came from distant lands lasted for ten days each and to the poor, destitute and the orphans for thirty days. The last, that is the seventy-fifth day, was devoted to the bestowal of Harsha's personal belongings.[15] Thus, out of these 75 days, only one was allotted for the distribution of gifts to the Buddhists and as many as twenty for distributing gifts to the Brāhmaṇas.

INFLUENCE OF FAMILY MEMBERS AND OTHER CONTEMPORARIES ON HARSHA

Thus, the character and personality of Harsha were moulded by the thought-currents and institutions of his age. How far was he influenced by the personalities of his family members and friends, it is difficult to assess. Yet some indications for this are available. If Bāṇa's statement that Prabhākara wanted Harsha to ascend the throne has some truth and was reflected in Prabhākara's behaviour during Harsha's childhood, then one can presume that it might have helped in making Harsha ambitious. It might have produced a latent feeling in Harsha's mind that Rājyavardhana was an obstacle between him and the paternal throne. Yaśomatī was proud of the fact that she was the daughter of a great warrior, the wife of a great conqueror and the mother of brave sons. She also expressed her pride in the fact that she was won by Prabhākara after paying the price of valour (*parākramakrayakrītā*),[16] was honoured with the *Mahādevīpaṭṭabandha* and had put her feet on the heads of her co-wives.[17] Therefore, conceivably Harsha inherited some germs of pride and self-conceit from her. Rājyavardhana, the elder brother of Harsha, was interested in the religion of Śākyamuni, but he was also a great warrior and, according to Śaṅkarārya, the commentator of Bāṇa, could be lured by Śaśāṅka by the offer of the hands of his daughter. If at all, Harsha might have learnt from him the lesson that it is the duty a prince to punish his

[14] Samuel Beal, *The Life of Hiuen-Tsiang*, London, 1911, Second edn., New Delhi, 1973, p. 187.

[15] *Ibid.*, pp. 186 ff.

[16] *HC* , *op.cit.*, pp. 153-54. Cf. the description of Dattadevī, the queen of Samudragupta, as *Paurusha parākramadattaśulkā* (J.F. Fleet, *Corpus Inscriptionum Indicarum,* Vol. III, revised by D.R. Bhandarkar and edited by B.Ch. Chhabra and G.S. Gai, New Delhi, 1981, p. 222).

[17] *HC* , p. 154.

enemies and enjoy the pleasures of life. Probably he also learnt from his elder brother something about the teachings of Śākyamuni. Rājyaśrī was too young when he became king to have exerted any appreciable influence on his character. Later on also she was no more than a pawn on the chess-board of the Maukhari politics. At the most she might have goaded him to take interest in Buddhism and be considerate towards the followers of this religion.

Among other characters of the period Siṁhanāda is known to have stimulated Harsha's ambition to become a world-conqueror,[18] and Skandagupta, the commander of elephant forces, taught him the necessity of always remaining cautious.[19] That Harsha was very cautious in his political behaviour (whether or not due to the advice of Skandagupta) is quite apparent. For example, when the news of Grahavarman's murder was received Rājyavardhana became highly angry and left 'the same day' to punish the enemy and as a consequence of his haste was deprived of his life.[20] On the other hand, when the news of Rājya's murder came, Harsha expressed his anger suitably but left to punish the enemy only after making due preparations and settling the affairs of the kingdom properly.[21] Divākaramitra probably taught him how a king might exploit the religious sentiments of his people for political ends, and Bhaṇḍi most likely helped him in political intrigues and art of diplomacy. Bāṇa was merely a court-poet whose sole aim was to get the patronage of the emperor. But in his company (and that of other poets) Harsha's literary tastes might have become more refined. Yuan Chwang entered the life of Harsha very late. Though in his *Records* the pilgrim tries to give the impression that it was due to his influence that Harsha became a Mahāyānist, but actually Harsha continued to remain a Śaiva throughout his life.[22] He showed due respect to Yuan Chwang but was himself too mature to be influenced by a foreign monk, younger to him by at least ten years. It should not be forgotten that he knew almost nothing about Yuan Chwang and met him quite late in life, and that too only for a short while. Dhruvabhaṭa, the son-in-law of Harsha, was also too young to influence the personality of his father-in-law.

HARSHA'S LOVE FOR CHINA AND THINGS CHINESE

However, Bhāskaravarman, the Kāmarūpa monarch and a friend of Harsha,

[18] *HHAH*, pp. 172-73.
[19] *Ibid.*, p. 173.
[20] *Ibid.*, p. 157.
[21] *Ibid.*, pp. 174-76.
[22] *Ibid.*, pp. 316-24.

belonged to the age-group of Harsha. Further, both of them were Śaivite and believed in the policy of religious toleration. Probably it was from Bhāskara's love for China and things Chinese that Harsha also became interested in them. According to the Chinese annals, Bhāskara requested their envoys for a picture or statue of Lao-tzŭ and the Sanskrit translation of a Tao manuscript and when Yuan Chwang visited his capital he entertained the latter with the T'ang period musical composition. That Harsha had become interested in China and Chinese culture *before* he met Yuan Chwang is also a fact for he had already sent a mission to T'ai-tsung before his first meeting with the Chinese pilgrim. His interest in China and Chinese culture probably explains his partiality for Yuan Chwang indicated by the pilgrim's boast that Harsha composed 'verses innumerable' in his praise and called a religious assembly for testing his Mahāyānist treatise 'the same day' he saw it. Harsha favoured Yuan Chwang unduly in the Kanauj assembly also and offered him 10,000 gold and 30,000 silver coins at the time of his departure for China. According to the Chinese annals, Harsha was overwhelmed by the fact that the Chinese emperor had honoured him by sending an envoy to him and received the Chinese embassy in the manner as if he had become a vassal of that country. All these accounts are obviously exaggerated but they do show that he and Bhāskara were as interested in China, Chinese scholars and Chinese culture as our modern elite are in western culture, ideas and goods.

The above study brings out, we believe, the main determinant psycho-sociological factors which shaped the personality of Harsha. Probably in case of no other ancient Indian monarch, except Aśoka, our sources provide an opportunity to make such an analysis.

FOURTEEN

The Feudal Factor and Caste

I

The early Indian social organisation was based on the theory of the *chāturvarṇya*[1] which later on became complicated by its transformation into caste system with further division of labour, functional specialization and social fragmentation. A significant development from about the seventh century A.D. onwards was the proliferation of castes. The *Brahmavaivarta Purāṇa* (Brahmakhaṇḍa, X. 14-136), usually assigned to the seventh century, counts 100 castes including 61 castes noted by Manu, but the *Vishṇudharmottara Purāṇa* (II, 81-82) (c. eighth century) says that thousands of mixed castes are produced by the connection of Vaiśya women with men of lower castes. This proliferation affected every segment of society—Brāhmaṇas, Rajputs, Vaiśyas, Śūdras and untouchables. Increasing pride of birth, characteristic of feudal society, and the accompanying self-sufficient village economy, which prevents both spatial and occupational mobility, gave rise to many new castes. The guilds of artisans which appear in inscriptions from the first century A.D. gradually hardened into castes for lack of mobility in post-Gupta times. The absorption of the tribal people into the Brāhmaṇical fold, which began in the Vedic times, was mainly based on conquests. Coupled with the process of large-scale religious land grants, acculturation assumed enormous dimensions and considerably added to the varieties of the Śūdras and so-called mixed castes.[2]

[1] Irfan Habib points out that the varṇas initially presaged very little of the caste system that was to grow later and that it is vain to expect a social institution like caste to exist before the producers in society were able to provide a "surplus" (*Caste and Money in Indian History*) (D.D. Kosambi Memorial Lectures, 1985), Bombay, 1987, pp. 4-5.

[2] R.S. Sharma, 'Problem of Transition from Ancient to Medieval in Indian History', in *The Indian Historical Review*, March 1974, Vol. I, Pt. i, p. 6; idem, *Early Medieval Indian Society: A Study in Feudalisation*, Kolkata, 2001, Ch. 1; On this, also see Shankar Goyal, 'Caste System as Reflected in the Works of Bāṇa and Yuan Chwang', in the *Proceedings*

The classical exposition of the caste system is found in the early Smṛti literature which was the Indian counterpart of the Roman law and jurisprudence of Europe. In the post-classical age, however, several factors threatened the very existence of this order. Among them are included political and social confusion created by the fall of the Gupta empire, the pressure exerted by the growing number of foreigners in the Indian society which changed the population texture of the country very fast, specially of the north-western and western regions, and the rise of Tāntrika and other heterodox sects whose attitude was against the very idea of caste organisation. All these factors threatened the traditional social organisation of the country and generated a sense of increasing chaos and decline. In almost similar circumstances in the early medieval Europe, the Church, organised during the later Roman empire, became a bulwork against social chaos. In India, the crisis was faced by making the traditional caste system more rigid with some modifications to meet the new situation. That is why from the sixth century onwards we find that the efforts at the regulation and enforcement of the *chāturvarṇya* accelerated and continued to be so throughout the early medieval period. The inscriptions of the Maukharis and Pushyabhūtis refer to the efforts made by their kings for the proper regulation of the varṇa system. The tightening of the caste rules in the commentaries, digests and the late Purāṇas and the increasing efforts at their enforcement by the rulers of the early medieval period, represent respectively the theoretical and practical aspects of these efforts. The contracting economy of the period with its emphasized agrarian and local character contributed a good deal to this process.[3]

II

The emergence of the *sāmanta* hierarchy in the post-Gupta age had a peculiar relationship with the growing rigidity of the caste system. On the one hand, it helped in the growing rigidity of the caste system, for in their small principalities petty feudal chiefs found it desirable to enforce the rules of caste rigorously with a view to maintaining the local agrarian set up. The insecurity caused by constant feudal wars also tended to strengthen localism and hereditariness of caste functions. On the other hand, however, feudalism tended to come into conflict with caste system by increasing the process of social mobility. As Sorokin has pointed out, social mobility makes the social structure elastic and breaks caste and class isolation. Also, by creating a

---

of the Papers from the Aligarh Historians Society, ed. Irfan Habib, 71st Session of the Indian History Congress, Gaur Banga University, Malda, 2011, pp. 124-47.

[3] For a detailed discussion on the growing rigidity in the social order, impact of feudalism and other developments on caste system and other related issues in the age of Harsha see Shankar Goyal, *Harsha : A Multidisciplinary Political Study*, Jodhpur, 2006, Ch. 9.

new class of feudal barons drawn from various sections of society, who were gradually accepted within the Kshatriya fold, feudalism posed a new problem for the supporters of rigid caste system. The terms *Brahma-kshatra* and *Vaiśya-kshatra* applied to some ruling dynasties of this period shows that there were some Brāhmaṇas and Vaiśyas who discarded their caste professions for martial pursuits. Though Harsha has not been called a *Vaiśya-kshatra*, yet theoretically he belonged to this category.[4] Yuan Chwang noted that ruling dynasties of the period belonged to all the four varṇas. This tendency ran in direction just opposite to the tendency of the growth in the rigidity of the traditional caste system.

As a matter of fact, the social theorists of the early Indian medieval period had to come to terms with the changing realities not only by making the caste system more rigid, but by giving it a new orientation. This they did by modifying the scheme of the privileges and duties of various castes. For example, with a view to regularizing the fact that a large number of Brāhmaṇas were agriculturists, the social theorists of the period recommended agriculture for the Brāhmaṇas in addition to their six-fold duties. Similarly, the fact that now the Śūdras were forced to work on the fields of their local feudal lords, was also regularized by giving them (the Śūdras) the right to cultivate soil in order to serve the upper castes. That is why we notice a pronounced tendency to lump together the Vaiśyas (mostly small land-owning farmers) and Śūdras in the literature of this period. It seems that in the older settled Brāhmaṇical areas the Vaiśyas lost a good deal of their land rights to the feudal lords. On the other hand, the Śūdras, who were landless labourers, were granted some land and rose in social status. Further, the decline of trade and towns diverted both Śūdra artisans and Vaiśya merchants to cultivation. In this manner poor Vaiśyas and rich Śūdras began to approximate each other.[5] This modified Brāhmaṇical order spread from Madhyadeśa into Bengal and south India as a result of land grants to the Brāhmaṇas, many of them migrating from the north from the fifth-sixth centuries. Although the Rajputs emerged as a significant factor in the politics and society of northern India from the seventh century, in Bengal and peninsular India their place seems to have been taken by the landed Brāhmaṇas. In the older inhabited areas the traditional theoretical fourfold varṇa system did not fit in with the new feudal and social ranks created by unequal distribution of land and military power. From the sixth century attempts began to square up feudal ranks with ritual ranks. The earlier texts regulate the economic life of the people on the basis of their varṇas. But the *Bṛhatsaṁhitā* of Varāhamihira, a work of the sixth century, prescribes varying sizes of houses not only in the varṇa order but also according to the grading of ruling chiefs.

[4] *Ibid.*, p. 260.

[5] Sharma, *op. cit.*, pp. 5-6.

This tendency becomes marked in later times in several medieval texts on architecture.[6]

III

In the seventh century Yuan Chwang found kings belonging to all the four castes. Apart from Kshatriya kings there were Brāhmaṇa kings in central India, kings of Vaiśya caste in Kanauj and Pārayātra and of Śūdra caste in Sindh and some other states. He states :

> The sovereignty for many successive generations has been exercised only by Kshatriyas : rebellion and regicide have occasionally arisen, other castes assuming the distinction.[7]

Thus, Yuan Chwang apparently thought that the sovereign *de jure* was usually of the Kshatriya caste, and it was that caste alone which could lawfully produce a king, but he found instances of men of other castes raising themselves to the throne.

The succession to kingship was generally regulated according to the law of primogeniture but the reigning king had the privilege to nominate his successor who could be different from his eldest son.[8] Sometimes ministers played some role in the selection of the next king. In case a king died childless he was usually succeeded by his younger brother. In the Maitraka dynasty succession of younger brother was a normal feature. Females had no place in the order of succession. Only Suvarṇagotra is said to have been ruled by females. The females did not play much role in the administration also. Rājyaśrī's importance in Kanauj was caused by exceptional circumstances. There is also no indication whatever that she had any say in the administration. In the *Kādambarī* and the Haraha's inscription there is reference to the coronation of the crown-prince (*yauvarājyābhisheka*). Chief-queens were also honoured with *Mahādevīpaṭṭabandhasatkāra*.

Kings of the post-Gupta times, although of smaller status (and perhaps because of this), began acquiring grandiloquent titles like Paramabhaṭṭāraka, Mahārājādhirāja, Parameśvara, Chakravartin, etc. They usually claim that their fame reached beyond the four oceans. Such a claim is made not only for paramount rulers like Harsha but also for minor rulers like Harivarman Maukhari. The Smṛtis tried to reinforce the importance of kings by likening their qualities to those of the gods. At one place Bāṇa calls Harsha the combined incarnation of all gods (*sarvadevāvatāramivaikatra*) and elsewhere even superior to Indra, Yama, Varuṇa, Kubera and Jina (Buddha). However, in the

[6] *Ibid.*, p. 6.

[7] T. Watters, *On Yuan Chwang's Travels in India* (henceforth *Travels*), I, Delhi, 1961, p. 170.

[8] G. P. Sinha, *Post-Gupta Polity (500-750 A.D.)*, Calcutta, 1972, pp. 3 ff.

Kādambarī he raises his voice of protest against such claims. In the *Harshacharita* Harsha has been addressed as 'Devānāṁpriya' also, but it was not his title.[9]

Strangely the transfer of many of the duties of kings to feudal lords tended to increase autocracy of the former in personal life. That is why the inscriptions of the period are full of criticism of the evil ways of the kings which rulers like Yaśodharman, and many a Maukhari and Pushyabhūti kings, usually claim not to have followed. Among the main duties of the king were included the conquest of the neighbouring states, protection of the people and the preservation of the varṇa system.

In the feudal polity the success of a king depended largely upon his personal ability and his devotion to work. Therefore, kings like Harsha worked dedicatedly. Yuan Chwang refers to the busy daily routine of Harsha and his tours of inspection. He says :

> He was just in his administration, and punctilious in the discharge of his duties. He forgot sleep and food in his devotion to good works. ... The king also made visits of inspection throughout his dominion, not residing long at any place but having temporary buildings erected for his residence at each place of sojourn, and he did not go abroad during the three months of the Rain-season Retreat. ... The king's day was divided into three periods, of which one was given up to affairs of government, and two were devoted to religious works. He was indefatigable, and the day was too short for him.[10]

Fortunately, the material for making a survey of the society of the period of Harsha are relatively ample and reliable. In the first place we have the *Records of the Western World* of the Chinese traveller Yuan Chwang who was a minute observer and a detailed recorder of what he saw. Secondly, we have the *Harshacharita* and other works of Bāṇa, the court-poet of Harsha, another contemporary writer of eminence and credibility. The importance of both these writers for the study of the society of the age of Harsha is immense — of Yuan Chwang because he was a foreigner but being a Buddhist by faith sympathetic to and well-versed in Indian lore, and of Bāṇa because in his works one finds an immense amount of information about the society of his age which was the age of his patron Harsha also. Apart from them numerous other literary works and inscriptions including the three grants of Harsha himself [11] provide archaeological data of the most reliable character.

[9] Goyal, *op. cit.*, pp. 270-72.

[10] *Travels*, I, pp. 343-44.

[11] Madhuban, Banskhera and the recently found Kurukshetra-Varanasi grants. For a recent study of these grants cf. Shankar Goyal, 'Harsha ke Abhilekha : Kuchha Samasyāyeṅ aur Sujhāva', in S. R. Dubey (ed.), *Ābhilekhika Adhyayana kī Pravidhi evaṁ Itihāsa-Lekhana*, Delhi,. 2004, pp. 183-89; idem, 'The Recently Discovered Kurukshetra-Varanasi Grant of

The revival of Hinduism, which had taken place under the imperial Guptas, was complete in the sixth and seventh centuries A.D. An outstanding development of this period is that Hinduism gradually displaced Buddhism, which could not regain the predominance it enjoyed in the age Aśoka and Kanishka.

Several grants of this period refer to the fact that the kings and rulers of the period were constantly busy regulating proper functioning of all the varṇas and the āśramas. Ancient Indian writers on social institutions regarded it as one of the main duties of the Hindu kings to look after the observance of the duties and obligations of the people according to laws and customs of the varṇas and the āśramas. A king was never expected to allow the people to swerve from their duties.[12] Bāṇa in his *Harshacharita* characterises Harsha as one who carried out all the rules for the varṇas and the āśramas like Manu.[13] While speaking of the cultural life and of the Śrīkaṇṭha janapada (modern Thanesar region), he says that 'the laws of caste usage are for ever unconfused'.[14] In Harsha's dramas and the works of the other contemporary authors we get a picture of society which was patently based on the varṇa organisation. We shall, therefore, begin our survey of Indian castes with their description as recorded by Yuan Chwang. He writes :

> There are four orders of hereditary clan distinctions. The first is that of the Brāhmins,... these keep their principles and live continently, strictly observing ceremonial purity. The second order is that of the Kshatriyas, the race of kings; this order has held sovereignty for many generations, and its aims are benevolence and mercy. The third order is that of the Vaiśyas or the class of traders, who barter commodities and pursue gain far and near. The fourth order is that of the Śūdras or agriculturists; these toil at cultivating the soil and are industrious at sowing and reaping. These four castes form classes of various degress of ceremonial purity. The members of a caste marry within the caste,... Relations whether by the father's or the mother's side do not intermarry, and a woman never contracts a second marriage.[15]

This description of Indian castes in the first half of the seventh century A.D. is important because it has been recorded by an intelligent and impartial

---

Harsha : Year 23', *Journal of the Epigraphical Society of India*, Mysore, Vol. XXXI, 2005, pp. 136-46.

[12] Kauṭilya's *Arthaśātra*, tr. R. Shamasastry, Book I, Mysore, 1951, Ch. III.

[13] *Harshacharita* of Bāṇa (hereafter referred to as *HC*), tr. E.B. Cowell and F.W. Thomas, 2nd edn., Delhi, 1968, p. 66

[14] *Ibid.*, p. 79.

[15] *Travels*, I, p. 168. Yuan Chwang, though a Buddhist, here puts the castes in the order given in the Brāhmaṇa books, but in the Buddhist scriptures the Kshatriyas are usually placed above the Brāhmaṇas.

foreign observer who lived among the people and studied and understood their language.

It is interesting that in the matter of marriage, there is a distinct difference in the remark of Megasthenes (c. 300 B.C.) and that of Yuan Chwang. In c. 300 B.C. Megasthenes had observed that the Brāhmaṇas were allowed to marry wives from the lower castes. "No one is allowed to marry out of his caste or to exchange his profession for another", he observes, "an exception is made in favour of the philosopher who for his virtue is allowed this privilege."[16] This agrees with the provision of *Manusmṛti* which allows the higher castes to marry into a lower one. In such a case the progeny, when the lower order was immediately next, belonged to the same caste as that of the father. Thus, in the seventh century caste system was still somewhat loose and higher castes were generally allowed to marry in the immediately lower caste without the lowering of the caste of the progeny. Yuan Chwang reports that Harsha's daughter was married to Dhruvabhaṭa of Valabhī and that while the former was a Vaiśya the latter was a Kshatriya. Bāṇa also records that Harsha's sister, a Vaiśya by caste, was married to Grahavarman Maukhari of Kanauj, a Kshatriya. Such marriages took place usually in castes only one degree apart, though rarely they took place even in castes two or more degrees apart. Bāṇa himself records that he had two Pāraśava brothers, i.e., sons of a Śūdra wife of his father. Here, the use of the word Pāraśava shows that the progeny is not treated as illegitimate though the caste of the sons was not that of the father. However, in case of a Brāhmaṇa marrying a Kshatriya wife or a Kshatriya marrying a Vaiśya wife the caste of the progeny was treated the same as that of the father. Dhruvabhaṭa's son by the daughter of Harsha obviously could not be treated as less than a Kshatriya. Ample epigraphic evidence is available to show that the Brāhmaṇas actually married Kshatriya wives, or even Vaiśya wives without loss of caste by the progeny. Thus, *anuloma* marriages seem to have been quite common in the age of Harsha.

IV

According to Bāṇa, Harsha was born in the family of Pushyabhūti, evidently, a Vaiśya name, while Yuan Chwang specifically calls him of Fei-she (Vaiśya) origin.[17] The *Āryamañjuśrīmūlakalpa* also clearly states that the Pushyabhūtis belonged to the Vaiśya caste.[18] According to R.S. Tripathi, the suffix bhūti additionally indicates that Pushyabhūti, the founder of the family, was a Vaiśya.[19] D. Devahuti, in her study of Harsha, also supports the view that

[16] Cf. J.W. McCrindle, *Ancient India as Described by Megasthenes and Arrian*, Calcutta, 1877, p. 86.

[17] *Travels*, I, pp. 344-45.

[18] K. P. Jayaswal, *An Imperial History of India*, Lahore, 1934, p. 28.

[19] R. S. Tripathi, *History of Kanauj*, Delhi, 1959, pp. 30-31.

Harsha was of Vaiśya extraction;[20] so does S.R. Goyal.[21] K.P. Jayaswal held the same opinion,[22] though on the basis of his own interpretation of a few verses occurring in the Buddhist text *Āryamañjuśrīmūlakalpa* [23] he had also tried to prove that the emperor Yaśodharman-Vishṇuvardhana of Malwa was the founder of the Pushyabhūti dynasty. His theory of the association of Yaśodharman-Vishṇuvardhana with Thanesar, however, was based on Fleet's wrong translation of a passage of the Mandasor inscription of this ruler.[24] We need not go into its details here.

Many scholars, including Cunningham,[25] Bühler [26] and B.N. Sharma,[27] believe that the Pushyabhūtis belonged to the Kshatriya class. Their belief is based on a passage occurring in the *Harshacharita* of Bāṇa according to which the two houses of the Pushyabhūtis and the Maukharis were like the Moon and the Sun (*Somasūryavaṁśāviva Pushyabhūti Mukharavaṁśau*).[28] It is argued that here Bāṇa is making a reference to the Kshatriyahood of the two dynasties. Therefore, like the Maukharis who were Kshatriyas of the Solar line, the Pushyabhūtis also must have been a branch of the Lunar Kshatriyas. But this passage of the *Harshacharita* does not at all prove that the Pushyabhūtis were Kshatriyas by caste. Here, Bāṇa is using a simile[29] which is intended to serve only one purpose and that is to illustrate that the Pushyabhūti and the Maukhari dynasties were as great and important as the Solar and the Lunar lines of the Kshatriyas. It should be remembered that it is one of the basic tenets of logic that a simile should never be stretched beyond the purpose it intends to serve.

Many scholars have tried to seek an allusion to the Kshatriya origin of Harsha in this passage since they are obsessed with the idea that in ancient India kings usually belonged to the Kshatriya class. Cunningham is a good example of such a faulty belief. Commenting on the statement of Yuan Chwang that Harsha belonged to the Fei-she caste, he opines that 'it is a mistake'. For, in the opinion of Cunningham, "being a celebrated ruler Harsha must have

[20] D. Devahuti, *Harsha : A Political Study*, 2nd edn., New Delhi, 1983, p. 72.

[21] S.R. Goyal, *Harsha Śīlāditya*, Meerut, 1986, pp. 55-57.

[22] Jayaswal, *op. cit.*

[23] *Ibid.*, p. 45, verses 614-18.

[24] J.F. Fleet, *Corpus Inscriptionum Indicarum*, Vol. III, Calcutta, 1888, p. 148. For a correct translation of this passage see D. C. Sircar, *Select Inscriptions*, Calcutta, 1965, p. 419, fn. 4.

[25] A. Cunningham, *The Ancient Geography of India*, Varanasi, 1963, p. 377.

[26] *Epigraphia Indica*, I, 1892, p. 68, fn. 4.

[27] B. N. Sharma, *Harṣa and His Times*, Varanasi, 1970, pp. 89-92.

[28] *HC*, P. V. Kane's edn., Delhi, 1965, p. 16.

[29] Tripathi, *op. cit.*, p. 30.

belonged to the Kshatriya class; probably he was a 'Bais Rajput', in which case he would be a Kshatriya but the word 'Bais' led Yuan Chwang into believing that he was a Vaiśya."[30] This is a remarkable reasoning indeed ! For, Cunningham deduces from the statement of Yuan Chwang what the Chinese pilgrim does not say and neglects altogether what he has explicitly said (that Harsha belonged to the Fei-she caste). Yuan Chwang mentions caste of several rulers in his account. According to him, the king Dhruvabhaṭa of Valabhī was of Kshatriya extraction,[31] the king of Sindha was a Śūdra,[32] Bhāskaravarman of Assam was a Brāhmaṇa[33] and the ruler of Pāriyātra was a Vaiśya.[34] Considering these facts, he can hardly be expected to have made a mistake in the case of Harsha, whose caste must have been a well-known fact in his day. As Watters states, we must remember that Yuan Chwang had ample opportunities for knowing the antecedents of the Pushyabhūti family, and must have had some grounds for making this assertion.[35]

Here, we would like to draw the attention of scholars to certain passages of the *Harshacharita* which have not been properly used so far.[36] These passages conclusively prove that the dynasty of Harsha did not belong to the Kshatriya caste. At one place, in the second *uchchhavāsa* of the *Harshacharita*, Bāṇa describes Pāriyātra, the dauvārika (chief of the door-keepers) of Harsha. Here, after describing other aspects of Pāriyātra's personality, he states that the dauvārika was 'gleaming with two jewelled ear-rings at his ear, as if they were the sun and moon brought to be asked whether even a king of the solar or lunar race were such as our king.'[37] From this passage it is quite clear that Harsha belonged neither to the Solar line and nor to the Lunar family of the Kshatriyas. Bāṇa clarifies this point further in the third *uchchhavāsa* also. Here, in one passage, noted first by Devahuti,[38] Pushyabhūti, the founder of the dynasty, helps Bhairavāchārya and in return gets a boon from the goddess Lakshmī to the effect that he would become the founder of a third dynasty as famous as the other two dynasties, Solar and Lunar: "Because of this magnanimity of thine... thou, like a third added to the Sun and Moon, shalt be the founder of a mighty line

[30] Cunningham, *op. cit.*

[31] *Travels*, II, p. 246.

[32] *Ibid.*, II, p. 252.

[33] *Ibid.*, II, p. 186.

[34] *Ibid.*, I, p. 300.

[35] *Ibid.*, pp. 344-45.

[36] Cf. Shankar Goyal, 'Social *Milieu* of the Pushyabhūtis : Significance of Some Hitherto Unnoticed Passages of the *Harshacharita*', in *Essays in Indian History and Culture*, Y. Krishan (ed.), New Delhi, 1986, pp. 167-70; idem, *op.cit.*, pp. 121-23.

[37] *HC*, tr. Cowell and Thomas, p. 49; also P. V. Kane's edn., p. 28.

[38] Devahuti, *op.cit.*, pp. 57-58.

of kings... Wherein shall arise an emperor named Harṣa,... world-conquering like a second Māndhātṛi,... ."[39] From this passage also it is certain that to Bāṇa Harsha was not a Lunar or Solar Kshatriya by birth. Here, it may also be emphasized that at no place Bāṇa has categorically stated that the Pushyabhūtis were Kshatriyas. At several places he praises their valour but without mentioning their caste. Therefore, we do not think that one should have any reservations in accepting the testimony of the author of the *Āryamañjuśrīmūlakalpa* and Yuan Chwang, both of whom categorically state that the family of Harsha was of the Vaiśya caste. After all, kings of the Vaiśya caste could also have been men of valour and prowess.

The fact that Harsha was a Vaiśya and did not belong to a tribe greatly influenced the subsequent history of the Pushyabhūti kingdom. It played a significant role even after his death, for after his death his family or dynasty remained unsupported by a tribal following as it happened in so many cases when a king belonging to a tribe was supported by his tribal followers in times of distress. Ajit Singh of Jodhpur, so loyally served by Durgadas and the Rathor tribe, is a case in the point.

It is significant that in 642-43 A.D. Harsha was at the height of his glory but he could not sustain it; his glory immediately evaporated after 643-44 A.D. Such critical times came in the history of the Chālukyas, the Guhilas and many others but they were able to overcome the crisis at least once or twice with the help of their tribe. But the family of Harsha failed to overcome its crisis even for a brief period obviously because it had no tribal base to fall back upon for its support.

V

In the seventh century the occupations of the first two castes remained much the same as in the pre-Harsha period. In the pre-Harsha period the place of the Brāhmaṇas in the society was indispensable as teachers, priests, purohitas and preceptors. All important religious ceremonies in the life of a man beginning from the cradle to his pyre (and even after his death) were performed by purohitas who received gifts and donations for religious performances. Therefore, gifts and donations had become the main source of livelihood of the Brāhmaṇas. Literary and epigraphic sources at our disposal provide us with innumerable instances of these ceremonial gifts. In this respect a very significant and interesting fact has been mentioned by Yuan Chwang which, as S.R.Goyal has argued,[40] contrary to the prevailing notion among historians, proves that Harsha was much more pro-Brāhmaṇa than pro-Buddhist. In the

[39] *HC*, tr. Cowell and Thomas, p. 97; cf. Kane's edn., pp. 53-54.

[40] For details vide S.R. Goyal, *Harsha and Buddhism*, Meerut, 1986, p. 101; On this, also see Shankar Goyal, *The 'Medieval' Factor and the Age of Harsha : A Cultural Study*, Jodhpur, 2016, Ch. 3.

Life of Yuan Chwang it is said that in the quinquennial assembly held at Prayāga, in which Harsha gave lavish gifts for seventy-five days to the priests, monks, etc. he was extremely partial to the Brāhmaṇas, for he gave gifts to "the religious community" (that is, the Buddhist monks) for a day only, while his bestowal of gifts to the Brāhmaṇas lasted for twenty days. Even bestowal of gifts to the heretics (Jainas, etc. ?) and to those who came from distant lands lasted for ten days each and to the poor, destitute and orphans for thirty days. The last, that is the seventy-fifth day, was devoted to the bestowal of Harsha's personal belongings. Thus, out of these 75 days only one was allotted for distribution of gifts to the Buddhists and as many as twenty for distributing gifts to the Brāhmaṇas.

The glorification of gifts to the Brāhmaṇas by the other three varṇas became a distinct feature of Hinduism in this age.[41] By gifts Manu unequivocally meant gifts to the Brāhmaṇas. He says that it was the supreme duty of man in the Kali Age to give gifts to the Brāhmaṇas.[42] Almost all the inscriptions and literary works of this period testify to the fact that the people in those times firmly believed that feeding the Brāhmaṇas was one of the acknowledged means of gaining divine favours and religious merit.

In her *The Unknown Hsüan-tsang* Devahuti has quoted an interesting passage from a Chinese text which deposes that the Brāhmaṇas learnt the four Vedas. The first is called 'the span of life' (*Āyurveda*), i.e. the nourishing of life and the development of one's nature. The second Veda is called 'sacrifice' (*Yajurveda*), i.e. sacrifice and prayers. The third is called 'evenness/balance/peace' (*Sāmaveda*). The fourth is called 'arts' (*Atharvaveda*), i.e. extraordinary ability and skills, exorcisms and medicine.[43] According to Devahuti, the Āyurveda was actually a part of the *Atharvaveda* and it is curious that here Yuan Chwang puts it as an independent Veda at the head of the list of Vedas. The pilgrim was no doubt familiar with the *Ṛgveda* as the first Veda.[44] Its complete omission by him in this context is not easy to explain. A possible explanation is that being a Buddhist Yuan Chwang was casual about the Vedas just as he was about the Brāhmaṇic, theoretical class profession equation which he records a little later and where he assigns agriculture to the Śūdras. The *Ṛgveda* was the most authoritative Veda for the Brāhmaṇas and we know that some of its hymns were directly criticized by the Buddha. That probably explains Yuan Chwang's deliberate disregard for it.[45]

According to Yuan Chwang, "Among the various castes and classes

[41] G.S. Ghurye, *Caste and Class in India*, 2nd edn., Bombay, 1957, Ch.1.

[42] *Manusmṛti*, VIII, 6.

[43] D. Devahuti, *The Unknown Hsüan-tsang*, Oxford, 2001, p. 126.

[44] *Ibid.*

[45] *Ibid.*, p. 128.

of the country the Brāhmaṇas are the purest'',[46] and they are ''highly esteemed.''[47] It was for their excellent reputation that in China the name ''Brāhmaṇa-country'' (P'o-lo-men-kuo) became ''popular for India''[48] The pilgrim was highly impressed by their devotion to learning. Harsha's dramas and Bāṇa's works also contain numerous references to their devotion to learning and of the examples of gifts to the Brāhmaṇas.[49] Harsha's three grants, including his recently discovered Kurukshetra-Varanasi grant, were also made to the Brāhmaṇas. Bāṇa's *Harshacharita* deposes that he donated to the Brāhmaṇas 'a hundred villages, delimited by a thousand ploughs' on the eve of his departure for the *digvijaya* (world-conquest).[50] All the personal belongings of the deceased king Prabhākaravardhana were given to the Brāhmaṇas.[51] They also consumed the departed spirit's first oblation.[52] All the important religious ceremonies were performed by a purohita who received gifts and donations for his religious performances.

The social status of the Brāhmaṇas was based on their learning and religious life. The Chinese pilgrim tells us that the Brāhmaṇas lived contentedly, strictly observing ceremonial purity.[53] He writes, 'among the various castes and classes of the country the Brāhmaṇas were the purest, and they were highly esteemed'. Once he met a Brāhmaṇa who was 'super abundant in reasoning and eminent in the Vedas and other śāstras'.[54] Bāṇa uses the epithet *Brahmamukha* for the Brāhmaṇas, because they 'had the Vedas on their lips'.[55] For the Brāhmaṇas it was absolutely necessary to learn the Vedas by heart. In the *Nāgānanda* the Vidūshaka is asked by the *cheṭī* to repeat the Vedic hymns to prove that he was a Brāhmaṇa.[56] In the *Priyadarśikā* the king tells the Vidūshaka that the qualities of a Brāhmaṇa are known by the number of the Vedas he knows.[57] Sometimes the Brāhmaṇas were known after the particular Veda over which they attained mastery.[58] The Banskhera grant was issued to

[46] *Travels*, I, p. 168.

[47] *Ibid.*

[48] *Ibid.*, p. 140.

[49] *Priyadarśikā*, Act II, tr. G.D. Nariman, A.V. William Jackson and C.J. Ogden, New York, 1923; *Ratnāvalī*, Act II, ed. and tr. C. R. Devadhar and N. G. Suru, 2nd edn., Poona, 1954; *HC*, tr. Cowell and Thomas, p. 65; *HC*, Kane's edn., p. 35; *Kādambarī*, tr. C. M. Ridding, Bombay, 1956, p. 55.

[50] *HC*, tr. Cowell and Thomas, p. 199.

[51] *Ibid.*, p. 164.

[52] *Loc. cit.*

[53] *Loc. cit.*

[54] S. Beal, *The Life of Hiuen-Tsiang*, New Delhi, 1973, pp. 74-75.

[55] *HC*, tr. Cowell and Thomas, p. 111, n. 1,

[56] *Nāgānanda*, Act III, tr. P. Boyd, London, 1872.

[57] *Priyadarśikā*, Act II.

[58] *Epigraphia Indica*, IV, 1896-97, pp. 208-11.

Bhaṭṭa Bālachandra and Bhaṭṭa Bhadrasvāmin. Of them the former was a Ṛgvedin Brāhmaṇa whereas the latter was a Sāmavedin. Similar such epithets are also given to the donees of the Madhuban and the recently discovered Kurukshetra-Varanasi grants.[59] The epithets in these and several other grants, most probably, denote the Brāhmaṇa's mastery of the respective Vedas. The faces of the cousins of Bāṇa are said to have been 'made pure by the study of the Vedas'.[60] Bāṇa tells us that he himself had 'studied the Vedas with the six Aṅgas'.[61] He informs us that after Prabhākaravardhana's death, Harsha was 'closely attended by old Brāhmaṇas who were well-versed in the Śruti, Smṛti and Itihāsa'.[62] The houses of Bāṇa's kinsmen are described as 'full of students and disciples who were making noise by continual recitation'.[63]

The Brāhmaṇas used to wear the sacred thread (*yajñopavīta* or *brahmasūtra*).[64] The *Brahmasūtra* was also put on by the Brāhmaṇa females. While describing the costume of Sarasvatī, Bāṇa says that 'her body was purified by the *brahmasūtra*'.[65] In the *Kādambarī* Mahāśvetā is also said to have put on the *brahmasūtra*. Significantly, the Brāhmaṇas were respected for their learning and high moral conduct. Their place in the society was also regarded as higher than that of the other varṇas because of their being born as Brāhmaṇas. In the *Harshacharita* we are told that 'respect was due even to one who was a Brāhmaṇa by birth and uninitiated by ceremonies'.[66]

By the seventh century distinctions within the Brāhmaṇa caste, presently known as Pañcha Draviḍas, Pañcha Gauḍas, etc., had not arisen, not to speak of the many minor sub-castes into which Brāhmaṇas in the post-Harsha period had become subdivided. The only distinction within the Brāhmaṇa community then in vogue appears to be that of *śākhā* or *charaṇa*, i.e. the school of Vedic ritual or recitation. The *gotra* was also almost always mentioned, and the *pravara* sometimes. In all the inscriptions and the copper plate grants of that period we nowhere find the Brāhmaṇas distinguishing themselves as Kannojias, Sārasvatas or Draviḍas. They are always described as belonging to a particular *gotra* and studying a particular *śākhā*.

The words then used to indicate the Veda or *śākhā* of a Brāhmaṇa

[59] *Loc. cit.*

[60] *HC*, tr. Cowell and Thomas, p. 73.

[61] *Ibid.*, p. 66.

[62] *Ibid.*

[63] *Ibid.*, p. 35.

[64] *Ibid.*, pp. 5 ff.; *Kādambarī*, tr. Ridding, p. 105. There are several references to *Yajñopavita* in Harsha's dramas also.

[65] *Ibid.*, p. 5.

[66] *Ibid.*, p. 7.

were in some respects different from those later used. Bahvṛcha was usually used then instead of Ṛgvedi, Chhāndoga instead of Sāmavedī, and Yajurvedī instead of Vājasaneyī. And it may further be noted that Bhāradvāja-sagotra was the usual expression then instead of Bhāradvāja-gotra now used.

In the seventh century the names of the Brāhmaṇas and most other upper castes generally ended in particular suffixes indicating their gotra. These suffixes are mentioned even in the Smṛtis. °Sarman was the principal suffix for indicating the Brāhmaṇa caste. Other suffixes or affixes were °bhaṭṭa, °deva, °svāmin, etc. They sometimes had the suffixes °varman and °gupta also probably to indicate that they followed the profession of warriors or traders. The first Kadamba ruler of south India had the surname °sarman (viz., Mayūraśarman) but his descendents adopted the surname °varman (e.g., Śāntivarman, Kākutsthavarman).

The Brāhmaṇas in ancient days as now followed a diversity of professions besides their principal professions of performing sacrifices and officiating at sacrifices (*yajana*), learning (*adhyayana*) and teaching (*adhyāpana*). Bāṇa describes his uncles as learned men studying themselves and teaching others, performing great sacrifices, keeping agnihotra and leading a religious life appropriate for gṛhastha Brāhmaṇas. And yet he includes among his friends and associates of his earlier days dancers and music teachers, actors and painters, poets and dramatists, servant girls and old women, goldsmiths and chemists, Hindu Sannyāsīs and Buddhist recluses, etc. In the *Mṛchchhakaṭika* at one place a Brāhmaṇa thief is introduced which shows that the Brāhmaṇas were good and bad both in those days as they were in other periods.

VI

The second varṇa in the social structure was that of the Kshatriyas. They had not yet become divided into 36 families of the medieval period. These families are described neither by Bāṇa nor by Yuan Chwang. Kings are, however, mentioned in a broad way as belonging to the Solar and Lunar dynasties, but the dynasties of the Chāhamānas, Solaṅkīs, Sisodiyās, Paramāras, Rāthoḍs, etc., are not mentioned anywhere. The Kshatriyas then formed like the Brāhmaṇas one group without probably much marriage restrictions in particular families. Caste organisation then was, in fact, somewhat loose, as the Kshatriyas freely married Vaiśya wives from great families. The instances of the Maukhari Grahavarman, a Kshatriya, marrying Rājyaśrī, the sister of Harsha, a Vaiśya, and that of the Valabhī king Dhruvabhaṭa, also a Kshatriya, marrying Harsha's daughter, mentioned by Yuan Chwang, prove this. But such marriages were not very common. Instances of *pratiloma* marriages or marriages of higher varṇa girls with grooms of lower grade do not occur in the inscriptions (but they probably were quite common in fact) and hence the old law of the *Manusmṛti* about it was apparently still in force.

The Kshatriyas also had their peculiar descriptive epithets or name-endings like the °varman and °trātā mentioned in the Smṛtis, other epithets may also be gathered from the epigraphic records, such as° sena and° bhaṭa which the Valabhī kings usually took up.° Siṁha, which was a most favourite epithet with the Rajputs of the medieval period, is not usually met with in the records of the seventh century though we have the name Droṇasiṁha among the Valabhī kings.

According to Yuan Chwang, the Kshatriyas were of 'the race of kings' and 'had held sovereignty for many generations'.[67] They were praised for their 'benevolence and mercy'.[68] The kings of the greater part of India were generally Kshatriyas whenYuan Chwang paid his visit. But Yuan Chwang has himself recorded some exceptions.

The Kshatriyas were noted for their patriotism, valour, courage and heroism. They were great warriors and fought many battles. The janapada of Sthāṇvīśvara was regarded as the land of heroes and of 'the sons of swords' (i.e., the Kshatriyas).[69] They worshipped their arms and it seems that it was customary with the heroes of the Kshatriya community. Bāṇa informs us that Prabhākaravardhana worshipped his sword named Aṭṭahāsa with perfumes, scents, frankincense and wreaths.[70]

In his general account of the caste system Yuan Chwang observes that it was no longer the exclusive right of the Kshatriyas to rule. As the pilgrim himself tells us, the kings of Matipur and Sindh were of Śūdra stock while the rulers of Kāmarūpa, Ujjain and Jajhoti were Brāhmaṇas by caste, Harsha himself was a Vaiśya and so was the king of Pāriyātra (in modern Rajasthan).[71] The Brāhmaṇas were regarded throughout India as the most honourable caste, but they did not always hesitate to take to cultivation as an honest means of livelihood. When once Yuan Chwang and his fellow travellers were running before a band of robbers they came across a Bhāhmaṇa ploughing the field.[72]

[67] *Travels*, I, p. 168.

[68] *Ibid.*, pp. 168 ff.

[69] *HC*, tr. Cowell and Thomas, p. 82. The Jats of Haryana, ancient Thanesar region, are still a warlike community.

[70] *Ibid.*, p. 91.

[71] S. Beal, *Si-Yü-Ki* or *Buddhist Records of the Western World*, I, Delhi, 1969, pp. 179, 190, 209; II, pp. 196, 271, 272.

[72] *Life*, p. 73; Shankar Goyal, *The 'Medieval' Factor and the Age of Harsha : A Cultural Study*, pp. 54-55.

VII

The third varṇa in the society was that of the Vaiśyas or 'a class of traders who bartered commodities and pursued gains far and near'.[73] Harsha's dramas contain several examples of business and trade. The traders are said to have gone as far as Ceylon. Bāṇa also speaks of this community while describing the richness and prosperity of the Śrīkaṇṭha janapada. The traders had formed a powerful community throughout the ages and had influenced the life of the people and the political atmosphere with the might of their wealth. But, just as all the Kshatriyas were not kings, all the Vaiśyas were not traders. The majority of them, however, must have pursued trade. Others must have taken to agriculture and other vocations also.

By the seventh century the later names of Vaiśya sub-castes had not yet come into being and communities such as Maheshvaris and Agrawals were then unknown. Their main distinctive appellations or suffixes were ° gupta and ° bhūti though some other words were also used such as ° vardhana. As regards profession some of the Vaiśya families had raised themselves higher than traders and merchants and had become kings by following the profession of arms. According to a number of scholars, the imperial Guptas were of Vaiśya caste while according to many others, including S.R. Goyal, R.B. Pandey and U. N. Roy, they were Brāhmaṇas.[74] One should remember that in ancient India the Smṛti rule that the suffix ° sarman should be used by Brāhmaṇas, ° varman by Kshatriyas, ° gupta by Vaiśyas and ° dasa by Śūdras was not always strictly adhered to. That is why, as noted above, the Kadamba Brāhmaṇas adopted both the suffixes ° sarman and ° varman, Brahmagupta, a Brāhmaṇa astronomer, was a Vaiśya, Kauṭilya, also a Brāhmaṇa, had the name Vishṇugupta and Kālidāsa, obviously a Brāhmaṇa poet, had the suffix ° dāsa in his name. The suffix ° vardhana, taken by Harsha's family, indicates Vaiśya caste for him and the testimony of Yuan Chwang that Harsha was a Fei-she, or Vaiśya, is conclusive. Some Vaiśya families in those days, therefore, gave birth to heroes and statesmen. The Guptas were spread over the whole of northern India and the names of warriors and statesmen in those days many a times ended in ° gupta showing their high qualification for military posts.

[73] *Travels*, I, p. 168.

[74] S. R. Goyal, *A History of the Imperial Guptas*, Allahabad, 1967, pp. 70-81; idem, *The Imperial Guptas : A Multidisciplinary Political Study*, Jodhpur, 2005, pp. 84 ff.; R.B. Pandey, *Prāchīna Bhārata*, Varanasi, 1971, p. 254; U. N. Roy, *Gupta Samrāṭ aur Unkā Kāla*, Allahabad, 1971, pp. 47-52. But for the theory that the imperial Guptas belonged to the Vaiśya caste cf. V.V. Mirashi, *Vākāṭaka Rajavaṁśa*, Varanasi, 1964, p. 56; P.L. Gupta, *The Imperial Guptas*, Varanasi, 1974, p. 234, and some others.

VIII

Lastly, we have to speak of the Śūdras whose occupation, according to Yuan Chwang, was agriculture.[75] But in the pre-Christian centuries agriculture was the occupation of the Vaiśyas while menial service alone was left to the Śūdra caste. According to some scholars, the ploughing of land in which action worms and insects are inevitably killed was gradually looked upon as sinful and was eventually prohibited to the Dvijas, a prohibition which is even mentioned in Manu. These classes hence withdrew gradually from agriculture and left it in the hands of the Śūdras. On the question of the Śūdras being engaged in agriculture it may be pointed out that many texts such as the Smṛtis of Manu, Yājñavalkya, Nārada and Devala, and the *Vāyu Purāṇa, Laghu-Āśvalāyana, Vṛddha-Hārīta, Mahābhārata*, etc. permit the Śūdras to follow the professions of the Vaiśyas in certain circumstances. In fact, irrespective of the Smṛti injunctions, all classes did indulge in professions other than those normally ascribed to them by the texts.

The general condition of the outcastes was not satisfactory. They were segregated and not allowed to mix with the three higher varṇas. In the early fifth century Fa-hien found that "Throughout the whole country the people do not kill any living creature, nor drink intoxicating liquor, nor eat onions and garlic. The only exception is that of the Chāṇḍālas. That is the name for those who are (held to be) wicked men, and live apart from others. When they enter the gate of a city or a market-place, they strike a piece of wood to make themselves known, so that men know and avoid them, and do not come into contract with them."[76] Yuan Chwang also mentions that butchers, fishermen, public performers, executioners and scavengers 'had their habitations marked by a distinguishing sign' and that 'they were forced to live outside the cities and were required to sneak along on the left when going about in hamlets'.[77] This description is confirmed by Bāṇa who in his *Kādambarī* informs us that 'the Chāṇḍāla maiden had a bamboo stick with

[75] *Travels*, I, p. 168. The classical varṇa theory in fact did not have any place for a fifth varṇa. As Romila Thapar points out, the basic structure of the fourfold category was theoretically not open to alteration (*Ancient Indian Social History*, Delhi, 1978, p. 129). The distinction that Manu and other lawgivers made between the four varṇas and untouchables like the Chāṇḍālas, however, gave rise in course of time to the concept of the fifth varṇa (cf. for details Vivekanand Jha, 'Caṇḍāla and the Origin of Untouchability', in *The Indian Historical Review*, Vol. XIII, Nos. 1-2, July 1986 and January 1987,pp. 1-36).

[76] J. H. Legge, *A Record of the Buddhist Kingdoms, etc.*, being an account of the Chinese monk Fa-hien's travels in India, Oxford, 1886, p. 43. It is just possible that the extreme regard for animal life had something to do with the exclusion of the Chāṇḍāla from the village and the town, for he was a professional hunter and fisherman.

[77] *Travels*, I, p. 147.

which she made a stroke on the floor to rouse the attention of the king'.[78] Bāṇa treats her as Mātaṅga (Chāṇḍāla or of low birth), 'unworthy of being touched'.[79] I-tsing also states that scavengers had to warn passers-by of their presence by striking sticks, and if anyone by some mischance touched one of them he had to wash himself and his garments.[80] As I-tsing never visited the South, his comments obviously apply to north India. The practice of compelling the untouchables to live outside the towns and villages must of course be traced back to the Vedic times, for the Brāhmaṇa texts speak of the Chāṇḍālas living beyond the skirts of towns and villages and of their habitations as not fit to be visited by the Āryans. The profession of the Chāṇḍālas was from the Vedic times much the same as it was in the seventh century A.D.

IX

Yuan Chwang speaks of the mixed castes also.[81] He is very brief in his description, but Bāṇa draws an elaborate picture of them. His knowledge of these people was very wide and he had a large circle of friends who belonged to these classes.[82] Among them the following persons deserve mention as they denote occupational groups and classes : (1) Two cousins of Bāṇa are called Pāraśava. We cannot determine with certainty what particular caste this word denoted. According to Manu,[83] Pāraśava means 'the son of a Brāhmaṇa from a woman of the Śūdra caste', and such a son was so designated because he was no better than a corpse (*śava*) for conferring religious and spiritual benefits which a son was expected to do. Such people, most probably, formed a debased class of the Pāraśava or degraded Brāhmaṇas. (2) The Bhāshākavi Īśāna belonged to the class of vernacular poets or composers of songs. (3) Veṇībhārata was another poet who belonged to the class of 'bards or panegyrists'. They most probably consisted of the poets singing songs in praise of families at ceremonial occasions. (4) A class of dealers in antidotes. Bāṇa mentions one such man named Mayūraka. The word *jāṅgulika* meant a *physician*, expert in removing the effects of poison. (5) A class of betel-bearers (*tāmbūladāyakas*). (6) A class of readers (*pustakavāchakas*) whose occupation is difficult to be precisely determined. He was perhaps employed to read some religious and literary works before the people. Bāṇa mentions one such person

[78] *Kādambarī*, tr. Ridding, p. 8.

[79] *Ibid.*, pp. 8-9.

[80] J. A. Takakusu, *A Record of the Buddhistic Religion as Practised in India and Malaya Archipelago (A.D. 671-695) by I-tsing*, Delhi, 1966, p. 139; also see Surendranath Sen, *India through Chinese Eyes*, Madras, 1956, p. 78.

[81] *Travels*, I, pp. 147, 168.

[82] *HC*, tr. Cowell and Thomas, pp. 32 ff.; Kane's edn., p. 19.

[83] IX, 178.

named Sudṛshṭi who read to him some pages of the *Vāyu Purāṇa.* (7) A class of glodsmiths whom Bāṇa refers to as Kalāda or Svarṇakāra or Hemakāra. They appear to have been engaged in making gold ornaments. (8) *Hairika* who was entrusted with the supervision of the work of goldsmiths. It is also suggested that the word may indicate a 'gem-cutter'. Most probably it denotes the class of people who were experts in gemmology. Then there were many others such as (9) painters (*chitrakṛts*), (10) model-makers or manufacturers of dolls, (11) drummers (*mṛdaṅgikas*), (12) flute-players (*vaṁśikas*), (13) story-tellers (*kathakas*), (14) leather-workers (*charmakāras*), (15) carpenters, and (16) blacksmiths, etc.

Such social groups or sub-castes were not new to the Indian society in the age of Harsha. We find many such occupational classes in the Ṛgvedic age and many of them are found even today. Some of these sub-castes or social groups were the products of different trades and occupations and also due to social violations in the codes of marriages and general ethics.

Besides the agriculturists there were many classes whose profession was labour of varied kinds and these classes were probably of mixed origin. These are described by Yuan Chwang as innumerable. Those who called themselves neither Brāhmaṇas nor Kshatriyas, neither Vaiśyas nor Śūdras were probably included by him in these mixed classes. "There are", he observes, "numerous classes formed by groups of people according to their kinds and these cannot be described."[84] Their number indeed, then as now, must have been counted by hundreds and hence the despairing remark of Yuan Chwang that they cannot be described. Mixed castes with special occupations have been described in several Smṛtis also and each division mentioned therein is again divided into subdivisions according to minor diversities of occupations, gradually increasing their number.

X

Towns and villages in the seventh century were usually enclosed by high walls. The thoroughfares within were narrow, and shops and stalls were ranged on either side of the high road. The dwelling houses had wattled bamboos or wooden fencing around them. The houses had wooden rooms plastered with *chūnam* and having tiled roofs. The houses were high and built either of boards or bricks and were thatched with grass. The walls were whitewashed with *chūnam* and the floors were plastered with cowdung.[85] I-tsing also says that apartments were not spacious in India.[86] The monk's cells, that have survived at Kanheri and Nalanda, etc., fully support this statement. It is not likely that

[84] *Travels*, I, p. 168.
[85] *Ibid.*, p. 147.
[86] Takakusu, *op. cit.*, p. 190.

small householders could afford to go for much bigger rooms. The furniture were naturally few. Small mats and wooden seats were in general use. Yuan Chwang refers to corded benches which were in universal use.[87] The modern *chārpāi*, so common in north India, is obviously the lineal descendant of Yuan Chwang's corded bench or identical with it. Pillows stuffed with cotton or other soft material were in common use.

A few *chārpāis*, a few earthenware pots, wooden dishes, metal utensils and a copper jar for storing water, and an earthen one for drinking water, probably completed the poor man's household goods, while the rich man had dishes of the costly metals, even of gold and silver. Though the houses were poorly furnished their dwellers were marked for their personal cleanliness. Their habits resembled those of the modern orthodox Indians. Early in the morning they carefully cleaned their teeth and tongue with a piece of tooth-wood (*dātun*) and thoroughly rinsed their mouth. Some went further and washed their nostrils by drawing in a quantity of water. No one could even offer salutation to senior persons without first going through this hygienic routine.[88] Though a bath after a meal was forbidden, a bath before it was obligatory. At mealtime people sat either on mats or on small wooden seats (modern *chowkī*) with legs crossed, at an interval of one cubit from each other to avoid physical contact. Food could also be served on the ground cleaned with cowdung. It was eaten with the right hand without a spoon or chopsticks. Only one plate was used on which the different items were served, but left-over food was thrown away; it was never served to another person. Nor was uncooked fish or vegetables were ever eaten. Yuan Chwang states, and his statement is confirmed by I-tsing, that "those utensils which are of pottery or wood thrown away after use and those which are of gold, silver, copper or iron get another polishing."[89] I-tsing adds that porcelain and lacquer works were not originally known in India and wooden articles were scarcely even employed as eating utensils, but they might be used only once if new.[90] After every meal the Indians used to wash their mouth and hands and clean their teeth and tongue elaborately with tooth-wood, and they did not come into contact with each other until they had thus purified their body. Thorough washing and cleansing were demanded after a call of nature had been attended to. The practice of rubbing the hands and feet with earth, that I-tsing noticed, still survives.[91] Those who sat together at a meal with their feet straightened out, and touching one another's and did

[87] *Travels*, I, p. 147.
[88] Takakusu, *op.cit.*, pp. 33, 90.
[89] *Travels*, I, p. 152.
[90] Takakusu, *op.cit.*, p. 36.
[91] *Ibid.*, pp.91-93.

not use a tooth-brush, were scorned.[92]

At an ordinary meal little pieces of ginger and a spoonful of salt were served first. Then followed some gruel made of dried rice and bean soup with hot butter to be mixed with the principal article of food with the fingers. Last came cakes, fruits, ghee and sugar.[93] Cold water was served both in the winter and the summer to quench the thirst.

A ceremonial feast was preceded by songs and music. *Pañchabhojanīyas* and *Pañchakhādanīyas* with appropriate drinks were served on such occasions. Custom demanded that a superabundance of every dish should be provided. A common householder would offer each of his guests food and condiments sufficient for three, while a really wealthy family would serve ten men's ration to one. The guest was at liberty to carry away the surplus if he so liked, and this practice, which I-tsing noticed at Tāmralipti, still survives in Bengal. The *Pañchabhojanīyas*, according to I-tsing, consisted of (1) rice, (2) a boiled mixture of barley and peas, (3) baked corn flour, (4) meat, and (5) cakes. The *Pañchakhādanīyas*, food to be chewed, were (1) roots, (2) stalks, (3) leaves, (4) flowers, and (5) fruits.[94] It is to be noted that milk and milk preparations were not included in either of the two groups, and while we come across meat as one of the *bhojanīyas*, fish is entirely omitted. We must not forget that the list was compiled by a Buddhist monk who lived mostly at Nalanda and might not have any experience of a feast at a Hindu house. As raw vegetables were not eaten, roots, stalks, leaves and flowers, four of the five *khādanīyas*, were doubtless cooked vegetables.[95]

Intoxicating drinks are mentioned by Fa-hien but he adds that none but the Chāṇḍālas indulge in them.[96] Yuan Chwang, however, not only refers to strong drinks of different kinds but asserts that the higher castes had their distinctive wines and beverages. Thus, "the wines from the vine and sugar-cane are the drink of the Kshatriyas; the Vaiśyas drink a strong distilled spirit; the Buddhist monks and Brāhmins drink syrup of grapes and of sugar-cane; the low mixed castes are without any distinguishing drink."[97]

Some interesting information about the daily life and character of the people of the various castes of Madhya Deśa is found in the *Ta T'ang Hsi Yü Chi* which Devahuti has partly reproduced in her *The Unknown Hsüan-tsang*. The Kshatriyas and Brāhmaṇas, Yuan Chwang tells us, were of simple manners, clean, frugal and fond of spotless white. The robes of

[92] *Ibid.*, p. 26.
[93] *Ibid.*, pp. 43-44.
[94] *Ibid.*, p. 43.
[95] *Ibid.*, p. 137.
[96] Legge, *loc. cit.*
[97] *Travels*, I, p. 178.

the king and the ministers were quite different. They wore flowers and jewel-adorned headgears and rings, bracelets and pendants. The rich merchants wore only bracelets. Most people went barefoot, few using foot-wear. They stained their teeth red or black, trimmed their hair and pierced their ears. They washed before eating, and cleaned their teeth after eating; everytime they performed the call of nature they took bath and used perfumes of sandal-wood or turmeric. They did not pass dishes, and they did not eat left-overs. The pottery and wooden (bark ?) vessels were destroyed after use; the vessels of gold, silver, copper and iron were rubbed and polished after every meal. The ordinary people were upright, and faithful in their promises. They were not crafty in money matters, or deceitful in their conduct. There were nine ways of showing outward respect. The most respectful was 'to make one's prostration on the ground and then to kneel and laud the virtues of the one addressed'.[98]

According to Yuan Chwang also,[99] cleanliness among Indians was their conscious habit, not the result of compulsion. They did not allow others to use their own eating utensils. Earthenware and wooden vessels (for food) were thrown away after their first use. Gold, silver, copper and iron vessels were polished every time. After eating they chewed the willow branch (*dātun* of an unidentifiable wood) to clean their mouths and they touched each other only after they finished washing. They washed each time after urination and after emptying their bowels. They smeared perfumes such as sandal (*chandana*) and turmeric on their body. They bathed before religious ceremonies and before they said prayers. Most of these habits have persisted among Indians till today. There were no fixed regulations as to the dress of mourning. It was customary to raise lamenting cries and weep together. The mourners rent their garments and loosened their hair, struck their heads and beat their breasts. The priests were not permitted to lament or cry for the dead, not even for their parents. They simply recited their prayers and recounted their obligations to the dead. There were three ways of doing the last rites of the dead:[100] by cremation, by water, and by desertion. In the first, the body was burnt; in the second, it was thrown into flowing water; and in the third, it was left in a wilderness to be devoured by beasts. No eating was allowed in the house till after the funeral. Those who attended the funeral had to wash themselves. No posthumous titles were given and no death anniversaries were observed. The old and infirm, and those who suffered from serious illness, or wanted to end their life for other reasons, drowned themselves in the Ganges in the hope of being born among the *devas*.

[98] Devahuti, *The Unknown Hsüan-tsang*, pp. 126-29.

[99] *Ibid.*, p. 126.

[100] Cf. also J. S. Grewal, 'Hiuen Tsiang's India', in *India—Studies in the History of an Idea*, Irfan Habib (ed.), New Delhi, 2005, pp. 65-66.

FIFTEEN

Feudalization of Polity in the Age of Harsha

BĀṆA'S CRITICISM OF THE CONTEMPORARY POLITY

Bāṇa was an orthodox Brāhmaṇa of the Vātsyāyana *gotra.*[1] He gives an eulogy of the four generations of his ancestors with which may be compared the similar praise of three of them in the introductory verses of the *Kādambarī.* The eulogies convey that they were all great teachers and diligent sacrificers thus fulfilling the main duties of a Brāhmaṇa householder after the Smṛti standards. Bāṇa himself was brought up in orthodox Brāhmaṇical atmosphere. Among his teachers mention is made in the *Kādambarī* of a certain Brāhmaṇa teacher Bhatsu whose feet were worshipped by the Maukhari rulers. When he went to meet Harsha he performed Brāhmaṇical sacrifices and worshipped lord Vīrūpāksha (Śaṅkara). When he met Harsha for the first time and the latter accused him of being a great rogue (*bhujaṅga*), he made the submission that he was a Brāhmaṇa born in the family of the Soma-drinking Vātsyāyanas. Every ceremony of his was duly performed when its time came and he had thoroughly mastered the Veda with its six *aṅgas* and had, as far as possible, heard lectures on the śāstras.

Bāṇa was also a great admirer of Harsha. According to him, Harsha's achievements were of epic proportion[2] and greater than those of the great *chakravartīs* of the Vedic age.[3] Both these facts—his orthodox Brāhmaṇical

[1] For the personal history of Bāṇa, see Shankar Goyal, '*Harshacharita* as a Source of History', in the *Proceedings of the Papers from the Aligarh Historians Society,* ed. Irfan Habib, 69th Session, Indian History Congress, Kannur University, Kannur, Kerala, 28-30 December, 2008, pp. 122-24; idem, *Harsha Revisited : A Re-interpretation of Existing Data,* Delhi, 2018, Ch. 1.

[2] *Harṣa-carita of Bāṇa* (hereafter *HC*), Eng. tr. of E.B. Cowell and F.W. Thomas, repr., Delhi, 1968, p. 76.

[3] *Ibid.,* pp. 74-75.

background and his admiration for Harsha—have created the impression that he was a firm believer in the Brāhmaṇical ideas and customs and did not anywhere view the contemporary polity and administrative system with a critical eye.

But that is not true. There are some passages in both of his works which certainly echo his voice of protest and dissent against some aspects of the political culture of his age.[4] Of course, it must be conceded that as a member of the orthodox Brāhmaṇa class and a court-poet of Harsha, he could not raise his voice of protest or dissent at a very high pitch; but he has certainly made it clear that he did not approve some aspects of the political culture and administrative structure of his age. His personal background makes his criticism of the contemporary polity all the more significant and reliable.

BĀṆA'S CRITICISM OF THE CONCEPT OF THE DIVINITY OF KINGS

First of all Bāṇa was highly critical of the belief in the theory of the divinity of kings—a theory which was widely current in ancient India and which kings deliberately tried to popularise. The *Manu Smṛti* (VII. 4-5; V. 96) says: "the Creator created the king with the essential parts taken from Indra, the Wind-god, Yama, the Sun, Agni, Varuṇa, the Moon and Kubera, the lord of wealth and, therefore, he surpasses all beings by his majesty; one should not disrespect (even) a boy-king with the thought 'he is a human being (like others)', for it is a great deity that stands (before people) in human form as a king" (VII.8). Kauṭilya (I. 13) makes a spy say among *pauras* and *jānapadas* : "kings are (in) the place of (that is, perform the functions of) Indra and Yama, since they visibly inflict punishment and bestow favours. Even divine punishment affects those who despise them (kings). Therefore, kings should not be despised." The *Matsya Purāṇa* (226.1) says that the king was created by Brahmā by taking portions of gods for wielding the power of punishment for the the protection of all beings. According to the *Agni Purāṇa* (226.17-20), as the king exercises the functions of nine deities viz. the Sun, the Moon, Vāyu, Yama, Varuṇa, Fire, Kubera, the Earth and Vishṇu, he has the form of all these deities. The *Śukranītisāra* (I. 73-79) echoes similar ideas. The *Nārada Smṛti* (Prakīrṇa Section, 20-31) argues that in the form of the king it is really Indra himself who moves about on the earth, that a king even when devoid of qualities deserves honour from the people, that kings exercise the functions of five deities, namely, Agni, Indra, Soma, Yama and Kubera. The *Mārkaṇḍeya*

[4] Shankar Goyal, 'Voices of Protest and Dissent in the Works of Bāṇa', *Śrījñānāmṛtam* (A Commemoration Volume dedicated to Professor Shri Niwas Shastri), ed. Vijaya Rani, Delhi, 1996, pp. 650-60.

Purāṇa (27.21-26) mentions the same five deities. The *Mahābhārata* (Śānti Parvan, 69) states that all the gods are invisible, but the king is a deity that can be seen. The *Vāyu Purāṇa* (57.72) remarks that in all past and future *manvantaras* universal emperors (*chakravartīs*) are born on the earth with parts of Vishṇu. The *Bhāgavata Purāṇa* (IV. 14.26-27) says that Vishṇu, Brahmā, Śiva, Indra, Vāyu, Varuṇa—these and other gods—exist in the body of the king and that the king is full of (the parts of) all gods. It was in consonance with this conception that ancient Kshatriya dynasties and their panegyrists tried to trace the descent of those dynasties from the Sun or the Moon and in later times from Fire. The *Pañchatantra* (I. 120) states that "Manu has declared that the king is made up (of parts) of all gods." The *Rājanītiprakāśa* points out that the idea of the king having in him parts of the deities applies only to the independent Mahārājas while the idea of a ruler doing the functions of five deities applies to vassal kings. The practice of addressing the king as "deva" in Sanskrit plays was originally the result of the same tendency of the deification of the royal office.

The theory of the divine nature of kingship finds mention in the epigraphs also. Of emperor Samudragupta, we are told by Harisheṇa that 'he was the incomprehensible spirit that was the cause of protection of good and destruction of evil,' that 'he was Apratiratha (=Vishṇu) roaming in the world' and that 'he was a mortal only in celebrating the rites of the observances of mankind, but otherwise was a god dwelling on the earth.'[5] The later genealogists usually describe Chandragupta II as Vishṇu himself (*svayaṁ-cha-Apratirathaḥ*).[6] In the records of north Bengal the Gupta kings are given the trilogy of titles (*Paramadaivata, Paramabhaṭṭāraka* and *Mahārājādhirāja*) which, with the slight change of *Paramadaivata* into *Parameśvara*, became the distinctive designation of paramount rulers in later times. With the object of claiming superhuman excellence for them, the coin-legends of the Gupta rulers attribute to them the conquest of heaven by good deeds following their conquest of the earth.

Bāṇa was also quite familiar with the theory of the divinity of kings but in his *Kādambarī* he expresses his opposition to it quite explicitly. In this work at one place Śakunāsa, the minister of Tārāpīḍa, teaches Chandrāpīḍa, the crown-prince, some basic principles of pragmatic politics. It is quite a lengthy discourse and may be regarded as representing the ideas of Bāṇa himself on the subject. In this discourse at one place Chandrāpīḍa is taught that only utterly foolish kings believe that they are god incarnate on earth:

[5] S.R. Goyal, *Guptakālīna Abhilekha*, Meerut, 1984, pp. 42, 45; idem, *The Imperial Guptas : A Multidisciplinary Political Study*, Jodhpur, 2005, pp. 166-70, for further details.

[6] *Ibid.*, p. 135.

> ...though subject to mortal conditions, they look on themselves as having alighted on earth as divine beings with a superhuman destiny; they employ a pomp in their undertakings only fit for gods and win the contempt of all mankind. They welcome this deception of themselves by their followers. From the delusion as to their own divinity established in their minds, they are overthrown by false ideas, and they think their own pair of arms have received (like the four arms of Vishṇu) another pair; they imagine their forehead has a third eye (like the third eye of Śiva) buried in the skin. They consider the sight of themselves a fovour; they esteem their glance a benefit; they regard their words as a present; they hold their command a glorious boon; they deem their touch a purification.[7]

This is obviously an instance of Bāṇa's dissenting voice against political beliefs current at that times.

Bāṇa was also critical of some aspects of the administration of his patron though due to obvious reason he expresses his disapproval only in a guarded language. For example, he gives a picture of people's sufferings and their lamentations when the huge army of Harsha was on march. At that time some persons were praising the ruler by saying that 'The king is Dharma incarnate'. But there were others who :

> despondent at the plunder of their ripe grain, had come forth wives and all to bemoan their estates, and to the imminent risk of their lives, grief dismissing fear, had begun to censure their sovereign, crying 'Where's the king ?' 'What right has he to be king ?' 'What a king!'[8]

Such observations made by despondent people at the risk of their lives, were indeed a great censure on the administration and it goes to the credit of Bāṇa that he mustered sufficient courage to present a true picture of people's sufferings in the biography of Harsha himself.

BĀṆA'S CRITICISM OF THE CUSTOM OF SATĪ PREVALENT IN THE ROYAL HOUSEHOLDS

Bāṇa was also highly critical of the custom of satī. The custom of satī goes back to the Ṛgvedic age.[9] In the historical period its earliest notice occurs in the Greek accounts of Alexander's invasion.[10] It became popular during the age of the imperial Guptas and continued afterwards. The Chaṅgunārāyaṇa inscription of Mānadeva[11] and the Eran stone pillar inscription of king Bhānugupta[12] offer earliest epigraphic evidences of the satī custom. When

[7] *Kādambarī*, Eng. tr. of C.M. Ridding, London, 1896, Indian repr., 1960, p. 95.

[8] *HC*, pp. 208-09.

[9] R.C. Majumdar and A.D. Pusalker, eds., *The Vedic Age*, London, 1951, p. 390.

[10] A.L. Basham, *The Wonder that was India*, London, 1954, p. 187.

[11] D.C. Sircar, *Select Inscriptions* (hereafter *SI*), Calcutta, 1965, pp. 378-79.

[12] S.R. Goyal, *Guptakālīna Abhilekha*, pp. 317-22; idem, *The Imperial Guptas*, p. 445.

king Prabhākaravardhana was on the death-bed, overcome with excessive and unbearable sorrow, queen Yaśomatī plunged into fire to avoid widowhood.[13] It seems that several other wives of king Prabhākaravardhana also committed satī. After the assassination of Grahavarman, Rājyaśrī, his devoted wife, prepared to enter the funeral pyre.[14] Her decision was changed only after the persuasions of the Buddhist sage Divākaramitra. In the *Nāgānanda* of Harsha it is said that after Jīmūtavāhana's death Malayavatī asked for the crown of her deceased lord so that "clasping it to her heart she might enter into the funeral pyre". In the *Kādambarī* when Mahāśvetā found that Puṇḍarīka was dead, she asked her friend Taralikā to rise and collect the wood to make a funeral pyre so that she might follow her lord.[15] In the same work Kādambarī decides to embrace death, "honouring the feet of Chandrāpīḍa with bent head" and "placing them in her lap".[16]

In the accounts of the self-immolation by Yaśomatī and attempt for the same by Rājyaśrī, Bāṇa does not say anything by way of his own opinion. Obviously, he could not make any adverse remarks against the actions of the mother and sister of his patron. But in the *Kādambarī* he does make Chandrāpīḍa, the hero of the work, criticize the satī custom in no uncertain terms. Almost in the language of a modern critic of the satī custom, Chandrāpīḍa persuades Mahāśvetā not to commit satī by arguing that :

> ...life is easily resigned by those whom sorrow has overwhelmed, but it needs a greater effort not to throw away life in heavy grief. This following another to death is most vain ! It is a path followed by the ignorant ! It is a mere freak of madness, a path of ignorance, an enterprise of recklessness, a view of baseness, a sign of utter thoughtlessness, and a blunder of folly, that one should resign life on the death of father, brother, friend, or husband. If life leaves us not of itself, we must not resign it. For this leaving of life, if we examine it, is merely for our own interest, because we cannot bear our own cureless pain. To the dead man it brings no good whatever. For it is no means of bringing him back to life, or heaping up merit, or gaining heaven for him, or saving him from hell, or seeing him again, or being reunited with him. For he is led helplessly, irresistibly to another state meet for the fruits of his own deeds. And yet he shares in the guilt of the friend who has killed himself. But a man who lives on can help greatly, by offerings of water and the like, both the dead man and himself; but by dying he helps neither.[17]

[13] *HC*, pp. 154-55.
[14] *Ibid.*, p. 254.
[15] *Kādambarī*, Eng. tr., p. 152.
[16] *Ibid.*, p. 217.
[17] *Ibid.*, p. 156.

To convince Mahāśvetā that the satī was not a time-honoured custom, Bāṇa makes Chandrāpīḍa give several instances in which wives of great men, semi-divine beings and gods did not give up their lives after the death of their husbands though their fidelity to their husbands was quite well-known :

> Remember how Rati, the sole and beloved wife of Love, when her noble husband, who won the hearts of all women, was burnt up by fire of Shiva, yet did not yield her life; and remember also Kuntī of the race of Vṛishṇi, daughter of Sūrasena, for her lord was Pāṇḍu the wise; his seat was perfumed by the flowers in the crests of all the kings whom he had conquered without an effort, and he received the tribute of the whole earth, and yet when he was consumed by Kindama's curse she still remained alive. Uttarā, too, the young daughter of Virāṭa, on the death of Abhimanyu, gentle and heroic, and joyful to the eyes as the young moon, yet lived on. And Duḥshalyā, too, daughter of Dhṛitarāshṭra, tenderly cared for by her hundred brothers; when Jayadratha, king of Sindhu, was slain by Arjuna, fair as he was and great as he had become by Shiva's gift, yet made no resignation of her life. And others are told of by thousands, daughters of Rākshasas, gods, demons, ascetics, mortals, siddhas and Gandharvas, who when bereft of their husbands yet preserved their lives.[18]

Thus, here Bāṇa raises his voice of protest against a social evil which was quite prevalent in his times[19] and was recognized as 'honourable' even in the family of his patron. It must have required some courage indeed!

BĀṆA'S LAMENTATION ON THE CONDITION OF GOVERNMENT SERVANTS

Another instance where Bāṇa becomes quite critical of the polity of his age, occurs when he makes Haṁsavega, the Kāmarūpa envoy to Harsha, enter upon a diatribe against government servants. It is a bitter invective probably unparalleled anywhere else in Sanskrit literature. The flattery of the royal courtiers, the royal servant socked in utter selfishness and the haughtiness and proud demeanour of king who behaved with utter contempt have been painted here with a rare fidelity.[20] In his view the government servants hardly deserved to be called human beings :

[18] *Ibid.*, pp. 156-57.

[19] Cf. also, J.K. Sharma, 'Women in Vardhana India', in *Panjab University Research Bulletin* (*Arts*), Volume XVIII, Number 2, October, 1987, pp. 139-40. However, Bāṇa's denunciation of the custom of satī was a singular act for no one else is known to have followed him. Nevertheless, it was not a universal custom. We learn from Bāṇa and, later on, from Daṇḍin, that a woman who was either pregnant or who had a son to support generally refrained from doing it.

[20] V.S. Agrawala, *The Deeds of Harsha*, Varanasi, 1969, p. 207.

—if a wretch of a servant belongs to the world of men, then a *rājila* snake is a cobra, and a withered stalk the best of rice. Better for a manly man is a moment of manliness; at the price of bowing the wise deem not even the joy of a world-sovereignty worth a bow.[21]

According to Bāṇa, a penitent government servant pours contempt on himself thinking that :

...to hell with such wealth, perdition seize such advancement, hail to such worshipful enjoyments, my service to such grandeur, away with such glory, joy go with such pomp, for the sake of which my head must seek the earth.[22]

A government servant has no independent personality. He is :

An eunuch whose love is but words, a worm of inodorous carrion, a mannikin of no account, a walking footstool all grey atop with the dust of feet, [252] in coaxing notes a human cuckoo, in gratifying cries a peacock, in bosom-rubbing a land tortoise, in mean fawnings a dog, in modulated notes a pipe, in strainings of body a harlot's person, in the rice-fields of manliness a straw, in jerkings of head a lizard, in curling himself up a hedgehog, in rubbing of feet a very footstool, in slappings with hands a ball, in beatings with sticks a lute board,—[23]

According to Bāṇa, such a person has nowhere to go :

Whither shall he go to find peace ? What is his life like ? What manly pride is his? What possible pleasures ? What dream of enjoyment ? This dreadful name of servant, like a torrent of mud, lays everything low.[24]

Why a normal goodly person becomes inclined to service ? And what are the feelings which drive him to accept such a situation? These questions are answered by Bāṇa thus :

When towards servitude inclined by overwhelming calamity, like a wicked mother, old in years; spurred on by greed like an unsatisfied wife; harassed by ill imaginings with their manifold cravings, begotten of youth, like bad children; beholding circumstances over-ripe, like an elderly daughter in his house, and suggesting recourse to another man; urged to exertion by all planets of distress, like poor kinsmen; pursued by foul deeds, like aged servants, of long standing and not to be shaken off : when thus, cherishing in his heart in vain the desire of grasping the whole round of delights, as though the power of all his senses were blighted, a man makes up his mind to enter a palace, as a malefactor a cowdung fire, to the burning torment of all his frame,—[25]

According to Bāṇa, only a person who is on evil days makes up his mind to enter a palace. He is like a person whose power of senses is blighted

[21] *HC*, p. 223.
[22] *Ibid.*, p. 222.
[23] *Ibid.*, pp. 222-23.
[24] *Ibid.*, p. 222.
[25] *Ibid.*, pp. 219-20.

but who still cherishes the whole round of pleasures. Withering like a festoon spray at the very portal, he has the distress of being shut out by the lackeys, and hangs on there. Entering at the door, if he enters at all:

> ...he is beaten by others like a deer, dashed away time after time, like the dummy in elephants' practice, by buffets from the hands of a group of lackeys, downbent through greed of wealth, like a tree branch over a treasure. No petitioner, he is turned away and shot forth [249] by the mean, till he flies into desperation : no thorn, he is plucked away, as he clings to the feet, and hastily hurled aside : no Kāma, he is annihilated by the scorching glance of a master angered by his unseasonable approach. Like an ape, he changes not colour when angrily reprimanded : like a Brāhman-slayer, he performs degrading offices, forbidden to touch, his shaven poll seared by daily obeisances: like Triśaṅku, he stands day and night with downbent head, excluded from both worlds : like a horse, he submits for a mouthful of food to be driven at will : like a fasting monk, he wastes his frame, retaining the desire of life in his heart : like a dog, he turns away from his proper spouse and in bondage to vile habits consumes himself : like a dead man, he receives his ball of meal in gruesome quarters : like a crow, he lives for nought a wastrel life, his manly vigour subservient to a greedy tongue : like a ghoul frequenting graveyard trees, he hovers about royal favourites made rough by their accursed success : like a child, he is innocently duped by the talk of parrot kings, conferring delight by a false tongue and showing affection only on their lips : like a vampire, [250] there is nothing he will not do under his master's spell: like a painted bow, he is for ever bent in the one act of distending a string of imaginary virtues, but there is no force in him : like a heap of dust sweepings gathered by a broom, he carries off toilet-leavings : like a phlegmatic patient, he is daily worried by acrid doorkeepers : like a Buddhist, he has attained to life-weariness through learning the vanity of things, and longs for the yellow robe : like the meal offered to the Divine Mothers, he is cast out into space even at night: like one under a taint, he aggravates a wretched existence by poor lodging : like a pumping machine, he has left all weight behind him and bends even for water : degraded below the worm, he worships even with his words the feet of those uncontented with his head alone. Abandoned by shame, as if she were alarmed by hard strokes from chamberlains' canes : avoided by self-esteem, as if stifled in a heart contracted by meanness : parted from magnanimity, as if angered by his condescension to low acts; through devotion to riches he heaps up troubles, increasing his contemptibleness under the idea of magnifying his means. Fool ! though there exists a wood fragrant with the scent of myriad flowers, he does homage to a mirage : though a noble, he trembles like a malefactor as he draws near : though of good presence, his being is fruitless as a painted flower : though learned, his speech is as blundering as a fool's : though capable, he folds his hands helplessly, like a leper. Roasted without fire at the elevation of his equals, dying without expiring [251] at the rise of his inferiors, tossed like a straw by insults, burned without respite by the fire of pain, though partial

> unportioned, though cold to pride yet scorching his kin, though of humble carriage yet making no way, though his weight is fallen from him yet gravitating downwards, though void of spirit yet a seller of human flesh, though free from intoxication yet not master of his actions, though no hermit yet giving up his soul to pensiveness, a burnt-poll bowing as soon as he gets up, a domestic fool for ever dancing to amuse the wise, a household firebrand burning his stock, a human ox bending his neck to get even a wisp of grass, a mass of flesh born only to fill his belly,...[26]

This diatribe of Bāṇa against government service is quite unique. He has analysed the feelings of those in service. He had himself made close observation of palace life during his wanderings and also at the court of Harsha and had noted the peculiarities of the conduct of the government servants, their greed and lowly demeanour. His observations throw a flood of light on the nature of the bureaucracy of the age of Harsha. As he could not criticize this aspect of Harsha's administration directly, he has put his observations in the mouth of the Kāmarūpa envoy. In a way it is an elaborate commentary on the line of his own thinking as revealed in his musings on receiving the message of Kṛshṇa, the brother of Harsha, to come to the royal court at once :

> I have indeed been misunderstood by the king, and this advice has been given by my disinterested kinsman Kṛiṣṇa; but all service is hateful, and attendance is full of evils, and a court is full of dangers.[27]

Thus, it is apparent that though an orthodox Brāhmaṇa and a great admirer of Harsha, Bāṇa was in no way blind to the evils of the polity of his time.

HARSHA'S ADMINISTRATION : RISE OF POLITICAL SĀMANTAVĀDA

In addition to some records belonging to the preceding and succeeding periods, contemporary literary sources, specially Bāṇa's works and the testimony of Yuan Chwang, throw a good deal of light on Harsha's administration. In Yuan Chwang we also find general statements about condition in India and information regarding the political set up and governmental machinery. Viewed in its totality the polity of Harsha seems to be based on the administrative pattern of the preceding Gupta age, but at the same time it appears to have been much more 'feudalized' and with lesser cohesion. Under the Guptas political unity was characterized by a balance between centralization and regional autonomy;[28] Harsha's empire was a looser federation much more based on diplomatic alliances than on the firm hold of the central authority. Harsha's superiority over his subordinate kings and feudatories depended on his strength which was lesser than that of the Guptas despite the fact that he is said to have had a very large army, for his army itself was not a 'monolith'

[26] *Ibid.*, pp. 220-22.
[27] *Ibid.*, p. 44.
[28] For details, vide B.N. Puri, *The Gupta Administration*, Delhi, 1991.

controlled by the emperor but a collection of the feudal military units contributed by the *sāmantas.* Actually, the growth of the *sāmanta* institution, the Indian version of feudalism, was the greatest single factor which differentiates the administrative organisation of Harsha from the administration of earlier periods.[29]

In the *Arthaśāstra* of Kauṭilya (1.6)the term *sāmanta* has been used in the sense of an independent neighbour and in the *Manu Smṛti* (VII. 258) and the *Yājñavalkya Smṛti* (II. 153) in the sense of those important persons with whose help the boundary disputes of the villages were settled. The Allahabad pillar inscription of Samudragupta shows that the subjugated princes were expected to pay all tributes, carry out royal orders, give their daughters in marriage and render homage to the conqueror.[30] Though the term *sāmanta* has not been used in this record, but it gradually became popular in this sense. In the *Raghuvaṁśa* (V. 28) the word *sāmanta* is used for a neighbouring potentate who is made a vassal. In the Barabar hill cave inscription of Anantavarman Maukhari his father is described as *Sāmantachūḍāmaṇiḥ.*[31] In the third quarter of the fifth century A.D. the term *sāmanta* was used in the sense of a vassal in south India also, for the phrase *Sāmantachūḍāmaṇayaḥ* appears in a Pallava inscription of the time of Śāntivarman (455-70 A.D.).[32] Mahārāja Vainyagupta (known date 507 A.D.) had two vassals under him namely *Pādadāsa Mahārāja* Rudradatta and *Mahārāja Mahāsāmanta* Vijayasena. The sixth century rulers of Bengal, such as Samāchāradeva and Jayanātha, also had several sāmantas under them. In his Mandsore stone pillar inscription Yaśodharman (known date

[29] Surprisingly, D. Devahuti in her work *Harsha : A Political Study* (Oxford, 1970, the second edition of which appeared in 1983) does not discuss the word or concept of feudalism which was the most conspicuous feature of the age of Harsha and without a reference to which polity and institutions of the period cannot be understood. She only refers to and briefly discusses 'typically Indian sāmanta institution' without making it the central theme of the history of the political life of that period. Her treatment of the administration of Harsha is descriptive, like any such chapter of any other book on Harsha. She studies Harsha's administration as a seperate topic, not as one of the factors which determined the shape and course of political developments. She discusses the principles of ancient Indian polity from the Vedas to the *Nītisāra* of Kāmandaka but does not take the trouble to show how are they relevant for understanding the polity of Harsha. For a detailed analysis of this view, vide Shankar Goyal, *Harsha : A Multidisciplinary Political Study*, Jodhpur, 2006, Ch. 1; idem, *The 'Medieval' Factor and the Age of Harsha : A Cultural Study*, Jodhpur, 2016, pp. 104 ff.

[30] S.R. Goyal, *Guptakālīna Abhilekha*, pp. 17-18; idem, *The Imperial Guptas*, pp. 149-55.

[31] J.F. Fleet, *Corpus Inscriptionum Indicarum*, III, Calcutta, 1888, No. 49.

[32] R.B. Pandey, *Historical and Literary Inscriptions*, Varanasi, 1962, No. 29.

532 A.D.) claims to have subjugated the sāmantas in the whole of north India. In the sixth century the rulers of Valabhī also bore the title *sāmanta, mahārāja* and *mahāsāmanta.*[33]

SĀMANTAVĀDA IN THE AGE OF HARSHA

In the age of Harsha the term sāmanta was widely used for the vassal chiefs. Śaśāṅka, the enemy of Harsha, was for sometime a mahāsāmanta before he became an independent ruler. Mahārāja mahāsāmanta Śrī Mādhavarāja II of the Śailodbhava dynasty, ruling over Koṅgoda, was a feudatory of Śaśāṅka in 619 A.D. Bāṇa speaks of various types of feudal lords—*sāmantas, mahāsāmantas, āptasāmantas, pradhāna-sāmantas, śatrusāmantas* and *pratisāmantas. Āptasāmanta* was probably one who willingly accepted the vassalage of the overlord. V. S. Agrawala takes the word *āpta* in the sense of hereditary.[34] Pradhāna sāmanta was the most trusted hand of the emperor. The meaning of the term pratisāmanta is not definitely known while the śatrumahāsāmanta were probably the mahāsāmantas of the former enemies who now rendered various services to the emperor. At one place Bāṇa refers to *anuraktamahāsāmanta* which might suggest that they of their own accord became attached to the overlord.

In his *Harshacharita* and *Kādambarī* Bāṇa gives some idea of the behaviour and obligations of the sāmantas. He mentions several modes of saluting the king by the defeated kings who were reduced to the position of sāmantas. These included salute by bowing the head and touching the feet of the emperor, taking the dust from the feet of the emperor on one's own head, and placing the head on the earth near the feet of the emperor and greeting him by removing one's own crown and head-dress (*śekhara* and *mauli*). Some served as the bearer of fans, others prayed for their own life tying a sword to their neck, and still others, deprived of all their possessions, showed their eagerness to salute the emperor with folded hands, and allowed their beard to grow till their fate was finally decided by the conqueror.[35]

The defeated kings, relegated to the position of sāmantas, were made to render various kinds of services to the king in the court. They held *chaurīs,*[36] served as doorkeepers in the court by holding a rod of cane in the hand, and served as reciters of the auspicious words such as 'victory' (*jaya*). They used to make repeated inquiries with the gatekeeper about the possibility of getting an audience with the emperor. The defeated sāmantas sent their minor sons

[33] *SI,* p. 394.

[34] V.S. Agrawala, *The Deeds of Harsha,* p. 257; also see his *Harsha Charita : Eka Sāṁskṛtika Adhyayana,* Patna, 1953, pp. 221 ff.

[35] *HC,* p. 48.

[36] *Ibid.*

to the conqueror obviously as protégés. When the Mālava princes Mādhavagupta and Kumāragupta were formally introducted by Prabhākaravardhana to Rājyavardhana and Harsha, they rose from their seats and saying "As your Majesty commands", saluted the Pushyabhūti princes by swaying their heads again and again to the earth. As Prabhākaravardhana's mother Mahāsenaguptā was most probably a sister of Mahāsenagupta, the father of these princes, this mode of showing submission assumes significance. Bhaṇḍi, who served as the commander of the Thanesar cavalry force, was also the son of Yaśomatī's brother, probably a sāmanta chief.

On the occasion of the installation of Yaśomatī as chief-queen, the wives of sāmantas consecrated her with water from golden pitchers and thus offered her their services. In the *Harshacharita* Yaśomatī claims that she used to be bathed in water by the wives of countless sāmantas. At the birth of Harsha also the wives of the neighbouring kings came in thousands to the palace from every side. In the times of trouble sāmantas helped the emperor. When Harsha entered the Vindhyan forest in search of Rājyaśrī an *aṭavi* sāmanta Vyāghraketu assisted him in finding out the whereabouts of Rājyaśrī with the help of a Śabara youth. We learn that on the advice of the pradhāna sāmantas, whose voice could not be disregarded, Rājyavardhana took food when he was afflicted with grief. If the counsel of such vassals could not be ignored in personal matters, how could it be disregarded in administrative matters which required their help and cooperation ?

Some sāmantas resided permanently in the court. The *Kādambarī* depicts a lively picture of thousands of subordinate crowned kings seated in the assembly hall of a palace—some playing dice, others practising the game of chess, and still others playing on the seven-stringed *parivādinī* lute. They talked of poems, indulged in jocular talks, solved political riddles and engaged themselves in various activities meant for entertaining themselves or the king.

FEUDAL NATURE OF KINGSHIP

Although hereditary monarchy was the familiar form of government in the seventh century, a faint hint of the pre-Gupta 'republics' was left in Kapilavastu, Buddha's birthplace, where, according to Yuan Chwang, 'each town had its own chief.' But this system seems to be more 'feudal' than 'republican' in character.

Kings of the post-Gupta times, although of smaller status (and perhaps because of this), began acquiring grandiloquent titles like Paramabhaṭṭāraka, Mahārājādhirāja, Parameśvara, Chakravartin, etc. They usually claim that their fame reached beyond the four oceans. Such a claim is made not only for paramount rulers like Harsha but also for minor rulers like Harivarman Maukhari. The Smṛtis tried to reinforce the importance of kings by likening their qualities to those of the gods. At one place Bāṇa calls Harsha the combined incarnation of all gods (*sarvadevāvatāramivaikatra*) and elsewhere even superior to Indra, Yama, Varuṇa Kubera and Jina (Buddha). However, in the *Kādambarī* he raises his voice of protest against such claims. In the *Harshacharita* Harsha has been addressed as 'Devānāṁpriya' also, but it was not his title.

Strangely the transfer of many of the duties of kings to feudal lords tended to increase autocracy of the former in personal life. That is why the inscriptions of the period are full of criticism of the evil ways of the kings which rulers like Yaśodharman, and many a Maukhari and Pushyabhūti kings, usually claim not to have followed. Among the main duties of the king were included the conquest of the neighbouring states, protection of the people and the preservation of the varṇa system.

In the feudal polity the success of a king depended largely upon his personal ability and his devotion to work. Therefore, kings like Harsha worked dedicatedly. Yuan Chwang refers to the busy daily routine of Harsha and his tours of inspection. He says :

> He was just in his administration, and punctilious in the discharge of his duties. He forgot sleep and food in his devotion to good works. ... The king also made visits of inspection throughout his dominion, not residing long at any place but having temporary buildings erected for his residence at each place of sojourn, and he did not go abroad during the three months of the Rain-season Retreat. ... The king's day was divided into three periods, of which one was given up to affairs of government, and two were devoted to religious works. He was indefatigable, and the day was too short for him.[37]

In the seventh century Yuan Chwang found kings belonging to all the four castes. Apart from Kshatriya kings there were Brāhmaṇa kings in central India, kings of Vaiśya caste in Kanauj and Pārayātra and of Śūdra caste in Sindh and some other states. He states :

> The sovereignty for many successive generations has been exercised only by Kshatriyas : rebellion and regicide have occasionally arisen, other castes assuming the distinction.[38]

Thus, Yuan Chwang apparently thought that the sovereign *de jure* was

[37] T. Watters, *On Yuan Chwang's Travels in India*, Vol. I (hereafter *Travels*), Delhi, 1961, pp. 343-44; Shankar Goyal, *Harsha : A Multidisciplinary Political Study*, p. 282; idem, *The Significance of Yuan Chwang in the Context of the Seventh Century : A Critical Assessment*, Delhi, 2018, p. 21.

[38] *Ibid.*, p. 170; for further details, also see J.S. Grewal, 'Hiuen Tsiang's India', in *India—Studies in the History of an Idea*, ed. Irfan Habib, New Delhi, 2005, pp. 64 ff.;

usually of the Kshatriya caste, and it was that caste alone which could lawfully produce a king, but there were instances of men of other castes raising themselves to the throne.

The succession to kingship was generally regulated according to the law of primogeniture but the reigning king had the privilege to nominate his successor who could be different from his eldest son.[39] Sometimes ministers played some role in the selection of the next king.[40] In case a king died childless he was usually succeeded by his younger brother. In the Maitraka dynasty succession of younger brother was a normal feature. Females had no place in the order of succession. Only Suvarṇagotra is said to have been ruled by females. The females did not play much role in the administration also. Rājyaśrī's importance in Kanauj was caused by exceptional circumstances. There is also no indication whatever that she had any say in the administration. In the *Kādambarī* and the Haraha inscription there is reference to the coronation of the crown-prince (*yauvarājyābhisheka*). Chief-queens were also honoured with *Mahādevīpaṭṭabandhasatkāra*.

Harsha was fond of pomp and show and occasionally indulged in the vagaries of a king. He was ambitious and clever and conducted his diplomatic relations shrewdly. His reign was characterised by a clever application of existing values and concepts rather than by bold and imaginatives handling of the changing social and political milieu.

FEUDAL-FEDERAL NATURE OF THE EMPIRE

The lesser kings called Mahārājas and Rājās owed allegiance to the emperor under different terms of agreement. Some were required to offer complete submission, others were installed in suitable government posts as the direct employees of the central authority and yet others were expected to offer valuable gifts and military, political and/or economic services. The sovereign based his demands on the needs of the empire as well as on the relative strength of the subordinate allies.

As we have shown elsewhere,[41] Harsha's subordinate kings may be classified into several broad categories. Even within each category individual

---

Shankar Goyal, 'Caste System as Reflected in the Works of Bāṇa and Yuan Chwang', in the *Proceedings of the Papers from the Aligarh Historians Society*, ed. Irfan Habib, 71st Session, Indian History Congress, Gaur Banga University, Malda, 11-13 February, 2011, pp. 124 ff.; idem, *The Significance of Yuan Chwang in the Context of the Seventh Century : A Critical Assessment*, p. 50.

[39] G. P. Sinha, *Post-Gupta Polity (500-750 A.D.)*, Calcutta, 1972, pp. 3 ff.

[40] For Harsha's acquisition of Kanauj sovereignty, cf. Shankar Goyal, *Harsha : A Multidisciplinary Political Study*, pp. 182-88.

[41] *Ibid.*, pp. 211-24.

rulers were bound with the central authority in a specific relationship. With Gujarat, probably the most honoured of the subordinate states, there was a matrimonial alliance. Udita, the ruler of Jālandhara in Punjab, held a ministerial office as well. The central Indian and Rajasthan rulers may have been only nominally under Harsha's suzerainty while the non-aryan *aṭavi* sāmantas of the Vindhya forests, loyal but internally autonomous, were obviously bound by a different kind of relationship. The Chinese sources record the presence of twenty important kings on a state occasion presided over by Harsha.The large number of feudatory states that had sprung up after the decline of the Guptas, had by now mostly been overpowered by Harsha but he had to allow their rulers to retain their titles and had to remain content in most cases with only a show of submission on their part.

MINISTERS AND OTHER DIGNITARIES

The administrative structure of Harsha's empire was highly feudalized. It seems that he himself began to bestow the titles of *mahāsāmanta, sāmanta*, etc. to honour some of the higher state employees to bring them on a level with those who were previously autonomous feudatories but after submission had been appointed to suitable government posts. Some of the courtiers are also called sāmantas.

As the title *sāmanta* was closely associated with land, Harsha seems to have paid at least some of his *sāmanta* employees by allocating to them the revenue and other benefits accruing from pieces of cultivated land. In times of weak central control such officials or dignitaries might begin to regard themselves as owners of the land. But if the monarch had any strength he could displace the wayward *sāmantas*. There were other *sāmantas*, however, who were paid directly by the treasury.

Those *sāmantas* or *mahāsāmantas*, who were not part of the civil service but continued to look after their territories as glorified governors, after submitting to the emperor probably paid the bulk of their land revenue annually, or upon every harvest, into the state treasury. But those *mahāsāmantas* and *mahārājas*, who were subservient to Harsha in the capacity of inferior allies, probably paid tribute at intervals in the form of wealth and facilities they could provide and the centre needed most, presumably in accordance with their treaty obligations. In times of war they certainly helped the emperor with their armies as the testimony of Yuan Chwang and of the Aihole inscription in connection with Harsha-Pulakeśin war proves.

The council of ministers generally known as the *Mantriparishad* may have consisted of some heads of departments along with those who acted solely as counsellors. Traditionally about twelve in number, they could have been of any religious persuasion and probably could belong to any *varṇa* from Brāhmaṇa to Śūdra. The *Mahābhārata* recommends the inclusion of all classes in the cabinet and specifies their respective numbers. According to Yuan Chwang, the ministers of Kanauj were asked by Po-ni to consider his advice to request Harsha to ascend the Kanauj throne. Yuan Chwang also informs us that Rājyavardhana lost his life because of the fault of his ministers.

From their titles it appears to have been common practice for the ministers to possess military qualifications in addition to administrative ones, though in some cases these titles may be purely decorative honours. According to Bāṇa, Bhaṇḍi led the army in the absence of Harsha but Yuan Chwang calls Po-ni a minister. In the *Harshacharita* Skandagupta is the commander of elephant wing of the army but in the Banskhera inscription he figures as Dūtaka Mahāprāmātāra. In the *Harshacharita* he also advises Harsha.

A designation that often appears in ancient records is that of Kumārāmātya which sometimes may have been a title of honour but more often than not appears to have carried some administrative responsibilities. Some of the *kumārāmātyas* figure as district or provincial functionaries, others as members of the central secretariat. Some of the highest government officers, such as the minister of interstate relations, were selected from among the *kumārāmātyas*. In modern times one finds a parallel in the Indian Civil Service.[42]

The most important diplomatic office was held by the minister of interstate relations, the *Mahāsandhivigrahādhikṛta*, literally, the great officer in charge of alliances and hostilities. No doubt he was an official of cabinet rank. Avanti was the occupant of this office when the *Harshacharita* was composed. The use of the word *mahā* in his title proves the existence of lower officers with the title *sandhivigrahā-dhikṛta*. Another functionary who is mentioned in the *Harshacharita* is the *Mahāpratihāra*, who was in charge of court procedure and of arranging royal audiences. In this work *pratihāras* of different ranks, of whom *dauvārika* was perhaps the most important, manned the royal palace consisting of an outer and an inner court. He accommodated feudatories and visitors waiting to be ushered into the king's presence. The palace consisted of four sections three of which were for public audience. An inner chamber was meant for special and more confidential meetings. Beyond that stood the double storeyed white palace.

[42] Cf. K.K. Thaplyal, 'Kumārāmātya—A Reappraisal', in *Reappraising Gupta History for S.R. Goyal*, eds. B. Ch. Chhabra, P.K. Agrawala, Ashvini Agrawal and Shankar Goyal, New Delhi, 1992, pp. 224-31.

Various other officers manned the private quarters of the royal household along with the *pratihāras*. There were separate quarters for the queens (*antaḥpura*) and princesses (*kanyā-antaḥpura*).

The king not only had a council of ministers but also a large secretariat consisting of varous departments such as those for revenue, public welfare, interstate relations, army and so forth. A general coordinator known as *Sarvādhyaksha* is known from south Indian inscriptions, whose duty was to despatch orders from the centre to the provincial and district officers. According to Yuan Chwang, there were separate custodians for maintaining official annals and state papers collectively called *nīla-piṭa*.

In the days of Harsha *purohitas* had lost much of their importance. But their presence, along with that of the astrologers etc., was needed for the performance of rituals and also on auspicious occasions.

There is ample evidence to show that the department of religion and social welfare was very active in Harsha's administrative system but we come across little nomenclature in this connection. The *pramātāra* mentioned in Harsha's inscriptions appears to have been connected with the legal aspect of land donation. Officers permanently employed for the purpose must have looked after the establishment and maintenance of free boarding, lodging and medical facilities along the highways for travellers and poor people, while regular employees would have arranged the frequently mentioned debates, assemblies, entertainments and so forth. Yuan Chwang also records the appointment of an inspector for Buddhist affairs by Harsha.

ADMINISTRATIVE UNITS

Harsha's empire was divided into administrative units of different sizes. Yuan Chwang usually mentions the dimensions of the seventy 'countries' he visited in India, but often in 'circuits', a method quite unhelpful in determining the area of the 'country' in question. Some of them were very large, other quite small. Harsha's inscriptions mention the traditional *grāma* (village), *vishaya* and *bhukti* but not the *deśa* of the imperial Gupta epigraphs, although the division may have existed in his time.[43] Anyway, in the Gupta period also *deśa* was more or less synonym for *bhukti*. *Pathaka*, a classification between the first two, occurs in Harsha's Banskhera plate and in some near contemporary epigraphs but not in those of the imperial Guptas.[44] The modern districts or commissioner's divisions and provinces may be considered the present-day counterparts respectively of the *vishaya* and the *bhukti* with regard to size. Some of the bhuktis were Tīrabhukti, Puṇḍravardhanabhukti,

[43] G.P. Sinha, *op. cit.*, p. 72.

[44] It is not mentioned in Harsha's Madhuban and Kurukshetra-Varanasi records also. However, it occurs in the Valabhī epigraphs.

Nogāvābhukti, Nagarabhukti, Vardhamānabhukti, Śrāvastībhukti, Ahichchhatrābhukti, etc. Sometimes the term *bhoga* also occurs as a territorial unit.[45] It was quite usually headed by a *bhogika* (the *bhogapati* of the *Harshacharita*). The governor of the *bhukti* was a nominee of the king. Sometimes he is designated *uparika* and is honoured by titles such as *mahārāja* and *rājasthānīya*. Rājasthānīya literally meant viceroy (one who functions as a king in place of the latter). He appointed the *vishayapatis*, sometimes styled as *kumārāmātyas*. *Pathaka* was probably equivalent to modern paraganas. Grāma was the smallest territorial unit. The village headman, *grāmeyaka* or *grāmādhyaksha*, though does not find mention in the inscriptions of the period, must have existed. He probably secured his office on the strength of heredity, informal village opinion and government approval. In the *Harshacharita* village *mahattaras* and *agrahārikas* come to request Harsha not to let their fields damaged by his army.

The village headmen worked in cooperation with a group of local representatives. A large number of their seals have been unearthed. The villages had their own local courts of justice, the *pañchāyata*. The *Harsha-charita* refers to the *pañchakula*, probably in this sense. The rule of high appeal extended to these institutions as well.

The *bhukti* and *vishaya* offices were called respectively *adhikaraṇa* and *adhishṭhāna* and were maintained by the keepers of records, the *pustapālas*. The legal aspects of the land transactions and possibly the revenue records concerning them were supervised by the *vishaya* and *grāmāksha-paṭalas*. The latter was helped by *karaṇikas* (clerks). *Grāmākshapaṭala* was probably the counterpart of modern *paṭavārī*. The *vishayapatis* worked in co-operation with representative bodies perhaps consisting of twenty members, most important of whom were the chief banker,chief trader, chief artisan and chief scribe, leaders apparently of their respective guilds. The *vishayas* had their own law courts. Some of their seals of authority have survived. There were also special courts, fixed and mobile, for members of specific professions but appeal might be made to higher courts, as far as the king.

REVENUE SYSTEM

In the age of Harsha village was the unit of agriculture. Land was measured, and an average village might consist of one square *krośa*, also called a thousand plough tract, equivalent to approximatly 1,333 acres. Other systems of measurement also might have been prevalent. A one plough tract yielded a monthly revenue of about one silver *paṇa*.

Land revenue was the most important of the traditional eighteen kinds

[45] G.P. Sinha, *op. cit.*, pp. 68-69.

of taxes, most of which are not specified. Certain offences were punished by fines. The Maurya and Gupta records provide us with a large list of taxes and taxable commodities and enterprises which probably also applied to Harsha's times. Harsha's all the three known grants—the Banskhera, Kurukshetra-Varanasi and Madhuban inscriptions—show that in addition to land produce the village was expected to provide numerous other taxes and services. The three epigraphs mention, in identical terms, two categories of taxes— *udraṅga*, i.e. land tax,[46] and *sarvarāja-kula-bhāvya pratyāya*, i.e. 'all the dues (*pratyāya*) which were due to royalty', and then lists the following taxes:

(1) *tulyameya* (a tax levied on articles of merchandise, according to their weight and measure),[47]
(2) *bhāga* (king's share of grain),
(3) *kara* (tax in kind),[48]
(4) *bhoga* (periodical offerings),[49] and
(5) *hiraṇya* (tax in cash).

Probably village workers of some types, for example those who measured grain, sweepers, etc., perhaps because of the indispensability of their services, were exempted from taxes, but were required instead to contribute their labour without payment though only 'sparingly'. Whole cities too might be asked to donate dairy produce, soldiers, free labour, etc. in lieu of taxes.

Yuan Chwang had all praise for Indian system of taxation. He gives a few details about the fiscal matters in the general description of India :

> As the government is generous official requirements are few. Families are not registered, and individuals are not subject to forced labour contributions. Of the royal land there is a fourfold division : one part is for the expenses of government and state worship, one for the endowment of great public servants, one to reward high intellectual eminence, and one for acquiring religious merit by gifts to the various sects. Taxation being light, and forced service being sparingly used, every one keeps to his hereditary occupation and attends to his patrimony. The king's tenants

[46] C.V. Vaidya cites several epigraphic evidences in support of the view that *udraṅga* was a land tax and *uparikara* was an extra tax (*History of Mediaval Hindu India*, Vol. I, Poona, 1921, pp. 131-32). D.C. Sircar takes *udraṅga* to be the principal tax (*Indian Epigraphy*, Delhi 1965, p. 360).

[47] G. Bühler takes *tulyameya* not as a tax but as an adjective to the taxes that follow, and translates it as 'to be given according to the weight and according to measure' (*EI*, I, p. 75).

[48] D.C. Sircar suggests the possibility of *bhāga-bhoga-kara* as one compound meaning 'tax in the shape of *bhāga* and *bhoga*' (*op.cit.*, p. 394).

[49] G. Bühler translates *bhāga-bhoga* as 'share of the product enjoyed by the king' (*EI*, I, p. 75).

> pay one-sixth of the produce as rent. Tradesmen go to and fro bartering their merchandize after paying light duties at ferries and barrier stations. Those who are employed in the government service are paid according to their work. They go abroad on military service or they guard the palace; the summonses are issued according to circumstances and after proclamation of the reward the enrolment is awaited. Ministers of state and common officials all have their portion of land, and are maintained by the cities assigned to them.[50]

Though this description is somewhat idealised, yet it gives an idea of how Harsha conducted the economic affairs of his realm.

LAW AND JUSTICE

Law and justice in the age of Harsha were carried out along the well-established lines but for a few innovations. The *pramātāra*, for example, figures only in post-Gupta inscriptions. Devahuti believes that he was probably associated with law and justice and explained the Dharmaśāstra to the king.[51] Other court procedures point to a continuity of tradition. Bāṇa refers to law courts as *adhikaraṇas.* Harsha's grants use the well-known legal terminology with regard to land rights.

As the executor of justice the king was the highest court of appeal but his legislative powers were always extremely limited. Dharmaśāstra literature, custom of the land, usages of vocational groups, ratiocination, and the opinion of the learned were considered to be the sources of law. When all failed to solve the problem, the king was required to exercise his own judgment in accordance with the sources. He was, moreover, expected to be easily accessible and, as a judge, to possess restraint.

Some designations mentioned in our sources apparently describe police duties. The term *daṇḍa,* with military, judicial or police connotations, is used in the latter sense in the *Harshacharita.* The Dussādhasādhanikas were probably police officers who were expected to perform those duties which were regarded as difficult (such as arresting hardened criminals). The words *sañchāraka,* "messenger", and *sarvagataḥ,* "one who could reach anywhere", indicate the presence of a confidential courier service which kept the king informed of public opinion, criticism, etc. Many palace guards are described as daṇḍadharas, vetragrāhīs, etc. in the *Harshacharita.* Inscriptions refer to *chāṭas* and *bhaṭas* who most likely performed police duties. The *Harshacharita* mentions *chāṭa-bhaṭas* as soldiers in the vanguard of the infantry.

[50] *Travels,* I, pp. 176-77; also see D. Devahuti, ed., *The Unknown Hsüan-Tsang,* Oxford, 2001, pp. 135-36.

[51] D. Devahuti, *Harsha : A Political Study,* pp. 213-14.

In the *Harshacharita* a reference is also made to jails. Rājyaśrī was put in prison bound with iron fetters. On special occasions prisoners were released from jails before the expiry of their term. Writing about the judicial processes Yuan Chwang says :

> As the government is honestly administered and the people live together on good terms the criminal class is small. The statute law is sometimes violated and plots made against the sovereign; when the crime is brought to light the offender is imprisoned for life; he does not suffer any corporal punishment, but alive and dead he is not treated as member of the community (lit. as a man). For offences against social morality, and disloyal and unfilial conduct, the punishment is to cut off the nose, or an ear, or a hand, or a foot, or to banish the offender to another country or into the wilderness. Other offences can be atoned for by a money payment.[52]

In the *Kādambarī* Bāṇa makes a reference to *divyas* or ordeals. Somewhat differently they are also mentioned by Yuan Chwang :

> These are by water, by fire, by weighing, and by poison. In the water ordeal the accused is put in one sack and a stone in another, then the two sacks are connected and thrown into a deep stream; if the sack containing the stone floats, and the other sinks, the man's guilt is proven. The fire ordeal requires the accused to kneel and tread on hot iron, to take it in his hand and lick it; if he is innocent he is not hurt, but he is burnt if he is guilty. In the weighing ordeal the accused is weighed against a stone; and if the latter is the lighter the charge is false, if otherwise it is true. The poison ordeal requires that the right hind leg of a ram be cut off, and according to the portion assigned to the accused to eat, poisons are put into the leg, and if the man is innocent he survives, and if not the poison takes effect.[53]

MILITARY ORGANISATION AND FEUDAL ATMOSPHERE IN THE ARMY

From the *Harshacharita* it appears that the king was regarded as the supreme military authority. Only two important military titles are mentioned in Bāṇa's work. They are *Senāpati* and *Balādhikṛta*. The *Daṇḍanāyaka* figures in many contemporary inscriptions although not in those issued by Harsha. Yuan Chwang gives a few details about the military organisation of the period. He informs us that :

> The National Guard (lit. warriors) are heroes of choice valour, and, as the profession is hereditary, they become adepts in military tactics. In peace they guard the sovereign's residence, and in war they become the intrepid vanguard.
>
> The army is composed of Foot, Horse, Chariot, and Elephant soldiers. The war-elephant is covered with coat-of-mail, and his tusks are

[52] *Travels*, I, pp. 171-72.
[53] *Ibid.*, p. 172.

> provided with sharp barbs. On him rides the Commander-in-chief, who has a soldier on each side to manage the elephant. The chariot in which an officer sits is drawn by four horses, whilst infantry guard it on both sides. The infantry go lightly into action and are choice men of valour; they bear a large shield and carry a long spear; some are armed with a sword or sabre and dash to the front of the advancing line of battle. They are perfect experts with all the implements of war such as spear, shield, bow and arrow, sword, sabre & c. having been drilled in them for generations.[54]

Thus, Yuan Chwang reproduces the traditional list which includes chariots. But in fact the chariots had gone out of use even in the Gupta times and boats had become an important wing of the army (cf. *mahānau* of inscriptions). Yuan Chwang himself nowhere else refers to the chariots in the armies of contemporary kings.

All the three grants of Harsha record the presence of great boats (*mahānau*) at 'the camps of victory', located, it seems, at sites along the rivers. In addition to river boats Harsha may have possessed some sea-going vessels for strategic as well as trade purposes, operating from the ports of Bengal, Orissa and Gujarat. But we have no evidence for that. The *Harshacharita* also refers to camels in the army of Harsha. But probably they were used in courier service and as beasts of burdon and did not constitute a separate wing of the army.

Harsha had a large standing army. He increased his army from 5,000 elephants, 20,000 cavalry and 50,000 infantry to 60,000 elephants and one lac infantry.[55] Yuan Chang does not give the increased figures of cavalry. These figures may appear exaggerated but, in view of the situation of the period, may not be altogether incorrect. Yuan Chwang states that when Bhāskara came to meet Harsha he brought 20,000 elephants and 30,000 ships (actually large boats) with him. Therefore, the figure of 60,000 for Harsha's elephants may be regarded as not unduly inflated. The elephant corps appears to have received the greatest attention, perhaps because the huge beast could be used to destroy the enemy fortifications. Pulakeśin II also had an exceptionally strong elephant division. The *Harshacharita*, and to some extent the *Si-Yü-Ki*, contain most interesting information on the ingenious use of elephants in war. Bāṇa also recalls the designations of various officers connected with this wing of the army. Cavalry was not neglected. Horses of good breeds were imported from well beyond the Indian frontiers and the science of steeds was a well-developed branch of knowledge. The infantry also played an important part in the battlefield. They could wield a variety of weapons including arrows, javelins and slings, while they protected their bodies with thick unguents and shields

[54] *Ibid.*, p. 171.
[55] *Ibid.*, p. 343.

made of leather.

In the period under review sāmantas were trained in the warfare from their very childhood. On coming of age, they developed a reckless war-mania, which found vent on ceremonial occasions. At the time of Harsha's march for *digvijaya*, his feudatory kings boast:

> No obstacle save resolution do the conquests of heroes know. ... How insignificant is the distance between the Snowy Range and Gandhamādana! The land of the Turuṣkas is to the brave but a cubit. Persia is only a span. The Śaka realm but a rabbit's track. In the Pāriyātra country, incapable of returning a blow, a gentle march alone is needed. [240] The Deckhan is easily won at the price of valour. Mount Malaya is hard by the Dardura rock,...[56]

The army camp of Harsha contained all the homely comforts from tasty dishes to harems. In his *Harshacharita* Bāṇa describes in detail the large kitchens of the king and great nobles, the use of luxurious articles by them in the camp, the carriages of the high born nobles' wives and the troops of their seraglio elephants. He notes:

> Donkeys ridden by throngs of boys accompanied the march. Crowds of carts with creaking wheels occupied the trampled roads. Oxen were laden with utensils momentarily put upon them. ... Here groups of elephant men, bachelors, knaves, donkey boys, camp followers, thieves, serving men, rogues, and grooms, sated with an easily acquired meal of plentiful readily pounded remnants of grain, expressed their approval of the camp in bold boisterous jubilation. There poor unattended nobles, overwhelmed with the toil and worry of conveying their provisions upon fainting oxen provided by wretched village householders and obtained with difficulty, themselves grasped their domestic appurtenances,... Here swiftly running in a line,... were the king's hired porters, carrying... golden footstools, waterpots, cups, spittoons, and baths, pushing every one aside in irrepressible pride at being in charge of their sovereign's property with himself at hand : also bearers of kitchen appurtenances with goats attached to thongs of pig-skin, a tangle of hanging sparrows and forequarters of venison, a collection of young rabbits, potherbs, and bamboo shoots, buttermilk pots protected by wet seals on one part of their mouths which were covered with white cloths, baskets containing a chaos of fire-trays, ovens, simmering pans, spits, copper saucepans, and frying-pans.[57]

The king carried out state business even while en route to a far off destination. From the *Harshacharita* it appears that Harsha's army covered about nine miles per day. The plight of the villagers at the time of the march of Harsha's army has also been vividly described by Bāṇa:

> Here, with cries of 'The labour is ours, but when paytime comes some other rascals will appear,' village servants, set to scare on the feeble oxen

[56] *HC*, pp. 210-11.

[57] *Ibid.*, pp. 201, 207-08.

> tripping at every step, were indiscriminately badgering the whole body of nobles. There the whole country side had come in eager haste from both directions out of curiosity to see the king, and fools of grant-holders, issuing from the villages on the route and headed by aged elders with uplifted waterpots, pressed furiously near in crowds with presents of curds, molasses, candied sugar, and flowers in baskets, demanding the protection of the crops: flying before their terror of irate and savage chamberlains, they yet in spite of distance, tripping, and falling, kept their eyes fixed upon the king, bringing to light imaginary wrongs of former governors, lauding hundreds of past officials, [238] reporting ancient misdeeds of knaves. Others, contented with the appointed overseers, were bawling their eulogies:— 'The king is Dharma incarnate'; others, despondent at the plunder of their ripe grain, had come forth wives and all to bemoan their estates, and to the imminent risk of their lives, grief dismissing fear, had begun to censure their sovereign, crying 'Where's the king ?' 'What right has he to be king ?' 'What a king !' [58]

CONCLUSION

In fine, the polity in the age of Harsha seems to represent a natural sequal to the Gupta polity. However, the administrative structure of Harsha was certainly less efficient than the Gupta administration but probably much better than the administration of the subsequent periods. In the age of the Guptas Fa-hien did not face dacoit menace anywhere; in the age of Harsha Yuan Chwang was looted by them at least on two occasions. Then there is Bāṇa's reference to the plight of villagers during the march of Harsha's army. But, despite all these indications of administrative laxity, it may easily be conceded that the polity in the age of Harsha looks much better than what we see in the Rajput kingdoms of the subsequent period.

[58] *Ibid.*, pp. 208-09.

SIXTEEN

Feudalization of Education in the Age of Harsha

FEUDALIZATION OF THE BUDDHIST MONASTERIES AND HINDU TEMPLES IN THE AGE OF HARSHA

In ancient India *āśramas* or hermitages known as *gurukulas* were the seats of learning. But in the medieval period feudalization of the Buddhist monasteries and Hindu temples resulted in the institutionalisation of education. For the feudal rights enjoyed by the Nālandā Mahāvihāra in the age of Harsha himself, evidence is provided by the Chinese sources. Hui-li, the biographer of Yuan Chwang, records that the king of the country, probably the local ruler of Magadha, or Harsha himself, had remitted the revenues of about 100 villages (the number had increased to 200 by the time of I-tsing), for the endowment of the convent. Two hundred householders of these villages, day by day, contributed several hundred piculs (1 picul=133 1/8 lbs.) of ordinary rice and several hundred catties (1 catty= 160 lbs.) of butter and milk.[1] In the same way clothes, food, beds and medicines were supplied to the inmates.[2]

In the seventh century lavish endowments were made to the Nālandā Mahāvihāra by kings Pūrṇavarman—probably a Maukhari ruler, Harsha, Bhāskaravarman and probably Aṁśuvarman of Nepal.[3] Seals of two Maukhari kings and of Bhāskaravarman have been found at Nālandā. Pūrṇavarman is said to have presented to Nālandā a figure of the Buddha standing upright and made of copper, 80 feet high. He also constructed a pavilion of six stages to cover it. Harshavardhana is usually identified with the king of mid India who is mentioned by Yuan Chwang as the builder of one of the largest monasteries there. The construction of the boundary wall around the whole establishment

[1] Samuel Beal, *The Life of Hiuen-Tsiang* (hereafter *Life*), New Delhi, 1973, pp. 112-13.

[2] *Ibid.* and n.3.

[3] H. Heras, 'The Royal Patrons of the University of Nālandā', *JBORS*, XIV, 1928; Shankar Goyal, *Harsha : A Multidisciplinary Political Study*, Jodhpur, 2006, pp. 249 ff.

has also been attributed to him. The construction of a large brass monastery built by him was still going on when Yuan Chwang visited Nālandā.

The feudalization of the *vihāras* and their emergence as self-sufficient economic units tended to politicise their administration.[4] It was but natural for kings, who gave lavish grants and endowments to the monasteries (and temples), to see to it that they behaved in a proper manner. Harsha himself is said to have 'brought the brethern together for examination and discussion, giving rewards and punishments according to merit and demerit. Those brethren who kept the rules of their Order strictly and were thoroughly sound in theory and practice he "advanced to the Lion's Throne" (that is, promoted to the highest place) and from these he received religious instruction; those who, though perfect in the observance of the ceremonial code, were not learned in the past he merely honoured with formal reverence; those who neglected the ceremonial observances of the Order, and whose immoral conduct was notorious, were banished from his presence and from the country.'[5] King Kumāra of Kāmarūpa threatened Śīlabhadra, the Head of the Nālandā Mahāvihāra, that he would demolish the institution in case his request for despatching Yuan Chwang was not complied with. In Kashmir also, the ruler of that kingdom is seen appointing some score of monks headed by Bhadanta Yaśa from among the monks to help Yuan Chwang when the latter stayed there.[6] Incidentally, in China also the government kept strict control over the Buddhist Church as is evident from the account of Yuan Chwang's life after his return from India.

The transformation of the organisation of the Buddhist monasteries on feudal lines changed the pattern of the Buddhist education. In earlier periods education in monasteries was intended for monks and nuns only. However, with the feudalization of the monastic life and economy, the monasteries emerged as great organised or corporate centres of higher learning where education was imparted not only to the monks and nuns but to the general public also. In the age of Harsha Nālandā Mahāvihāra was the foremost of such institutions. The emergence of the Brāhmaṇical *agrahāra* villages and temples as centres of learning was the Hindu counterpart of the feudalization of educational system. The early medieval temple colleges at Salotgi, Ennariram, Tirumukkuda, Tiruvorriyur, Malakapuram and at many other places and also the Kadiyur Agrahāra, the Sarvajñapura Agrahāra, etc., were big corporate educational institutions which had their own land and buildings,

[4] Cf. S.R. Goyal, *Harsha and Buddhism*, Meerut, 1986, pp. 133-35; Shankar Goyal, *op.cit.*, pp. 250-51.

[5] T. Watters, *On Yuan Chwang's Travels in India* (henceforth *Travels*), I, Delhi, 1961, p. 344.

[6] *Life*, p. 69.

paid regular salaries to their teachers and sometimes even gave maintenance allowance to students. They could not come into existence without the feudal land grants and endowments. The tradition of these temples and *agrahāras* was continued by the *maṭhas* of the early medieval āchāryas. The feudalized Buddhist monasteries of the Gupta and post-Gupta periods, specially of the age of Harsha may, therefore, be regarded as the forerunners of the later-day corporate educational institutions.[7]

THE GLORY THAT WAS NĀLANDĀ

Leave aside the discussion on the feudalization of the Buddhist monasteries and Hindu temples in the age of Harsha, education was unquestionably widespread and scholarly life was alive. Yuan Chwang's visit, aimed at accumulating Buddhist learning, which involved studies not only in religion but also in grammar, logic, epistemology, and certain sciences, is itself a proof of it. Apart from Nālandā, in northern India, Kashmir, Valabhī and Banaras were the great centres of learning in Yuan Chwang's time, with many lesser ones no doubt, such as, Kanauj, Prayāga, Jālandhara, etc., connected with state and religious activities. But, apparently, the Chinese pilgrim's detailed account of the Nālandā establishment throws much light on various aspects of education in India.[8] Young men, he states, were educated in the *śāstras* of 'the five sciences' : grammar, the arts and mechanics, the medical lore, ethics, and the science of 'the interior'. The Brāhmaṇas studied the four Vedas which, as given by Yuan Chwang, do not exactly represent the real four Vedas. The first, he tells us, related to the preservation of life and the regulation of the natural condition. The second related to the rules of sacrifice and prayer. The third related to decorum, casting of lots, military affairs, and army regulations. The fourth related to the different branches of science, incantations, and medicine. Efficient teachers taught these works to young people. There were some who remained aloof from society and searched for wisdom, relying on their own resources.[9] Constant vigilance and a spirit of enquiry and doubt on the disciple's part appear to have been as important a requirement as regard and veneration for the teacher.[10] The curriculum at Nālandā comprised Buddhist and Hindu religious and secular subjects and is probably indicative of the general practice at such establishments over a very long period of time

[7] Shankar Goyal, *The Significance of Yuan Chwang in the Context of the Seventh Century : A Critical Assessment*, Delhi, 2018, p.81.

[8] *Life*, pp. 110-12; *Travels*, II, pp. 164 ff.; Samuel Beal, *Si-Yü-Ki* or *Buddhist Records of the Western World* (hereafter *Records*), II, Delhi, 1969, pp. 102 ff.

[9] *Records*, I, pp. 77-80; *Travels*, I, pp. 154-61.

[10] *Records*, I, p. 79; II, pp. 170-71; *Travels*, I, p. 160; II, p. 165; *Mahāvagga*, i. 25. 20, and i. 36.12.

in ancient India.[11]

But of all the establishments in the age of Yuan Chwang Nālandā was "the most celebrated seat" of moral and intellectual endeavour and a radiating nucleus of Buddhist culture and thought. It was a university in the real sense of the term and it welcomed all who flocked to it from all parts of the country and the world. When Yuan Chwang visited the university it was at the height of its glory. There he lived for five years and provided us with an elaborate picture of the glory that was Nālandā. He tells us that only those "who were deeply versed in old and modern learning" succeeded in getting admission. Out of ten applicants two or three were admitted.[12] In spite of such severe test the number of students was ten thousand which speaks of the importance of Nālandā as a great seat of learning. The number of learned priests and scholars was very huge. There were one thousand teachers who could explain "twenty collections of *sūtras* and *śāstras*"; five hundred could explain thirty collections; and the learned priests had mastered fifty collections. The teachers were the "men of great ability and learning" and "they were looked upon as the models" all over India.[13] They followed a very strict code of conduct and engaged themselves in learning and discussion. They were "very strict in observing the precepts and regulations of the Order."[14] The chief priest Śīlabhadra had studied all the *śāstras* and could explain everything. The pilgrim was highly impressed when he met him, a man of encyclopaedic learning, and "whose perfect excellence was buried in obscurity."[15] Śīlabhadra was born in the Brāhmaṇical royal family of Samataṭa. He had travelled far and wide in quest of knowledge. During his itinerancy he came to Nālandā where he met Dharmapāla who ordained him as a *bhikshu*. It was here at Nālandā he rose to prominence for "his profound comprehension of the principles and subtleties of Buddhism."[16] Yuan Chwang states that some of the distinguished scholars were associated with Nālandā, who "had kept up the lustre of the establishment and continued its guiding work." Of them he mentions Dharmapāla, Chandrapāla, Guṇamati, Sthirmati, Prabhāmitra, Jinamitra, and Jñanachandra for their "merit and learning" and they were the "authors of several treatises

[11] *Life*, p. 112; *Records*, I, pp. 78-79; *Travels*, I, pp. 154-60; *Harshacharita*, text, ed. Kasinath Pandurang Parab, 5th edn., Bombay, 1925, pp. 236-37; tr. E.B. Cowell and F.W. Thomas, Delhi, 1968, p. 236; J.A. Takakusu, *A Record of the Buddhistic Religion as Practised in India and Malaya Archipelago (A.D. 671-695) by I-tsing*, Delhi, 1966, pp. 176-77; also see, H.D. Sankalia, *The University of Nālandā*, Madras, 1934.

[12] *Travels*, II, p. 165; *Records*, II, p. 170.

[13] *Ibid.*

[14] *Ibid.*

[15] *Ibid.*

[16] *Ibid.*, p. 109.

widely known and highly valued by contemporaries."[17] Whatever Yuan Chwang speaks of Nālandā is also confirmed by I-tsing[18] who studied there for a considerably longer period. The excavations at Nālandā further bear true witness to its magnificence and glory as a great seat of learning in the seventh century A.D.

YUAN CHWANG ON LANGUAGE AND SCRIPT IN INDIA

Yuan Chwang tended to presume that there was only one language and one script in India but his own evidence points to regional variations in both the language and script. He describes the Indian script as consisting of forty-seven letters. This alphabet had spread in different directions and formed diverse branches. Mid India preserved the original character of the language in its integrity. Concerned only with Sanskrit, the language of the educated, he seems not to have taken interest in the spoken languages of the people. But he does talk of 'dialects'. In Utkal, the words used by the people, and their pronunciation, were different from what he found in central India. The pronunciation of words in mid India was clear and pure, and fit as a model for all. In Andhra too, the language and arrangement of sentences differed from those of mid India. The people of the frontiers had contracted many incorrect modes of pronunciation.[19]

[17] *Ibid.*, p. 165.

[18] J.A. Takakusu, *op.cit.*, pp. 65, 154, 167.

[19] J.S. Grewal, 'Hiuen Tsiang's India', in *India—Studies in the History of an Idea*, ed. Irfan Habib, New Delhi, 2005, p. 67.

SEVENTEEN

The 'Medieval' Factor in Indian Art

NATURE OF THE GUPTA CLASSICISM

It is almost a general conviction that the establishment of the Gupta empire, particularly over greater part of north India, facilitated "the efflorescence of Indian genius in all its aspects" fostered by "the resurgence of a conscious national ideal."[1] That is why the art of the Gupta period is referred to as the 'classical art' of India and the Gupta age is called the classical or golden age of Indian history. The term 'classical' usually means 'of the first rank or authority', 'an age in which literature, architecture and fine arts reach a high level of excellence to form a standard or model for later times'.[2] This assertion can be precisely applied to the Gupta age. It cannot be denied that in some spheres of culture—religion, philosophy, literature, sculpture, coinage, etc. the Gupta age was indeed the classical epoch of our history, at least in the north,[3] since in the Deccan and south India it was the post-Gupta period that saw the evolution of a high level of civilization.[4] The Gupta art is 'classical' because of its intrinsic quality of high order, which was shared throughout the country but was never parallelled earlier or later, and which, serving as a veritable index, helps us appreciate the nature of achievements accruing to anterior or posterior artistic

[1] S. K. Saraswati, *A Survey of Indian Sculpture*, Calcutta, 1957, p. 120.

[2] Cf. Romila Thapar, *A History of India*, Vol. I, Harmondsworth, Penguin, 1966, p. 157.

[3] Romila Thapar (*op.cit.*, p. 137) and recently S.R. Goyal ('The Myth of the Golden Bird : An Investigation into the Belief of Material Opulence of Ancient and Early Medieval India in the Light of Her Gold Coinage', his Presidential Address delivered to the 90th Annual Conference of the Numismatic Society of India at Santiniketan on December 1-3, 2006, *JNSI*, Vol. LXIX, Pts. i and ii, 2007, p.15) have restricted the classicism of the Gupta period to northern India alone.

[4] Romila Thapar, *op. cit.*

practices in the country.[5] Kālidāsa, the greatest poet-dramatist of the age, describes the art of the period as 'fine art' (*lalita-kalā*).[6] It reflected a passion for refinement that was obvious in every aspect of life; "it eliminated ponderousness and volume and concentrated more and more on elegance, producing ultimately a surpassing grace and delicacy which distinguish Gupta work from that of all other ages."[7]

Apart from acute passion for refinement the Gupta art, specially sculpture, was characterized by several other features. Firstly, in the Gupta sculpture human figures are not merely a manifestation, rather the representation of Nature with all its grandeur. "The Gupta sculptor used the human figure as the vehicle for the transmutation of Nature into art." Naturally, therefore, his main concern was the human figure and how to make the various features of its form relevant to what exists in the vegetal and animal worlds; in other words, in Nature at large. In fact, the articulation of all natural phenomena in terms of the human figure was the basic artistic proposition before the Gupta sculptor, whereas the sculptors of Bharhut and Sāñchī were content with representing the human figure as a complement of flora and fauna.

Secondly, Gupta sculpture is, more consciously and explicitly than most schools of plastic art, a synthesis between the external form and the inner meaning, like the Kālidāsian imagery of the union of Speech and Thought (*vāg-artha-viva saṁpṛktau*).[8] According to V.S. Agrawala,[9] the introvert vision underlying the outer forms of Gupta art is writ eloquently in the faces of the Buddhist and Brāhmaṇical images, which combine an intense religious feeling with a tranquil and classical charm. Only such an expression can represent the achievement of a true harmony of thought and action in the actual lives of men. In accordance with this new outlook, each seeker looked for reality within himself. The spiritual content of the Gupta Buddha image is sharply distinguished from the open, smiling countenance of the Kushāṇa Bodhisattva. The art creations of the golden age are expressions of the spiritual harmony and blissful realization that were the hallmark of the superior motifs of thought and life comprised in the Gupta culture.

[5] D.C. Bhattacharyya, in R.C. Majumdar and K.K. Dasgupta (eds.), *A Comprehensive History of India*, Vol. III, Pt. II, New Delhi, 1982, p. 1173. For a discussion on the classicism of the Gupta age see B. Ch. Chhabra, P. K. Agrawala, Ashvini Agrawal and Shankar Goyal (eds.), *Reappraising Gupta History for S. R. Goyal*, New Delhi, 1992; S.R. Goyal and Shankar Goyal (eds.), *Indian Art of the Gupta Age*, Jodhpur, 2000.

[6] *Raghuvaṁśa*, VIII. 67.

[7] V.S. Agrawala, *Studies in Indian Art*, Varanasi, 1965, p. 245.

[8] *Raghuvaṁśa*, I.1.

[9] V.S. Agrawala, *op.cit.*

"The ideal of Gupta culture was harmony and synthesis. ...This attitude so widely reflected in literature and religion exercised a very wholesome effect in the realm of art. On the one hand, it invokes beauty with all its perfection of physical form and ornamental and decorative make-up, and on the other, it pays full homage to the ideal of spiritual realisation as seen in the figures of Śiva, Vishṇu, Buddha, Bodhisattva, etc. ...Serenity, repose, calmness, joy, unruffled fixity of the mind, control over the objects of senses, perfect knowledge, compassion, discrimination and wisdom — these are some of the great principles of life and character which the divine images make manifest. ..."[10]

Another feature of the Gupta classical art is its wide geographical range. "From Dahparbatiyā in Assam to Mīrpurkhās in Sind, monuments of Gupta sculpture are scattered all over the country-side. Great centres of the art included Sārnāth, Mathurā, Pāṭaliputra, Devagarh, Bhītargaon, Udaigiri, Nāgod, Bhumarā, Ajantā, and the Gandhāra province, where a great mass of remarkable sculpture, in stone and in stucco or baked clay, was produced. Outside India, the school exercised far-reaching influence on the art of China and the Far-East, moulding them into something of an all-Asian pattern."[11] Elsewhere, the same scholar states that the Gupta art not only filled the entire country from one end to the other, but also inundated the surrounding regions in a peripheral overflow. It was truly a nation-wide movement in the sphere of art with many a centre functioning in each direction and each region displaying a spontaneous exuberance. Wheresoever the Bhāgavata religion spread its benign influence backed by an impassioned literary appeal, art monuments sprang up in its train as visible reflectors of the popular surcharge. The influence of the art of Madhyadeśa is patent in every detail of sculpture and architecture, whether the monument was raised in the east or in the west.[12] What was achieved in the Gupta age at Mathurā and Sārnāth did not remain confined to these two places alone. The experience gained at these centres was presumably shared by various other places throughout India, and all the regions naturally produced sculptures which qualitatively approximated the creations of the Madhyadeśa. Thus, in the classical Gupta art all parts of India shared some basic norms and forms. Local preferences did exist, but there was hardly any symptoms of assertive tendency on their part. Moreover, these elements of regional moods were well integrated in the art form in such a way that the product did seldom lose its homogeneity. This was because of the existence,

[10] *Ibid.*, p. 208.
[11] *Ibid.*, p. 248.
[12] *Ibid.*, p. 202.

during that period, of an overall political, and as such cultural, authority in operation throughout the country.

The Gupta sculpture is usually found integrated with the architecture of structural temples and cave-shrines. In the Kushāṇa period the image was predominant and the modest shrine was only just beginning to appear. It more or less resembled the form of a *gandha-kuṭī* improvised with three plain slabs held in position by a flat top from which the temple art seems to have evolved.[13] In the Gupta period the image of the deity, now fully evolved, found its counterpart in a fully evolved temple with flat roof, porch and plinth. The two match admirably. Subsidiary images and reliefs of attendant figures also find their due place in the scheme of temple-decoration.[14] The stucco figures and terracottas connected with these temples show an equally high degree of workmanship. Both in stone and in modelled bricks, an infinite variety of scroll-motifs is found. The most significant example of this decoration may be seen in the casing slabs round the Dhāmekh Stūpa at Sarnath, perhaps the most successful example of large surface-decoration in this technique in ancient India. Contemporary literature refers to scroll-work as *patrāvalī, patralatā, patrāṅguli*, etc.[15] The fashion for deep-cut scroll-work found its culmination in the stone *jālī*.[16]

FACTORS IN THE TRANSITION FROM CLASSICISM TO MEDIEVALISM

The question of the transition from classicism to medievalism in culture, art and history of India[17] is indeed a part of the general problem of the periodisation of Indian history. There is so far no generally agreed upon scheme of periodisation, but in view of the obvious weaknesses of other schemes, historians generally follow the European practice and divide Indian history into ancient, medieval and modern periods. But there is some confusion about the duration of the classical period within the broader limits of ancient period. Usually the age of the imperial Guptas is equated with the

[13] Cf. P.K. Agrawala, *Gupta Temple Architecture*, Varanasi, 1968, Ch. I; idem, 'Art and Architecture in the Gupta Period', in S.R. Goyal and Shankar Goyal (eds.), *op.cit.*, pp. 50-100.

[14] V. S. Agrawala, *op.cit.*, p. 248.

[15] *Ibid.*, p. 253.

[16] For a recent study of Gupta sculpture see S.N. Chaturvedi, 'Gupta Sculpture—Facets and Factors', in S.R. Goyal and Shankar Goyal (eds.), *op.cit.*, pp. 101-26.

[17] For a detailed discussion on the rise of medievalism in Indian history see Shankar Goyal, *History and Historiography of the Age of Harsha*, Jodhpur, 1992, pp. 240-72; idem, *Harsha : A Multidisciplinary Political Study*, Jodhpur, 2006, pp. 238-68; idem, *The 'Medieval' Factor and the Age of Harsha : A Cultural Study*, Jodhpur, 2016, pp. 130-46; also see below fn. 20.

classical age of India,[18] but from the cultural point of view there is no unanimity about its upper and lower limits. Its upper limit is sometimes extended to c. 750 A.D. and the lower one is so stretched as to include even the Maurya age in it. It is not surprising since in Europe also historians and chroniclers use the term 'ancient' as almost synonymous with the age of the classical Graeco-Roman civilization. We may, therefore, concede that in India also the same situation existed and that the age of the imperial Guptas marked the efflorescence and culmination of earlier tendencies many of which go back to the Maurya period and that much of its glory continued for about two centuries or more after the fall of the Gupta empire. Romila Thapar expresses a similar opinion in a recent study through her statement that "the classicism of the Gupta period is not an innovation emanating from the Gupta rule but the culmination of a process that began earlier."[19]

But what about the beginning of the medieval period? Did the ancient period end with the end of the classical age or continued right upto the establishment of the Delhi Sultanate as some historians believe? The advent of the Muslims in India is generally seen as marking the end of the ancient period, and works on ancient Indian history by eminent historians such as R.D. Banerji, R.C. Majumdar, K.A. Nilakanta Sastri and R.S. Tripathi carry its narrative roughly up to 1206 A.D. Many other dates have also been suggested with regard to the starting point for the medieval period—the establishment of the Kushāṇa dynasty (Rapson), rise of the Guptas (Marshall), 647 (V.A. Smith), 916 (H.C. Ray), and 997 (K.M. Munshi) being some of them. But to us it appears that no exact date can be fixed for

[18] Cf. K.M. Munshi, Foreword to *The Classical Age*, R.C. Majumdar and A.D. Pusalker (eds.), Bombay, 1953, pp. xiv-xv; Romila Thapar, *op. cit.*, Ch. 7; idem, 'Aśokan India and the Gupta Age', in A.L. Basham (ed.), *A Cultural History of India*, London, 1975, pp. 38,46; R.C. Majumdar (ed.), *A Comprehensive History of India*, Vol. III, Pt. I (A.D. 300-985), New Delhi, 1981, p. 105; R. N. Dandekar, in R.C. Majundar (ed.), *op.cit.*, p. 279; A. K. Narain, 'Religious Policy and Toleration in Ancient India with Particular Reference to the Gupta Age', in Bardwell L. Smith (ed.), *Essays on Gupta Culture*, Delhi, 1983, pp. 17-51; S.R. Goyal, *Gupta Sāmrājya ka Itihāsa*, Meerut, 1987, Ch. 17. *Contra* D. N. Jha, *Ancient India–An Introductory Outline*, New Delhi, 1977, pp. 96-116; idem, *Ancient India in Historical Outline*, New Delhi, 1998, pp. 149-73; idem, *Early India–A Concise History*, New Delhi, 2008, pp. 157-82; idem, *Prāchīna Bhārata, Sāmājika, Ārthika aura Sāṁskṛtika Vikāsa kī Paṛatāla*, Delhi, 2009, Ch. 8. For a criticism of Jha's formulations vide Shankar Goyal, 'A Critique of Professor D.N. Jha's Evaluation of the Classicism of the Gupta Age', in B. Ch. Chhabra et al (eds.), *op.cit.*, pp. 61-73; idem, *The Image of Classical India*, Jodhpur, 1997, Ch. 3; idem, *Marxist Interpretation of Ancient Indian History*, Poona, 2000, pp. 72-88.

[19] Romila Thapar, *The Penguin History of Early India*, New Delhi, 2003, p. 281.

cultural periods. The real problem is not of the actual dates but of the determination of the period of operation of those factors and forces that impart an age its distinctive character. The operation of such factors and forces is usually slow and overlapping, for some of them emerge somewhat late, some fade away earlier than others and some continue to operate quite late in the next period. A cultural trend might have had a long history before it finally emerges in a definite form and likewise might continue to exist in a diluted or changed form for sometime even after it apparently ceased to exist. That being so, one cannot hope to have fixed dates in the periodisation of history; one can only try to determine the main period of operation of those tendencies which differentiate an epoch from the preceding and succeeding ones. Processes of transition in polity, society, economy, art and culture take long to fructify and cannot be associated with a fixed date. All that we can do is to try to find out whether and when these processes converged at some point of time.[20]

In India the transformation of the classical heritage into medieval culture did not take place all at once. It was brought about slowly in the course of several centuries intervening the decline of the Gupta empire and the establishment of the Delhi Sultanate. That is why the culture of this period, specially in the two post-Gupta centuries, on the one hand, seems to have much in common with the classical culture of the Guptas and, on the other, appears to be nearer to the culture of the Sultanate period with the difference that in the post-Gupta centuries, unlike the Sultanate period, the Muslims were not the dominant political power in northern India. We, therefore, believe that the beginning of the medieval period in Indian history may broadly be traced from the fall of the Gupta empire itself, though it may be readily conceded that the period of about two centuries, roughly from the fall of the Gupta empire (550 A.D.) to the rise of the Pratihāras (c. 750 A.D.) sheds light on the classical and medieval periods both, by a sort of *dehalī-dīpaka-nyāya* (the maxim that a lamp placed on the threshold illumines both the inside and outside of a room) and thus belongs to both.

[20] Cf. R. S. Sharma, 'Problem of Transition from Ancient to Medieval in Indian History', in *IHR*, March 1974, Vol. I, No. 1, p.1; idem, *Perspectives in Social and Economic History of Early India*, New Delhi, 1983, Ch. XVI; idem, *Early Medieval Indian Society : A Study in Feudalisation*, Kolkata, 2001, Ch.1; cf. also N.R. Ray, 'The 'Medieval' Factor in Indian History', being his Address as the General President of the Twenty-ninth Session of the Indian History Congress, Patiala, 1967, pp. 1-42; V. K. Thakur, 'Transition from the Ancient to the Medieval Period', in D. Devahuti (ed.), *Problems of Indian Historiography*, Delhi, 1979, pp. 79-82; B.N.S. Yadava, 'The Accounts of the Kali Age and the Social Transition from Antiquity to the Middle Ages', in D.N. Jha (ed.), *Feudal Social Formation in Early India*, Delhi, 1987, pp. 65-112; Shankar Goyal, *The 'Medieval' Factor and the Age of Harsha*, Jodhpur, 2016, pp. 1-24; also see above fn. 17.

In Europe one of the main factors that led to the transition from classical to middle ages was the immigration and invasions of the barbarian nomads. On the one hand, it resulted in the barbarization of the classical culture and, on the other, imparted a new vigour to the European society. The immediate consequence of the nomadic pressure, culminating with that of the Huns, was the breaking up of the Roman empire. With this began the process that slowly resulted in the formation of the regional kingdoms of the Franks, Germans, Lombards, Slavs, Normans, etc. in the early medieval period. The role of the central Asian nomads and other foreign invaders in Indian history, in the centuries preceding and following the fall of the Gupta empire, was almost similar.

As in Europe, the pressure of the foreign tribes not only shattered the imperial fabric of India, it also corrupted her classical values, modified her social and economic institutions and generated a sense of pessimism leading to the theory of social decline in the Kali Age which the post-Gupta literature and epigraphs so vividly describe. On the positive side, the arrival of the foreign tribes imparted a new vigour and vitality to the Indian society, just as the Germanic tribes had done in the decadent Rome. In this connection the effeminate and irreligious character of the kings of the sixth century A.D., who have been so roundly denounced by Yaśodharman of Malwa (known date 532 A.D.), with vigour and vitality of the Gurjara-Pratihāras of Kanauj offers an interesting comparison. Indeed, the age of the imperial Gurjara-Pratihāras has been compared with the period of the Carolingian Renaissance of the medieval Europe. As a matter of fact, not only the Gurjara-Pratihāras but several other Rajput dynasties contained Scythian, Hūṇa or Gurjara blood in their veins though many of them, in course of time, became mixed up with the indigenous people, specially Brāhmaṇas (who, as a result of the growing feudal tendencies, were emerging as one of the most important elements of the ruling aristocracy of the country) and the ancient republican tribes of the Punjab and Rajasthan (which had lost political power only recently in the Gupta age) and probably also the aboriginal tribes of Rajasthan, Bundelkhand, etc. (which, when Hinduized, were readily accepted within the pale of the orthodox society).

Other main factors that played a significant role in the transformation of the classical society in Europe as well as India were feudalism and regionalism. As in the early medieval Europe, in India also the rise and growth of feudalism in the post-Gupta age was concomitant and connected with the growth of regional tendencies in life.[21] To some extent foreign tribes

[21] We, however, believe that it was the Gupta age itself that witnessed strong feudalization of the state apparatus which was not found earlier. In a recently delivered paper in the panel on the Economic Change in Indian History organized by the Aligarh

which established their own cultural zones (such as the Gurjaradeśa) and feudal system (which thrived on the localization of industries, emphasis on agrarian economy and decline of trade and commerce) stimulated this tendency. In the classical age the farflung corners of the country were linked up through a network of roads and rivers and traders moved from one part of the country to another and also to foreign lands. Consequently, regionalism and insularity were cut across by the hook up of regional economy with the national economic structure. But in the post-classical period the absence of a centralized authority increased localism and insularity in economic life.

The formation of regional cultural units such as Andhra, Assam, Bengal, Gujarat, Karnataka, Kerala, Maharashtra, Orissa, Rajasthan, Tamilnadu, etc. and the emergence of regional languages and literatures started from sixth-seventh centuries. Faint beginnings of regional and cultural personality-consciousness are found in other parts of the country also. Bengal was divided into two main units, Gauḍa and Vaṅga, and later the whole region was named after Vaṅga. Yuan Chwang mentions several nationalities. The *Mudrārākshasa* of Viśākhadatta speaks of different regions whose inhabitants differed in customs, clothing and language while the *Kuvalayamālā* (eighth century) notes the existence of 18 major nationalities and describes the anthropological character of 16 peoples, pointing out their psychological features and citing the samples of their languages.

The post-classical Indian society was greatly disturbed by the new religious thought-currents also. In this period, as in the classical age itself, Indian rulers generally followed the policy of religious toleration and did not confine their patronage to any one particular religion or sect. In the social sphere, the spirit of toleration manifested itself in the spirit of accommodation usually shown by the members of various sects towards each other, and in the worship of syncretic deities emphasizing the union or identity of the deities of two or more sects, though below the surface one may notice dissensions among various cults which were actually religious manifestations of the socio-economic conflicts of the time.

In the post-classical period the majority of the people of India apparently followed various sects and cults of the Paurāṇika Hinduism. The study of the Vedas and Vedic religion was still popular and the orthodox

---

Historians Society held at Delhi we have argued that the two and a half centuries of the Vākāṭaka ascendancy in parts of central India and the northern Deccan, with its non-monetary, small scale village settlements and relatively declining urban economy, also presents a *milieu* in which we find some elements of feudalism (Shankar Goyal, 'Feudal Elements in the Vākāṭaka Economy', in the *Papers from the Aligarh Historians Society*, Irfan Habib (ed.), 70th Session, Indian History Congress, Delhi University, Delhi, 15-17 May, 2010, pp. 195-219).

Hindus loved to trace all their sects to the ultimate authority of the Vedas, though the cult of sacrifice existed only as a casual accompaniment of the Paurāṇika Hinduism. The influence of Jainism was restricted to certain areas, specially Rajasthan and Gujarat, while Buddhism which was declining very fast, almost totally disappeared from the Indian scene by the close of the twelfth century.

The Paurāṇika Hinduism itself was divided into a number of cults and sects. Among them were included Śaivism, Vaishṇavism and Śāktism, not to mention a large number of minor sects and sub-sects, centring round the worship of gods like Sūrya, Gaṇeśa, Kārttikeya, Brahmā, etc. Of these, probably Śaivism was the most popular one specially among the ruling aristocracy. It had become divided into several branches — Śaiva, Pāśupata, Kāpālika, Kālāmukha, Kaula and many others. Many of these sects became monastic in character. The chief feature of Vaishṇavism of this period was the worship of the *avatāras* (incarnations of Vishṇu), specially Kṛshṇa, Rāma and Ādivarāha. Śakti or Devī was also worshipped under various names — Durgā, Kālī, Chaṇḍī, Bhairavī, etc.

The popular or conventional form of the Hindu sects was characterized by the worship of numerous deities in temples built by kings, *sāmantas* and rich people. They were endowed with grants of land, tolls and taxes. Temple- and monastery-building activities, which acquired momentum in the later Gupta age, reached their climax during the eleventh and twelfth centuries. Great temples and monasteries of this period possessed large estates and enormous wealth, with the result that the priestly class, as in medieval Europe, acquired a powerful hold over the people. Even the Jaina priestly class appears to have been organised on quasi-feudal lines.

EMERGENCE OF MEDIEVAL TRENDS IN INDIAN ART

The disintegration of the Gupta empire and the rise of feudalism, impact of foreign invaders, regionalism, insularity, growth of Smārta-Paurāṇika religion and Tāntrika tendencies were concomitant with and brought about a change of scene in the sphere of art as well.

The rise of feudalism influenced the post-Gupta art in several ways. It undermined the economic role and social status of the mercantile and commercial classes of *śreshṭhīs* (bankers) and *sārthavāhas* (caravan-leaders) and of the urban class of *nāgarakas* (cultured citizens). The economic, social and political position of the new class of *sāmantas* of varying status was strengthened. The number of feudal chiefs went on multiplying with the crystallization of feudalism after 550 A.D. The ancient religious art at Bharhut, Sāñchī, Karle, Kanheri, Junnar, Amarāvatī, Nāgārjunīkoṇḍa, etc., was patronized mainly by the mercantile and commercial classes, artisan and craft guilds as well as the royal families. But the art of the period from c. 550 A.D. onwards was supported mainly by the kings of different principalities, feudatories, military chiefs, etc., who alone usually could own and donate land to religious institutions.

Art in the Gupta period, when feudal tendencies had just begun to appear, reflected the vitality and zest of revived Brāhmaṇism which was associated with the emerging socio-economic structure and supported by the rising class of patrons. In the fourth-fifth centuries Vātsyāyana made *nāgarakas* (and not *sāmantas*) the centre of his *Kāmasūtra*. But in the sixth-seventh centuries "the arts patronized by the rich (both the old commercial class and the new feudal lords) reflect aristocratic tastes in their embellishment and in the dignified countenance and elaborate coiffures of both male and female figures. The aristocratic lovers of Badami, Ajanta, Ellora, Deograh, Nachna, etc., indulging in *madhupāna* (drinking of wine) or enjoying music and dance, attended by women with *chauris* or wine-jars, certainly betray the feudal outlook of the age."[22] Commenting on the art of Ajanta, Coomaraswamy observes : "Despite its invariably religious subject-matter, this is an art of "great courts charming the mind by their noble routine"; adorned with *alaṁkāras* and well-acquainted with *bhāva-bheda*. The *Harṣacarita*, *Kādambarī*, and the works of Kālidāsa and other classic Sanskrit dramatists, and the later Ajaṇṭā paintings all reflect the same phase of luxurious aristocratic culture."[23]

The Rajput chiefs of the post-Gupta period, many of whom were Hinduized foreigners or Hinduized tribals, strove hard to glorify themselves. For being accorded a high status in the caste hierarchy they depended upon the support of the priest class, and their keenness in this regard led to the practice of extensive gifts (*dāna*) to the Brāhmaṇas. The epigraphic evidence supports the fact that the kings of the leading dynasties from the sixth century onwards performed ceremonial *dānas* such as *hiraṇyagarbha*, *shoḍasha mahādāna*, *saptasāgara mahādāna*, *dharitrīdāna* and even *brahmāṇḍadāna*. The wealth and power bestowed by them made the priests of the period greedy and lover of luxury. This psychology was in perfect consonance with and to a great degree the cause of craze for the sensual indulgence which dominated the literature and art of the period. *Pūrtadharma*, which involved the building of temples, tanks and works of public utility, was emphasized as the highest mode of religion in the Purāṇas. The importance of *pūrta* for

[22] Devangana Desai, 'Art under Feudalism in India (c. A.D. 500-1300)', *IHR*, March 1974, Vol. 1, Pt. i, p. 13.

[23] A. K. Coomaraswamy, *History of Indian and Indonesian Art*, Delhi, 1972, p. 90 and n.

the art activities of the period cannot be gainsaid. In the Upanishads *pūrta* was meant for fools who go to the lower worlds, whereas *tapas* was the highest virtue. In the Purāṇas, on the other hand, temple-building is said to be more meritorious than the performance of the Vedic sacrifices. *Pūrtadharma* was thus the dominant ideology behind the large-scale building of temples in this period. Inspired by this ideology, numerous land-owning *sāmantas*, princes and kings of the period, who wanted to acquire *puṇya* (merit) and *kīrti* (fame), built temples and donated lands and villages for their maintenance.

In the post-Gupta age architectural activity in the form of structural temples was also inspired by competition among various cults and sects nurtured by the affluence of their royal, feudal or mercantile patrons. These temples installed images of the cult icons and of the *pārśvadevatās* and the *parivāradevatās*. For this the artist's services were obtained who got praise and payment, and also future commissions, only if he did his work to the satisfaction of the patrons.

The Smārta-Paurāṇika religion of the post-Gupta age was influenced by the magical elements such as *maṇḍalas*, *yantras*, *nyāsas* and *mantras*[24] which soon became widespread through the patronage given by the kings to Tāntrikism and in the later centuries some of the Tāntrika sects, especially the Pāśupatas, were invited by the kings of various regions to settle in their kingdoms. In the fifth-seventh centuries many Brāhmaṇas received lands in Nepal, Assam, Bengal, Orissa, central India and the Deccan, where Tāntrika texts, shrines and practices appeared about this time. Tāntrikism permeated every sect and religion—Jainism, Buddhism, Śaivism and Vaishṇavism, and from the seventh century onwards continued to hold ground throughout the medieval period.[25] As a matter of fact Tāntrikism influenced the mental attitude of almost all the sects and cults of the period in varying degrees. This contributed to the esoteric character of the art as well, though esoteric elements thus introduced into art were appreciated only by a limited few who were initiated into the doctrine.

After the collapse of the Gupta empire, political disintegration gave rise to numerous petty states in north India which in turn resulted in the rise of regional schools of art. Specially in the post-650 A.D. period, when feudal tendencies were ascendant, numerous local centres of art grew up. For about a thousand years, roughly from about the third century B.C. to the end of sixth century A.D., Indian art admits, despite local variations due to local tastes, to a common denominator at each different stage of its evolution.

[24] Even the Gangadhar inscription of the first quarter of the fifth century A.D. refers to *tantra* and *ḍākinīs* (S.R. Goyal, *Guptakālīna Abhilekha*, Meerut, 1984, p. 347).

[25] Devangana Desai, *op. cit.*, p.12.

But now regional spirit began to assert itself. About the middle of the eighth century A.D., the process of regionalization seems to have been completed, and thenceforth is noticed the rise and growth of a number of 'provincial' schools of art, spread over the length and breadth of the country. The 'classical' idiom was now interpreted in terms of the varied local ethnic-cultural backgrounds. Local themes and visions predominated the art of this period, though its all-India tradition persisted. The temples at Bhubaneshwar in Orissa, Osian in Rajasthan and Aihole and Pattadakal near Dharwar indicate new experiments in the ground plans, *śikhara* designs, etc., according to regional patterns.

No longer satisfied with the flat-roofed shrines of the early Gupta period, new fashions in architecture concerned themselves with the development of the *śikharas* and *maṇḍapas*, and bold architects began to convert the entire mountain blocks into monolithic shrines resembling Kailāsa and Meru. Both royalty and the people were motivated by the same spirit. The Kailāsa temple of Ellora was the outcome of the grand conception of the Rāshṭrakūṭa emperors in the eighth century. The ideal divine abode of Śiva and Pārvatī on the mount Kailāsa was recreated on earth, as if in the form of the Kailāsa temple. Even within particular style regional variations developed. The *Nāgara* style of temple architecture, prevalent in the region between the Himalayas and the Vindhyas, developed regional variations. Such variations were caused by local conditions, different directions in development as well as assimilation of extraneous trends whenever these made themselves felt.

In the realm of sculpture and painting the post-Gupta centuries witnessed the emergence of a distinct 'medieval' trend with many regional variations. Plasticity of the fully rounded and modelled form had been the most significant characteristic of classical Indian sculpture and painting both. But now movement started towards summarizing the rounded volume in the direction of flat surface and linear angles.[26] Being essentially three dimensional, sculpture resisted for long the intrusion of this medieval trend while painting, which is essentially two dimensional, offered much less resistance. According to N.R. Ray, this medieval element was the accumulated result of a continuous ethnic fusion of northern racial elements that poured into the plains of north India from central Asia in the centuries preceding and following the fall of the Gupta empire.[27]

In sculpture the images of the post-Gupta centuries project the emotional experience and ideology of the time and place. The refined and modest conventions of the Gupta period were replaced in the early medieval

[26] N.R. Ray, *loc. cit.*

[27] *Ibid.*

age by colossal creations. Art now fulfilled its purpose by the comprehensive narration of cosmic themes taken from the life-stories of gods and demons, and by interpreting the spiritual message of the age through a significant symbolism.[28] Thus, the Tāntrika atmosphere pervades the figures of dancers in the Paraśurāmeśvara temple and the fierce forms of gods and goddesses in the Vaitāla temple at Bhubaneshwar. In the rock-cut sculptures of Ellora (seventh-eighth centuries) one finds the divinities engaged in violent struggle against their enemies. The myths narrated in the Purāṇas and the epics provide new themes.

Thus, during the early medieval period art movements in the different regions tended to separate from one another, and a dialogue between one artistic zone and the other for sharing a common artistic vision and for undertaking a journey towards a common goal was minimized. In fact, the art scene was gradually seized upon, as if by 'a sort of bankruptcy in creativity'. The art expressions tended to become more and more merely gestures without conviction, performance without feeling. Sculptural expressions tended towards non-communicability denuding the sculpture of all the qualities of excellence of the earlier periods : it lost much of the aesthetic charm and became highly mechanized. It was no longer illuminated by the spiritual experience of the sculpture and ceased to be intelligible to the people at large. Art, particularly sculptural art of this period, despite its prolific productive spree patronized by the affluent religious treasuries, failed to share the hope, aspiration and contemplation of the people in general. This amounted to the loss of the two most essential and vital characteristics of classicism, viz., the roundness of the form and its flowing linear rhythm. Consequently, now the sculptural productions tended to become more and more denuded of the essence of classicism. Of course, an uncomfortable search for a direction remained, but what emerged out of it was in no way as brilliant as what had preceded. There arose a different approach towards art which is what is referred to as the 'medieval factor' or 'medievalism' in Indian art.

[28] V.S. Agrawala, *op. cit.*, p. 257.

Genealogy and Chronology of the Imperial Guptas

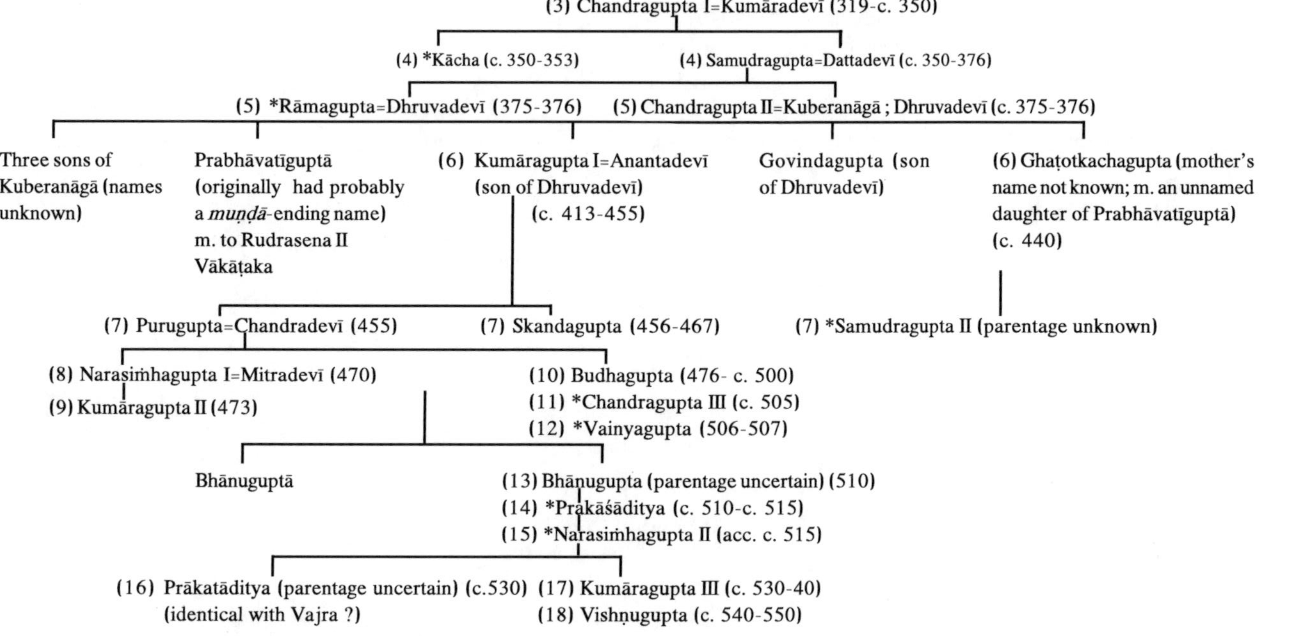

Note : The place of Bhānugupta in the genealogy of the dynastry is altogether unknown. The relation of kings whose names are marked with an asterisk with their immediate predecessor is not known from the epigraphs, but other lines of evidence make it quite reasonable to assume that the latter was the father of the former. The chronological order of a ruler is indicated by his number, but in cases where wars of succession took place and for sometime two or more princes ruled simultaneously, the same number is given to all of them.

Genealogy and Chronology of the Vākāṭakas

Vindhyaśakti I
(c. 250 to 275)
|
Pravīra *alias* Pravarasena I
(c. 275 to c. 335)
|

Gautamīputra I = d. of Bhavanāga
|
Rudrasena I
(c. 335 to 350-55)
|
Pṛthivīsheṇa I (c. 350/55 to 380/85)
|
Rudrasena II=Prabhāvatīguptā, d. of Chandragupta II
(c. 380/85 to 385/90)
|
(Yuvarāja) Divākarasena
(c.385/90 to 405/10)

Dāmodarasena
(c.405/10 to 410/15)

Pravarasena II = Ājñākabhaṭṭārikā
(c.410/15 to 445-50)
|
Narendrasena = Ajjhitabhaṭṭārikā
(c.445/50 to 470/75)
|
Pṛthivīsheṇa II
(470/75 to 495/500)

Sarvasena I (c. 325-355)
|
Vindhyaśakti II *alias* Vindhyasena
(c. 355 to 400)
|
Pravarasena II (c. 400 to 425)
|
Sarvasena II
(c. 425 to 455)
|
Devasena
(c.455-480)
|
Harisheṇa
(c. 480-510)

Genealogical Table of the Pushyabhūtis of Thanesar

Genealogical Table of the Later Guptas up to Ādityasena

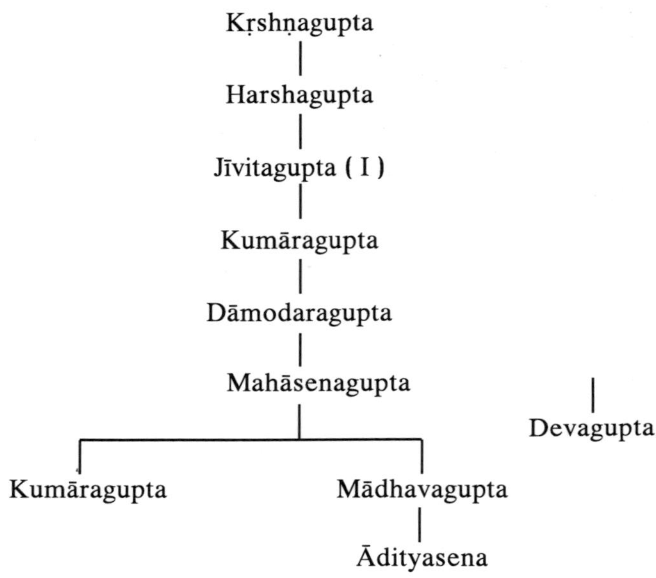

Genealogical Table of the Maukharis of Kanauj

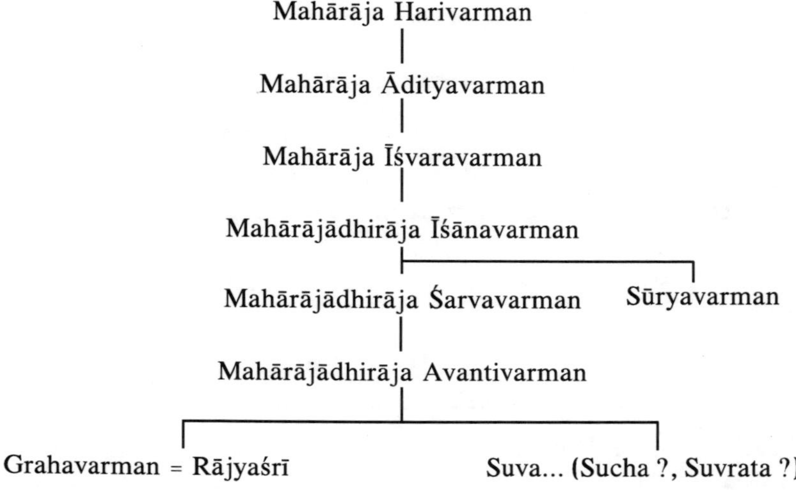

Genealogical Table of the Maitrakas of Valabhī (up to Dharasena IV)

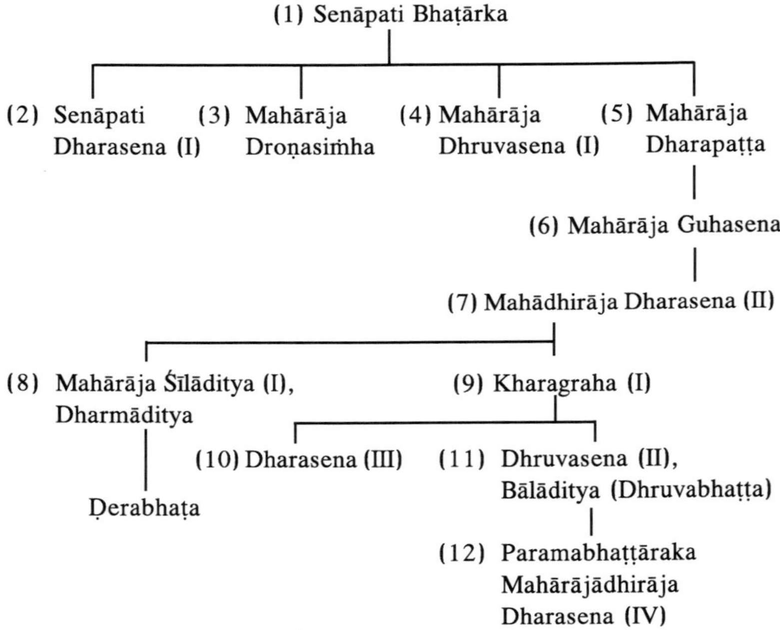

Genealogical Table of the Chālukyas of Vātāpi up to Pallava Interregnum (c. 642-54)

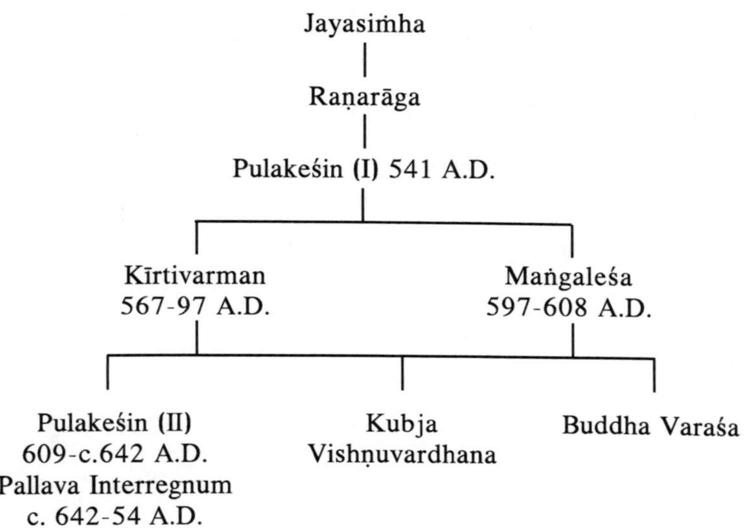

Genealogical Table of the Pallavas of Kāñchī (up to Narasiṁhavarman I)

Siṁhavarman, c. 550-75 A.D.
|
Siṁhavishṇu, c. 575-600 A.D.
|
Mahendravarman (I), c. 600-30 A.D.
|
Narasiṁhavarman (I), c. 630-68 A.D.

Bibliography

Agni Purāṇa, ĀSS, Poona, 1900.

Agrawal, Ashvini, *Rise and Fall of the Gupta Empire*, Delhi, 1989.

Agrawal, Jagannath and Goyal, Shankar, eds., *S.R. Goyal : His Multidimensional Historiography*, New Delhi, 1992.

Agrawala, P.K., *Gupta Temple Architecture*, Varanasi, 1968.

Agrawala, V.S., *Harsha Charita—Eka Sāṁskṛtika Adhyayana* (in Hindi), Patna, 1953.

—, *Kādambarī—Eka Sāṁskṛtika Adhyayana* (in Hindi), Varanasi, 1958.

—, *India as Known to Pāṇini*, Varanasi, Second edn., Varanasi, 1963.

—, *Prāchīna Bhāratīya Loka Dharma*, Ahmedabad, 1964.

—, *Studies in Indian Art*, Varanasi, 1965.

—, *The Deeds of Harsha*, Varanasi, 1969.

—, 'Coin Data in Divyāvadāna', *Indian Numismatic Chronicle*, Vol. III, pp. 148-50.

Aitareya Brāhmaṇa, ed. B.G. Apte, Poona, 1931.

Aiyangar, S.K., *Ancient India and South Indian History and Culture*, Vol. I, Poona, 1941.

Allan, J., *Catalogue of the Coins of the Gupta Dynasties and of Śaśāṅka, King of Gauḍa (in the British Museum)*, London, 1914.

—, *Catalogue of the Coins of Ancient India*, London, 1936.

Altekar, A.S., *The Coinage of the Gupta Empire*, Varanasi, 1957.

—, *State and Government in Ancient India*, Delhi, 1977.

—, 'Some Alleged Nāga and Vākāṭaka Coins', *JNSI*, V, 1943, pp. 111-34.

Arthaśāstra of Kauṭilya, Eng. tr. R. Shamasastry, Bangalore, 1950; edn. of R.P. Kangle, in 3 Parts, Bombay, 1960, 1963, 1965.

Āryamañjuśrīmūlakalpa, ed. and trans. by K.P. Jayaswal as *An Imperial History of India*, Lahore, 1934.

Aśvaghosha, *Buddhacharita*, Oxford, 1893.

Atharvaveda, tr. W. D. Whitney, Cambridge, Mass., U.S.A., 1905.

Bagchi, P.C., *She-Kia-Fang-Che*, Calcutta, 1959.

Bakker, Hans T., *Ramtek*, Leiden, 1989.

—, *The Vākāṭakas : An Essay in Hindu Iconology*, Groningen, 1997.

—, ed., *The Vākāṭaka Heritage : Indian Culture at the Crossroads*, Groningen, 2004.

Banerji, R.D., *The Age of the Imperial Guptas*, Banaras, 1933.

Banskhera Copper Plate of Harsha, *Epigraphia Indica*, IV, pp. 208-11.

Basak, R.G., *History of North-Eastern India (c. A.D. 320-760)*, Calcutta, 1934.

Basham, A.L., *The Wonder that was India*, London, 1954.

—, ed., *A Cultural History of India*, London, 1975.

Beal, S., *Si-Yü-Ki* or *Buddhist Records of the Western World*, Delhi, 1969.

—, *The Life of Hiuen-Tsiang*, New Delhi, 1973.

—, *Chinese Accounts of India*, Vol. II, Calcutta, n.d.

Beni Prasad, *The State in Ancient India*, Allahabad, 1928.

Bindoff, S.T., 'Political History', in *Approaches to History*, ed. H.P.R. Finberg, London, 1962.

Brahmavaivarta Purāṇa, ed. Jivanand Vidyasagar, Calcutta, Saraswati Press.

Bṛhatsaṁhitā of Varāhamihira, ed. H. Kern, Calcutta, 1865.

Buddha Prakash, *Aspects of Indian History and Civilization*, Agra, 1965.

Byrski, M.C., 'Some Remarks about King Harṣavardhana Śīlāditya', *Bhāratī*, 5, i, 1961-62, pp. 75-85.

Chakrabarti, Kunal and Sinha, Kanad, eds., *State, Power and Legitimacy : The Gupta Kingdom*, Delhi, 2019.

Chakravarti, Ranabir, *Exploring Early India up to c. AD 1300*, 3rd edn., Delhi, 2016.

Champakalakshmi, R., *Trade, Ideology and Urbanization : South India 300 BC to AD 1300*, New Delhi, 1999.

Chatterjee, Bhaskar, ed., *History and Archaeology, Professor H.D. Sankalia Felicitation Volume*, Delhi, 1989.

Chatterji, G.S., *Harshavardhana* (in Hindi), 2nd edn., Allahabad, 1950.

Chattopadhyaya, B.D., *The Making of Early Medieval India*, New Delhi, 1997.

—, 'Trade and Urban Centres in Early Medieval North India', *IHR*, Vol. I, No. 2, September 1974, pp. 203-19.

Chattopadhyaya, S., *Early History of North India*, Calcutta, 1958.

Chhabra, B.Ch., Agrawala, P.K., Agrawal, Ashvini and Goyal, Shankar, eds., *Reappraising Gupta History for S.R. Goyal*, New Delhi, 1992.

Chhabra, B. Ch. and Gai, G.S., eds., *Corpus Inscriptionum Indicarum*, Vol. III, *Inscriptions of the Early Gupta Kings and their Successors*, revised by D.R.Bhandarkar, New Delhi, 1981.

Choudhary, G.C., *Political History of North India from Jaina Sources*, Amritsar, 1954.

Craig, Gordon, 'Political History', in *Daedalus*, Cambridge, Mass., Winter 1971, pp. 323-38.

Cunningham, A., *The Ancient Geography of India*, Varanasi, 1963.

—, *Coins of Mediaeval India*, Varanasi, 1967.

Daedalus : The Historian and the World of the Twentieth Century, Cambridge, Mass., Spring 1971.

Dandekar, R.N., *A History of the Guptas*, Poona, 1941.

Daṇḍin, *Daśakumāracharita*, ed. M.R. Kale, Bombay, 1917.

Dange, S.A., *India from Primitive Communism to Slavery*, Bombay, 1949.

Dasgupta, S.N., *A History of the Sanskrit Literature*, Vol. 1 : *Classical Period*, Second edn., Calcutta, 1975.

De, S. K., *History of Sanskrit Literature*, Calcutta, 1947.

Deo, S.B. and Joshi, Jagatpati, *Pauni Excavations (1969-70)*, Nagpur, 1972.

Desai, Devangana, 'Art under Feudalism in India (c. A.D. 500-1300)', *The Indian Historical Review*, Vol. 1, No. 1, March 1974, pp. 10-17.

Devahuti, D., *Harsha : A Political Study*, 2nd edn., Oxford University Press, New Delhi, 1983; 1st edn., Oxford, 1970.

—, ed., *Problems of Indian Historiography*, Delhi, 1979.

—, ed., *The Unknown Hsüan-tsang*, New Delhi, 2001.

Devra, G.S.L., *Rajasthan Itihāsa ke Abhigyāna Rūpa*, Jaipur, 2010.

Dey, Nundo Lal, *Geographical Dictionary of Ancient and Medieval India*, London, 1927.

Dhavalikar, M.K., 'The Golden Age and After : Perspectives in Historical Archaeology', his Presidential Address delivered to the Diamond Jubilee Session of the Indian History Congress, Calicut, 1999.

Dubey, D. P. and Dubey, A.K., 'Uttar Pradesh, Bihar and Uttarakhand', in *25 Years of Indian Epigraphy* (A Bird's Eye-view of the Progress of Epigraphy in Different States of the Country), ed. Shrinivas V. Padigar, Dharwad, 2016, pp. 301 ff.

Dubey, S.R., ed., *Ābhilekhika Adhyayana kī Pravidhi evaṁ Itihāsa-Lekhana*, Delhi, 2004.

Dubreuil, J., *Ancient History of the Deccan*, tr. from French by V.S.S. Dikshitar, Pondicherry, 1920.

Dutta, B.N., *Studies in Indian Social Polity*, Calcutta, 1944.

—, *Dialectics of Land Economics in India*, Calcutta, 1952.

Dutta, Mala, *A Study of the Sātavāhana Coinage*, Delhi, 1990.

Ettinghausen, M.L., *Harṣa Vardhana : Empereur et Poète, etc.*, London, 1906.

Finberg, H.P.R., ed., *Approaches to History*, London, 1962.

Fleet, J.F., *Corpus Inscriptionum Indicarum*, III, Calcutta, 1888.

—, *Dynasties of the Kanarese Districts*, Bombay, 1899.

Ganguly, D.K., *The Imperial Guptas and their Times*, New Delhi, 1987.
Gankovsky, Yu. V., *The Peoples of Pakistan*, Moscow, 1978.
Ghoshal, U.N., *Studies in Indian History and Culture*, Second revised edn., Calcutta, 1965.
Ghurye, G.S., *Caste and Class in India*, 2nd edn., Bombay, 1957.
Giles, H.A., *The Travels of Fa-hsien*, London, 1923.
Goff, E.G., 'Is Politics Still the Backbone of History ?', *Daedalus*, Cambridge, Mass., Winter 1971, pp. 1-19.
Gokhale, B.G., *Samudra Gupta : Life and Times*, Bombay, 1962.
Gopal, S. and Thapar, R., eds., *Problems of Historical Writing in India*, New Delhi, 1963.
Goyal, Shankar, *History and Historiography of the Age of Harsha*, Jodhpur, 1992.
—, *Aspects of Ancient Indian History and Historiography*, New Delhi, 1993.
—, *History Writing of Early India*, Jodhpur, 1996.
—, *The Image of Classical India*, Jodhpur, 1997.
—, *Recent Historiography of Ancient India*, Jodhpur, 1997.
—, *Ancient Indian Numismatics*, Jodhpur, 1998.
—, *Marxist Interpretation of Ancient Indian History*, Poona, 2000.
—, *Problems of Ancient Indian History : New Perspectives and Perceptions*, Jaipur, 2001.
—, *Contemporary Interpreters of Ancient India*, Jaipur, 2003.
—, *Harsha : A Multidisciplinary Political Study*, Jodhpur, 2006.
—, *Ancient India : A Multidisciplinary Approach*, Jodhpur, 2006.
—, *175 Years of Vākāṭaka History and Hitoriography*, Jodhpur, 2009.
—, *The 'Medieval' Factor and the Age of Harsha : A Cultural Study*, Jodhpur, 2016.
—, *Harsha Revisited : A Re-interpretation of Existing Data*, Delhi, 2018.
—, *The Significance of Yuan Chwang in the Context of the Seventh Century : A Critical Assessment*, Delhi, 2018.
—, ed., *Political History in a Changing World*, Jodhpur, 1992.
—, ed., *S.R. Goyal : His Multidimensional Historiography*, New Delhi, 1992.
—, ed., *Prāchīna Bhārata kā Ādhunika Itihāsa-Lekhana*, Jodhpur, 2000.
—, ed., *Reconstructing Indian History for S.R. Goyal*, Vols. I, II, Jaipur, 2003.
—, ed., *History and Politics*, Jodhpur, 2015.
—, 'Social *Milieu* of the Pushyabhūtis : Significance of Some Hitherto Unnoticed Passages of the *Harshacharita* ', *Essays in Indian History and Culture*, ed. Y. Krishan, New Delhi, 1986, pp. 167-70.
—, 'Śaśāṅka and Buddhism', in the *Proceedings of the Indian History and Culture Society*, 10th Annual Conference, 1986, Varanasi, 1988, pp. 45-50.

—, 'Political History : The Loss of Innocence', in *Political History in a Changing World*, eds. G.C. Pande et al, Jodhpur, 1992, pp. 290-99.

—, 'Political Ideology of the Early Imperial Guptas', in *Reappraising Gupta History for S. R. Goyal*, eds. B. Ch. Chhabra, P. K. Agrawala, Ashvini Agrawal and Shankar Goyal, New Delhi, 1992, pp. 215-23.

—, 'A Critique of Professor D.N. Jha's Evaluation of the Classicism of the Gupta Age', in *Reappraising Gupta History for S.R. Goyal*, eds. B. Ch. Chhabra, et al, New Delhi, 1992, pp. 61-73.

—, 'Coins of Prabhākaravardhana Pratāpaśīla and Harsha Śīlāditya', *Journal of the Numismatic Society of India*, Vol. LIV, Pts. 1-2, 1992, pp. 65-69.

—, 'Rise of Medievalism in Indian History', *Vishveshvaranand Indological Journal*, Vol. XXX, Pts. 1-2, June-Dec. 1992, pp. 233-60.

—, 'Recent Historiography of the Age of Harsha', *Annals of the Bhandarkar Oriental Research Institute*, Vol. LXXII-LXXIII, 1993, pp. 331-61.

—, 'The Rājyavardhana Murder Case', *Heritage of India : Past and Present* (Professor R.K. Sharma Felicitation Volume), eds. P.K. Mishra and S.K. Sullerey, Delhi, 1994, pp. 579-90.

—, 'Historiography of the Imperial Guptas : Old and New', *VIJ*, Vol. XXIX, Pts. I-II, 1991 (1995), pp. 239-74.

—, 'Voices of Protest and Dissent in the Works of Bāṇa', *Śrījñānāmṛtam* (A Commemoration Volume dedicated to Professor Shri Niwas Shastri), ed. Vijaya Rani, Delhi, 1996, pp. 650-60.

—, 'Prabhākaravardhana : A New Assessment', in *Sri Venkateswara University Oriental Journal*, Volume XLIII, Parts 1 and 2, 2000, pp. 9-31.

—, 'Harsha's Relations with the Deccan and the Far South: Some Problems and Suggestions', in the *Proceedings of the Twenty-second Annual Session of the South Indian History Congress*, Thiruvananthapuram, 2002, pp. 135-37.

—, 'Political History as an Integral Study of Political Life and Institutions', *Annals of the Bhandarkar Oriental Research Institute*, Vol. LXXXIV, 2003, pp. 135-42.

—, 'Acquisition of the Maukhari Empire by Harsha', *Journal of the Asiatic Society*, Vol. XLV (2), 2003, pp. 53-62.

—, 'Factors in the Making of Early Medieval Society in India', *Journal of Indian History and Culture*, Vol. XI, 2004, pp. 25-52.

—, 'Psycho-Sociological Analysis of Harsha's Personality', *Journal of Indian History*, Vols. LXXVI-LXXVIII, 2004, pp. 7-14.

—, 'Harsha ke Abhilekha : Kuchha Samasyāyeṁ aura Sujhāva' (in Hindi), in *Ābhilekhika Adhyayana kī Pravidhi evaṁ Itihāsa-Lekhana*, ed. Sita Ram Dubey, Delhi, 2004, pp. 183-89.

—, 'A.S. Altekar and the Bayana Hoard', *JNSI*, Vol. LXVII, Pts. i-ii, 2005, pp. 80-84.

—, 'The Vākāṭakas in the History of the Deccan : A Fresh Appraisal in the Light of Recent Discoveries and New Interpretations', The Loyola College Endowment Lecture delivered at the XXVI Annual Session of the South Indian History Congress, held at the Bangalore University, March 3-5, 2006, pp. 1-21.

—, 'The Recently Discovered Kurukshetra-Varanasi Grant of Harsha : Year 23', *East and West*, Vol. 57, 1-4, 2007, pp. 193-203.

—, 'Religious Analysis of Harsha's Personality', *Proceedings of the Indian History Congress*, 68th Session, Delhi, 2007 (Delhi, 2008), pp. 136-48.

—, 'The Myth of the Vākāṭaka Coins', *IHR*, Vol. XXXIV, No. 2, July 2007, pp. 1-15.

—, '*Harshacharita* as a Source of History', in the *Papers from the Aligarh Historians Society*, ed. Irfan Habib, 69th Session, Indian History Congress, Kannur University, Kannur, 2008, pp. 122-52.

—, 'The Authenticity of the Plays Ascribed to Harsha', *Proceedings of the Indian History Congress*, 69th Session, Kannur University, Kannur, 2008 (Kolkata, 2009), pp. 86-93.

—, 'Caste System as Reflected in the Works of Bāṇa and Yuan Chwang', in the *Papers from the Aligarh Historians Society*, ed. Irfan Habib, 71st Session, Gaur Banga University, Malda, 2011, pp. 124-47.

—, 'Harsha-Pulakeśin II Struggle : A Collated Study of Epigraphic and Literary Evidence', in *JESI*, XXXVII, 2012, pp. 100-05.

—, 'An Investigation into the Feudal Nature of the Vākāṭaka Economy : A Study of the Epigraphic Evidence', our Presidential Address, The Epigraphical Society of India, published in the *Journal of the Epigraphical Society of India*, Vol. XXXVIII, 2012, pp. 1-38.

—, 'Feudalization of Polity in the Age of Harsha : An Analysis', in *History and Politics*, ed. Shankar Goyal, Jodhpur, 2015, pp. 143-67.

—, 'Yuan Chwang's India and the Problem of the Extent of Harsha's Empire and Sphere of His Influence', in the *Papers from the Aligarh Historians Society*, ed. Irfan Habib, 77th Session, Indian History Congress, Kerala University, Thiruvananthapuram, 2016, pp. 104-16.

—, 'Some Observations on India's Intercourse with Iran in the Seventh Century A.D.', in the *Papers from the Aligarh Historians Society*, ed. Irfan Habib, 78th Session, Indian History Congress, Jadavpur University, Kolkata, 2017, pp. 11-16.

—, 'Harsha : A Retrospective', our Presidential Address, Section I : Ancient India, 78th Session, Indian History Congress, Jadavpur University, Kolkata, 28-30 December, 2017, *PIHC*, Delhi, 2018, pp. 27-41.

—, 'The Rāmṭek Prabhāvatīguptā Memorial Fragmentary Inscription', in *Epigraphic Studies*, Selected Papers from the Panel on Epigraphy at the 16th World Sanskrit Conference, 2015, Sanskrit Studies Centre, Silpakorn University, Bangkok, Thailand, ed. D.P. Dubey, New Delhi, 2018, pp. 129-37.

Goyal, S.R., *A History of the Imperial Guptas*, Allahabad, 1967.

—, *Gupta evaṁ Samakālīna Rājavaṁśa*, Allahabad, 1969.

—, *Prāchīna Nepāla kā Rājanītika aura Sāṁskṛtika Itihāsa*, Varanasi, 1973.

—, *Prāchīna Bhāratīya Abhilekha Saṁgraha*, Vol. I, *Prāk-guptayugīna*, Jaipur, 1982.

—, *Guptakālīna Abhilekha*, Meerut, 1984.

—, *A Religious History of Ancient India*, 2 Vols., Meerut, 1984, 1986.

—, *Harsha and Buddhism*, Meerut, 1986.

—, *Harsha Śīlāditya*, Meerut, 1986.

—, *Gupta Sāmrājya kā Itihāsa*, Meerut, 1987.

—, *Maukhari-Pushyabhūti-Chālukyayugīna Abhilekha*, Meerut, 1987.

—, *Māgadha-Sātavāhana-Kushāṇa Sāmrājyoṅ kā Yuga*, Meerut, 1988.

—, *Gupta aura Vākāṭaka Sāmrājyoṅ kā Yuga*, Meerut, 1988.

—, *Maukhari-Pushyabhūti-Chālukya Yuga*, Meerut, 1988.

—, *Indigenous Coins of Early India*, Jodhpur, 1994.

—, *An Introduction to Gupta Numismatics*, Jodhpur, 1994.

—, *The Dynastic Coins of Ancient India*, Jodhpur, 1995.

—, *The Coinage of Ancient India*, Jodhpur, 1995.

—, *Dakshiṇa Bhārata kā Itihāsa*, Jodhpur, 1995.

—, *Ancient Indian Inscriptions : Recent Finds and New Interpretations*, Jodhpur, 2005.

—, *The Imperial Guptas : A Multidisciplinary Political Study*, Jodhpur, 2005.

—, *A History of the Vākāṭaka-Gupta Relations*, Jodhpur, 2006.

—, *Paurāṇika Sects and Cults*, Jodhpur, 2016.

—, *A Comprehensive History of Hinduism*, Jodhpur, 2018.

—, 'Political History : A Reconsideration', in *Jijñāsā*, Volume 2, Number 2, April 1975, pp. 9-26.

—, 'Need of a New Approach to the Writing of Political History of Ancient India', in *Political History in a Changing World*, eds. G.C. Pande et al, Jodhpur, 1992, pp. 1-17.

—, 'The Myth of the Golden Bird : An Investigation into the Belief of Material Opulence of Ancient and Early Medieval India in the Light of Her Gold Coinage', his Presidential Address, The Numismatic Society of India, published in the *Journal of the Numismatic Society of India*, Vol. LXIX, Parts I and II, 2007, pp. 1-24.

Goyal, S. R. and Goyal, Shankar, eds., *Indian Art of the Gupta Age*, Jodhpur, 2000.

Grewal, J.S., 'Hiuen Tsiang's India', in *India — Studies in the History of an Idea*, ed. Irfan Habib, New Delhi, 2005, pp. 60-81.
Gupta, P.L., *Gupta Sāmrājya*, Varanasi, 1970.
—, *The Imperial Guptas*, Varanasi, 1974.
—, 'Fabrication of Ancient Punch-marked Coins', *Indian Numismatic Chronicle*, Vol. III, pp. 133 ff.
Gupta, S.P., ed., *Readings in Political History of India*, Delhi, 1976.
Habib, Irfan, ed., *India — Studies in the History of an Idea*, New Delhi, 2005.
—, ed., *Religion in Indian History*, New Delhi, 2007.
Handa, Devendra, ed., *Oriental Numismatic Studies*, Volume I, New Delhi, 1996.
Harshacharita of Bāṇa, ed. Kasinatha Pandurang Parab, 5th edn., Bombay, 1925.
—, ed. P.V. Kane, 2nd edn., Delhi, 1965.
—, tr. E.B. Cowell and F.W. Thomas, 2nd edn., Delhi, 1968.
—, ed. Jagannath Pathak, 6th edn., Varanasi, 1998.
Hauser, Arnold, *The Social History of Art*, Vol. I.
Heras, H., 'Relations between Guptas, Kadambas and Vākāṭakas', *JBORS*, XII, 1926, pp. 455-65.
—, 'The Royal Patrons of the University of Nālandā', *JBORS*, XIV, 1928.
Herzfeld, E., *Paikuli : Monuments and Inscriptions of the Early History of the Sassanian Empire*, Berlin, 1924.
Hiralal, *Inscriptions of the Central Provinces and Berar*, Nagpur, 1932.
Hitti, Philip K., *History of the Arabs*, first published in 1937, revised 10th edn., Palgrave Macmillan, 2002.
Huart, C., *Ancient Persia and Iranian Civilization*, tr. M. R. Dobie, London, 1927.
Jain, Bal Chandra, *Inventory of the Hoards and Finds of Coins and Seals from Madhya Pradesh*, Varanasi, 1957.
Jan Yun-Hua, 'Hui Chao's Records on Kashmir', *Kashmir Research Biannual*, No. 2, 1962.
Jayaswal, K.P., *History of India, 150 A.D. to 350 A.D.*, Lahore, 1933.
—, *Hindu Polity*, Bangalore, 1943.
Jha, D.N., *Revenue System in Post-Maurya and Gupta Times*, Calcutta, 1967.
—, *Ancient India : An Introductory Outline*, New Delhi, 1977; revised and enlarged edn. as *Ancient India in Historical Outline*, New Delhi, 1998.
—, *Early India — A Concise History*, New Delhi, 2008.
—, *Prāchīna Bhārata, Sāmājika, Ārthika aura Sāṁskṛtika Vikāsa kī Paratāla*, Delhi, 2009.
—, ed., *Feudal Social Formation in Early India*, Delhi, 1987.

—, ed., *The Feudal Order*, New Delhi, 2002.
—, his Presidential Address to the Ancient India Section of the 40th Session of the Indian History Congress, Waltair, *PIHC*, 1979, pp. 15-45.
Jha, D.N. and Shrimali, K.M., eds., *Prāchīna Bhārata kā Itihāsa*, Delhi, 1981.
Jha, J.S., ed., *K.P. Jayaswal Commemoration Volume*, Patna, 1981.
Jha, Vivekanand, 'Caṇḍāla and the Origin of Untouchability', *The Indian Historical Review*, Vol. XIII, Nos. 1-2, July 1986 and January 1987, pp. 1-36.
Joshi, L.M., *Studies in the Buddhistic Culture of India*, Delhi, 1967.
Joshi, M.C., *Princes and Polity in Ancient India*, Jodhpur, 1986.
Joshi, Munish Chandra, Gupta, S.K. and Goyal, Shankar, eds., *King Chandra and the Meharauli Pillar*, Meerut, 1989.
Kādambarī of Bāṇa, tr. C.M. Ridding, London, 1896; Indian repr., Bombay, 1956.
—, ed. P.V. Kane, Bombay, 1920.
—, ed. Pt. Ramtej Shastri, Varanasi, 1952.
Kalhaṇa, *Rājataraṅgiṇī : A Chronicle of the Kings of Kashmir*, 2 Vols., tr. Sir M.A. Stein, Westminster, 1900 ; tr. R.S. Pandit, Allahabad, 1935.
Kālidāsa, *Kumārasambhava*, in *Kālidāsa Granthāvalī*, ed. Sitaram Chaturvedi, Aligarh, 1950.
—, *Raghuvaṁśa*, in *Kālidāsa Granthāvalī*, ed. Sitaram Chaturvedi, Aligarh, 1950.
Kaliyugarājavṛttānta of *Bhavishyottra-purāṇa*, quoted in *History of Classical Sanskrit Literature* by M. Krishnamachariar, Madras, 1937.
Kāmandakīya-nītisāra, ed. Ganapati Sastri, Trivandrum, 1912.
Kāmasūtra of Vātsyāyana, ed. D.L. Goswami, Banaras, 1929.
Kane, P.V., *History of Dharmaśāstra*, Vol. III, Poona, 1973.
Kapur, Nandini Sinha, 'State Formation in Vidarbha : The Case of the Eastern Vākāṭakas', *IHR*, XXXII, 2, July 2005, pp. 13-16.
Kathāsaritsāgara, ed. Durga Prasad and Parab, Bombay, 1930.
Kaumudī-mahotsava by Vijjikā (?), ed. Shakuntala Rao Shastri, Bombay, 1952.
Kāvya-mīmāṅsā of Rajaśekhara, eds. C.D. Dalal and R.A. Sastry, Baroda, 1934.
Keith, A.B., *Sanskrit Drama*, Oxford, 1924.
—, *History of Sanskrit Literature* (Hindi edn.), Delhi, 1960.
Kosambi, D.D., *Myth and Reality : Studies in the Formation of Indian Culture*, Bombay, 1962.
—, *An Introduction to the Study of Indian History*, 2nd revised edn., Bombay, 1975.
—, *The Culture and Civilisation of Ancient India in Historical Outline*, 7th edn., New Delhi, 1982.

Krom, N.J., 'The First Hindu Coin from Java', *JNSI*, Vol. XXX, 1968, pp. 200-01.

Kulke, Hermann, 'Some Thoughts on State and State Formation under the Eastern Vākāṭakas', in *The Vākāṭaka Heritage : Indian Culture at the Crossroads*, ed. Hans T. Bakker, Groningen, 2004, pp. 1-9.

Kulshreshtha, Sarojini, ed., *Baḍhate Kadam-Badalte Āyāma : Parameshwari Lal Gupta (80 Varsha)*, Varanasi, 1995.

Kurukshetra-Varanasi Copper Plate Inscription of Harsha, *East and West*, Vol. 57, 1-4, 2007, pp. 193-203 ; *Epigraphia Indica*, XLIII, i, pp. 40-51.

Kuṭṭanīmata of Dāmodara, ed. M. Kaul, Calcutta, 1944.

Kuvalayamālā, ed. L.B. Gandhi, Baroda, 1927.

Law, B.C., *Historical Geography of Ancient India*, Paris, 1954.

—, ed., *Buddhistic Studies*, Calcutta, 1931.

Legge, J.H., *A Record of the Buddhist Kingdoms, etc.*, being an account of the Chinese monk Fa-hien's travels in India, Oxford, 1886.

Liu, Xinru, *Ancient India and Ancient China, Trade and Religious Exchanges A.D. 1-600*, Oxford, 1988.

Lorenzen, David N., 'Professor S.R. Goyal's Suggestion on Political History Writing in the Light of Historians and Political History of the Gupta Empire', in *Political History in a Changing World*, eds. G.C. Pande, S.K. Gupta and Shankar Goyal, Jodhpur, 1992, pp. 53 ff.

Macdonell, A.A., *A History of Sanskrit Literature*, Delhi, 1962.

Madhuban Copper Plate Inscription of Harsha, *Epigraphia Indica*, I, pp. 67-75.

Mahābhārata, Critical Text, 7 Vols., Poona, 1877-97.

Mahajan, Malati, 'Flora from Place Names in Inscriptions Found in Maharashtra', *Studies in Indian Place Names*, III, 1982, pp. 25-38 and IV, 1984, pp. 90-99.

Mahalingam, T.V., *South Indian Polity*, Madras, 1967.

Maity, S.K., *Gupta Civilization*, Calcutta, 1974.

—, *The Imperial Guptas and their Times* (cir. A.D. 300-550), New Delhi, 1975.

Majumdar, R.C., *The Classical Accounts of India*, Calcutta, 1960.

—, *Readings in Political History of India*, ed. S.P. Gupta, Delhi, 1976.

—, ed., *The History of Bengal* (Vol. I : Hindu Period), Dacca, 1943.

—, ed., *A Comprehensive History of India*, Vol. III, Pt. I (A.D. 300-985), New Delhi, 1981.

—, 'Ideas of History in Sanskrit Literature', *Historians of India, Pakistan and Ceylon*, ed. C.H. Philips, London, 1961.

Majumdar, R.C. and Altekar, A.S., eds., *A New History of the Indian People*, Vol. VI : *The Vākāṭaka-Gupta Age (Circa 200-550 A.D.)*, Lahore, 1946.

Majumdar, R.C. and Dasgupta, K.K., eds., *A Comprehensive History of India*, Vol. III, Pt. II, New Delhi, 1982.
Majumdar, R.C. and Pusalker, A.D., eds., *The Vedic Age*, Bombay, 1951.
—, eds., *The Age of Imperial Unity*, Bombay, 1953.
—, eds., *The Classical Age*, Bombay, 1954.
Mālatīmādhava of Bhavabhūti.
Mammaṭa, *Kāvyaprakāśa*, Eng. tr. Ganganatha Jha, Allahabad, 1925.
Mānavadharmaśāstra or *Manusmṛti*, ed. J. Jolly, London, 1887.
Mārkaṇḍeya-purāṇa, ed. K.M. Banerjea, Calcutta, 1862.
Matsya-purāṇa, Poona, 1907.
Mayūra, *Sanskrit Poems by Mayūra*, ed. G. Quackenbos, New York, 1917.
McCrindle, J.W., *Ancient India as Described by Megasthenes and Arrian*, Calcutta, 1877.
Mirashi, V.V., *Corpus Inscriptionum Indicarum*, Vol. IV, *Inscriptions of the Kalachuri-Chedi Era*, Ootacamund, 1955.
—, *Corpus*, V, *Inscriptions of the Vākāṭakas*, Ootacamund, 1963.
—, *Vākāṭaka Rājavaṁśa kā Itihāsa tathā Abhilekha* (in Hindi), Varanasi, 1964.
—, *Literary and Historical Studies in Indology*, Delhi, 1975.
—, *Indological Research Papers*, Vol. I, Nagpur, 1982.
Mishra, P. K. and Sullerey, S.K., eds., *Heritage of India : Past and Present*, Delhi, 1994.
Mookerji, R.K., *Harsha*, London, 1926.
—, *The Gupta Empire*, Bombay, 1947.
Moosvi, Shireen, 'The Making of India', her General President's Address, in the *Proceedings of the Indian History Congress*, 77th Session, University of Kerala, Thiruvananthapuram, 2016, Aligarh, 2017, pp. 1-17.
Mṛchchhakaṭikam, ed. R.D. Karmarkar, Poona, 1937.
Mudrārākshasa, ed. Alfred Hillebrandt, Part I, Breslau, 1912.
Mukherjee, B.N., ed., *Śrī Dineśacandrikā*, Delhi, 1983.
Mukherjee, S.N., ed., *India : History and Thought*, Calcutta, 1982.
Mukhopadhyay, S.K., *Evolution of Historiography in Modern India : 1900-1960*, Calcutta, 1981.
Murray, H.J.R., *A History of Chess*, published in 1913, repr., Oxford, 1962.
Nāgānanda of Harsha, tr. P. Boyd, London, 1872.
—, ed. R.D. Karmarkar, Poona, 1919.
Nāgojī, *Kāvyapradīpodyota*, ed. D. Chandorkar, Poona, 1898.
Nālandā Seals, *Epigraphia Indica*, XXI, pp. 74-76.
Narain, A.K., 'Writing a New History of Ancient India : A Study of Problems, Sources and Methods', in *Problems of Historical Writing in India*, New Delhi, 1963, pp. 1-10.

Nītisāra of Kāmandaka, ed. Rajendralal Mitra, Calcutta, 1884.
Om Prakash, *Prāchīna Bhārata kā Itihāsa*, New Delhi, 1987.
Padigar, Shrinivas V., ed., *25 Years of Indian Epigraphy*, Dharwad, 2016.
Padmagupta, *Navasāhasāṅkacharita*, ed. V.S. Islampurkar, Bombay, 1895.
Pañchatantra, tr. A. Williams, *Tales from the Pañchatantra*, Oxford, 1930.
Pande, G.C., Gupta, S.K. and Goyal, Shankar, eds., *Political History in a Changing World*, Jodhpur, 1992.
Pandey, R.B., *Historical and Literary Inscriptions*, Varanasi, 1962.
—, *Prāchīna Bhārata*, Varanasi, 1971.
Panikkar, K.M., *Śrī Harsha of Kanauj*, Bombay, 1922.
Pargiter, F.E., *The Purāṇa Text of the Dynasties of the Kali Age*, London, 1913.
Patañjali, *Mahābhāshya*, Rohtak, 1961-63.
Pathak, V.S., *Ancient Historians of India*, Bombay, 1966.
—, 'Biographies in Early Mediaeval Sanskrit Literature (With Particular Reference to the *Harshacharita*)', in *Bhāratī*, Varanasi, 1963-64, pp. 65 ff.
—, 'Motifs on Gupta Coins and Sassanian Wares', *Numismatic Digest*, Vol. X, 1986, pp. 87 ff.
Philips, C.H., ed., *Historians of India, Pakistan and Ceylon*, London, 1961.
Pirenne, Jacques, *The Tides of History*, Allen and Unwin.
Priyadarśikā of Harsha, ed. Jivanand Vidyasagar, Calcutta, 1874.
—, tr. G.D. Nariman, A.V. William Jackson and C.J. Ogden, New York, 1923.
Problems of Historical Writing in India, Proceedings of the Seminar held at the India International Centre, New Delhi, 1963.
Puri, B.N., *The Gupta Administration*, Delhi, 1991.
Raghuvaṁśa of Kālidāsa, ed. G.R. Nandargikar, Bombay, 1897.
Radhesharan, *Samrāṭ Samudragupta*, Rewa, 1969.
Rāmacharita of Sandhyākara Nandī, eds. R. C. Majumdar, R. G. Basak and N. G. Banerji, Rajshahi, 1939.
Ramesh, K.V., *Chālukyas of Vātāpi*, Delhi, 1984.
Rao, M.S. Nagaraja, ed., *Shri C. Sivaramamurti Commemoration Volume*, Delhi, 1987.
Ratnāvalī of Harsha, ed. K.M. Joglekar, Hedvi, 1907.
—, ed. and tr. C.R. Devadhar and N.G. Suru, 2nd edn., Poona, 1954.
Raychaudhuri, H.C., *Political History of Ancient India*, Calcutta, 1953; with a *Commentary* by B.N. Mukherjee, Oxford, 1996.
Ray, N.R., 'The 'Medieval' Factor in Indian History', being his Address of the General President of the 29th Session of the Indian History Congress, Patiala, 1967.

Ṛgveda, ed. F. Maxmüller, 1890-92; edn. of T. H. Griffith, Banaras, 1896-97; Poona edn., 4 Vols., 1933.
Roy, B.P., ed., *Churning the Indian Past*, Patna, 2003.
Roy, U.N., *Gupta Samrāṭ aura Unkā Kāla*, Allahabad, 1971.
Śabdakalpadruma of Radhakant Dev, 5 Vols., Delhi, 1961.
Sampurnanand, *Samrāṭ Harshavardhana* (in Hindi), Bombay, V.S. 1977.
Sankalia, H.D., *The University of Nālandā*, Madras, 1934.
Saraswati, S.K., *A Survey of Indian Sculpture*, Calcutta, 1957.
Sastri, K.A.N., *A History of South India*, Madras, 1966.
Schwartz, Benjamin, 'A Brief Defence of Political and Intellectual History with Particular Reference to Non-Western Cultures', *Daedalus*, Cambridge, Mass., Winter 1971, pp. 98-112.
Sen, S.P., ed., *Historians and Historiography in Modern India*, Calcutta, 1973.
Sen, Surendranath, *India through Chinese Eyes*, Madras, 1956.
Shamasastry, R., ed., *The Arthaśāstra of Kauṭilya*, 3rd edn., Mysore, 1922.
Sharma, B.N., *Harṣa and His Times*, Varanasi, 1970.
Sharma, D., 'Harṣa : A Buddhist', *Indian Historical Quarterly*, XXXII, Nos. 2 and 3, 1956, pp. 168 ff.
Sharma, I.K., *Coinage of the Sātavāhana Empire*, Delhi, 1980.
Sharma, J.K., 'Women in Vardhana India', *Panjab University Research Bulletin (Arts)*, Vol. XVIII, No. 2, October 1987, pp. 129-44.
Sharma, R.S., *Śūdras in Ancient India*, Delhi, 1958.
—, *Indian Feudalism*, Calcutta, 1965.
—, *Perspectives in Social and Economic History of Early India*, New Delhi, 1983.
—, *Urban Decay in India (c. 300-1000 A.D.)*, New Delhi, 1987.
—, *Ancient India*, New Delhi, 1995.
—, *Aspects of Political Ideas and Institutions in Ancient India*, 4th revised edn., Delhi, 1996.
—, *Early Medieval Indian Society : A Study in Feudalisation*, Kolkata, 2001.
—, *India's Ancient Past*, Oxford, 2015.
—, ed., *Indian Society : Historical Probings in Memory of D.D. Kosambi*, 3rd edn., New Delhi, 1984.
—, 'The Origins of Feudalism in India', *JESHO*, I, Pt. 3, 1958.
—, 'Coins and Problems of Early Indian Economic History', *JNSI*, Vol. XXXI, Pt. i, 1969, pp. 1-8.
—, 'Decay of Gangetic Towns in Gupta and Post-Gupta Times', *PIHC*, 33rd Session, 1972, pp. 92-104.
—, 'Problem of Transition from Ancient to Medieval in Indian History', in *The Indian Historical Review*, New Delhi, Vol. 1, No. 1, March 1974, pp. 1-9.

—, 'The Kali Age : A Period of Social Crisis', in *India : History and Thought*, ed. S.N. Mukherjee, Calcutta, 1982, pp. 186-203.
Sharma, T.R., *A Political History of the Imperial Guptas*, New Delhi, 1989.
Shastri, A.M., *Early History of the Deccan : Problems and Perspectives*, Delhi, 1987.
—, *Inscriptions of the Śarabhapurīyas, Pāṇḍuvaṁśins and Somavaṁśins*, New Delhi, 1995.
—, *Vākāṭakas : Sources and History*, New Delhi, 1997.
—, ed., *The Age of the Vākāṭakas*, New Delhi, 1992.
She-Kia-Fang-Che, ed. P.C. Bagchi, Calcutta, 1959.
Shrimali, K.M., *Agrarian Structure in Central India and the Northern Deccan (c. A.D. 300-500) : A Study of Vākāṭaka Inscriptions*, New Delhi, 1987.
—, *Prāchīna Bhāratīya Dharmoṅ kā Itihāsa*, Delhi, 2017.
—, *Itihāsa, Purātattva aura Vichāradhārā*, Delhi, 2021.
—, 'Pattern of Settlements under the Vākāṭakas', *PIHC*, 44th Session, Burdwan, 1983, pp. 101-12.
—, 'Religions in Complex Societies : The Myth of the 'Dark Age' ', in *Religion in Indian History*, ed. Irfan Habib, New Delhi, 2007, pp. 36-70.
—, his Foreword in *Hye Ch'o kā Yatrā-Vṛttānta : Āṭhavīn Sadī kā Bhārata*, Hindi tr. of *The Hye Ch'o Diary : Memoir of the Pilgrimage to the Five Regions of India* (1984) by Jagdish Chandrikesh, New Delhi, 2007.
Shrivastava, B.N., *Harshavardhana and His Times*, Varanasi, 1974.
Singh, M.V., *India Rediscovered*, New Delhi, 2006.
Sinha, B.P., *The Decline of the Kingdom of Magadha*, Patna, 1954.
—, *Dynastic History of Magadha*, New Delhi, 1977.
—, *Readings in History and Culture*, Delhi, 1978.
—, *Twilight of the Imperial Guptas*, Delhi, 1993.
—, ed., *A History of Bihar*, Vol. I, Patna, 1974.
Sinha, G.P., *Post-Gupta Polity (500-750 A.D.)*, Calcutta, 1972.
Sircar, D.C., *Select Inscriptions*, Calcutta, 1943.
—, *Geography of Ancient and Medieval India*, Delhi, 1960.
—, *Land System and Feudalism in Ancient India*, Calcutta, 1965.
—, *Indian Epigraphy*, Delhi, 1965.
—, *Landlordism and Tenancy in Ancient and Medieval India*, Lucknow, 1969.
—, *Studies in the Political and Administrative Systems of Ancient and Medieval India*, Delhi, 1974.
Smith, Bardwell L., ed., *Essays on Gupta Culture*, Delhi, 1983.
Smith, V.A., *Early History of India*, 4th edn., Oxford, 1924.
Soḍḍhala, *Udayasundarīkathā*, ed. C.D. Dalal and E. Krishnamacharya, G.O.S., Baroda, 1920.

Somadeva, *Kathāsaritsāgara*, tr. C.H. Tawney, 2 Vols., Calcutta, 1880-84.

Sonepat Seal of Harsha, *Corpus Inscriptionum Indicarum*, III, ed. J.F. Fleet, pp. 231-32.

Spink, Walter M., 'The Vākāṭaka Caves at Ajanta and their Successors', in *Reappraising Gupta History for S. R. Goyal*, eds. B. Ch. Chhabra et al, New Delhi, 1992, pp. 247-62.

Subandhu, *Vāsavadattā*, Bibliotheca Indica, Calcutta.

Subhāshitaratnabhāṇḍāgāra, ed. K. P. Parab, 5th edn., Bombay, 1911.

Takakusu, J.A., *A Record of the Buddhistic Religion as Practised in India and Malaya Archipelago (A.D. 671-695) by I-tsing*, Delhi, 1966.

Thakur, V.K., *Urbanisation in Ancient India*, New Delhi, 1981.

—, *Historiography of Indian Feudalism*, Patna, 1989.

—, *Social Dimensions of Technology : Iron in Early India c. 1300-200 B.C.*, Patna, 1993.

—, *Social Roots of Buddhism*, Patna, 2000.

—, ed., *Towns in Pre-Modern India*, Patna, 1994.

—, ed., *Peasants in Indian History I : Theoretical Issues and Structural Enquiries*, Patna, 1996.

—, ed., *Science, Technology and Medicine in Indian History*, Patna, 2000.

—, 'The Marxist View of Ancient Indian History', *JBRS*, Vol. LXII, Pts. 1-4, 1976.

—, 'Transition from the Ancient to the Medieval Period', *Problems of Indian Historiography*, ed. D. Devahuti, Delhi, 1979, pp. 79-82.

—, 'Decline or Diffusion : Constructing the Urban Tradition of North India during the Gupta Period', *IHR*, XXIV, Nos. 1-2, 1997-98, pp. 20-69.

Thapar, Romila, *A History of India*, Vol. I, Harmondsworth, 1966.

—, *Ancient Indian Social History*, Hyderabad, 1978.

—, *The Penguin History of Early India*, New Delhi, 2003.

—, *The Past Before Us : Historical Traditions of Early North India*, New Delhi, 2013.

—, *Readings in Early Indian History*, Oxford, 2013.

—, 'Aśokan India and the Gupta Age', in *A Cultural History of India*, ed. A.L. Basham, London, 1975, pp.38-50.

Thaplyal, K.K., *Inscriptions of the Maukharīs, Later Guptas, Puṣpabhūtis and Yaśovarman of Kanauj*, Delhi, 1985.

Trautmann, T., 'Lichchhavi-Dauhitra', in *JRAS*, 1972, I, i, pp. 1 ff.

Tripathi, L.K., 'Coins as Source of Economic History', *JNSI*, XXXIII, i, 1971, pp. 1-14.

Tripathi, R.S., *History of Kanauj to the Moslem Conquest*, Delhi, 1959.

Trivedi, H.V., *Catalogue of the Coins of the Nāgas of Padmāvatī*, Gwalior, 1957.

Vaidya, C.V., *History of Mediaeval Hindu India*, Vol. I, Poona, 1921.
Vākpati, *Gauḍavaho*, ed. S.P. Pandit, Bombay, 1887; 2nd edn. by N.B. Utgikar, Poona, 1927.
Vāyu Purāṇa, ĀSS, Poona, 1905.
Vikramāṅkābhyudaya, ed. G. Bühler, Bombay, 1875.
Vikramāṅkadevacharita of Bilhaṇa, ed. G. Bühler, Bombay, 1875.
Vishṇu-purāṇa, Eng. tr. H.H. Wilson, Calcutta, 1961.
Warder, A.K., *An Introduction to Indian Historiography*, Bombay, 1972.
Watters, T., *On Yuan Chwang's Travels in India*, Delhi, 1961.
Whalley, Paul, 'Place Names in U.P., of Agra and Oudh', *Journal of the Uttar Pradesh Historical Society*, II, Pt. 2, 1921, pp. 19-29.
Williams, Joanna Gottfried, *The Art of Gupta India*, New Delhi, 1983.
Winternitz, M., *History of Indian Literature*, 3 Vols., Delhi, 1981, 1983, 1985.
Yadava, B.N.S., 'The Accounts of the Kali Age and the Social Transition from Antiquity to the Middle Ages', in *Feudal Social Formation in Early India*, ed. D.N. Jha, Delhi, 1987, pp. 65-112.
Yājñavalkya-smṛti, Banaras, 1924.
Yamazaki, Toshio, 'Some Aspects of Land-Sale Inscriptions in Fifth and Sixth Century Bengal', *Acta Asiatica*, Bulletin of the Institute of Eastern Culture, No. 42, August 1982, pp. 17-36.
Yazdani, G., ed., *The Early History of the Deccan*, London, 1960.

Journals

Annals of the Bhandarkar Oriental Research Institute, Poona.
Bhāratī, Varanasi.
Bulletin of the Gorakhpur University, Gorakhpur.
Bulletin of the School of Oriental and African Studies, London.
Daedalus, Cambridge.
East and West, Rome.
Epigraphia Indica, New Delhi.
History Today, New Delhi.
Indian Antiquary, Bombay.
Indian Coin Society Newsletter, Nagpur.
Indian Culture, Calcutta.
Indian Historical Quarterly, Calcutta.
Indian Historical Review, New Delhi.
Indian Numismatic Chronicle, Patna.
Indica, Bombay.
Itihāsa-Samīkshā, Jaipur.
Jijñāsā, Jaipur.

Jñāna-Pravāha, Varanasi.
Journal of the All-India Philosophy Association, Jodhpur.
Journal of Ancient Indian History, Calcutta.
Journal of the Asiatic Society, Kolkata.
Journal of the Asiatic Society of Bengal, Calcutta.
Journal Asiatique, Paris.
Journal of the Bihar and Orissa Research Society, Patna.
Journal of the Bihar Purāvid Parishad, Patna.
Journal of the Bihar Research Society, Patna.
Journal of the Bombay Branch of the Royal Asiatic Society, Bombay.
Journal of the Epigraphical Society of India, Mysore.
Journal of the Ganganath Jha Research Institute, Allahabad.
Journal of Indian History, Trivandrum.
Journal of Indian History and Culture, Chennai.
Journal of the Numismatic Society of India, Varanasi.
Journal of Oriental Institute, Baroda.
Journal of Oriental Research, Madras.
Journal of the Royal Asiatic Society of Bengal, Calcutta.
Journal of the Royal Asiatic Society—Bombay Branch, Bombay.
Journal of the the Royal Asiatic Society of Great Britain and Ireland, London.
Journal of the U.P. Historical Society, Lucknow.
Kashmir Research Biannual.
Memoirs of the Archaeological Survey of India, Delhi.
New Indian Antiquary, Bombay.
Numismatic Digest, Nasik.
Panjab University Research Bulletin (Arts), Chandigarh.
Prāchī-Jyoti, Kurukshetra.
Proceedings of the Indian History Congress.
Proceedings of the Indian History and Culture Society.
Proceedings of the Oriental Conference.
Proceedings of the Papers from the Aligarh Historians Society, Aligarh.
Proceedings of the South Indian History Congress.
Quarterly Review of Historical Studies, Calcutta.
Shodha Samaveta, Ujjain.
Social Scientist, New Delhi.
Śodha Patrikā, Udaipur.
South Indian Epigraphy, Annual Reports.
Sri Venkateswara University Oriental Journal, Tirupati.
Studies in Indian Place Names.
Vishveshvaranand Indological Journal, Hoshiarpur.

Index